D0022798

Property of
St. John Fisher College
Lavery Library
Rochester, N.Y. 14618

# Creating a Classroom Community of Young Scientists

# Creating a Classroom Community of Young Scientists

## Second Edition

JEFFREY W. BLOOM

Routledge
Taylor & Francis Group
New York   London

Routledge is an imprint of the
Taylor & Francis Group, an informa business

Routledge
Taylor & Francis Group
270 Madison Avenue
New York, NY 10016

Routledge
Taylor & Francis Group
2 Park Square
Milton Park, Abingdon
Oxon OX14 4RN

© 2006 by Taylor & Francis Group, LLC
Routledge is an imprint of Taylor & Francis Group, an Informa business

Printed in the United States of America on acid-free paper
10 9 8 7 6 5 4 3 2 1

International Standard Book Number-10: 0-415-95236-0 (Softcover) 0-415-95235-2 (Hardcover)
International Standard Book Number-13: 978-0-415-95236-1 (Softcover) 978-0-415-95235-4 (Hardcover)

No part of this book may be reprinted, reproduced, transmitted, or utilized in any form by any electronic, mechanical, or other means, now known or hereafter invented, including photocopying, microfilming, and recording, or in any information storage or retrieval system, without written permission from the publishers.

**Trademark Notice:** Product or corporate names may be trademarks or registered trademarks, and are used only for identification and explanation without intent to infringe.

**Library of Congress Cataloging-in-Publication Data**

Bloom, Jeffrey W.
     Creating a classroom community of young scientists / Jeffrey W. Bloom.-- 2nd ed.
          p. cm.
     Includes bibliographical references and index.
     ISBN 0-415-95235-2 (hb : alk. paper) -- ISBN 0-415-95236-0 (pb : alk. paper)
     1. Science--Study and teaching (Elementary) 2. Elementary school teachers--In-service training. I. Title.

LB1585.B63 2006
372.3'5--dc22                                                                                           2006001764

**Visit the Taylor & Francis Web site at**
**http://www.taylorandfrancis.com**

**and the Routledge Web site at**
**http://www.routledge-ny.com**

# Dedication

This book is dedicated to my two sons, Ethan and Gregory, who are a never-ending source of insight, wonder, delight, and inspiration.

# Contents

## Part I: Getting Started

## Part II: Teaching Science for Children's Meaningful Learning

## Part III: Appendixes

# Preface to the First Edition

In attending deeply to children and trying to empathize with them, as in studying other cultures, one is constantly reminded that these beloved strangers are behaving in ways that are only intelligible if their world is recognized as differently structured, laid out according to different landmarks. Much of the time we are busy trying to talk children out of their perceptions, giving them the correct answers, the ones that are widely shared and fit neatly into familiar systems of interpretation.… It takes adult effort to turn bright, open children into a sullen underclass or into compliant factory workers, to keep life in shades of black and white and avoid new learning. (pp. 56–57)

All too often those who can teach or lead with authority are armored against new learning, while those who are open to new learning are made diffident about expressing what they do know by the very fact that they deem it tentative. The best learners are children, not children segregated in schools but children at play, zestfully busy exploring their own homes, families, neighborhoods, languages, conjuring up possible and impossible worlds of imagination. (p. 73)[1]

This book has been in the making for many years. The idea arose from my dissatisfaction with the currently available elementary science methods textbooks, which, from my perspective, do not adequately address current research and tend to be overwhelming to both elementary pre-service and in-service teachers. As a result, I began developing a "handbook," which I photocopied for my own students. As the years passed, schools began ordering copies of the handbook for their own teachers. The impetus to put this current version in print came from a chance meeting with the vice president of Irwin Publishing. His enthusiasm for and genuine interest in the idea acted as a catalyst.

My own interests in science extend back to early experiences in elementary and, especially, junior high school. However, as a university student and young professional, my interests began to extend beyond science into art, philosophy, social issues, literature, psychology, and different cultures. While still maintaining my interest in science, I began to develop understandings of the nature of the human experience and how science is only a part of that experience. Although science is a very powerful tool for explaining our world, it does not and cannot offer explanations for all of what we experience as human beings. In fact, I have to realize that we, as human beings, think about and make sense of our world from many different perspectives. These multiple perspectives are what make the human experience so rich. And so, it is from this point of view (of multiple perspectives and understandings) that I have undertaken this project.

In thinking about what to write as a preface to this book, I wanted to thank all of those people who have contributed in some way to my interest in science, children, and the broad context of knowing about our world. At the same time, I wanted to tell my story in a way that sets the tone for this book. Of course, such a story must begin with the early influences on my thinking.

My mother and father did not complete much formal education. However, not only did they value learning, but they had a passion for learning. My father was fascinated with electronics and mechanics. My mother read with a passion. As a young child, both of my parents went out of their way to support any glimmer of an interest I had in anything. As will be seen in the following paragraphs, their influence on my developing curiosity and interests in learning was extremely important.

During the summer after grade 6, I read a book called *Lady with a Spear*, by Eugenie Clark. Dr. Clark was and still is a renowned expert on sharks. Her book told of her childhood experiences and the development of her interest in sharks. I was completely captivated by the book, and especially by her work with sharks. After finishing the book, I wrote to her asking for more information about sharks. A couple of weeks later, I received a letter from her. She was quite supportive, but suggested that I write to Dr. Jack Casey at a laboratory closer to my home. A couple of weeks after writing to Dr. Casey, I received a package with several preserved shark embryos he had just removed from a shark they had captured, along with several small books on sharks. As a child, these responses made a big impression on me, and set into motion several years of my own research on sharks. Although neither Eugenie Clark nor Jack Casey realized their impact on one young boy, their generosity cannot go unmentioned.

Before long my basement was filled with containers of preserved sharks, skates, and fish. After dissecting many sharks and hours of researching sharks in a local college library, my junior high school science teacher, William Lebing, made an outrageous comment: "You've dissected enough. You've got to work with live sharks. We'll fill up this classroom with water, if we have to." Although filling the classroom with salt water was not a possibility, his comment extended the realm of possibility. William Lebing had a way of captivating and motivating his students. His support and approach that made science relevant has had a long-lasting impact on me and many other students.

With the possibility of working with live sharks at the forefront of my imagination as I entered high school, my mother and I wrote to a local legislator, Richard Schweiker, for help in getting a live shark. Within a couple of weeks, arrangements were made for Woods Hole Oceanographic Laboratory to provide me with a shark. A short time later, my father, my high school chemistry teacher (Donald Byerly), Donald Byerly's brother, and I were making a 20-hour trip to Woods Hole. After a tour of Woods Hole, we returned with a 42-inch smooth dogfish shark in the trunk of my father's car. My father, an expert at jury-rigging, had cut the side out of a 50-gallon oil drum and had rigged up an overinflated tire with a hose, air stone, and valve to supply air to the shark. After a couple of days with the shark in a "not large enough" tank in the basement, it began to behave strangely — flipping on its back. I called a local aquarium showplace, the Aquarama in Philadelphia, but they offered little assistance. Driving to school with Donald Byerly on the morning of the third day, we talked about the shark's condition. I finally said that there wasn't much left to do but pray for it. Donald Byerly's response was simple: "It won't help." In reflecting on this simple and rather flatly stated remark, I see it as a transition point in what was the impetus for a rather extensive process of conceptual change (a topic that will be discussed later in this book). I'm sure he had no idea of the impact of his remark. However, my worldview began to change over the next several years. His remark initiated a process of questioning my assumptions about life — a process I continue to value throughout my personal and professional life. As I teach and conduct research, I place the notion of openly questioning my own assumptions and the assumptions of others at the forefront of my work. Donald Byerly was another great science teacher, who cared about his students to the extent of spending time outside of school helping them.

The story of my work with live sharks did not end here. Several weeks after the death (on the third day) of my shark (who was relegated to a container of formaldehyde), I received a call from the Aquarama. Although their intent was probably driven by visions of publicity, they invited me to work on sharks at their facility. I was given a thousand-gallon tank and all of the sharks I wanted. For the next two and a half years, I spent several days a week working with sharks and helping them with feeding and collecting specimens for their displays. I also connected with a group of researchers studying sharks, and accompanied them on several shark-tagging expeditions. Bruce Bell (the curator at the time) and Bill Connell (the aquarist) were extremely accommodating and supportive. They helped bring a boy's dreams alive. After graduating from high school, Bill Connell, who had taken over the position of curator, called and asked if I'd be interested in working there for the summer. For the next three months, I cleaned tanks, fed (including falling into the shark tank while trying to hand-feed one of the sharks) all of the fish and reptiles, helped with scuba diving demonstrations in their two-story tank, and climbed on the backs of alligators to put antiseptics on cuts they had received from stones children had thrown at them. My experiences working at and working for the Aquarama were extraordinary. Not only did I learn a great deal, but my enthusiasm for science and my appreciation of the natural world were expanded.

The "questioning my assumptions" theme was put into high gear during my university years. The diversity of fellow students from around the world combined with the increasingly intensified issues of the Vietnam War of the late 1960s and early 1970s forced me to re-examine many of the my own preconceptions. My interest in sharks took a backseat to the political and psychosocial issues facing young people at the time. My father's death in 1969 punctuated the intensity of the changes taking place around and within me. Other interests started to emerge through work in a variety of courses. Bill Beidler, a philosophy professor specializing in Eastern philosophy, provided a source of sanity in an increasingly confusing world. He also opened up possibilities of understanding the world from different perspectives. His intelligence, openness, generosity, and kindness have made a lasting impression. He also rekindled my interest in photography as an art form.

Bob Bryden's (biology professor) infinite patience and understanding of students in the midst of social-political turmoil went a long way toward maintaining my own interests in biology. He also provided his students with opportunities to do science through extended field experiences. He managed to demystify many biological concepts and instill a genuine interest among his students. Other professors, whose names I cannot recall, also had an incredible impact. Somehow Guilford College, a small Quaker college in North Carolina, attracted a faculty (and a student body) who valued inquiry and the questioning of assumptions and beliefs.

After arriving at the University of Rhode Island to take further courses in zoology, I had the great fortune to work with Frank Heppner, an ornithologist. Frank is an extraordinarily creative teacher and researcher. His weekly wine and lunch discussion sessions with graduate students explored questions in the research literature, which often led to rather bizarre hypothesizing. The notion of scientific inquiry took on a new meaning for all of us. From chasing flocks of birds with cameras mounted in remote-controlled planes to wind tunnel studies of bird flight and reaction times, we were immersed in genuine inquiry. His last class of his freshman zoology course was attended by all graduate students. For the technology of the time, his automated multiple-slide projector and quadraphonic sound hour-long show captivated everyone. Of course, his arriving on stage for his first class on a Harley Davidson and dressed as a Hell's Angel was not to be missed by anyone. As a "Hell's Angel" he tried to convince the packed auditorium of students that his bike was alive. Although the students couldn't counter his arguments, he managed to engage hundreds of students in "talking" science. Robert Shoop put all graduate students through the test of scientific inquiry during a week-long field trip to the University of Georgia's ecology lab at the Savannah River Plant. Working in groups, everyone had to identify a problem, collect and analyze data, and present their findings to the staff of the lab — all in three days. With virtually no sleep and all of the problems of nothing working out as planned, we experienced an intensified version of inquiry, including perseverance, persistence, technical problem solving, and so forth. These experiences at the University of Rhode Island extended my own understanding of the nature of science and rekindled my enthusiasm for science.

During the year I worked at the New York Ocean Science Laboratory, which was my first full-time employment, I began to develop an interest in teaching. The interest arose after reading a couple of books on teaching, one of which was *39 Children* by John Holt. I began reflecting on my own experiences in science classes and how I thought science could be presented in a better way. Quite naively, I began pursuing teaching positions. The following year, I started teaching middle school science at Brooklyn Friends School in New York City. Of all of my colleagues there, Elise Mandell, the French teacher, became my mentor. She was an exceptional teacher, with files on every imaginable topic. Our talks at the end of the day usually resulted in her digging through her files for materials relevant to what I was doing. Her enthusiasm for teaching, her love of children, and broad-ranging interests became a model toward which to strive. The children in the school were wonderful (especially in retrospect). Although they were a challenge, they taught me a great deal about teaching, learning, patience, and caring.

During my two years at Brooklyn Friends, I had the great fortune to meet a Tibetan Buddhist teacher, Chögyam Trungpa. His unlimited generosity and compassion and his caring for children taught me a great deal. He saw teaching as a way of allowing children to take more control and responsibility and as a way of helping children appreciate themselves and their world. In addition, he emphasized a kind of critical inquiry that questioned all of our assumptions about ourselves and our world. His impact remains close to my heart.

During the summer after my first year at Brooklyn Friends, I took a five-week workshop in education at Naropa Institute in Boulder, Colorado, with one of the greatest minds to grace the Western world. Gregory Bateson, a renowned anthropologist, had a vast knowledge of many disciplines. Although he had the credentials to be an arrogant authority, Gregory Bateson was an extremely kind, gentle, and down-to-earth human being. In failing health, he continued to care more about others and to try to help them see beyond the limits of their own preconceptions. Many of his ideas are imbedded in this book. In particular, I am completely indebted to him for the notion of "contexts of meaning" or as he referred to it, "multiple perspectives." My notion of "context maps" has been derived from his work with open systems theory and multiple perspectives–loop processes.

During my next three teaching positions, my students continued to teach me a great deal. All of whom found their way into my heart. I am indebted to them all. While developing and teaching in a gifted program, I met another great teacher, Vicki McLean. She was the master of commanding respect from children (and colleagues), while maintaining a cheerful, upbeat, and gentle demeanor. Her understanding of children and the process of learning taught me a great deal.

My entry into a doctoral program is entirely due to Howie Jones at the University of Houston. He made theory come alive. His insight into teaching science through informal contexts extended my ideas about how to approach science in the classroom. Rick Duschl, with whom I worked on my dissertation, pushed me to examine the philosophy of science and to critically examine my own ideas. His rigorous thinking became a model for all of his students.

In my years of working in teacher education, I have much to owe to all of my bachelor of education and master's degree students. My first two years of teaching B.Ed. students at Queen's University taught me a great deal. It was a painful process for all of us (and I must ask their forgiveness), but I came to realize that the way science has been presented to them throughout their schooling has done a great deal of damage. Embarking on a career in which one must teach science requires a different way of thinking about and approaching this subject. Their course evaluations led me once again to re-evaluate my assumptions about teaching, learning, and science. All of my students since then (at both Queen's University and Acadia University) have continued to be a great inspiration and to be a never-ending source of challenges to my own preconceptions.

Without the support of grants from the School of Graduate Studies and Research at Queen's University, the Acadia University Faculty Association (AUFA), and the Social Sciences and Humanities Research Council of Canada, I would not have had the opportunity to investigate children's learning to the extent that I have been able. The most recent grant from AUFA has allowed me to make further contacts with colleagues, including Karen Gallas, and to set up a functional office during my sabbatical. My sabbatical from Acadia University has allowed me to focus almost entirely on the task of writing this book.

Many of my colleagues have been extremely helpful in my quest for further learning about teaching, the nature of science, the integration of subject areas, and research. I cannot name everyone, but a few people have had a significant impact on my thinking and/or have extended themselves beyond the call of duty: Hugh Munby (Queen's University), Nancy Hutchinson (Queen's University), Mary Schoeneberger (to her memory; from Mount Saint Vincent University), George Posner (Cornell University), David Piper (Acadia University), Zoubeida Dagher (University of Delaware), and Jay Lemke (Brooklyn College of CUNY). Many other people's work has had considerable impact on my thinking. Most of these individuals will be cited throughout this book. However, I would also like to extend thanks to Torgny Vigerstad for the many hours of discussion about the nature of science and about specific science concepts. It is always revitalizing. Trudy Sable for her invitation to serve on her master's thesis committee and for sharing her exceptional insight into the culture of the Mi'kmaw people of Nova Scotia and the nature of native science.

During my years of research on children's learning in science, I have had the distinctive opportunity to work with some exceptional teachers. Their insight into teaching and children has been most helpful. In addition, I want to thank the Shambhala Middle School in Halifax, and the students I "taught" during a research project. They taught me more than they know. A couple of teachers have contributed a great deal to my continued learning about classrooms, teaching, and children. Anu Lukezich not only allowed me to conduct research in her classroom, but involved me in teaching alongside of her. Her wisdom and insight are greatly appreciated. Karen Gallas, a truly incredible teacher and researcher, allowed me (a stranger) to spend a day in her most remarkable classroom. If only all teachers could be like her.

At various points in writing this book, Skip Hills and Peter Chin have provided valuable insights into science and teaching. Our casual conversations stimulated more thought into many of the issues examined in a number of chapters.

I also want to thank the students who read and critiqued the proposal and sample chapter of this book. They include George Armstrong, Joanne Bulmer, Liz Burrill, Wanda Jewers, Tammy Kane, Pamela MacDonald, Dawn MacKinnon, Kim Nelson, Jennifer Offman, Theresa Ryan, Nicki Shaw, Lynda Shoveller, Tim Swinamer, Kelly Buchan, Freda Larade-van Feggelen, Kai Misenko, and Rosemary Ward. In addition, a number of students have graciously allowed me to use examples from their journals. These students include Natalie Lacy, George Dorian, Peter MacDonald, Cathy Fourdraine, Susan Murray, Valerie DaCosta, Katherine MacLeod, and Suzanne Hobden.

In the final writing of this book, three individuals (previous students) critiqued the manuscripts of chapters: Alana Eaton, Andrea Martin, and Heidi Mack. Each of these individuals did an exemplary job. I especially want to thank Alana Eaton, who stuck with the task through to the end.

Writing the bulk of this book during sabbatical has allowed me to devote most of my concentration to this task. However, finding a space and support for writing is essential. I want to extend my thanks to Rena Upitis, Dean, Faculty of Education, Queen's University, for providing me with an office, telephone, and Internet hookup. Queen's

University not only provided physical support for this task, but a great deal of support for finding ways for me to set up a personal budget line for photocopying, telephone calls, and postage. Without this support, as well as the support of my colleagues at Queen's, the task would have much more difficult.

Kathy Roth's (of Michigan State University) comments on both the proposal and the final manuscript of have also been a great help. In addition, the comments of other colleagues, including Zoubeida Dagher (of the University of Delaware) and others who acted as blind reviewers, on the initial proposal contributed a great deal to the final product.

Working with a good publisher is a blessing. Irwin Publishing has been an extraordinary company with which to work. Jeff Miller, Acquisitions Editor, has not only been supportive and flexible from the very beginning, but has provided very insightful and knowledgeable comments. Working with an editor like Grace Dalfonso, who is on the same "wave-length," has been a delight. Of course, this whole project would not have occurred had it not been for the initial interest and support of Michael Byron Davis, Vice President.

Last, but not least, I want to extend my appreciation to my wife, Barbara, for her continued encouragement and support for this project, as well as her insightful comments on various aspects of early versions of the manuscript.

All of the people mentioned and many more have been important influences on my thinking about children, learning, and teaching. Although the stories of my interactions with these people may be interesting in themselves, the significance extends beyond the specific effects on my own growth as a professional. These stories point to the ways in which teachers, students, colleagues, and others can affect children's and one's own growth and development. Seemingly insignificant comments and events can have a lasting impact. The stories also point to what Maxine Greene discusses as giving children a vision of possibility. Although today's social and political situation is different from that of the threat of nuclear war (Cold War era) and the Vietnam War era I experienced as a child and young adult, present-day youth face many challenges. Confusion and a sense of hopelessness are problems for all levels of society, and especially for the increasing population of impoverished families. As educators, it is important for us to provide our students with visions of possibility and hope, of kindness and compassion, and of courage and self-worth. Teachers must rise to these challenges, which extend far beyond the scope of teaching science. However, as you may gather as you read through this book, science and the integrated curriculum through the notion of multiple perspectives or understandings can provide a way for children to develop a greater sense of their own power. The power to realize their human potential and to strive for the possible, whether that possibility is in science, art, writing, athletics, a trade, or whatever path they choose to follow.

## Notes

1. Mary Catherine Bateson, *Peripheral Visions: Learning along the Way* (New York: Harper Collins, 1994).

# Preface to the Second Edition

It has been eight years since I worked on the first edition of this book. During this time, I have moved several times, encountered many new situations, and worked with many more teachers, university students, and colleagues. All of these changes and encounters have provided new and exciting opportunities for further learning. As teachers, I hope you see all of the opportunities you have to learn from each and every new situation, each child, and all of your colleagues.

This edition contains a lot of new material, with a particularly strong emphasis on inquiry and teaching and learning for more relevant, meaningful, and complex understandings. As I have worked with teachers and children over the past several years, I have come to a point where I think it is critically important that we approach teaching and learning very differently. If we do not change our expectations and visions of what is possible with children, I fear for the future of our world. Learning needs to be a joy, but what I see is a lot of people (children and adults) who are basically bored. Learning is a process of intense engagement with all kinds of materials, events, and ideas, but what I have been seeing is children and adults going through the motions to accomplish whatever the minimum is for getting through school or the workplace. In the meantime, politics and the basic fabric of our local and global societies seem to be crumbling, while the natural environment that supports all life is under increasing threat. Unless we change the way we teach and think about schooling, we could enter into an unrecoverable, downward spiral. I only hope that the ideas in this book will have some impact on those of you who read it. However, I hope the major impact will be on the real bottom line: children! They start their life full of energy, curiosity, creativity, and incredible ways of thinking and making sense of the world. I only hope that the ideas in this book will help to perpetuate and refine their curiosity, creativity, and thinking.

Since the first edition was published, the original publisher went out of business. However, I must thank Michael Davis, the former vice president of Irwin Publishing (the publisher of the first edition), for his help in arranging for the new edition. He is still committed to this book. Michael is the reason this book was published in the first place, after we first met in Nova Scotia, when he encouraged me to work on this project.

As I mentioned in the preface to the first edition, Gregory Bateson was a huge influence on me as a beginning teacher, as well as throughout my career as a teacher, then as a science educator and researcher. However, his legacy has continued through the more recent influences of his daughters, Mary Catherine Bateson (an incredible thinker, researcher, educator, and writer in her own right) and Nora Bateson (a thoughtful and creative filmmaker, living in British Columbia). In addition, I have been greatly influenced by Tyler Volk. Tyler is a global ecologist at New York University, who also was influenced by Gregory Bateson, and has taken Bateson's work a step further in his book *Metapatterns: Across Space, Time, and Mind*. I think this work takes the abstractions of Gregory Bateson's notion of metapatterns to greater heights of abstraction, as well as to the immediate practicality of how and what we can teach children and how we can think about teaching and learning.

I also want to thank all of my students from my period at Morgan State University. They taught me a lot about teaching in urban environments and about the African American experience. Their intelligence, great spirit, curiosity, and critical thinking were (and continue to be) a great inspiration. All of my students in Arizona have continued to be great teachers. However, my Navajo, Hopi, and other Native American students and colleagues have been particularly influential. Their intelligence, kindness, and spirit have been quite influential on my thinking about teaching, learning, and living in the world.

Much of the new material in this edition arose out of projects funded by a U.S. Department of Education grant: *The Arizona Teaching Excellence Coalition* (AzTEC). This grant involved a statewide partnership among faculty in the sciences, mathematics, technology, and education at Arizona State University, the University of Arizona, Northern Arizona University, a number of Arizona community colleges, and schools and school districts across the state. This partnership provided for an exciting exchange of ideas. Many thanks are extended to all who participated in this grant, and especially to Jim Middleton of Arizona State University, who provided the initial effort and extraordinary vision for this project.

I also want to thank Michelle Messersmith, Alexis Baca-Spry, Sarah Ogden, and, once again, Alana Eaton (who, as a former student and new teacher, reviewed every word of the first edition) for their helpful comments and suggestions on the second edition. Of course, I am eternally grateful to Catherine Bernard and Brook Cosby of Routledge for their help in getting this project started and for their helpful comments on this edition. Brook has provided particularly insightful suggestions.

# Part I
## Getting Started

# Chapter 1
# Introduction

This book is intended to help teachers—both pre-service and in-service—develop exciting science programs in their classrooms. For those of you who are science-phobic or who do not like science, this goal may seem to be either contradictory or daunting, at the very least. However, this book is designed to be user-friendly, as well as to provide an approach to teaching science that is exciting for teachers. The approach described in this book is one that provides you with the basic groundwork for designing and implementing a science program that takes into account the latest research in teaching and learning.

One of the major themes throughout this book is based on the notion of teachers' professional communities. Whether we are beginning or experienced teachers, we may lose sight of what it means to be a member of a professional community. Entering a community of professional practice involves a great deal of new learning, part of which may be found in this book. However, a great deal of this learning is acquired through our interactions with master teachers and other educational experts, as well as with our colleagues (fellow students or other teachers). In addition to such interactions, we also have to take on responsibility to learn from our interactions with children and parents, from engaging in learning experiences within subject matter areas (in terms of this book, the emphasis is on science) to reading widely in a variety of fields (e.g., science, education, psychology, literature, philosophy, etc.). More discussion on this theme of professional communities will appear later in this chapter, as well as other chapters, with particular emphases in Chapters 10 and 11.

Young children love doing science. From the time they are born, children begin making sense of their world. The majority of their questions are scientific questions (e.g., "What's thunder?" or "Why do the leaves change color?"), along with a hefty number of philosophical questions. Unfortunately, by the time children reach high school, their enthusiasm for science has waned. Something happens that turns children off to doing and learning science. This book provides you with an approach that will capture children's imaginations, stimulate their curiosity, and, hopefully, provide a strong foundation for their continued interest in and appreciation for science and the world in which they live.

## 1.1　Beginning the Journey

Science in your classroom can be a point of departure for developing active inquiry, problem solving, critical thinking, and independent work, as well as for incorporating understandings from many different perspectives, such as art, music, poetry, storytelling, social sciences, math, and sports. You need to reflect upon your past experiences with science—writing lab reports and following "the scientific method," memorizing lists of facts and names, thinking that science has all the right answers. How did these experiences affect your attitude toward science? Such experiences of science do not represent what science really is or how it works. Science can be exciting and dynamic. There is no such thing as the one and only scientific method. Scientists approach problems from all sorts of different angles and with an assortment of methods. The whole point of science is to try to understand how the world works. Trying to understand how the world works is what children do naturally, and it is what you need to take advantage of when teaching science. Just remember: Avoid being the knowledge authority (the one who disseminates knowledge). Instead, cultivate a sense of excitement for exploring and inquiring about our world and for generating and testing possible explanations.

The amount of scientific knowledge has increased exponentially over the past several decades. Even teachers with a background in science cannot be expected to be experts in each content area they teach. Even if you have a strong background in a particular area of science, too much knowledge on your part can create problems when you try to implement a child-centered, inquiry-based classroom. In such cases, the tendency is to provide children with the "correct" answer, rather than to stimulate them to inquire further and develop their own explanations. What you need to do is to develop patience and the skills necessary to facilitate inquiry. At the same time, you need to develop your own ability to take risks. The risks you will most likely face include (a) implementing an inquiry-based science unit or lesson, (b) not having all the answers to children's questions, (c) allowing children to explore their own areas of interest and their own inquisitiveness, (d) helping children develop investigations and experiments that could fail, and (e) taking the time to delve deeply into science when you feel pressure from the administration to cover the curriculum or "teach to the test." If you are up to taking these risks and turning your own and your students' mistakes into positive experiences, you can be rewarded by a classroom permeated by excitement for learning.

It is important for you to realize from the start that you, as a teacher, are the expert and the knowledgeable decision maker about how to teach. You know the particular circumstances in your classroom and the specific characteristics of your children. In order to develop and maintain a child-centered classroom effectively, you have to be in a position to make decisions that will facilitate learning. Taking this position means that you cannot rely on what someone else says should be done, including using prepackaged activities and units, when you have 20 or 30 individuals running around with a wide variety of interests, strengths, and weaknesses. Such an approach may sound overwhelming, but as you gain experience and confidence, your classroom can become a fantastic arena for all kinds of learning.

There appear to be three basic aspects of the teaching profession that can be designated as those that define an excellent teacher:

1. **Passion**—Being passionate about learning, teaching, and working with children.
2. **Caring**—Caring for and about children.
3. **Reflection**—Critically and analytically reflecting on one's own teaching and on children's learning.

These three aspects go a long way toward providing the basic grounding for being a good teacher. Your passion for learning, caring for your students, and reflection will show through to the children. As a role model, you will provide the guiding framework for your students to emulate through your passion, caring, and reflection.

However, a fourth aspect of being an excellent teacher involves *an understanding of the subject matter*. In order to work effectively with children's inquiries, discussions, questions, and so forth, teachers need to have a fairly good understanding of the fundamental concepts involved in the topics being investigated in the classroom. Although we cannot know everything, we need to develop an understanding of the subject matter that will allow us to respond to children in meaningful ways. If a child asks a question about some aspect of an investigation, rather than saying, "I don't know" (which is better than responding with a wrong answer) or responding with a simplistic answer, a knowledgeable teacher can respond with a question, series of questions, or additional activities that can help guide the child's thinking toward formulating his or her own answer. In a way, a passionate, caring, and reflective teacher applies that passion, caring, and reflection to the subject matter. A truly excellent teacher is passionate about learning and inquiring, cares about the way the subject matter is presented, and reflects on how to present the subject matter.

There are a few final notions to keep in mind as you read through this book and as you embark on or develop your teaching career:

1. **Do not underestimate your students**. Experience and language skills tend to be the factors that separate grade 1 and grade 6 students. Given the same level of experience with a particular topic, grade 1 and grade 6 students frequently make the same kinds of inferences and construct similar concepts and meanings. The major difference between the two age groups is the level of sophistication of their language. So, do not be afraid to elevate your expectations.

2. **Do not be misled by students' first reactions to questions**, such as "I don't know." School can adversely affect children from an early age. They back off from answering questions, taking risks, or offering answers that may not be correct. Do not fall into the trap of supplying the quick-fix answer when they say they do not know. Rephrase the question. If that does not work, ask a series of questions that may help them make the appropriate connections. For instance, a student once asked what a specific object was on the inside of a frog she was dissecting. I asked her what she thought it was. She said she did not know and looked at me as though I was crazy for asking. Then I asked her what the structure was connected to and where that led. Before long, she came up with the answer herself. You need to create a safe environment that supports guesses, mistakes, and outrageous ideas.

3. **Children construct their own knowledge and meanings**. No matter what a teacher does, no two students will have the same understanding of a lesson. Children make connections and construct knowledge based on their personal experiences, previous knowledge, emotions, values, aesthetics, beliefs, metaphors, and so on. This diversity of knowledge and meaning construction needs to be encouraged and shared among children.

4. **Let children take control over their own learning**. If children become interested in a project, an experiment, or other task, do not prescribe how they should proceed. Children (and adults) learn by making mistakes. Mistakes should be rewarded! As children make mistakes, help them evaluate what went wrong and help them come up with possible solutions. Too much teacher talk and teacher domination will adversely affect children's learning, ownership over their work, and motivation. Letting go of your control is difficult to do. It will take a lot of hard work on your part (a) to notice what you do and how the children react, (b) to reflect on your experiences, and (c) to come up with and initiate alternative strategies.

5. **The key to a successful classroom** (one that is exciting, where children take responsibility for their own learning and interactions,

where creativity thrives, etc.) **is in the atmosphere you create in the classroom and in the implicit and explicit structure you help to create**. An effective concept for guiding your work at setting up such a classroom is that of the classroom as a community of young scientists and learners. In this kind of classroom, children are seen and treated as significant contributors to the community and to the social construction and negotiation of knowledge. This applies as well to grade 1 as it does to grade 6. (Again, do not underestimate children!)

## 1.2   Philosophy and Theoretical Framework

The approach described in this book is based on several currently popular areas of research and theoretical development. The history, philosophy, and sociology of science impacts how we view the nature of science and how we can better represent science in our classrooms. Children's engagement in inquiry, evaluation of knowledge claims, and interactions with one another within a community of young scientists and learners are based on what we know about how science works.

Cognitive psychology has contributed a great deal to our understandings of how children learn and construct knowledge, both individually and as a social process. The notions of constructivism and social constructivism describe how children construct their own meanings and understandings. The research in cognitive psychology has far-reaching implications for how we set up learning situations and how we, as teachers, interact with children, as well as for how children interact with one another.

The new field of complexity sciences, which have emerged from chaos and complexity theories, has begun to have a significant impact on our understandings of teaching and curriculum, learning, classroom talk, and even the content of what to study. This second edition has incorporated some of this material. Basically, chaos theories deal with how patterns are either embedded in or emerge from seemingly chaotic events. Complexity theories focus on how complex systems generate and maintain themselves. In terms of classrooms, these theories have implications for (a) how a classroom community can be established and maintained, (b) understanding and facilitating classroom discussions, (c) understanding children's learning, and (d) the way we view subject matter content in terms of the patterns that are shared across disciplines. In a way, seemingly chaotic events like a classroom argument can appear to be chaotic, but definite patterns emerge, which lead to increasingly complex conceptual development (see the argument example in Chapter 5). From such a perspective, we might consider the notion of a teacher's role as *inviting chaos and trusting complexity*. In other words, we may provide opportunities for students to engage in activities and discussions that may initially seem to be chaotic. However, if the students are *actually engaged*, we can trust that they will delve into complex thinking and learning. The fundamental point that we need to consider is how we can focus our work with children on understanding *systems*. A system can be thought of as any cycle or complex set of interacting cycles, such as the solar system, an ecosystem, an earthworm or any biological organism, weather systems, a mechanical system (cars, bikes, etc.), a political system, the global ecological system, a social system (family, community, organization, nation, etc.), a culture, and so forth. If we focus on understanding systems, we find that all systems share many of the same patterns that help to maintain or sustain them. So, if a child explores and develops an understanding of family as a system (about which he or she will already have a good understanding), understanding another system, such as an ecosystem, will involve many of the same concepts and patterns as those of the family system. See Appendix D for more information.

Teaching as reflective practice and teacher as researcher, including teacher self-study, are major areas of research among teacher educators, as well as teachers. These areas of research suggest that in order to be an expert teacher and to continue to grow professionally, teachers need to develop their skills of looking at their own practice and at how individuals and groups of children interact and learn. Teaching is not a profession where you can take a recipe and implement it in the classroom. Every classroom and every child is different. Situations change from week to week, day to day, and even more frequently. You need to rely upon your own intelligence, insights, observations, and intuition in order to deal with each situation effectively.

A teacher's ability to reflect upon his or her own experiences in the classroom is essential. Such reflection goes beyond merely remembering the day's events and wallowing in your mistakes or riding high on your successes. You have to think about what took place during the day, what could have contributed to the events, how contributing factors affected specific events, and how you could have modified such factors or introduced new strategies to create more effective learning. Mistakes have to be seen as fortunate opportunities to grow and learn. Activities that work well also should be analyzed for why they were effective. Developing this ability to reflect is critical to becoming a self-reliant, confident, and dynamic professional—to becoming a master teacher. To facilitate this process, you should keep a professional journal. Record your thoughts every day or whenever the opportunity arises. If you do not have time to reflect upon a particular event, or if you are too wound up emotionally in the event, record your observations of what took place in as much detail as you can, then go back and reflect upon the experience at a later time.

Critical, analytical, and reflective thinking not only lies at the core of becoming a good teacher, but also forms the basis for your students becoming active and independent learners. "Students as active and independent learners" sounds great, but it is not an easy thing to accomplish. If you are not an active and independent learner yourself (able to think critically and reflectively), you will continue to be frustrated when you try to get your students to become independent learners. Critical thinking involves being open to new ideas (open-minded), but at the same time being skeptical. Among the many aspects of critical thinking are (a) questioning the accuracy of particular statements, (b) determining what is and is not relevant to a particular problem or issue, (c) determining the ambiguity of particular statements and claims, (d) identifying underlying assumptions, and (e) detecting biases. Many children love to argue. What you need to do is help them become critical thinkers and critical arguers. They need to be able to recognize what is a strong argument, as well as what is a weak argument, so that they can argue against ideas rather than attack a person.

Each of the previous areas of research is incorporated into the fabric of this book. However, you will need to practice adopting this framework. Reading the book alone will not make you a good science teacher. Working with inquiry, helping children construct understandings, and reflecting upon your own teaching need to be practiced. Activities and questions throughout this book will provide you with opportunities to start practicing each of these skills. Fundamentally, you will need to take risks, try new approaches, make mistakes, and learn from those mistakes. Whether you are a practicing teacher or someone who has just started the path to becoming a teacher, this book can be used as a desktop companion to develop an exciting and fruitful science program in your present or future classroom.

This book does not provide a survey of different theoretical or practical approaches to teaching science or of different perspectives on children's learning. Neither Piaget's theory of developmental stages nor behaviorist notions of learning are addressed. Rather, this book is based on a fairly cohesive set of theoretical and research-based perspectives. These perspectives represent the current direction and thinking in the science education community. But, more than that, these perspectives can allow you to develop a cohesive approach to teaching and doing science that can be both exciting and rewarding.

## 1.3  Goals and Emphases

The major goals for children in an elementary science program are described in the following paragraphs. This list is by no means exhaustive. As you read through this book, explore science, and work with children, you may want to add your own goals. As a beginning teacher, you may find this list a bit daunting. What you may want to do is focus on a few goals at a time (i.e., work on achieving three or four goals during your first year of teaching).

1. **Children should develop an understanding of the nature of science**. They should be involved in doing science, such as (a) designing and conducting experiments or observational studies and (b) evaluating, arguing about, and negotiating their own explanations and knowledge claims. From such experiences, they should develop

understandings of how to evaluate the claims of experts in terms of how knowledge is constructed and what is valid knowledge.

2. **Children should be involved in "talking" science**. As referred to in the previous goal, children should become adept at talking science with other students. This process includes the social skills of conducting talks, listening, and communicating effectively. In addition, children should be able to evaluate and constructively criticize the explanations and knowledge claims of others.

3. **Children should be engaged in inquiry**. The major emphasis of their engagement in science should involve investigating scientific phenomena through a variety of inquiry techniques. Such inquiry should involve hands-on activities a majority of the time, but should always involve them in thinking about their work.

4. **Children should construct thorough and elaborate understandings of science concepts**. Although in some cases currently accurate and accepted scientific understandings may be difficult for children to learn, their engagement in inquiry and personal and social construction of understandings should lead them to understandings that are based upon their own evidence, examples from personal experiences, and rational thinking.

5. **Children should develop integrated understandings of various phenomena**. All too often children are presented with the notion that science is the only way to understand something. However, artists, poets, historians, and mathematicians may have very different ways of understanding the same phenomena. Children naturally integrate as they make sense of their worlds, and teachers should be ready to encourage children to explore these perspectives further.

6. **Children should develop understandings of the patterns and concepts that are common to all subject matter areas and across cultures and areas of personal experience**. As mentioned previously, children need to engage in exploring the patterns that share connections across contexts and that lead to understanding biological, physical, social, political, and cognitive systems.

7. **Children should become producers of knowledge, rather than consumers of knowledge**. Children's active engagement in exploring science and other subject matter areas should be focused on generating explanations and insights, then communicating their learning in public venues. Sitting passively and consuming knowledge should not be the primary approach.

A few other goals that you may want to ponder are provided below. Some of these goals may fit in with the more global goals described above, but others may not.

■ To help children develop *complex, relevant, and meaningful understandings*

- To develop children's appreciation and *respect for our environment*
- To nurture *curiosity* about how the world works
- To encourage children to develop an understanding of the *patterns and relationships* in the environment
- To help children learn how to *observe*
- To teach children to *communicate* their observations
- To encourage children to *explore their own concepts* of how things work
- To help children to develop *enthusiasm* and *interest* in science
- To expose children to the *scientific explanations* of how things work
- To encourage children's *questioning*
- To encourage the development of *analytical* and *critical thinking*
- To help children develop skills in *negotiating* their knowledge claims and explanations with other students
- To help children develop skills in *establishing support* for and *clearly articulating* their understandings, knowledge claims, and explanations
- To nurture *independent learning* and thinking
- To help children develop their own "*stories*" about events and objects in their world
- To help children understand aspects of their world from *different perspectives*
- To help children make connections between different perspectives
- To help children *evaluate the appropriateness* of different perspectives or understandings for specific contexts (such as science, art, social, religious, and other cultural and conceptual contexts)

## 1.4 How to Use This Book

Several themes or strands are woven throughout the chapters in this book, including reflective thinking, social constructivism, inquiry, the classroom as community, complex learning, and integrating across the curriculum. Although specific chapters are devoted to the first four of these themes, they are addressed as the basis for the approach discussed in this book. In addition, the notion of reflection is dealt with more explicitly in each chapter. Reflective questions are usually inserted in the margin sidebars. There are no correct answers to these questions. Considering these questions is important in that they will help you develop the skills of asking and thinking about instructional questions. In addition, formulating answers to these questions will help you to define your own teaching philosophy and approach, which should be an ongoing process throughout your career.

You may find it useful to read Chapter 10 and the first section in Chapter 11 before reading the rest of this book. These two chapters will help you formulate an orientation to how to think about developing your skills of critical and analytical reflection and about orienting yourself to how to participate in the professional community of teachers. In general, it is important to consider that to be an excellent teacher you must strive for excellence as often as possible, rather than to just go through the motions or do just what is necessary to maintain your job as a teacher. In other words, you need to take advantage of every opportunity to learn about subject matter, about teaching, about learning, and about yourself as a teacher.

In a number of places, activities are suggested. These activities are designed to provide you with experiences that will deepen your own understanding of science, learning, and teaching. Look at these activities as opportunities to raise your passion for learning, inquiring, and discovery.

Additional comments are also added throughout many of the chapters. These comments provide more detailed information about scientific content or about educational research and theory. At the end of most chapters are lists of additional readings and advanced readings. For those of you who wish to read more about the topics considered in each chapter, these readings offer a good place to start. The advanced readings are generally more theoretical or based on current research. Such readings offer exciting possibilities for extending your own understandings of what you need to consider as a teacher. However, you may want to develop some further experience of teaching science in the classroom before delving into these readings.

The following 10 chapters in this book represent the core ideas to developing an exciting and effective science program in your classroom. The appendices that appear after these chapters are intended to supply you with some useful information, from safety in the classroom to how to make equipment and where to find sources of supplies and equipment.

National science standards are addressed in Appendix B (United States) and Appendix C (Canada). Since local standards and curriculum vary from state to state and province to province, more general considerations are discussed with examples from the *National Science Education Standards* in the United States and from the Canadian *Common Framework of Science Learning Outcomes K–12* (Common Framework). (Note: Measurements are given first in the International System of Units, using the SI symbol, followed by the equivalent U.S. Conventional System of measurement in parentheses.) However, you also should look at Chapter 7 for a discussion of accountability and high-stakes tests, which are connected with the whole notion of standards.

In general, I hope that this book will become a desktop companion. Some chapters may provide a lot of information, some of which may be more difficult than others. However, as with any learning, the more experience we accumulate, the more we are able to understand. So, revisiting some of these chapters over the next several years of your career may provide you with further insights and inspirations. You also may find that the appendices will provide you with useful information throughout the school year.

In addition, I have a website that focuses on teaching and learning science. This site (at http://elsci.coe.nau.edu/news.php) has online inquiry activities for children, information on teaching science, a wide array of articles and information on science teaching and learning, as well as online discussion forums.

## 1.5  Some Questions to Consider

The following questions may help to provide a focus for thinking about the material and activities in this book. These questions can serve as a guide for thinking about not only what is contained in this book, but also what we encounter in classroom experiences and while reading the newspaper, watching the news, or engaging in any kind of activity that may relate to working with children or learning on our own.

- What are the implications for how children learn?
- What are the implications for our own learning?
- What are the implications for curriculum and schooling?
- What are the implications for the notion of a classroom as a community of learners and inquirers?
- What are the implications for how we represent science?
- How can this (idea, etc.) be used to refine my own philosophy of teaching and learning?
- How can this (idea, activity, etc.) be incorporated into my classroom activities?
- What are the assumptions underlying this idea, and how does it fit with my assumptions about teaching, learning, curriculum, or schooling?
- Does this (idea, approach, etc.) create a conflict with my own beliefs or ideas about teaching, learning, or schooling, and how can I come to terms with this conflict?
- How am I developing as a practitioner in the community of teachers?

Teachers, we don't need no thought control.
    —Pink Floyd,
    "The Wall"

◆ What common assumptions about teaching and learning are the focuses of this quote from Pink Floyd's song "The Wall"?

◆ How could you develop a classroom where these assumptions are replaced by a different set of assumptions?

## 1.6  Two Quotes to Think About

From Mary Catherine Bateson's book *Peripheral Visions: Learning Along the Way*:

All too often those who can teach or lead with authority are armored against new learning, while those who are open to new learning are made diffident about expressing what they do know by the very fact that they deem it tentative. The best learners are children, not children segregated in schools but children at play, zestfully busy exploring their own homes, families, neighborhoods, languages, conjuring up possible and impossible worlds of imagination.... Some traditions emphasize this, expecting those who have leisure to fill it with explorations of the arts or natural history. (p. 73)

We reach for knowledge as an instrument of power, not as an instrument of delight, yet the preoccupation with power ultimately serves ignorance. The political scientist Karl Deutsch defined power as "the ability not to have to learn," which is exemplified by the failure of empathy in a Marie Antoinette or the rejection of computer literacy by an executive. Ironically, in our society both the strongest, those who have already succeeded, and the weakest, those who feel destined for failure, defend themselves against new learning. (p. 75)

- So, what do you think?
- Where do I, you, we fit within these perspectives?
- How do we, as a people in this society, view learning?
- How do children in our experiences view learning?
- What are the implications for how we can teach (or rather, create learning opportunities for children)?

*Chapter 2*
# Initial Explorations

It may seem paradoxical, but the first thing you need to do when learning how to teach science is to have fun. Our previous experiences with science in school may have involved a lot of memorization–a dry textbook–and lecture-oriented approach to learning. Our laboratory experiences may have required that we perform experiments and write lab reports that confirmed the predetermined correct answer. This book hopes to provide you with an alternative approach to teaching science. The first step to taking a different view of science involves engaging in some activities that will allow you to experience science in a new way. In fact, what you need to do is be a child again. You need to return to a perspective in which you see the world with curiosity and excitement.

The rest of this chapter is devoted to engaging in several activities that will allow you to explore science freely. As you engage in these activities, you need to reflect on the experiences as both a learner and a teacher. After each activity, a list of reflective questions will ask you to look at your experiences and the implications of these experiences from both perspectives (as learner and as teacher). Engaging in these activities will help you to develop a better sense of what *doing* science is like, how you can learn a great deal about your world from your own investigations, and, hopefully, how you can develop a higher comfort level with science and reinvigorate your curiosity.

Although these activities can be done alone, you may find that working in a group is very helpful and much more enjoyable. In fact, working in a group is highly recommended, since talking to others as you work allows each group member to build on each other's ideas and questions. After you have completed the activity in your group (or alone), you may want to do activities again with a group of children or an entire class. Listening to and watching the children explore each activity can provide you with a better sense of how children approach exploring and learning in science. Working with children also may provide an interesting comparison to your work in a group of adults.

## 2.1 Pond Water Investigation

Whether you live in a big city, the suburbs, or the country, you should be able to find a pond, lake, or stream. You will need to collect some pond water and bring it back to a place where you can examine it in more detail. The equipment you will need is listed below:

- A 4-l (1-gal) wide-mouthed glass jar (you can obtain these from restaurants that use pickles, hot peppers, etc.).
- A plastic or metal kitchen strainer with a handle about 20 to 25 cm. (8 to 10 in.) in diameter. This is optional; a strainer is very helpful but not necessary.
- An 8-l (2-gal) bucket with a handle.

When you arrive at the pond, fill the bucket with 3 l (3 qt) of pond water. Run the strainer through the pond, going through any plants that may be in the water. Do not be gentle about doing this. What you are trying to do is knock off any organisms that may be clinging to the plants. Empty the contents of your strainer into the bucket. You can run the strainer into the bottom of the pond. When you lift up the strainer, it may be full of muck, sand, and gravel. Before taking the strainer from the pond, hold the top of the strainer just above the surface of the water and shake it back and forth. You need to get most of the muck to pass through the strainer. When you have completed this step, empty the contents into the bucket. You also should pick up some rocks and hold them in the bucket. Rub across the rocks with your hand, then shake them vigorously in the bucket of water. Rubbing and shaking the rocks will dislodge small organisms (e.g., flatworms, hydra, and small arthropods) that are clinging to the rocks. Then, return the rocks to the pond. Take a handful of aquatic plants from the pond and shake them vigorously in the bucket of water to dislodge other organisms. Return the plants to the water. You can repeat shaking rocks and plants a few times. Pour the bucket of water, emptying the entire contents, into the jar. Finally, carefully pull a few of the aquatic plants from the pond (try to get the roots) and place them into the jar. Put the lid on the jar and take it back home or to school. When you arrive, you can loosen the lid of the jar to allow for some airflow, but prevent excessive evaporation.

**FIGURE 2.1**    **FIGURE 2.2**    **FIGURE 2.3**

**FIGURE 2.4**    **FIGURE 2.5**    **FIGURE 2.6**

Before exploring the contents of the jar, you should let it stand for at least a few hours, if not overnight, to allow the silt and mud to settle to the bottom. In the meantime, you can gather some of the other equipment you will need (see Figure 2.1 to Figure 2.6).

1. Magnifying glass
2. Small specimen dishes, petri dishes, or plastic margarine containers
3. A kitchen baster
4. Eye droppers
5. Forceps
6. A binocular dissecting scope (this scope and a compound microscope are optional, but very useful if you have access to them)

In contrast to many of the science activities you may have experienced in the past, this activity has very few guidelines. The task is to explore your jar of pond water. Summon up all of your curiosity and enthusiasm and see what you can discover. The following questions and pointers may help guide you through the activity:

■ Keep a written record of your comments and questions as you explore the pond water. You should write down all of your reactions and descriptive comments about what you see and discover. Taking detailed notes is helpful in order not to forget what you have observed and thought about as your study proceeds over time. You also will be able to track changes to the pond water envrionment, as well as your own thinking.

■ You probably will come up with many good questions as you work. Try to formulate some possible answers and explanations to these questions. Do not look in books for the answers. See if you can generate some plausible answers through your observations and any experiments you might be able to do.

■ You may feel a need to name the organisms. The tendency in our school experiences is to get the correct name. However, you may find it more enjoyable and more meaningful to develop your own names. Make these names descriptive of the organism. Even the

Latin and Greek names given by biologists, which are now referred to as the scientific names, are based on descriptive characteristics. For example, "amoeba" comes from the Greek word *amoibe*, which means "change" and "-a" refers to "having the characteristic of," so amoeba is a creature with the characteristics of changing shape or a "shape-changer" (what appears foreign and mysterious in scientific language is actually fairly accessible and simple, once you translate the Greek and Latin roots). In addition, you may want to make a quick sketch of each animal next to the name you have given it.

■ If you find that you would like to magnify an organism more than what you can do with one hand lens, try placing two or three together in layers. You may also find that putting the lens(es) right up against your eye and moving closer to the object will intensify your magnified experience.

■ Some of the following questions may help get you started, but do not feel limited to these questions: How do the organisms you see manage to survive? How are they adapted for their own way of life? How do they breathe (i.e., get air)? How do they get food? How do they move?

■ Where do they live in the pond (top, bottom, middle, throughout)? Why do they live in these areas? How are they adapted to live there? (How are they different from other organisms that live elsewhere in the pond? How are they similar to other organisms living in the same location? What is their role or niche in the ecosystem?)

For many people, the idea of handling or seeing organisms with which we are not too familiar results in feelings of aversion or disgust. Such reactions seem to be a fairly common and normal experience. However, many of these types of reactions tend to be a consequence of how we were socialized by our parents, teachers, and friends when we were children. In our society, both men and women tend to be socialized to react and behave in certain ways. It is especially unfortunate that many women (and some men) have been socialized to react negatively to a wide variety of our co-inhabitants of earth. The problem with such reactions is that we can continue to perpetuate such a socialization process. The result can be quite damaging to the young children we have as students in our classrooms, especially when we consider the very small number of girls and women who pursue science in high school and university. If you react adversely to "yucky" events in the classroom, you can influence the girls and boys. As a teacher, you are a very strong role model, so moving beyond these reactions is very important. The best way to move beyond these kinds of reactions is to engage continually in activities where you will confront the objects of your disdain. With time and patience, you will get used to such experiences and may even find them intensely interesting. Part of the responsibilities involved in becoming a member of the professional community of teachers is to examine how our actions and their underlying assumptions affect children. Our avoidance of

---

✳

✦ How did you react to this activity? Did you feel conflicted by previous expectations of doing science? Did you have any particular emotional reactions to mucking around in the pond water?

✦ Did you feel frustrated by the lack of structure of this activity? Or did you feel a sense of freedom to explore as you wish?

✦ Why do you think you felt the way you did by the activity?

✦ What questions did you generate? Could you come up with some plausible answers?

✦ What metaphors did you generate to describe or explain your observations?

✦ What did you find to be the most difficult part of the task?

✦ What did you find to be the best part of this activity?

✦ How do you think children would react to a similar activity?

✦ What further explorations of pond water would you like to do?

> **Example 2.1**
>
> You may think that you can simply avoid doing anything "yucky" in your own classroom. However, such a tactic may detract from your science program. In fact, what may happen is that the yucky activity will find you. Consider, for example, the following event that happened to a grade 1 teacher.
>
> The grade 1 teacher was in her classroom preparing for the children to arrive. As they entered the room, a little girl walked into the room with a dead cat cuddled in her arms. The girl brought the cat up to the teacher to show her.
>
> **STOP HERE: What would you do if this happened to you?**
>
> The teacher took the cat and placed it in a cardboard box and called to all of the children to sit in a circle on the carpet. She asked them if they thought the cat was dead, as the box was passed around the circle. Each child came up with an opinion and an explanation to support his or her claim. After each child had a chance to talk, they discussed the various points of view and decided that the cat was indeed dead. Then they discussed what they thought should be done. An agreement was reached to bury the cat, which they proceeded to do.

doing certain kinds of activities or reacting negatively to specific events can have a long-lasting effect on children. So, as we begin to enter our professional community, we can begin to address these concerns in ways that will allow us to have a more positive effect on children.

In Example 2.1, the teacher supported the children's curiosity and engaged them in a meaningful discussion of what one child had discovered. Although the discussion could have been extended in a number of possible directions, the teacher allowed the children to control the direction of this impromptu activity. In addition to how the teacher may have felt about the dead cat being brought into her classroom, she acted unfazed by this event and turned it into an inquiry activity. Although dead animals may present health risks, which are fairly minimal with most fresh road kills, you do need to be careful. You should have a supply of vinyl gloves or rubbing alcohol (for washing hands or for pouring over the animal), and make sure that if children handle a dead organism, they do not touch their faces before washing their hands with soap and water or alcohol. See Appendix A (Section A.1.8) for further safety information.

> When I took your class, I didn't like to touch worms or "creepy-crawlies." Now, since the initial activities we took part in [like those in this chapter], I have developed a reputation for being "the bug lady." In our own home we now have praying mantids, stick insects, toads, newts, crayfish, as well as worms, crickets, and the usual gerbils and

a budgie. Tomorrow, I am taking our latest "brood" of stick insects to school to give out to the children and teachers whom I have converted! Having a stick insect, for example, in the classroom has been very exciting. The students were at first very reluctant to have a stick insect walk on them, but soon were clamoring to have the experience! I "grossed out" many of my colleagues by carrying one around on my arm, but now they all want one! The students have developed a genuine curiosity, not to mention an appreciation for these and have generated some very good questions on their own. I guess I am trying to say that, by engaging in exactly this kind of unstructured activity and inquiry, I have discovered a passion for creatures that before I barely ever thought about. The activities opened many opportunities for me to help my students experience the joy of discovery, too!

**Alana Eaton, Alberta, grade 5 teacher**

## 2.2 Investigating Earthworms

This activity requires that you gather some earthworms to bring back to a place where you can observe them. When you go to collect earthworms, you need to bring along a small container (1 l/1 qt) and a shovel or small gardening spade (if you do not have a spade, a large spoon or even your hands will do the job quite nicely). Gently dig in a garden area. Put enough soil (best if mixed with some dead leaves) to fill half of your container. As you find earthworms, place them in the container. You only need a few, but the bigger they are, the better. When collecting the worms, you need to be careful not to break them in half. If an earthworm is partly visible in the soil, you can either dig around it so that the worm falls loosely into the hole you are digging or grasp one end of the worm and gently pull. If you feel resistance from the worm, do not pull too hard or it will tear apart. Just keep a gentle but firm pressure. It will eventually relax its hold and come loose.

If you plan on keeping your earthworms for more than a few days, you should place them in a larger container with a larger amount of your soil and leaf mixture. You also can add some dry oatmeal to the mixture. Keep the soil moist, but not soaking wet. In addition, it is best to keep your earthworms in a cool (preferably) not higher than 16°C/60°F), dark place. Your container for keeping the earthworms should have a tightly fitting lid with a few small holes punched in it.

The materials you will need to do this activity include the following:

■ Magnifying lenses
■ Moist paper towels
■ A shallow baking pan or similar container

As with the previous activity, you should feel free to investigate your own questions and follow your curiosity. Before you begin, there is one common misconception that should be addressed. Many people think that if you cut an earthworm in half, it will survive and grow into two earthworms. In fact, if you cut an earthworm in half, it will die. It may take some time, as both parts will continue to wriggle, but it will die. If you are concerned about killing your earthworms, you also should not keep them submerged in water for more than a very short period of time. They will drown. (Think about it: What do earthworms do during or after a rainstorm?) On the other hand, keeping them out of moist soil for more than 30 min can result in your worms drying out and dying. As you work with your earthworms, you should sprinkle or spray them with a little bit of water every 10 min or so. Other than these precautions, you should feel free to explore your earthworms in any way you wish.

Again, you should keep track of all your questions, comments, insights, and so forth, as you continue to explore. Some of the following questions may help you get started:

- How do the earthworms manage to move?
- How are they adapted for their own way of life?
- How do they breathe (i.e., get air)?
- How do they get food?
- What senses do they have?
- What types of environments do they prefer?
- What internal organs do they have (what can you see through their skin)?
- How do they communicate (if they can)?

As you generate questions, can you think of any experiments that will help you formulate answers? For instance, suppose you come up with a question such as, Do they prefer light or dark? How can you design a simple experiment to formulate an explanation? The idea here is to work through the process of how to find out answers to your questions. Throughout the process you should keep track of the difficulties you encounter and how you dealt with them. As you read through this book, you can refer back to your earlier notes to see where you had difficulties and how you may have been able to deal with them in different ways. Designing and doing experiments, along with keeping records of your questions and reflections on the experience, are very important in developing your skills as a teacher. However, the bottom line to everything we do involves children. So, in order to work effectively with children and their inquiries, it is essential that we have experienced the inquiries in which they will engage. By doing an earthworm investigation, for example, we will be able to help our students conduct a similar investigation more effectively. Such a process also allows you to experience the difficulties and successes in ways that children do. This kind of experience can be extremely valuable when you begin to engage children in similar sorts of investigations and activities. Your planning will be enriched greatly by your firsthand experiences with such activities.

- ✦ How did you react to this activity? Did you have any particular emotional reactions to working with and handling earthworms?
- ✦ Did you feel frustrated by the lack of structure of this activity? Or did you feel a sense of freedom to explore as you wish?
- ✦ Why do you think you felt the way you did about the activity?
- ✦ What questions did you generate? Did you come up with some plausible answers? What were the difficulties?
- ✦ What metaphors did you generate to describe or explain your observations?
- ✦ What did you find to be the most difficult part of the task?
- ✦ What did you find to be the best part (e.g., most engaging, etc.) of this activity?
- ✦ How do you think children would react to a similar activity?
- ✦ What further explorations of earthworms would you like to do?

The following activity requires finding an area where you can get into woods and fields. If you live in an urban area, finding such a location may be more difficult; however, a local park with a wooded area will do just fine. If you have difficulty finding a wooded area, you can still do this activity in any area with grass and plants.

The materials you should take with you include the following items, although you can do this with no extra materials at all.

- Hand lenses (magnifiers—more than one is useful if you want extra magnification)
- Small plastic containers with and without lids (e.g., empty margarine containers)
- Digging implements (e.g., trowel, spoon)
- A two-way magnifier (not essential, but a great tool)
- Magnifier boxes (square or cylindrical plastic boxes with a magnifier lid)

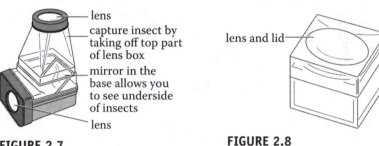

lens
capture insect by taking off top part of lens box
mirror in the base allows you to see underside of insects
lens

lens and lid

**FIGURE 2.7**

**FIGURE 2.8**

Although you may want to take this excursion on a warm, sunny day, going in any kind of weather can be a great deal of fun. Whatever the weather, you need to dress appropriately. If you plan to go on this trip after a rainstorm, you may want to bring along a large plastic garbage bag on which to sit and lie down. The only weather you may want to avoid are thunderstorms. With all of your materials in hand, you are ready for your trip. For a number of reasons, as explained earlier in this chapter, as well as for safety, you should do this activity with a group. The following points and questions will help you through the activity:

- As you walk through your field site, you should look for one or more of the following types of environments: a dense stand of evergreen or other types of trees; an open field with a dense covering of high grasses or low shrubs or both; an open, but heavily treed area.
- Choose one of these areas and find a place deep into the stand of trees or in the field.
- Lie down in a comfortable spot—you may feel somewhat resistant to this, but try to force yourself.

- Close your eyes, relax, and try to focus your attention on what you can hear, feel with your skin, and smell. Stay in this position for at least 4 or 5 min. (This activity is called *acclimatizing*.) More information on these types of activities can be found in Steve van Matre's books on earth education (see Appendix L).

- After this, stay in the same position, but open your eyes. Try to keep your focus on hearing, feeling, smelling, but add your vision to your experience. Remain in this position for several more minutes.

- You may find that you feel so relaxed that you want to do this for a longer period of time. Feel free to do so.

- If you did this in a wooded area, you may want to experience the contrast. Go to the field and try it again.

- Now that you have had a chance to introduce yourself to the local field site, take some time to explore the plants and animals around you. You may find it interesting to compare the plants and animals you find in an open field to those found in wooded areas.

- Explore freely, looking for whatever creatures or plants you find interesting.

- Keep track of your observations, questions, comments, explanations, and discoveries.

- Capture some insects or other creatures and look at them with various magnifying devices.

- Try developing explanations that answer the questions you ask. Some of the following questions may help get you started:
  - How are these organisms adapted to surviving in the habitat in which you found them?
  - How do organisms found under the surface of the soil differ from those on the surface of the soil or on tops of plants?
  - How do the organisms found in the field differ from those in the wooded areas?
  - How do these differences relate to the way they are adapted for survival in different habitats?
  - How are they adapted to finding and eating certain kinds of food?
  - How are they adapted for protection?
  - How are they adapted to moving in their habitats?

- Again, feel free to make sketches and develop your own descriptive names for the organisms you find.

## 2.4   Moon Study

This investigation involves a set of phenomena that are around us every day, but to which we rarely pay much attention. At the same time, the moon and its relationships to the earth and the sun are often misunderstood, which makes it all the more intriguing to study. In these investigations, you will

- ◆ What are your reactions to these experiences?
- ◆ How did your sensory experiences during these acclimatizing activities differ from how you ordinarily feel walking through such areas?
- ◆ Did you feel more "in touch" with your environment during and after these experiences?
- ◆ How do you think children would react to such experiences?
- ◆ In what other ways could you do these or similar acclimatizing activities? Can you think of any ways of adapting these activities?

- ◆ What discoveries did you make?
- ◆ Were you able to come up with plausible explanations for the questions you asked?
- ◆ How did this process compare to other field trips you have taken as part of a science course?
- ◆ How did you feel as a participant in this activity versus other field trips you have taken?
- ◆ Can you describe how different aspects of this type of field study result in different reactions from participants? Did you feel more in control? Why? Did you generate more ideas, questions, and explanations than in other types of field trips? Why? How do you think children would respond to such an approach?

need to devote a little bit of time every day to make and record observations, then spend some time trying to make sense of your observations. In addition, you should keep a log of what you experience psychologically and record analytical reflections about your experiences (see Chapter 10 for help with analytical reflection). So, while you will learn a great deal about the moon, earth, and sun relationships, you also will gain a great deal of insight into the experience of science (i.e., how science works, what scientists experience in doing science, etc.). The next chapter on the nature of science may help you make more sense of what you experience (e.g., frustration, anger, joy, insights, tedium, and so forth).

In order to conduct this investigation, you may find it helpful to have the following materials:

- A clipboard with paper or a notebook
- A pen or pencil (a yellow-colored pencil may be nice to use as well)
- A compass (or an ability to find the North Star)
- A clinometer (or make one with a protractor, piece of cardboard, string, and paper clips—see Appendix I for instructions)
- Graph paper (this is not absolutely necessary, but you may want to construct some graphs)
- Modeling clay or three balls of different sizes (Styrofoam balls are great, and they can be mounted on stands or hung from string or wires)
- Flashlight or other light source

As you proceed with your study, try to *avoid looking up answers to questions* in books or on the Internet (you can do this when you have completed the investigation). In a way, this study is one of personal discovery. The real power of engaging in this activity involves how you make sense of your observations and other data you collect, and especially how you reconcile what you see in the data with what you have previously believed (or currently believe) to be true.

### 2.4.1 General Guidelines

1. When you see the moon in the early evening, go out to make observations at exactly the same time for at least three nights in a row.
2. Spend 5 to 10 min every day making observations. To get a more complete understanding, do this for at least four weeks.
3. Develop a data collection sheet you can print out or copy for each observation. You may want to include the following categories:
   - Moon and sun rise and set times (which you can find from a local newspaper or at a variety of online sites).
   - Drawing of the moon showing phase (yellow pencil is good for this) and location of distinctive features (e.g., craters, mountains). Include an estimate of how much of the moon is visible, which you can record as a percentage.

- A drawing showing where the moon is in relation to easily identifiable star formations.
- Moon's position as an estimated angle from the eastern horizon. Use your clinometer for this or estimate using your arm to point at the moon (90° is where your arm is pointing straight up), while you are facing south.
- Other observations.
- Working explanations of and models that explain the data you are collecting.
- Personal experiences and analytical reflections.

4. Ask lots of questions (beyond those listed below) and investigate them.

### 2.4.2  Questions to Investigate

- In which direction does the moon move around the earth?
- How do the phases of the moon occur?
- What happens to the face of the moon during the month? (Does the face of the moon always face the earth? Does it always face the sun? Does it face different directions at different times?)
- How long is a lunar day?

### 2.4.3  Collecting and Analyzing Data

The data you collect can provide the information necessary to answer the questions above, as well as other questions you may ask along the way.

1. **Using the clinometer:**
   - When you see the moon, use a compass or find the North Star and turn your back to it so that you face south.
   - Hold the clinometer at arm's length in front of you so that the middle hole along the base of the protractor is at eye level. Make sure the paper clip on the string that hangs from this middle hole is aligned with the vertical line below the hole.
   - Move the other paper clip on a string so that it lines up with the position of the moon. You probably have to visualize a line extending from the paper clip, since the moon may be higher than the string or may be slightly behind you.
   - Look at where the string crosses the lines (that indicate degrees) on the protractor, then record that number on your data collection sheet as the moon's position in degrees from east. If it is dark out and you cannot see the lines and numbers on the protractor, hold the string in place against the protractor, then go to a light source to read the number of degrees.
   - Collect this data at exactly the same time for three days in a row.

2. **Drawing a sky map of the moon and nearby stars:**
   - With a clipboard and paper or a notebook, face south, then move to the east or west as necessary to face the moon. Indicate the direction on your star map sketch. Draw dots for the stars (bigger dots can represent brighter stars). Add a sketch of the moon, in relationship to a particular pattern of stars. It is helpful to use stars that will be easily recognizable from night to night, and which may point to the moon or be located near the moon.
   - On the following one or two nights, go out with your original sky map and draw the moon in relation to the original pattern of stars.
   - Be sure to put the date (and time, too) next to the moon for each observation.
   - You may find it helpful to make your moon sketches as accurate as possible to show the phase (how much of the moon is visible and which way the points of the crescent go).

3. **The more data you can collect, the better:**
   - Although there are a few questions provided as initial starting points, other questions may arise as you make observations and begin analyzing and making sense of the data. So, the more data you have, the more information you will have at your disposal.

4. **Analyzing your data:**
   - Devise approaches to make sense of your data. The process is much like doing logic puzzles, but your big challenge may involve conflicts between what the data suggest and what you have always believed to be true. Try a variety of approaches, including graphs, charts, sketches, and so forth.

5. **Generating explanations and models:**
   - One of the most important aspects of doing science has to do with generating a number of *possible explanations* from your data and with developing *models* that demonstrate a particular phenomenon in ways that are consistent with the data. In fact, you may find it very interesting to develop a model of the sun, earth, and moon based on your previously existing beliefs, and then compare it with a model that explains your data.
   - Try making models with a light source (flashlight or lamp) as the sun and different size balls or modeling clay balls as the earth and moon. Other types of models can include sets of drawings, graphs, or charts of sun and moon rise and set times, and so forth.

### 2.4.4 Other Questions to Ponder and Explore

- How fast is the moon traveling? (Find the average distance between the earth and the moon.)

- If you live near the ocean or any tidal waters, compare the sun and moon rise and set times to the data from a local tide table. Is there a correlation between the positions of the sun and moon and high and low tides? When are the high tides the highest?

- Look up information on our moon and the moons of other planets in our solar system: their masses, the distances from their home planet, the speed of their revolution (which could be calculated from the distance from the planet and the length of time to complete one revolution). Is there a relationship between the moons' speeds and distances? Is there a relationship between the mass and speed or between the mass and distance?

- How is the cycle of the moon similar to cycles in our everyday lives, in mechanical systems (like those in cars and mechanical toys), in social systems and settings, in a school day or year, and in literature? Why are there cycles (what do cycles do)?

## 2.5  Exploring Light, Lenses, Mirrors

For those of us who can see, we rely very heavily on light. We use lenses in a variety of ways (from those in our eyeballs to those in glasses and contact lenses and those in cameras, movie projectors, binoculars, telescopes, microscopes, and hand lenses). We use mirrors for our everyday personal care and in microscopes, telescopes, and technical equipment. Dentists and mechanics use mirrors to see in areas not directly visible. The extent of how light behaves, how it affects our behavior, how it influences animal behavior, and how we use and manipulate light is far reaching. A whole book or even books could be devoted to exploring light. However, in the exploration below, we will touch on a few aspects of light that can be studied with rather simple and readily available materials.

Before beginning, gather together the materials you will need to investigate light. The items with an asterisk (*) are the most essential items these materials include.

- One or more hand lenses*—Ideally two or three of the same size and one or more of different sizes.
- One or more mirrors*—One or more flat mirrors are essential, plus a concave or convex mirror (makeup mirrors are concave; junkyards may have right-side car mirrors that are convex).
- Ruler*—Preferably a 30-cm. (metric) ruler or a 12-in. ruler.
- Paper or notebook*—Graph paper may be helpful as well.
- Candles*—Birthday candles (larger ones may be useful, too).
- Stopwatch or wristwatch.*
- Protractor.*
- Container(s)*—At least 10 cm. (4 in.) deep and at least 15 cm. (6 in.) wide.
- Flashlight.

- ✦ What kinds of emotional reactions did you have during this study? Do scientists encounter the same types of emotional reactions during their work? Ask a scientist. How do they deal with these emotions? How did you deal with these emotional reactions?

- ✦ What difficulties did you encounter? How did you approach (or not) these difficulties? How do such difficulties relate to the process of doing science? How can such difficulties add to activities and discussions in the classroom?

- ✦ How did this activity help you learn about the moon, the earth, and the sun? What ideas of yours about the moon changed by engaging in this activity? What did it feel like to encounter data that conflicted with your previously held ideas? How did your learning differ from that gained from textbook and lecture approaches?

- Aluminum foil, fairly rigid cardboard, and glue (spray type) can be used to make a simple mirror—Spray glue on a square of cardboard, then carefully place aluminum (shiny side up) on the cardboard. Use a roller or smooth, straight object to try to make a smooth surface of aluminum foil (you may want to try a second "mirror" using the dull side of the aluminum).
- A variety of lenses—Scrounge for discarded lenses from optical manufacturers and opticians and from discarded cameras, telescopes, binoculars, microscopes, etc.
- A variety of mirrors—Scrounge from junkyards (car mirrors) and trash piles (discarded home mirrors). Ask home and auto glass stores for discarded or defective mirrors; remove mirrors from discarded toys, SLR cameras, and so forth. You can cut glass and mirrors using a glass cutter that can be purchased from a hardware store (or have them cut the mirror for you). Be sure to use duct tape or another type of heavy tape to cover the edges.

### 2.5.1 General Guidelines

- The activities below are starting points. You should try your own variations, ask questions, and try to investigate these questions (What if I tried …? is a great type of question to explore).
- Take notes, record your data, keep track of insights and questions, generate possible explanations, and sketch possible models.
- Keep notes on the difficulties you encounter and your emotional reactions and other experiences.

### 2.5.2 Explorations

**1. Hand lenses:**
- Go outside into the sunlight on an area of dirt, asphalt, or cement, or take along a ceramic plate or metal tray. Place a piece of paper on the ground or in the plate or tray (if it is windy, hold down the paper with a rock or two). Take along a glass or bottle of water (to extinguish fires).
  - Use one hand lens to focus the sunlight on the paper and wait until it starts burning.
  - Try this again, but measure the time it takes to start burning.
  - Try again and measure the distance between the paper and the hand lens, when the light is focused sharply on the paper.
  - Do this with different size hand lenses. Or, if you have two hand lenses of the same size, hold or tape them together and repeat the previous steps.
  - Make a sketch of your setups and record your data.
  - What patterns are evident from your data?
- Place a coin or other small object on a table. Hold a hand lens over the object so that it is in focus. Measure the object as it

appears through the lens, then measure the actual object. How much is the object magnified?

- Measure the distance between the hand lens and the object, when it is in focus.
- Now, repeat the same procedure by placing two hand lenses together. If you have different size hand lenses, try these procedures with them. Try putting three hand lenses together and repeating.
- What patterns do you see in the data you have collected? What do these patterns suggest about how hand lenses work? How are these patterns similar to those collected when you set paper on fire?

■ Set up a mirror so that some object is visible in the mirror. If you were to use a hand lens to focus on the object in the mirror, how far away do you think you would need to hold the hand lens?

- Use a hand lens to focus on the object in the mirror. Measure the distance from the mirror to the hand lens and from the mirror to the object.
- Try changing the distance between the object and the mirror. Does this distance make any difference?
- How can you explain your results?

**2. Mirrors:**

■ Go outside into the sunlight and about 20 or 30 m (or yards) from the side of a building where you can place the mirror on the ground and support it with a rock or book. Adjust the position of the mirror so that the sun reflects against the side of the building.

- Observe the sun's reflection on the side of the building.
- What do you notice?
- Stand with your back to the sun and watch your shadow.
- Do you see your shadow move?
- How can you explain the difference between the movement of the sun's reflection and the movement of your shadow?

■ Put a piece of paper on the top of a table, then prop up a mirror on top of the paper and place an object to the right or left of the mirror and nearer to you from the plane of the mirror. Position yourself so that you can see the object in the mirror. Now, place another object directly in line between you (using one eye will be helpful) and the reflection of the object in the mirror. With this object in place, look down the line and place a pencil mark on the paper directly below where you see the object in the mirror. Move over to the original object, then line up this object with the reflection of the other object and place a pencil mark directly below where you see the object in the mirror. (See Figure 2.9.)

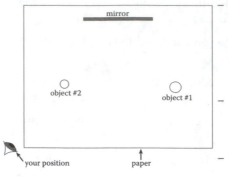

**FIGURE 2.9**

- Using the mirror (without moving it), draw a line along the bottom of the mirror (so that you have a line representing the plane of the mirror).
- Using a ruler, draw lines from the middle of each object to the marks you drew below the mirror.
- Use a protractor to measure the angle between the line from object 1 to the point marked below the mirror. Repeat this measurement for object 2.
  - What is the relationship between the angles?
  - Try moving the objects to different positions and repeat the process.
  - What pattern or principle can you construct that shows this relationship?
- Can you position several mirrors in a way that you can see an infinite (or at least a large) number of reflections of a particular object?
- Can you make a spy scope out of mirrors, cardboard, and other materials to look around corners or over walls?

3. **Refraction:**
   - Fill a container with water, then place a coin in the middle. Look directly down at the coin, then move to an angle. Does the position of the coin appear to change? Repeat this, but use a ruler to line up your line of vision with where you see the coin in each position.
     - After observing the coin from an angle, hold the ruler in place, then return to looking at where the coin is from above. Draw a sketch as seen from the side. When you make the following measurements, it may be helpful to have a partner do the actual measurements. If you can, use your protractor to measure the angle between the plane of the surface of the water and the line from where your eye is to where you see the coin from an angle (use the ruler to show the line). Then, without moving from your original position, have your partner line up the ruler between the coin's actual position and your eye, then measure the angle between the plane of the water's surface and the ruler. Add these angle measurements to your sketch.
     - What is the difference between the two angles (coin as observed and actual position of the coin)? Try taking measurements from different angles. What pattern do you see in the data? How can you explain your results?

- How do these results compare to those you obtained with the mirrors?

**4. Candles:**

- Find a place (probably outside) at night where it is as dark as possible. Place a candle in a clear glass container and light it. Place the container with the lit candle on the ground.
  - How far away will you have to go before you can no longer see the light from the candle?
  - If you do not know the distance of your normal walking stride, mark where the toe of one shoe is, then take a normal step and mark where the toe of the other shoe is. Measure the distance between the two marks. Now, start walking away from the candle in a straight line, while counting the number of paces.
  - Did this distance surprise you? How can you explain your results?
  - Does the size of the candle make a difference? Does the amount of darkness (or the amount of ambient light) make a difference?
  - Repeat this during the day. Are your results the same? Develop an explanation for your results.
  - Try setting up a series of mirrors in a completely dark hallway or room. Measure the distances between the mirrors to re-create the distances you measured outside. Place a candle opposite a mirror, then sit in various locations so that you can still see the candle in the mirrors. Can you determine how far away you need to be before you can no longer see the light of the candle in mirrors?

- ✦ As you worked through these activities, what kinds of reactions did you have to the experience? How did these reactions compare to those of the previous activities?
- ✦ Were the nature of the difficulties and problems encountered in these activities similar to those encountered in the previous activities? How did you deal with these difficulties? Do scientists confront similar problems?
- ✦ Did you come up with additional questions to investigate? How did you go about investigating these questions?

## 2.6 Summary

Hopefully, the activities in this chapter have introduced you to a new and enjoyable way of exploring science. Although these activities are relatively unstructured, they allow you to take control over what you are interested in exploring and over the ideas and explanations generated. Take some time to critically reflect on how your experiences with this approach affected your learning and your attitudes toward science. Taking a less structured approach to doing science allows for children's creativity to emerge, as well as allows for them to follow a more genuine or more authentic approach to science. A more genuine approach follows questions that arise during the inquiry process. Following such questions not only is more genuine or authentic, but also allows children to develop a sense of ownership over the inquiry and the ideas that arise from their investigations. Throughout the rest of the book you will be exposed to a number of similar approaches (of varying structure); however, all of these approaches have certain principles in common.

- ✦ How do you think curiosity (from emerging questions) can drive your curriculum? How can you organize or structure your classroom to stimulate curiosity and support children's curiosity and their continued inquiry?

- ✦ It is important to communicate (verbally and in one's actions) to students that curiosity is valued and that children need to follow their curiosity in exploring and investigating their questions. What do you need to do to communicate these expectations? What specific actions do you need to do repeatedly and with consistency to communicate these expectations?

- ✦ Even though we may share an understanding of what curiosity is on a superficial level, it may be surprising to find that we may not have a clearly defined idea of curiosity, and that different people may have different ideas about curiosity. Ask others (colleagues, fellow students, children, scientists, artists, etc.) what they think curiosity is. Develop a list of all of your and others' ideas. After you have developed this list, think about the implications this list has for how you teach and how you can stimulate, support, and take advantage of children's curiosity.

- ✦ Now that we have developed a better understanding of curiosity, reflect on your own curiosity. How did curiosity manifest when you were a young child (if you can remember specific instances)? How did it manifest during your high school and university years? Did specific teachers or schooling, in general, stimulate and support your curiosity? If so, how? If not, how?

- ✦ As a teacher, you need to be curious about all subjects, about your own teaching and identity as a teacher, and about children (how they learn, how they think, children's difficulties and strengths, etc.). What is the current status of your curiosity? (Are you curious about anything? What do you do about it?) How can you restimulate and value your own curiosity?

The notion of taking ownership over ideas and the direction of investigations is one of these common principles. These beginning activities have allowed you to experience this principle. As adults, we can react to such activities in a variety of ways, including aversion, frustration (e.g., feeling a need for more structure and getting the correct answers), and so forth. Young children may not react this way, while older children may react in ways similar to adults. Most schooling seems to socialize people into expecting that learning situations must be structured, controlled by the teacher, and focused on getting the correct answer. In order to change such expectations among your own students, you may have to make your new expectations very clear, then patiently persevere and persist in such an approach until you have resocialized your students.

# Part II
## Teaching Science for Children's Meaningful Learning

*Chapter 3*
# The Nature of Science

- ✦ How have you experienced curiosity?
- ✦ Do schools promote and support children's curiosity?
- ✦ What are you curious about now?

Curiosity calls attention to interesting, odd, and sometimes important items in the drama that is revealed to us through our senses. Idle, or purposeful, curiosity is the motor that interests children in science; it is also the principal motor that energizes and steers the education of professional scientists and conduct of their subsequent scientific work.

—**Herbert Simon (2001, p. 5)**

- ✦ How would you explain what science is?
- ✦ What is the purpose of science?
- ✦ What does a scientist look like? Make a quick sketch.
- ✦ What do scientists do?
- ✦ How would you differentiate between science and technology? How are they related?
- ✦ From what sources have you developed your understanding of the nature of science and scientists?
- ✦ How have these sources affected your perceptions of science?
- ✦ How do schools portray science?

The task of teaching science needs to go beyond a formula or textbook-based approach. Such a task requires that we stimulate children to explore, explain, theorize, and test their explanations and theories. In order to create such a science program in our classrooms, we need to develop some understanding of the nature of science, so that we can represent science in ways that are more authentic. The intent here is to make science more relevant and accessible to teachers and children by making connections to how science works and how it affects and is affected by society. However, before we delve into a discussion of the nature of science, it may be useful to explore our own ideas of what science is and who scientists are. Take a few minutes to think about some of the questions listed in the sidebar before proceeding.

## 3.1 Introduction

Throughout our lives we are bombarded with information and images of science. We hardly go through a day without hearing or seeing some reference to science. When we watch TV, we see advertisements, news stories, and programs that refer to science in some way. We read newspapers and magazines that refer to science. Our school experiences, especially in science classes, have portrayed science in certain ways. All of these experiences and more have contributed to our understanding of what science is.

What are some of these messages and images of science? In advertisements, we hear that "scientists have proven" that some product is effective. On news programs, we hear about a new scientific discovery or about some problem about which a scientist is interviewed. On other programs, we may see scientists depicted in certain ways: in lab coats, as "mad" scientists, as highly intelligent, and so forth. Some television programs, such as *CSI*, will talk about how the evidence proves someone's guilt or innocence, or will have one character ask a colleague if he or she has a theory (not a hypothesis). In school, most of us have experienced an overwhelmingly large and unfamiliar vocabulary or language of science. We have had to memorize volumes of facts. Laboratory exercises have focused on confirming what our teachers have told us to expect. We have had to follow the scientific method and write laboratory reports based on each step of this process. All of these messages from the media and through school affect how we understand the nature of science and scientists.

Research into people's, including children's, ideas of science has shown many misconceptions about what science is and how it works. We see science as a body of knowledge—facts, laws, theories, and so forth. This body of knowledge is often seen as a static and unchanging set of truths. We see science as accessible only to a few very intelligent people. We may even see science as having an inside track on the "truth." If a scientist says something is true, then it must be so. Furthermore, the scientific method is portrayed as the one way scientists work. They formulate a problem, generate hypotheses, design an experiment, test their hypotheses, and make conclusions. We see science as an objective enterprise. The scientists' method allows them to describe some aspect of nature without human bias. In addition, science describes an external reality that exists apart from the human experience. Do all of these perspectives accurately describe the nature of science?

What is the nature of science? This question is difficult to answer, because it continues to be a hotly debated issue. However, for the purposes of this book and of teaching science in the elementary school, we can take a more general look at science and scientists. The following section provides some key ideas, which may shed some light on how science works and the many ways in which it can be defined.

## 3.2  The Nature of Science

As we read through the following points, we should keep in mind that some members of the scientific community may not agree with all of these characteristics. We also should think about how these points have or have not been depicted in our own experiences with science in school. In addition, we also need to ponder how we can translate these points into our own approach to teaching science.

- **Science is subjective; there is no objective truth**. Many scientists may find this statement goes against the grain of what they believe. We often hear of how science provides us with a view of objective truth; however, we are all inescapably human. We bring to our inquiry our own set of biases, preconceptions, and assumptions.

  There is no objective experience.... All experience is subjective.[1]

- **All observation is based on theory—scientists see what they believe**. Scientists enter into inquiry with a knowledge of particular theoretical frameworks. Their observations are based on what they already know. The same holds true for everyone. We see what we expect to see, or we see things in terms of our prior knowledge and beliefs. (See Example 3.1.)

- **Science is a social enterprise**. Scientists do not work in a vacuum. They interact with peers in their workplace, at conferences and meetings, and through publications in journals. Within this context, scientists argue about each other's claims and experimental results.

---

**Example 3.1**

A population (i.e., evolutionary) biologist was working along the shoreline of one of the Galapagos Islands. He noticed two snails mating; however, the two snails appeared to be two completely different species. "What's going on?" he wondered. In his understanding of the definition of species, he believed that members of a species usually only mate with individuals of the same species, and that only individuals of the same species can produce fertile offspring. His observation was immediately couched in his previous theoretical knowledge. After careful observation over the next few weeks, these two very different snails produced fertile offspring. What this scientist found was not an earthshaking revolution in the theory, but that the two snails were in fact members of the same species. Each snail grew and lived in different locations along the tidal and subtidal zones. The change in their shapes was due to the influence of where they grew from the time they were born. The scientific term for this phenomenon is *phenotypic plasticity* (i.e., the ability of an organism to change its external, visible characteristics during development based on external conditions).

---

Scientists do not always reach a consensus; however, certain claims reach the status of accepted knowledge through the consensus of a smaller, but usually more politically powerful, set of peers.

■ **Science is embedded in a social and political context**. Scientists operate within the social and political context of their times. Grants are approved or rejected by government agencies, private foundations, and corporations, which have their own political agendas; therefore, the focus of research is affected by the agendas of the granting agencies.

Science is always influenced by society, but it operates under a strong constraint of fact as well. The Church eventually made its peace with Galileo because, after all, the earth does go around the sun. In studying the genetic components of such complex human traits as intelligence and aggressiveness, however, we are freed from the constraint of fact, for we know practically nothing. In these questions, "science" follows (or exposes) the social and political influences acting upon it.[2]

■ **Science cannot prove anything; it can only disprove something**. The notion of proof is one of the most common misconceptions about science. Scientists can support their claims with a great deal of observational and experimental evidence, but they cannot make the statement that they have proven something. On the other hand, when scientists produce enough evidence to contradict a previously held knowledge claim, they can *disprove* that claim.

Science never proves anything.... Science sometimes *improves* hypotheses and sometimes *disproves* them. But *proof* would be another matter and perhaps never occurs.... Science *probes*; it does not prove.[3]

■ **Scientific knowledge is tentative and can change**. Because science cannot prove anything, all knowledge is viewed as tentative. Although some fact or theory may have wide acceptance today, there is always the possibility, at some point in the future, that a new explanation will be formulated to replace the previously held knowledge.

■ **Science is based on certain assumptions or beliefs that what we observe is true**. As human beings, we have limited perceptual abilities. We already know that dogs can hear higher frequencies than humans. We only see a certain range of wavelengths of light. We can see only difference or change at a certain frequency of occurrence. When we watch a film or television, we see the rapid succession of still frames at 16 frames or more per second. We do not see the single frames. Instead, we perceive smooth motion. Are there other phenomena that we cannot perceive, of which we cannot even

◆ **Can you think of any examples of how science is a social enterprise or how it is influenced by social and political factors?**

conceive? This element of doubt is the basis for this claim that science is based on a certain set of beliefs or assumptions. We assume that what we perceive is true. Ultimately, we come to realize that all knowledge is tentative and cannot be proven.

- **Basically, there are two types of science**: (a) *normal science*, which extends our knowledge of and supports existing theoretical domains (the most common), and (b) *revolutionary science*, which develops explanations that overthrow previously entrenched theoretical frameworks and builds new theoretical frameworks. Most scientists in their day-to-day work operate within a normal science framework. They add new knowledge of cells to the existing framework of cell theory or elaborate on an existing explanation of a chemical process. Occasionally, a scientist may find evidence that contradicts the basis of an existing theoretical framework. Over time, this evidence and additional evidence produced by other scientists will lead to the overthrowing of the previously accepted theoretical framework.

- **Science is a process of inquiry**. Science can be seen as a body of knowledge only because of its process. Scientists inquire into the nature of how the world works, whether that is how the brain functions or how the universe came to be. Through inquiry, scientists construct principles, laws, and theories to explain our phenomenal world.

- **There is no one scientific method**. All through our school careers, we read in textbooks and hear from teachers a description of the scientific method. In fact, scientists approach their inquiry in many different ways. Some scientists may spend a great deal of time "playing" around with ideas and the objects of their inquiry. Questions may arise, which may be followed by more formal experiments or observations. Formal hypotheses may or may not be generated. Scientists may spend a lot of their time devising experimental apparatus to enable them to test some idea. They may go back and forth between creatively fantasizing about some phenomena, in an attempt to describe some of the possible explanations, and more formal experiments. However, it seems that reputable scientists try to conduct inquiry based on rigorous methodology that can produce repeatable and accurate results (i.e., reliable and valid).

- **Science relies on observation, experimentation, and logical or rational thinking**. As is evident from the previous discussions, scientists rely on formalized observation, such as in field settings, and experiments to generate data. The data are then analyzed and interpreted in terms of enhancing a particular theoretical framework or in terms of constructing a new theoretical framework. Some theoretical scientists, however, may never step into a laboratory or a field setting. Much of what these scientists do is in the form of thought experiments. One of the best known of these theoretical scientists was Albert Einstein. He formulated the theory of relativity

- ✦ **Can you think of any other scientific revolutions, where one way of understanding phenomena was replaced at least partially by another?**
- ✦ **Have you gone through a similar process of changing from one set of beliefs (about anything) to another? What led to the change? How did it feel?**

**Example 3.2**

Until the early part of the 16th century, Ptolemy's explanation of planetary motion, developed in the 2nd century, was accepted as truth. The earth was the center of the universe and everything revolved around it, including the sun. The stars were in a celestial sphere. In the 16th century, Copernicus became dissatisfied with this theory. The measurement of planetary motion, based on Ptolemy's theory, over the past few centuries showed a discrepancy. In order to come up with a more predictable mathematical model of planetary motions, Copernicus placed the sun at the center of the universe with the planets, including earth, revolving around it in circular orbits. He still believed in the celestial sphere, but his new theory of planetary motion led to the eventual overthrow of Ptolemy's explanatory theory. Of course, Copernicus seemed to be greatly concerned with being ridiculed by other scholars of his time, as well as with the reaction of the Church, which held humankind (and therefore the earth) to be at the center of the universe. We can see how Copernicus hedged his bets by referring to a number of historical sources to support his argument for a sun-centered universe:

At rest, however, in the middle of everything is the Sun. For in this most beautiful temple, who would place this lamp in another or better position than that from which it can light up the whole thing at the same time? For the Sun is not inappropriately called by some people the lantern of the universe, its mind by others, and its ruler by others. [Hermes] the Thrice Great labels it a visible god, and Sophocles's Electra, the all-seeing.[4]

Refinements to the Copernican theory continued within the framework of normal science over the next three centuries, and still continue to date.

**Notes**

**Ptolemy** was a Greek astronomer and geographer, who was born where Egypt is now in about 85 A.D. He has been given credit for the development of the notion that the earth is the center of the universe and solar system, with all of the planets and the sun revolving around the earth.

**Copernicus** (the Latin form of his Polish name, Kopernik, which he adopted later in his life) was born in Poland in 1473. In the early 1500s, he proposed a view of the solar system and universe, which countered the prevailing Ptolemaic view. This new view stated that the sun is the center of the solar system and that there is no one center of the universe (he had other, more specific explanations as well).

through a process of thought experiments using mathematical models. In the case of paleontologists who study fossils, they cannot do experiments. Instead, they rely on the historical evidence found in rocks and fossils. Their work is based on extracting clues to past life and the evolutionary development of species from the fossil record.

- **Scientists formulate explanations and theories, based on factual information, to explain phenomena**. As we have seen, the goal of scientists is to formulate explanations and theories that explain some phenomenon. Theories are not vague ideas of how something works; they are highly structured explanatory frameworks based on accumulated evidence from experiments and observations. They are frameworks in that they organize current interpretations of data in ways that provide consistent understandings. However, people commonly equate the notion of theory with belief. In contrast, beliefs are personal, social, cultural, or religious frameworks of understanding that are based on personal experiences and interpretations, or on some sense of faith. This faith may be based on some authority (e.g., God, gods, or some person). From a certain perspective, science is based on belief, which involves a belief that what we observe through experiments or rigorous observations is true. However, the difference between the belief structure underlying scientific theories and personal, cultural, or religious beliefs is that science relies on reliable and valid evidence as the basis for scientific theories. For instance, the theory of evolution is based on a vast amount of geological and fossil evidence, as well as on experiments with heredity and population biology. On the other hand, cultural and religious beliefs are based on a combination of faith and historical teachings and writings. It is interesting that evolution is a controversial issue in the United States, and to a lesser degree in Canada, but other scientific theories tend to be accepted, such as cell theory, gene theory (a critical basis for evolutionary theory), theory of gravity, and so forth.

- **Science is one of many ways of explaining the world**. Many other ways of explaining the world exist, such as art, religion, and poetry. Also, various cultural groups have ways of explaining the world. Each way of explaining the world is powerful within the particular social and cultural context. Science is extremely useful in explaining phenomena in an industrialized and technological society. Art and poetry are extremely useful in explaining the realm of human emotional, aesthetic, and social experience. Cultural beliefs and religions are extremely useful in providing a framework for personal and social action and for a personal sense of well-being.

- **Scientists are "normal" human beings with the same range of intelligence as any other educated professional**. Our experiences in science courses, when almost everything coming from the teacher's mouth sounds like a foreign language, begin to make us feel marginalized in

We need to consider the difference between understanding or knowledge and belief. The controversy over evolution seems to be based on some sense that understanding evolution is a threat to one's religious beliefs, or that knowledge can threaten belief. Evolution is the fundamental framework that holds together all of biology and geology.

- ✦ If our intent is to help children develop understandings of science, then not studying the fundamental theoretical frameworks of science will prevent them from developing accurate understandings. What are the implications of this statement for how we need to approach science teaching?
- ✦ Does there need to be a conflict between science and religion? Can we ask children to understand science without asking them to change their own beliefs?

- ✦ Is there any one truth?
- ✦ Is any one of these ways of knowing and explaining better than any other?

the area of science. This feeling can be reinforced by our experiences of hearing scientists speak on news programs and other shows. Science can seem so inaccessible. We react either with awe, "Oh, they're very smart; they must know the right answers to this problem," or with disregard, "Yeah, they're just pulling the wool over everyone's eyes; they don't really know what the problem is; I don't believe a word they're saying." In school, many of us have been pushed to the fringes, where we either hate science or feel very anxious about taking a science course. These reactions are unfortunate, because, in fact, science is accessible and can be a great deal of fun. Many of the people who have become scientists have found science to be intriguing and stimulating. Such people, however, are not necessarily more intelligent than anyone else. Maybe they have good memory skills and find it easy to learn the vocabulary. Or maybe they have found something so interesting in science that they manage to survive the dreadful course work. If we take away the content-specific language, science becomes much more accessible. Many nonscientists (i.e., people not trained in science) have made remarkable contributions to the field. Gregor Mendel (the father of genetics) was a farmer, turned teacher, turned monk. David Levy (a Canadian with a degree in English) co-discovered what is now known as the Shoemaker-Levy 9 comet. Susan Hendrickson (a high school dropout and female version of the fictional Indiana Jones) has a fossil dinosaur skeleton named after her (Tyrannosaurus Sue) (see http://www.pbs.org/wgbh/nova/orchid/amateurs.html for additional examples). A group of high school children in a poor suburban Phoenix school designed an underwater robot. They entered their robot, not in the high school division, but in the university division of the 2004 Marine Advanced Technology Education Center Remotely Operated Vehicle Competition. They won first prize and beat engineering students from MIT and other universities (see http://www.npr.org/templates/story/story.php?storyId=4603454).

■ **Scientists are subject to biases and ways of thinking similar to anyone else.** This point relates to the common idea that science is objective. In fact, scientists bring with them all of their human biases, emotions, and values. All of these factors influence the way scientists work, the problems they choose, the design of their experiments, and their explanations of the data. As we have seen in the example of Ptolemy and Copernicus, both of these scholars were

❋

◆ **What have your views of scientists been?**

◆ **How did you feel in science classes?**

◆ **What experiences have contributed to your feelings about science?**

---

**Example 3.3**

In an interview, a biologist, Dr. Baker, was asked the following question: "Which scenario do you think is worse: (a) an oil spill off a coastal, marshland area, or (b) a developer filling in a marsh and building a housing development?" This was his response:

And, I suppose on a scale, well, I suppose that in terms of the total number of dollars involved, something like a major oil spill is probably a bigger mess. On the other hand, it may affect fewer people directly if they happen to be along the coast of Brittany. There won't be too many affected by that, whereas many developments occur in areas where a lot of people, the quality of life of a lot of people, is affected; as the discussions in Toronto in what's happening as to the access to the shoreline there and because of the developments along there; and how that's decreased the quality of life of everybody in the city who enjoyed that shoreline.

This scientist's reasoning is economic and social in character. There is no mention that the oil spill will initially kill a lot of the life in the marsh, or that half of the oil will sink to the bottom and half of it will be eaten by bacteria. There is no mention that marshes are a major source of nutrients for coastal and oceanic ecosystems or are a major source of atmospheric oxygen. He does not mention that the oil spill is temporary damage, while the building in of the marsh is more or less permanent.

influenced by the prevailing views of their times. See Example 3.3 for a contemporary example.

- **Science and technology are separate, although related, disciplines.** There is a continuing debate about the difference between science and technology; however, a simple way to discriminate between them is that science tries to explain how, whereas technology applies knowledge. From this definition, we may assume that science always precedes technology, that science provides the knowledge base for technology. This pattern may occur often, but technology can sometimes precede science. The invention of the wheel was not preceded by an explanation of Newtonian physics of this simple machine (the wheel is thought to have originated around 3200 B.C. in Sumer, now southern Iraq, while Newton lived in Europe in the 1600s A.D.). Although the invention of the electron microscope was based on scientific knowledge, its use allowed new scientific knowledge to be constructed. In a similar way, the development of the Hubble telescope was based on scientific knowledge, but has allowed scientists to extend their knowledge in ways previously unavailable. To muddle the differentiation between science and technology even further, how do we characterize a biologist who is developing a new, faster growing, more nutritious grain? How do we classify a physicist who works on the design of nuclear power plants, or a biochemist making new drugs? Where do medical doctors fit into this scenario?

We have repeatedly stressed how little "method" there really is in science. There is no set of prescribed rules which, when followed, will lead unerringly to the truth. Instead, progress is made by reliance on the judgment of individuals choosing among a complex set of possible strategies that are often in conflict with each other, and depends more on intuition than on explicit procedures.

We have often pointed out the subjective element in science. This appears first in the realization that even "scientific facts" contain a more or less culturally conditioned component. It appears also in the creative processes of individual discovery and in the role of the consensus of scientists who decide, on the basis of commonly shared but subjective criteria, what problems are important, what experiments are decisive, and what theories are correct.[5]

■ Last, but certainly not least, is **curiosity**. Good scientists, as well as any inquirer, have an insatiable curiosity about their field, as well as other areas. Curiosity is the flame, the fuel that drives inquiry. "I wonder how …," "What would happen if …?" "How does … work?" Children are born curious about their world, much to the chagrin of parents, who spend time keeping their fingers out of electrical sockets and probing hands out of other dangerous situations. However, children learn a tremendous amount about their worlds by being curious before they enter school. Read Richard Feynman's book *"Surely You're Joking, Mr. Feynman": Adventures of a Curious Character.* It is a must-read! (Feynman worked on developing the first atomic bomb in Los Alamos, New Mexico, then went on to win the Nobel Prize in Physics in 1965.) When you stop laughing, think about how such a child would be dealt with in schools. What do we do to children's curiosity, so that by the time they reach high school, their curiosity has been beaten out of them? How can we change this tendency and make schools a place where the flames of children's curiosity are fanned?

This list of statements is certainly not the entire picture of what science is, nor is it without controversy. Many scientists would not agree with some of these statements. Even philosophers and sociologists of science may disagree about some of these points. In the following section, we will look at what some scientists have to say about their views of science.

## 3.3 Views of Science: Scientists and Thinkers about Science

In this section, we will look at how scientists and other writers and thinkers about science view the nature of science and scientific work. It is basically a collection of excerpts from writings and personal communications. You may find it best to read one excerpt at a time, ponder the questions that follow, then take a break and return to the next excerpt at a later time. As we read

※
+ As well as being influenced by society, both science and technology affect society.
+ Rather than explain this statement, you may want to ponder how we see science and technology affecting our everyday lives.
+ How have science and technology affected your life?
+ How have science and technology affected our society?
+ How have science and technology affected other societies, such as less industrialized countries and tribal cultures?
+ How have science and technology affected government policies?
+ What other effects do you see on human values, beliefs, social patterns, culture, jobs, media and communication, and other avenues of human endeavor (e.g., art, literature, music, poetry, etc.)?

through these excerpts, we should think about how the statements relate to what has been discussed in the last section. In addition, we may find that some excerpts add a new perspective to our view of science. The intent of this section is to provide you with a variety of short readings through which you may begin to redefine your views of science and to think about the implications for teaching science in the classroom. Although the previous sections presented a list of characteristics of science, this section opens up the possibility of redefining how you feel about the scientific endeavor.

## Stephen Jay Gould: Noted Author and Paleontologist, Harvard University

As a romantic teenager, I believed that my future life as a scientist would be justified if I could discover a single new fact and add a brick to the bright temple of human knowledge. The conviction was noble enough; the metaphor was simply silly. Yet that metaphor still governs the attitude of many scientists toward their subject.

In the conventional model of scientific "progress," we begin in superstitious ignorance and move toward final truth by the successive accumulation of facts. In this smug perspective, the history of science contains little more than anecdotal interest.… It is as transparent as an old-fashioned melodrama: truth (as we perceive it today) is the only arbiter and the world of past scientists is divided into good guys who were right and bad guys who were wrong.

Historians of science have utterly discredited this model during the past decade. Science is not a heartless pursuit of objective information. It is a creative human activity, its geniuses acting more as artists than as information processors. Changes in theory are not simply the derivative results of new discoveries but the work of creative imagination influenced by contemporary social and political forces. (p. 201)[6]

Stephen Jay Gould had a regular column in the magazine *Natural History* and wrote many popular books. One of his most notable, and somewhat controversial, accomplishments was the notion of punctuated equilibrium, which suggests that evolution does not happen gradually. Instead, it occurs rapidly during relatively brief periods (in response to major environmental changes) following longer periods of stability. From his statement, we get a sense of how his views of science changed from the time he was a child. However, the first experience that triggered his interest in science was a trip to the American Museum of Natural History in New York City. His first look at a gigantic dinosaur sparked his imagination and started him on his path to a career in science.

## Lewis Thomas: Physician and Noted Author

In basic research, everything is just the opposite. What you need at the outset is a high degree of uncertainty; otherwise it isn't likely to be an important problem. You start with an incomplete roster of facts, characterized by their ambiguity; often the problem consists of discovering the connections between unrelated pieces of information. You must plan experiments on the basis of probability, even bare possibility, rather than certainty. If an experiment turns out precisely as predicted, this can be very nice, but it is only a great event if at the same time it is a surprise. You can measure the quality of the work by the intensity of astonishment. The surprise can be because it did turn out as predicted (in some lines of research, one per cent is accepted as a high yield), or it can be confoundment because the prediction was wrong and something totally unexpected turned up, changing the look of the problem and requiring a new kind of protocol. Either way, you win. (p. 138)[7]

In talking about basic science, as opposed to applied science, Lewis Thomas talks of the importance of surprise in the work of science. We get the sense that having experiments work the way we expect them to is not what we really want to have happen in science. Experiments that fail may in fact be more important than those that produce expected results.

The typical pattern in science classrooms and school laboratories is to perform experiments that confirm what we already know. We rarely, if ever, do a laboratory experiment as part of a science course where we have very little idea of what to expect. Such experiences of school science avoid the view of science as a process of inquiry and theory building, or as a process of discovery.

◆ What are the implications of Einstein's statement about everyday and scientific thinking for our work as teachers?

◆ What are the implications for the teaching of Einstein's statement that science understandings are expressions of what we perceive in the simplest possible terms?

◆ How can we use the notion of "simple expressions of science understandings" as a basis for teaching writing skills?

◆ What are the implications for how we portray and do science based on Einstein's notion that scientific statements of understandings are judged on their adequacy or inadequacy and are devoid of emotions and values?

◆ Even though scientific statements may not contain emotions or values, how do (or should) emotions and values play a role in science?

### Albert Einstein: Nobel Prize Recipient in Physics

The whole of science is nothing more than a refinement of everyday thinking. It is for this reason that the critical thinking of the physicist cannot possibly be restricted to the examination of the concepts of his own specific field. He cannot proceed without considering critically a much more difficult problem, the problem of analyzing the nature of everyday thinking. (p. 59)

The aim of science is, on the one hand, a comprehension, as *complete* as possible, of the connection between the sense experiences in their totality, and, on the other hand, the accomplishment of this aim *by the use of a minimum of primary concepts and relations*. (Seeking, as far as possible, logical unity in the world picture, i.e., paucity in logical elements.) (p. 63)

Science searches for relations which are thought to exist independently of the searching individual. This includes the case where man himself is the subject. Or the subject of scientific statements may be concepts created by ourselves, as in mathematics. Such concepts are not necessarily supposed to correspond to any objects in the outside world. However, all scientific statements and laws have one characteristic in common: they are "true or false" (adequate or inadequate). Roughly speaking, our reaction to them is "yes" or "no."

The scientific way of thinking has a further characteristic. The concepts which it uses to build up its coherent systems are not expressing emotions. For the scientist, there is only "being," but no wishing, no valuing, no good, no evil; no goal. (p. 114)[8]

Einstein's notion that scientific thinking is a refinement of everyday thinking is particularly intriguing in terms of our work with children. Children already think in ways that serve as the basis for thinking scientifically. They make inferences, construct their own explanations and theories, and perform informal experiments. All we need to do is to help them refine the skills they already use. In the second paragraph, Einstein suggests that our understandings need to be based upon what we perceive and must be as simple as possible (i.e., understandings need to be elegantly simple). In our work with children, we may want to consider how we can help them develop such elegantly simple explanations. In the last two paragraphs, Einstein discusses two basic characteristics of science: (a) the relations developed through science, as stated in laws and principles, are judged as either adequate or inadequate, and (b) scientific concepts are devoid of emotions and values. Having children engage in discussions of whether their own or someone else's explanations are adequate or make sense is an important aspect of doing science. Although engaging in science in ways that do not include emotions and values may be the ideal, it may be more important to have children recognize the role that emotions and values play in doing science. So, when a scientist or a child thinks, "I really think that getting this kind of a result is going to be important," it is important to recognize that this thought can influence how we make sense of our results. By recognizing this influence, the affect of the thought can be minimized. On the other hand, an emotional connection or reaction in classroom work can lead to intriguing insights and to integrated activities. So, for a child who is investigating earthworms and says, "I don't think the worm is very happy in this tray," the emotional connection can lead to an understanding of what factors affect earthworm behavior. Such connections can lead to writing activities, such as stories about earthworms.

### Michael Polanyi: Noted Canadian Scientist and Philosopher of Science

I have spoken of the excitement of problems, of an obsession with hunches and visions that are indispensable spurs and pointers to discovery. But science is supposed to be dispassionate. There is indeed an idealization of this current today, which deems the scientist not only indifferent to the outcome of his surmises, but actually seeking their refutation. This is not only contrary to experience, but logically inconceivable. The surmises of a working scientist are *born of the imagination seeking discovery*. Such effort *risks* defeat but never *seeks* it; it is in fact his craving for success that makes the scientist take the risk of failure. There is no other way. Courts of law employ two separate lawyers to argue opposite pleas, because it is only by a passionate commitment to a particular view that the imagination can discover the evidence that supports it.[9]

+ Can you think of any experiences you've had with science where the teacher or the students expressed passion about their inquiry?

+ What approaches to teaching science seem to prevent the emergence of passion and creativity?

+ How do you think science can be presented in a way that allows children to be passionate and creative about what they are doing?

In Polanyi's description of one aspect of science, we get a sense of passion. The passion of scientists, like that of artists, poets, and dancers, provides the fuel to face risks and to persist in difficult endeavors. We also get a sense of science as an imaginative undertaking. The work of a scientist appears to require creativity to see beyond the bounds of what is known.

---

### Ursula Franklin: Professor Emeritus, University of Toronto, Department of Metallurgy and Material Science

In her ... book *The Politics of Women's Biology*, Ruth Hubbard, a just-retired Harvard biologist, points out that scientists are the socially sanctioned fact makers. However, scientists constitute a very small and homogeneous social group which in the past was almost entirely male, almost entirely white and schooled in similar settings using similar or identical texts. Yet, as their insights and the results of their research become "facts," they shape the whole society. On the other hand, when those who work outside the in-group of scientists—say women who nurse, cook, or garden—bring forward observations and insights, however well tested and verified, these contributions rarely achieve the status of facts.

I raise these issues to point out that the knowledge we try to convey and the understanding we try to build is often very fragmented. The ways and means by which knowledge is accumulated and understanding is developed always structure the process of inquiry itself. Therefore, it should not come as a surprise that dominant views on gender, race, and ideology have profoundly influenced scientific questions and scientific facts. In other words, the teaching of science and technology will be truncated and incomplete if it does not contain discussions about why certain problems are of interest and fundable at particular points in time while other questions don't seem to matter.

We also need to make it clear that experimental science in its reductionist and abstracting mode is but one source of understanding of the world around us. For instance, ecological problems show very clearly the limitation of traditional science as a basis for understanding and acting on some of the world's most urgent tasks.[10]

---

✦ **How does Dr. Franklin portray the relationship between science and society?**

✦ **Can you think of any examples that support her points?**

✦ **In what situations have you seen or otherwise experienced reductionism and positivism in relation to science?**

Ursula Franklin's notion of the fragmentation of knowledge (i.e., that our understandings of the world are in pieces and generally not as cohesively linked as we would like to think) and of reductionism (i.e., the tendency to reduce the explanations of phenomena to their smallest components, usually at the expense of not seeing the whole context or the interaction among the parts) in science is a significant aspect of much of what we encounter in traditional science. From this perspective, a scientist may have a thorough understanding of a particular hormone in the body and how it functions directly on various parts of the body; however, she or he may have no knowledge of how that hormone interacts with other hormones and other factors. Positivism, which claims that all real knowledge is observable and must be verifiable (usually associated with the tendency of scientists to claim that the best knowledge is scientific), is frequently expressed along with reductionism. Both reductionism and positivism tend to be used in ways that help to avoid the issue of fragmentation of knowledge. In other words, by being sure that you have the "right" answer, you do not see that what you are saying may not be the entire picture. Or, even though we do not understand how all the parts of a system work (e.g., the human body), we make it seem as if we do know. Much of what we encounter in the medical system is a picture that doctors know what particular symptoms mean, when they may only know a few possibilities. In fact, some arguments may dismiss any attempts at seeing the whole picture by simply stating that the new information is not valid.

☞

✦ **Positivism** refers to an approach taken in science and other disciplines that knowledge can only be constructed from direct observation and experimentation, and that such knowledge has the quality of being absolute (i.e., there is one right answer or one truth).

✦ **Reductionism** refers to an approach in science and other disciplines that examines the smallest parts of more complex wholes. From this perspective, *the whole is the sum of its parts*. Current thinking, especially for those involved in chaos and complexity sciences, suggests that *the whole is more than the sum of its parts*. In other words, the understanding of the parts will not give us a complete understanding of the whole. Without considering the whole system and the contexts in which it is situated, understandings of the parts will not provide a complete picture of the whole system.

### Kary Mullis: Nobel Prize Recipient in Chemistry (1993)

The laws of science are demonstrable. They are not beliefs. When experiments in our century showed that Newton's gravitational laws were not quite accurate, we changed the laws—despite Newton's good name and holy grave in Cambridge. Relativity fit the facts better. This is the way science has been done now for almost four centuries, and because of science—not religion or politics—even people like you and me can have possessions that only a hundred years ago kings would have gone to war to own. Scientific method should not be taken lightly.

The walls of the ivory tower of science collapsed when bureaucrats realized that there were jobs to be had and money to made in the administration and promotion of science. Governments began making big investments just prior to World War II. Scientists and engineers invented new firearms, sharper things, better engines, harder things, airplanes that could fly faster, radars to detect them, antiaircraft guns to shoot them down, antibiotics for the pilots who got shot down, amphetamines to keep everybody awake long hours, daylight savings time to lengthen the hours, and finally one big bomb that in a shocking finale brought World War II to a breathtaking and hideous end.

Scientists had revealed that they weren't just a bunch of screwballs who had nothing to do with the world. They were not, and never had been, useless little guys sitting in ivory towers playing with slide rules. Just a few of them, with motivation and some tools, could make a bomb that would have put the fear of the Christian God into Attila the Hun.

Science was going to determine the balance of power in the postwar world. Governments went into the science business big time.

Scientists became administrators of programs that had a mission. Probably the most important scientific development of the twentieth century is that economics replaced curiosity as the driving force behind research. Academic, government, and industrial laboratories need money for salaries for staff: the primary investigator and his technicians, postdocs, graduate students, and secretaries. They need lab space, equipment, travel expenses, overhead payments to the institution, including the

❋

✦ How does Kary Mullis's description of science as demonstrable and not a belief compare to the commonly held views of science in today's society? How does the portrayal of science by the media differ from Mullis's contention?

✦ Can you list examples of how politics has been influencing science and the communication of science? Do politicians censor or manipulate scientific findings to address their own needs and goals?

✦ How can we incorporate into our teaching the ways in which science affects society and politics and the ways in which society and politics affect science? Why do you think this is important for children to learn?

✦ What kinds of "social inquiry" activities can you think of that would allow children to explore the influences between science, society, and politics?

salaries and expenses of administrators, financial officers, more secretaries, maintenance of grounds around the institution, security officers, publication costs for scientific reports in scientific journals, librarians, janitors, and so on. It's expensive, and there is a lot of pressure on a professional scientist trying to maintain or expand a laboratory domain. Most of the money comes from institutions like the National Science Foundation, the National Institutes of Health, the Defense Department, and the Department of Energy. There is serious competition for these funds. And the question we should ask is, "What the hell are you doing with our money that is so important to us?"[11]

Kary Mullis states unequivocally that science is demonstrable and not a belief. In other words, science is based on facts that can be demonstrated to be true. When a scientific claim is disproved, it is replaced. He also describes science in its current state as deeply embedded in politics. Economics has replaced curiosity as the driving force behind science. The goals of science have changed based upon the needs and goals of politicians.

### Richard Feynman: Nobel Prize Recipient in Physics (1965)

When I was a kid I had a "lab." It wasn't a laboratory in the sense that I would measure, or do important experiments. Instead, I would play: I'd make a motor, I'd make a gadget that would go off when something passed a photocell, I'd play around with selenium; I was piddling around all the time. I did calculate a little bit for the lamp bank, a series of switches and bulbs I used as resistors to control voltages. But all that was for application. I never did any laboratory kind of experiments.

I also had a microscope and loved to watch things under the microscope. It took patience: I would get something under the microscope and I would watch it interminably. I saw many interesting things, like everybody sees—a diatom slowly making its way across the slide, and so on.

One day I was watching a paramecium and I saw something that was not described in the books I got in school—in college, even. These books always simplify things so the world will be more like they want it to be: When they're talking about the behavior of animals, they always start out with, "The paramecium is extremely simple; it has a simple behavior. It turns as its slipper shape moves through the water until it hits something, at which time it recoils, turns through an angle, and then starts out again."

It isn't really right. First of all, as everybody knows, the paramecia, from time to time, conjugate with each other—they meet and exchange nuclei. How do they decide when it's time to do that? (Never mind; that's not my observation.)

I watched these paramecia hit something, recoil, turn through an angle, and go again. The idea that it's mechanical, like a computer program—it doesn't look that way. They go different distances, they recoil different distances, they turn through angles that are different in various cases; they don't always turn to the right; they're very irregular. It looks random, because you don't know what they're hitting; you don't know all the chemicals they're smelling, or what.

One of the things I wanted to watch was what happens to the paramecium when the water that it's in dries up. It was claimed that the paramecium can dry up into a sort of hardened seed. I had a drop of water on the slide under my microscope, and in the drop of water was a paramecium and some "grass"—at the scale of the paramecium, it looked like a network of jackstraws. As the drop of water evaporated, over a time of fifteen or twenty minutes, the paramecium got into a tighter and tighter situation: there was more and more of this back-and-forth until it could hardly move. It was stuck between these "sticks," almost jammed.

Then I saw something I had never seen or heard of: the paramecium lost its shape. It could flex itself, like an amoeba. It began to push itself against one of the sticks, and began dividing into two prongs until the division was about halfway up the paramecium, at which time it decided that wasn't a very good idea, and backed away.

So my impression of these animals is that their behavior is much too simplified in the books. It is not so utterly mechanical or one-dimensional as they say. They should describe the behavior of these simple animals correctly. Until we see how many dimensions of behavior even a one-celled animal has, we won't be able to fully understand the behavior of more complicated animals.[12]

---

Scientists … are used to dealing with doubt and uncertainty. All scientific knowledge is uncertain. This experience with doubt and uncertainty is important. I believe that it is of very great value, and one that extends beyond the sciences. I believe that to solve any problem that has never been solved before, you have to leave the door to the unknown ajar. You have to permit the possibility that you do not have it exactly right. Otherwise, if you have made up your mind already, you might not solve it.… It is of paramount importance, in order to make progress. That we recognize this … doubt. Because we have the doubt, we then propose looking in new directions for new ideas.… So, what we call scientific knowledge today is a body of statements of varying degrees of certainty. Some of them are most unsure; some of them are nearly sure; but none is absolutely certain.[13]

---

One of the greatest experimental scientists of the time who was really doing something, William Harvey, said that what Bacon said science was, was the science that a lord chancellor would do. He spoke of making observations, but omitted the vital factor of judgment about what to observe and what to pay attention to. (p. 173)

♦ In Richard Feynman's story, where did he encounter the limits of reductionism as found in school textbooks?

♦ Can you think of examples (of the limits of reductionism) that you have encountered similar to the one described here?

♦ What are the implications of this story for how you can work with children in the classroom?

✳

✦ In the first statement by Richard Feynman, what are the implications of "judgment about what to observe" for how we can help children conduct investigations?

✦ In the other statements about the nature and qualities of science, what are the implications for how we can represent science in our classrooms?

What science is: the result of the discovery that it is worthwhile rechecking by new direct experience, and not necessarily trusting the race experience from the past. I see it that way. That is my best definition.…

There is the value of the worldview created by science. There is the beauty and the wonder of the world that is discovered through the results of these new experiences. (p. 185)

Another of the qualities of science is that it teaches the value of rational thought, as well as the importance of freedom of thought; the positive results that come from doubting that the lessons are all true. You must here distinguish—especially in teaching—the science from the forms or procedures that are sometimes used in developing science. It is easy to say, "We write, experiment, and observe, and do this or that." You can copy that form exactly. But great religions are dissipated by following form without remembering the direct content of the teaching of the great leaders. In the same way it is possible to follow form and call it science but it is pseudoscience. In this way we all suffer from the kind of tyranny we have today in the many institutions that have come under the influence of pseudoscientific advisers. (p. 186)

As a matter of fact, I can also define science another way: Science is the belief in the ignorance of experts. (p. 187)[14]

### Charles Darwin: Noted Naturalist and Father of Evolutionary Theory

In 1838, that is, fifteen months after I had begun my systematic enquiry, I happened to read for amusement Malthus on *Population*, and being well prepared to appreciate the struggle for existence which everywhere goes on from long-continued observation of the habits of animals and plants, it at once struck me that under these circumstances favourable variations would tend to be preserved, and unfavourable ones to be destroyed. The result of this would be the formation of new species. Here, then, I had at last got a theory by which to work; but I was so anxious to avoid prejudice, that I determined not for some time to write even the briefest sketch of it. In June 1842 I first allowed myself the satisfaction of writing a very brief abstract of my theory in pencil in 35 pages; and this was enlarged during the summer of 1844 into one of 230 pages, which I had fairly copied out and still possess. (p. 40)

I think that I am superior to the common run of men in noticing things which escape attention, and in observing them carefully. My industry has been nearly as great as it could have been in the observation and collection of facts. What is far more important, my love of natural science has been steady and ardent.

This pure love has, however, been much aided by the ambition to be esteemed by my fellow naturalists. From early youth I have had the strongest desire to understand or explain whatever I observed,—that, to group all facts under some general laws. These causes combined have given me the patience to reflect or ponder for any number of years over any unexplained problem. As far as I can judge, I am not apt to follow blindly the lead of other men. I have steadily endeavoured to keep my mind free so as to give up any hypothesis, however much beloved (and I cannot resist forming one on every subject), as soon as facts are shown to be opposed to it. Indeed, I have had no choice but to act in this manner, for with the exception of the Coral Reefs, I cannot remember a single first-formed hypothesis which had not after a time to be given up or greatly modified. This has naturally led me to distrust greatly, deductive reasoning in the mixed sciences. On the other hand, I am not very skeptical,—a frame of mind which I believe to be injurious to the progress of science. A good deal of skepticism in a scientific man is advisable to avoid much loss of time,—[but] I have met with not a few men who, I feel sure, have often thus been deterred from experiment of observations, which would have proved directly or indirectly serviceable. (p. 52)[15]

[Charles Darwin—born February 12, 1809, and died April 19, 1882—was considered throughout his early schooling as a run-of-the-mill student, but he had an insatiable curiosity aided by his keen observation abilities and dogged pursuit to construct explanations of what he saw. The following is from biographical writings of his son, Francis.]

He could not help personifying natural things. This feeling came out in abuse as well as in praise—e.g. of some seedlings—"The little beggars are doing just what I don't want them to." He would speak in a half-provoked, half-admiring way of the ingenuity of the leaf of a Sensitive Plant in screwing itself out of a basin of water in which he had tried to fix it. One might see the same spirit in his way of speaking of Sundew, earthworms, &c. (p. 72)

In the non-biological sciences he felt keen sympathy with work of which he could not really judge. For instance, he used to read nearly the whole of *Nature*, though so much of it deals with mathematics and physics. I have often heard him say that he got a kind of satisfaction in reading articles which (according to himself) he could not understand. I wish I could reproduce the manner in which he would laugh at himself for it. (p. 78)

A few of his mental characteristics, bearing especially on his mode of working, occur to me. There was one quality of mind which seemed to be of special and extreme advantage in leading him to make discoveries. It was the power of never letting exceptions pass unnoticed. Everybody notices a fact as an exception when it is striking or frequent, but he had a special instinct for arresting an exception. A point apparently slight and unconnected with his present work is passed over by many a man almost unconsciously with some half-considered explanation, which is in fact no explanation. It was just these things that he seized on to make a start from....

✦ In these two examples of Charles Darwin, what characterized his work?

✦ Have you experienced any of these characteristics in any area of interest? How have they influenced you?

✦ If you have worked with children, have you seen them manifest any of these characteristics?

✦ How could you help children develop some of these characteristics?

✦ In reading both the quote by Darwin and the description of Darwin by his son, Francis, we get a sense of a man who was critical, but accepting, of his weaknesses (e.g., not being skeptical). The combined nature of these attributes appears to have lead to an interesting mix of humility and confidence. However, he was quite hesitant about publishing his theory of evolution. He knew what happened to scientists who challenged the Church's doctrine. When he returned to England from his scientific voyage on the HMS *Beagle*, his standing in the scientific community was raised dramatically. He knew this new-found status could crumble. What sense of Darwin do you get from these two examples about how he must have felt and dealt with his dilemma about going public with his new theory of evolution? Can you find examples of other scientists who have experienced similar fears or have received repercussions from the community of scientists or the government?

Another quality which was shown in his experimental work, was his power of sticking to a subject; he used almost to apologise for his patience, saying that he could not bear to be beaten, as if this were rather a sign of weakness on his part.... I think his doggedness expresses his frame of mind almost better than perseverance. Perseverance seems hardly to express his almost fierce desire to force the truth to reveal itself. He often said that it was important that a man should know the right point at which to give up an inquiry. And I think it was his tendency to pass this point that inclined him to apologise for his perseverance, and gave the air of doggedness to his work.

He often said that no one could be a good observer unless he was an active theorizer. This brings me back to what I said about his instinct for arresting exceptions: it was as though he were charged with theorizing power ready to flow into any channel on the slightest disturbance, so that no fact, however small, could avoid releasing a stream of theory, and thus the fact became magnified into importance. In this way it naturally happened that many untenable theories occurred to him; but fortunately his richness of imagination was equaled by his power of judging and condemning the thoughts that occurred to him. He was just to his theories, and did not condemn them unheard; and so it happened that he was willing to test what would seem to most people not at all worth testing. These rather wild trials he called "fool's experiments," and enjoyed extremely.... The love of experiment was very strong in him, and I can remember the way he would say, "I shan't be easy till I have tried it," as if an outside force were driving him. (pp. 94–95)[16]

✦ How do you react to Marie Curie's view of her life and work?

✦ Why do you think she put up with such hardship in her work?

✦ In terms of the social context during the late 1800s and early 1900s, how do you think her work provided her with a sense of liberty and independence?

### Marie Sklodowska Curie: Nobel Prize Recipient in Physics (1903) and Chemistry (1911)

[In describing Marie Curie:] She was enjoying science the way other people love music—for the delight and profound enjoyment that it gave her. As she recalled later, "This life, painful from certain points of view, had, for all that, a real charm for me. It gave me a very precious sense of liberty and independence." (p. 18)

Sometimes I had to spend a whole day mixing a boiling mass with a heavy iron rod nearly as large as myself. I would be broken with fatigue at that day's end.... If we had had a fine laboratory, we should have made more discoveries and our health would have suffered less. And yet, ... it was in this miserable old shed that the best and happiest years of our life were spent, entirely consecrate [sic] to work." (p. 23)[17]

### Jane Goodall: Noted Zoologist and Author

When I began my study at Gombe in 1960 it was not permissible—at least not in ethological circles—to talk about an animal's mind. Only humans had minds. Nor was it quite proper to talk about animal personality. Of course everyone knew that they did have their own unique characters—everyone who had ever owned a dog or other pet was aware of that. But ethologists, striving to make theirs a "hard" science, shied away from the task of trying to explain such things objectively. One respected ethologist, while acknowledging that there was "variability between individual animals," wrote that it was best that this fact be "swept under the carpet." At that time ethological carpets fairly bulged with all that was hidden beneath them.

How naive I was. As I had not had an undergraduate science education I didn't realize that animals were not supposed to have personalities, or to think, or to feel emotions or pain. I had no idea that it would have been more appropriate to assign each of the chimpanzees a number rather than a name when I got to know him or her. I didn't realize that it was not scientific to discuss behavior in terms of motivation or purpose. And no one had told me that terms such as childhood and adolescence were uniquely human phases of the life cycle, culturally determined, not to be used when referring to young chimpanzees. Not knowing, I freely made use of all those forbidden terms and concepts in my initial attempt to describe, to the best of my ability, the amazing things I had observed at Gombe.

I shall never forget the response of a group of ethologists to some remarks I made at an erudite seminar. I described how Figan, as an adolescent, had learned to stay behind in camp after senior males had left, so that we could give him a few bananas for himself. On the first occasion he had, upon seeing the fruits, uttered loud, delighted food calls: whereupon a couple of the older males had charged back, chased after Figan, and taken his bananas. And then, coming to the point of the story, I explained how, on the next occasion, Figan had actually suppressed his calls. We could hear little sounds, in his throat, but so quiet that none of the others could have heard them. Other young chimps, to whom we tried to smuggle fruit without the knowledge of their elders, never learned such self-control. With shrieks of glee they would fall to, only to be robbed of their booty when the big males charged back. I had expected my audience to be as fascinated and impressed as I was. I had hoped for an exchange of views about the chimpanzee's undoubted intelligence. Instead there was a chill silence, after which the chairman hastily changed the subject. Needless to say, after being thus snubbed, I was very reluctant to contribute any comments, at any scientific gathering, for a very long time. Looking back, I suspect that everyone was interested, but it was, of course, not permissible to present a mere "anecdote" as evidence for anything.

The editorial comments on the first paper I wrote for publication demanded that every *he* or *she* be replaced with *it*, and every *who* be replaced with *which*. Incensed, I, in my turn, crossed out the *its* and *whichs* and scrawled back the original pronouns. As I had no desire to carve a niche for myself in the world of science, but simply wanted to go

- ✦ Have you experienced the same sort of limitations, as described by Jane Goodall, on how you can think in science?
- ✦ If a biologist tells you that you cannot describe a dog as happy when she is wagging her tail, what would you think?
- ✦ How do such limitations affect the way we can develop understandings of the world?
- ✦ What are the implications of allowing children to express their emotional understandings on their learning and involvement in science?

on living among and learning about chimpanzees, the possible reaction of the editor of the learned journal did not trouble me. In fact I won that round: the paper, when finally published, did confer upon the chimpanzees the dignity of their appropriate genders and properly upgraded them from the status of mere "things" to essential Being-ness.[18]

Suppose a child looks at a small bird chasing a hawk across the sky and says something like, "Look! That little bird is angry …. he's chasing that big bird." From a traditional biologist's point of view, we cannot say that the bird can experience anger. If we were to say this to the child, how do you think the child would react? Making such a statement to a child seems to have two basic outcomes. One, you invalidate the child's observation and interpretation, making him or her feel much less likely to engage in trying to explain his or her observations. Two, we disconnect the child from his or her world. By stating that the bird is angry, the child is making a statement that draws a connection between the bird and the child. The child understands what anger is and how it feels. Seeing similar behavior in a bird helps the child feel some sense of connection with his or her living world.

| Gerty Radnitz Cori: Nobel Prize Recipient in Chemistry (1947) |
|---|
| Art and science are the glories of the human mind…. I see no conflict between them. In the past, they have flourished together during the great and happy periods of history…. Contemplation of the great human achievements through the ages is helpful to me in moments of despair and doubt. Human meanness and folly then seem less important.[19] |

| Barbara McClintock: Geneticist, Nobel Prize Winner in Physiology or Medicine (1983) |
|---|
| [In describing Barbara McClintock:] When a MISS BARBARA MCCLINTOCK of St. Louis announced her 1936 engagement in the newspapers, the chairman of the University of Missouri's botany department was horrified. Mistaking his new thirty-four-year-old assistant professor for the woman in the newspaper [a different "Barbara McClintock"], he summoned Dr. Barbara McClintock to his office. Then he threatened her, "if you get married, you'll be fired." <br><br>Barbara McClintock: <br><br>[The University of Missouri was] awful, awful, awful. The situation for women was unbelievable, it was so bad. (p. 144) <br><br>[Talking about her childhood:] I didn't play with girls because they didn't play the way I did. I liked athletics, ice skating, roller skating, and bicycling, just to throw a ball and enjoy the rhythm of pitch and catch; it has a very wonderful rhythm. |

✦ How do you see art and science as the "glories of the human mind"?

✦ How do you think art and science are connected and not in conflict?

✦ Gerty Cori mentions that she experienced moments of despair and doubt, and that contemplating artistic and scientific achievements helped her in these moments. We tend to think of great people as not experiencing such emotional problems. Richard Feynman (who worked on the original design of the atomic bomb) experienced similar despair and doubt as he drove across the river from New York City. He looked at the city and the bridges thinking it was all going to be destroyed by what he helped to create. Can you find other examples of scientists talking about their difficulties? How did they or did they not deal with such difficulties?

✦ Do children experience emotional problems in school? How can we help them deal with these problems?

My parents supported everything I wanted to do, even if it went against the mores of the women on the block. They wouldn't let anybody interfere. (p. 148)

[Talking about her career:] [We] did very powerful work with chromosomes. It began to put cytogenetics, working with chromosomes, on the map in the late 1920s–early 1930s.... It was just a little group of young people. The older people couldn't join; they just didn't understand. The young people were the ones who really got the subject going because they worked intensely with each other. It was a group activity because they discussed everything and were constantly thinking about what they could do to show this, that, or the other thing.... The fun was solving problems, like a game. It was entertaining. (p. 153)[20]

The following quote by James Burke looks at the bigger picture of the role of scientific knowledge and how it fits in with other ways of knowing. We also get a clear sense of how all knowledge is socially constructed.

## James Burke: Award-Winning BBC Television Writer, Producer, and Presenter

In spite of its claims, science offers no method or universal explanation of reality adequate for all time. The search for the truth, the "discovery of nature's secrets," as Descartes put it, is an idiosyncratic search for temporary truth. One truth is replaced by another. The fact that over time science has provided a more complex picture of nature is not in itself final proof that we live by the best, most accurate model so far.

The knowledge acquired through the use of any structure is selective. There are no standards or beliefs guiding the search for knowledge which are not dependent on the structure. Scientific knowledge, in sum, is not necessarily the clearest representation of what reality is; it is the artifact of each structure and its tool. Discovery is invention. Knowledge is man-made.

If this is so, then all views at all times are equally valid. There is no metaphysical, super-ordinary, final, absolute reality. There is no special direction to events. The universe is what we say it is. When theories change the universe changes. The truth is relative.

This relativist view is generally shunned. It is supposed by the Left to dilute commitment and by the Right to leave society defenseless. In fact it renders everybody equally responsible for the structure adopted by the group. If there is no privileged source of truth, all structures are equally worth assessment and equally worth toleration. Relativism neutralizes the views of extremists of all kinds. It makes science accountable to the society from which its structure springs. It urges care in judgment through awareness of the contextual nature of the judgmental values themselves.

- ✦ Although the first story about Barbara McClintock's encounter with her department chair was situated in a social context of the mid-1900s, do the same sorts of issues occur with women in science today?
- ✦ Has the situation changed, in terms of the social pressures exerted on girls, from the time of McClintock's childhood (1902–1920) to the present day?
- ✦ What does McClintock's description of her group work suggest about how science is done?
- ✦ What are the implications of such group work for how we conceive of setting up our classrooms?
- ✦ What are the implications for her notion of problem solving as fun to how we can approach teaching?

❋

✦ How does Burke's perspective of science differ from what you have learned and experienced?

✦ If we are to take this perspective seriously, what are the implications for how we approach teaching science in the classroom?

✦ If we want to make scientific knowledge more accessible, what are the implications for teaching science?

✦ Can you think of any examples of how making scientific knowledge more accessible is important in today's society?

A relativist approach might well use the new electronic data systems to provide a structure unlike any which has gone before. If structural change occurs most often through the juxtaposition of so-called "facts" in a novel way, then the systems might offer the opportunity to evaluate not the facts which are, at the present rate of change, obsolete by the time they come to public consciousness, but the relationships between facts: the constants in the way they interact to produce change. Knowledge would then properly include the study of the structure itself.

Such a system would permit a type of "balanced anarchy" in which all interests could be represented in a continuous reappraisal of the social requirements for knowledge, and the value judgments to be applied in directing the search for that knowledge. The view that this would endanger the position of the expert by imposing on his work the judgment of the layman ignores the fact that science has always been the product of social needs, consciously expressed or not. Science may well be a vital part of human endeavor, but for it to retain the privilege which it has gained over the centuries of being in some measure unaccountable, would be to render both science itself and society a disservice. It is time that knowledge became more accessible to those to whom it properly belongs.[21]

## Henry Bauer: Professor of Chemistry and Science Studies at Virginia Polytechnic Institute and State University

Misconceptions about science are rampant. But they are rampant among scientists as well as humanists and social scientists, among science writers as well as the general public. They are rampant even among those who purport to measure or survey scientific literacy. (pp. 1–2)

The "theory-ladenness of facts"—to what degree do we observe what we believe we shall observe, by contrast with what may (or may not) be really there? For our present purpose, it is sufficient to recognize that these are the salient acknowledged elements of the popular view of being scientifically methodical: empirical, pragmatic, open-minded, skeptical, sensitive to possibilities of falsifying, thereby establishing objective facts leading to hypotheses, to laws, to theories; and incessantly reaching out for new knowledge, new discoveries, new facts, and new theories.

The burden … will be how misleading this view—which I shall call "the myth of the scientific methods"—is in many specific directions, how incapable it is of explaining what happens in science, how it is worse than useless as a guide to what society ought to do about science and technology. (pp. 19–20)

Geologists and physicists tend to approach even scientific problems in disparate ways. They learn differently what it is to be scientific, what the scientific method is; and so too do chemists and biologists and other scientists come to different and even contradictory views of what science is. Yet these characteristic differences are but little recognized, and the mis-

**Different Sorts of Science**

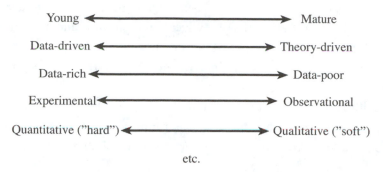

| | |
|---|---|
| Young | ⟷ Mature |
| Data-driven | ⟷ Theory-driven |
| Data-rich | ⟷ Data-poor |
| Experimental | ⟷ Observational |
| Quantitative ("hard") | ⟷ Qualitative ("soft") |

etc.

**And Different Types of Science Might Be**

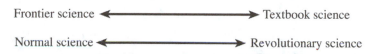

| | |
|---|---|
| Frontier science | ⟷ Textbook science |
| Normal science | ⟷ Revolutionary science |

**And Scientists, as in Other Professions, Vary in Being**

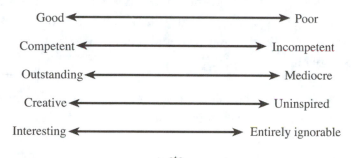

| | |
|---|---|
| Good | ⟷ Poor |
| Competent | ⟷ Incompetent |
| Outstanding | ⟷ Mediocre |
| Creative | ⟷ Uninspired |
| Interesting | ⟷ Entirely ignorable |

etc.

**FIGURE 3.1  BAUER'S DEPICTION OF SCIENCE AND SCIENTISTS.**

conception remains widespread that there exists a single method whose utilization marks the whole of science. In point of fact, … there is not any single thing that one can usefully and globally call science; rather, there are many different sorts of science. Once one has said that science is the study of nature, and that scientific knowledge is valid only so long as it is not contradicted by nature, one has said essentially all that is truly common, without qualification, among all the sciences. Beyond that, one finds nothing but variation. (p. 28)[22]

### Fred Begay: Navajo Nuclear Physicist, Los Alamos National Laboratory, New Mexico

"Skills in abstract reasoning are developed in the Navajo home," he said. "My parents were Hataalii, Navajo and Ute chanters and spiritual leaders. My family education was based on the laws of nature and our own cognitive science process. These are the same skills needed to study physics and mathematics."

✦ Bauer suggests that misconceptions about science are rampant. Can you develop a list of such misconceptions that we encounter in our everyday lives and from science textbooks, books, and curriculum materials?

✦ The notion of "the myth of the scientific method" may be quite shocking. How does this idea affect your own conceptions about science and science teaching?

✦ A more useful notion may be that there are a great variety of methods used by different science disciplines and individual scientists. Try doing a brief investigation and find out how scientists generally do science in some or all of the following: molecular biology, cellular biology, animal behavior biology, ecology, quantum physics, astronomy, geology, paleontology, chaos and complexity, chemistry, and any others you may want to include.

Begay, who spoke only Navajo and Ute until the age of 10, was sent to a BIA school in Colorado where he spent eight years learning to be a farmer.

"They thought we weren't intelligent enough for academic learning," he said. "Actually, we were just cheap labor and ran the farms to grow food for the school. Can you imagine how many students out there are turned away who can do good work?"

Although he was not traditionally prepared for higher education, Begay said he felt at home in the classroom when he began his studies at UNM. "In some ways I was better prepared than some of the others, although I didn't know it at the time," he said.

Navajo math is based on module eight arithmetic, as is computer science, rather than the module ten arithmetic taught in most American schools. From their earliest years living in traditional eight-sided hogans, young Navajo brains are accustomed to fractal geometry, as this "new" branch of math now appearing in schools is known.

"Fractal art can be used on the computer to explore and visualize both the Navajo and modern principles of scientific concepts, such as lasers and magnetism," Begay said. "It's the best way to get kids interested, since every child is a scientist and they are naturally curious about natural phenomena."[23]

Native Americans and other minority groups are not well represented in science. However, as is apparent in the above excerpt of a news release, Fred Begay's traditional Navajo upbringing provided an important background in the foundations for understanding quantum physics, computers, and mathematics. In fact, the long-standing Native American understandings of nature are very similar to the relatively recent scientific fields of quantum physics, ecology, and the even newer fields of chaos and complexity theories. However, the tendency has been to ignore or even dismiss the understandings of a variety of underrepresented cultures.

## Donald Radler: Editor, *UniSci News*

Science is the design or conduct of reproducible experiments to test how nature works, or the creation of theories that can themselves be tested by such experiments. Science is also the orderly observation of events that cannot yet be manipulated, and, ultimately, the testing of many different such observations as the basis for theories to explain the events.

This makes science the one human activity that seeks knowledge in an organized way. It's not the knowledge that's organized, it's the seeking. Science doesn't guess, doesn't hope, doesn't wish, doesn't trust, doesn't believe.

Science seeks.

It's the search that makes science so powerful and so exciting. Science does add to our store of knowledge, but some of the knowledge it adds turns out to hurt more than it helps. Science does lead to new products, some of which prove not to be so good, either. It's the seeking that makes science what it is.

Seeking is a uniquely humble human experience. It doesn't say I know, it says I need to find out. It doesn't declare one thing better than another, it merely describes each thing as it finds it. It doesn't tell anyone how to do anything, it merely discovers how nature does things.

Humble, nonjudgmental, nondirective. What other human enterprise has this cluster of attributes, this quiet dignity? And the best that there is of this enterprise goes on at universities, where much of the research is basic science, a simple search for truth. UniSci is pleased to have American universities as its "beat," and the research they perform as the material it covers.

We hope we cover it well. We also hope that our coverage will enhance the respect that society has for the scientific method and the scientific bent of mind, and its willingness to support them, particularly at the level of basic research.[24]

From these excerpts about science, we have seen a number of views about the nature of science, as well as some of the issues that affect science. However, the key concern is how we can use these ideas in our classrooms. As we develop the idea of the classroom as a community of young scientists throughout this book, we should think about how this sense of community can serve as a jumping-off point for exploring scientific communities. Older students can read excerpts such as those in this chapter, then discuss the issues and compare these statements to what takes place in their classroom communities. Scientists and those with professions involved in science can be invited to classrooms, where students can ask questions that stem from their discussions of the issues contained in their readings.

In addition, many of the relationships between science, society, and politics are crucial for the development of an informed citizenry. Every day, claims are made in the name of science. In newspapers, magazines, and movies and on TV, all sorts of claims are made about new products, environmental or medical issues, and so forth. On the flip side of making claims are efforts to hide scientific results. Politicians, corporations, and even the news media will consciously not discuss scientific claims that hold the potential to undermine a particular political or corporate point of view. An exciting way to involve our students in this area of science-society-politics is to have our students investigate and critique claims or uncover evidence that contradicts particular political or corporate stances. As they proceed with such investigations, you can discuss with your students ways in which they could share their findings, such as a video documentary, a newsletter, or a web page.

## 3.4 Activities

The following activities may be an interesting way to extend your understanding of science and scientists. Although some of the activities may require a significant time commitment, you may find them to be most rewarding. You may want to consider doing the more involved activities as something fun to do (i.e., the volunteering activity) during the summer or at some other time.

1. **Interview a scientist**:
   - Arrange to meet with a scientist (e.g., a university professor, a researcher in a government laboratory, a researcher in an industrial laboratory). Be sure to make it clear that you want to conduct a short interview about his or her experience and views of science.
   - Tape-record the interview (make sure you ask permission and ensure that no names or identifying information will ever be disclosed).
   - Write down a few questions you want to ask before your meeting. You may want to ask about his or her research as a way of getting started.
   - Listen to your tape-recorded interview and analyze the tape in terms of this scientist's views of science and approach to his or her work.
   - Did he or she express any opinions of how science should be taught in the classroom? How do these opinions fit with your own views?
   - How would you summarize this scientist's views of science?

2. **Observe a scientist**:
   - Find a scientist who is willing to let you observe his or her work in the laboratory or at a field site. Spend as much time as you can.
   - Take notes of your observations in as much detail as possible. When you return home, review your notes and elaborate on them while your memory is still fresh.
   - Take a tape recorder along to capture some of the conversations. Afterwards, listen to the tape to help you extend your notes.
   - Ask questions about what is going on, but be careful not to be a nuisance. Be sensitive to the situation and ask questions when there seems to be a lull in activity.
   - What kinds of problems did the scientist and co-workers encounter?
   - How did they deal with the problems?
   - How would you summarize the scientist's engagement with science and his or her approach to doing science?
   - What implications do you see for the teaching of science?

**3. Volunteer:**

- This activity may require more of a time commitment but can be very rewarding. Find a scientist with whom you can volunteer. Some examples of volunteer work might include cleaning and organizing the lab, taking care of animals or other organisms, entering data into the computer, and assisting with data collection. Be sure to tell the scientist that you are interested in learning more about science and how science works. Explain how you want to enrich your own teaching of science by experiencing science firsthand.
- Negotiate a workable time commitment.
- Include some of the same techniques as in the previous two activities for recording your observations and any conversations.
- Keep track of your observations and insights.
- Ask yourself the same questions as in the previous two activities.
- What else have you learned?

## 3.5 Examples of Children's Ideas

In this section, we will explore children's views of science and scientists. As we look through the examples, we may want to ponder how they came up with these images and understandings. How do their views compare with your own views? (Also, the names of the children are pseudonyms, which have been coded to correspond to their grade level; i.e., names beginning with the fifth letter of the alphabet, *E*, refer to students in grade 5, *F* names are in grade 6, and *G* names are in grade 7.)

A revealing way of finding out children's images of scientists is to ask them to draw a scientist. Examples 3.4 through 3.6 depict grade 5 students' drawings of scientists. In Example 3.4, the children have drawn "mad" scientists. Their hair is messy. In general, they are depicted as crazy. Eugene's scientist has a strange smile, no doubt from something chemical he has tried on himself.

Example 3.5 shows a continuation of the mad scientist. Elvin's scientist in a lab coat, along with Elise's scientist, has exploded some mixture of chemicals. Everett's and Eileen's scientists are less ominous, but are depicted as wearing the stereotypical lab coats.

The drawings in Example 3.6 are not as ominous as those in the previous examples, but they still depict scientists in white lab coats. Here, Elliot depicts a sense of "wonder." Ellen's woman scientist "wants to learn more about things." Effie's and Eleanor's scientists are working toward goals in the applied field of medicine.

The previous examples tend to depict some of the common misconceptions about scientists that are held by children (and many adults). Some of these common views depict scientists as looking weird (mad, evil, etc.), as men (however, there are a few women scientists in these examples), as chemists, and as wearing lab coats. However, the reality is that scientists look like

**Example 3.4: Grade 5 Children's Drawings of Scientists**

Earl: "A mad scientist going crazy."

Emily: "A mad scientist holding test tubes. She has messy hair and is in a lab coat."

Evan: "I drew Frankenstein."

Eugene: "I have drawn a picture of a mad scientist that has done a bunch of experimentation on himself."

**Example 3.5: Grade 5 Children's Drawings of Scientists**

Elvin: "A man with a burn on his face because his experiment blew up."

Elise: "The scientist was scared of the booms and potions."

Everett: "I have drawn a scientist with bottles."

Eileen: "I drew a scientist with a white coat on."

**Example 3.6: Grade 5 Children's Drawings of Scientists**

Elliot: "Wonder"

Ellen: "The scientist is a girl who wants to learn more about things."

Effie: "This scientist is mixing chemicals to find a cure for cancer."

Eleanor: "For the scientist, I drew a man with medical equipment."

everyone else. Although unfortunately most scientists are men, the percentages of women and minorities are increasing. Obviously there are more areas of science than chemistry, where lab coats are more common in the laboratory. However, some chemists never step foot in a lab, such as theoretical or quantum chemists. Even scientists who work in labs may tend to wear jeans and T-shirts rather than lab coats. So, where do all of these faulty ideas about scientists come from? There is no clear evidence as to where these ideas arise, but these kinds of depictions of scientists are common in cartoons, TV shows, movies, and books. However, in terms of children, the notion of a mad or weird scientist is far more intriguing and sparks the imagination more than a scientist dressed in jeans and a T-shirt digging in the soil for hours. Our challenge is to find a way of sparking children's imagination, while at the same time providing a balanced view of scientists.

The excerpts from interviews with children about science (Examples 3.7 and 3.8) provide another way of examining children's ideas about the nature of science. These interviews were conducted after an inquiry unit; however, many of their ideas about science still maintain some of the popular notions. As you read through the excerpts, think about how their ideas fit with the notions of science discussed so far in this chapter.

- ✦ **How do the views expressed in the children's drawings (Examples 3.4 to 3.6) compare to your views—both before and after having read this chapter?**
- ✦ **Do the children's representations match the diversity of people involved in science (i.e., diversity of sex, race, ethnicity, etc.)?**
- ✦ **How do the children's views compare to those of the writers cited in Section 3.3 of this chapter?**
- ✦ **From where do you think the children developed their views?**
- ✦ **What do their views suggest about what we should address in our teaching of science?**
- ✦ **What can we do to address issues of diversity among scientists?**

**Ask a group of children or a class to draw a picture of a scientist.**

- ✦ **How do your results match those depicted in this chapter?**

**Follow up this activity with a group discussion about their drawings. Ask them about the kinds of people who work as scientists, what the day-to-day experience of scientists is like, and so forth.**

- ✦ **Are their answers consistent with their drawings?**
- ✦ **Did any of the children challenge the stereotypical view of scientists or think of examples that counter such a view?**

---

**Example 3.7: Children's Responses to the Question "What Is Science?"**

*Frank:* Science is probably working with different things to make reactions. I heard on a TV show every reaction has an equal and balanced reaction, so I guess that's probably what science is, just testing reactions.

*Gina:* Study of some things? You know, anything really, everything is kind of a science. Yeah, I mean, you can't go, you can't go into a room and not know the English language and try and converse, use words at least, unless the other person knows. I mean you have the science of speaking, and how your tongue moves around your mouth. And, you know how it forms words. You know, and I guess it's the science of studying people. Yeah, everything can be a science if you make it. No matter how, you know, even writing on the chalkboard, if you use one part of the chalk, what effect is it going to make?

*Greg:* Science is like, well, a lot of people think that everything has an explanation somehow, and science is how you, like using science is how you reach the explanation. So, like, to figure out like there's a … instead of being magic, it's almost like magic, but there's a scientific reason, that it floats up and goes down, because of the air in it. It's like there's a scientific reason for everything.

*Gail:* Well, I think scientists like to explore new things; like do experiments and see what happens. Right now I'm working with like a mouse, see if I can tame it and see.

*Eric:* I don't think I can.

*Grace:* Well, I guess it's experimenting. Mostly it's experimenting with the natural world. It's not like … and it's also experimenting with new things that can be developed. Well, the science I've done is like leaves and trees and water and lots of stuff like that.

*Graham:* Science is mostly discovering different things. Like today in science Greg and I took apart a curling iron and the part that heats up, we stripped it and whatever, stripped the wires, and then, I forget the word, but we put the wires together on a plug and we plugged it in, and it heated up. And I had to clock, well, I sort of made this up, like this experiment. I had to clock, so I held a match up to it after 4 minutes it heated up. How many seconds would it take to heat up to light the match. And one time it took 10 seconds and another time it took 39 seconds. So, it's mostly just discovery. Like underwater expeditions discover new things, like, I don't know, sunken ships or different animals.

*Teacher:* With that experiment you were doing, why was there such a big difference between the two times?

Graham: I don't know. I thought it had something to do maybe with the way the match was coated with the strike-anywhere stuff, the way I held it, because the first time, I just put the thing right to it and it lit. And the second time, I just put the tip to it, but after that I just put the side of it and it just flared. And then Frank's doing something with—I didn't get to see what—but he's doing something with chemicals.

Gloria: Um, science is, well, science is everything, 'cause, because, um, well, it's just like even a, a piece of wood is part of science because it has atoms in it, and people study atoms and that's part of science. And, science like studying things and learning about things and it's hard to define science because it's everything.

Fred: Science is a method of learning. It has to do with hypothesizes [sic] and guesses. It's just a way of learning I guess.

❋

◆ How do the students' understandings of science differ from what we have been discussing so far in this chapter?
◆ Which of the students' statements seem to be more accurate?
◆ How could you address some of the more vague or inaccurate understandings of the nature of science in your classroom?

---

**Example 3.8: Children's Responses to the Question "How Does Science Work?"**

Frank: Well scientists probably learn it from people from the past like Albert Einstein working with the theory of relativity and stuff.

Gina: I think, well, you can learn from the books, but by observing and doing, you can learn a lot more than from reading from the book, and I think they do a lot of that. You know, if they want to learn how, if they're studying floating, then maybe they'd go to a pool and just float there, or go on a ship, do things like that, so you can learn from hands-on and doing.

Greg: Yeah, they experiment. I guess they sort of test things. Like, like how they figured out to do this. [Here, he is referring to a toy Cartesian diver, a "Squidy," he just worked with during the interview.] They had to figure out they'd have to put air in it so it would float. And then they had to experiment to make it so it would sink by just pressing.

Gail: They have lots of equipment. I don't know. It depends on what kind of scientist it is. There's kind of different kinds; I don't know, ecol…, people that like, dig on bones and stuff, archeologists. They kind of, are they scientists? Like they're kind of like scientists, I guess. What happened millions of years ago, I guess. One time we were up at Needham, and there's guys there. And they had something so they, like they had all sorts of like things all over the place. And we couldn't see them. They had one up at Needham and they had one somewhere else.

> *Eric:* Well, what kind of scientists? Uh, biologists probably study the way of life of other species, and figure out how things grow.
>
> *Grace:* I guess by, well, scientists learn a lot of important things like, they invented space ships so you could go into space and stuff like that. And they can see the planets and stars. Well, they can't see the stars. They can see planets and the moon and everything. And they invented stuff for the astronauts to wear so they can still breathe when they're on the moon.
>
> *Graham:* They do an experiment like I did or something like that and then they take notes and—I did that—see what happens. I used three matches trying to do it. Only two of them lit 'cause one of them didn't work. I don't know why. I couldn't get it lit on the strike-anywhere either. I don't know what was wrong with it. Maybe it was, I don't know, maybe it was wet or something. So, they like take notes and they take notes and they explain. Right in the beginning they write down what they think will happen, and at the end they write down what happened. But they guess sort of thing, and then they try it out.
>
> *Gloria:* They, well, science, you can, if you're studying something, you pick what you're going to study and you make a hypothesis or, if you, like, if you're studying a helium balloon, you make a hypothesis it's going to float and then you observe it and if it does float, then your hypothesis is correct, and that's science, studying something, or just learning about things.
>
> *Fred:* It's a number of different experiments, and it works by experimenting and seeing what will happen. Sometimes science is just nature.

✦ Which of the statements about how science works are reasonably in lne with what we have read so far in this chapter?

✦ What types of activities could you do in the classroom to represent the process of doing science in a better way?

## 3.6 Summary

In order to represent the nature of science in ways that are more authentic, we need to move away from the more traditional approach that relies heavily on following the textbook. Science is a process for developing explanations of our world. From the perspective of different scientists (Section 3.3), we may have noticed a sense of *passion*. Many scientists, like many professionals, operate from a basis in passion—a passion for understanding, a passion for making discoveries and gaining insights, and a passion for solving problems. The question we need to consider is, How can we support and encourage the passion of children?

We also need to address children's stereotypical views of scientists, such as the mad scientist, scientists in lab coats, white male scientists, etc., to include a diversity of scientists. More importantly, we need to encourage participation in science by girls and children of different racial, cultural, and ethnic backgrounds. However, a major difficulty in encouraging such participation is that the traditional white male approach to science may clash with other approaches to science. For instance, the traditional interpretation of ecological relationships and animal behavior is based on competition and aggression. More recently, however, a number of women biologists and others have been suggesting that many ecological relationships and animal behaviors are based on cooperation. Such a view is more consistent with Native North American understanding as well. As discussed earlier, science does not necessarily have an inside track to the truth, nor is the knowledge necessarily unchangeable. We can see here how the concept of competition is beginning to share center stage in ecological relationships with the concept of cooperation. Another strategy we might consider is allowing children to use a variety of ways to express their understandings, so that artistic, dramatic, and poetic expressions can be accommodated and even encouraged. For instance, while studying a local forest ecosystem, you can have children write and act out skits about something they have learned through their investigations. They also can create artistic representations of important concepts they have learned or of key observations. Even sketching trees or flowers from different angles (from a distance, from a 45° angle, and from underneath) can lead to interesting insights about the structure of trees. Poetry can be used to express appreciations for nature, as well as to express issues and the nature of the forest ecosystem dynamics.

Our own previous experiences with science may not have been very exciting or intriguing. When science is taught as a body of knowledge (i.e., the typical textbook approach to learning a lot of facts and principles), science tends to be "deadened." From such an approach, we experience science as difficult, boring, and static. The approach presented in this book tries to enliven science and enliven learning. Learning in school, including science, should help children to see a world of possibility, see learning as exciting and intriguing, and see their worlds as full of life. In taking such an approach, we need to avoid dogma. Saying that some explanation is right because that is what the book says tends to deflate children's curiosity and excitement. Children need to engage in inquiry and the construction of their own explanations based on their results. They need to engage in developing their own theories and to argue with each other about why one theory or explanation is better than another. However, such an inquiry approach requires a great deal of work by teachers. As opposed to teaching from a book, which is much easier, teaching through inquiry involves more critical and creative thinking by teachers. You need to engage in the inquiry yourself and think of ways to help children extend their inquiry. At the same time, you and your students need to have fun. Having fun happens when you make discoveries, solve problems, see things in new ways, and take ownership over the knowledge being developed. The rest of this book will provide you with a background and practical ways of doing just this kind of an approach.

The following are some suggestions for incorporating the nature of science into instruction:

Find a group of children (in your own classroom, if you are a teacher, or any group of children you can get together). Interview them:

✦ What is science?
✦ How is it different from or similar to other fields (i.e., art, history, math, etc.)?
✦ How does science work?
✦ What are scientists like?
✦ What do scientists do when they go to work?
✦ What other questions can you ask?

Be sure to tape-record the children's responses or take extensive notes. (Note: Be sure to use a consent form to be signed by the children's parents, and the children as well. Talk with your university instructor or school principal about consent forms.)

✦ What patterns do you see from the children's responses?
✦ What are the implications for how we should be teaching science?

- Have students complete some tasks that represent their understandings of science and scientists, such as drawing a scientist and open discussions.
- Discuss with the children how they could work like scientists. Try to identify some of the key characteristics and post them around the classroom. You could precede this discussion by having them interview scientists, looking at videos of scientists working, and so forth.
- Doing a unit on the nature of science may not be a particularly fruitful approach. However, spending some time on the previous activities could lead to a strand that you revisit throughout all of your instruction.
- After these activities, have children reflect on what characteristics of their investigations were like those of scientists.
- Try to incorporate the history of science as appropriate. If you are studying adaptation, you could have students find out more about Charles Darwin and other biologists (including women and those from different cultural, ethnic, and racial groups), as well as the understandings of Native Americans and other indigenous peoples. If you are studying the solar system, have students investigate Ptolemy, Galileo, indigenous people's astronomy, and so forth. However, be sure to focus not only on how they worked, but what these people were like as individuals and what the social and political contexts in which they lived were like. You can have them write and present skits or plays on these individuals. In having them write their plays and skits, you may want to suggest or have them suggest some creative twists, like What if Darwin traveled through time to visit us now? What if Galileo could use the Hubble telescope?
- Another way of creating a critical focus on the nature of science could include a weekly "bad science report" or "warped science critique," where students can bring in examples of bad science, misconceptions about science, and so forth. Such critiques could involve examples from TV shows, movies, news, and other media representations.

Such approaches to incorporating the nature of science into instruction is important, if not crucial, to educating our children for participation in society and the political process. Although this area of science education seems to be overlooked throughout much of schooling, the nature of science is highlighted in the national standards of both the United States and Canada, as well as other countries. Appendixes B and C provide a short description of the standards and how they relate to the content of this book.

## Additional Reading

Read popular books by or about scientists. Some examples of scientist-authors and science writers whom you may find enjoyable are

- Richard P. Feynman (especially those about his own life, like *"Surely You're Joking, Mr. Feynman:" Adventures of a Curious Character*)
- Stephen Jay Gould
- Lewis Thomas

Abram, D. (1996). *The spell of the sensuous: Perception and language in a more-than-human world*. New York: Pantheon.

Ackerman, D. (1990). *A natural history of the senses*. New York: Vintage Books/Random House.

Bauer, H. H. (1994). *Scientific literacy & the myth of the scientific method*. Urbana, IL: University of Illinois Press.

Biklen, D., & Cardinal, D. N. (Eds.). (1997). *Contested words, contested science*. New York: Teachers College Press.

Brockman, J. (2004). *Curious minds: How a child becomes a scientist*. New York: Vintage Press.

Cromer, A. H. (1997). *Connected knowledge: Science, philosophy, & education*. New York: Oxford University Press.

Driver, R., Leach, J., Millar, R., & Scott, P. (1996). *Young people's images of science*. Philadelphia: Open University Press.

Mullis, K. (1998). *Dancing naked in the mind field*. New York: Pantheon/Random House.

Quammen, D. (1996). *Natural acts: A sidelong view of science and nature*. New York: Avon Books.

Raup, D. M. (1991). *Extinction: Bad genes or bad luck?* New York: W. W. Norton & Company.

Stangroom, J. (2005). *What scientists think*. New York: Routledge.

Weiner, J. (Ed.) (2005). *The best American science and nature writing 2005*. New York: Houghton Mifflin. (A volume of these writings is published every year with different editors, but all from Houghton Mifflin Publishers.)

Wolpert, L. (2000). *The unnatural nature of science*. Cambridge, MA: Harvard University Press.

## Advanced Reading

Some of these books are older classics, while others are more recent. They cover material about science from good science writing to science education.

Burke, J. (1985). *The day the universe changed*. Boston: Little, Brown & Company.

Burke, J. (2000). *Circles: 50 round trips through history, technology, science, culture*. New York: Simon & Schuster.

Capra, F. (2002). *The hidden connections: Integrating the biological, cognitive, and social dimensions of life into a science of sustainability*. New York: Doubleday.

Casti, J. L. (1994). *Complexification: Explaining a paradoxical world through the science of surprise*. New York: Harper Collins.

Darwin, F. (1995). *The life of Charles Darwin*. London: Guernsey Press. (Original work published 1902.)

Duschl, R. A. (1990). *Restructuring science education: The importance of theories and their development*. New York: Teachers College Press.

Einstein, A. (1995). *Out of my later years*. New York: Carol Publishing. (Original work published 1956.)

Gould, S. J. (1981). *The mismeasure of man*. New York: W. W. Norton & Company.

Hawking, S. (1988). *A brief history of time: From the big bang to black holes*. New York: Bantam Books.

Irwin, A., & Wynne, B. (Eds.). (1996). *Misunderstanding science? The public reconstruction of science and technology*. New York: Cambridge University Press.

Kuhn, T. S. (1970). *The structure of scientific revolutions* (2nd ed.). Chicago: University of Chicago Press. (Original work published 1962.)

Latour, B., & Woolgar, S. (1986). *Laboratory life: The construction of scientific facts*. Princeton, NJ: Princeton University Press.

Millar, R. (Ed.). (1989). *Doing science: Images of science in science education*. New York: Falmer Press.

Roth, W. M., & Calabrese Barton, A. (2004). *Rethinking scientific literacy*. New York: Routledge.

Schwab, J. J, Westbury, I., & Wilkof, N. J. (Eds.). (1978). *Science, curriculum, and liberal education: Selected essays*. Chicago: University of Chicago Press.

Schwartz, J. (1979). *Einstein for beginners*. New York: Pantheon Books.

Sheldrake, R. (1995). *Seven experiments that could change the world: A do-it-yourself guide to revolutionary science*. New York: Riverhead Books.

Simon, H. (2001). "Seek and ye shall find": How curiosity engenders discovery. In K. Crowley, C. D. Schunn, and T. Okada (Eds.), *Designing for science: Implications from everyday, classroom, and professional settings* (pp. 5–20). Mahwah, NJ: Lawrence Erlbaum Associates.

Stevenson, L., & Byerly, H. (1995). *The many faces of science: An introduction to scientists, values, and society*. Boulder, CO: Westview Press.

## Other Resources

Donald Simanek's "Science Quotes" (Lock Haven University of Pennsylvania): http://www.lhup.edu/~dsimanek/sciquote.htm

Lynn Fancher's "What Is Science?" (College of DuPage): http://www.cod.edu/people/faculty/fancher/Science.htm

Jerry Stanbrough's (Batesville High School, Indiana) "About Science Notes" (with link to "Science and Scientific Method" quotes): http://www.batesville.k12.in.us/physics/PhyNet/AboutScience/

World Village "Science": http://quotes.worldvillage.com/i/b/Science

## Notes

1. Gregory Bateson, *Mind and Nature: A Necessary Unity* (New York: Bantam, 1979), p. 33.
2. Stephen J. Gould, *Ever Since Darwin: Reflections in Natural History* (New York: W.W. Norton, 1977), pp. 238–239.
3. Bateson, *Mind and Nature*, pp. 29, 32.
4. C.A. Ronan, *Science: Its History and Development among World's Cultures* (New York: Facts On File Publications, 1982).
5. M. Goldstein & I. Goldstein, *How We Know: An Exploration of the Scientific Process* (New York: Plenum Press, 1978), p. 260.
6. Gould, *Ever Since Darwin*.
7. Lewis Thomas, *The Lives of a Cell: Notes of a Biology Watcher* (New York: Bantam, 1974).
8. Albert Einstein, *Out of My Later Years* (New York: Citadel Press, 1995).
9. Michael Polanyi, *The Tacit Dimension* (New York: Doubleday & Company, 1966), pp. 78–79.
10. Ursula Franklin, The Real World of Mathematics, Science and Technology Education, *MSTE News*, 1(2), Suppl. 4. (From an address given at an invited colloquium of the MSTE Group, Faculty of Education, Queen's University, Kingston, Ontario, May 16–17, 1991.)
11. Kary Mullis, *Walking Naked in the Mind Field* (New York: Pantheon Books, 1998), pp. 112–114.
12. Richard Feynman,*"Surely You're Joking, Mr. Feynman!": Adventures of a Curious Character* (New York: W.W. Norton, 1985), pp. 91–92.
13. Richard Feynman, *The Meaning of It All: Thoughts of a Citizen-Scientist* (Reading, MA: Helix/Perseus Books, 1998), pp. 26–27.
14. Richard P. Feynman, *The Pleasure of Finding Things Out* (Cambridge, MA: Helix/Perseus Publishing, 1999).
15. Francis Darwin, *The Life of Charles Darwin* (London: Senate, 1995).
16. Darwin, *The Life of Charles Darwin*.
17. Sharon Bertsch McGrayne, *Nobel Prize Women in Science* (Washington, DC: Joseph Henry Press, 1998).
18. Jane Goodall, *Through a Window: My Thirty Years with the Chimpanzees of Gombe* (Boston: Houghton Mifflin, 1990), pp. 14–15.
19. Bertsch McGrayne, *Nobel Prize Women in Science*, p. 98.
20. Bertsch McGrayne, *Nobel Prize Women in Science*.
21. James Burke, *The Day the Universe Changed* (Boston: Little, Brown and Company, 1985), p. 337. (Based on a television series of the same name.)
22. Bauer, H. H. (1992). *Scientific literacy and the myth of the scientific method*. Urbana, IL: University of Illinois Press.
23. Los Alamos National Laboratory, News and Public Affairs, Physicist Begay Honored for Mentoring Minorities in Science (news release), http://www.lanl.gov/news/releases/archive/99-169.shtml, downloaded September 2005.
24. Taken from http://unisci.com/science2.shtml (no longer being published)

## Chapter 4
# Children's Learning and Sense Making

In the past, and still evident in many classrooms today, teachers' attention has focused on the explicit, written curriculum to the exclusion of how children come to understand and learn. However, recent work on children's thinking and learning has led to changes in the way we view teaching. This view of teaching places emphasis on the individual child, which has given rise to the phrase "child-centered instruction." This chapter will examine a number of areas of research that impact on our thinking about children's learning and understanding. The two major areas of research on children's learning involve constructivism and social constructivism (see definitions at the beginning of the following two subsections). These two areas will serve as the basic framework for this chapter and the rest of the book. Several related areas of research will also be discussed. These additional areas include (a) categorization as a basic process of learning, (b) the construction of meaning, (c) play as a fundamental learning strategy, (d) story as a framework of learning, and (e) how children tap into the basic patterns of complex learning. While reading this chapter and examining the examples, think about how children think and develop complex connections.

In order to teach effectively from a constructivist and social constructivist perspective, we need to develop a thorough understanding of how children think and learn (i.e., from such a child-centered perspective). We cannot rely on a step-by-step procedure to deliver instruction, but must consider each child's personal understandings before providing activities that build on these understandings.

As we read through this chapter, numerous examples and activities will allow us to examine children's learning and thinking in more detail. However, as many of the activities suggest, the key to developing a working understanding of how children learn is to talk to and work with children. If you have the opportunity to do some of the activities with children, either formally in a classroom or informally with an individual or small group, your understanding of how children think and learn will be enhanced greatly.

## 4.1 Constructivism

Constructivism is a theory of learning. It contends that children (and adults) construct knowledge from their personal experiences, whether those experiences are in or out of school. Constructivism is a departure from the behaviorist view of learning, which was, and still is, a dominant influence on teaching and curriculum in schools. From the behaviorist perspective, learning occurs as a response to a particular stimulus. Children's prior experiences and ideas are not considered. The teacher introduces an idea or concept and children remember it. Evidence of this learning can be obtained through observable behavior, such as responses on a test or observable classroom activity.

On the other hand, constructivism contends that children enter the classroom with a vast amount of knowledge gained from their personal experiences of living in the world. Even a five-year-old entering school for the first time brings into the classroom a great deal of knowledge and many explanations for how the world works. Within the metaphor of construction, children's prior knowledge acts as a foundation upon which to build further understandings. When children encounter new information and ideas in school, they try to make sense of these ideas in relation to what they already know. In a class of 30 children, the result can be 30 different understandings. Each child's individual and prior understandings affect how the new information is incorporated. In some cases, the new information may not make any sense to the child, when compared to his or her previous understandings. The result can be that the new information is not taken seriously and is not incorporated into the child's new constructions of knowledge. In other cases, the new information and experiences are not related to anything the child has experienced before. In such cases, children start to make sense of these new experiences. However, constructivism does not make the claim that all learning is observable. So, as children work with new ideas, they may not be able to explain what they have learned. Their images and personal experiences with specific activities and ideas have not been put together in ways that can be expressed in language.

In Example 4.1 (lines 3, 5, and 7), Cindy notices that the front of the worm is red and draws on her previous knowledge to infer that the color may indicate the location of the worm's hearts. Later in the excerpt, she mentions that

As we read through the first two sections on constructivism and social constructivism, the distinction between them may not always be clear. There is, in fact, a lot of overlap. For the purpose of this book, we may want to make the distinction that constructivism addresses how individuals construct their own personal understandings within a broader context of social interactions (i.e., social constructivism). The overlap between these two theoretical frameworks is particularly evident in many of the examples of instruction provided in the section on constructivism, where social constructivist approaches are suggested.

> **Example 4.1: Excerpt of a Conversation with a**
> **Grade 3 Girl While Looking at Earthworms**
>
> *Cindy:* What are you going to do with the worms?
>
> **Teacher: Just look at them.**
>
> *Cindy:* What's wrong with that, it's all red at the front?
>
> **Teacher: I don't know.**
>
> *Cindy:* Is that where its hearts are or something?
>
> **Teacher: Is that what you think?**
>
> *Cindy:* 'Cause there's little red dots or something.
>
> **Teacher: Red ... right there? What do you think?**
>
> *Cindy:* I don't know. I think they are about the middle, aah, this one inches, it couldn't get off.
>
> **Teacher: What else do you think is inside the worm?**
>
> *Cindy:* Well I don't know what's inside of it to make it move. You know it probably has stuff like we do like when something hurts us we curl up, and they probably do that too so; and having so many hearts I don't know what's going to happen and they...
>
> **Teacher: They have many hearts you think?**
>
> *Cindy:* Yeah.
>
> **Teacher: How many?**
>
> *Cindy:* Have you heard about that? They have like seven so that if they get cut off ... like that one ... they have another heart so they can live.

**Refer to Example 4.1:**

- ✦ What does Cindy's understanding of earthworms look like?
- ✦ What aspects of her understanding are accurate and what aspects are inaccurate?
- ✦ Can you identify points at which she infers new knowledge?
- ✦ How can we help Cindy extend her learning?
- ✦ What experiences can we provide, which will allow her to explore the earthworm circulation?

worms have seven hearts. Although there are five pairs of "hearts" (called aortic arches), she has prior knowledge that earthworms have more than one heart. In the final comment, she makes another inference suggesting that because earthworms have multiple hearts, they can be cut in two parts and still survive. This idea is intriguing, even though earthworms will die if cut in half. Her thinking suggests that hearts are essential for the survival of an organism. Her thinking makes intuitive sense in that if an organism has several hearts, then the remaining hearts can compensate for those lost when it is cut in half.

Such thinking is a characteristic of the nature of our understanding of constructivism. Children are active learners and sense makers. They make inferences based on their current understandings and what seems to make sense to them. As we can see in line 13, Cindy appears to base at least some of her inferences on her understanding of her own body and suggests that an earthworm "probably has stuff like we do."

As with any situation that arises in the classroom, there are many possible approaches to extending children's learning. Earthworms tend to be somewhat translucent, so there are opportunities to view their internal organs without cutting them open. By placing an earthworm on a piece of moist foam rubber, you can gently press the earthworm against a piece of clear glass or plastic, which helps make the internal organs more readily visible. With the aid of a magnifying glass, a child can examine the internal organs more closely. He or she may even be able to see the pulsating of the hearts. Traditionally, earthworms are not dissected until much higher grades; however, you probably will find that young children may be fascinated by the opportunity. With some guidance and assistance, some children will find the experience very helpful in constructing better explanations of their observations of the living earthworm. If you do not wish to have the children dissect an earthworm, especially with Native American students (whose cultural beliefs would be undermined by such activities), models and simulated dissection software are available. Experiences with dissection are of particular importance to children's inquiry and construction of knowledge and understanding. If at all possible, such experiences are much more meaningful than simply looking up or providing the information. However, at some point later in their inquiry, you may want to introduce some appropriate books. Once children have experienced many of the concepts through their own inquiry, the introduction of reading material will allow them to make more meaningful connections to the information provided in books. The introduction of reading material at the beginning of a unit may limit children's curiosity and a sense of ownership over their own ideas and explanations.

In the previous example, a grade 1 girl draws on previous knowledge gained from talking with her mother. Here the information is presented in a rather straightforward way, with no added information about the context. What she says is simple recall of information she heard from someone else. The question at this point is what experiences can be provided to allow the child to develop a more elaborate understanding.

◀▶

**The dissection of animals has become much less popular in the past decade or so.**
**How do you stand on the issue? What is your rationale? What does actual dissection offer that simulated dissection cannot?**
**Dissection should have a purpose that arises from children's curiosity and questions during inquiry. It should be a natural extension of the inquiry. Another guideline to consider is whether the children will learn more about the topic and develop a greater appreciation for life by doing the dissection. In general, it seems that the actual organism, rather than a virtual one, provides a sense of the texture, flexibility, and three-dimensional qualities. In addition, the virtual dissection (even one that is videotaped) is more difficult to explore in terms of looking at how one part is connected to another in order to get a sense of the entire system of interconnections. However, the virtual dissections are good alternatives.**

---

**Example 4.2: Grade 1 Girl Talking about Earthworms: Sex**

**Teacher:** **Tell me, what do you know about worms?**

*April:* They, umm, they both, they're girls and boys.

**Teacher:** **They're both?**

*April:* Yes.

**Teacher:** **How do you know that?**

*April:* Because my mum told us.

---

When considering the questions in the sidebar, we need to look first for opportunities to engage children in the process of inquiry. Looking for sex organs in earthworms through dissection may not be the best way to proceed, because of the difficulty in identifying the organs. However, children can take a few earthworms home for several days and record their observations. (They should moisten the soil in their earthworm container every evening, and observe them after that.) If they see two earthworms next to each other on the surface (as depicted in Figure 4.1), you can then pose several questions to them:

- What could the earthworms be doing?
- Why is it that they are in this position?
- Can their position next to each other, facing opposite directions, tell us anything about the sex of the earthworms and how they mate?

**FIGURE 4.1**

The following discussions among the students can allow them to express their ideas and argue with each other about which ideas make more sense. (More details on conducting such discussions will be provided in Chapter 5.)

---

**Example 4.3: Grade 1 Girl Talking about Earthworms: What Eats Them**

**Teacher:** **What else do you know about worms?**

*Ann:* I know that they like damp cold places and on rainy days they come up but … but that's exactly when robins are looking for food, so worms can get caught very easily.

**Teacher:** **Uh huh, so what do robins do with them?**

*Ann:* They take them to their babies so the babies can eat them.

---

✦ **How can we help April elaborate on her knowledge about the sex characteristics of earthworms?**

✦ **What experiences can we provide?**

In the above example, Ann discusses the relationship between birds and earthworms. Her experiences of seeing earthworms coming to the surface of the soil on rainy days allows her to draw a connection to when robins look for food. She extends her idea of robins catching earthworms to include the maternal behavior of feeding their babies. What is noticeable in this excerpt is the elaboration of her understanding. Rather than simply stating the core information, Ann elaborates on this information by placing it in context. In fact, her description takes on the characteristics of a story about earthworms and robins. Compared to April's statement about earthworms being both sexes (in the preceding example), there is much more a sense of *richness of understanding*, with connections to Ann's personal experiences and observations of earthworms.

In Example 4.4, we can see how Emily is actively trying to make sense of her observations in a process of constructing knowledge. She draws on her understandings of specific ideas, such as "veins" and "nerve," to provide both a structural and functional explanation for what she sees. At the same time, she refers to "sniffing" and "cats' whiskers" as analogies for the function of the front tip of the earthworm. What we see here is the process of developing a rich set of connections to varied information related to one aspect of the earthworm's behavior. The entire sequence is embedded in the contexts of her prior knowledge about specific organs and structures of the earthworm crawling around in a pan of dirt.

Again, there are many possible approaches to these questions. Dissection (real or simulated) and exploration of a model are obvious ways to allow children to explore the internal organs and generate explanations. In addition,

✳

+ **From an instructional point of view, how can we extend a child's, such as Emily's, learning?**
+ **What experiences can we provide that will allow Emily to explore her ideas in more depth?**
+ **How can we facilitate her inquiry into the senses of earthworms?**
+ **Can you think of any experiments that will allow students to develop more in-depth explanations?**

---

### Example 4.4: Grade 5 Girl Discussing Earthworms

*Emily:*    I think that's the veins, or that coily thing, I think it gets thicker as it goes back.

**Teacher: Right.**

*Emily:*    I think, I think the skinnier part is the head and the, 'cause you, the little thing at the end that looks kind of like a point.

**Teacher: Uh huh.**

*Emily:*    I think that's kind of a sensor.

**Teacher: Oh.**

*Emily:*    Something like that so they can find their way around.

**Teacher: That's interesting. You know that's probably exactly what that does, too.**

*Emily:*    Well, it looks like it because it's going around and around. It looks like it's kind of sniffing to see what's there.

**Teacher: Uh huh. Right. Do they have noses or does it just act like a nose?**

*Emily:*    I think it's kind of like cats' whiskers, you know.

**Teacher: Uh huh.**

*Emily:*    They don't smell but they feel.

**Teacher: Feel. Yeah.**

*Emily:*    They've got kind of a nerve.

**Teacher: Uh huh.**

*Emily:*    Maybe, maybe that line in there; maybe that's a nerve …

**Teacher: That could be too.**

*Emily:*    … connecting to the head.

---

there are a number of experiments you and your students can devise. As will be discussed in Chapter 6 on designing experiments, you should involve students in the design of their experiments. However, for the benefit of this discussion, some examples might be helpful. You might try placing a tiny bit of petroleum jelly on the tip of the earthworm, then observe and record descriptions of its movements and behavior. In terms of other senses, you can draw a circle about 16 to 25 cm. (8 to 10 in.) in diameter with a marker or crayon on a piece of flat glass or plastic. Very gently pick up and place an earthworm in the center of the circle and time how long it takes for the earthworm to move out of the circle. Now place a second earthworm in the middle of the circle and poke it with your finger until it writhes. Remove this earthworm and very gently place a third earthworm in the center of the circle and time how long it takes this one to move out of the circle. Although you may not always get the expected results, if each group of children is doing the experiment, you may have enough data to work with as a class. What should happen is that the third earthworm will move out of the circle much more rapidly. What could account for this behavior? Obviously, the second earthworm (the one that was poked) left behind some kind of chemical message. From this point, you can start a discussion of how this could be important to the survival of earthworms.

The major point here is that when we are teaching, we need to find out what our students already know (see Chapter 7 for assessment methods that will help uncover students' prior knowledge). Of course, we cannot get a complete picture of their prior knowledge, but we can get an idea of some of the major understandings they already have. The information we gather on what children already know should serve as a basis upon which to build our instructional strategies. As we go through a unit in class, we have to be on the alert for further evidence of how our students' previous understandings are affecting their current sense making. The process of teaching from this perspective becomes one of monitoring children's understandings and introducing new activities to challenge or extend their previous conceptions. These activities should be within a framework of inquiry. Such inquiry should provide the kinds of experiences from which students can formulate their own explanations and understandings.

**Although constructivism, for the most part, has its origins in Piaget's research on children's epistemology (i.e., structure of knowledge), many contemporary researchers and practitioners distance themselves from his work. Much of this resistance to acknowledging connections to Piaget may be due to the heavy emphasis North Americans have placed on his developmental stage theory. The implications of constructivist research suggest that such stages of development tend to be suspect, in that they tend to limit teachers' expectations and consequent learning activities. From a contemporary constructivist perspective, a child's prior knowledge and experience with particular phenomena are more critical to his or her intellectual development than are age-dependent stages.[1]**

## 4.2 Social Constructivism

Social constructivism maintains that knowledge is constructed but contends that all learning occurs within the context of culture. Individuals learn through communicating and interacting with one another. An individual in isolation will not learn. From the moment a baby is born, he or she starts learning about the world through his or her interactions with parents and others. Without any direct instruction, very young children learn the very abstract symbol system of communication: language. Along with language, children start constructing concepts about their world and the norms and values of their cultures.

Much of the work in the area of social constructivism has its roots in the writings of Lev Vygotsky, a Russian scholar, from the early part of the 20th century. In his most popular notion of the "zone of proximal development," he suggests that children can move from their current level of development to their potential level of development under the guidance of an adult or more capable peer. In other words, a child may develop higher levels of skill and knowledge through his or her interactions with others. Over the past couple of decades, the necessity of a more capable peer or adult continues to be debated, and that certain kinds of interactions among peers at the same level may provide the impetus for further skill and knowledge development.

Social constructivism goes further than saying that all learning is context dependent. Attempts to teach children generalized skills, which can be applied to different situations, are not possible—at least, no evidence exists that teaching such skills leads to any significant transfer or applicability to other contexts. In other words, the teaching of particular thinking skills must be embedded in some context, some real situation. Teaching a skill such as deducing as a unit of instruction is not of much value in and of itself. However, if deducing is introduced as a skill in working with a particular contextually embedded problem, then children will have the opportunity to see the relevance of the skill in terms of the achievement of a specific goal. Essentially, all thinking is considered to be problem solving. Such thinking is goal directed, whether it is trying to make sense of something or figuring out how many sports cards or magazines can be bought with a certain amount of money.

One implication of social constructivism is that the most advantageous learning occurs when the material we want to cover is situated in a real and relevant context. So, if we are studying earthworms (to continue with the previous examples), we should be looking at earthworms within one or more contexts. A number of possible contexts might include gardening or farming, evolution and the development of different lineages of organisms, comparisons of how things move or reproduce, and so forth.

Social constructivism also suggests that learning occurs between and among individuals. Having an individual sit and look at an earthworm and fill out worksheets is not going to be as productive as having a group of children work together in a group. Group work can allow children to learn from each other, argue about which of their ideas make more sense, and negotiate their own knowledge claims.

As we read on into the next chapter on children's talk, we will delve more deeply into the specifics of looking at children's learning in social contexts. For now, we may want to consider some of the questions in the sidebar about the implications of social constructivism for learning and teaching.

## 4.3 | Contexts of Meaning

This particular use of the word *context* refers to the associated meanings attached to any particular object or topic. Each context can have a different meaning or perspective; for example, if we think of *frog*, we may hold several different perspectives. We may see the frog as an amphibian within a biological frame of understanding. We also may see the frog in terms of (a) the frog prince, (b) the sounds of frogs peeping at night during a romantic interlude by a pond, (c) the game of leap frog, (d) frog's legs to eat, (e) Kermit the Frog, or (f) music in the genre of "Solitudes" recordings (e.g., sounds of waves breaking along an ocean beach, sounds of a forest, etc.). *Meaning*, therefore,

---

✳

- ✦ Compare instances from your own schooling when you have had to work alone and in groups.
- ✦ What did you have to do in a group?
- ✦ How did having to defend your own ideas affect your thinking and learning?
- ✦ How did this experience compare with working alone?
- ✦ In which experience did you feel that you learned the most?
- ✦ Can you provide reasons for your answers?
- ✦ If you are planning a unit on outer space, for example, how might you go about organizing the classroom to encourage children's working in groups?
- ✦ How could you set up the unit in a way that makes it more relevant and realistic, in a way that engages children to work on realistic problems?
- ✦ What sorts of activities would help facilitate the children's inquiry, sense making, problem solving, and negotiation of knowledge claims

involves not only the school-type knowledge we have already examined, but also personal experiences, emotions, values, aesthetics, metaphors, imagery, interpretive frameworks, elaboration, stories, and fantasy. As we proceed through some examples of children's work and talk, each of these components of contexts of meaning will be explored in more depth. As we look at the examples, we need to keep in mind that these components do not necessarily occur as separate entities. We will find that children's thinking is quite complex, with a great deal of overlap among these different aspects of contexts of meaning. As we proceed, you may want to consider the implications of contexts of meaning for teaching and meaningful learning in science, for integrating instruction across the curriculum, and for how we can encourage and support children's creativity.

Typically, when we look at children's learning in the classroom, we focus on what we might call school-type knowledge. We do not pay too much attention to children's emotional reactions, values, or stories of their personal experiences. In elementary school, we may allow children to express these, but we do not place much value on them in terms of what our students are supposed to be learning in school. In reality, children draw on a wide range of human experiences and reactions when they interact with their world. The meanings children bring into the classroom include not only the prior knowledge (school-type knowledge) we have seen from a constructivist perspective, but also a richness of human experiences that come together to contribute to the overall *texture* and substance of our understandings. In the following paragraphs and examples, we will examine the nature of contexts of meaning as an extended view of constructivism.

In the short excerpt in Example 4.5, from a student teacher's work with a small group of children, Danny and Deanne discuss a beetle's antennae as they observe the beetle moving around in a container. The children's use of analogies (i.e., he "listens" and "what cats do with their whiskers") provide a powerful way for the children to figure out and make sense of their observations. Although the children's use of analogies is important to their sense making, the analogies can also help us, as teachers, to extend the children's inquiry. From this point, we can extend their inquiry into other things that act as cats' whiskers do (recall Emily's discussion of earthworms in Example 4.4). We also can encourage a line of inquiry into how animals sense their environment, and how different animals are adapted in different ways for their particular habitat and way of surviving.

Metaphors, including analogies, similes, etc., are effective tools for making sense of what children experience in and out of the classroom. From an early age (certainly before they enter school), children make use of metaphors in their everyday conversations, play, and sense-making activities. Unfortunately, we, as teachers, often overlook the significance of these uses of language. Example 4.6 provides a list of some metaphors used by students in grades 1 and 5 during their conversations while observing earthworms. As

◆ Can you think of any other structures that act like cats' whiskers?
◆ How are these different structures similar?
◆ What would it feel like to have cats' whiskers or any of these other structures?
◆ How do these structures contribute to the way in which each particular type of animal is adapted for survival?

◆ How can each of the previous metaphors be used as a starting point to examine a scientific understanding of a particular type of animal's adaptation to its habitat and way of life?
◆ How can each of these metaphors be used to initiate an integrated activity (e.g., art, poetry, story writing, social studies, and math)

---

**Example 4.5: Two Grade 4 Children's Discussion as They Observed a Beetle**

*Danny:*  His antennae, those are what he listens with, the beetle hears from his antennae. He feels around.

*Deanne:*  That's what cats do with their whiskers.

---

you read through these examples, think about the instructional implications, then try answering the questions that follow.

---

**Example 4.6**

Some metaphors used by children in describing earthworms and other animals. Children with names beginning with *A* are in grade 1, and with *E*, in grade 5.

| Name | Metaphor | Situation |
|------|----------|-----------|
| Adam | "Sticked their noses into the ground and tried to drill it around" | Describing how an earthworm might dig into the ground |
| Adam | "They feel like stickers" | While touching an earthworm |
| Alex | "Like springs and stretch" | Describing earthworm movement |
| Amy | "I wonder if their skin is really clothes" | Describing the function of skin |
| Amy | "It feels like your sheets are all cool" | While holding an earthworm |
| Andy | "Looks like a dragon's mouth" | Describing the "head" of an earthworm |
| Ann | "Play dirt games [underground]" | Describing earthworms' behavior |
| Earl | "Goes in like … jelly and then spreads this end out" | Describing earthworm movement |
| Elaine | "Legs [move] like a barber's [pole]" | Describing a millipede's movement |
| Elliot | "I wouldn't ride on him; too slimy" | Reaction to touching an earthworm |
| Evan | "Antennas are sort of like eyes and ears" | Describing the function of an insect's antennae |

---

Children's talk is full of wonderful ideas, images, metaphors, and stories. As we can see in Example 4.7, Amy starts talking about a dried starfish. She runs through naming the parts, with a reference to the familiar human term *tummy*. As she continues to talk, she adds little bits of elaboration, like the "feet … they sometimes move … and then that must have died like … that movement." She was sitting at a table filled with a variety of natural objects. As she noticed a spiral-shaped shell, she made a connection with its shape, "like an ice cream cone," which quickly became a dramatic story, complete with sound effects and her own emotional reaction and value statement. In her last statement, she starts another storyline, as she imagines sliding down the spiral to her home. The story adds a description of how the spiral gets "smaller and smaller." Then she immediately jumps into a description of her own personal experiences with the shells that she has at home. What we see here is a delightful mix of imaginative stories, emotions, and anthropomorphic frameworks.

---

**Example 4.7: A Grade 1 Girl's**
**Discussion about a Starfish and a Shell**

**Teacher:** **Ah, what's he called?**

Amy:    A starfish, that's the head, that's the arms, and those are the feet, and this is the tummy.

**Teacher:** **Really?**

Amy:    Yeah, that's the tummy, that's usually the head, that's the arm and that's the arm, and that's usually the feet; they sometimes move and then that must have died like, that movement [as she begins looking at a spiral shell], this looks like an ice cream cone, slurrrrppp, hmmm, that's good.

**Teacher:** **Yeah, it does look like an ice cream cone.**

Amy:    Or you could go in there and go for a swirl to get down to your house—niiiiiiiyehhhhhhhhhhhh, get smaller and smaller, oh I have one of these; I have lots of shells. I've got one like that. It's so huge. You can see reflections in those, one two three, three of them.

---

Anthropomorphism is the placing of human characteristics on other objects or living creatures. The "tummy" of the starfish is an example of this type of framework. Science educators have often criticized anthropomorphism as contributing to the development of inaccurate understandings in science. Recently, however, some educators and researchers are seeing that there may in fact be some benefit to the use of anthropomorphism. As we can see in this example, the use of *tummy* allows Amy to see a connection with the starfish. They share something in common. In a time when humankind is devastating the environment, encouraging a view of how all living things are connected can be beneficial. In addition, anthropomorphism can act as a guide for children's inferences. We saw an example of this in Example 4.1, when Cindy says, "it [the earthworm] probably has stuff like we do." From this kind of anthropomorphic connection, children can begin to infer some characteristics of another organism based on knowledge of their own bodies.

In Example 4.8, the story of this girl's personal experiences of walking through forests is brought to life with her emotional reactions. The smell of skunks is not something she likes. On the other hand, she has developed a relationship with her "squirrel friends," whose chatter she sees as their anthropomorphic communication with her, even though their chatter could be a reaction to her presence and a warning of potential danger. This connection with squirrels appears to have helped her develop a stronger appreciation for other animals of the forest—an appreciation that has developed into definite views about hunting.

☞

**Children often come up with connections to events in their world that do not fit with scientific knowledge, such as the squirrels talking with the child in Example 4.8. Rather than dismissing these connections, we need to consider the power of such comments for connecting with the natural world and as a means to develop integrated understandings.**

---

**Example 4.8: A Grade 5 Girl's Discussion of Forests, Based on a Context Map She Constructed***

*See discussion of context maps in section 7.4.

**Teacher: What about things that you don't like. Can you name one thing that you don't like about the forest?**

*Erin:* Well that's a hard one because I like just about everything about the forest. But I don't like sometimes when I'm walking in the woods and I smell something that has a skunk spray on it.

**Teacher: OK. That is not a very nice smell, is it?**

*Erin:* No.

**Teacher: OK. Can you just look at your context map that you drew, and can you just tell me why you joined some of the words together? Say, pick out a few of the words you joined, like *squirrels* and *nice*.**

*Erin:* Well, because I think squirrels are really really nice. I have a bunch of squirrel friends down in the woods and I put the little "are" on there [referring to "squirrels 'are' nice"] because whenever I'm down in the woods, the squirrels always come around and chatter to me.

**Teacher: Ah. OK. What about this one? Animals and hunting.**

*Erin:* Well, because animals are probably why they hunt. I mean they go out to hunt animals, so I put down here "do not like" hunting.

---

**Example 4.9**

A colleague of mine was driving home with his young daughter one night. While sitting in the back seat, the girl watched the moon out of the window. She said to her father, "See? The moon is following us." When they got home, the father and daughter sat on the front steps and looked at the moon. The father, being a good science educator, asked her what she thought the moon was made of. After several minutes of discussing the scientific knowledge of the moon, the daughter looked up and said, "But who's going to watch over me now?" Taken aback, the father realized that he had just taken something (i.e., a sense of security) away from his daughter and questioned what he had done.

In the example below, a grade 2 girl, Beth, mentions that the earthworm is "wagging its tail," while observing and discussing her observations. In this instance, Beth places the characteristic of other animals (we call this zoomorphism, instead of anthropomorphism) onto the earthworm.

---

**Example 4.10: A Grade 2 Girl's Talk about Earthworms**

**Teacher:** **What do you think they eat?**

*Beth:*        Worms eat?

**Teacher:** **Yeah.**

*Beth:*        Little teeny weeny bugs.

**Teacher:** **Mmm hmm.**

*Beth:*        Very small.

**Teacher:** **Very small things.**

*Beth:*        Wagging his tail.

---

As in the previous examples (Examples 4.8 and 4.9), Beth's comment does not fit with our scientific knowledge: earthworms do not have tails. Nevertheless, the comment is wonderfully rich in possibilities. Such a notion can lead in many directions—for both scientific inquiry and integrated activities. From the idea of the earthworm wagging its tail, Beth could be encouraged to write a children's story about her pet earthworm. The whole idea of wagging tails can be explored, comparing the meaning of tail wagging in different animals (e.g., the meaning behind a cat wagging its tail is quite different from a dog wagging its tail). The concept of tail can also be investigated. What animals have tails? What do their structures look like? How are the structures similar and different? How are the functions of tails in different animals similar and different? From this last question, the inquiry could lead back to a child, such as Beth, realizing that earthworms do not have a tail (even though they look like tails). If the child has been encouraged to explore his or her initial meaning in more detail and to produce a story or some other product about this understanding, the impact of finding out the scientific meaning may not have such devastating effects (as in losing the companionship of the moon).

In Example 4.11, we see the effect of Edie's previous knowledge through her work in an independent study on her understanding of life in the ocean. Her understanding of sponges, which many children may not even consider to be alive, is reasonably detailed. We also get a sense from reading her comments that she has developed a detailed contextual understanding. Nevertheless, even with this reasonably complex understanding, she has a specific judgment (i.e., "everything is kind of odd") and a personal emotional reaction to the life of a sponge (e.g., "oh, I'd hate to be a sponge").

☞

**Refer to Example 4.9. The introduction of scientific knowledge can change the meaning children bring to a situation.**

**How would you handle situations in which children talk about their personal connections with natural events?**

**How can the science be addressed without taking something away from the child?**

**Can both perspectives be accommodated?**

> **Example 4.11: A Grade 5 Girl's Description of Life in the Ocean**
>
> **Teacher: Okay. What if you went to the deepest part of the oceans and went to the bottom, what would you see?**
>
> *Edie:* You'd see octopuses and you'd see; what else is at the very bottom of the ocean? Maybe you'd see a shark or a whale, they'd be close to the bottom. You'd see some fish, some … and you'd see seaweed and coral and there are caves in the very bottom where the octopus live and you'd see these little, well, I did an independent study in the sea, I don't know what you'd call them, oh, sponges, you know the little, some about that tall, what a boring life—you just sit there planted at the bottom of the sea.
>
> **Teacher: What are they, sponges?**
>
> *Edie:* They look like a sponge, and they're alive but they don't move, they feed on plankton, they don't have an eye, they don't have a nose, they don't have a mouth, they just kind of sit there and everything is kind of odd.
>
> **Teacher: Are they plants or animals?**
>
> *Edie:* Just sponges. Oh, I'd hate to be a sponge.

A similar instance of a child who connects or imagines what it would be like to be a particular animal appears in the example below.

> **Example 4.12: A Grade 5 Boy's Imagining of What It Would Be Like to Be an Earthworm**
>
> *Evan:* Have you ever tried thinking about what it would be like to be a bug?
>
> **Teacher: To be a bug? No. What do you think it would be like?**
>
> *Evan:* I don't know. It would just be dark, I think.
>
> **Teacher: It would be dark?**
>
> *Evan:* Yeah, I think. Oh, here's a living thing, [whispers] a centipede.
>
> **Teacher: Right.**
>
> *Evan:* [Talking as if to a puppy] Here little centipede. There you go. Come here.
>
> **Teacher: Be careful. Go gently, down deep. Oh there.**
>
> *Evan:* Oh, there's a worm. Hi, little worm.
>
> **Teacher: What's he? Oh, it looks like another centipede, millipede.**
>
> *Evan:* I … oh, whoa! I gotta get this one. Yeah! Ooh, like I was saying, what does it, oh?
>
> **Teacher: Here. Go put him in here and let's …**
>
> *Evan:* Which way is your head? I think this one. What does it feel like to be a worm under the ground all the time. You just have these little testicles [sic] and they pick up stuff and [sighs], it must be dark or something like that.

> **Teacher:** Yeah. Do you think they can tell whether it's dark or light?
>
> *Evan:* Ummm, great for fishing.
>
> **Teacher:** These. Yeah.
>
> *Evan:* I don't know. Just, I just think it would be dark. It would be a bit boring.
>
> **Teacher:** Okay, that's probably good enough.
>
> *Evan:* I think it would be lonely.
>
> **Teacher:** Lonely?
>
> *Evan:* Lonely.
>
> **Teacher:** Um hm.
>
> *Evan:* I don't know. It just feels weird to be a human being.
>
> **Teacher:** It feels weird to be a human being?
>
> *Evan:* I don't know. It depends.
>
> **Teacher:** Yeah.
>
> *Evan:* There are some times when I just get really, really confused. But how come everything, every subject in my life has to do with a Led Zeppelin song I just realized but that has absolutely nothing to do with it.
>
> **Teacher:** Yeah [laughs]. So what's so confusing? Oops, you missed.
>
> *Evan:* What's so confusing, I just, I don't know, I just, just feel different. Have you ever noticed on days when …
>
> **Teacher:** Let's just put this back up here.
>
> *Evan:* When it's like really really sunny? It's a picture that I have. It's like on days when it's really really sunny. You know, like for instance, when I go outside, I have a totally new feeling and that must happen to lots of people, but on days when it's really really sunny; when I go outside or inside, I can hardly tell whether I'm inside or outside. But, come on, like, I can remember my trip to Florida. It was pouring. It was really sunny and—oh, this one's escaping—it was really sunny and it was really nice, like, something like that even school days, when it's sunny, it's still nice like that.
>
> **Teacher:** You feel better on sunny days?

In this excerpt, Evan embarks on a lengthy story about what life would be like as an earthworm and the similarities to his life as a human being. Within this rambling storyline are notions of earthworms' utility to people (i.e., "great for fishing") and his talking to a millipede as if it were a pet dog. Making connections to what it would be like to be a particular organism is a transposition of self to the object of discussion. The child "becomes" the object or organism. Such transpositions or connections are not generally acknowledged as being of value from the perspective of the science community; however, many tribal or aboriginal cultures may view this connection as a positive one. In fact, seeing the connectedness among all of creation is a basis for beliefs of many tribal cultures, as well as Eastern religions and some Christian interpretations of the Bible. From the Mi'kmaw (a North American Indian nation located along the coast in eastern Canada) perspective, the connectedness is much more substantial than the connections we've seen in children's thinking; however, they share a basis in seeing a commonality between people and other animals.

---

**Example 4.13**

The Mi'kmaw notion of connectedness between animals and people. People also had "animal helpers" or personal alliances with animals, whom they could call upon for assistance, protection, or guidance. Both their "spirits" were interchangeable, and inseparable in essence. Whatever happened to one, no matter what form either one was manifesting, affected or transferred to the other, i.e., when the moose leg bone gets broken, the man's leg also breaks.[2]

---

◆ **If you have a Native child in your classroom, what are the implications for instruction about animals?**

◆ **How would you approach such differences in belief?**

◆ **For other children who express human–animal transpositions (e.g., giving animals human traits), how could you approach instruction in ways that do not devalue their ideas?**

These are difficult questions, with no particular right answer. On the one hand, you may want to have children work with the scientific understandings, but on the other hand, you need to be sensitive to the cultural beliefs and personal understandings of children. The notion of contexts of meaning may offer some guidance. If we see science as useful in a particular context and other ideas as useful in associated contexts, then we may be able to address each understanding in relation to the appropriate context. For instance, in the case of the earthworm examples, above, we can support children's exploration of their own understandings and personal connections through a set of individualized activities. At the same time, we can explore how such a personal understanding is appropriate in the context of the child's experience or of the particular culture. Following this, we can discuss how scientists might understand and explain the earthworm. In such a discussion, we can also explore how such scientific explanations might be useful (within a certain context). From this point, we can embark on scientific inquiry.

Children's imagery has been evident in some of the previous examples of children's talk about different topics. The metaphor of an earthworm "drilling" into the ground suggests a cartoon-type image of earthworms spinning themselves around as they burrow through the ground. We can capture children's images of science topics by having them create drawings. Most children love to draw, and it provides a way to get at what children are thinking about without relying on children's talking or writing. Such a technique is useful with young children who have not acquired writing skills. In addition, older children who feel restrained by writing, because of real or perceived weaknesses in writing, can communicate their ideas more freely. Example

4.14 provides a sample of six children's drawings in response to the request to draw a picture of the beginning of life on earth.

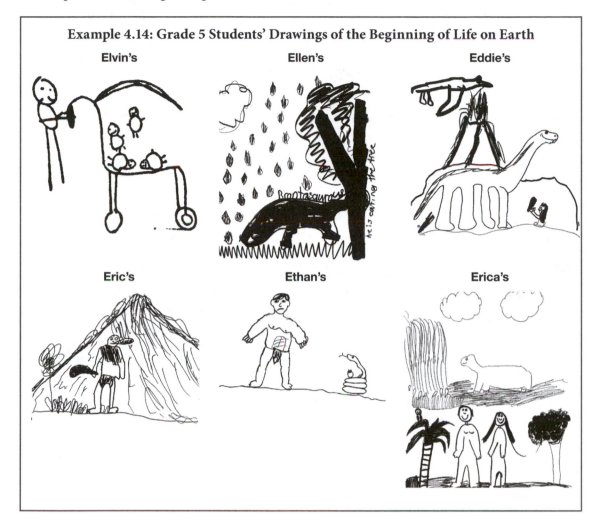

**Example 4.14: Grade 5 Students' Drawings of the Beginning of Life on Earth**

Elvin's    Ellen's    Eddie's

Eric's    Ethan's    Erica's

As we can see, the children have quite different views about the beginning of life on earth. Elvin's image is more immediate, showing a baby in a carriage. Pushing the carriage is the baby's mom. Certainly, this image is an accurate depiction of the beginning of individual human life. Ellen and Eddie depict dinosaurs; however, Eddie mixes up the timeline of events and has a primitive human fighting a dinosaur (dinosaurs predated early humanoids by over 60 million years). Eric shows a primitive human standing in front of a volcano. In Eric's drawing, we might question whether he is associating the volcano with the early, prelife nature of the earth, which was characterized by a lot of volcanic activity. In the last three drawings, there is some consistency of an evolutionary view of the development of life, even though some conceptual details are inaccurate. Ethan's view of the beginning of life on earth is a religious one, including Adam and two major symbols of the snake and the apple. On the other hand, Erica's hedges her bets and includes the religious symbolism of Adam and Eve at the bottom of her drawing, as well as a dinosaur at the top.

These drawings not only reveal inaccurate scientific understandings (e.g., humans and dinosaurs in the same picture), but also show how personal and cultural beliefs affect children's images and understandings of topics that have scientific explanations attached.

One of the problems facing people in our society around such issues as evolution vs. creationism is the view that the issue is an either/or situation—either you believe in creationism or you believe in evolution. Maintaining such a view often results in conflict. There is, in fact, a difference between what we mean by belief and what we mean by understanding. A student can believe one thing, but have multiple understandings of alternative ideas (see Chapter 3 for a discussion of belief vs. theory; in this discussion *understanding* would involve theories, which are constructed frameworks of particular scientific understandings). From this perspective, we should be able to place each alternative understanding within a separate context and provide instructional activities to address one or more of these understandings. What kinds of discussions and activities could you try in order to implement such an approach?[3]

As we can see from the previous examples, imagery and metaphor allow us as teachers to gain insight into children's understandings and to help them develop broader and more informed understandings. These ways of representing knowledge and understanding can be used by children in much more abstract ways as well. In Example 4.15, a grade 5 girl represents her understanding of life on earth after being asked to respond to task instructions: "Aliens from outer space have just landed in your backyard and have asked you to explain to them what life on earth is all about. You can draw or write anything you want to help them understand." When you examine the drawings, think about what she might be trying to communicate.

Many teachers avoid the topic of evolution, either out of some fear of what some parents might say or do or out of their own confusion about their understanding of both perspectives.

✦ How do you stand on the issue of evolution versus creationism (or intelligent design)?

✦ Would you address evolution in the classroom?

✦ If a student were to generate a symbolic representation, such as the one in Example 4.15, how could you extend this approach to the whole class?

✦ How could such use of symbols be used to implement integrated inquiry across the curriculum?

---

**Example 4.15**

Effie's (grade 5) response to what life on earth is all about (see Figure 4.2):

From left to right beginning at the top, the objects are a car, a dinosaur skeleton, a rocket, a movie projector, an airplane, a ship, signs, a camera, a newspaper, pyramids, a cat, a school, a book, a shopping bag, a hamburger, an apartment building, a glass of water, people holding hands, a football, a loaf of bread, an aquarium, a piggy bank, and a Canadian flag.

---

When asked to talk about her drawing, the girl explained that

cars, ships, planes show how we travel; a skeleton of a dinosaur shows prehistoric life; space travel shows that we go beyond earth; signs that

**FIGURE 4.2**

we use, camera and movies, daily news, pyramids show our history; a cat shows that we care about animals; a school shows that we are educated; books show what we know; a shopping bag shows that we shop; a burger shows what we eat; a skyrise apartment shows how we live; a glass of water shows water; a chain of people shows that we sometimes live in harmony; a football symbolizes the games that we play; a loaf of bread shows what we eat; a fish shows an animal that lives in water; a piggy bank shows that we save money; and a Canadian flag tells who we are.

Her drawings are symbolic representations of her understandings. The use of metaphor and imagery in this case has been extended to a formal symbolic form of representation.

So far in this chapter, we have seen that children's thinking can be quite complex and abstract, even at very young ages. What we tend to see taking place in classrooms are activities and instruction that underestimate children's capabilities. By not paying much attention to children's abstract thinking, such as metaphors and imagery, we miss opportunities to see the full extent of children's thinking. In many cases, such abstract thinking does not appear within the context of the official topic under study. Consequently, when children do express more abstract ideas, they are overlooked. The key point is that we as teachers need to be on the alert for children's expressions of understanding.

We may find that some students may take a very different view of school. For one reason or another, they do not relate to school. Basically, school is not relevant to their own needs or perceptions. In such cases, children's "street" knowledge may be far more organized and abstract than what they understand of the topics being studied in school. In these instances, the meaningfulness of their street experiences is more relevant to what they perceive of their life. How can you cross this barrier between school and their everyday lives outside of school to make classroom learning more relevant? In Example 4.16 (another example of children's responses to aliens about life on earth), although not a child of the street, Evan's depiction of school is that it is not personally relevant. His feeling about school is evident from the central position of his crossed out school with "NO WAY! FORGET IT!" written around the image. The flashy images from popular media and music appear to be of much more potential interest than school.

✳

**Before thinking about your answers to the following questions, some background information may be helpful. Evan is from an upper-middle-class, professional family. From all evidence, his family life is supportive, loving, and stable. He is quite bright, but does very poorly in school. He is not disruptive, but tends to be withdrawn in class. His understanding of the sexual imagery appears to be at a superficial level. His real love is music. He reads music magazines and researches musical groups. He wants to be a writer.**

**◆ What sorts of strategies could you use to reach out to Evan and make his experiences in school more relevant?**

**◆ What science and integrated activities and investigations could you present to him?**

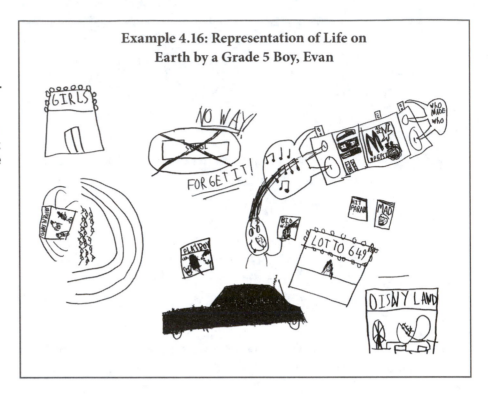

Example 4.16: Representation of Life on Earth by a Grade 5 Boy, Evan

We have also seen that the notion of contexts of meaning can be useful in extending our understanding of how children construct knowledge and understanding. Such understandings contain multiple perspectives, which can be used to provide learning opportunities that extend their existing perspectives. These learning opportunities can include further science inquiry or the development of projects across the curriculum. Example 4.17 shows the combined results of students' context maps (i.e., webbing tasks, not concept maps; see Section 7.4). What different perspectives on floating do you see represented?

As we can see in Example 4.17, some of the ideas expressed by the children relate to scientific perspectives, while others involve fantasy, the nature of science, aesthetics (e.g., horses cantering on the middle left of the example), and so forth. Each of these perspectives could be explored as integrated topics. By integrating across the curriculum, using ideas that children have generated, we are allowing our students to feel more ownership over what is done in the classroom. When children feel a sense of ownership, they are more motivated and see more relevance to what takes place in the classroom.

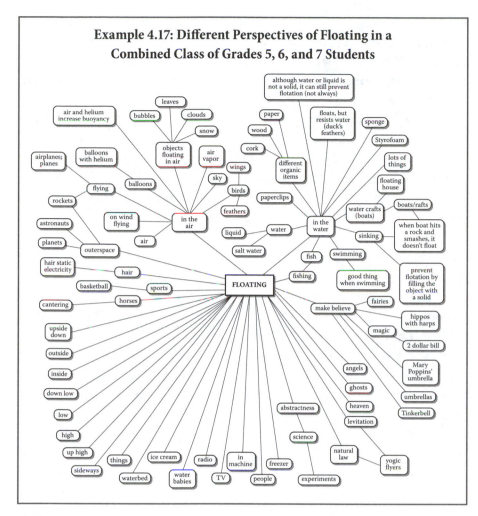

**Example 4.17: Different Perspectives of Floating in a Combined Class of Grades 5, 6, and 7 Students**

◆ From the perspectives you have identified in Example 4.17, suggest some possible science inquiry activities to further students' understandings of the science concepts evident in the example.

◆ What activities can you suggest to help the students explore the non-science-related perspectives?

## 4.4   Categorization

A major theme of cognitive research involves the notion of categorization. The significance of categorization for teaching science is its relationship to what we mean by *concept*. The term *concept* is used throughout educational settings, but we rarely hear anything about what it means. Although *concept* can be defined in different ways, the following is an attempt to capture the essence of its meaning in ways that are helpful to teachers. A concept can be thought of as relating to a category. For instance, if you think of a word, such as *bird* (STOP HERE: What was the first image you had when you read the word *bird*?), you associate it with a variety of relevant information. Such information can include examples of birds (e.g., robin, starling, pigeon, penguin, emu) and characteristics of birds (e.g., feathers, warm-blooded, wings, flight). When you first read the word *bird*, what image did you have? Often this first image might look like a very common bird, such as a robin. This type of example is called a prototype. It is the prototypical or most representative bird in terms of your own experience and understanding. The prototype contains the characteristics you most closely associate with the idea of bird.

In terms of characteristics or features of birds, we can think of the features of birds as either defining features or characteristic features. Defining features are those that define birds and are not shared by any other category, such as mammals (e.g., feathers are a defining feature of birds). Characteristic features, on the other hand, can be shared across categories, such as with mammals and birds (e.g., warm-blooded is a characteristic feature of both birds and mammals).

We categorize everything—the people we meet, the people we live with, our students, animals, plants, technological devices, etc. As we learn more about a particular category, we add new information to and reorganize our categorical system. In other words, we construct new knowledge based on our existing framework or categorical system. However, as we have seen in the previous section on contexts of meaning, we associate much more than the school-type knowledge with our categorical systems or concepts. Personal experiences, fantasy, emotions-values-aesthetics, metaphors, and so forth, all become a part of our understanding of particular concepts.

From an instructional point of view, we could emphasize having children elaborate on a particular conceptual area or categorical system, such as birds. Such an approach may be useful but does not address the concerns of multiple perspectives or broader relations between categorical systems. If we study birds in depth without looking at their relationship to other animals or to other broader concepts, we end up with a rather narrow understanding. For example, as we study birds, we also can address how the anatomy of birds compares with that of other animals. Such comparisons lead to a variety of concepts related to evolution (e.g., adaptation, homology). We can look at how the forelegs of different animals have similar bones, but are shaped differently for different activities (e.g., the pelvic fins of fish, the front legs of frogs, the arms of humans, and the wings of birds). Other concepts, such as flight, can be compared. What are the similarities and differences between the flight of birds, insects, airplanes, etc.? As we introduce children to such cross-categorical relationships, we can help children construct more meaningful and more richly interconnected understandings of their world.

Let us take a look at some examples of children's thinking in relation to their categorical understanding. In the first example, a grade 1 girl, Ann, struggles with how to classify earthworms.

※

◆ What kinds of activities could you provide for Ann that would allow her to elaborate on her categorical or conceptual understanding?

◆ What cross-categorical themes could be developed around her ideas?

◆ What kinds of activities could be developed to address such themes?

---

**Example 4.18: Grade 1 Girl Talking about Earthworms: Classification**

**Teacher: What other things do you know about worms? Anything else?**

*Ann:* Well I know that they are not mammals.

**Teacher: They are not mammals. Do you know what they might be?**

*Ann:* They are not mammals but I don't know what you would call something if they are not mammals.

**Teacher: Hmm, why wouldn't they be a mammal?**

*Ann:* Becau[se] if they weren't, I don't think that worms have eggs, and if they have eggs that means that they're not a mammal.

In this example, Ann does not have an extensive understanding of animal classification (from the perspective of the standard biological taxonomy), but she has some understanding of the characteristics of mammals. Here, she is not sure if earthworms lay eggs or not. However, she does know that if they do lay eggs, they cannot be mammals. Her thinking is really quite complex. She recognizes what she does and does not know, yet still looks for certain defining or characteristic features, which will guide her decision making. When students are thinking like this, the major drawback is information. Her categorical scheme is thin.

In the next example, we see a different sense of category. Here, children have been playing with bubbles for about an hour over a couple of days. The teacher enters into the discussion with two children. What cross-categorical relations are being addressed in this sequence?

---

**Example 4.19: Grade 4 Students' Examination of Bubbles**

**Teacher:**  **What shapes do you see in there?**

*Dan:*      Triangles.

*Debbie:*   Squares and kind of like the shape of the stop sign.

**Teacher:**  **You mean an octagon.**

*Debbie:*   Yeah, that's right!

**Teacher:**  **Look at how they are connected.**

*Dan:*      By straight lines.

*Debbie:*   Wow! All the bubbles are joined by a straight line.

---

✦ What are the implications of addressing such cross-relations for children's learning?

✦ What was the role of the teacher?

✦ How does the teacher's role in this sequence differ from what typically occurs in classrooms?

✦ How could the insights gained in this sequence be extended through other inquiry activities?

When we consider what prior knowledge children bring with them into the classroom and their abilities to see relations and make sense of their observations, we may see that what typically occurs in classrooms is at a much lower level than children's capabilities. Children are capable of constructing much more elaborate and in-depth conceptual understandings than we frequently assume. The notion of working with categorical understandings and the cross-relationships between categories can be a useful framework for thinking about and organizing instruction. As we proceed with our thinking about teaching, the construction of conceptual (categorical) understandings may help us clarify our goals and actions when working with children's inquiry.

## 4.5    Play

Children play. This comment appears to be rather obvious, but we frequently overlook this important activity in children's lives, especially when they are in the classroom. Children (and even adults) learn a great deal through play. Through play children learn language, social relations and skills, and a lot about how the world works. In terms of learning science, play can provide children with opportunities to develop basic understandings of how particular phenomena work, to generate questions, and to develop links to integrated topics.

Scientists play, too, although their play is much more focused on particular concepts and theories. A biologist studying fish behavior may play around with different ideas that might explain how a certain kind of fish manages to find food (this could be done alone sitting on his or her porch at home or with a group of other biologists) or with different variables that might affect how the fish behave. The biologist plays with ideas and materials to explore possible explanations.

In a similar way, children play with objects and ideas within the context of sense making. As a teacher, you can introduce a topic, such as magnets, by placing a variety of metallic and nonmetallic objects along with a variety of objects on the students' tables. As they play with these materials, they start to see how magnets behave and begin to develop a foundation of understanding based on their personal experiences. Initially, however, children may not be able to verbalize much of their understandings, but the experiential memory of these events provides them with the background from which to build further understandings. As they continue to play, they may see certain patterns and generate a variety of metaphors, explanations, and questions. From this point, further inquiry activities can be introduced. In some instances, children may even think of their own experiments and activities as a natural extension of their play.

Refer to Example 4.20.
+ What kinds of ideas are evident in these two examples?

---

**Example 4.20: A Preschooler's Play**

My 2½-year-old son had been playing with cars on the deck in the backyard for several days. On this particular day, he was sitting in the middle of the deck playing. We had been doing some renovations to the house and a rain trough was lying at an angle against one of the railings. At one point, he stopped playing, idly looking around. All of a sudden, he stopped moving his head and focused on the trough. He stared at it for a few seconds, his eyes got bigger, and he ran over to the trough with a car in hand. His new ramp added a new dimension to his play.

On another occasion, he found a cylindrical magnet when he broke open a magnetic marble. He started playing with it on the side of the refrigerator. When he let go of the magnet, it rolled across the front of the refrigerator and around the corner. His eyes lit up and he came running to tell us what he had just discovered.

---

Children's play is an important way of learning. The nature of the play may change with the age of the child, but the idea of playing around in science can lead to significant learning and further inquiry. As teachers, we need to be aware of how useful such activities can be. Again, we may not be able to see the immediate and full effects of such play on children's learning.

Play is also closely related to the notion of story, which we explored to some extent in the section on contexts of meaning. In many situations, play takes on the form of story. Children playing with cars or dolls embed their play in an unfolding story. The story provides a context for their play and sets up ground rules for their actions.

Vivien Gussin Paley (an elementary school teacher) has written a number of wonderful books about children's play and "living" stories. These insightful books are a must for elementary school teachers.

Play and stories can be a major part of children's work on class projects as well. The nature of the play and stories, however, can be focused around the topic of inquiry. Such use of story, once again, provides a relevant context for the children's work. In Example 4.21, groups of students (in a mixed grade 5, 6, and 7 class) embedded their work on boat designs in the context of a story. The stories of these two groups focus on the extra features of their boats. The intent of the activity was for each group (playing the role of consulting firms) to submit a boat design to the local government agency for potential use as a tour boat to local natural history sites. Each group had to include a scientific explanation and rationale for why their boat design was appropriate. They were to include the calculations for how many passengers (i.e., load) the boat could hold, explanations for how the boat manages to float, and so forth. The example includes two excerpts of the groups' final presentations to their parents, who acted as the government agency committee reviewing the proposals.

Hopefully, you have had an opportunity to play around with some science materials and ideas, either in the warm-up activities in Chapter 2 or on your own. After having read the previous parts of this chapter and knowing what you know now, take some time to reflect on these activities and think about the following questions. Discuss your ideas and answers with your peers.

◆ In terms of the notion of play, what did you notice about how you felt during this experience?

◆ How did you create a context for some of your activities and ideas?

◆ What kinds of questions did you generate?

◆ What kinds of explanations did you generate for your observations?

◆ How could the questions and explanations you generated be extended to more focused inquiry?

◆ What ideas did you generate that could lead to integrated activities?

---

**Example 4.21: Boat Design Stories**

**Group 1**

*Gina:* We're the members of Sea-Sable Enterprises, and we have a really neat boat; and it's a glass bottom, so on the whole voyage to Sable Island you can see the bottom and see the lovely fish, which is an advantage, because you can view the marine life as you go on your voyage. It is equipped with a few things that are nice. [Small laugh.] It offers a movie screen for the trip. You know, it'll show kids movies or something, in case your kids get bored. And we have a bar at the back that serves pretzels and drinks and other …

*George:* Necessities.

*Gina:* Yeah. And there's two doors. Those are your exits. And you have double seating all along. And, like, its capacity is about … How many people, Eric?

*Eric:* Forty people, including cargo.

| | |
|---|---|
| *Gina:* | There is a female and male washroom equipped, and the captain quarters are up here. Um, the motor is strong and it's powered by battery, so it's not as bad for the environment. |
| **Group 2** | |
| *Greg:* | No-no-no-no. [To audience.] This, you've already seen this on a ramp; generally drawn on a scale map, looking square, so you can tell. This is our launch pit, right here, and here is our arcade, where it's two dollars entry, but the games, unlike regular arcades, are only a nickel each, except for our virtual reality system, which is a dollar. And this is our casino. It has a license, don't worry. This is our kitchen for our restaurant, which is here, adjoining the bar. Oh, I meant, did I mention that the legal drinking age is twelve? |
| *Frank:* | Only to certain, only to certain non-very alcoholic. |
| *Greg:* | Such as stuff like that. And this is our poolroom, not swimming pool. It's a billiards room, I should say. And this is our movie theater. And, oh, our mosh pit can be filled up and with water and made into a swimming pool for … |
| *Frank:* | Recreational purposes. |

As we can see in the example, the students spent a great deal of time thinking about the story aspect of their boats. Although it did take some time away from their inquiry, the story created relevance and became a great motivating factor.

## 4.6 Complex Learning

Up to this point, what we really have been pointing to is the nature of children's complex thinking and learning, as well as the need to take such complex learning even further. However, the standard approach to schooling in general has been one that distills learning to its simplest form and fragments knowledge by separating subjects and even separating bits and pieces of information within a subject. As Mary Catherine Bateson suggests,

> We are drowning in disconnected information today. In spite of the tighter and tighter interlinking of the world by trade and communication, our understanding is ever more fragmented by specialization. In order to act with sensitivity in the world we need a unified vision, a capacity to understand the coupling of human societies with each other and with ecosystems and the biosphere. (p. 45)[4]

The increasing pressures to "teach to the test," to teach to specific standards, and to cover a tremendous amount of information within a year of schooling increases the tendency toward fragmentation. One piece of information is disconnected from other pieces and from the contexts in which such information is situated. For example, we may have learned in school that genes from each parent determine eye color. Everyone seems to accept this bit of knowledge. However, when we discuss adaptation of organisms, the acceptance of genes by many people becomes more questionable. And, when evolution is discussed (particularly in the United States), a divisive split occurs between those who believe in creationism and those who do not. However, the concepts of how genes work are fundamental to each of these situations.

A recent conversation provides another example. An avid gardener built a greenhouse and investigated thoroughly the science behind the greenhouse for gardening throughout the year. At the same time, he said, "This is the coldest winter we've ever had. So much for global warming!" He continued to criticize environmentalists' pressure to create legislation that addresses global warming. However, he farms organically, buys fuel-efficient cars, and recycles. Again, there is a disconnect between one specific context or use of information and another. The fragmentation of knowledge leads to a lack of cohesiveness of understandings and disconnections between ourselves and others, between ourselves and our environment, and between our views of one situation and another.

At the same time, business leaders are complaining that they have to spend millions of dollars to train employees how to think, and even how to complete very simple mathematical or literacy tasks. They have even tried to develop creative and critical thinking skills, but have had no success.[5] In order to think critically, to analyze particular situations, to conduct inquiry, to think creatively, and to solve problems, we need to have richly interconnected understandings, not only within a subject area, but also across subject areas, as well as to our personal experiences, beliefs, and cultural traditions. However, we need to move toward seeing and understanding the patterns that connect one idea to another, one culture to another, and so forth. This notion of seeing and understanding patterns is the primary focus of the rest of this section.

A pattern can be as simple as a shape or a physical form or as complex as patterns over time or as patterns within relationships. Just about every subject matter area or occupation is fundamentally concerned with patterns. Sociologists study patterns of behavior in groups. Scientists study patterns of the natural world. Anthropologists study patterns in culture. Artists study and express patterns found in a variety of contexts. Psychologists study or work with patterns of the mind and behavior. Mechanics understand the interconnected patterns of multiple systems that serve to operate an automobile, then use these understandings to solve problems. In a similar way, medical doctors use their understandings of physiological and anatomical patterns to solve problems. However, because of the fragmentation (i.e., specialization) in medicine, doctors often have difficulty solving particularly complex problems.

If we look back at the examples earlier in this chapter, we can see how children seem to naturally think in complex ways and rely on their

◆ Can you think of other examples of how fragmented knowledge has led to rather perplexing conflicts?

◆ In what ways do you feel disconnected to particular situations in your life (with people, with the environment, with other cultures, with science, etc.)?

◆ Do you have any passions or interests where you feel you have a rich understanding and feel connected? Can you describe how your knowledge in this area is different from that in areas where you feel disconnected?

recognition of patterns to make sense of what they experience. In Example 4.4, Emily recognizes the earthworm's pattern of behavior as a kind of searching: "It's going around and around. It looks like it's kind of sniffing to see what's there.... I think it's kind of like cats' whiskers." Here she makes the connection with moving "around and around" as the same kind of cycle she has seen with how cats move their whiskers. So, in this sense, the cat and the earthworm share a cyclical pattern of sensory behavior. As a teacher, we can help children explore this pattern or concept in much greater depth and extent. Fundamentally, this sensory cycle is a cycle of exploration or of gathering further information. So, the question is, What other cycles can we think of or find that operate for the same sort of purpose? Some examples may include

- **Searching the Internet**, where we type in search terms, get results, look through and evaluate the results, type in different search terms, etc. (library searches follow a similar pattern, too).
- **Oxygen sensors in car engines** receive information from the gas-air mixture, make adjustments to the mixture, receive information from the mixture, etc.
- **An artist (painter)** looks at a scene or object, receives sensory information, which is translated into selection of colors and brush strokes, looks further at the scene, etc.
- **In conversations** we listen to what someone says, then think about what is said and respond.

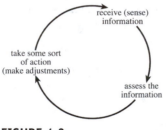

**FIGURE 4.3**

In such information-gathering cycles, we notice that there is a repeating sequence, as depicted in Figure 4.3.

In general, cycles serve the purpose of maintaining some sort of system or situation. So, in all of our examples, including the one described by Emily in Example 4.4, there is some sort of situation being maintained, at least for some period of time. The earthworm and the cat maintain their awareness of the environment, we maintain conversations, the car maintains the proper mixture, the artist maintains his or her creative cycle of perception and representation, and we, hopefully, maintain a fruitful search cycle on the Internet or in the library.

So, if we explore a pattern, such as cycles, in such a way, the result can be a much greater understanding of how cycles work and where they occur. At the same time, we are providing opportunities to integrate these understandings across the curriculum; whether it is in solving math problems, engaging in art projects, investigating and analyzing social or political situations, or conducting science investigations, the same basic ideas of cycles are involved. Through such an approach that takes advantage of children's natural abilities to see and utilize patterns in making sense of their worlds, we can pro-

Pick a period of time (a day, a week, etc.) and do your own scavenger hunt for cycles. Look for cycles in your own life, in mechanical things, in the biological world, in your social world, on TV, in novels and stories, in movies, in politics, and so forth. Write down and draw or diagram the cycles you find. Remember the fundamental purpose or effect of cycles is to maintain some situation or system.

Although all cycles maintain some situation, what other specific effect(s) or purpose(s) does each of your cycles have, such as information gathering and use, stabilizing, perpetuating or maintaining, balancing, etc? Keep in mind that any particular cycle may have several effects or purposes.

◆ What steps or sequences do you see in each cycle?

◆ How do these steps function in the cycle?

◆ What similarities and differences do you see among your cycles?

◆ Do some cycles stop? What causes them to stop? Are the causes similar among different cycles that do stop?

After you have worked through this activity, reflect on how this investigation and analysis of cycles has affected your understandings of the world we live in.

◆ How could you incorporate this approach into teaching science? How could you extend this approach to integrate investigations in math, art, social studies, writing and reading, etc?

vide for more relevant and meaningful learning experiences. This approach also brings up an interesting paradox. By focusing on more complex learning (seeing the connections across subject areas and areas of personal experience, etc.), learning (or teaching) may become simpler. Simpler, in this sense, has to do with children's natural abilities of making sense in ways that are meaningful and relevant. It is not a big stretch to extend and refine this process. However, it is a more complex task for teachers to begin thinking about the connections of patterns across subject matter areas.

Appendix D provides further information on a variety of patterns that are basic to multiple subject matter areas. However, a list of these patterns here may be helpful:

- **Spheres**—As actual forms, as well as metaphors
- **Sheets**—As forms and metaphors
- **Tubes**—As forms, connections (relationships in space), and metaphors
- **Layers**—As forms and metaphors
- **Borders** (and **pores** or openings)—As forms and metaphors
- **Binaries or greater numbers** of components in **relationships**
- **Centers**—As organizing factors
- **Arrows**—As directions and relationships in time
- **Time and calendars**
- **Breaks**—Transitions, changes, etc.
- **Cycles**[6]
- **Gradients**
- **Clusters**
- **Triggers**—Initiating factors
- **Emergence**—Birth or arising of something new
- **Webs**—Networks of interconnections
- **Rigidity and flexibility**

In addition to these fundamental patterns, we also can view a lot of concepts as applicable across subject areas, such as adaptation and acclimatization, force, energy, power, homeostasis or balance, communication, movement, growth, and so forth. This particular list of concepts also brings up an important point about how meanings may differ in specific subject matter areas. For instance, *adaptation* from a general perspective may mean some sort of mechanism that provides for adjustments to a specific environment or situation. However, in biology it has a specific meaning tightly tied to genetics. An individual animal adjusting to a change in temperature or altitude is *not* an example of adaptation, but rather an example of acclimating. However, if genetic changes occur over generations of a particular species that provide a mechanism for adjusting to a wider range of temperature variation, then this is an example of adaptation. In other contexts, adaptation may be used to describe any kind of adjustment, whether it is a jazz, dance, or dramatic performance or a literary metaphor or a mechanical system.

The major problem that occurs with learning is that the everyday or common definitions of many of these terms differ from the scientific definitions. As a result, many students use the common definitions in science, which leads to numerous misunderstandings. As teachers, we should take the time to discuss how meanings change from one context or subject to another. We can engage children in critiquing the misuse of terms in advertisements, books, movies, and so forth, then have them create intentional misuses through a variety of tasks (e.g., comic strips, advertisements, poetry, etc.). You also can play with answering questions using different definitions. For example, a child or you may ask, "What does earthworm movement look like?" A response may be, "Brown." Changing the context, in this example, from the perspective of childhood humor and in terms of the context of physiology of bowel movement, we get a very different and unexpected response. At the same time, children can develop their skills in decoding meanings and contexts. Through playing with language, we help our students develop critical understandings of how meanings change at one level, yet they may share the same basic meaning at another level. So, adaptation involves adjusting to a situation in all contexts at a very basic level, but in specific contexts it has a different meaning at another level of detail.

From this brief discussion, we can see how a focus on complexity can begin to develop more interconnected and less fragmented understandings. Ideas and patterns that are evident and important in understanding concepts in one subject matter area can be applied to other areas. Once an idea or pattern, such as cycles, is understood in one context, the understandings can be applied to other areas. In approaching the teaching and learning of the patterns and concepts described previously, it may be important to start with exploring the everyday instances of these patterns in children's lives, then proceed to exploring them in different subject matter contexts. For example, after a brief discussion of cycles (i.e., discussions of what a cycle is), you can have children do a scavenger hunt for cycles, which could include examples from other times in their day (e.g., waking up, eating breakfast, brushing teeth, doing homework, going to bed, etc.). Once they have generated a list, you can have them discuss (as a class or in small groups, which then share their results with the class) how each example is similar and different and what it is about cycles that is important (e.g., what are the functions of cycles?). If a pattern or concept arises out of an inquiry activity in science, as in the earthworm example discussed in Example 4.4, you can use that instance to move toward an exploration of the children's experiences of cycles, including a scavenger hunt. The basic idea here is to develop the personal connections to these patterns and concepts first. In doing so, personal meaning and relevance can be established, which can help in continued meaningful and relevant learning as you expand into specific subject matter areas.

If we examine national and local standards, we will see how these basic patterns and concepts are found not only in those concerned with science, but also in those concerned with language, mathematics, social studies, art, and physical education and health. However, the major difference is that the standards tend to promote teaching bits and pieces of fragmented knowledge, while in looking at the bigger picture of fundamental understandings that cross subject matter areas, we see how these understandings interconnect. In the United States, however, the *National Science Education Standards* emphasize the understanding of systems. In essence, the approach being suggested by complex learning in this chapter is one of systems thinking. Instead of learning about one specific concept or idea, we are considering ways of learning about the interconnections and interrelationships of systems. These systems can be physiological, ecological, social, mechanical, psychological, or political. But, even further than these individual types of systems, we can develop understandings of how all of these systems are similar, and maybe even how they are interconnected. For example, a political system makes certain demands on the economic system, which in turn affects ecological systems, which can then lead to effects on individual physiological systems, and then back again to political, economic, and ecological systems.

As mentioned earlier in this section, business leaders are quite concerned about the inabilities of their employees to think creatively and critically and to transfer their understandings from one context to another. In fact, the evidence up to this point suggests that transfer of learning in schooling and other educational efforts does not happen. However, the approach to complex learning as described in this section offers hope for transfer. In fact, the approach itself (i.e., exploring patterns and concepts in different contexts and subject matter areas) is one where transfer is built in. In other words, by investigating how one pattern or concept appears in multiple contexts as a matter of routine, we are addressing the processes of transfer within the very way we approach developing our understandings of the world.

> *Transfer of learning* is when children (or adults) are able to apply what they have learned to different contexts. Evidence to date shows no correlation between teaching and the ability to transfer or utilize knowledge in other contexts. This lack of evidence is true with children in school and with adults in the university or the workplace. See Chapter 7 for a more detailed discussion of transfer.

## 4.7 Summary of Implications for Teaching

The following is a list of the major points in this chapter:

- Children do not enter the classroom as blank slates. They come with a great deal of personally constructed understandings.
- Children construct new knowledge based on what they already know.
- Children's understandings include a wide variety of perspectives that cross curricular boundaries.
- Children construct knowledge individually and socially.

✔

♦ **Find a group of children with whom you can work. If you are a teacher, you can do some of these activities with your class. If you are a pre-service teacher, a school may be amenable to allowing you (and your partner, if you have one) to borrow a group of children for 45 minutes to an hour. You may also find neighborhood children or your own children and their friends with whom you can work.**

♦ **Gather up some materials (e.g., a pail of dirt with earthworms or other creatures; a 4-liter or gallon jar of pond water, along with a kitchen baster, magnifying lenses, and small containers; an old radio, clock, or other electronic or mechanical device, along with a variety of tools; some spinning tops, along with some straight, round sticks; cardboard; tape; and scissors). Take the materials and just let the children play with them.**

♦ **It is very helpful to take a tape recorder along to tape children's conversations (a video recorder is even better at capturing their activities and facial expressions). Afterwards, review the recordings and think about the kinds of thinking, ideas, and questions that arose among the children.**

※

**Refer to the above activity:**

♦ **What conceptual understandings can you identify?**

♦ **Which understandings were accurate and which ones were not?**

♦ **How could some of these ideas and questions lead to further inquiry or integrated activities?**

♦ **How could you provide further inquiry activities to challenge some of their inaccurate understandings?**

■ The social construction of knowledge reflects social and cultural beliefs and assumptions.

■ The meanings children associate with different topics involve emotions-values-aesthetics, metaphors, personal experiences, school-type knowledge, imagery, fantasy, stories, interpretive frameworks (including beliefs), and elaboration.

■ Conceptual understanding involves the elaboration of how we categorize our observations of the world.

■ Play and story provide a way of establishing an experiential basis for further learning and of creating a context for our understandings.

■ Children naturally think and make sense of their worlds in complex ways, which we can help to refine and extend for more complex and integrated understandings.

We have also seen that children's thinking is quite complex and abstract. Even very young children are capable of understanding relatively complex and difficult concepts. The basis for understanding more difficult and abstract concepts is not so much an issue of age as it is an issue of prior experience with the conceptual topic. As teachers, we need to find out what children know, then develop learning experiences that build on the children's previous understandings. However, when we find out what children understand, we will frequently find that their understandings are not scientifically accurate. At this point, we need to develop strategies and experiences that challenge their understandings. This approach is described as teaching for conceptual change. The basic points in this approach are

■ Children's personal understandings are often resistant to change.

■ In order for children to change their understandings, they need to be confronted with conflicting evidence.

■ A change in understanding is the child's choice.

There is a vast amount of evidence to support the point that children's understandings tend to be resistant to change. Instruction can have little or no effect. In fact, even if we confront children with conflicting evidence, they may disregard the evidence or incorporate it into their existing understandings in such a way that the new evidence does not contradict their existing understandings. Supplying such contradictory evidence is the only approach that seems to have any potential for allowing children to decide what they believe to be the best explanation. As we read through the following chapters, we will have an opportunity to see how this approach can be implemented.

## Additional Reading

Donaldson, M. (1978). *Children's minds*. London: Fontana Press (Harper Collins).
    Intriguing little book. It is a classic that presents research evidence that counters the claims made by Piagetian researchers about developmental stages.
Eisner, E. (1994). *Cognition and curriculum reconsidered* (2nd ed.). New York: Teachers College Press.
    Examines the different ways people represent and communicate understandings and the implications of this view on curriculum.

Harlen, W. (1993). *Teaching and learning primary science* (2nd ed.). London: Paul Chapman Publishing.
Wonderfully written book about teaching science from a constructivist perspective. Includes chapters on children's ideas, thinking, learning, and language.

Paley, V. G. (1986). *Mollie is three: Growing up in school*. Chicago: University of Chicago Press.
One of many great books by this teacher/researcher. Very insightful look at children's and teachers' thinking.

Stein, S. (1986). *The evolution book*. New York: Workman Publishers.
A book of information about and teaching activities on evolution. A great resource for teachers.

Volk, T. (1995). *Metapatterns: Across space, time, and mind*. New York: Columbia University Press.

## Advanced Reading

Bell, B. (2005). *Learning in science: The Waikato research*. New York: Routledge-Falmer.

Bloom, J. W. (1990). Contexts of meaning: young children's understanding of biological phenomena. *International Journal of Science Education, 12*, 549–561.

Bloom, J. W. (1992). The development of scientific knowledge in elementary school children: A context of meaning perspective. *Science Education, 76*, 399–413.

Bransford, J. D., Brown, A. L., & Cocking, R. R. (Eds.). (2000). *How people learn: Brain, mind, experience, and school*. Washington, DC: National Academy Press.

Davis, B., Sumara, D., & Luce-Kapler, R. (2000). *Engaging minds: Learning and teaching in a complex world*. Mahwah, NJ: Lawrence Erlbaum Associates.

Duckworth, E. (1996). *"The having of wonderful ideas" and other essays on teaching and learning* (2nd ed.). New York: Teachers College Press.
A Piagetian researcher and educator's examination of children's ideas. Nice treatment of teaching from the child's perspective, but does not address the importance of language and talk.

Gilbert, J. K., & Boulter, C. J. (Eds.). (2000). *Developing models in science education*. Boston, MA: Kluwer Academic Publishers.

Harcombe, E. S. (2001). *Science teaching/science learning: Constructivist learning in urban classrooms*. New York: Teachers College Press.

Haskell, R. E. (2001). *Transfer of learning: Cognition, instruction, and reasoning*. San Diego: Academic Press.

Hodson, D. (1998). *Teaching and learning science: Towards a personalized approach*. Philadelphia: Open University Press.

Watts, M., & Bentley, D. (1994). Humanizing and feminizing school science: Reviving anthropomorphic and animistic thinking in constructivist science education. *International Journal of Science Education, 16*, 83–97.

## Notes

1. For an argument and evidence against Piagetian research on developmental stages, see Margaret Donaldson's classic research in the book *Children's Minds* (London: Fontana Press (Harper Collins), 1978).

2. Trudy Sable, *Another Look in the Mirror: Research into the Foundations for Developing an Alternative Science Curriculum for Mi'kmaw Children* (unpublished master's thesis, St. Mary's University, Halifax, NS, 1996), p. 85.

3. For information and activities on evolution, see Sara Stein's *The Evolution Book* (New York: Workman Publishers, 1986) and Lisa Westberg Peters' *Our Family Tree* (New York: Harcourt's Children's Books, 2003).

4. M. C. Bateson, *Willing to Learn: Passages of Personal Discovery* (Hanover, NH: Steerforth Press, 2004).

5. R. E. Haskell, *Transfer of Learning: Cognition, Instruction, and Reasoning* (San Diego, CA: Academic Press, 2001).

6. These first 11 metapatterns are from T. Volk, *Metapatterns: Across Space, Time, and Mind* (New York: Columbia University Press, 1995).

*Chapter 5*
# Children's Talk

This chapter extends the examination of children's learning from the previous chapter, with particular emphasis on social constructivism. Where constructivism is concerned with an individual's construction of knowledge, social constructivism is concerned with how groups construct knowledge through argument, negotiation, and other aspects of conversation. Children's talk is a major aspect of social constructivism (which also includes teacher-to-children talk, communication between parents and children, communication within social groupings, and communication within a culture), which is of particular importance in creating a community of inquirers in the classroom. Such talk within the classroom provides a means for children to construct further understandings and allows teachers and other children to challenge the ideas and explanations of others. In addition, children's talk allows us, as teachers, to monitor and assess our students' understandings.

In this chapter, we will explore the nature of classroom talk as it typically occurs, then we will move on to how we can modify classroom talk so that children can develop greater responsibility for discussions and can construct deeper understandings. We also will examine an extended argument about density in a small class of grades 5, 6, and 7 students. The final part of the chapter will return to a general examination of what we need to do as teachers to facilitate productive science talks in the classroom. Throughout this chapter, continue to keep in mind how children think, construct understandings, make sense of scientific phenomena, and develop complex connections within and across subject matter areas.

## 5.1 The Traditional Approach to Classroom Discussions

Typically, talk in classrooms is dominated by the teacher. If we go into a classroom and measure the time that teachers talk versus the time that students talk, we would probably find that teachers talk about two-thirds of the time. If we look at the pattern of this talk, we would find that the teacher usually initiates any particular talk sequence with a question. The teacher's question is followed by a student response, which in turn is followed by an evaluative comment by the teacher. This pattern is usually referred to as the initiate-respond-evaluate (IRE) sequence.

In Example 5.1, the teacher asks a question, then calls on a student. The student responds with an answer, which is followed by an evaluative statement by the teacher and another question. The teacher calls on another student, who supplies an answer. The teacher follows with an evaluative comment. There are several questions we need to ask ourselves about this pattern of interaction (if you can, take a few moments to think about each question before reading on):

- **What is the goal of this pattern of interaction?**

  The goal of this pattern tends to involve the acquisition and recall of particular content. In other words, the teacher asks questions to ascertain whether children can respond with the correct answer. The concern is not with helping children construct their own understandings or with encouraging children to formulate explanations and to challenge each other's ideas. When we follow such a pattern, we generally are not concerned with the extent of each individual's idiosyncratic understandings, or even with the depth or extent of their subject matter understandings. This particular approach also is most common in teaching-to-the-test, where pieces of informa-

---

**Example 5.1: A Traditional (Hypothetical) IRE Classroom Talk Sequence**

**Teacher:** **Does anyone remember what we call this kind of machine [while holding up a bottle opener]? Yes, Jimmy?**

*Freddie:* It's a bottle opener.

**Teacher:** **Yes, that's right, but what is the name of the simple machine? OK. Francine?**

*Francine:* It's a lever.

**Teacher:** **Good, that's right.**

---

tion are paramount and thorough understandings are not of particular value.

- **What messages about classroom interactions and learning are being communicated?**
  Such interactional patterns tend to reinforce an orderly approach to classroom talk. The teacher asks the questions and children raise their hands. The dialogue tends to go from teacher to child to teacher, and so on. The notion of learning is one of being able to recall the right information. Successful participation in such interactions is based on rote learning. The concern is not with complex understandings, but with repeating fragmented and disconnected knowledge.

- **What is the nature of control and power in such a sequence?**
  This question is related to the previous one. Whether the teacher asks the questions or answers student questions, the teacher controls the flow and content of what is discussed in class. The teacher does most of the talking and determines what is acceptable and what is not. Students have very little control over what is and is not discussed.[1]

The IRE sequence tends to limit student input and control, as well as the extent of learning. As a commonly used strategy, such limitations do not fit well with acknowledging how children learn from a constructivist or social constructivist perspective. However, it's occasional use with some modifications can be helpful in extending certain kinds of student learning. In Example 5.2, look for the difference in how this sequence extends an avenue for further exploration and learning.

In this example, the basic IRE sequence is evident; however, the teacher expands on the evaluative segment by making a connection to a historical figure and Benjamin Franklin's view of why he invented things. Essentially, the evaluative segment can be used to connect students' comments to a

---

**Example 5.2: A Modified (Hypothetical) IRE
Sequence of Teacher–Student Interaction**

**Teacher:** **Class, we've been talking about devices that make things easier for us to do. Can you think of any examples that we haven't talked about before? Yes, Andrea.**

*Student:* I was watching this mystery on TV last night. I think it took place in England. This guy was working in a bookstore with books up to the ceiling. He used a ladder on wheels at the bottom and a track on the top to move around and get to the high books.

**Teacher:** **Great example. That ladder idea was invented by Benjamin Franklin. I think he said that his inventions were the result of his own laziness. He must have been pretty lazy, because he invented a lot of things!**

---

broader or different context. The student's comment is not just good or bad, or right or wrong. It is connected to some other situation, event, or idea. The teacher can provide links to broader contexts.

## 5.2 An Alternative Approach to Classroom Discussions

From a different perspective, when children talk to one another about the work they are doing, they become involved in trying to make sense of their observations and figuring out how to make their experiment or activity work. As we saw in Chapter 3, on the nature of science, a fair amount of time may be spent trying to get the apparatus or experiment to work properly. In Example 5.3, several children are trying to set up mirrors so that they can look into one mirror and see an infinitely repeatable image of themselves. They had been working at this activity for half an hour or more before the teacher joined them.

Carrie and Cynthia have begun to develop a great deal of experiential knowledge of how mirrors work. Although they may not be able to articulate an explanation of certain concepts, they have begun to develop a fundamental, almost intuitive, understanding of reflection and angles. In addition, they have engaged in an authentic inquiry task arising from their own interests and questions. When they were successful at setting up the mirrors to reflect their own images repeatedly, they sought out other children, such as Chloe, with whom to share their insights.

In the previous example, the children engaged in inquiry independently of the teacher. They worked together to make sense of what they were doing. However, if we return to the premise of social constructivism—that children construct knowledge through their interactions with others—we need to think of alternative approaches to prescriptive, teacher-controlled classroom talk. Several points need to be kept in mind:

1. **Children are people**, with values, goals, intentions, personalities, and so forth. This point appears to be very obvious; however, when we look at the roles they are forced to play in classrooms, we begin to see that we tend to offer them little opportunity to take control, to take on responsibility, and to express themselves authentically and in ways that they choose. We tend to demand conformity and adherence to our expectations of how students should behave, talk, and act. Rarely do we allow children truly to be themselves. When we ask questions, we expect certain answers. When children express an idea, we choose whether it is appropriate or not. Their expressions of humor are often squelched. When children are working on an activity, they may carry on side conversations about movies, video games, etc. We call this being "off task" and consider it inappropriate. This term was introduced within the context of authoritarian classrooms based on corporate models, where efficieny and obedience were of

## Example 5.3: Two Grade 3 Girls' Discussion as They Work with Mirrors

*Carrie:* We've got to put that one up there. No, put that one closer or else it doesn't do anything.

**Teacher: So what's it doing?**

*Cynthia:* It's making 3000 pictures on the …

*Carrie:* It's making, you can see it in all the pictures, only they're at different angles. Don't put it like that because then it won't stay like that.

**Teacher: I just want to see.**

*Carrie:* There, put that there just in case it falls backwards. Try to make it not fall any, which way …

*Cynthia:* I found all the old books under there.

*Carrie:* What are you doing?

*Cynthia:* I'm going to be seven, I mean eight paces away.

*Carrie:* I can see 1, 2, 3, 4, 5, 6, 7, 8; I can see 8 of me too.

**Teacher: Eight of you?**

*Carrie:* Yeah, because if you look in here, like you can see, you can see one of you in the small mirrors because they are reflecting up into there.

**LATER**

*Cynthia:* It looks like a maze and it keeps going. I can see those boots, I can see those boots.

*Carrie:* Oh yeah, those old boots. Oh where? I don't see any. Oh yeah, I see them now.

*Cynthia:* There they are.

*Carrie:* I see them, I see them, and also you can see more of yourself because when you look in here, you know how we've taken some of this mirror away.

**Teacher: Right.**

*Carrie:* And some of that mirror away, because of that then you can see more of you, because …

**Teacher: Right.**

*Carrie:* Because you can, because it's like that [laughs], yes you can because it's like that.

**Teacher: Because you cut off part of the mirrors to get more mirrors in.**

*Carrie:* Yeah, because you cut off that, aah. Here, I want to show you, you've got to come over here, Chloe. I want to show you, Chloe, I want to show you. You see if you look here, you see lots of pictures of you, because of all the mirrors. You've got to lay down like that, way down here.

*Cynthia:* That's the place for you to look through. See, you can see lots. You don't have to break it.

✳

In terms of side conversations and other off-task actions:

◆ Do such conversations prevent us from accomplishing what we need to do?

◆ What are the benefits to the social situation and to one's own state of mind when carrying on side conversations?

paramount importance. Yet, at the same time, how often do we have side conversations when we work in a particular job? We need to think about how we can create the kind of classroom atmosphere that allows children to express themselves authentically and to feel as if they can take risks.

2. **Children need to be involved in co-constructing knowledge and understanding.** Rather than following a typical IRE or teacher–student pattern of classroom talk, we need to encourage children to talk to each other about their ideas.

3. **Children need to be encouraged and guided through a process of talking effectively and productively.** This process is not one of the teacher evaluating and filtering what they say, but of the teacher helping children to ask for clarification and to challenge and elaborate on each other's ideas and explanations.

4. **We need to allow children to take more control of what is said, when it is said, and how it is said.** During discussions, we need to provide opportunities for children to feel a sense of ownership over the ideas being expressed and over the way in which the discussion takes place. The traditional demand of always raising hands before speaking generally should not be a part of classroom talks, where the intent is to model authentic inquiry and give children more control over their learning. Such a demand tends to stifle children's spontaneity and the flow of the conversation. Although the discussion may wander and appear to go out of control, we need to keep in mind that the children are making connections to different contexts. However, we can help children in developing listening skills, which include (a) recognizing when someone has "the floor," (b) recognizing when someone has finished talking, (c) listening to and understanding what someone else is trying to say, and (d) how not to attack another person, but to "attack" ideas in positive ways (e.g., not saying "That's a stupid idea," but rather "I don't agree with that idea" or "That idea doesn't make sense" or "Do you have any evidence to support that idea?).

5. **The teacher should listen to what children say and think about what they mean and how their thinking can be extended.** As teachers, we tend to talk too much. We jump in with comments and criticisms. If we stand back and listen to what children are really saying and let them continue developing the theme of their conversation, we allow children to extend their own understandings. When we do participate, we should try to be a co-participant in the ongoing discussion or a mentor in how to be a participant in discussions.

6. **The teacher should act as a model of how to challenge, clarify, and elaborate on ideas.** As a co-participant, co-learner, and co-inquirer, we can ask challenging questions or present situations that challenge the claims of others. When children make statements that are

unclear to us, we can ask them to restate or clarify their claims. We also can elaborate on ideas and add our particular understandings and insights.

7. **We need to realize that not all children will readily participate in class discussions**. Some children will resist participating for a number of reasons, such as shyness, fear of being wrong, disinterest, and so on. If we persist in engaging children in authentic classroom talk, those who are quiet may begin to enter into the discussions over time.

8. **Teachers need to help children understand the nature and purpose of classroom talk**. In the classroom, we rarely explain to children what our goals and purposes are. We seem to play a game of "guess the rules and goals." If we want children to listen to each other, ask challenging questions, ask for clarification, elaborate on ideas, apply their previous understandings, and construct new understandings and explanations, we need to explain these goals to them. When a child is not listening to someone else's idea, we need to remind him or her that we need to listen to what others say in order to challenge or build on what has been said.

The previous points briefly describe a generalized view of classroom talk. However, we need to examine more closely what we want students to do and learn during classroom talk, more specifically, science talk. As discussed in Chapter 3, on the nature of science, what we essentially want to do is have children working and talking as young scientists. Scientists do not readily accept what a colleague claims. In general, they do not sit around in an orderly fashion and raise their hands, while carrying out a very controlled and reasonable conversation. Rather, colleagues ask tough questions, demand evidence to support claims, and expect reasonably clear and articulate explanations. Sometimes, when they do not believe the claims or premises of colleagues, they may become quite angry and engage in heated arguments. Scientists are human beings, with emotions, beliefs, and all the rest. The major difference in the way scientists talk and work is that they demand supporting evidence and strong methodology.

Classroom science talk should reflect the spirit and nature of science, as well as more general characteristics of any community of inquirers. So, as we continue to formulate our framework for teaching science, we need to take into account some further, more specific principles, which are described below. Each of the following points can be taught and discussed explicitly with children. In this case, teaching can include (a) stating and discussing these points with students, (b) modeling these points in classroom discussions, and (c) coaching children during classroom discussions.

Try audio- or videotaping yourself or another teacher during a typical classroom session. Listen to the tape and look at the patterns of classroom talk.

+ How does the amount of teacher talk compare to student talk?

+ What kind of patterns of talk do you notice (e.g., IRE)?

+ How does the teacher control the content and flow of the talk?

+ How much cross talk occurs between students?

+ Once you've had an opportunity to think about the above questions, think about how you could conduct the same sort of discussion differently.

1. **The co-participants (teacher and students) in classroom science talks should develop the skills of listening to the claims, arguments, and explanations of others.**
   a. Respect each other's ability to make a meaningful contribution.
   b. Respect the ideas and feelings of others.
   c. Thoughtfully consider what another says.
   d. Active listening requires that some action be taken, such as weighing the statement against one's own ideas, responding to the speaker with a question or comment, testing the idea through an activity of some sort, and so on.
   e. Responses to what someone else says should probe, challenge, or extend the idea.
   f. Know when to jump into the conversation without interrupting or talking "on top of" someone else.

2. **The co-participants in classroom science talks should develop the skills of thinking and talking critically about the claims, arguments, and explanations of others, as well as of our own.**
   a. Ask for clarification of points and claims.
   b. Ask probing questions that ask for further explanations and examples.
   c. Ask for supporting evidence for the claims made by others.
   d. Add comments that show relationships between ideas or to different contexts.
   e. Add comments that elaborate on a particular theme.
   f. Offer alternative explanations or theories.
   g. Evaluate explanations and ideas on the basis of whether they make sense.
   h. Evaluate whether explanations are consistent with the evidence.
   i. Evaluate the accuracy of explanations and ideas.
   j. Evaluate the relevance of explanations, evidence, and other ideas.

These points are by no means exhaustive. They are only a basis from which to begin working with classroom science talk. *The process of acquiring these skills may take some time. We cannot expect to walk into a classroom and have students acquire these skills.* As we model these skills in our contributions to classroom discussions and point out how these skills are effective and important as we use them, children will begin to adopt these new ways of working in the classroom. As you continue to talk science and engage children in discussions that allow them to build theories, they will start refining their skills. In Example 5.4, Karen Gallas provides a wonderful example of how grades 1 and 2 students engage in some very complex discussions of very difficult material.

**Example 5.4: Grades 1 and 2 Students
Discussing Whether Voice Is Matter**

In an earlier part of the discussion the children had collaboratively concluded that air is matter, because matter takes up space.

*Tom:*     If voice is, um, matter, um, is, like, would we be getting squished right now, if it's like, taking up room?

*Lester:*   No, it wouldn't exactly be getting like squished.

*Ellen:*    Because air's taking up space, and it's not squeezing us.

*Zach:*     And it takes up more space than we do.

***Teacher:*  Could you say your question again, Tom?**

*Zach:*     How could it not really like …

*Tom:*     If, if …

*Zach:*     Squeeze us …

*Tom:*     If voice is matter …

*Zach:*     To death?

*Tom:*     Why isn't it, like, smushing us against the walls?

*Michael:* Because air is matter, but when there's like, like take a big wind, for instance. When hurricanes or tornadoes come along, they take up a lot of air, and space, and they are air. But it's just a big quantity of air.

**LATER**

*Ian:*      But how can you tell voice is matter if … It seems like air doesn't take up space, but it actually does. So, so you can't, you can't exactly tell with air where, like, where it is. There's not like, one piece of air going in a different place. That's not the same as with voice. So, it doesn't seem like it would take up room. It's not like every day you see a chunk of air floating around in the sky.

*Ellen:*    Not if it's really cold and you're breathing, and it gets really cold. [Sounds of many children breathing in and out.]

*Ian:*      Yeah, so. You don't see a chunk of voice flying around if someone says something. It's not like you see these words coming up in a chunk of voice flying up into the air. [Pointing into the air] "Ohhhh, there's your voice."

**LATER**

*Zach:*     I think voice is matter because like, when you talk, you can feel something like hot on your hand. If you put your hand near your mouth and if you don't talk, you don't have something hot on your hand.

*Ian:*      I just tried that experiment and what I found out, see, I said, "I can" and I found out that when I … That hot stuff that I felt on my hand is just breath. I was just breathing.

*Eli:*      But Zach, if that is true, then why can't we really see it happening? Why can't we really see it happening?

*Michael:* I don't know. It's like air, you can't see air happen.

*Zach:*     You can see it on frosty days.

*Michael:* Yeah, you can. You see your breath. And your breath is air.[2]

✦ **What are your reactions to the children's talk in Example 5.4?**

✦ **Who is in control of the flow and content of the discussion?**

✦ **At what points do you see the children challenging each other's ideas?**

✦ **What socially constructed knowledge and understandings are evident from the children's talk?**

The excerpts in Example 5.4 took place later in the school year. It should be apparent that the children had acquired some of the skills of talking and listening. Although they did talk over each other (lines 6 to 10), they were keenly aware of what everyone was saying. The teacher, Karen Gallas, only interjected one request for a child to repeat a question. During the remainder of the discussion (in these excerpts), the children controlled the content and flow of the discussion. Throughout this sequence, the children are contending with the idea of whether voice and air are the same thing. As the discussion proceeds, the argument becomes much more pointed. In lines 30 to 35, Ian challenges Zach's claim with evidence from his experiment. Eli then jumps in with a challenging question. In the last three lines, Michael makes a claim, which is countered by Zach, and followed by another claim that breath is just air. The major point here is that children can engage in very sophisticated theory-building arguments. When they feel ownership over the ideas and the process, they take such tasks seriously.

What we see here, which we generally do not see in school classrooms, is passion. The children are passionate about their arguments and ideas. If passion is evident in our students' school activities, then what is occurring is authentic. Real and relevant learning is taking place in ways that are consistent with what we might expect of any person or group of people who are genuinely interested in what they are doing. Each person has a stake in his or her ideas. As a result, children take the process seriously. In contrast, when the traditional guessing game format of classroom discussions takes place, students tend not to have a stake in the ideas they put forth. However, if some students are motivated by the dangling carrot of high achievement, they may have a stake in being right, but not necessarily in the ideas and understandings themselves.

## 5.3  An Example of a Classroom Argument

In this section, we will have an opportunity to look at an extended discussion and argument about density in a small class of grades 5, 6, and 7 students. The argument began shortly after the students had completed an activity in which they predicted which objects would float and which would not. The argument ensued while discussing the issue of why ebony did not float. As you read through the excerpts of the argument, consider the following questions:

- What role does the teacher take in the argument?
- Who has control of the argument (students or teacher)?
- What argument strategies do the students use? How effective are these strategies in carrying out an argument?
- What are the students' conceptual understandings?
- Can you identify underlying principles or themes of their understandings that interfere with their constructing more scientifically accurate understandings? Identifying such principles or themes is difficult, but it is critical when addressing students' idiosyncratic understandings.

The following student argument occurred near the beginning of a teacher's work with this class. In contrast to Karen Gallas's classroom science talk (see Example 5.4), the students had not learned the social skills of conducting an argument as were evident among Gallas's students. Learning and internalizing these skills takes time. Although the following argument is rough around the edges in terms of the children's social skills, the argument was successful in extending the children's thinking.

Before we proceed, you need to keep in mind that students' arguments can become very complex. We may find ourselves confronted with concepts about which we have very little understanding. (Take a moment to reflect on an argument you have had recently.) It is very important to keep in mind that we should not view this as a problem. We cannot allow our fear of not knowing limit our students' engagement in talking science. *Allowing our students to engage in arguments is an essential ingredient in the process of knowledge construction and theory building.* If we feel as if we have just jumped in over our heads, we can join in the process of trying to make sense of the phenomenon. *The biggest mistake we can make is to assert our own misunderstandings.* The approach being suggested in this book is that we, as teachers, do not have to play the role of knowledge authority. Several alternative roles for teachers are suggested by the following metaphors: co-participant in a learning community, facilitator, guide, mentor, and orchestrator. So, when we find the following argument delving into complex scientific concepts, we should see this as an opportunity to reflect on our own feelings about science and teaching and take the opportunity to make sense of new concepts. To assist in this process, explanations of the concepts suggested by the students will be included in more detail as they arise.

The argument began as Greg expressed his problem with the idea that ebony sinks: "But then, uh, …? Then, if you scaled up the big piece of wood, then you have to scale up the water too. You have to make the water, so, then it would float." He suggests that by placing the little block of ebony in a bigger body of water, we could get the block to float. Frank, however, expressed his disagreement. This idea and brief disagreement marks the beginning of an argument that resurfaced and continued throughout the following four class meetings.

We can see in this excerpt how the teacher interacts in the discussion. He suggests a challenge near the beginning ("But even if we took one out into the lake…"), which is finished by another student. At this point, the teacher thought the point had been made that ebony also would sink in a larger body of water. However, as we will see in the following excerpts, the point was not made. Since the term *density* had been brought up by students earlier in class, the teacher asked for a definition or explanation of density ("What does dense mean?"). Later, the teacher offers an alternative way of thinking about density ("these blocks… are about the same size"). Gina's response about molecules appears to be accepted by the other students, but becomes the concept that

❋

✦ In this example, how would you describe the students' understandings of density?

✦ What instructional options should we consider implementing as a follow-up to this discussion?

> ## Example 5.5: Beginning of the Density Argument in Class 2
>
> *Note*: Italicized speech indicates the speaker's emphasis. Teacher's talk is in boldface type.
>
> **Teacher: But even if we took one out into the lake, that little piece, and put it in the lake …**
>
> *Frank:* It would sink.
>
> **Teacher: It would sink.**
>
> *Greg:* Yeah, yeah.
>
> *Fred:* But if you put it in a …
>
> *Greg:* No, it wouldn't. It would go along to the bottom.
>
> **Teacher: [To class] What does dense mean? What does density mean?**
>
> *Frank:* Density?
>
> *Graham:* [Not quite loud enough for the whole class] Like someone next to me has a dense head. Ha, ha, ha.
>
> *Frank:* It means the …
>
> *Greg:* Pushed together!
>
> *Gina:* [Interrupting Frank] It means the amount of molecules that are in the thing. Like the molecules are closer together and they …
>
> *Student:* They compress!
>
> **Teacher: What you said, I have another way of talking about it, you know? Now, these blocks of wood are about the same size, right?**
>
> *Student:* It's put together tighter, it's like squeezed.
>
> *Greg:* Yeah.
>
> **Teacher: If you take these two pieces of wood that are about the same size, what are we saying?**
>
> *Gina:* There's more molecules per, per square millimeter.
>
> **Teacher: So, when you do this, you take how much weight is in the volume, right? That's the density. How much weight is in the volume? How can we figure out the volume, the density of water?**
>
> *Gina:* Does all water have the same amount of molecules in it? Like, if you just took water from the tap and …
>
> *Gina:* No, because water has salt in it. Never mind.
>
> *Frank:* Uh, $H_2O$. No, that's the molecule. Uh, water, I'm not sure.
>
> *Frank:* Well, it can be a lot. It can be a little.
>
> *Greg:* If you took all this, if you took all this water and put it in a container *smaller*, it would still weigh the same, but it would have a different density, because the volume is, uh, smaller.

guides the other side of the argument (in opposition to Greg's perspective). What we see in this sequence of dialogue is the teacher's attempt at exerting some sense of control over the conceptual content of the discussion. At the same time, the beginnings of a much more extensive disagreement about density are being hashed out by the students. Gina continues to contend with a molecular explanation of density, while Greg suggests that putting a certain quantity of water into a smaller container would increase the density of water.

## What the Teacher Was Thinking

At this point in the discussion, the teacher did not expect students to talk about molecules. He had not considered the possibility that the students would bring this concept into the discussion. He also felt hesitant about exploring it in more depth: Would this concept be too difficult for some of the students? In terms of Greg's point about volume, the teacher was not too sure what was going on. The teacher did not feel that the Piagetian notion of conservation of volume applied to the children's thinking in this situation (i.e., the contention that children, at an early point in their development, do not understand that when you pour water from a tall, thin container into a short, wide container the volume of the water remains the same). Somehow the way in which Greg was talking about the issue of volume did not fit with the Piagetian notion. As a result of his uncertainty, the teacher decided to introduce further inquiry activities around the notion of density. Immediately following this part of the argument, the students measured the density of ebony and a number of other objects using the formula for density: density = mass (weight) ÷ volume.

At the beginning of class 3, the students picked up where they had left off and the argument continued. Greg restated his basic claim that the block of ebony would float in a larger volume of water: "Well, the theory of volume is that objects are as dense as they are compacted, so … Also, the smallest thing could float, if it was in a larger volume, because it was the same small thing." Both Fred and Gina disagreed, while Gina reaffirmed her claim that density is determined by the number of molecules in a particular volume. After the teacher asked for an explanation of how density can be measured, Gina continued to elaborate on her understanding of molecules and density:

> Like if you compared … one piece of ebony to one piece of pine that were the same size … and you put them on a scale, that ebony might weigh more, and you would know that the molecules are denser in the ebony.… But I don't know how they could find out how much denser, like how many molecules.… Wait, Greg, Greg [as Greg tries to interject another comment]. If the pine … it has the same measurements, it'll seem like it has the same amount of molecules, so that wouldn't work.

At the end of this sequence, Greg appeared to agree with Gina about the difference in density between the same-size blocks of pine and ebony: "I agree. You're right there and I'm wrong."

☞

**Density is commonly depicted as a formula:**

mass (weight on earth) ÷ volume = density

**In other words, density is the amount of mass in a specific volume. For example, if we measure the dimensions and the weight of a block of wood as shown below, and apply our measurements to the formula, we get a ratio of the mass (how much stuff) to the volume (how much space the stuff occupies).**

**The density is expressed as 0.75 g/cm³. By comparison, if we calculate the density of water, 1 cm³ of water weighs 1 g. The resulting density of water is 1.0 g/cm³. Because the density of the block of wood is less than the density of water, the block will float when placed in the water.**

**The molecular explanation for density is not analogous to visualizing a container filled with ping-pong balls (representing molecules). Let us compare two common substances: water and gasoline. As many of us have probably seen in movies (e.g., *True Lies*, where Arnold Schwarzenegger is swimming under water while the surface is covered with burning gasoline), gasoline floats on water. If we look at the molecular structure of water, two hydrogen atoms are attached to one oxygen atom (i.e., $H_2O$). The molecular weight of hydrogen is 1.01. The molecular weight of oxygen is 16.00. So, the molecular weight of water is 18.02. For a basic grade of gasoline, the molecular structure contains 8 carbon molecules and 18 hydrogen molecules. Carbon's molecular weight is 12.01. The molecular weight of gasoline is shown in Figure 5.1.**

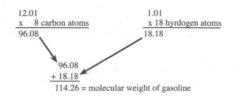

**FIGURE 5.1**

As we can see, a gasoline molecule (114.26) weighs much more than a water molecule (18.02). If we poured a quantity of gasoline that weighed 114 g, it would occupy a volume of about 162 cm³. The resulting density for gasoline is approximately 0.702.

☞

**Not all science educators agree that providing opportunities for children to argue about and explore scientific explanations is more important than having them develop accurate understandings. The bias in this book is that in order to (a) stimulate and excite children about science, (b) allow greater depth and breadth of understanding, and (c) represent an authentic view of the nature of science, we may have to sacrifice correct content. In addition, there is some compelling evidence that some understandings of content are extremely difficult to change through any kind of instructional intervention.**

**This evidence appears in the extensive research of phenomenological primitives, which act as extremely basic guiding frameworks for students' thinking.[3]**

The issues involved in our own understanding of science concepts are important to consider. Many teachers see their own lack of knowledge as a major problem and either teach science in a tightly controlled way or avoid teaching science altogether. However, our own lack of understanding does not have to be seen as a major problem. Yes, we should work on developing our own understandings, but at the same time, we should not see this as a limiting factor in how we teach. We need to remember that teachers should avoid placing themselves in the position of being the knowledge authority. Rather, teachers should be facilitating inquiry and access to other sources of knowledge (e.g., scientists, books, magazines). We also can view situations in the classroom, which delve into complex conceptual areas, as opportunities to inquire and learn along with our students. The key ability we need to develop is a kind of conceptual radar. We need to be able to spot the points at which our knowledge is unclear, then spend some time investigating this content outside of class. As we develop a clearer understanding of this content, we can always return to the topic at a later date. Keep in mind, however, that the accuracy of the children's understandings may not be as important as allowing them to explore and argue about their understandings in greater depth.

Catching the subtleties of children's arguments is always a challenge; however, there are a couple of strategies you may find helpful. First, as children develop their own skills at conducting classroom science talks, the group can begin to detect points of confusion. As the students begin to point out areas of confusion, the teacher, in turn, can make a note of these areas and investigate them further. The second strategy is to keep at least one tape recorder available for taping classroom discussions. Listening to the tape at a later time can reveal many points missed during the intensity of the classroom action.

As we consider some of these difficult questions throughout the upcoming argument excerpts, we will begin to see the students' understandings unfold and extend even further. The particularly interesting aspect of allowing children to control the content and flow of classroom discussions is that we are afforded the opportunity to see a more complete view of their developing understandings. As we have seen so far, the students' ideas are extended by their interactions with each other. They respond to other students' comments by elaborating and defending their own positions. If we, as teachers, cut off the discussion, we risk not getting a fuller picture of their understandings and risk smothering their own passion and ownership of the ideas.

The argument continued briefly during class 4, while the children rehashed some of their previous points. We will now skip to class 5 and pick up the argument as it arises partway through class.

---

**Example 5.6: Continuation of the Density Argument in Class 5**

*Gina:* No, little cup of water, and you pour a little cup of water into a big bucket it still weighs the same.

*George:* It's true.

*Gina:* If you pour a little cup of water into a big basin, you'll have the same amount of water in the big basin, than in the little cup of water.

**Teacher: Yeah, but is the density the same?**

*Gina:* Yes.

*[Other voices saying "Yes"]*

*Greg:* Yes, because it changes in a smaller volume, because the density gets …

*Gina:* Well, I'm sorry [with indignation] …

**Teacher: But, if you change the volume, you change the weight, too.**

*Gina:* Well, maybe slightly, but I'm sorry to say, when I drink a glass of water, I don't notice any difference. I don't feel any heavier, or I don't feel the water's thicker than when I take a big bucket of water and drink it.

*Greg:* That's because the water comes *out* [with adamant emphasis on *out*]. It's different when you drink a cup of water.

*Gina:* See, see, he just said the density's gonna be the same, no matter what you do. But you're *wrong*, Greg. You're *wrong* [assuredly].

*Greg:* No, what we said was density, density changes in a smaller volume.

*Gina:* You're *wrong*.

*Greg:* No, what we said is the density, I don't know, it changes in a smaller volume [persuasive emphasis on *changes* and *smaller volume*].

*Gina:* *That's not true* [equally adamant emphasis on each word].

*Greg:* Yes, it is. It's the same …

*Gina:* You're *wrong*.

**Teacher: [To Greg] Well, we're not convinced.**

*Greg:* That's what you said.

**Teacher: Convince us. I'm not convinced, and she's not convinced.**

*Gina:* You're wrong, Greg.

*Greg:* No, I'm not.

*Gina:* *O-oh, yes*, you are [stands up].

*Eric:* [To Gina] He's right, you know.

---

## Example 5.7: Continuation of the Density Argument in Class 5

*Gina:*     *You can't compress water* [with raised voice, almost yelling]!

*George:*    You can so. You can compress water.

*Gina:*     You can't take a big thing, and compact it into a little thing. You *can't.*

*Greg:*     The density will change.

*Gina:*     Right, if you *could.*

*Greg:*     That's just an example. The pressure *will change* …

*Gina:*     If you *could,* it would happen, but you *can't. Wait a second!* [Goes to the board] Wait. Wait.

*Greg:*     No, *I'm right.* I'm right.

*George:*    If you took a glass …

*Gina:*     If you took a big tall container and a big thin container [as she makes drawings of these containers on the board], the density doesn't change. The water level in here is just higher than it is over here. If you have the same size thing, and a huge thing over here [this entire segment is at a near yell] …

*Greg:*     You can compress it.

*Gina:*     No! I can't pour a full thing of *this* into a small thing of *this* [demonstrating with two different size containers she picks up from a table].

*Eric:*     *Yeah, I know, but if you had a lot of pressure, you can* [seriously and with raised voice while standing next to Greg at the blackboard].

*Greg:*     You can. How do you think they …

*Gina:*     *How are we gonna get that pressure* [loudly]?

*Eric:*     We aren't …

*Graham:* You're wrong.

*Greg:*     Yeah, Gina. We just have …

**Teacher:** **Okay, let Greg talk for a minute.**

*Greg:*     If, I'm not saying that we *can*; but, it's true. People do put this amount of water into a little thing like …

*Gina:*     No! If you're not saying they can, then how *do* they [raised voice]?

*Greg:*     You can.

*Gina:*     No, you *can't* [raised voice].

*Greg:*     Yes, you *can* [raised voice and smiling].

---

In this fast-paced exchange of words, the students' passion is quite evident. From the perspective of any passerby, the classroom might have looked as if it were completely out of control. In fact, the students were completely involved in this argument. Those students who were not talking were engaged in following the flow of the argument. At this point, the expressed conceptual understanding is still centering around the issue of volume. In the next example, which continues immediately after the previous sequence, a picture of the students' understandings begins to unfold. How does the "volume of a body of water" notion develop? What other factors are involved in Greg's idea?

What we see happening in the previous sequence is the introduction of the concept of pressure. Greg's initial idea of placing a block of ebony in a larger body of water appears to be connected to his idea that pressure changes the density of water. The idea of pressure affecting a body of water also seems to be connected with the idea of gravity. A larger body of water is exposed to more gravity, which he seems to think will create more pressure on the water, therefore increasing its density. Intuitively, Greg's argument makes a great deal of sense. As we have discussed previously, these intuitive understandings are quite resistant to change. If we were to tell Greg that he was mistaken and explain the more accurate conception, it is unlikely that he would modify his understanding. Under the authoritarian control of a teacher, students such as Greg may succumb to acknowledging agreement. In reality, however, they have not reconciled their understandings with the official knowledge; therefore, any sense of real understanding does not occur.

Although the argument appears to be almost exclusively between Gina and Greg, most of the other students listen intently, interjecting occasional comments. We can see evidence of their listening in Example 5.8, where other students add significantly to the argument. From his observations of the students and his postargument discussions with individual students, the teacher felt that the class was involved. However, other strategies could have been implemented. Certainly, the teacher could have asked other students to reiterate the status of the argument.

The last day of the argument saw an increase in the number of students participating. Even the less dominant students were making significant contributions to the content of the argument. Frank's reasoning where he extends the rocket example (starts with "Yeah, and some air....") is thoughtful and appropriate to the development of the ideas being expressed. When we allow children to engage in such arguments, they draw on a wide range of personal experiences and understandings in a process of social sense making. As mentioned previously, such discussions, which are not overtly controlled by the teacher, allow the children to feel a sense of ownership and control. Although the classroom behavior may seem like periodic chaos as children express their passionate connection to their own ideas, it is an indication of their serious engagement in talking science.

In terms of the specific understandings expressed by these students, their ideas were based on several simple and intuitively plausible models or images. The molecular perspective is based on the idea that molecules are consistent in size, shape, and weight across substances. From a very young age, children hear about molecules, but what images do they have of molecular structure? From Gina's argument in particular, molecules may appear as little balls. Density is determined by how tightly compacted the molecules are. Such an explanation may work within any given substance, but, as we have seen, molecules vary greatly in size, shape, and weight across substances. The pressure side of the argument sees pressure as unidirectional. Gravity exerts pressure on the body of water, which in turn pushes down on the water, increasing its density. Both sides of this argument are amazingly sophisticated.

We also have seen how the teacher changed tactics, from attempts at conceptual control in the beginning to fostering the debate. As the argument

◆ What other strategies could have been used for involving other students and for monitoring their understandings?

The concept of pressure is also somewhat complicated. When we refer to air pressure or water pressure, we need to realize that pressure exerts a force in all directions. If we dive underwater to the deep end of a pool, we can feel the effects of the pressure on our eardrums. The pressure of the water is pushing against us from all directions. We experience the same effect of air pressure all of the time. The pressure of the air is pushing on us from all directions. In water, the pressure increases as we descend. At about 10 m (33 ft) deep, the pressure is double what we experience standing in the air at sea level. At this depth, we commonly refer to 2 atm of pressure. At 20 m (66 ft), we would experience 3 atm of pressure, and so on, in increments of 10 m (33 ft).

**Example 5.8: The Final Day of the Density Argument in Class 6**

*Greg:* Right. I know how you can put pressure on water, Gina. And I have this person to back me up. You know, you know those things that you drink where you use a pump and you get a little rocket? And you pump it up and then it shoots into the air?

*Fred:* Yeah.

*Greg:* Well, that you're putting pressure on the water because you're pumping air into this little container.

*Gina:* No, but, but it's not compacted. The thing is …

*Graham:* Yes it is, Gina.

*Greg:* Yes it is.

*Gina:* No. What's going on is it's, so it has to put all that pressure that you're giving it up into the rocket.

*Graham:* Yes. But, that still, you're, this is like, you're still, you still put pressure inside the container.

**Teacher: Wait, wait a second. Let, okay, let Graham …**

*Graham:* But, you're still putting the pressure inside of it. You still have it in there.

*Gina:* You're still putting pressure on it.

*Greg:* Exactly.

*Gina:* But the molecules won't compact.

*Graham:* Yes they will.

*Gina:* 'Cause they have to shoot out.

*Graham:* Yes. But, after, after a certain amount of …

*Frank:* Yeah, and some air. But, it's because, it's because there, when the rocket, if it was compressing against the water, the only thing that would come out was air. And when you shoot the rocket, water comes out. So it must be compressed. But air, but water can be stretched apart, put into a bigger volume.

*Gina:* It's not stretched apart. It just fills up the bottom.

*Frank:* No. But when it's steamed.

*Gina:* What it can't do, what it can't do. Okay. All right.

*Graham:* Yeah, steam, steam, damn it, steam.

*Frank:* If something can be compressurized or whatever you can call it, it can probably be compacted.

*Graham:* Same with evaporation. Evaporation. It's just …

*Frank:* 'Cause when it's steamed, it's just barely anything.

*Gina:* But, can I say something? It's not …

*Greg:* No you can't.

*Fred:* No, of course. Because you're going to be wrong.

*Gina:* It's not just, it's changing its shape. It's not compressurized. See, the water, if you have it in a big container, it's not going to just, and you pour it into that container, which is higher because it can't compress into that low of a spot right there. And you pour it into here, it's not just going to stay as one big thing. But, it's not going to be from being compressurized, it's just going to flow out.

*Graham:* Without force.

*Greg:* No, without force, Gina, but with force it will.

*Frank:* It will.

*Fred:* With force, it will.

*Graham:* It will compress.

picked up momentum, he began joining the discussion as a co-participant and facilitator. As a co-participant, he asked clarifying or challenging questions. As a facilitator, he provided opportunities for quieter students to speak. However, the transition from controller to co-participant was not an easy one for this teacher. Throughout the argument, he faced many dilemmas (see Chapter 10 for further discussion of dilemmas). His major dilemma, however, was his conflict between controlling the students or letting them move forward with the argument. On the one hand, he had his old images of what classrooms should look like. On the other hand, he felt that students should take control and that such arguments were reflective of what scientists might do in their laboratories and meetings. He also was curious about where the argument would lead, if he just stepped back, watched, and listened.

This argument started off with seemingly simple points, but quickly became very complicated. Even with very young children, classroom discussions can become far more complex than we might expect and may extend beyond the limits of our own knowledge. This increase in complexity is exciting and offers children opportunities to elaborate on their understandings. The point that needs to be emphasized again is that *we should not allow our own feelings of limited knowledge hinder the extension of classroom discussions*. In scientific communities, arguments may not result in an agreement on a particular explanation. Multiple explanations and considerable doubt may reign for years. Engaging our students in authentic discussions and theory building are the kinds of activities that are important. The understandings, whether accurate or inaccurate, set the foundation for in-depth learning in the future. The students who engaged in the previous argument are not likely to forget what was discussed. When they encounter these concepts again, they will have a more thorough understanding of the issues involved in molecular structure, pressure, and density.

Before reading further, try to answer the following questions:

- In the density argument, what do you think served as the initial attractor or center?
- Can you find the specific instance of a bifurcation point or break that set up a new theme in the argument?
- Can you describe a typical feedback loop or cycle in the argument?

The initial attractor that set this argument in motion seems to involve the sinking of ebony. A conflict (a conflicting binary) between the expectation that wood floats and the observation of ebony sinking set the argument in motion and maintained the argument over several weeks. In planning this particular activity, ebony was included as a potential conflicting situation (attractor or center). It was viewed as a potential, but unpredictable, stimulus for engaging students in further inquiry and discussion. The bifurcation points (breaks) or points where new themes arose in the argument are the points where one student challenged another's ideas, such as Gina claiming that Greg's idea of ebony floating in a bigger body of water would not

Gravity is a downward force. If we consider two objects, say a lead ball and a glass marble, and drop them at exactly the same time from exactly the same height, which one hits the ground first? The answer is completely counterintuitive. As it turns out, the size or weight of the object does not affect how fast the object falls. All objects will fall at the same rate of acceleration. However, a large, flat object will fall more slowly, because of the increased upward force of friction from the air. Without an atmosphere, the objects would fall at the same rate. The same idea holds true for a body of water. The surface area of the body of water makes no difference. The same force of gravity is exerted at each point on the surface.

The chemistry of water is very complex. It breaks the rules of behavior of other substances. We expect that if you increase the temperature of a fluid, it will become less and less dense. When it boils and vaporizes, the fluid becomes even less dense. On the other hand, when we decrease the temperature, we expect the fluid to get more dense as the molecules slow down and move closer together. When a fluid freezes and becomes a solid, the density is even greater. Water, however, does not follow this rule completely. As the temperature of water increases, its density becomes less, but when water is cooled, it reaches its greatest density at 4°C (about 39°F). As the temperature decreases past 4°C, its density starts to decrease. Finally, when water freezes, its density is lower than any water in a fluid state: ice floats. In addition, water is considered to be nearly incompressible. However, as we have seen, the density of water does vary, which indicates that its volume changes (although slightly) at different temperatures. So, water at the bottom of a deep lake is colder (but never colder than 4°C) and denser (i.e., more compressed) than the water at the surface. If the temperature of the water at the bottom of the lake drops below 4°C, its density decreases and it rises toward the surface. In the winter, the entire lake may be at the same temperature, which allows the mixing of water from the bottom with that from the surface.

☞

The entire argument, as with most uncontrolled arguments and discussions, are dynamic systems involving complex thinking. An increasing number of people in education and the social sciences are beginning to use *chaos and complexity theories*, which have been borrowed from the sciences, to investigate and make sense of discourse and cognition. Chaos theories deal basically with seemingly random or chaotic phenomena that either have embedded patterns or give rise to emergent patterns. A typical example of a chaotic system is a tornado. Complexity theories may look at some of the same phenomena, as well as others, to make sense of how they are self-generating, self-sustaining, and self-maintaining systems (referred to as autopoietic systems). The chaotic system of a tornado also can be examined as a complex, autopoietic system. However, our own bodies and the biosphere are complex systems as well. The basic concepts in chaos theories include (a) *strange attractors* or simply *attractors*, which are some sort of factors that initiate and maintain a dynamic system, and (b) *bifurcation points*, which are additional attractors that split or break the pattern of a particular system and set up a new system (e.g., a tornado that splits into two or more). In addition, both chaotic and complex systems need some sort of energy to drive the systems, which in the case of social systems may be emotional energy, curiosity, passion, etc., as well as feedback loops or cycles that help to maintain the systems by cycling information, energy, and materials. The other intriguing aspect of chaotic systems is that they are not predictable. Although you may be able to predict the probability or likelihood of some sort of event occurring, you cannot predict with certainty or predict specific outcomes. In addition, the patterns (or metapatterns, as fundamental patterns or patterns of patterns) described in Appendix D can help provide additional tools for understanding such complex systems: (a) the notion of *center* includes the concept of attractor and other factors that help to maintain organization; (b) *breaks* include the concept of bifurcation point, as well as any type of transformation or change; (c) *cycles* include feedback loops and other repetitive sequences; and (d) *binaries* are pairings and relationships that may lie at the core of social system attractors or centers and may be involved in breaks or bifurcation points and in cycles. All the metapatterns listed in Appendix D are essentially descriptors of the embedded and emergent patterns of chaotic and complex systems.

**Refer to Examples 5.5 to 5.8.**

✦ How did reading through this argument affect your feelings about teaching science?

✦ How do you feel about facilitating students' arguments and discussion that may lead into areas in which you do not have a thorough understanding?

✦ How would you deal with this situation?

✦ From the previous argument and a more complete picture of the students' understandings, what activities might you suggest to address some of their inaccurate understandings?

work. Other bifurcation points occurred throughout the argument as new terms or evidence were brought up students. The cycles or feedback loops are evidenced in the continual back and forth of stating of claims, discounting of claims, introduction of new evidence or logical claims, and so forth. Certainly the energy to drive this system involved passion situated in the students' sense of ownership over the ideas. With this energy, the system produced unpredictable, but increasingly complex, ideas. In such a situation, we may be able to predict with high probability that a conceptual conflict will occur and that it may lead to the development of complex ideas, but we can never predict exactly how the complex system will manifest or what specific ideas will emerge.

## 5.4 Extending Our Understandings of How to Work with Children's Discussions

Although we may initially feel that working with children's classroom discussions may be easy, we discover quickly that it requires quite a bit of work. If we enter a classroom thinking that we can just get the children talking, then sit back and listen, we most likely will find that the discussions will not work. In order to facilitate such discussions successfully, we need to be prepared. This preparation should include

1. Developing our own understandings of the concepts
2. Developing our own understandings of the inquiry processes involved in investigating these concepts
3. Understanding the goals for inquiry and discussion
4. Coming up with potential stimulators for discussion (attractors or centers), which can commonly involve some kind of conflicting situation (binary)

In order to develop our own understandings and processes of inquiry, we have to spend time prior to the unit investigating the topic ourselves. Although we do not need to be experts, we do need to have an understanding of the basic concepts. Such preparation is somewhat like developing a map of the territory. (Further information on preparation is available in Chapter 8.) We should have some idea of where discussions could go and what types of ideas we expect children to consider. As in the density argument (in the previous section), the teacher was caught off guard by the students' discussion of molecules. Such surprises are exciting and extend the learning of all of the co-participants. Although our own limited understandings should not prevent teaching science and exploring more complicated areas, we should work on developing our own understandings so that we can facilitate student discussions more effectively. As co-participants and facilitators, we should be able to ask appropriate questions, present challenges to the knowledge claims of students, and detect possible inaccurate understandings. Detecting inaccurate understandings is essential to formulating our responses. Although we can play devil's advocate and challenge accurate claims, we need to know when children's understandings are inaccurate. When we detect such inaccuracies, we can respond in one of two general ways:

1. Ask a challenging question or present a challenging situation
2. Develop a plan to add an inquiry activity that challenges these understandings

We will look more closely at questioning strategies and presenting challenges in the following pages.

Understanding our goals for inquiry and discussion are critical components of our preparation. We need to have a clear picture of the kinds of thinking and talking we want our students to develop. As discussed earlier in this chapter, we want to encourage children to take ownership over the process of science talks. At the same time, we want children to ask clarifying, probing, and challenging questions of each other. However, the focus of such discussions should be geared toward

1. Exploring a topic
2. Making connections to new ideas and information
3. Developing or modifying the children's theories and understandings

✦ **In your everyday life experiences, can you find instances of chaotic and complex systems?**
✦ **How can you plan to set up a complex event (a discussion, an investigation, or an argument) in your classroom?**

For example, Karen Gallas engages her students in a very different kind of talk than did the teacher in the density argument. She formalizes such discussions by scheduling science talks on a variety of topics every month or so. During these talks, a broad, open-ended question is used to initiate the discussions. Her goal here is not necessarily to have students understand the scientific explanations. Rather, her goal is to engage her students in authentic science talk, in which students co-construct specific understandings. In addition, she expects her students to challenge one another's claims, negotiate understandings, provide supporting evidence, and so forth.

---

**Example 5.9: Some of the Questions Karen Gallas Uses to Initiate Science Talks in Her Grades 1 to 3 Classes**

- How did the moon begin?
- Why is the earth a rounded shape?
- Why does science exist?
- How are earthquakes made?
- How did people learn to talk?
- How do mirrors work?
- Why do the seasons change?
- Does the universe end?
- Is there life on other planets?
- Will we ever be able to live on another planet?
- Are dragons real?
- What is too slow for the eye to see?
- How do legs move?
- How did animals begin?
- How did people begin?
- How do babies grow inside the mother?
- How do plants grow?
- How do shells grow?
- How do people grow?
- Why do people die? [4]

---

Many of the questions Karen Gallas asks of her young students have no obvious right or wrong answer (e.g., Is there life on other planets?). Other questions tend to ask for functional explanations, such as, How do legs move? Whatever their purpose, all of these questions stimulate children to build their own theories and understandings as a group.

One of the most important requirements for successfully implementing classroom discussions is creating a nonthreatening atmosphere in the classroom, where students feel safe to take risks (e.g., be wrong) and say what is on their mind. In order to create such an environment in our classrooms, we need to be sensitive to the needs and personalities of each of our students. The basic ground rule that takes the individuals into account and helps maintain a safe environment is

> No one should make fun of or put down another person or the ideas of another person. However, ideas can be challenged. "That's a stupid idea" is not appropriate. "That idea doesn't make sense to me" is appropriate. This rule was not enforced in the extensive density argument that we saw in the previous section. The students had not experienced science talks previously. Although most of these students did not seem to be limited by the nature of the interactions, even greater participation might have been possible with the enforcement of this rule. Accomplishing effective science talks will take some time and practice before students internalize the rules and game plan.

Although we initially need to focus on our own skill development, we should keep in mind that we are acting as models for our students. As time proceeds in our classrooms, we want our students to acquire the same skills. The first set of skills to consider is questioning strategies, or what questions do we ask? The following list provides a general list of the types of questions we can use during classroom discussions. As we develop our questioning skills, we may extend this list. The basic rule of thumb is to ask authentic questions. We do not want to ask questions that exert our control over the substance and direction of the discussion, or to ask questions that make the students feel that we are playing a guess-the-right-answer type of game (i.e., I know the right answer; can you come up with it?).

### 5.4.1  Questioning Strategies

1. Ask **probing questions**. Find out more about a student's understandings. What does the student's understanding look like? What does a particular knowledge claim mean?
   Examples:
   - Can you explain what you mean by ...?
   - How does ... work?
   - How does ... (some idea) you just mentioned relate to ... (another idea) you mentioned earlier?
   - What could account for our results?

2. Ask questions that **challenge a particular knowledge** claim.
   Examples:
   - You've said that ... works in ... (this way), but what happens if you ... (do this)?
   - You've said that ... works in ... (this way), but what happens ... (in this contrary example)?

3. Ask questions that **request examples** of a particular process or phenomenon.
   Examples:
   - Do you have any examples of this ...?

- Have you experienced …?

4. Ask questions that ask for **supporting justification or evidence**. Are the explanations consistent with the evidence?

Examples:

- I'm (we're) not convinced; can you convince us?
- What evidence do you have to support your idea of …?
- How can you justify your claim that …?
- Is this explanation consistent with the evidence we've generated in our experiments (or observations)?
- Does … (this evidence from our experiments or observations) contradict our explanation?

5. Ask questions that request **further elaboration**.

Examples:

- How does … relate to other … (similar phenomena)?
- What happens when … (something is added or taken away, changed, etc.)?

6. Ask questions that request **alternative explanations**.

Examples:

- Can we think of any other ways to explain … (this particular phenomenon)?
- How else could … (this phenomenon) happen?
- Which explanation or explanations seem to make more sense?
- Which explanation or explanations fit best with our observations or experimental results?

7. Ask questions about the **sensibility of observational or experimental results and explanations**.

Examples:

- Is … (this result) what we expected?
- What is surprising about our results?

8. Ask questions that **explore patterns and relationships**.

Examples:

- Can we think of how … (this object or process) is similar to … (different object or process)?
- If we were from another planet, how could we tell whether … (an assortment of objects, like a crab shell, a snail shell, a bone, etc.) came from a living thing?
- What patterns or shapes can we find in … (particular objects)?
- Where else can we find these patterns or shapes? (That is, if looking at living or once living objects, can we find them in human-made objects and vice versa?)
- What is significant about this shape or pattern? (That is, "Why?" What functions does it serve?" or What's the advantage of this pattern or shape?")

### 5.4.2 Avoiding Common Pitfalls to Teaching through Inquiry and Discussion

The next list of skills shows the typical patterns of teacher behavior that interfere with genuine inquiry. These skills are presented as problems to avoid. As we read through each of these skills, we should think back about our own experiences as a teacher and student. How often did we experience these problems? What effect did they have on classroom discussions?

1. **Avoid changing the topic during a class discussion**. Students may be prevented from expressing their ideas. Further development of ideas can be hindered. Students may perceive such actions as authoritarian control of what is and is not appropriate in terms of their reasoning or their ideas. Allow students to work through a line of discussion. However, we may want to move onto another topic or activity. You can avoid perceptions of authoritarian control by providing students with time to explore a particular issue before moving on.

2. **Avoid using positive evaluative comments in response to children's comments**. Saying "good," "interesting," and so forth may send a message that certain answers or comments are better than others. Such comments reinforce a focus on getting the right answer. On the other hand, such comments come almost automatically, and do not provide much meaningful feedback. As an alternative, we might consider adding onto such automatic comments with some elaboration, such as "Good, that explanation makes a lot of sense, but can we add any evidence to support it?" or "Great explanation, but I'm not entirely convinced. What do you think you need to do to make it more convincing?" In these two examples of alternative responses, we are supporting the students, and at the same time, we are pushing them to do further thinking.

3. **Avoid asking difficult or challenging questions of certain students and not of others**. If we ask the same few students critical questions, they may feel that such questions are negative evaluations of their ideas. If critical questions are asked, they should be used for everyone. In addition, the asking of challenging questions should be discussed and expected from everyone.

4. **Avoid leading questions and comments**. Such questions and comments can prevent students from developing their own understandings. This strategy can also be interpreted as a controlling strategy and can degenerate into a guessing game for the right answers. Instead of asking a question like "What is a food web?" we could ask, "Can we make a food web that describes the interrelationships in our school yard?" The first question asks for a right answer, whereas the second question asks the students to apply their understandings, which they can defend or challenge within the class.

5. **Avoid asking recall questions**. Such questions can prevent students from developing their own ideas.

6. **Avoid asking "Does everyone agree?" questions**. Students may interpret such questions as a signal to agree with the teacher. This interpretation is especially relevant when students are unfamiliar with the rules of and approach to talking science. Instead, we can ask students if they disagree or if they can think of any examples to support or challenge a particular claim.

7. **Avoid being the authority of knowledge**. If we become the knowledge authority in the classroom, we prevent students' genuine inquiry and discussion about topics. We should not claim to have a corner on the truth. This problem may be one of the most difficult to overcome. When we have an understanding of something, it is often very difficult to resist telling students the right answer. Instead, we can encourage students to look for support from other sources, such as experts in the field, books, or magazines.

8. **Avoid providing factual information**. When we provide factual information, either verbally or in writing, we can prevent students from evaluating this information. Students may also feel obliged to agree with the teacher. Whenever possible, provide students with others sources of factual information and encourage them to evaluate this information.

9. **Avoid supporting the reliability or truth of particular resources**. This point is related to the previous one. By stating that a particular source of information has the correct answer, we discourage students from evaluating both the information itself and the source of the information.

10. **Avoid talking too much**. As mentioned previously, teachers tend to dominate classroom talk (about 67% of classroom talk is done by the teacher). Make a point to listen to what the students are saying. Allow students to express their ideas and understanding as fully and completely as possible. By dominating classroom talk, we can prevent the development of understandings and take ownership over the inquiry and discussion away from the students.

11. **Avoid being at the center of attention**. By requiring that all interaction go through the teacher, we prevent student-to-student discussion and argument. We also take away the potential for students to feel a sense of ownership and control over their thinking and actions.[5]

When you begin trying to conduct classroom science talks, you will quickly notice how often mistakes are made. We try to control the flow of the discussion. We act as the knowledge authority and provide the correct answer. There is no doubt that teaching through classroom science talks is difficult. The key tool to developing these skills lies in our ability to reflect on our teaching practice. Reflecting on our teaching allows us to pick up on our mistakes. If we do not recognize the mistakes, we will miss important learning opportunities. We should view mistakes as wonderful opportunities to grow professionally. The following questions in the sidebar may help to focus attention on the kind of reflection in which we need to engage as we work with students during classroom talks.

## Additional Reading

Bentley, D., & Watts, M. (1995). *Communicating in school science: Groups, tasks, and problem solving.* London: Falmer Press, pp. 5–16.

> An important book about the general topic of communication (written and oral). Informative examination of creating the kind of environment that fosters communication in group work, for understanding, in solving problems, and for assessment.

Gallas, K. (1995). *Talking their way into science: Hearing children's questions and theories, responding with curricula.* New York: Teachers College Press.

> This book is a must for all teachers. As a teacher-researcher, Karen Gallas describes her classroom in which she conducts regular science talks about very complex ideas with very young children. It's an extraordinary book, not to be missed.

Newton, D. P. (2002). *Talking sense in science: Helping children understand through talk.* New York: Routledge-Falmer.

Sutton, C. (1992). *Words, science and learning.* Buckingham, UK: Open University Press.

> An accessible, yet thorough, look at language use in teaching and learning science.

Ward, A. (1997). *Classroom conversations: Talking and learning in elementary school.* Toronto: ITP Nelson.

> An informative book about using and facilitating classroom talk across the curriculum.

## Advanced Reading

Bloom, J. W. (2001). Discourse, cognition, and chaotic systems: An examination of students' argument about density. *Journal of the Learning Sciences, 10,* 447–492.

> This article provides an analysis of the density argument discussed in this chapter.

Cazden, C. (1988). *Classroom discourse: The language of teaching and learning.* Portsmouth, NH: Heinemann.

> Examines research in teacher-to-student and student-to-student discourse—a very informative book.

Edwards, D., & Mercer, N. (1987). *Common knowledge: The development of understanding in the classroom.* New York: Routledge.

> Examines research in classroom discourse and learning. Offers a lot of practical knowledge of use to teachers. This is an important book to add to your library.

Elliot, J. (1976/77). Developing hypotheses about classrooms from teachers' practical constructs: An account of the work of the Ford Teaching Project. *Interchange, 7,* 2–26.

> Offers a more in-depth discussion of the pitfalls when teaching through inquiry and discussion.

Lemke, J. (1990). *Talking science: Language, learning, values.* Norwood, NJ: Ablex Publishing, 1990.

> This book takes an in-depth look at classroom talk in secondary science classrooms. However, many of the insights are very important for teachers at any level. Those without a science background may find some of the classroom science talk examples difficult, but this should not be seen as a major problem.

Marton, F., & Tsui, A. B. M. (Eds.). (2004). *Classroom discourse and the space of learning.* Mahwah, NJ: Lawrence Erlbaum Associates.

## Other Resources

Olson, R. *Talking science: Techniques and technology for science talks* (a video series). University of Southern California, Wrigley Marine Science Center. Retrieved from http://wrigley.usc.edu/spotlight/talkingscience_video.html

> Although intended for adults, this video series can provide useful information for helping your students become better speakers and presenters.

Steane, D. (2004). The terrarium as science text. *Talking science (EQ Australia).* Retrieved from http://www.curriculum.edu.au/eq/spring2004/article2.html

Some of the following questions will focus on general concerns of conducting classroom discussions, while others focus on specific experiences with children's discussions. If you have an opportunity to conduct a science talk with a class or small group of children, think about some of these questions.

✦ As you read through this chapter and its examples of classroom talk, how did you feel about this approach to teaching science?

✦ How does this approach differ from what you have experienced as a teacher and a student?

✦ When conducting classroom talks, what problems did you see?

✦ Are these problems related to your previous expectations of what classrooms should look like?

✦ How much ownership and control over the discussion did the children have?

✦ How much did you talk (compared with the children)?

✦ Which of your questions or comments seemed to facilitate the discussion?

✦ Which of your questions or comments seemed to hamper the discussion?

✦ How could you improve the quality of the classroom discussion?

## Notes

1. An in-depth analysis of teacher and student control strategies is available in Jay Lemke's book *Talking Science* (Norwood, NJ: Ablex Publishing, 1990).
2. From Karen Gallas, *Talking Their Way into Science: Hearing Children's Questions and Theories, Responding with Curricula* (New York: Teachers College Press, 1995), pp. 63–66.
3. See A. diSessa, Toward an epistemology of physics, *Cognition and Instruction*, 10, 105–225, 1993.
4. From Karen Gallas, *Talking Their Way into Science*, pp. 104–105.
5. For further information, see J. Elliot, Developing hypotheses about classrooms from teachers' practical constructs: An account of the work of the Ford Teaching Project, *Interchange*, 7, 2–26, 1976/77, and D. Ireland & T. Russell, The Ottawa Valley Teaching Project, *Curriculum Studies*, 10, 266–268, 1978.

*Chapter 6*

# Teaching and Learning through Inquiry

What is inquiry? This seemingly simple question has been the source of much discussion (and, of course, disagreement) among science educators over the past decade or so. It is a major focus of the national standards in the United States and the emphasis of science education efforts around the world. Inquiry also is the basis for all of science. Looking at the word *inquiry*, we see it is similar to *inquisitiveness*. If we are inquisitive, we have questions (another word with a common root to inquiry). So, questions and the process of questioning are the core of teaching and learning through inquiry.

How many of us as adults ask questions based on curiosity or any kind of desire to really understand something? How many children before they enter school ask questions based on curiosity? It seems that the answers to these two questions are very different. Children ask questions all of the time, and sometimes to the great annoyance of parents! Yet, by the time we get out of high school, most of us are no longer very curious about anything. Something happens during our schooling years that seems to beat the curiosity (and creativity, which seems to be associated with curiosity) out of us.

Children are naturally curious. They ask questions from the time they begin to talk. Even before they can talk, they are exploring their worlds. With no sense of danger, they engage in an exploration of everything they can get their hands on and lips around. This exploration is important to their learning, but presents great challenges to parents. Some parents are overly restrictive, while others are much too lax. This continuum from restrictive to lax is

- ◆ What are some possible reasons for why children lose their curiosity?
- ◆ What kinds of things do teachers do that may squash curiosity?
- ◆ What underlying assumptions or beliefs about schooling can lead teachers to suppress or encourage curiosity?
- ◆ What experiences have you had that suppressed or encouraged curiosity in school?
- ◆ What can we do to stimulate and encourage curiosity?
- ◆ What can we do to help children maintain their curiosity throughout the rest of their lives?

similar to what teachers do in classrooms. Unfortunately, it seems that somewhere in children's lives in schools curiosity is all but obliterated. The first step to encouraging curiosity is to stimulate our own curiosity about almost everything (e.g., science, psychology, mathematics, art, our own thinking, etc.). From here, we will not only serve as role models for curious characters (i.e., children), but also gain a greater understanding of what it means to be curious and how we can encourage and stimulate children's curiosity and how this will impact children's learning.

As we proceed to look into what inquiry is, how it works, how we learn through inquiry, and how we can teach through inquiry, there are several important points to keep in mind. When we consider the role of questions, there are two major sources of questions in the classroom: (a) those asked by the teacher and (b) those asked by children. In either case, we can return to looking at the words: *inquiry* to *inquisitiveness* to *question* and finally to *quest*. The whole notion of inquiry is embarking on a quest for answers. The most engaging, relevant, and meaningful inquiry for children arises from their own questions, ideas, and interests. However, we will often need to introduce questions, topics, and projects, especially at the beginning of an investigative unit or subunit. In these situations, we need to generate potential questions and present them in ways that can hook or engage the students. We might think of this process of asking questions as problematizing instruction. How can we ask questions that create meaningful and relevant inquiries and engage children's curiosity? Although we could make an attempt of generating a big list of problematized questions, this may not be particularly helpful.

Frequently, the most engaging questions are those that arise out of the specific circumstances we encounter in and around our schools. For instance, you and your children may see a car accident outside of the school. A number of questions can arise, such as the following: Why did the accident occur? Did something about the intersection affect the accident? How does speed and the weight of the cars affect the amount of damage? What road conditions affect the potential for accidents? I am sure children would generate many more, and probably more interesting, questions. From this point, the children in your class can become forensic scientists. They can measure and sketch the skid marks, assess the damage to the cars, sketch the intersection and any factors around the intersection (e.g., overhanging trees, parked cars and buses, etc.), and assess the road conditions (e.g., flatness of the road, wetness, etc.). Back in the classroom, the children can figure out the speed and movement characteristics of the cars. From here, you can embark on experiments that measure the effects of force (mass × acceleration) on collisions, and basically investigate Newton's three laws (i.e., inertia, force, and opposing forces). What are the effects of friction, mass (or weight), speed, and so forth, on the dynamics of collisions? You and your children can devise ways to measure damage in collisions (e.g., build a sliding or rolling car to which you can add weights and put on a front that crumples, like folded up aluminum foil, then measure how much the foil crumples in various collisions). In

Read Richard Feynman's *"Surely You're Joking, Mr. Feynman!": Adventures of a Curious Character* and Kary Mullis's *Dancing Naked in the Mind Field*. These are great books that relate stories of two Nobel Prize recipients getting into all sorts of trouble as a result of their insatiable curiosity. (Be prepared to do a lot of laughing.) When reading these books, ponder the implications for teaching and learning. If you and other teachers had children like these in classrooms, how would they be treated? What are the boundaries to what you would allow to take place? What do we tend to do that puts too many restrictions on children's curiosity?

this example, the inquiry is based on an event of immediate relevance to the children. The real skills as a teacher are to be curious and see the potential in all kinds of situations.

However, if nothing so dramatic happens, you may need to generate problems or inquiry topics that capture children's imagination and curiosity. You can set up a "curiosity corner" in which you and your students can share curious objects, photos, and so forth. This curiosity corner can lead to encouraging individuals or the whole class to begin a variety of inquiries. In one case, a teacher I know had such a table. One day a boy brought in a Star Wars toy, and before long the table became a Star Wars display. At that point, the teacher decided that a unit on space was an obvious next step. You also can have a weekly "question quest." This weekly event could be combined with a snack time, when you and your children can sit in a circle on the floor and ask questions about anything that has happened during the week or that is of interest. Although you can have both of these situations occurring as a general pattern throughout the year, you also can initiate inquiries on a variety of topics. To begin such inquiries, there are two basic approaches. In one approach, you may want to start with an open-ended exploration, such as playing with magnets and a variety of magnetic and nonmagnetic objects, playing with and observing earthworms, or going outside and digging around in the soil. For whatever topic, such explorations can generate lots of questions and insights from the children, which in turn can lead to a variety of inquiries. The approach can be more structured, but at the same time can be designed to capture children's imagination. Portfolio projects also can be designed for engaging children in relevant and meaningful inquiries. These projects (as discussed in Chapters 7 and 8) are simulated real-life situations. Essentially, the unit is set up in such a way that each group of students becomes a company that works toward putting together a bid for a particular project. In this situation, you can start with a letter from a government agency or a big company asking for bids for a particular product. In terms of the example in Chapter 7, a fictional letter from the Department of Tourism in Nova Scotia asked each student company for a bid on a boat design to take tourists to natural history sites along the coast. When implemented, the children were immediately engaged in working on an initial prototype, followed by a series of investigations, and finally to building their model with supporting evidence. Of course, there are many variations on the more structured approach to initiating inquiry. Fundamentally, you need to take a creative leap. Maybe you can make all kinds of outrageously designed paper airplanes. Ask your students to predict which ones will fly or fly well, then ask if they can build a paper airplane that will stay in the air the longest, fly the farthest, fly the straightest, or do the most tricks. Another possibility may involve a particular community issue or project. If your school is located in a community, where many families struggle to feed their children, you can discuss with your children the possibility of starting a community garden for growing vegetables. You can investigate the best conditions for growing vegetables, then proceed to preparing the garden and growing vegetables. On the other hand, your children may be interested in building a school pond as a community natural history site. From the inception, your students can determine what is required, the costs, the sources of materials, and then build the pond. Afterwards, the pond can be a center for pond investigations and the assessment of water quality and the ecosystem's health.

Taking such an approach not only captures children's imaginations and curiosity, but also provides them with a sense of ownership that is embedded in a meaningful and relevant context. Throughout our teaching, we need to constantly focus on

- Stimulating and supporting **curiosity**
- Embedding all teaching activities in **meaningful** and **relevant** contexts
- Providing opportunities for children to take on a sense of **ownership** and **control** over the content, direction, and functioning of inquiry projects (and of the classroom as well)

## 6.1   Types of Questions and Inquiry

When we or our students ask questions, it is important to recognize what kinds of questions are being asked. If we know what kind of question is being asked, we can determine the kinds of activities that are needed in order to work toward answers. For each of the question types below, the subheadings indicate the kind of activity associated with the questions. As teachers, we need to know these categories of questions, so that we can help children plan and develop activities to find potential explanations and answers. At the same time, we should help children discriminate between the types of questions they are asking, so that they can develop the skills of determining how they can proceed.

### 6.1.1   Questions That Lead to Experiments

- Do earthworms like (prefer) light or dark?
- What factors affect the period (time) of a pendulum swing (or how can I make a pendulum that swings for a long time)?
- Does the size of a paper airplane's wing make a difference in its flight time and distance (or how can I make a paper airplane that flies the farthest and stays aloft the longest)?

These types of questions can be used to start designing experiments that can provide the data necessary to answer the questions. These questions point to the possibility of manipulating a variety of factors (variables). In turn, these factors can be varied, measured, or controlled. As teachers, our task is to help children design such experiments.

### 6.1.2 Questions That Lead to Observational Studies

- How do crickets chirp?
- How long is the life cycle of a roach?
- In which direction does the moon move around the earth?

In contrast to experimental-type questions, these types of questions point to investigations that can be answered by collecting data through observations. In some cases, variables or factors can be manipulated (to see what happens, such as "Let's see what happens if we add salt to a glass of Coca Cola"), but in a strict sense they are not controlled experiments. Your challenge is to help students design observational studies that will yield good (valid and reliable) data.

### 6.1.3 Questions That Lead to Large Multiapproach Studies and Projects

- What can we do to prevent flooding in our community?
- How can we build a rocket that will go a mile high?
- What can we do to clean up the pond and create a natural area?

These types of questions lead to larger-scale investigations that will probably include all of the question types provided here. Such questions are very powerful, since they have potential (a) for complex, relevant, and meaningful learning and (b) for producing knowledge that students can make public. The challenge here is to help students break up the big task into smaller tasks and organize the whole project.

### 6.1.4 Questions That Ask for Explanation Building

- How do bicycles work?
- How do the phases of the moon occur? (starts with an observational study)?
- What causes hurricanes (or typhoons)?

The types of questions can lead to students formulating numerous possible explanations, which can be investigated or tested. Although some questions can be investigated through external sources, it is generally more engaging to have students develop sets of possible explanations prior to looking at external sources of information.

### 6.1.5 Questions That Lead to Problem Solving or Logical Thinking

- When earthworms engage in reproductive acts, they are always found on the surface of the ground facing in opposite directions, with about the front quarter of their bodies touching side to side. Why are they only found in this position? What does this suggest about their sexes?
- How much water does an oak tree leaf contain?
- How fast does a robin fly?

Although many of these questions can be investigated through external sources, they can be answered by collecting certain kinds of data or by a kind of logical, puzzle-solving approach. In other cases, there may be no source for the answers.

### 6.1.6  Questions That Lead to Theorizing

- How did plants begin?
- What is sound?
- What are germs?

These types of questions are great initiators of science talks and other types of theorizing.

### 6.1.7  Questions That Lead to Philosophizing

- Why is there life on earth?
- Why do we have weeds?
- Why are there diseases like AIDS?

There are no real right answers for these questions. So, the discussions can reveal a great deal about how students think and what beliefs and knowledge influence their thinking.

### 6.1.8  Questions That Require Technical Information (i.e., in Order to Proceed with an Investigation, Analysis, Explanation, etc.)

- What can we use to measure the speed of a marble?
- What formulas do we need to find the volume and surface area of a sphere?

Although students should be encouraged to think of ways to solve these problems, you may need to provide them with the information or a source for the information, in order to help them proceed with their investigations or other tasks.

### 6.1.9  Questions That Require Certain Conceptual or Factual Information in Order to Proceed

- How do earthworms move? (Once students determine that earthworms must have muscles, they may need to be provided with two bits of information: (a) muscles can only contract with force and (b) muscles need to be in oppositional pairs. Using an example of this with one's biceps and triceps may be helpful.)
- We are trying to figure out how to make two switches control the same lightbulb in our model house so that either switch will turn the bulb on and off, but we cannot figure it out. How can we do it?

With these types of questions, you may find it helpful to provide certain background concepts in order for students to formulate their own explanations.

### 6.1.10 Questions That Require Research from External Sources

- What keeps a heart beating?
- What is the size, distance from the sun, and mass of Mars?
- What does the liver do?

With these kinds of questions, you may need to guide them to external sources of information, such as books, web pages, e-mail addresses of scientists, and so forth.

You may find that Appendixes D, H, I, and J, in particular, provide useful information on investigations that arise from these questions.

## 6.2  Patterns of Inquiry in the Classroom

As mentioned earlier in this chapter, there are two basic approaches to inquiry: inquiry directed by the teacher and inquiry based on children's questions. These two patterns of inquiry are quite different in the way they manifest in the classroom. Teacher-directed inquiry tends to be linear, following a preset sequence of investigations. On the other hand, inquiry that follows from students' questions can take many directions (even beyond what the teacher might expect). Figure 6.1 provides a visual depiction of what these patterns may look like as they appear over time in the classroom.

The key differences between these two patterns have to do with the degree of student *ownership* and *engagement* and with the *complexity* of students' understandings that result. When students feel that they are pursuing their own questions and following their curiosity, they are more engaged. They begin to develop higher standards for their work, so that mediocre work is not satisfactory. Teacher-directed inquiry tends to foster attitudes of going through the motions or just doing what is necessary (e.g., "Tell us what you want and we'll memorize it, then regurgitate it back"). On the other hand, when students are investigating their own questions and working toward a goal, they tend to put in more effort and strive for excellence. As a result, their thinking becomes more focused. They take their work seriously and think more deeply and critically about their investigations. They also are producing knowledge and contributing to the classroom inquiry community. Such an approach goes beyond teaching to meet the mandated curriculum by

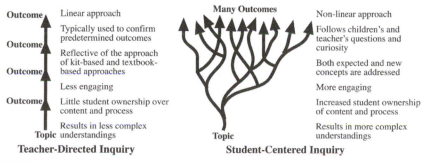

**FIGURE 6.1**

teaching life skills that will be required in most occupations and professions, as well as in everyday life.

## 6.3   A Cycle of Inquiry

Figure 6.2 presents a cyclical model of inquiry. However, you should notice that there are many lines (dotted and solid) that move back or jump forward in the cycle. In other words, this model represents an ideal process, but in reality, inquiry does not happen in a set sequence. And certainly inquiry is not linear. It does not move from a start point to an endpoint in a straight line. However, all too often inquiry in schools is presented as a linear process. For example, we may think that questions are the beginning of inquiry, but frequently inquiry starts with playing around with or exploring some thing or idea. We may see some event or pattern and then wonder why it happens that way or wonder what would happen if we change something.

In general, starting with some sort of exploration, which can be open-ended to relatively structured, can be helpful in generating questions to investigate. While students are exploring, you can take note of their comments and questions. In addition, you should have students write down their questions, discoveries, insights, and tentative explanations as they explore. A student in each group can take on the role of recorder to keep track of this information.

As students begin to define questions, you can help them plan ways of investigating these questions. From the types of questions discussed previously (see Section 6.1), you and your students can determine what type of investigation is needed. Later in this chapter, we will explore how to design investigations, but for now the idea is to engage children in the design process, rather than handing them a set of instructions to follow. Although it is much easier for the teacher to hand out a predesigned set of instructions, some of the most important learning involves this design process. Learning how to design investigations fosters the abilities necessary for lifelong learn-

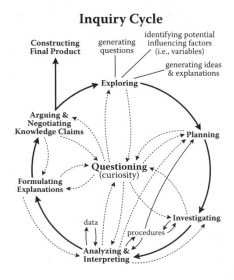

**FIGURE 6.2**

ing. Whether students become artists, mechanics, or scientists, the thinking involved in such learning is critically important for almost any field of endeavor, from decoding political or advertising claims to dealing with medical doctors.

The rest of the cycle moves through implementing investigations, analyzing and interpreting data, formulating explanations, and engaging in discussions on which explanations are a best fit with evidence from the data. Finally, we need to pursue possibilities for communicating the results in as public a forum as possible. Throughout this process, students need to be encouraged to critically assess their designs and data collection procedures. Could errors in the measurement or recording of observations affect the data? Did factors (or variables) that were not accounted for affect the results? Could the apparatus be redesigned to reduce the effects of extraneous factors? These types of questions work toward developing critical thinking skills and a sense of competence as young researchers.

## 6.4  Observational Studies

In contrast to experimental studies, observational studies tend not to manipulate variables. The focus is on describing and analyzing observed events. Such studies can range from studying the moon, sun, and earth relationships to studies of the natural history of ants in your classroom ant farm. The skills are different from those of experimental studies, but the focus is still on exploring, answering questions, and confirming or disproving previously formulated explanations and theories.

Observational studies also can be done in conjunction with experimental studies. If your students are studying ants, they may ask questions that lead to experiments. At the same time, they can be investigating the natural history (their life cycle, behavior, and day-to-day activities) and anatomy of ants. Ants can be observed both outside in their anthills and inside the classroom in ant farms the students have constructed. As the children become involved with experiments and observations, they will generate additional ideas and questions to explore further.

We also need to discriminate between two basic types of observations: (a) simple observational tasks and (b) larger, more involved observational studies. Simple observational tasks will probably occur frequently. As described in one part of Example 9.2, the students in Jane's classroom took turns making observations of moldy bread. Then they moved on to comparative observations of a number of different substances on which mold was growing. In other situations, students may add observations to their notes during experiments. In observational studies, however, the students use a variety of observational techniques to gather data on a continuing basis. The lists of example topics and questions (which appear in Section 6.4.1) are more characteristic of such extended observational studies.

Earthworm communication can be investigated in a number of ways. However, you may like to try a fairly simple experiment. You will need several clean smooth surfaces, like flat dinner plates or 10- to 12-in.-diameter (28- to 30-cm-diameter) pieces of glass (with the edges smoothed), a supply of earthworms, a second empty container with soil in which to place your "used" earthworms, and a stopwatch or a clock with a second hand. Steps:

✦ Gently remove and place an earthworm in the center of your plate or glass.

✦ As soon as the earthworm is placed on the plate, start timing how long it takes the earthworm to reach the edge.

✦ Set the first plate aside and place your used earthworm in the second container.

✦ Gently place another earthworm in the center of a second plate.

✦ Poke the earthworm with your finger until it starts squirming around violently.

✦ Remove this used earthworm immediately after it squirms and place it in the second container.

✦ Gently remove a fresh earthworm and place it in the center of the second plate, on which you poked the previous earthworm.

✦ Time how long it takes this earthworm to reach the edge. You may need to repeat this several times to get an average time.

✦ If you found (it does not always work as planned) that the earthworms placed on the plate of the poked earthworms moved off the plate more quickly, how can you explain how this happened?

## 6.4.1  The Focus of Observational Studies

Observational studies focus on describing and analyzing events, behaviors, patterns, and so forth. Some examples of topics and questions that may lead to observational studies are listed below. As with any inquiry, the questions listed under each topic can be generated by any participant in the inquiry community, including both the teacher and the students.

The kinds of questions listed in the example topics above lead to observational studies. However, there are many other questions, which can lead to experimental studies. Can you think of any such questions?

The previous examples can be embedded in larger investigations and projects. For instance, children may be involved in investigating the natural history of earthworms or ants from birth to death. Some investigations may involve experiments, such as determining how earthworms communicate or what environmental factors they prefer. However, the larger, ongoing investigations may require a lot of observation of the behavior, interactions, and movements of these creatures.

Earthworms:
■ How do they move?
■ How do they reproduce?
■ What do they eat?
■ How do they burrow in the ground?

Redwing blackbirds:
■ Do they have a territory?
■ How do they mark and defend their territory?
■ How big is their territory?
■ How do they communicate?

Fish:
■ How do they swim and move around?
■ How do they mate and reproduce?
■ How do they find food?
■ Do they have a territory?

Gerbils or mice:
■ In what different ways do they move?
■ What senses do they use and for what purpose?
■ How do they eat and drink?
■ What behaviors do they display and when and why?

Behavior:
■ How do people act and react in different social situations?
■ When birds sit on a wire, they appear to be evenly spaced. Do people have similar personal spaces or territories?
■ How do different animals communicate and about what do they communicate?
■ How many different ways are there to communicate?

Ponds:

- What types of things live in the pond?
- What types of things live around the pond?
- How many different habitats are in and around the pond?
- What factors, surrounding areas, and other creatures affect the pond and the life in and around it?

Weather:

- Over the period of a few months, how does the angle of the sun correspond to changes in the temperature and other weather patterns?
- Can you find any corresponding relationships between the types of clouds, humidity, precipitation, and wind?

Moon:

- In which direction does the moon travel around the earth?
- What causes the phases of the moon?

In addition to the types of observational studies listed above, many physical phenomena that are typically considered the focus of experimental studies can begin with observational studies. Children can explore the behavior of pendulums, cars or marbles on a ramp, or magnets. They can explore what objects float or sink; how to create simple circuits with a battery, lightbulb, wire, and switches; or the behavior of light as it passes through lenses, reflects off of mirrors and other objects, or refracts and reflects as it hits water. As such observations proceed, they may move into more experimental designs. For example, as a group of children are exploring how the light from a flashlight changes direction when it hits the surface of water in a plastic aquarium, they may move toward measuring the angle at which the light hits the surface of the water (angle of incidence) and the angle from the surface to the bottom of the aquarium (angle of refraction). The results from this experiment can then lead to discussions of how the archerfish, which shoots insects off of branches hanging over the water, can manage to hit its target. Are archerfish amateur mathematicians as they calculate the angle of refraction? How do osprey and other aquatic birds of prey manage to dive from the air into the water and catch fish?

One of the more important goals for observational studies is identifying and understanding *patterns and relationships*. Just recording observations may be interesting, but children should be encouraged to take the process further. Table 6.1 outlines some of the basic types of patterns children can begin to identify and understand through their observational investigations. In addition, more specific patterns are discussed in Appendix D, as well as in parts of Appendixes G and H.

The fundamental goal for observational studies (as well as most schooling) is to help children develop deeper understandings of themselves and the world in which they live. Even very young children can begin to establish the patterns of thinking that will allow them to develop such understandings.

☞

**Patterns allow us to connect different events. In other words, we can understand how different events, objects, people, and so forth, are interrelated in some way. Table 6.1 depicts some of the examples of how patterns connect different types of ideas in science. However, patterns that connect can be explored through the arts, literature, film, history, anthropology, and even in how different people can connect with each other (both within and across cultures). A painting by Monet connects the patterns of color, light, and texture, which in turn provides us with the opportunity to experience certain feelings and emotions arising from our connection with the painting. Children should be encouraged to explore the range of patterns that connect within the context of an integrated curriculum—one that can begin with a science topic and connect across disciplines.**

**TABLE 6.1** Types of Patterns and Relationships

| Pattern or Relationship | Definition | Example |
|---|---|---|
| Spatial | A pattern that involves the spatial arrangement or location of certain kinds of objects or parts of objects | Tails are located at the rear end of something<br>Solar system distances<br>Animal territories |
| Temporal | A pattern over time; a sequence of events that take place in time | Tails wag (a tail moves as a sequence of events in time)<br>Moon phases |
| Formal | More abstract understandings of relations among objects or parts of objects | Homology: The wing of a bird is like the flipper of a dolphin (both appendages come from the same evolutionary origin)<br>Analogy: The tail of a lobster and the tail of a fish (they have different origins but serve some of the same purposes) |
| Interrelationships | How different objects, events, or parts are interrelated or connected | How the sun is interconnected to plants, earthworms, cows, hawks, etc.<br>How are earthworms and humans similar?<br>How are farms and industries connected to marshes downstream?<br>How are lakes similar to human beings or to cities? |

### 6.4.2 Starting an Observation Session

Typically, any observational investigation will move from the general to the specific. For instance, if your students are starting an investigation of ants, they may begin with general observations of an anthill. As they observe the anthill, they may begin to notice certain behaviors and come up with specific questions. These observations and questions can lead to more specific studies.

---

**Example 6.1: A Possible Sequence from General to Specific Observations**

As the students observe an anthill in the school yard, they notice that when one of the children knocks off a part of the hill, a lot of the ants start scurrying around and seem to be trying to fix the damage. This observation could lead to questions like

- Are all of the ants that are scurrying around involved in making repairs, or are they there for another purpose?
- How long does it take to make the repairs?

As the students investigate these questions, they may come up with additional questions like

- How many ants does it take to fix the damage?
- If the damage is bigger, will more ants be needed to make the repairs?

---

With some observational studies, particularly those at an outdoor site, you may want students to begin with acclimatizing activities (as described in Chapters 2 and 10). Acclimatizing activities (lying down with your eyes closed; listening, feeling, smelling the environment; then opening your eyes and taking in the visual dimension) help to sensitize and slow down the students. Running around, talking wildly, or even being caught up in our own thoughts makes it difficult to observe as much as we could if we are more relaxed. After such a general acclimatizing introduction, you can introduce more specific acclimatizing activities, such as looking at ants through a paper towel tube, which helps to focus one's attention and exclude distractions from peripheral vision.

---

**Example 6.2: Examples of Specific Acclimatizing Activities**

- Get down onto the ground and look up at a plant or shrub. (Change your typical vantage point of looking down.)
- Pick up some soil, put it into your palm, and put your nose into it. Breathe in slowly and take in the smell. When you have breathed in completely, try breathing in more. Compare soil from different locations.
- Feel a tree or a rock with skin on different parts of your body (fingers, palm, forearm, cheek, etc.).
- Look at a tree in the distance, but concentrate on the space around and within it, rather than on the tree itself.
- Take a blank sheet of paper and collect as many different colors in the environment as you can. Rub plants, soil, and so forth, on the paper. How many different colors can you collect? How many different shades of a color can you find? Draw a scene of the area without using pencils, pens, markers, and so forth.

---

### 6.4.3 Observational Techniques and Tools

The following techniques and tools are useful in collecting information about different topics. Some of these techniques can be used in almost any study, while others have more specific uses. See Appendixces H, I, and J for more detailed information on the following and additional techniques and tools.

*6.4.3.1 Observational Notes*  Observations should not be limited to the traditional approach of trying to be objective. Rather, notes should be as elaborate, detailed, and descriptive as possible. As opposed to purely objective observations, children should be encouraged to include what is typically considered to be anthropomorphic (giving animals and objects the characteristics of human beings), zoomorphic (giving one animal or object the characteristics of other types of animals—see the discussion of naming organisms during pond investigations in Chapter 2), and emotional descriptions. Such types of descriptions often point to significant patterns and concepts that could otherwise be missed. The extent of elaboration is obviously related to the age and writing skill development of your students (younger children may need to focus on other techniques, such as mapping, drawing, and technological aids). In some cases, with both older and younger children, you, as the teacher, can take notes for the students. A large piece of newsprint or other paper can be used to write down the observations of the group. These observations can be posted on the wall for everyone to see and use when needed.

---

**Example 6.3: A Child's Observations of an Earthworm**

In this example, the observations were not written down. However, you can see the level of detail and elaboration in these observations, and how they lead to some inferences on the part of the girl.

Now it's turning green … a little bit. It looks like they kind of change colors as they move…. Huh! The dark pink and there's red and there's green and there's a brown and there's that purple color. There's even that orange…. I think that's the vein and then there's that … egh … yellow…. Yeah…. Just like … dark spots on the inside…. I think that's the veins … or that … coily thing…. I think it gets thicker as it goes back…. I think, I think the … skinnier part is the head and the … 'cause … the little thing at the end that looks kind of like a point…. I think that's kind of a sensor … something like that so they can find their way around…. Well, it looks like it because it's going around and around. It looks like it's kind of sniffing to see what's there. I think it's kind of like cats' whiskers … you know…. They don't smell but they feel…. They've got kind of a nerve…. Maybe, maybe that line in there … maybe that's a nerve … connecting to the head….

---

*6.4.3.2 Mapping*   When we think of maps, we probably see an atlas or a road map. However, maps can be constructed to show all kinds of different information. We can draw a map of the area surrounding a pond we are studying. We can draw a map of a bird's territory, with the locations of each type of the bird's behavior indicated on the map (e.g., chirping can be shown on the top of certain bushes). We can map the movements of an insect or other animal. We can draw a contour map to indicate elevations. Maps can be used to show the locations of vegetation, the presence of specific kinds of animals, the locations of different kinds of habitats, and so forth. In each case, drawing maps can be very useful in looking for and analyzing patterns, interconnections, behavior, and so forth. The point is that the construction of maps should have a purpose. Telling children to draw a map of the area of a pond, without some discussion and agreement on the part of the children, is not going to result in much motivation to complete the task. However, when children see the need to do this task, not only will they be more motivated, but they will take the task seriously. The map in Example 6.4 could be one

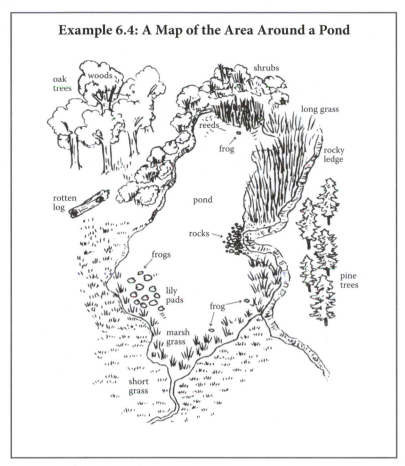

**Example 6.4: A Map of the Area Around a Pond**

oak trees

woods

shrubs

long grass

reeds

rocky ledge

frog

rotten log

pond

rocks

frogs

pine trees

lily pads

frog

marsh grass

short grass

drawn at the beginning of a study of a pond. Such a map can allow children to identify different habitats and, at the same time, see the spatial relations between them. As the children explore and observe further, they can add details or draw more specific maps. In addition, if they take water samples, collect organisms, and collect other data, such as temperature, pH, depth, and so forth, the sampling locations can be marked on the map, so that when they return, they can collect data at the same locations.

Example 6.5 shows a map of a bird's territory. The interesting aspect of this map is the addition of the bird's vocalizations to the map. Such a map allows students to start to make inferences about the relationships between behavior and movement.

*6.4.3.3 Drawings and Sketches* Drawings and sketches are always helpful in focusing children's attention on details they may otherwise overlook. a sketch of an insect they have found may help them focus their attention on particular parts and to see patterns in the way these parts are arranged. As drawings are accumulated during a study, they can be kept as a record of each organism, object, or event. As they begin to analyze their information, children can classify or sort each drawing in ways that will allow them to see further patterns and relationships.

*6.4.3.4 Technological Aids* There are many readily available technological devices that can be used to help children record information and to view this

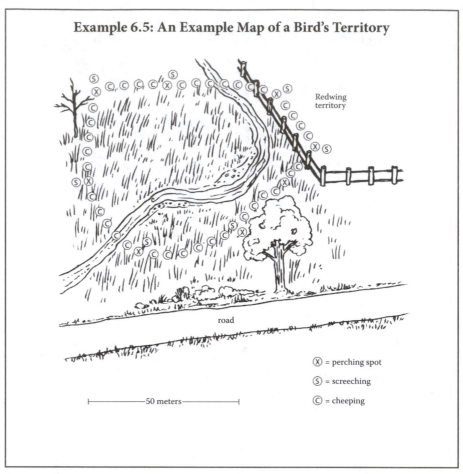

**Example 6.5: An Example Map of a Bird's Territory**

Redwing territory

road

50 meters

Ⓧ = perching spot

Ⓢ = screeching

Ⓒ = cheeping

information at later times. Audio tape recorders, digital video camcorders, and digital cameras can add a great deal to your students' investigations. Although your school may not have all of this equipment, you may be able to use your own (if you have them) or borrow them from parents of the children in your class (you may have to borrow the parent along with the equipment!). If digital equipment is not available, you can use film cameras, scanners, and VHS or other types of video cameras (see Appendix J). Audio tape recorders can be used to record particular sounds in the environment. If you are investigating birds or frogs, tape recorders can be used to tape the sounds of different species. Listening to the tapes can allow students to discriminate between the different sounds. In combination with software available for most computers, you can digitize the sounds and have them shown as sonographs (or graphic images of the sounds showing the change in frequency over time). With the computer, children can make changes to the sound and re-record the change. Will a frog respond to croaking if you take out certain frequencies?

Digital camcorders are great tools for many different types of investigations. Children can videotape a bird in flight, then play it back frame by frame. Each frame can be printed onto an overhead transparency. The final product can show a detailed account of the bird's movements. How does a cat (that is being held so that it is belly up) manage to land on four feet when dropped? Videotape it, then view it frame by frame or in slow motion. Why does a superball bounce all over the place? With a magic marker, draw a circle around a superball, then videotape its bounce. How do people react to different situations? Videotaping people on subways, buses, or other crowded situations can be quite revealing. Children can analyze body language, facial expressions, and so forth. (Keep in mind that videos or photos of people cannot be displayed publicly without informed consent from those people. Without such consent, these videos and photos can only be used in the classroom and cannot be placed on the web.)

Digital cameras can be used to capture specific situations or record a specific location or event. Children may take pictures of various parts of their ant farm in order to keep a record of each specific location. A series of photographs of a terrarium or a field site will allow children to analyze change in the same location over time. Digital cameras add the dimension of getting an immediate record on an event, rather than waiting for film to be developed. In addition, if you have a macro photographing option on your digital camera, you can take photos of very small objects or creatures from very close-up.

## 6.5   Experimental Studies

Designing and conducting experiments are important skills in conducting inquiry. When children ask questions or formulate explanations or theories about specific phenomena, the next step in the inquiry process is to explore for possible answers or test possible explanations. Many of the rudimentary skills of experimenting are a part of children's natural curiosity. Children's play often involves trying out some idea (i.e., doing informal experiments) to see what happens.

Children start experimenting with their worlds as soon as they can manipulate their environment in some way. Even young babies experiment. They make some expression and watch their parents' reactions. As they grow older, they experiment with language. As their thinking becomes more elaborate and complex, they extend experimenting into all aspects of their play. They may build a structure out of blocks, then see what happens if they push against it. The "what if" question appears to be the basis for most of children's experimenting—"I wonder what will happen if …." From this perspective, experimenting is an integral part of human learning.

In the classroom, we want to help children refine their skills of experimenting. *Children need to develop the skills of designing and conducting their own experiments.* Teachers typically hand children the formula for doing an experiment, but such an approach not only takes the ownership of the inquiry away from the children, but also detracts from their learning of the skill and from pursuing explanations and answers to their questions. So, as we discuss the designing of experiments in this section, we need to keep in mind that we should not present experiments as a prescriptive process. Rather, we should use our knowledge of experiments to help guide children. The implication of such an approach is that as children engage in designing experiments, they

> **Example 6.6: Children's Everyday Experiments**
>
> A grade 5 boy was looking at earthworms. He had been handling an earthworm for some time when he asked,
>
> > Do you mind if I tie you in a knot? [talking to the worm]. Okay … let's see if they can get out of a knot.… Hey, it won't go! [laughs]. Now this … okay.… Oh, that looks so weird. Yeah. It looks so weird, to see the knot go around. Well, I don't … if the human body got tied in a knot I think that it would be impossible to get out of because … we've got these joints and worms are so flexible.
>
> An idea came to mind and the boy did a little experiment (or manipulated observation) to see if he could find out an answer. Although this experiment is not very complex, it demonstrates how children do experiments as a natural extension of their involvement in and curiosity about the world.
>
> *Note*: Although the idea of tying a knot with an earthworm may seem cruel, the boy was very gentle. He never pulled on the two ends of the earthworm to tighten the knot, which could have split it in half. As children become curious, they come up with some ideas that could be cruel to animals. Before beginning work with animals, it is always best to have a discussion with your children that focuses on how they think they should care for the animals.

should be allowed to make mistakes. Experiments may not work or yield good results. As children experience these problems, teachers need to engage them in analyzing their experimental designs and in discussing how they can refine their procedures and measurement techniques.

In Example 6.7 children are contending with problems in their experimental design, which involves the development of important thinking skills. Although the notion of *variable* was not mentioned explicitly, the children

> **Example 6.7: An Example Classroom Discussion Sequence about Experiments**
>
> The following is an example of what a classroom discussion about a faulty experiment with pendulums might look like:
>
> **Teacher: So, what do you think of your results? Did it work out as you expected?**
>
> *Child:* No. The results didn't seem to be the same.
>
> **Teacher: What do you mean by "not the same"?**
>
> *Child:* Well, the numbers were all over the place.… They don't make any sense.
>
> **Teacher: What do you think went wrong?**

| | |
|---|---|
| *Child:* | I don't think we did it right. |
| **Teacher:** | **Can we determine what we could do better, so that we can get more consistent results? What did we do wrong? What could we do differently?** |
| *Child:* | I don't think we were pulling the weight back the same distance every time. |
| *Child:* | Yeah, and I think the lengths of the string were different. One group was measuring their length from the top of the weight … where the knot is on the string … to the top of the string. And, another group was measuring the length from the bottom of the weight to the top of the string. And, we measured from the middle of the weight. |
| **Teacher:** | **Yeah, I think those things could be a problem. So, how should we refine our experiment?** |

and the teacher were discussing problems with controlling variables. Variables are any of the factors that can affect the result of an experiment, including the factor that is measured as the result (i.e., the dependent variable) and the factor that is manipulated (i.e., the independent variable). For example, some, but not all, of the variables or factors that can potentially affect pendulums are:

- Length of string
- Weight (mass) of bob
- Thickness of string
- String material
- Shape of bob
- Angle from which bob is released
- Frequency of swings (number of swings per specified period of time)
- Distance of swings

**FIGURE 6.3**

Each of these variables, as well as others, has the potential for affecting or being affected by other variables. When designing an experiment, we need to account for as many variables as possible. The process of accounting for variables involves not only listing all of the variables we can think of, but also how these variables will be used. How to use variables means basically assigning each variable to one of four categories:

1. The variable we want to measure as the result of our experiment (i.e., dependent variable)
2. The variable we want to manipulate to see what affect it has on the event (i.e., independent variable)
3. The variables we do not want to have interfering with our results (i.e., control variables)

4. The variables that may interfere with the experiment, but which cannot be controlled (i.e., extraneous variables)

When introducing experiments to children, you may want to consider allowing them to design their own experiments without a lot of teacher input. In order for children to develop an understanding of this process, it is important for the teacher to provide opportunities for them to think about and struggle with the designing of experiments, which is where real learning occurs. They should be allowed to make mistakes, but at the same time it is important for the teacher to guide them through a process of reflecting on and analyzing what aspects of their design worked and what aspects did not work. Then they should be allowed to revise their design and try again. This approach is time-consuming, which can be frustrating, but it is extremely important. To give children all of the answers and to provide them with a design does not allow them to internalize the process, nor does it allow them to experience science. We learn best by making mistakes, especially when we make an explicit effort to understand what could have been done better. Were our measurements accurate? Were we consistent in varying the independent variable? Did we control for all the variables? Could our apparatus (e.g., car ramp, pendulum stand, etc.) be designed better?

Basically, there are three types of situations in which we can do experiments with our students:

1. Just messing around to see what happens. In this situation, children can be openly exploring a phenomenon without any particular preconceived ideas (i.e., hypotheses) or explicitly formulated questions. They are just trying out different things and seeing what happens.
2. Answering a question. In this case, the children have a question in mind. They design an experiment to see if they can get results that will help them formulate an answer.
3. Testing or confirming an explanation or theory. Here, the students may have been arguing about a particular explanation for an event they have observed. In order to see if any of the explanations are valid, they can design an experiment to see which explanation is best.

In the second case, children may or may not have an idea (or hypothesis) about the result. Although not absolutely necessary, you may want to ask the students if they have any expectations about what will happen. We should remember that although most of our science experiences have emphasized formulating hypotheses, somewhat surprisingly scientists do not always generate hypotheses.

Another aspect of doing experiments with which we need to be concerned is observable or measurable results. Both measurement and observation can be somewhat tricky. No measurement can be absolutely accurate. There always is a lot of room for mistakes. For instance, if you were to give 25 students in your classroom a stopwatch and had them time how long it takes you to run 50 yards or meters, you would probably get 25 different results. The same holds true for observable results (i.e., those that cannot be measured). If each student in your class describes the results of introducing a mirror to a bird's cage, you will get different descriptions from each student. So, how do you deal with this? The best way with measurable results is to calculate the average value. The average value can be calculated either across all of the trials done by the students in the class or across a number of trials done by one group. Doing an experiment once may not yield very reliable results; therefore, several repetitions can be very useful. Keep in mind that students should be guided through activities that will allow them to come to this conclusion, rather than being told to do several trials. Starting them off with some measurement tasks, followed by a group discussion, may help them to realize that they need to do repetitions.

In experiments where the results are in the form of observations, you need to lead the children through a discussion of how each person describes an event in a different way. Students may come to several conclusions about how to handle such situations. They may feel that they need to negotiate amongst themselves what all of their observations have in common. Did some students see something that others missed? They also may feel that they need to agree beforehand on what makes a good description. From a traditional scientific perspective, scientists say that good observations should be objective and not contain any words that can be misleading, such as those used in anthropomorphism. However, as we have seen earlier in this chapter and in previous chapters, science is not really objective. Subjective and anthropomorphic statements can be very powerful descriptors. So, rather than take the life out of their scientific explorations, such descriptors can and should be encouraged. We can help children develop their own language to make sense of science. After making such descriptive observations, your students should be able to discuss the meaning of these observations and be willing to negotiate a common understanding among all members of the class.

Students also need to learn how to record and organize their data, observations, and results. Although a photocopied handout of data recording sheets may make your job easier, and the students will have an easier time of going through the motions (filling in the sheet and moving to the next task), they will miss critical learning opportunities. Your students will not learn important skills of organizing their data. With a teacher handout, the students also can get the message that there is only one way to organize their information. However, each individual or group may have a unique approach to organizing their work in a way that is effective for them. Discussing organization and record keeping with the class may allow students to see different options. Such a discussion should focus on what information the children need to record and in what ways their record-keeping chart can be organized so that they can see and use the information more easily. In this way, students can design their own record-keeping sheets and learn valuable organizational skills in the process.

**DOING EXPERIMENTS**
This set of activities is designed to allow you to practice designing some simple experiments by yourself or with a group.

✦ Design an experiment or series of experiments to find out which environmental characteristics earthworms or insects prefer. Do they prefer light or dark? Do they prefer cool or warm? List other environmental characteristics that you could also test.

✦ Design an experiment or series of experiments to find out the optimum angle of departure (the angle of a ramp from which cars will "fly" off) and relative force (distance up a ramp or angle of descent) a toy car needs to jump across a ravine 30 cm. or 1 ft. across and land right side up (i.e., on all four wheels). Be on the alert for other factors (or variables) that you may need to consider.

✦ Once you have tried one or both of these experimental activities, try doing them with a group or class of students. Try to set up the activities in a way that engages and motivates the children.

**REFLECTIONS**
✦ What problems or difficulties arose during these experiments? How did you solve these problems?

✦ What explanations, insights, or ideas for further investigation did you come up with during these activities?

✦ How did the children respond? Why do you think they responded the way they did?

✦ How did you deal with the children's inquiry and any difficulties that arose?

✦ How would you do these kinds of experiments differently the next time you introduce children to experiments?

The most meaningful experiments that occur in classrooms are probably those that originate from children's questions and ideas. Although you, as the teacher, will introduce a number of experiments, you should look for opportunities to engage your students in experiments based upon their questions and ideas. The skill you need to develop is how to recognize the types of questions that can lead to experiments (or other investigative techniques). The list of question types in Section 6.1 provides a guide to how certain questions lead to specific types of investigations. In addition, the questions in Table 6.2 provide further specific examples of the types of questions that can lead to experiments or other techniques of inquiry.

Preparation for both planned and impromptu experiments is important for active inquiry communities in the classroom. You should have essential measuring tools and other equipment readily available in convenient storage areas in the classroom. In addition, you will find that having a variety of storage bins with an assortment of "junk" (e.g., small scraps of wood, paper towel rolls, steel and aluminum cans, screws, bolts, wire, etc.) is invaluable. In the middle of an investigation, a group of children may find that they need to modify their experimental apparatus or test out a new idea. An assortment of odds and ends of different kinds can help facilitate their inquiry. (See Appendixes H, I, and J. Appendix H provides information on how to collect and analyze data. Appendix I provides information on making and using a variety of equipment and materials that support inquiry. Appendix J provides details on using a variety of different technologies.)

**TABLE 6.2** Questions and Comments That Can Lead to Experiments and Other Modes of Inquiry

| Question or Comment | Mode(s) of Inquiry |
| --- | --- |
| What do cockroaches eat? | Experiment Observation |
| My parachute comes down too fast. What can I do? | Experiment |
| Do earthworm have babies? | Observation |
| How can I get my [toy] car to go around the loop [of the ramp]? | Experiment |
| Why do those redwing blackbird fly around from branch to branch screeching? | Field observation |
| Wow! I just hit the little marble with this big marble and the little one flew off across the room. | Experiment |

## 6.6  Inquiry and Learning

Inquiry that is based primarily on children's questions and curiosity will naturally lead to more complex investigations and learning. As discussed earlier in this chapter, the typical teacher-centered approach tends to be linear and tends not to incorporate children's questions and emergent explanations and theories. When we attempt to focus on children's questions and ideas, the avenues of investigation can increase dramatically, which can result in covering significantly more conceptual material. In such cases, the classroom work

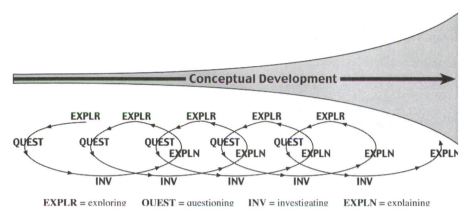

EXPLR = exploring    QUEST = questioning    INV = investigating    EXPLN = explaining

**FIGURE 6.4**

may range from investigations done by the whole class to multiple different investigations taking place at the same time. When multiple investigations that follow from each group's questions occur, each group should be provided time to share their results with the whole class. Such ongoing sharing of results can stimulate whole-class discussions and critiques (i.e., critiques of the results, experimental techniques, etc.), as well as provide opportunities for all students to learn from the work of their peers.

Figure 6.4 depicts the cyclical pattern of exploring, questioning, investigating, and explaining as it leads to ongoing conceptual development that becomes increasingly more complex. This pattern of ongoing cycles of inquiry leads to ever-increasing conceptual development over time. During these cycles, our emphasis should be on helping students develop extensive understandings that are consistent and make sense. As children proceed through exploring to generating questions and then through investigations, they should be encouraged to develop explanations for their results. At this point of explaining, they need to present their knowledge claims, defend these claims with evidence from their investigations, and eventually communicate their results and explanations in terms of some sort of final product. These final, or even numerous semifinal, products can include displays, demonstrations, booklets, video documentaries, web pages, and so forth.

## Additional Readings

Atkinson, S., & Fleer, M. (Eds.). (1995). *Science with reason.* Portsmouth, NH: Heinemann.

Callahan, C., Kitchell, H., Pierce, P., O'Brien, P., & Hall, J. S. (1998). *Organizing wonder: Making inquiry science work in the elementary classroom.* Portsmouth, NH: Heinemann.

Carin, A. A., Bass, J. E., & Contant, T. L. (2004). *Teaching science as inquiry* (10th ed.). New York: Prentice Hall.

Duckworth, E., Easley, J., Hawkins, D., & Henriques, A. (1990). *Science education: A minds-on approach for the elementary years.* Hillsdale, NJ: Lawrence Erlbaum Associates.

Fulton, L., & Campbell, B. (2003). *Science notebooks: Writing about inquiry.* Portsmouth, NH: Heinemann.

Gallas, K. (1995). *Talking their way into science: Hearing children's questions and theories, responding with curricula.* New York: Teachers College Press.

Harlen, W. (Ed.). (1985). *Primary science... taking the plunge: How to teach primary science more effectively.* Oxford: Heinemann.

Harlen, W. (1993). *Teaching and learning primary science* (2nd ed.). London: Paul Chapman Publishing.

Katz, L. G., & Chard, S. C. (1989). *Engaging children's minds: The project approach.* Norwood, NJ: Ablex Publishing.

Lowery, L. F. (Ed.). (2000). *NSTA pathways to the science standards: Elementary school edition.* Arlington, VA: NSTA Press.

Olson, S., & Loucks-Horsley, S. (Eds.). (2000). *Inquiry and the National Science Education Standards: A guide for teaching and learning.* Washington, DC: National Research Council.

Pearce, C. R. (1999). *Nurturing inquiry: Real science for the elementary classroom.* Portsmouth, NH: Heinemann.

Polman, J. L. (2000). *Designing project-based science: Connecting learners through guided inquiry.* New York: Teachers College Press.

Reardon, J., & Saul, W. (1996). *Beyond the science kit: Inquiry in action.* Portsmouth, NH: Heinemann.

Rosebery, A. S., & Warren, B. (Eds.). (1998). *Boats, balloons, and classroom video: Science teaching as inquiry.* Portsmouth, NH: Heinemann.

Roth, W.-M. (1995). *Authentic school science: Knowing and learning in open-inquiry science laboratories.* Boston: Kluwer Academic Publishers.

*Inquiry: Thoughts, views, and strategies for the K-5 classroom* (Foundations: A monograph for professionals in science, mathematics, and technology education), available online from http://www.nsf.gov/pubs/2000/nsf99148/htmstart.htm

Other inquiry-based learning materials available from Teach-nology at http://www.teach-nology.com/currenttrends/inquiry/

*Chapter 7*

# Assessing Children's Thinking, Learning, and Talk

When most people think of assessment, the first image that usually comes to mind is tests. This chapter, however, will not discuss tests at all. Rather, alternative approaches to assessing students' thinking and learning will be examined in some detail. By using alternative assessment strategies, the idea is to develop an extensive understanding of each individual student in our classes. As we proceed through the school year, we want to find out what children understand, how they think and develop understandings, how they relate to classroom activities, how they work with one another, what their individual strengths are, and how they view themselves. Any one method of assessment is not adequate to develop such a broad and in-depth understanding of our individual students. This chapter will provide a basis for approaching assessment in the class through a variety of approaches. As you read through each section, you should consider which approaches fit with the kinds of information you would like to accumulate for your students.

Assessment from the perspective of this book should be viewed as a natural part of the teaching and learning process. Many of the techniques described are parts of the instructional process. In fact, these techniques can be used in multiple ways. They can serve as instructional activities, as planning activities for you as the teacher, as diagnostic tools for identifying what students need to work on, and as a means of formulating information about children's growth and development that can be communicated to parents.

Setting long-term goals for our students is the foundation for developing your approach to assessment. Such goals need to identify the kinds of thinking, learning, and interacting you want to develop throughout the year. Many of these goals can be developed from the points discussed in the previous chapters. Although many goals may be suggested or mandated by school curricula, you should develop your own personal goals first, then look for points at which your goals and the curricular goals overlap or diverge. Later in this chapter, we will look more closely at working with school or government curricula and national standards. The following list of goals is meant to provide you with some ideas of the types of things you may want to consider including in your personal list of goals. You may wish to adapt these for your own use or develop your own set of goals. Ultimately, the decision must rest with you. You need to think about what is important to you in terms of your own philosophy of education and to the children in your class.

Some possible goals for teaching science in elementary school are listed below.

### 7.1.1  General and Affective Goals

Children will

- Enjoy doing science
  - Develop an enlivened view of science
  - See science as a useful and powerful way to inquire about their world
  - See science as one of many ways to make sense of and communicate about their world
  - Develop a passion for learning and inquiring
- Develop an appreciation for the world and a respect for the environment
  - Develop a sense of how they fit into the natural and industrialized world
- Be encouraged and supported in their inquisitiveness
- Develop understandings of the nature of science
  - Engage in active inquiry
- Work toward developing understandings that make sense, rather than memorizing the correct answers
- Not readily accept authoritarian knowledge claims without adequate supporting evidence
- Feel confident in their own abilities
- Appreciate their classmates
- Work cooperatively

### 7.1.2  Conceptual Understandings

Children will

- Develop elaborate understandings of science concepts
  - Develop a variety of alternative explanations of scientific phenomena
  - Develop understandings of broad patterns of relationships among biological and physical phenomena
  - Use relevant examples to support their explanations and understandings of scientific phenomena
- Test their ideas and explanations through observations and experiments
- Develop understandings of the interrelationships between science, technology, and society

### 7.1.3 Classroom Discourse Skills

Children will

- Engage in authentic discussions and arguments about their ideas and explanations
  - Learn to control and actively participate in classroom talks
  - Develop skills in negotiating knowledge claims and explanations
  - Develop skills for carrying out effective classroom discussions
  - Critique and challenge the ideas of others when these ideas do not make sense
- Communicate their explanations, understandings, and challenges clearly
- Use evidence to support their claims

### 7.1.4 Inquiry and Thinking Skills

Children will

- Be actively inquisitive about all sorts of phenomena and ideas
  - Formulate questions that will lead to further inquiry and theorizing
- Critique the quality and reliability of their own and other's explanations
- Analyze the reliability and accuracy of their experiments and observations
- Make use of inferences in developing their understandings
- Develop connections and relationships between different ideas
- Develop skills of collecting and recording data and observations

### 7.1.5 Psychosocial Skills

Children will

- Take responsibility for their own learning
- Take on leadership roles during inquiry and classroom talk sessions
- Be sensitive to the needs and feelings of their classmates

■ Develop an understanding and appreciation of their own strengths

### 7.1.6 Integrated Perspectives and Understandings

Children will

■ Develop elaborate integrated understandings across many disciplines

- Develop multiple understandings of various topics and aspects of their world
- Evaluate the appropriateness of different understandings and perspectives for specific contexts
- Develop a sense of how different ways of knowing (i.e., different perspectives) are appropriate to different contexts

Such goals serve as a guide both for developing assessment strategies and for developing inquiry and instructional activities. These goals do not describe specific content or concepts to be learned, but rather describe general areas of development that can be addressed throughout the school year. They serve as the glue that holds together your instructional approach. By clearly defining such expectations, the approach you take will be consistent and cohesive.

Throughout schooling, children all too often are kept in the dark about their teachers' expectations. Children need to be aware of these expectations or goals. Listing each goal at the beginning of the year may be somewhat overwhelming to the children. However, you may find that discussing goals at appropriate points during instruction may be helpful. As the goals continue to be addressed over the following days and weeks, the students can be reminded of the importance of these expectations.

+ **How do the goals listed above fit with your own ideas about teaching and learning?**
+ **How do these goals fit with the ideas emphasized in previous chapters?**
+ **Which of these goals do you want to keep for your own use?**
+ **What goals do you want to add for use in your classroom?**

## 7.2 Some Necessary Background

Before we start talking more specifically about assessment, we need to look at a few terms commonly used in teaching that directly relate to assessment. These terms include *goals*, *objectives*, and *concepts*, among others. When we use such terminology in our work as teachers, we may run up against a problem. This problem involves assuming that we actually know what we mean by a word like *goal* and what the goal we have created really means. Every profession throws around jargon, but the actual meanings are often lost. In turn, losing such a clear sense of meaning can adversely affect our work with children, our communication with parents and colleagues, and our assessment of children's thinking, learning, and behavior.

### 7.2.1 Goals

When we think of goals, we usually think of something we want to achieve in some way. We want to become a millionaire or we want learn how to swim. In education, we think of goals as a general description of what we want our students to achieve. However, it may be helpful to expand this notion to seeing goals as a description of possibilities. If we think of goals as possibilities, we evoke a sense of imagination and intrigue (in the positive sense). In this sense, we can reinvigorate our view of teaching and learning. From this point of view, our initial task becomes one of asking, What do I see as the possibilities for my students? How far can I take them? How far can they take me? What do I want my students to be when they grow up? How do I want them to feel about themselves and each other? How do I want them to feel about science? Such general questions are a good starting point for stimulating a vision of your classroom.

However, we cannot stop here. We can have a great vision, but then we are left not knowing how to get there. Once we have generated one or more goals, we need to start defining each goal and thinking about how we can go about achieving each goal. For example, we may come up with a goal that says, "I want my classroom to be a democratic community with students involved in running the community, taking responsibility, and feeling a sense of ownership over the classroom." But, what do we really mean by this statement? We could say that students will vote on issues that arise. However, if we think about this notion of voting, what is the end result of voting? A majority makes a decision, but that leaves the minority feeling disenfranchised or marginalized. So, what other ways can we operationalize democracy? Working through consensus is an alternative where students must engage in stating positions, justifying positions, listening to alternative positions, negotiating, giving up something in order to get something satisfactory, and so forth. In addition, such a process requires our own and our students' recognition that a consensus may not be reached and that we may need to table an idea or issue and not reach an immediate resolution. However, the benefit is that no one is marginalized and students can begin to develop a deep sense of ownership over the community.

Of course, the example goal just discussed contains many more terms that need to be defined, such as what "running the community" means, what "taking responsibility" means, and what "ownership" means. Look carefully at the discussion of democracy in the previous paragraph. What does this discussion do, in terms of defining and operationalizing democracy? In this case, we tend to assume democracy means voting, but voting may have unintended results. In our attempts to define what we mean, it is important to look at the assumptions connected to the terms we are using.

Once we have clarified our goal, we need to begin the process of actualizing it. The types of activities that characterize a democratic community, such as stating and justifying a position, listening to alternative positions, and so forth, are a guideline for how we can begin to engage children in such a community. From this point, we need to begin to teach children how to engage in each of these activities.

We can now see three aspects of goals: (a) the visionary statement of possibilities, (b) a definition and description of the meaning of the goal, with

Generating a list of goals as possibilities and as a description of your vision may take a long time. In fact, it may never end throughout your career. You may develop an initial list, then change or modify some goals, add new ones, and delete others. As you proceed from year to year in the classroom, it may even be a good idea to involve students in adding, modifying, and deleting goals. However, take this opportunity to begin the process. Generate a list of visionary goals or a list of possibilities. In beginning the process, think about goals in a number of areas, such as

- What should students' learning look like?
- How do you want your students to feel about themselves and each other?
- How do you want your ideal classroom to be (how should it function, how should it feel, how students will be involved in running the classroom, etc.)?
- What will students' thinking look like, and so forth?

Take one of the goals you created from the previous sidebar activity and define the goal; then describe how this goal can actually take place (operationalize it).

Behaviorism is a theory of psychology first developed by John Watson in 1925, then elaborated upon and brought into popularity by B. F. Skinner during the 1930s (however, he did not consider himself to be a behaviorist). Basically, behaviorism is concerned with observable and measurable behaviors, like a written statement, nodding a head, and so forth. Mental events, such as thinking and emotions, are not considered from a behaviorist approach.

special attention on assumptions that may interfere with accomplishing the goal, and (c) a list of characteristics or actions that operationalize the goal. The last of these three aspects points to what we might consider to be more specific objectives.

### 7.2.2 Objectives

Traditionally, the notion of objectives in education has been closely linked to a behaviorist theoretical framework. Objectives were referred to as behavioral objectives or objectives that were observable in a student's behavior or actions. Although the term *behavioral objectives* is rarely used any more, many of the behaviorist assumptions have continued to be associated with objectives. However, since the notion of having an objective as a more specific aspect of a general goal is useful, we need to redefine what we mean by objective in terms of our contemporary understandings of learning and classrooms.

As mentioned above, objectives are the specific aspects of a larger goal. From the previous discussion of goals, we can think of stating a position and justifying a position as two objectives of the larger goal of creating a democratic classroom community. These two objectives are very similar to two objectives we may have for a goal of engaging children in scientific arguments, such as stating a knowledge claim and justifying a knowledge claim. If we examine these two pairs of objectives, we again come up against the problem of what do we mean by "stating a position" or "knowledge claim" and by "justifying a position" or "knowledge claim"? If we do not have clear understandings of these objectives, we are going to have a hard time planning, teaching, and assessing them. In fact, the need to have precise understandings holds true for just about everything we teach in the classroom.

Stating a position or making a knowledge claim may seem rather obvious, but there are specific aspects that need to be considered. A position or knowledge claim should contain a clear proposition, such as a child saying, "I think we should have more time for quiet reading before lunch" or "I think the moon moves from west to east around the earth." In contrast, "I don't care about reading" or "The moon doesn't move" both make statements, but in the first case, the position is not particularly connected to what might be a discussion of when and for how long to have quiet reading time. In the second case, the statement is not clear as to what is meant by the moon not moving. So, position statements or knowledge claims need to have a clear proposition that is situated in a relevant context (e.g., when and for how long to read and in which direction the moon moves around what object).

Justification, as an objective, also needs to be defined in more detail. In order to justify a position or knowledge claim, a student needs to supply evidence (i.e., from experiments, observations, etc.) or a clearly stated rationale that supports the position or claim. For instance, the claim that the moon travels from west to east around the earth could be supported by a statement such as "When I observed the moon on Monday, it was near the west end of Orion, and on Wednesday it was past the east end of Orion; so therefore it moves from west to east." A rationale for quiet reading time may be stated as, "I think we should have quiet reading time before lunch, because I'm too tired after lunch and I think we can concentrate better before lunch." In both of these examples, support for claims is clearly stated with supporting evidence or reasons.

However, schooling tends to emphasize subject matter content as the focus of objectives, particularly on plans that need to be submitted to the principal. A typical objective, with a behaviorist orientation, is stated something like, "Each student will be able to draw a diagram showing how the moon revolves around the earth from west to east." In this example, the concept understanding is described in a way that is demonstrable through a student's behavior. Although this understanding is certainly important, it is described in a way that is devoid of context, relevance, and meaning. There are no connections to related concepts, human history and culture, or personal experiences. In addition, such a statement does not take into consideration how the student arrived at this understanding (from observations, etc.) and does not capture any related concepts. A more appropriate way of thinking of objectives in terms of subject matter content is to devise a map of the conceptual territory. Such a map can contain not only the specific understandings, but also how these understandings are achieved, how they are related to each other, and how they relate to other subject matter areas and to personal experiences. This type of description or map is particularly important when teaching through inquiry that is more authentic or personally meaningful and relevant. If students are engaged in inquiry that follows their curiosity and questions, it is difficult to predict exactly what will be taking place every day. However, with a map of the territory, you can identify where they are and how you can help them take the next step. So, in terms of science and other subject matter content learning, a list of specific objectives may not be very helpful, whereas a map or web of interlinking concepts will be much more useful.

### 7.2.3 Concepts

*Concept* is another term used throughout schooling, but do we really know what it means? Dictionary definitions are generally not of much help, as they define concept as a broad, abstract idea or a basic understanding of something. In fact, such a vague understanding of concepts has tended to create a rather narrow and decontextualized view of learning. As educators, we need to have a clear, detailed understanding of concepts, so that we can help children develop rich conceptual understandings, and so that we can assess conceptual learning.

We can think of concepts as patterns of specific events or objects. However, this definition does not go far enough. Most psychologists will agree that concepts are ideas that are comprised of several components, which are depicted in Figure 7.1. In this figure, which is depicted as a sphere, the defining feature and a prototypical image or model appears in the center. Other

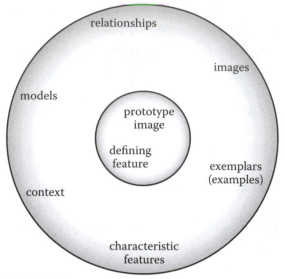

**FIGURE 7.1**

characteristics of concepts appear around the periphery, including characteristic features, exemplars or examples, images, relationships, models, and the context in which the concept is embedded. So, if we are focusing on students' learning concepts, we need to focus on the specific types of information that become a part of such understandings. Lev Vygotsky (the father of social constructivism) described such learning as "thinking in complexes":

> In a complex, individual objects are united in the child's mind not only by his subjective impressions but also by *bonds actually existing between these objects.* (Vygotsky, 1962, p. 61)

More recently, a group of science education researchers described this type of learning as "meaningful learning":

> Meaningful learning occurs when the learner seeks to relate new concepts and propositions to relevant existing concepts and propositions in his/her cognitive structure. (Novak, Mintzes, & Wandersee, 2000, p. 3)

An example of a partial conceptual map of the territory appears in Figure 7.2. Since the connections can be very extensive, this map shows only some of the conceptual and contextual material. However, this is a beginning that depicts some of the possibilities. In this map, we see other concepts appearing, such as those of gravity, motion, mass, and so forth. Because our world is so complex, we can never avoid bringing in multiple concepts. And we should not try to avoid such complexity. Without the complexity, learning becomes fragmented and devoid of context, which in turn makes the material less meaningful and less relevant, and actually more difficult to learn. It is interesting to consider that *learning for complexity (complex connections and understandings) is easier than trying to learn something that has been simplified.*

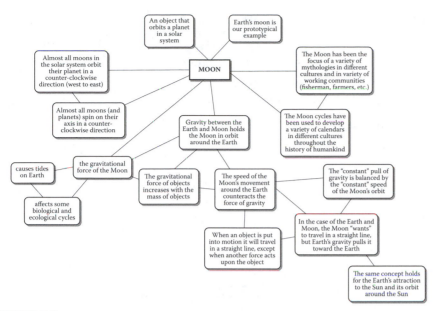

**FIGURE 7.2**

In addition to the material shown in this map, you can add inquiry questions, activities (experiments, observational studies, developing of models, artistic representations, language arts activities, etc.), and possible assessment strategies for each aspect shown on the map. For instance, you can add a box with "Activities A" and attach it with a line to one of the boxed conceptual statements. On a separate sheet labeled "Activities A," you can list the possible inquiries and other activities that can be implemented to address that conceptual area.

### 7.2.4 Theories

In Chapter 3, scientific theories were discussed in some detail. However, science educators also talk about children's theories and theorizing. These theories are often referred to as naïve theories. However, scientific and children's theories are similar in that they are frameworks for making sense of both everyday and more abstract ideas. A theory is a way of organizing the facts, concepts, and principles that are relevant to a specific topic. So, when we look at children's theories, they contain facts or other ideas that children assume to be true, as well as a variety of rationalizations, inferences, and concepts.

In terms of our working with and assessing children's theorizing, we need to examine how their ideas hold together (and make sense), how accurate their information is, what information is missing, and what kind of justifications they use. In children's discussions, we need to be keenly aware of what they say while assessing their theories, so that we can help guide them in refining their ideas and in articulating their ideas more clearly.

If we do not pay attention to what we really mean by particular goals, objectives, concepts, and theories, we will have great difficulty assessing students' understandings, thinking, talk, behavior, actions, relationships, and so forth. Although detailing all aspects of what we want to do in terms of

The statement that "learning for complexity is easier than trying to learn something that has been simplified" seems to be a paradox. However, paradoxes often point to powerful insights, which in this case may involve insights about learning.

◆ Can you think of a situation where you found it easier to understand something that involved material that was more complexly linked to your own experiences and to other contexts and subject matter areas?

◆ Conversely, can think of a situation where you found it difficult to understand something that appeared to be very simple with few connections to any other context?

◆ What are the implications of learning for complexity in terms of teaching and assessment?

creating a classroom community, developing children's thinking and social skills and developing children's understandings is a lot of work; we need to begin this process. The good news is that once we have done one particular area, we have it for use in the future. Each year you can set a goal for yourself to create one or two in-depth units or one in-depth set of goals and associated information for a particular aspect of your classroom community. Within a few years, you will have a fairly comprehensive set of detailed plans for teaching and assessment.

## 7.3 The Purpose of Assessment

### 7.3.1 Before Teaching

Before embarking on or even planning a unit, we need to assess children's understandings in order to plan more effectively. In such cases, we may find specific inaccurate concepts, which will allow us to develop activities to address these concepts. We also may illuminate particular areas of interest, which can be included in the unit. Some of these interests may not fall within the scope of science, and thus point to ways to develop integrated activities for individuals or groups of children. Children's difficulties in writing or reading may become evident, which will allow us to develop individualized strategies to help them develop these skills. Whatever information we can gather about our students' thinking, understandings, skills, and so forth, will help us to design activities and strategies to address these concerns. From a constructivist perspective, such pre-unit assessment is essential. Our awareness of children's prior knowledge is necessary for designing appropriate instructional activities that help children build on their previous understandings and challenge their inaccurate understandings.

### 7.3.2 During Teaching

During a particular unit, we can continue to assess children's classroom talk, understandings, thinking, and actions. By continuing the assessment process, we can monitor our students' development and adjust activities and other instructional strategies to meet the needs of individuals and the group. Frequently, teachers will plan an agenda of activities for an entire unit and keep to this agenda no matter what arises in the classroom. The problem with this type of an approach is that problematic concepts and difficulties with particular skills are ignored. Or, on the other hand, if students understand particular concepts, it may not be necessary to continue with an agenda of activities. In either case, the teacher can say, "I did a great job of covering all of the material." However, the students may not have learned anything, or they may have been bored to tears. The point is that we need to keep on top of what children are learning and thinking in order to keep our classroom learning community fresh and exciting.

### 7.3.3 After Teaching

Assessment of our students' learning and their development of specific skills at the end of a unit is also helpful. Not only do we need to communicate such growth to parents, but we also need to have some idea of the effectiveness of our instructional strategies. In addition, a detailed final assessment can help us design strategies to address specific difficulties in skill or learning development of individual children. We also may find students who have well-developed strengths and need to be encouraged to go further with their thinking and inquiry.

Assessment before, during, and after instructional units also provides opportunities to monitor the effectiveness of our classroom activities. By continuously monitoring the effectiveness of our instructional strategies, we can make adjustments to our strategies. For example, if we are in the midst of a sequence of activities with our students and we notice that they are having difficulty with a particular concept, we can put aside some time to plan further inquiry activities directed at this troublesome concept. So, rather than continue with our own agenda, we can readjust our plans in ways that address the needs of the students.

---

**Example 7.1: Monitoring Instructional Effectiveness**

In this example, the teacher had developed a plan of three activities around the notion of density. The first activity asked the students to predict which of an assortment of different objects would float. These objects included a variety of blocks of wood (including ebony, rosewood, teak, pine, oak, balsa, etc.), a block of paraffin, a ping-pong ball, a variety of objects made of different metals (including steel, aluminum, lead, brass, and copper), a glass ball, beeswax, cork, graphite, and plastic. After testing each object, the students measured the density of several of these objects. The second activity asked the students to find a way of getting the block of ebony to float and the block of rosewood to sink without manipulating the blocks of wood in any way. The idea of this activity was to change the density of the medium (e.g., adding salt to the water would allow the ebony to float, and placing rosewood in alcohol would result in its sinking). After finishing these two activities, the teacher noticed that the discussion among the students pointed to a great deal of confusion about density. Although he had not planned on doing any further activities on the concept of density, he went home and designed another activity. This new activity asked the students to build a boat out of aluminum foil, then determine the volume and weight of the boat. From these measurements, the students determined the relative density of the boat. The challenge was for the students to determine how much weight their boats could carry without sinking. The point of this activity was to provide a way for students to visualize the notion of density as the amount of mass (i.e., weight) in a particular volume.

---

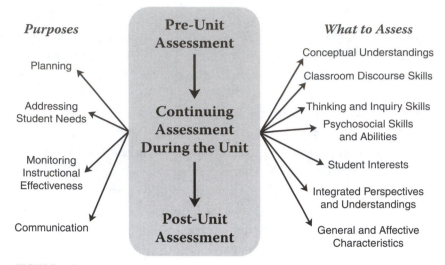

**FIGURE 7.3**

There is another critical purpose of assessment that tends to be overlooked. This aspect of assessment involves children in assessing themselves and their own work. Although portfolios address this concern to some extent, children need to be helped in assessing the quality of their own and others' work, including classroom talk (i.e., discussions and arguments), written work, inquiry, and other products of their work in inquiry communities. The same criteria used by you, as the teacher, need to be used by children in this process. In the beginning, children need to be guided in this process, by asking questions that help them focus on what to assess. Some examples may include

- Is the writing clear? Can other people understand what you are trying to say?
- Did you include a good justification for your claim or position?
- Does this evidence really support your claim?
- Is there a way to say this that makes the point easier to understand?

Such an approach to assessment becomes much more relevant if classroom work is geared toward final products that are to be shared publicly, as in a performance, a display, a book to be added to a public library, and so forth. Their work then becomes something that is not just for the teacher, but for a display of their own efforts and knowledge.

In addition to assessment of work, children should be involved in assessing themselves in terms of the effort they put into classroom work. Self-assessment of this sort has been used in some schools to address problems with at-risk students, but such an approach can be a powerful way for all students to build self-knowledge and responsibility for self and others, as well as develop the fundamental attitudes necessary for the growth of a classroom community of learners and inquirers. An example of this particular approach focuses on identifying where one fits in four levels of effort, which are described below.

1. Off track:
   - At this level, one is not putting any effort into what is taking place in the classroom or in work related to school.
   - The reasons for this can range from deep psychological resistance to schooling to a range of other factors, including having had a big fight with one's parents before school, too little sleep the night before, not feeling well, and so forth.

2. Going through the motions:
   - At this level, one is doing only what is necessary to get by during school. There is not much motivation or desire to do more than what is absolutely necessary. Unfortunately, such attitudes seem to be increasingly common not only among students in all levels of schooling, but also throughout many occupations.
   - The reasons can include socially communicated expectations that minimal effort is enough to get by or even to succeed; a variety of factors such as those listed under "off track" (e.g., not feeling well, etc.); a curriculum that is not relevant, meaningful, or interesting; and too much other work or too many more pressing demands that supersede the work in the classroom.

3. Putting in effort:
   - At this level, one is really trying to engage more deeply and completely in the work and activities of the classroom. There is a sense, at this level, of trying to do a good job and take the work seriously.

4. Striving for excellence:
   - At this level, one is motivated to do the best work possible and to go way beyond expectations. However, in addition to putting in this level of effort for one's own benefit, the person also sees that part of his or her responsibility includes helping others. So, someone working at this level also offers help so that others can understand the material, figure out problems, and engage in classroom activities and discussions.

The strategy for using these four levels of effort as a framework for self-assessment involves the following points:

- An initial interactive discussion of the purpose of this self-assessment and the meanings of each level of effort.
  - Emphasize discussions of how, for what, and when students have experienced each level, as well as how working at each level has felt.
  - As the teacher, include yourself in the discussion as a co-participant. Be sure to discuss how, for what, and when you have experienced these levels of effort. By co-participating in this way, you are modeling the kinds of attitudes and talk that are necessary in this activity and in learning communities.

- Be sure to emphasize that no one can strive for excellence in everything at all times. For a variety of reasons, we may be off track one day. We may have so many other demands that we must make choices about where we are going to put our effort and where we are not going to put in much effort. "Off track" or "going through the motions" is not necessarily negative. However, if one seems to be stuck at one of these levels in everything one does, that might be problematic.

- Begin the activity by designating one corner or part of the room for each level of effort. Then everyone, including the teacher, places themselves in one of the corners. It is helpful to designate either a specific time period (over the past week or today) or a specific activity or subject as the focus for the assessment of effort.

- At this point, when everyone is in a corner, students need to be encouraged to challenge one another to justify why they placed themselves where they did. One student may feel that another student belongs at a higher level or at a lower level. The person challenged then needs to provide reasons why he or she placed himself or herself at that particular level.

  - At first, students may be hesitant to challenge others. If this is the case, you can talk about why you placed yourself where you did, then ask random students to explain why they placed themselves where they did.

  - Some students may attack others verbally. When this happens, discuss alternative ways of challenging that will not hurt someone else's feelings. Be sure to mention that the results of doing this activity will have no effect on anyone's grade in the class. This activity requires the development of a safe environment, where students can feel that they can take risks and be honest and straightforward. Although having such a classroom environment to begin with is helpful, the activity itself can help to develop this type of safe environment.

- This activity should be done regularly. In the beginning, you may want to do this activity at the end of each day, then gradually move to once a week.

- As a teacher, you may want to try assessing yourself at the end of each day. Reflect on why you made the choices you did and why you were engaged at whatever level effort in different activities.

- In general, this self-assessment can be a powerful way to transform children's self-perceptions, the social dynamics of the classroom, and the relationships within the classroom. However, the process does take time. Be patient and keep pushing children to participate positively in the process.

Try assessing your own effort in various classes or in your workplace on a regular basis. Do your levels of effort change? Why do they change? How and why do you make decisions to put in differing degrees of effort? What affects the levels of effort you put into various situations? Thinking about these questions is important in understanding yourself, in developing understandings of what students are thinking and feeling in terms of the effort they put into school, and in developing goals for how we may change the amount or distribution of effort we put into our work. Going through this process will help us work with our students as they contend with these same issues.

## 7.4 Some Approaches to Assessment

In this section, we will examine a variety of approaches to assessment. Throughout the discussions and examples of each approach, we need to keep in mind how these approaches can be used for planning, addressing student needs, monitoring instructional effectiveness, and communicating with parents. At the same time, we need to consider the kinds of information about children's thinking, actions, and understandings we can extract from each approach, particularly in terms of assessing the complexity of children's understandings and thinking. In addition, these approaches can provide the data needed to support your claims about student learning and achievement. As such, they address the political issue of accountability.

### 7.4.1 Context Maps

Context maps are similar to what many elementary teachers refer to as webbing. Such maps are brainstorming tasks, but ask students to look for how their different ideas are connected to each other. The notion of context refers to generating different contexts of understanding or different perspectives. For example, a context map on frogs may include (a) scientific understandings of what a frog is, (b) musical understandings of their "singing" in choruses or duet, (c) romantic understandings sitting near a lake with a loved one, (d) literary (which can include romantic) understandings, such as in the story of the "Frog Prince," and (e) personally related understandings of eating frogs' legs or keeping frogs as pets.

The first time you introduce context maps to students, it is helpful to work an example with the entire class. Select an easy topic, such as *school* or *home*, then write this word in the center of the chalkboard or on a big piece of paper. Ask students to name anything that comes to mind when they think about this topic. Write each word or phrase on the board around the topic word in a circular fashion. Encourage the students to generate any kind of response, including emotional reactions and so forth—anything goes! When a variety of ideas have been written down (or you run out of room), ask the students to think of how any of their ideas are related to one another. As they describe such relationships, draw a line that links two or more ideas. After a linking line has been drawn, ask the students for an explanation of this relationship. Write this explanation along the linking line. When a few examples of linking relationships have been completed, you can stop the example and

**Which of the ideas expressed in Example 7.2 do you find surprising?**

◆ How do you see these ideas fitting in with the notion of floating?

◆ How did this girl organize the information in her map?

◆ What does this organization suggest about her thinking and understandings?

◆ What integrated topics are suggested in the example context map?

◆ Which ideas seem to be the most important to this girl?

discuss this technique with the students. When they begin their own individual context maps, you can suggest that they may add drawings to their maps and arrange the maps in any way they like. For very young children, you may suggest that they use drawings to represent their ideas. In general, children love constructing context maps. Usually, the most difficult part is constructing and labeling the relational links. However, with encouragement and continued practice, their ability to identify and describe these relationships will improve.

An examination of the resulting context maps will provide us with information on the variety of perspectives and understandings that children hold about a particular topic. Some of this information will provide us with clues to how we can integrate the curriculum for the particular unit based on the children's ideas. In Example 7.2, the students had been asked to construct context maps on *floating*.

The information contained in context maps not only suggests a variety of ideas and perspectives on a particular topic, but it also suggests which ideas may be important for each student. If one idea (i.e., item on a map) is connected by a lot of linking ideas, that particular idea may be of more

**Example 7.2: A Grade 7 Girl's Context Map on Floating**

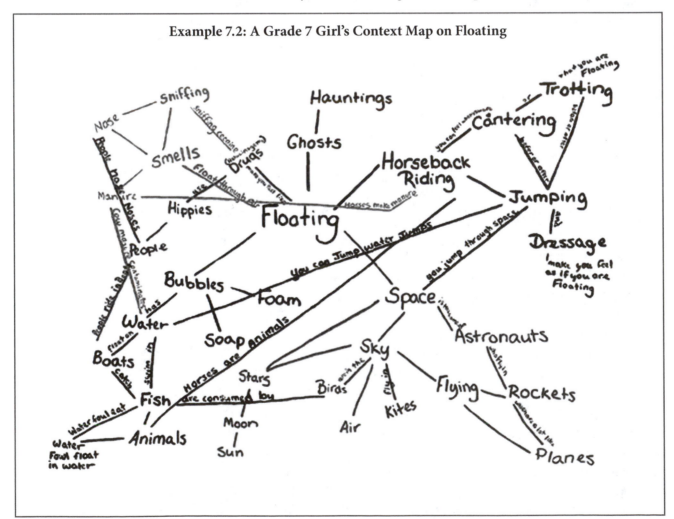

importance to the individual student. For example, in Example 7.2, both "jumping" and "sky" have six connecting links attached to them, and "horseback riding," "water," and "fish" are attached to five links. What do these terms suggest about this girl's understanding of floating and the meanings she associates with floating? The experience of horseback riding appears to have a metaphoric connection to floating. We also may think that this girl has an interest in horses, which in fact she does. Such a connection provides an ideal opportunity to develop integrated activities for the individual student. We could offer this child a variety of ways to explore and represent her ideas of horses and floating. Some examples could include poetry, art, dance or movement, stories, and so forth.

From a more scientific perspective, water (including fish) and flying in the sky also appear to be significant aspects of what this girl associates with the notion of floating. In developing a unit of instruction on floating, we may have considered only floating in water. However, the notion of floating in other mediums, such as air, may offer additional ways of extending our students' understanding of floating.

In addition, we can see that the girl who constructed the context map in Example 7.2 organized her information into six basic clusters. Each cluster contains related ideas. Her connecting links show the relationships between the items in each cluster. Such well-organized and clearly identified relationships between closely related ideas suggest thoughtfully and thoroughly constructed understandings.

In addition, this student has developed less closely related links, which connect different clusters, such as "jumping" (horses) to "water," and "jumping" to "space." Connecting less closely related ideas suggests an ability to see broader relationships among diverse perspectives. Helping children to see and develop such broad relationships can be important in several ways. The typical approach to schooling emphasizes learning within the boundaries of specific disciplines. Extending understandings beyond disciplines rarely takes place; however, when we emphasize such cross-disciplinary relationships, we provide opportunities for children to make deeper, more personal, and more complex connections with the topic and their own learning. The whole process of working with these kinds of relationships can *enliven* children's experience of learning about their world. We can tap into their interests and provide opportunities for our students to develop a passion for learning and representing their understandings. In addition, such broad relationships allow for the emergence of creative insights into patterns that connect different ideas and perspectives. The notion of "jumping through space" can lead to understandings of gravity, force, balance, and so forth. Such scientific understandings can be connected to the aesthetics of movement, gracefulness, coordination, and the communication between horse and rider.

Now, having seen how to make sense of the previous context map, try your hand at analyzing the context maps of Examples 7.3 and 7.4.

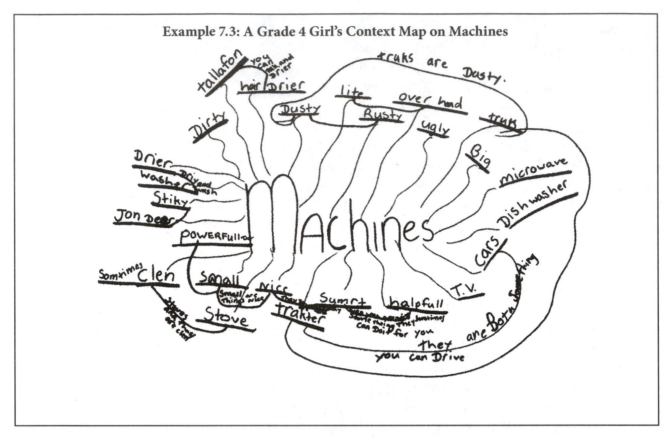

**Example 7.3: A Grade 4 Girl's Context Map on Machines**

✔

◆ **Which of the ideas expressed in Example 7.3 do you find surprising?**

◆ **How do you see these ideas fitting in with the notion of machines?**

◆ **What integrated topics are suggested in this context map?**

◆ **Which ideas seem to be the most important to this girl?**

In using context maps, you may find that doing your own maps in conjunction with those of your students before a unit may help define some of the potential ways of integrating instruction. You also may use context maps as an ongoing instructional tool. As you begin a unit, the class can start a context map on a wall in the classroom. As the unit proceeds, individuals and groups of students can add to the maps. Each item can be written and illustrated on a sheet of paper, then taped to the wall. Different colored yarn with labeled relationships attached to each piece of yarn can be used to make connections between different ideas. Such a group context map can be extended across the ceiling to other walls, and take on a three-dimensional quality. In addition, constructing such a group context map provides opportunities for students to negotiate the organization of the information. As time goes by, students may feel that certain ideas need to be clustered. The items and connecting lines can be moved to accommodate their new insights. As students complete individual or group investigations and projects, their resulting displays can be added to the developing context map.

### 7.4.2   Concept Maps

As opposed to context maps, concept maps focus on the details of specific concepts or groups of concepts and are more highly structured. Consequently, children (and teachers) find them much more challenging to complete. The benefits of concept maps include developing a well-defined picture of our own and our students' understandings. The process of constructing a concept map also pro-

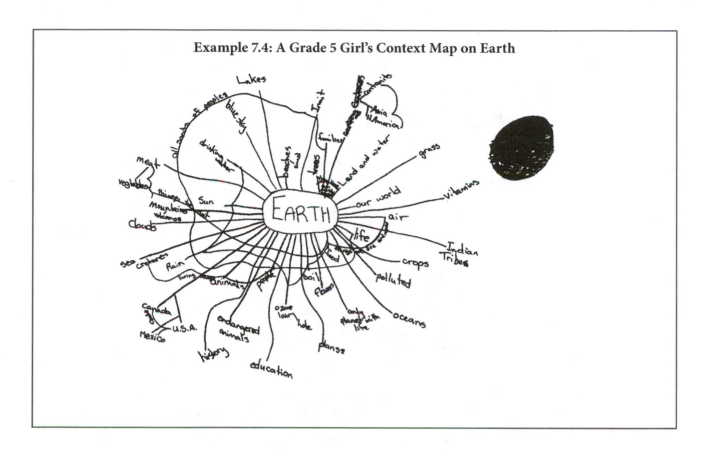

**Example 7.4: A Grade 5 Girl's Context Map on Earth**

vides a way to organize conceptual understandings. When complete, concept maps can be read like a sentence. Each term (or node on the map) is connected by one or more lines to other terms. Each of the connecting lines is labeled with a word or phrase that links the two terms. For example, if "elephants" is connected to "trunks," and "trunks" to "noses," this part of a concept map might read: "elephants" have "trunks" that are "noses."

As a planning task, teachers quickly find out where their own knowledge is lacking. This point is important. When we begin to develop a concept map that represents our knowledge of a particular topic, we find gaps and questions about what we know and what we do not know. Then we can work on developing these understandings. Example 7.5 depicts part of a concept map developed during the planning of a unit on density.

Concept maps can be used in the classroom to help children organize their knowledge, as well as a way to assess their specific understandings. In general, teachers and researchers have approached the construction of concept maps in two slightly different ways. The first way is to provide students with a list of terms that are associated with a particular concept. With this list in hand, children are instructed to construct a concept map using all of the terms. The other way allows the children to generate their own list of terms, then construct their concept maps from this list. In Examples 7.6 and 7.7, we see the lists of terms (on the left side of each example) generated by the children prior to constructing their maps.

◆ Which of the ideas expressed in Example 7.4 do you find surprising?
◆ How do you see these ideas fitting in with the notion of earth?
◆ What integrated topics are suggested in the example context map?
◆ Which ideas seem to be the most important to this girl?

## Example 7.5: Part of a Concept Map on Floating Constructed by a Teacher in Planning a Unit

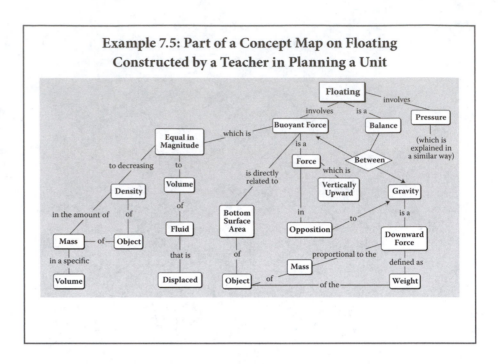

## Example 7.6: Frank's (Grade 6) Concept Map on Floating

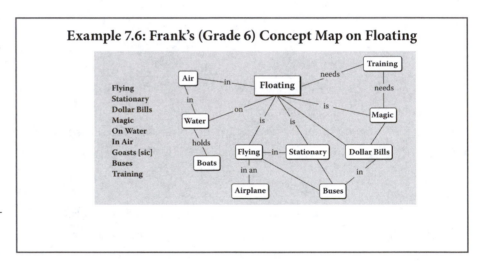

**Refer to Examples 7.6 and 7.7.**

✦ **How do the children's concept maps compare to the teacher's concept map in Example 7.5?**

## Example 7.7: Eric's (Grade 5) Concept Map on *Floating*

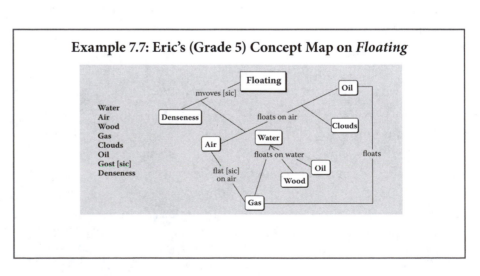

In both examples, the students have constructed concept maps on *floating* prior to the unit. Frank's map (Example 7.6) is organized more clearly than Eric's (Example 7.7); however, both Frank and Eric have constructed relatively complex maps. The complexity of concept maps involves the inclusion of cross-links. A concept map that has all of its items linked along straight lines is much more simplistic than a map that branches out and links items from different branches and clusters. Such complexity is indicative of understanding how different aspects of concepts are related. As students develop their understandings, we would expect to see them develop more complex concept maps.

We also see in these examples how Eric has attempted to place more emphasis on the scientific concepts, while Frank has included more information on the notion of magic. Eric has included the notion of denseness, but has not explained density or connected it in a meaningful way to other items. We also see that "oil" is connected to floating on air, which it does not do, but then this student may be referring to similarities between floating oil and the broader notion of floating "on air."

Although we may not expect a student's concept map to look like the teacher's or another expert's map, we do want children to develop more complex understandings and ways of representing these understandings. Concept maps offer a way for both teachers and students to see how their understandings develop in terms of the accuracy of their ideas, the complexity and coherence of their understandings, and the extent of their knowledge.

As with context maps, concept maps can be used to assess children's understandings before, during, and after a unit of instruction. They also can be used as a planning tool for teachers. Constructing a concept map prior to a unit provides a way for teachers to strengthen their own personal understandings of the concepts they will be addressing in a unit. With a more thorough understanding of the conceptual material, teachers will find it easier to respond to children's questions with questions of their own. When teachers respond with questions, they can help children uncover further understandings or reach a solution to a problem. For example, in one classroom, some grade 6 children were in the midst of dissecting a frog when they asked the teacher what some yellowish objects were in the abdomen of their frog. The teacher responded, "What does it feel like? Touch it." The students felt the objects, then said, "It feels greasy … oh! It's fat!" The teacher never gave the answer, but provided a means for the students to figure it out for themselves.

In addition, concept maps can be used as an instructional tool. Groups of children can construct concept maps. Throughout the group effort, children will have to argue about and negotiate knowledge claims in order to construct an agreed-upon concept map.

### 7.4.3 Written Tasks

Throughout the school year, children are asked to do all kinds of written tasks. All of these tasks offer teachers opportunities to assess children's

---

Try constructing your own context map on a science topic with which you are more familiar. Some examples may include plants, weather, digestion and eating, and bones. As you work through the process, keep the following points and questions in mind:

✦ How easily did ideas arise?

✦ Do you find constructing the links across ideas more difficult? Why or why not?

✦ How would you characterize the nature of your cross-links?

✦ Were some cross-links more obvious or subtle than others?

✦ How many different kinds of ideas did you generate?

✦ How could each different kind of idea be used to develop integrated activities?

✦ How many different subject areas could you integrate based on your map?

✦ After completing a context map, do you feel that you have a better understanding of the integrated nature of the topic? Why or why not?

✦ Do you feel that you might be better prepared to teach a unit on this topic after having completed a context map?

✦ How can context maps be used to address or accommodate gender, ethnic, and cultural perspectives?

understandings and thinking. The possibilities are endless. This book cannot deal with the full extent of possible tasks; however, two basic types of tasks will be examined below, and should provide you with guidelines for how to use written tasks as a means of assessment.

*7.4.3.1 Explanations, Descriptions, and Definitions* Much of what we deal with in schools has to do with how particular concepts or ideas are explained, described, and defined. Although the idea of definitions may seem to be rather boring, with a tendency toward rote learning, looking at the construction of *definitions as a process* can be valuable. Frequently, children have much more relevant definitions for objects or events than those found in textbooks or dictionaries. For example, the *Oxford English Dictionary* (2003, online) defines machines as follows:

> *n.* I. A structure regarded as functioning as an independent body, without mechanical involvement. II. A material structure designed for a specific purpose, and related uses. III. A mechanical or other structure used for transportation or conveyance. IV. An apparatus constructed to perform a task or for some other purpose; also in derived senses. V. Various extended uses. VI. Compounds [i.e., compound forms of machine].

Definition IV tends to be the one used in science textbooks. On the other hand, children tend to have very different ways of defining or describing their understandings of machines, which are more aligned with definitions I, II, and III, but also differ from any of these definitions. As we can see in Example 7.8, children have extended the meaning and definitions of machines to include a number of important concepts, which are connected to their everyday experience with machines. Children identify machines as things that need to be controlled in one way or another. They also associate various values and aesthetics with machines. Some students see the human body as an example of a machine.

In the Example 7.9, Gloria's definition of floating became much more concise after the unit. Before the unit, her definition focused on her own experiences with floating and with her imaginative view of what would happen without gravity. After the unit, she focused entirely on the interaction of two forces: buoyancy and gravity. Although this definition is incomplete, she shows a move toward a more precise scientific explanation. Her addition of a diagram adds to the meaning of her explanation.

As with all approaches to assessment, the tasks we ask children to do also can serve as instructional activities. When children generate definitions for various concepts, their ideas will vary quite a bit. As children work in groups (or as a class), they can use their definitions as the beginning for a group-constructed and -negotiated definition. As they work through a unit, the group can continue to modify, extend, or change their definitions to fit with their new discoveries and insights. Rather than becoming a static product, definitions become a process of negotiating their understandings.

## Example 7.8: Grade 5 Students' Definitions of Machines
### (Note: Children's spellings have not been corrected)

### Andrea

| Pre-unit descriptions | Post-unit descriptions |
| --- | --- |
| A machine is something that's not natural. We don't need a machine, it just makes things faster and easier, or it gives us pleasure. It works on its own except if it needs button pushing or controlling. That's what I think a machine is. | A machine is something that was not here at the beginning of the world. It is something made by man to help, entertain or save time. A machine can work mechanically, electrically, or even with the help of the human hand. Some machines we have in our home that we might not even think is a machine are eggbeaters, TV, and things that help us do things that we might not have been able to do. I think machines are very helpful, but sometimes they need harmful things like gas which when it has been used, comes out as exaust and pollutes the air. |

### Ken

| Pre-unit descriptions | Post-unit descriptions |
| --- | --- |
| It moves. It costs money. They crack down blow up parts works disks wires steel rusty not perfect good help you. | A machine is a moving object or a tool. A machine is built up with gears, metal, steel cranks and a lot of other parts. Most machines are built to help a man or a woman with their work. Machines are big if the work is big or if the work is small the machine will be small. Most of the machines are tools to machines are built to help even a simple moving turning crank is a machine. So that defines MACHINES. |

### Lori

| Pre-unit descriptions | Post-unit descriptions |
| --- | --- |
| A machine is an electric or standard piece of steel, wood, plastic, etc. It costs different prices depending how it works. You can look, ride, see, listen, etc. to machines. Machines can be very useful to you. A machine can be faster than your hands. | A machine is an object that moves. A machine does not have to have wires or axles to work. You can make a machine out of string, wheels and wood. Machines can be made by hand or made by other michines in factories. I think a machine was first made by man. The man made it to make things easier for everybody including himself. A machine can do almost anything you make it to be. I think that machines are machines because of the movement. In a big way we are machines because we move by muscles and bones. |

### Mel

| Pre-unit descriptions | Post-unit descriptions |
| --- | --- |
| Good, cool, robotic, no heart, no feeling, no brain, stupid, boring, no fun, bucket of bolts, stupid looking, dump car. | A machine is a structure or tool created by man. It is not a rock or a book. All biological beings are machines because they have certain movements, functions, or actions. A person is a great example of a machine. We are biologically formed. We gather import and lura out much to be the best. We eat to charge. We sleep to recharge. We go to let our bladder empty all the uneeded materials. We die when we have reached our peak and then the cycle starts with us again. We reproduce to keep our species alive. If we didn't have machines Earth would not exist in space or would people for we ar biological machines. |

♦ How do the children's definitions change from before the unit to after the unit?

♦ What scientific concepts have been incorporated into the children's definitions both before and after the unit?

♦ How has the complexity of the children's definitions changed from before to after the unit?

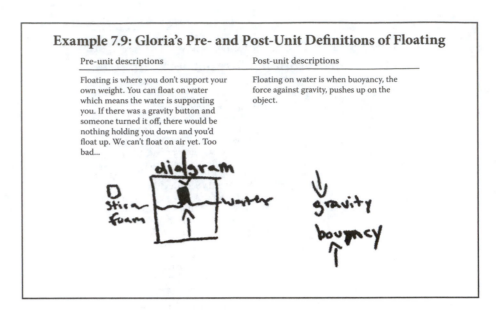

**Example 7.9: Gloria's Pre- and Post-Unit Definitions of Floating**

| Pre-unit descriptions | Post-unit descriptions |
| --- | --- |
| Floating is where you don't support your own weight. You can float on water which means the water is supporting you. If there was a gravity button and someone turned it off, there would be nothing holding you down and you'd float up. We can't float on air yet. Too bad... | Floating on water is when buoyancy, the force against gravity, pushes up on the object. |

*7.4.3.2 Descriptive Communications* Asking children to communicate their views, knowledge, and understandings of certain topics can be very revealing. We can learn much not only about their specific conceptual understandings, but also about their broader knowledge of the contexts in which these specific concepts are embedded. In addition, as we have seen in Example 4.15 (Effie's symbolic representation of what life on earth is all about), the way in which students represent their understandings can be brought to light. In Examples 7.10 and 7.11, we see how other students represent their understandings of life on earth. In each of these examples (including Example 4.15), the children have represented their understandings in very different ways. The views they have chosen to represent were also quite different. Effie represented her knowledge symbolically, Everett poetically, and Elliot through contrasting pairs of situations or ideas. In addition, each child has focused on different content. Effie chose to focus on social and historic material. Everett looked at aesthetic and scientific ideas. Elliot focused more on the psychological experience of life on earth.

As a pre-unit assessment, such tasks can provide a great deal of information that can be used to design more meaningful activities. If we were to design a unit around the topic of life on earth without using pre-assessment tasks, we might not select the kinds of subtopics that would address our students' interests, approaches to representation, and contexts in which they embed their ideas. However, by using such tasks, we can develop activities that will address the children's interests, approaches, and experiential contexts as well as their strengths and abilities.

The basic idea behind such activities is to provide a fairly broad and open-ended question that will elicit children's understandings as embedded in larger contexts. This idea is based on the assumption that specific ideas and concepts are only meaningful when they are embedded in one or more larger contexts. For example, if we are working with the concept that the seasons are dependent upon the angle of the earth's axis in relation to the sun, then

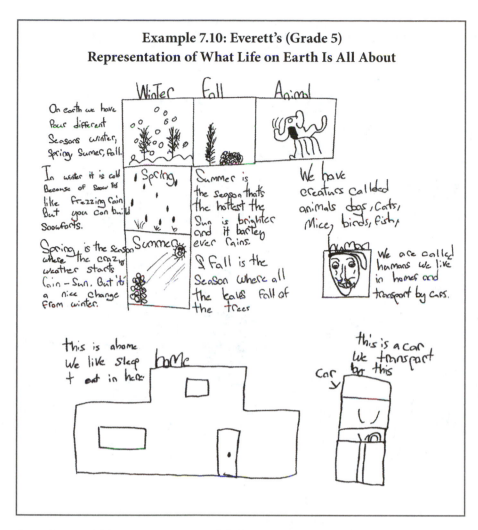

**Example 7.10: Everett's (Grade 5)
Representation of What Life on Earth Is All About**

Winter  Fall  Animal

On earth we have Four different Seasons winter, Spring, Sumer, fall.

In winter it is cold Because of Snow its like Frezzing rain But you can build Snowforts.

Spring is the season where the crazy weather starts rain - Sun. But it's a nice change from winter.

Spring

Summer

Summer is the season that's the hottest the Sun is brighter and it barley ever rains.

Fall is the Season where all the leaves fall of the trees

We have creatures callded animals dogs, Cats, Mice, birds, fish,

We are called humans we live in homes and transport by cars.

this is a home We live sleep + eat in here.

home

this is a car we transport by this

Car

◆ **What aspects of life on earth appear to be most important to Everett?**

◆ **In what ways does Everett represent his knowledge?**

◆ **How has he integrated his scientific knowledge with other disciplines?**

this idea could be more meaningful if it were connected to children's experiential contexts. For Everett (Example 7.10), this context could include his aesthetic reactions to his experiences of the seasons. For Elliot, the context could include people's psychological reactions to the seasons. Of course, we should not limit these contexts to what might be evident from the children's work. We also need to include new experiences of how to make sense of why the angle of the earth's axis is so important. Activities to provide experiences with this notion need to be developed and implemented in the classroom. We also should include other activities that develop relationships with other contexts. How is life in equatorial countries different from that in more northern or southern countries? How do different cultures relate to changes in the seasons, and historically, how did different cultures relate to changes in the seasons? How do changes in the seasons affect patterns of weather? In turn, how do changes in weather affect plants and animals? How do such changes affect human beings and human societies? How do changes in the tilt of the earth affect locations at different latitudes (i.e., locations at the equator, in the southern hemisphere versus the northern hemisphere, in far northern regions, etc.)?

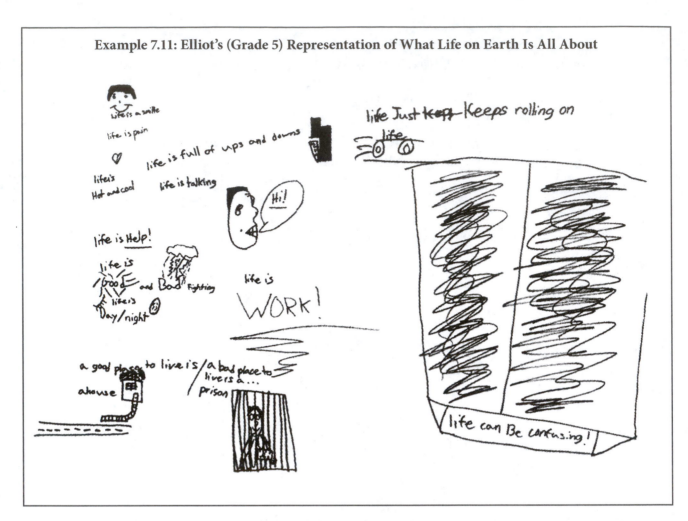

**Example 7.11: Elliot's (Grade 5) Representation of What Life on Earth Is All About**

life is a smile
life is pain
life is full of ups and downs
life is Hot and cool
life is talking
Hi!
life is Help!
life is Good and Bad Fighting
life is Day/night
life is WORK!
a good place to live is a house
a bad place to live is a... prison
life Just Keeps rolling on life
life can Be confusing!

### 7.4.4 Drawings and Diagrams

Drawings and diagrams allow children to express their ideas visually. These techniques are especially useful when students may have difficulty expressing ideas in words or when diagrams help provide a context for expressing their ideas. As we have seen in Example 4.14, the students' drawings of the beginning of life on earth provided information on the beliefs framing their ideas about the history of the earth. Such information is very useful in determining the nature of the activities you may need to design to address the children's ideas. For instance, one child shows a primitive human being in the same picture as a dinosaur. Since humans were not yet on the scene during the time of dinosaurs, you could design activities that would allow children to develop a more accurate understanding.

In Example 7.12, Josh drew a picture of the sun with the space shuttle and a satellite in response to a request to draw an eclipse of the sun as it would appear from outer space. This particular task is interesting in two ways. The teacher expected to see the sun on one side with the moon between the earth and the sun, showing the moon blocking the sun from shining on the earth. However, the instructions were vague. An eclipse of the sun could occur from any vantage point with any object blocking the sun. This particular point is

◆ What aspects of life on earth appear to be most important to Elliot?

◆ In what ways does Elliot represent his knowledge?

◆ How does Elliot's view of life on earth differ from Everett's (and Effie's in Example 4.15)?

◆ In each of these examples, what could we communicate to parents about how their children think and about their children's understandings?

very important. As teachers, we need to be very clear in our instructions. Although the teacher realized the problem after the tasks were completed, there is a possibility of thinking that a student does not have an accurate understanding. It is all too easy to quickly assess a task without understanding the student's perspective. In this case, the student interpreted the task instructions differently than the teacher and produced an accurate depiction based on his interpretation.

✦ From Examples 4.15, 7.10, and 7.11, what instructional activities could you develop to address these children's interests, ways of representing understandings, experiential contexts, and strengths?

✦ How would you assess the complexity of these children's understandings?

✦ Could these activities be used with the entire class?

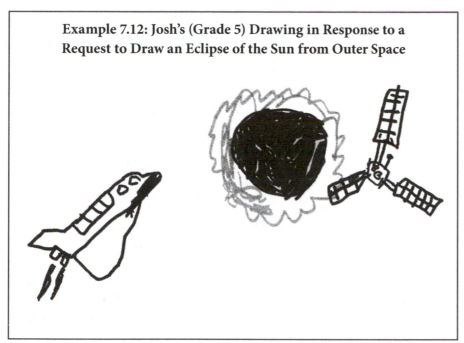

**Example 7.12: Josh's (Grade 5) Drawing in Response to a Request to Draw an Eclipse of the Sun from Outer Space**

The drawing itself is interesting in that Josh shows an eclipse of the sun by another object (moon, earth, etc.). In addition, he provides further contextual clues, in the form of a satellite and the space shuttle, to indicate that the eclipse is being viewed from outer space.

Drawings also can be provided by the teacher as a starting point for completing the drawing. In Example 7.13, Frank, a grade 6 boy, added to a drawing of a sailboat an explanation of why the sailboat floats. You can see in the pre-unit drawing that he had very little to add—mentioning only "air in hull, wood floats, wind pushes sail." In the post-unit drawing, his understanding was much more elaborate and included the concept of density.

Although we see an increase in the complexity and understanding of floating in Frank's post-unit drawing, his fourth item, "air in hull" (explained at the bottom of the drawing), is not exactly clear. As it turns out, many students attributed air for any object's ability to float. If we get responses such as this from our students, we need to be careful not to assume that our understanding of what they say is the same as theirs. When we get work of various kinds from students, we may want to ask them to explain their ideas. A short interview about their work and ideas may reveal areas of confusion, as well as areas where their understandings are much more complex.

**Example 7.13: Frank's (Grade 6) Explanation of Floating Based on a Provided Drawing**

| Pre-Unit Explanation | Post-Unit Explanation |
|---|---|
| Using the picture below, explain how you think the sailboat floats. Feel free to draw lines and arrows or anything else on the picture to help with your explanation. | Using the picture below, explain how you think the sailboat floats. Feel free to draw lines and arrows or anything else on the picture to help with your explanation. |

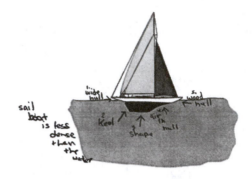

Asking our students to make or complete diagrams and drawings is useful both as a learning tool for them and as a way for teachers to keep tabs on children's learning. During group work, students can use their diagrams as a means of explaining their points to other group members. Such activities can be extended to where groups can negotiate their explanations while developing visual representations of their understandings. Once again, we can see how the process of assessment flows between our observations as teachers and the students' engagement in learning tasks.

### 7.4.5 Models and Modeling

The development of models that explain particular phenomena are important as both a learning activity and an assessment tool. Although models can be extensions of drawings and diagrams, they also can be physical working models of particular events. Whether we know it or not, we develop mental models of how things work throughout our lives. Some people may tend to develop visual models, while others develop kinesthetic (moving) or descriptive models. These models may serve as directions on how to get from one place to another; some people draw mental maps, whereas others construct a sequence of steps. As with naïve theories, many of the models children develop are naïve in the sense that they may not accurately reflect current scientific understandings. However, the basic process of building models is important. Our task as teachers is to help children refine these model-building skills.

In terms of assessment, children can be asked to build a model of the sun, earth, and moon that demonstrates (and explains) how the seasons, eclipses, and other phenomena occur. Such a model not only is helpful in assessing the depth, extent, and complexity of children's understandings, but also is an important learning activity. The process of building models helps to clarify and solidify one's understandings. (More detailed examples of modeling and their uses in inquiry are described in Appendix H.)

### 7.4.6 Classroom Talk

In Chapter 5, we had an opportunity to examine children's classroom talk as a medium for the social construction of knowledge. From this examination, we can see how our listening to children's talk in the classroom can help us gain a more extensive picture of children's understandings and of the development of their skills of conducting discussions. Rather than delve into a detailed examination of the material in the previous chapter, this section will provide a brief outline of some of the points we can use as a guideline for assessing children's classroom talk. The following questions may prove to be useful in helping you focus on key issues in assessing children's talk. However, we need to work on becoming good listeners in general, which involves knowing what we are listening for (as described earlier in this chapter in terms of goals, objectives, and so forth).

*7.4.6.1 Assessing Children's Talk*   Does the student

- **Participate in classroom discussions?**
- **Offer important contributions** to discussions?
- Take on a **leadership role** in monitoring the flow and dynamics of classroom or group discussions?
- **Respect other students' abilities** to make meaningful contributions?
- **Respect the feelings and ideas of his or her classmates?**
- **Think about and consider the value of other students' contributions?**
- **Take the initiative to critique, challenge, or question** (based on the last eight questions in this list) other students' explanations and knowledge claims by
  - Asking for **clarification?**
  - Asking **probing questions?**
  - Asking for **supporting evidence?**
  - Asking for **elaboration** on a topic or explanation?
  - Asking for **alternative explanations?**
  - **Critiquing the sensibility** of knowledge claims and explanations?
  - **Critiquing** explanations on their **consistency with evidence?**
  - **Critiquing the relevancy** of explanations and evidence?
- Express his or her ideas **clearly?**

> ✦ **Try building your own working model of the sun, earth, and moon in a way that explains how the phases of the moon occur, how the seasons occur, and how eclipses occur. Use a variety of balls (e.g., Styrofoam, modeling clay, etc.) and a lamp with no lamp shade as the sun to create the model. Observe the moon over several nights and collect data on its position in the sky over this time period (see Chapter 2, Section 2.4). Which way does the moon move around the earth? Look up other information as needed, such as sizes of the earth, moon, and sun and their distance from one another. Then try to develop a working-scale model.**
>
> ✦ **How did this task affect your understandings of the moon, sun, and earth relationships?**
>
> ✦ **What difficulties did you have? How can these difficulties help you to develop more thorough understandings?**
>
> ✦ **Try having one or more children develop a similar model (or models of other phenomena). What insights into their thinking and understanding did you gain from this activity?**

- **Use examples** to back up her or his claims?
- **Describe relationships** between different ideas?
- Offer knowledge claims and explanations **consistent with evidence** he or she has generated through inquiry or with evidence from external sources?
- Try to **make sense of the results** of his or her inquiry?
- Generate or is open to **alternative explanations**?
- **Elaborate on ideas**, rather than give one-word or short-phrase answers?
- **Accurately explain** his or her ideas in terms of contemporary scientific understandings?[1]

As with the entire notion of assessment, the process intersects with our instructional practices. Students need to be coached and guided through the criteria contained within the previous list of questions. Initially, these questions can help us to identify what types of skills need to be developed by our students. As time proceeds, we can use these questions to monitor student development and learning, as well as to identify individual strengths that can be developed to more sophisticated levels.

*7.4.6.2 Interviews* As you may have gathered from reading about the previous approaches to assessment, asking children to explain their work is frequently very helpful in clarifying and extending our understandings of children's thinking and learning. Asking children to explain their work should be standard practice. We need to probe underneath the surface of children's written products. Children's less developed abilities in writing or the particular circumstances (e.g., emotional state) can adversely affect their work. So, taking the time to ask children to explain what they have done and what they were thinking about can provide us with a much better picture of their understandings. Interviews can be conducted in a variety of ways. The easiest and most practical way is to develop a routine of circulating among your students while they are working and stopping to talk to individuals and groups. Ideally, this approach should not be seen by the students as obtrusive or intimidating. As you enter into talks with children, they should see you as being genuinely interested in what they are doing. Such interviews are informal and conversational and should not be a barrage of questions. the questions you ask should flow from the conversation. In Example 7.14, a teacher informally interviews a grade 5 boy about earthworms as he begins his inquiry.

Interviews can also focus on a specific task about an event or object. In Example 7.15, the teacher is talking with a student while she tries to solve a particular problem. This interview took place after a unit on floating and density. Any number of situations can be devised to explore children's understandings in this way. The idea is to provide a situation or task that will stimulate a child to solve a problem or formulate an explanation.

Interviewing children requires four basic skills:

## Example 7.14: Informal Interview with a
## Grade 5 Boy about Earthworms

**Teacher:** That's okay. There's more in there. Dig down. Ah, there's a nice big worm. Where'd he go to?

*Elliot:* Ah, he's over there. Don't want to, this time [laughs]. That looks more like a worm. Okay … [It sounds like Elliot is whispering to the worm. After one whisper:]

**Teacher:** What's bad? Yeah, why don't we put him back so we don't have to look at him. There [laughs]. Do you know much about worms?

*Elliot:* No.

**Teacher:** No? You've seen them around though.

*Elliot:* Oh yeah.

**Teacher:** When do you see them?

*Elliot:* Rainstorms.

**Teacher:** Rainstorms. Right.

*Elliot:* Digging in the garden. Oh I see moving. I wonder if they have eyes.

**Teacher:** You wonder if they have eyes?

*Elliot:* Yeah.

**Teacher:** I don't know. What do you think?

*Elliot:* I don't know. I think they just feel their way around.

**Teacher:** Yeah.

*Elliot:* They seem to know when you're coming.

**Teacher:** Yeah, yeah, it's strange. Ooh! Accident.

*Elliot:* Oh oh!

**Teacher:** Pulling back.

*Elliot:* There's something there.

**Teacher:** Ooh!

*Elliot:* Isn't that interesting, he knows it.

**Teacher:** I wonder how he knows.

*Elliot:* So do I [laughs]. He's crawling on the other guy. Where's, oh …

**Teacher:** Oh, the other one's getting; he's not too happy, either. He's backing up. I wonder if they can communicate with each other.

*Elliot:* It doesn't seem like it. See, he seems to know that there's something ahead so he's moved back, but I don't think those things have eyes because they've got those little "ten eyes."

**Teacher:** How do you think worms manage to move?

*Elliot:* Well, I think they, like, pull themselves out like this and they pull themselves back together and they get the traction out of; they're really moving, 'cause they've got, like … and they're made out of, almost like pieces and they've got, like, extra … for pushing themselves along. That's what it seems like they do. They, see, look. They go like this, then they spread.

**Refer to Example 7.14.**

◆ How does the teacher approach the interview?

◆ How do the teacher's questions flow out of the conversation?

◆ How does the student react to the teacher's approach?

◆ What kinds of information do you get about Elliot's thinking and understandings?

◆ What types of activities might help further Elliot's inquiry and understandings about earthworms?

◆ What additional questions could have been asked based on what Elliot said?

✳

Refer to Example 7.15.

✦ How does the teacher's approach in this interview differ from the approach in Example 7.14?

✦ What kinds of information do you get about Gloria's thinking and understandings?

✦ What additional questions could have been asked based on what Gloria said?

## Example 7.15: An Interview Based on a Task

In this example, Gloria was being interviewed while trying to solve the problem in the diagram below. She was trying to figure out the density of the block shown floating halfway submerged in the water.

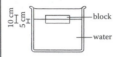

**Teacher: Okay. Here you've got this block floating in the container of water and it's halfway down in the water.**

*Gloria:* That's 10 cm.... It's a 10-cm. block.

**Teacher: It's 10 cm. down deep.**

*Gloria:* Yeah, 10 cm. And it's 5 cm. in the water, so the density is 0.5.

**Teacher: Okay, how did you come up … what was …?**

*Gloria:* Because it's halfway in the water … and if it was zero, then it would be completely floating on the water.

**Teacher: It wouldn't be in the water at all.**

*Gloria:* No, it would be on top of the water. So it has to be 0.5 to be halfway in the water.

1. Developing effective probing questions
2. Talking to students in ways that help them feel comfortable and willing to talk
3. Sensitivity to children's experience and their particular situation
4. Listening carefully to what they are saying without overlaying our expectations and preconceptions

Developing questions requires that we have some understanding of the particular conceptual content of the unit we are teaching, as well as more general understandings of the types of questions important to science. In Example 7.14, the teacher had certain questions in mind prior to the interview. In this particular excerpt, the teacher was interested in the student's understandings of how the earthworm is adapted for movement and for sensing its environment. Although the teacher did not expect students to have a great deal of knowledge about earthworms at the beginning of the inquiry, he wanted to find out how students approached constructing explanations about earthworm movement and senses. These questions, as well as others the teacher wanted to explore, arose out of the natural flow of the conversation.

The second and third skills require that we pay attention to children's body language and expressions. We also need to be aware of their personal situations and backgrounds. We may find that a certain student is having a bad day, for one reason or another. Pursuing an interview with such a child may not be fruitful. In addition, when talking with children, we may want to continue asking probing questions, but we get a sense that if we ask more questions, the students will stop responding and withdraw. Reaching such a point is counterproductive to the kind of classroom atmosphere we want to create. When we reach such a point, we need to back off from our own agenda. At the same time, we need to probe into their ideas. There is a fine line between probing too far and not far enough. With practice, our ability to sense the limits of children's patience and willingness to respond will develop.

As may be evident, interviewing is an instructional process as well. Interviews should become a natural part of classroom activity. Individuals or groups can be interviewed informally as they work. Although the atmosphere of interviews should be informal, more obvious interviews can be conducted during or after units of instruction. As other students proceed with tasks, you can have a child or a group come to a different location to talk about their work. In both cases, the intent should be to uncover information about children's thinking and understanding, as well as to help children develop their thinking skills and further their understandings. We should not be creating a situation in interviews where the children feel that they are under pressure and being judged.

## 7.5   Observations and Performance Assessment

Throughout every school day, we should be observing children's actions, talk, and work. What they do and say are important for developing more complete pictures of the characteristics and learning of our students. Observations of the day-to-day actions of our students allow us to extend our understandings beyond the specific information we gather about their learning and thinking. Some examples of the kinds of information we can get through daily observations include

- Are the students genuinely interested in the topic?
- Are they self-motivated?
- Do they show concern for others?
- Are they able to work with other children?
- Are they able to organize their work and time?
- Do they demonstrate leadership abilities?
- Are they attentive to what others (i.e., teacher and fellow students) are saying?
- Are they curious about the topics being investigated?
- Do they have positive self-images?
- What natural abilities do they show in class?
- Do they take on responsibilities?
- How do they approach problem solving and conducting inquiries?

- ✦ How do you think you can answer these questions? (What kinds of things do you need to notice?)
- ✦ What other questions can you add to this list?

In addition to the more general characteristics of children, we can use observations to assess specific aspects of children's thinking and understanding. Recently, performance assessment has become a popular tool for evaluating children's understanding of science concepts and skills. Such an approach to assessment requires that students perform certain tasks that ask them to apply their understandings. Rather than assess the static nature of a child's understanding through a test or other paper-and-pencil task, performance assessment allows teachers to observe how children use their knowledge during specific tasks. For instance, if the class has just completed a unit on velocity, the teacher may ask students to determine the velocity of a battery-operated toy car as it travels across the floor. By observing how the children approach the task and formulate an answer, the teacher can see whether the children have understood the concept and where their understandings may need more development. The situation is similar to that shown in the interview about determining the density of the half-submerged block of wood (Example 7.15). In this example, the student was asked to apply her knowledge to a problem she had not seen before. In order to formulate an answer, she needed to have an understanding of the concept. If she had memorized the formula for density, but did not understand the concept, she would have had difficulty solving this problem. In performance assessment, we need to have specific ideas of what we want to assess.

### 7.5.1  Portfolios

There are two basic types of portfolios:

1. A **personal development portfolio** is a collection of an assortment of student work.
2. A **knowledge claim portfolio** is a more focused collection of evidence that students put together in order to support a particular knowledge claim.

The first type tends to focus on individual students. The second can focus on individuals or groups. However, both types are based on similar ideas and goals:

- Children should control what goes into their portfolios. Children need to develop skills of making decisions about what constitutes good evidence for a claim. They need to be in control of what their portfolio looks like and what it contains.
- Both types of portfolios develop skills of communicating clearly and effectively.
- Organization and presentation skills are developed.
- Both types demonstrate skills of developing coherent and cohesive arguments.
- Both types have the goal of supporting a particular claim:
  - In personal development portfolios, the claim may be to provide evidence of an individual's learning and achievement. The child may need to ask himself or herself, "What do I want to include that will show what I know and understand?"

---

*Sidebar:*

- ✦ **Think of a topic, such as electricity (e.g., designing parallel and series circuits) or mirrors and reflection (e.g., designing a simple periscope that demonstrates how the angle of incidence equals the angle of reflection), and devise a simple performance assessment.**
- ✦ **What do you expect to see?**
- ✦ **If you have an opportunity, try your performance assessment with a child or group of children.**

- The knowledge claim portfolio contains information that supports a particular conceptual claim. Here students need to think about what kind of information is most convincing for the argument they are trying to make.

---

**Example 7.16: Examples of Knowledge Claim Portfolios**

1. Two different groups can develop portfolios to support opposite points of view:
   a. Develop a portfolio of supporting evidence that the earth is flat.
   b. Develop a portfolio of supporting evidence that the earth is spherical.
2. Each group is asked to design a proposal for a new aircraft design. The task is to develop a working prototype model that will demonstrate the aircraft's ability to meet the criteria desired by a particular company or government agency. Each consulting firm (i.e., group of students) needs to design a plane that will carry heavy loads the greatest distance. The submitted portfolio should provide scientific explanations and experimental evidence to support why that group's design is best suited for the task. The prototype, which can be made of cardboard, balsa wood, or aluminum foil, should demonstrate some of the basic principles of the criteria.

---

Knowledge claim portfolios provide the context for instruction. With students working in groups (which may be simulated consulting firms), a unit can begin with the distribution of letters to each group requesting the submission of bids for a particular product. The example letter that follows was used by a teacher in initiating and framing a unit on floating. The students' work (including inquiry activities, experiments, and design issues) on their proposal for a boat design became the basis for their portfolio.

Although this letter was geared to students in grades 5 to 7, similar letters can be constructed to address the abilities of particular students and specific topics. With a little creativity, portfolio-based units can be designed for just about any topic. Once the topic and letter are introduced, the teacher and students can negotiate a plan of action. In order to successfully complete such a portfolio, the students will need to acquire certain knowledge. You may find that allowing students to work on prototypes at the beginning will stimulate a lot of interest, and hopefully will allow them to discover that they need certain information and knowledge they do not have. Once the need for further knowledge is determined, you can introduce inquiry activities focusing on the concepts they will need to understand. The bulk of these activities should be designed before implementing the unit.

Once these inquiry activities have been completed, the students can proceed with their own experiments and product design. At the end, you can

**Example 7.17: Request for Boat Design**

**Economic Development**
**Nova Scotia Tourism and Culture**
**Provincial House, Halifax, Nova Scotia B0B 0N0**
**Mrs. Dee Tours, Minister of Tourism and Culture**

## Request for Design Plans

Dear Applicant:

Nova Scotia Tourism and Culture is requesting submissions of boat design portfolios for a tourism development project. We are asking for detailed submissions for a boat that will be used for transporting tourists to a variety of sites known for their unique natural history in Nova Scotia. Among the sites we wish to access are Sable Island, Saint Margaret's Bay, Cape Breton, the coves and inlets of the Eastern Shore, and the Bay of Fundy.

In order to assist you in the development of your submission, I will outline some of the basic requirements for the vessel we wish to use. In addition, I will also provide you with a description of what your submission portfolio should contain.

## Vessel Specifications

1. We want a vessel that is capable of carrying the largest number of passengers safely to all of the sites. As a result, the vessel will need to accommodate a reasonably heavy load. The boat should be no longer than 25 meters.
2. Since the waters off Nova Scotia, especially around Sable Island, can get very rough, we need a vessel that is very stable.
3. We need a vessel that is efficient. In other words, we need a vessel that will travel quickly with the least amount of fuel usage.

## Submission Portfolio Requirements

1. **A drawing of the vessel hull**
   - This drawing should be neat and should show the length, width, and height of the hull. Each of these dimensions should be labeled clearly. Be sure to include and label any special design features that relate to stability and efficiency. You can include a design of the deck, cabin, and other details of the hull design as well.
2. **A scale model of the vessel**
   - The model can be made of aluminum foil. Pipe cleaners can be used to provide additional support for the hull. The model should match the drawing as closely as possible. You should be able to demonstrate the carrying capacity (ability to carry a

heavy load), stability, and the vessel's ability to move quickly through the water. This scale model should be no longer than 25 centimeters.

3. **Drawings of the vessel hull in the water, with and without a load**

   - Both of these drawings should appear on the same sheet of paper and show the water line. In addition, each drawing should show, in scientific terms and using arrows, all of the forces acting to keep the vessel afloat. Be sure to label all arrows.

4. **Experimental results**

   - Include the results of the experiments and investigations you performed (such as number of grams of weight it took to sink your vessel hull, stability experiments, etc.). Be sure to include in your portfolio any tables, graphs, design sketches, or other material you think will demonstrate that you have carefully considered the problem.

5. **Summary and recommendations**

   - Recommended number of passengers, with supporting evidence for your claim
   - Recommended maximum seas (size of waves), with supporting evidence for your claim
   - Ease of motion through water, with supporting evidence for your claim
   - A detailed explanation of why your boat design floats as well as it does, with supporting evidence
   - Any other information that you feel will help support your design plan submission

As you can see, we are interested in both the *science* and *technology* of your boat design. The technological aspect involves the construction of the vessel. The science aspect involves the explanations for how your boat floats, maintains stability, and moves efficiently through the water. Since this boat will be used as a science exploration vessel for tourists, we want to use your explanations of the science of how your boat works in an onboard display for the tourists to read. Best of luck!

Sincerely,

Dee Tours, Minister of Tourism and Culture

put together a government or corporate committee to listen to the oral (and visual) presentation of each group. This committee could consist of parents, students from other classes, or professionals from the field in which the unit is based. The final presentations serve as opportunities for the students to communicate their results in a realistic setting. In addition, if parents are involved, they will have a chance to see what their children have learned and how they present themselves. The students also should evaluate each other's work.

Individual portfolios also can be introduced to address integrated interests and topics. During the same unit as the previous example, students were given another letter asking for artistic or literary portfolio submissions around the topic of floating. Such alternative and individual portfolios allow students to explore their own interests. In addition, such portfolio projects provide for the representation of understandings from different disciplinary angles. In this example, floating could be represented through music, dance/movement, poetry, painting or drawing, story, humor, and so forth. A certain amount of time in class can be set aside for your students to work on this portfolio project, with some intention that they will work on this project at home as well.

The introduction of knowledge claim portfolios and the related integrated product portfolios sets up a certain kind of authentic and realistic professional culture in the classroom. Instruction, classroom activities, communication, and assessment are all bound together by the portfolio framework. The children see a goal to work toward. The goal, in turn, provides students with a need to know certain information. The inquiry and other research activities become relevant to the task they have before them. And students tend to see such portfolio units as stimulating and fun.

## 7.6   What to Look for and Keeping Track

Although this chapter has described some of the necessary background for assessment and a number of tools for assessing our students, we need to examine one more fundamental question. That question has to do with what may be the most significant outcome of education, or the real bottom line. If children go through school, should they not graduate with the ability to use what they have learned in a variety of circumstances? The technical term for this ability is the ability to *transfer* what they have learned. In other words, children (or any of us, for that matter) should be able to learn something in the classroom, then use that knowledge in situations that range from solving a similar problem or completing a similar task to thinking critically or creatively in a completely different situation. Unfortunately, the evidence shows that formal attempts to teach for transfer (both in schools and in business training situations) are not successful, especially at higher levels of transfer (see Figure 7.4). When examining these levels, it is evident that complex learning that spans disciplines, as has been discussed throughout this book, is essential to transfer.

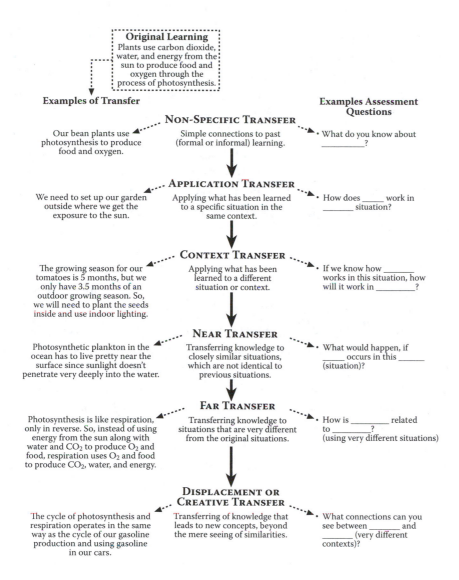

**Original Learning**
Plants use carbon dioxide, water, and energy from the sun to produce food and oxygen through the process of photosynthesis.

**Examples of Transfer**

**Examples Assessment Questions**

**NON-SPECIFIC TRANSFER**
Simple connections to past (formal or informal) learning.

Our bean plants use photosynthesis to produce food and oxygen.

• What do you know about _____?

**APPLICATION TRANSFER**
Applying what has been learned to a specific situation in the same context.

We need to set up our garden outside where we get the exposure to the sun.

• How does _____ work in _____ situation?

**CONTEXT TRANSFER**
Applying what has been learned to a different situation or context.

The growing season for our tomatoes is 5 months, but we only have 3.5 months of an outdoor growing season. So, we will need to plant the seeds inside and use indoor lighting.

• If we know how _____ works in this situation, how will it work in _____?

**NEAR TRANSFER**
Transferring knowledge to closely similar situations, which are not identical to previous situations.

Photosynthetic plankton in the ocean has to live pretty near the surface since sunlight doesn't penetrate very deeply into the water.

• What would happen, if _____ occurs in this _____ (situation)?

**FAR TRANSFER**
Transferring knowledge to situations that are very different from the original situations.

Photosynthesis is like respiration, only in reverse. So, instead of using energy from the sun along with water and $CO_2$ to produce $O_2$ and food, respiration uses $O_2$ and food to produce $CO_2$, water, and energy.

• How is _____ related to _____? (using very different situations)

**DISPLACEMENT OR CREATIVE TRANSFER**
Transferring of knowledge that leads to new concepts, beyond the mere seeing of similarities.

The cycle of photosynthesis and respiration operates in the same way as the cycle of our gasoline production and using gasoline in our cars.

• What connections can you see between _____ and _____ (very different contexts)?

**FIGURE 7.4**

So, the implications of complex and transferable learning for assessment include rethinking what we assess, how we assess, and how we try to make sense of what children say and do. If we look at the examples of children's ideas throughout this chapter, as well as Chapters 4 and 5, we see a lot of evidence of higher levels of transfer. They draw on ideas from a variety of contexts and make connections across diverse perspectives. So, why is the evidence for transfer so lacking? Part of the problem lies in the disconnected and fragmented nature of how teaching is done. The transfer we see in the examples in this book are from childen's personal meaning making, or from what they find meaningful and relevant. Therefore, in terms of teaching and assessment, we need to pay close attention to complex contexts that are meaningful and relevant to our students.

Take a minute to re-examine Example 7.2, the floating context map. Although the intent of the unit was to examine floating and its associated concepts of density, pressure, and buoyancy, this girl demonstrated a richly

✔

**Refer to Example 7.18**
Look back at some of the examples of children's work and talk throughout Chapters 4, 5, and 7. Use this grid to assess the children's ideas. Keep in mind that many of the items in the rubric are not applicable to these examples, so work with the ones that are most applicable (particularly in the first section of the rubric).

✦ How did this grid or rubric help you focus on key points?

✦ Did you come across information from the children's work that is not included in the rubric, but which you could add to your own rubric?

✦ Did using this rubric help you to see things in the examples that you did not see the first time you looked at these examples?

✔

✦ Based on the rubric in Example 7.18, can you identify additional items, which you view as important in terms of children's growth, development, and learning in school?

You may want to focus on the following areas:

✦ Classroom discourse and other communication skills

✦ Social or interpersonal skills in a classroom community

✦ Problem-solving skills

interconnected view of *floating*. The highly technical terms and numerous connections within the cluster of ideas around riding horses show a depth of understanding (i.e., the use of technical terms) that is connected across clusters or contexts. What is particularly interesting is that this context map shows very little evidence of the actual science content explored during the unit. So, in spite of the teacher's efforts, this girl developed a complex, interconnected map of what was meaningful to her. If we were to truly take advantage of what is meaningful to students, we could have students explore how the science behind the floating of boats is similar to and different from horseback riding, ghosts, odors (smells), flying, rockets and weightlessness in space, and so forth.

The tasks of focusing on how to assess or analyze children's thinking, talk, work, and products, and then of keeping track of this information, can be quite daunting. However, if we take the time to think about what specific types of skills, knowledge, and abilities we want to assess, we can develop rubrics that can help us focus on what we consider to be important and to keep ourselves organized. At the same time, these rubrics can save us a lot of time by simplifying the process of recording our assessments. Example 7.18 is an example of a partial assessment rubric that focuses on the complexity of learning, the transferability of learning, and inquiry. In addition to identifying fairly specific criteria about the nature of children's learning, the rubric provides two types of assessment: (a) three levels on the accuracy or quality of each item and (b) four levels on how evident each item is in the work of the student. Such a rubric can be used to assess student work over a specific period of time. By developing a few codes for specific topics, subject areas, assignment or activities, and so forth, you can keep track of a student's work over a particular period of time. For example, you can use numbers to correspond to specific activities and assignments, then abbreviations for subject areas (e.g., S = science, M = math, SS = social studies, A = art, etc.). You may want to use a different rubric every week or every month. Over the span of a few months, you can see areas where there has been a lot of growth or areas that seem to be deficient.

In addition to using the grid to record your assessment data, you may want to take additional notes on the back of the sheet or on an additional sheet. You also should have a folder for keeping samples of each child's work. Although you can decide what should be included in this folder, you may find it beneficial to allow children to decide what should be included in the folder as well. Allowing children to decide what goes in their folder allows them (a) to develop further responsibility for their learning and work at school, (b) to take more control over their lives at school, and (c) to develop self-evaluative skills. However, at the beginning of the year, you may want to negotiate with them as you help them develop these skills. Over time, most of the decision-making power can be handed over to your students. You may want to use the same approach with the rubrics you create. Develop a rubric using simpler language and with fewer items, then have your students assess their own and

**Example 7.18: Sample Assessment Grid for Complex Learning, Transfer, and Inquiry**

| | Accuracy or Quality | | | Evidence of | | | |
|---|---|---|---|---|---|---|---|
| | 0 | 1 | 2 | 0 | 1 | 2 | 3 |

*Complexity*

1. **Depth**—Detailed understandings, use of technical terms, etc.
2. **Breadth**—Covers or includes a lot of material, identifies fundamental patterns, relationships, etc.
3. **Interconnections I**—A lot of connections within a conceptual area
4. **Interconnections II**—A lot of connections across conceptual areas within a subject
5. **Interconnections III**—A lot of connections across subject areas and other contexts

*Transfer*

6. **Nonspecific**—Simple connections to past experiences
7. **Application**—Applies learning to specific task or situation in the same context (conceptual area)
8. **Context**—Applies learning to different situations or contexts (conceptual area, setting, etc.)
9. **Near**—Applies learning to similar but not identical situations or contexts (subject matter areas)
10. **Far**—Applies learning to very different situations or contexts (subject matter areas)
11. **Displacement/creative**—Applies learning in ways that lead to new concepts, insights, processes, etc.

*Inquiry*

12. **Curiosity**—General inquisitiveness
13. **Questioning** —Generates researchable questions
14. **Planning I**—Designs procedures for experiments or observational studies
15. **Planning II**—Identifies variables or influencing factors
16. **Planning III**—Identifies potential problems, issues, results, etc.
17. **Planning IV**—Organizes and develops a data-recording system (chart, etc.)
18. **Investigating I**—Uses appropriate tools, equipment, etc.
19. **Investigating II**—Collects data (measurements, observations, etc.)
20. **Investigating III**—Records data clearly, accurately; makes procedural/contextual observations
21. **Analyzing**—Analyzes data with appropriate graphs, charts, diagrams, simple statistics, etc.
22. **Interpreting**—Interprets data in ways that fit evidence from data and that make sense
23. **Analyzing/adjusting procedures** —Analyzes procedures, makes changes, re-collects data, etc.
24. **Formulating explanations I**—Develops multiple possible explanations
25. **Formulating explanations II**—Develops clear explanations that are consistent with data (evidence)
26. **Formulating explanations III**—Selects best explanation based on evidence, etc.
27. **Formulating explanations IV**—Develops models to help explain results
28. **Communicating results**—Uses visual aids, clarity, organization, etc.
29. **Argument and negotiation**—Engages in discussions of knowledge claims in productive ways

*Note:* Accuracy or quality: 0 = not accurate/poor quality; 1= partly accurate/reasonable quality; 2 = completely accurate/high quality.
*Evidence of:* 0 = not evident; 1 = rarely evident; 2 = occasionally evident; 3 = highly evident.

others' work prior to turning it in to you. Although this approach can be rather cumbersome for students to do for every assignment, you may want to have them use the rubric for big group or individual projects.

At this point, you may be asking, "But what about my state or provincial curriculum standards?" The previous approaches look at the nature of children's conceptual learning and other skills. In the United States, many of these more general criteria fit within the National Science Education Standards, but they generally do not appear in state or provincial (in Canada) curricular documents. So, how do we make sure we assess children's specific learning of required content? Before answering this question, we must deal with some issues involved in the potential tensions between an approach to learning that emphasizes complex learning and learning through inquiry, problem solving, and projects and an approach that focuses on teaching to the particular curriculum standards from the state or province in which you are teaching. Teaching through inquiry and placing a high value on complex learning involves two potential conflicts or tensions with government-enacted curricula: (a) it may take more time to cover material using an inquiry approach, and (b) allowing children to engage in inquiry may take you (and them) to areas of investigation that were not necessarily expected. At the same time, it is critically important that children learn in meaningful, relevant, and complex ways, if we expect them to flourish as adults in an increasingly complex world. So, back to the question of how do we address the required curriculum content. We do need to keep in mind that most places view the required curriculum as a guideline, not as a limiting factor (which it tends to become). In other words, we, as teachers, should not view the required curriculum as something that necessarily needs to be followed as a step-by-step framework. Instead, you can keep track of what you have accomplished throughout most of the year using a rubric, such as in Example 7.19. As you near the end of the year, you can assess your progress and, if necessary, spend the rest of the year addressing what was missed.

##  Additional Issues of Assessment as Driven by Curricular Documents and National Standards

With the current trend to reform science teaching at all levels of education, teachers may be faced with addressing benchmarks and other indicators in their instructional planning (see Appendixes B and C for a summary of U.S. and Canadian standards) and evaluation of students. Although this new wave of science education reform is welcomed by many parents, teachers, administrators, teacher educators, and politicians, the implementation of these reform efforts does involve some controversy. The *National Science Education Standards* from the National Research Council in the United States, the *Benchmarks for Science Literacy* from the American Association for the Advancement of Science, and the *Common Framework of Sci-*

| Example 7.19: Sample Assessment Grid for Required Curriculum or Standards | | | | | | | | | | | | | | |
|---|---|---|---|---|---|---|---|---|---|---|---|---|---|---|
| **Curriculum Standards** | | **Students** | | | | | | | | | | | | |
| | | Abby | Bobby | Carl | Chloe | Elliot | Greg | Jimmy | John | Kathy | Latoia | Melanie | Sarah | Valerie |
| 4 life[a] | Food chain as system of energy transfer | | | | | | | | | | | | | |
| 4 life[a] | ID omnivore, carnivore,etc. | | | | | | | | | | | | | |
| 4 life[a] | Structural adaptations | | | | | | | | | | | | | |
| 4.1.PO2[b] | Classify animals by group characteristics | | | | | | | | | | | | | |
| 4.3.PO1[b] | Describe ways various resources are used to meet needs of a population | | | | | | | | | | | | | |
| | | | | | | | | | | | | | | |
| | | | | | | | | | | | | | | |
| | | | | | | | | | | | | | | |
| | | | | | | | | | | | | | | |

*Note:* Use a coding system to indicate degree of competency (e.g., 0 = not met; 1 = minimal; 2 = basic; 3 = exceeds; 4 = vastly exceeds).

[a] Taken from the Ontario curriculum for grade 4.

[b] Taken from the Arizona state standards for grade 4.

*ence Learning Outcomes K–12* in Canada are all based on current research and theory in learning and teaching. Many of the ideas contained in these documents represent a significant advance in our thinking about teaching and learning science. However, as with any global attempt to reform education, there are problems that need to be considered. The problems are not so much with the national standards themselves, but with how these standards may drive assessment and, likewise, the way instruction and curricula are implemented. After reading each item in the following list of problems and controversies, you should take a few minutes to consider your position on the issues.

- The implementation of national or local standards often is accompanied by the introduction of standardized achievement tests. Much research has shown that standardized testing is not a good measure of student *learning or understanding*. Achievement tests may measure a certain piece of the puzzle of student learning, but do not provide a complete picture of what students know.
  - From what has been discussed so far in this chapter and the book, what ways of assessing children can you use to formulate a better picture of your students' understandings?
  - How might you use your own assessment procedures to allow your students to enter into standardized tests with greater confidence in their understandings?
- Standardized tests do not address the full extent of what we might consider to be our instructional goals. Such tests do not address issues of engaging children in theorizing, in critically assessing knowledge claims, in inquiry, and so forth.

- In communicating with your students' parents, how can you provide a balanced report on their progress and learning?
- We also need to consider what makes certain content more important than others. What do we really want students to come away with from our classes? What understandings are going to be beneficial to the vast majority of students who will not enter science as a career?
  - How would you answer these questions?
- Standardized tests emphasize the importance of specific conceptual and factual content. Given the extensive amount of research showing children's difficulty in developing accurate understandings about numerous scientific concepts, standardized tests may force teachers to "teach for tests" and force students to memorize the correct answers.
  - How do you feel about this conflict between teaching for understanding versus teaching for tests? (This question may point to the central issue.)
  - How might you use your own assessment procedures to prepare students for greater understanding, which address the content on the tests, without resorting to rote memorization?
- Standardized tests tend to discriminate against certain types of students: (a) those whose first language does not match the language of the test, (b) those whose cultural and belief backgrounds suggest different explanations for phenomena, (c) those whose learning disabilities may interfere with taking any kind of test, (d) those whose personalities and emotional makeup do not react well to the stress of testing, and (e) those whose family situations (places not conducive to study, insufficient food, poor sleeping arrangements, etc.) may provide huge obstacles to performing well in school or on tests.
  - How do you feel about these problems with testing?
- The generally unacknowledged side effect of standardized testing is the incredible amount of stress and anxiety that is placed on our students, which, in a way, is a form of psychological violence. Students who otherwise are beginning to enjoy school and are making significant gains in psychosocial and other areas of learning suddenly backslide as the time for standardized testing approaches.[2]
  - How do you feel about the effects testing has on children?
  - What can you do to counterbalance this effect?
- National and local standards frequently emphasize minimal knowledge and understandings—the least common denominator. In classroom situations, you may find that the children move into areas beyond the standards or into areas not included in the standards. On the other hand, standards tend to drive the curriculum and limit what teachers do in the classroom.

- How do you feel about the tendency for standardized tests to drive the curriculum?
- How can you develop your own curriculum in ways that address your concerns, while still addressing the concerns of national and local standards?

The current national standards tend not to delineate specific details of concepts to be learned. If we view these standards as guides to general concepts, we may find that what we ordinarily do in class will address these standards. For instance, in the National Science Education Standards (in the United States), Content Standard C under Life Science (p. 127) states, "As a result of activities in grades K-4, all students should develop understandings of the characteristics of organisms, life cycles of organisms, organisms, and environments." One item under "the characteristics of organisms" states

Organisms have basic needs. For example, animals need air, water, and food; plants require air, water, nutrients, and light. Organisms can survive only in environments in which their needs can be met. The world has many different environments, and distinct environments support the life of different types of organisms. (p. 129)

Hopefully, classroom instruction will delve much more deeply into these conceptual areas and provide a more relevant and interesting context for their exploration. However, with this standard as a guide, teachers and students can investigate numerous topics that address these and other concepts. In terms of assessment, teachers can use multiple approaches to investigate children's broader, as well as in-depth, understandings of these topics and concepts. In addition, if students are engaged in constructing more extensive and cohesive understandings, their understandings should translate into greater success on required standardized tests. However, students should be taught how to take such tests, such as answering the easiest questions in each section first, then answering those that are slightly more difficult, and so on. They also need to be aware of the time, so that they are over halfway through the test when they reach the halfway point of time available.

Another point to keep in mind, when working with local and national standards, is the incompleteness and decontextualized nature of the specific content standards. In the previous example, some biologists would include reproduction as a basic necessity of life. This particular need is not one of the individual organisms, but one of the species. From a perspective of what kinds of concepts are important, in terms of more unifying conceptions, the notion of the requirements for the survival of species is of greater significance than those for the survival of individual organisms.

Some additional points to keep in mind include

- Authorities in assessment and evaluation generally agree that student performance on high-stakes tests can be raised by teaching to the test, but that teaching to the test has little affect on student learning and understanding.

- Teaching to the test tends to be boring, irrelevant, and meaningless for both teachers and students. Developing positive attitudes toward learning and supporting curiosity as the basic attitudes for lifelong learning are undermined by such approaches to teaching.

- Teaching to the test ignores the needs, concerns, interests, and questions of children, as well as the needs and concerns of the community and any of the cultures represented in specific classrooms and schools.

- Issues of accountability:

  - Many of the problems with children's learning and achievement (these may be very different things) go beyond what any teacher or school can control. Larger social conditions and factors may have an effect on children's performance, such as English language ability, cultural beliefs and concerns, socioeconomic factors in the local community, family dynamics in the community (e.g., single-parent families, two parents working multiple jobs, drug and alcohol abuse, family violence, etc.), and so forth. At the same time, teachers are expected to raise test scores for all children. Teachers are also implicitly expected to play the role of parents, psychologists, and social workers.

  - Accountability is typically based upon student test scores and, to some extent, on teacher evaluations, which are done by principals or other school district personnel. Evaluations may be based on theoretical frameworks that conflict with the theoretical frameworks guiding a particular teacher's work. In such a case, the teacher can receive a very low evaluation, even though he or she has created a dynamic and effective learning community in the classroom.

  - The hierarchical pressures of accountability can put pressure on teachers to conform to specific teaching approaches and strategies. In some cases, school district administrators and principals communicate contradictory messages. For example, in one school district, the superintendent told teachers that he wanted them to engage children in inquiry. At another time, he demanded that they raise test scores, so that "all students will achieve above average" (what is wrong with this statement?), and that teachers need to spend most of their time teaching language and mathematics in elementary schools. As a result, the vast majority of teachers felt that it was too risky to teach science through inquiry or to teach science at all.

- Although professionals, including teachers, need to be accountable (or responsible), the way in which accountability measures are taken is of great concern for educators. Although we may not be able to control the accountability measures taken, we can take action.

- Communicate with parents about these issues. Parents have much more political clout. In one community, on Long Island, New York, the parents refused to send their children to school on the high-stakes testing days—policies and practices changed.

- Do thorough assessments, using multiple methods, of your students' learning and skill development. Keep examples and other evidence of this learning.

- Keep track of what conceptual content and skill development was addressed in your classroom, what the children learned, and how these two areas correspond to school district and state or provincial standards or curriculum mandates.

■ Schools and teachers who have focused on teaching for understanding have generally had large increases in test scores. However, most teachers and school administrators tend not to be willing to take the risk to focus on less but more in-depth content coverage.

■ In addition, the pressure on teachers to raise test scores tends to be more intense at the elementary school level. Elementary school teachers need to have expertise in all subject matter areas, while teachers at higher grade levels only need expertise in one subject matter area. In addition, high-stakes tests tend to focus on mathematics and language abilities, which sets up a competition for time between these subject matter areas and those of science, art, social studies, and physical education.

## 7.8 A Final Activity

Try using a variety of approaches to assessment with a group of children. Focus your efforts on one particular topic, which can be a topic they have already studied or one they have not studied. If you are a teacher, you can try using these approaches with your class. If you are an education student, you can work with a small group of children. After completing a variety of assessment tasks, think about the questions in the sidebar.

✦ **What information about children's understandings did each approach to assessment provide?**

✦ **Did the different approaches overlap in providing you with a consistent view of the children's understandings?**

## Additional Reading

Atkin, J. M, Coffey, J. E., Moorthy, S., Sato, M., & Thibeault, M. (2005). *Designing everyday assessment in the science classroom.* New York: Teachers College Press.

Enger, S. K., & Yager, R. E. (2000). *Assessing student understanding in science: A standards-based K–12 handbook.* Thousand Oaks, CA: Corwin Press.

Falk, B., & Blumenreich, M. (2005). *The power of questions: A guide to teacher and student research.* Portsmouth, NH: Heinemann.

Fulton, L., & Campbell, B. (2003). *Science notebooks: Writing about inquiry.* Portsmouth, NH: Heinemann.

Harlin, R., Shea, M., & Murray, R. (2005). *Drowning in data? How to collect, organize, and document student performance.* Portsmouth, NH: Heinemann.

Hassard, J. (1999). *Science as inquiry: Active learning, project-based, web-assisted, and active assessment strategies to enhance student learning.* Tucson, AZ: Good Year Books.

Hein, G. E., & Price, S. (1994). *Active assessment for active science: A guide for elementary school teachers.* Portsmouth, NH: Heinemann.

Jones, M. G., Jones, B. D., & Hargrove, T. Y. (2003). *The unintended consequences of high-stakes testing.* Lanham, MD: Rowman & Littlefield Publishers.

Kohn, A. (2000). *The case against standardized testing.* Portsmouth, NH: Heinemann.

Kuhs, T. M., Agurso, S., Johnson, R., & Monrad, D. (2001). *Put to the test: Tools and techniques for classroom assessment.* Portsmouth, NH: Heinemann.

Lipman, P. (2003). *High stakes education: Inequality, globalization, and urban school reform.* New York: Routlege.

Meier, D., & Wood, G. (2004). *Many children left behind: How the No Child Left Behind Act is damaging our children and our schools.* Boston: Beacon Press.

Perrone, V. (Ed.). (1991). *Expanding student assessment.* Alexandria, VA: Association for Supervision and Curriculum Development.

> Accessible treatment of a variety of issues and approaches to assessment across the disciplines.

Sacks, P. (2001). *Standardized minds: The high price of America's testing culture and what we can do to change it.* New York: Perseus Books.

Sirotnik, K. A. (Ed.). (2004). *Holding accountability accountable: What ought to matter in public education.* New York: Teachers College Press.

Swope, K., & Miner, B. (Eds.). (2000). *Failing our kids: Why the testing craze won't fix our schools.* Milwaukee, WI: Rethinking Schools, Ltd. (Also see other titles from this publisher.)

Young, S. F., & Wilson, R. J. (2000). *Assessment and learning: The ICE approach.* Winnipeg, Manitoba, Canada: Portage and Main Press.

## Advanced Reading

Darling-Hammond, L., Ancess, J., & Falk, B. (1995). *Authentic assessment in action: Studies of schools and students at work.* New York: Teachers College Press.

> Examines authentic assessment practices in five different schools.

Fuhrman, S. H. (2004). *Redesigning accountability systems for education.* New York: Teachers College Press.

Gardner, J. (2005). *Assessment and learning.* Thousand Oaks, CA: Sage Publications.

Johnson, R. S., Mims-Cox, J. S., & Doyle-Nichols, A. (2006). *Developing portfolios in education.* Thousand Oaks, CA: Sage Publications.

Mintrop, H. (2003). *Schools on probation: How accountability works (and doesn't work).* New York: Teachers College Press.

Mintzes, J. J., Wandersee, J. H., & Novak, J. D. (Eds.). (2000). *Assessing science understanding: A human constructivist view.* San Diego: Academic Press. [Cited here: Novak, J. D., Mintzes, J. J., & Wandersee, J. H. *Learning, teaching, and assessment: A human constructivist perspective.*]

Perrone, V. (1989). *Working papers: Reflection on teachers, schools, and communities.* New York: Teachers College Press.

> Thought-provoking book on a number of issues related to education. Chapters 11 and 12 present some interesting insights about testing.

Roth, W.-M., & Calabrese Barton, A. (2004). *Rethinking scientific literacy.* New York: Routledge-Falmer.

Vygotsky, L. (1962). *Thought and language.* Cambridge, MA: MIT Press.

White, R., & Gunstone, R. (1992). *Probing understanding.* New York: Falmer Press.

> Provides a detailed description of how to use a variety of techniques to access children's understandings.

## Notes

1. The last eight questions in this list are based on criteria for scientific explanations from Project SEPIA—Richard Duschl, Vanderbilt University, and Drew Gitomer, Educational Testing Service.
2. See Chapter 1 by Kathe Jervis in Vito Perrone's *Expanding Student Assessment* (Alexandria, VA: Association for Supervision and Curriculum Development, 1991) for an account of the effects of testing on a grade 3/4 classroom.

*Chapter 8*

# Planning and Implementing Instruction

This chapter provides an approach to instructional planning that is consistent with social constructivist and inquiry approaches that can foster meaningful, relevant, and complex learning. However, planning instruction can occur in many different ways. There is much room for creativity. As you plan instruction, you need to be sensitive to your own style of working and teaching, your knowledge of the students, and your own understandings of the topic. Therefore, you should feel free to adapt the approach suggested in this chapter to your own particular needs.

When designing instructional units, it is important to take into account a constructivist view of learning science (see previous chapters for more detailed information). Such a view of learning requires an approach with which you may not be familiar. In moving away from a teacher-directed approach to one that tries to engage children in authentic inquiry, you need to take a very different view of curriculum and instructional planning. In some ways, the task is more complicated and more involved than the more traditional approach, but you should find the planning process and the implementation of the unit personally rewarding. You also should find the whole process an adventure in personal learning and understanding. In addition, watching your students grow in a number of dimensions should be professionally satisfying.

The diagram in Figure 8.1 provides an overview of the planning process, which will be described in more detail in the following sections. Although there is a particular sequence that can be followed, the process of planning instruction does not necessarily occur in a linear fashion. As ideas arise, you need to record them and spend time elaborating on them. You also may find that as you progress in your planning, you will need to return to an earlier stage. Be flexible! For instance, you may be developing a unit on ecology. After outlining a number of activities, you discover that you do not understand a particular concept. At this point, you need to return to developing your understanding.

In Figure 8.1, there are two basic places to start the planning process: (a) at choosing a topic or theme or (b) at defining a possible real product or goal. In a way, these two are related, but the idea of starting with the goal product is particularly intriguing in that such a final product can provide a real focus

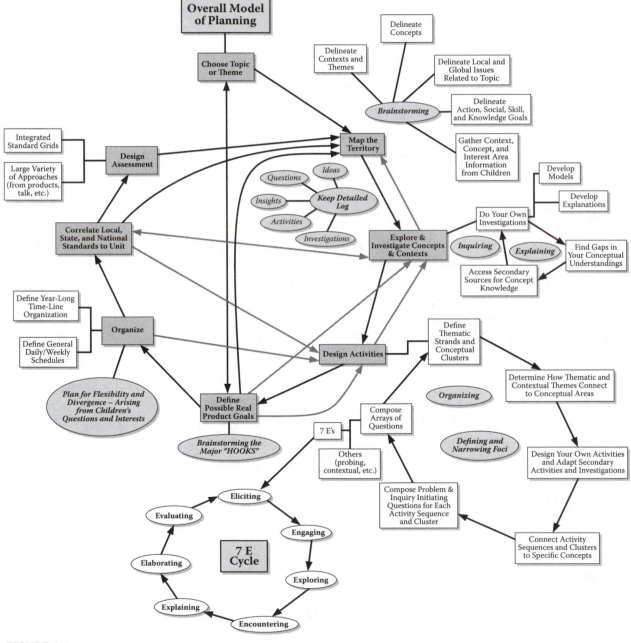

**FIGURE 8.1**

> **Example 8.1**
>
> A teacher may be working with the topic of gravity. She has a series of activities and questions prepared for the children to discuss. Partway through a discussion of the effects of gravity on earth and what it might be like if there were no gravity, a child asks, "What if we were able to build a room at the very center of the earth? What would it be like?" In an instance where such a question was asked, the teacher acknowledged the question as a good question, but continued with the original line of questioning. An opportunity was missed for engaging children in exploring a question of interest to them.

for everything else you do. For instance, you may want to delve into mechanics. An interesting focus may be the construction of model cars with a big race at the end of the unit. The race becomes the focus for how you conceive of the conceptual material, the timeline, potential inquiries and problem-solving activities, and so forth. The race also is the major hook for engaging students. The rest of the planning process as depicted in this figure is basically a set of particular types of activities that loop back and forth.

Throughout this process, you need to keep in mind that it is important for you to develop a thorough understanding of the concepts and activities. Without this understanding as a basis, you run the risk of creating a lifeless and static sequence of activities that will not engage your students in active inquiry. While you may have a sequence of activities planned, you must be prepared for unexpected questions and insights from the children. Without an adequate understanding on your part, you are likely to miss opportunities that take advantage of children's curiosity and help them explore important questions.

**Refer to Example 8.1.**

✦ **If this question were to arise in your own classroom, what are some possible ways to take advantage of this opportunity?**

## 8.1 Some Basic Guidelines and Principles to Consider

1. Remember that children come into the classroom with a variety of different experiences, knowledge, and personally constructed ideas and explanations for how things work.

2. Your planning should reflect the need to help children construct, reconstruct, and refine their ideas (see Chapter 4 for more detailed information).

3. Socially negotiating students' understandings and knowledge claims is probably the most powerful way of learning (see Chapter 5 for more information).

4. The way your curriculum and classroom manifest should accurately represent (as much as possible) the way science really happens and what science is about (see Chapters 3 and 6 for more details).

a. All knowledge is tentative and potentially changeable (do not be dogmatic)—what you need to communicate is how to deal with the knowledge that is currently accepted.

b. Science is about attempting to explain as clearly as possible the underlying mechanisms of phenomena.

c. Mistakes, experiments that do not work, equipment that does not work, and so forth, tend to be the rule rather than the exception. Such occurrences provide great opportunities for engaging students in analyzing what went wrong and how to improve project constructions and experimental designs.

d. Most scientists work collaboratively.

e. Scientists argue and negotiate their knowledge claims (in their labs, at conferences, and through their publications).

f. Scientists substantiate their knowledge claims with experimental or observational evidence, or with well-thought-out logical arguments.

5. Provide for flexibility. Changes in direction, new questions to explore, children's enthusiasm (or lack of it) for pursuing a particular question or topic, and so forth, need to be considered and addressed.

6. Children's conversations and writings are important. Push them to be clear and to substantiate their claims.

## 8.2  How and Where to Start

The following items may be followed sequentially, but you may find the process more fluid and flexible. Do not restrict yourself to working sequentially—when insight or inspiration arises, take advantage of it! As discussed previously, your actual starting point can be a combination of choosing a topic and defining a possible goal or final product. After this point, the rest of the process can proceed through the sequence, while looping back and forth to other steps in the sequence. Planning should not be a linear process.

1. **Map the territory—identify major theories, concepts, principles, facts, etc.** Initially, start by developing a brief map or outline of the topic, including relevant concepts, theories, contexts, patterns, and so forth (see Chapter 7). In the beginning, this map may be fairly sketchy and vague, but it is a starting place to capture your initial ideas. From this point, you need to go back and forth between the next step of exploring and investigating the concepts yourself and this first step of mapping the territory. As you develop some expertise in the topic, you should start identifying the major theories, concepts, principles, facts, and uncertainties. You may find it helpful to construct an outline or concept map to organize your own understandings. Be sure to keep track of any activities, experiments,

questions, and so forth, that relate to any of these concepts, principles, and uncertainties.

2. **Explore and investigate—develop your own understandings and expertise.** Before the actual planning, you need to make a commitment to becoming an expert in the particular topic you have chosen to study. First, you should gather all the materials you need to do the experiments and observations on the topic (you will probably need more materials as time goes on). Next, you should start exploring on your own. Try some experiments from books. Make up some of your own experiments. Keep a notebook handy so that you can record the important ideas that arise, such as

   a. **Questions** about how something works, what something is, and so forth
   b. Your own **explanations** and **ideas**
   c. Ideas for **new experiments or observations** you might try later
   d. Other **materials or equipment** you need
   e. **Observations** you have made
   f. **Instructional ideas**
   g. **Anything else** that might help you understand the material and design instruction

This initial exploration is important because it allows you to identify the boundaries of your knowledge (what you need to find out more about) and to gain an understanding of how your students might experience the activities. After you have played around with the materials and phenomena for a while, you should then start to consult content sources. Such sources can include

- Books designed for teachers.
- Books for children.
- Web sites.
- High school and university textbooks. (Do not let the technical terms throw you; see Chapter 10 for a discussion on how to deal with scientific content.)
- Videos from television (e.g., "Nova," "Best of National Geographic," "Smithsonian Treasures," "Nature," "New Explorers"). These and many other programs can provide good information on a variety of science topics. Be careful, however, of some science shows that misrepresent or sensationalize science (e.g., "In Search Of").
- Magazines and journals (e.g., *Discover, Canadian Geographic, Audubon, National Geographic, Natural History, Scientific American, National Wildlife*).
- Experts (amateur or professional, who may include parents with hobbies or expertise in a particular area, high school teachers, university professors, scientists in industry, technicians of

various sorts, other teachers in your school who teach through inquiry, etc.).

**Engage in doing the activities yourself.** As you gain further understandings of the material, you should continue to try different kinds of activities. Try designing experiments that address some of the questions you have generated. The idea is to follow up on your curiosity, just as you hope your students will. Do not be afraid of making mistakes. Just explore and refine your understandings. The mistakes you make are just as important as the successes. Mistakes should be celebrated with children as well. They provide great opportunities for learning. Remember always to keep a sense of humor! Recall the "Far Side," the popular cartoon series by Gary Larson that reflected his weird outlook on common circumstances and phenomena. Think also of Murphy's law, which states that if anything can go wrong, it will. People have amassed a number of related and corollary laws as well. You and your students might find it fun to start making up your own versions of Murphy's law. If experiments do not work as expected, analyze your design, measurement techniques, procedures, apparatus, and so forth. Could you refine any of these designs and techniques? This refinement process is a major part of what science is all about. Scientists are always confronted with these sorts of problems.

Example 8.2 illustrates that doing science with children does not mean that everything will work smoothly and with expected results. Doing genuine inquiry means making mistakes, coming up with new ways of exploring something, and reveling in the excitement of a fresh approach and new insights. Of course, coming up with no strikingly good answer is always a possibility as well.

---

**Example 8.2: A Biologist's Confrontation with Problems Collecting Data and Theorizing**

A biologist was studying flocking behavior of geese. He and his graduate students decided to build a remote control airplane with two movie cameras mounted in it, so they could follow flocks up close. After many crashes, redesigning, and reconstructing, they were able to get the plane and cameras in operation. Then came the task of finding flocks of geese. Attempts at getting close enough to a flock included driving across farmers' fields (often pursued by angry farmers) and one particularly frightening instance of getting lost and ending up in the middle of an airport runway. When they finally got airborne, the plane's radio signals were jammed by the signals from a large military transport plane that was flying by their location. After they found the crash site and developed the film, they had a painfully

---

hilarious showing of the plane's-eye-view of spinning into the ground with some great close-ups of blades of grass at the end. After many more attempts, they finally gave up when they discovered they had no idea where the plane was in relation to the flocks of birds. Although this particular technique was abandoned, they did not abandon their study of flocking behavior.

Years later when the biologist bought an early-model personal computer, someone gave him a simple logic game. When four dots were placed on the screen in different patterns, the dots would move based on some relation the player was supposed to figure out. After placing the dots in a particular pattern, they started moving across the screen just like the hundreds of bird flocks he had observed. With this discovery, he visited a mathematician friend and began work on a computer program to simulate bird flocking behavior. The program took into account a variety of factors, such as optimal flight speed, avoidance of collisions, optimal distance from another bird, and attraction to roost. When they finished, certain factors could be varied by the user (e.g., starting point, individual bird locations) before starting the simulation. The result — all of the flocking behavior he and his students had observed could be recreated on the computer screen!

3. **Design activities—develop clusters and sequences of activities around specific conceptual areas.** Although (and hopefully) you will not be able to plan for all of the possible directions that your students may take in their inquiry, you should try to identify some of the key concepts involved in your topic and design some clusters or sequences of experiments and activities to accompany each concept.

   Some conceptual material requires a sequence of activities that allows students to build upon previous experiences and understandings, while other material lends itself to a clustering of activities with no particular sequence. With activity clusters, you are more interested in providing students with a lot of opportunity to work with different activities related to a particular concept. Each of the activities in a cluster deal equally well with the same concept.

   However, no sequence is necessary. Providing students with a cluster of activities (instead of the traditional one-shot or one-experiment-per-concept approach) allows them to develop more elaborate and detailed understandings.

   When designing these activities, you should keep in mind the importance of providing experiences that allow your students to challenge and re-examine their own and their classmates' ideas and explanations. This pattern can be the most critical and probably the

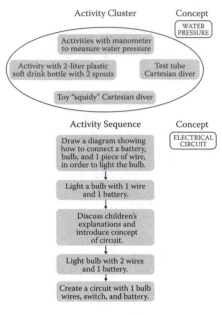

Activity Cluster     Concept

WATER PRESSURE

Activities with manometer to measure water pressure

Activity with 2-liter plastic soft drink bottle with 2 spouts

Test tube Cartesian diver

Toy "squidy" Cartesian diver

Activity Sequence     Concept

ELECTRICAL CIRCUIT

Draw a diagram showing how to connect a battery, bulb, and 1 piece of wire, in order to light the bulb.

Light a bulb with 1 wire and 1 battery.

Discuss children's explanations and introduce concept of circuit.

Light bulb with 2 wires and 1 battery.

Create a circuit with 1 bulb wires, switch, and battery.

**FIGURE 8.2**

most challenging part of your planning task. What makes this task more difficult relates to the overall notion of moving away from a highly structured and teacher-directed approach of delivering instruction to an approach that engages children in real inquiry and in acting like scientists. Essentially, this process is one of problematizing instruction. In other words, what you want to do is start each activity or set of inquiry activities with a question that situates the activities within the context of a problem. The following are a few examples of a specific topic for one or more inquiry activities and how they can be problematized:

**TABLE 8.1** Examples of Problematized Topics

| | |
|---|---|
| Earthworm movement | How do earthworms move through the soil? |
| Relationship between orbital speed and distance | All the planets orbit the sun, but they are different distances from the sun. Does the distance make a difference in how fast an object has to move to stay in orbit? Can we find a way to test this with the materials we have in our room? |
| Factors that affect plant growth | If we want to start an indoor garden, what factors are going to make the biggest difference to how fast and big our plants will grow? What are some factors that could affect their growth? How can we test the effects of each factor? |

There are numerous ways of approaching this task, depending on how you would like to see your children's inquiry unfold. If you would like the unit to start off with children's exploration of a particular phenomena or set of objects, and then follow up on their questions and ideas, the preparation of the unit is going to be different from one that starts off with a specific conceptual objective. The following sections provide examples of possible scenarios.

**Planning to start with a specific conceptual objective:**

You are planning a unit on sinking and floating, or buoyancy (with ships as the instructional device). You would like to present your students with the challenge of developing a working model and a supporting portfolio for a ship. In such a case, you might start off the unit with this challenge, then have students discuss what it is they need to learn. You may want them to start off with some explorations of sinking and floating, but the focus is on constructing the knowledge necessary to complete the portfolio. In order to prepare for this unit, you need to

- Identify all of the concepts children will need in order to complete their projects successfully. (Example of a specific concept or conceptual objective: Students will construct an understanding of buoyancy as an upward force as compared to gravity, which is a downward force.)
- Develop sequences of activities that allow children to confront the problems these concepts present.
- Work through each of these sequences yourself.

Establishing a portfolio culture in the classroom as a means of planning, instruction, and assessment is discussed in Chapter 7.

**Planning to start with exploration:**

You are planning a unit on animals with a focus on anatomical structures and functions. Having brainstormed a lot of concepts and possible directions this inquiry could take, you decide to start the unit by having children explore owl pellets and then build the unit around their questions and comments. What you need to do in order to prepare for this unit is to

- Identify the major concepts that potentially may be addressed in the unit.
- From your list of potential concepts, identify those that are most important (you may want to look at your state or provincial curricular documents) and that you want to be sure to cover at some point in the unit.
- Brainstorm the many possible directions the children's questions may lead. (The best way to do this is to involve a small group of children—your own or neighborhood children—in working with owl pellets while you tape-record their conversations.)
- Work with an owl pellet yourself, follow up on your own ideas and questions, try putting together a skeleton from the bones you pick out, and so forth.
- Develop sets of activities to help children explore their questions and ideas further.
- Address the concepts you want the children to work on during the unit. At a certain point after your students have been exploring their own questions, you can begin to introduce activities around questions that lead to the concepts that you wish to address.

No matter how thorough your planning, you will confront questions and situations the children bring up, which you will need to address. These unexpected problems are very important and should not be dismissed. Children come up with relevant concerns, which have to be addressed either immediately or in the very near future. Get the

A Cartesian diver is some version of an inverted tube filled partially with water. If the tube is inverted (open end pointing down) and placed in a container of water (keeping a finger over the open end until the tube is in the container of water), the tube should float so that the very tip is just about at the surface of the water. The top of the container is sealed with a piece of rubber sheeting (like a cut-up piece of balloon), pulled tightly over the container, and held in place with a rubber band. If you push down on the rubber sheeting, the diver will sink. Let go, and the diver will rise to the surface.

As the pressure is increased inside the container (by pushing down on the rubber sheeting), the water in the Cartesian diver is pushed upward in the tube. The air in the tube is compressed. By reducing the volume of the air, the density is increased (more mass in a smaller volume). With the increased density, the diver sinks. Release the pressure and the density in the tube increases, resulting in the diver rising back to the surface. (Figure 8.3)

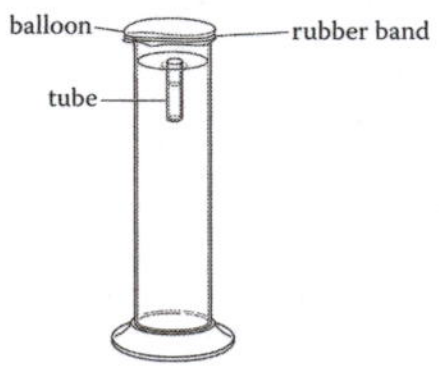

students involved in discussions of how to explore these questions, and then go back and do further investigations on your own.

Developing a set or sequence of activities is very challenging. *There is no set sequence* (although you may find that some sequences are better than others). In fact, you may find it very helpful to develop a number of different sequences for the same concept. You can draw on different activities or sequences, depending upon the questions asked and the explanations the children provide during one experiment or activity. *The trick to doing these sequences of activities is that each subsequent activity needs to confront the ideas generated from the previous activity.* For example, if you are developing a unit on buoyancy (sinking and floating) and you want to work with the concept of pressure (water and air) as it affects the buoyancy of certain objects (for instance, submarines), you might decide to start the sequence with a Cartesian diver (as an alternative to the cluster in the example above). You can start this with a setup using inexpensive and easily available Cartesian divers in a variety of styles (e.g., "Squidy," which is a Cartesian diver covered with a rubber shape of a squid). These Cartesian divers are placed in a 1- or 2-liter plastic soft drink bottle filled almost to the top with water. When you squeeze on the bottle, the Cartesian diver sinks. The expectation is to have the children play with the apparatus while the students in each group generate explanations and negotiate with one another which explanations are the most feasible. However, you want students to go further with this process. *At this point, having a set or sequence of activities comes into play.* Some students may have their own ideas for further investigative activities. These ideas should be supported. You may allow them to try their own investigations, then assist them in evaluating the effectiveness and validity of their activities. Some students may need more guidance in developing and implementing their ideas. In both situations, your knowledge of supporting activities will allow you to help students work through their experimental designs. Furthermore, some students may have no idea how to proceed. In this case, you may want to ask some questions that will help them focus on the problem, such as what factors do you think influence the action of the Cartesian diver? (See Section 5.4 in Chapter 5.) Depending on what ideas they come up with, you need to guide them to a question about a specific aspect of their idea that they need to investigate or substantiate.

Another situation that may arise is that *the students formulate an explanation that is inaccurate.* In this event, you need to suggest an activity that challenges their explanations. Choose an activity that you have designed and have them do it, while they generate and negotiate explanations in relation to their previous explanation. This process can continue until you and your students are satisfied with

balloon — rubber band
tube —

**FIGURE 8.3**

the explanations and understandings that have been constructed and negotiated. Such a process cannot be predetermined entirely in your unit and instructional planning. Engaging your students in the processes of constructing and negotiating explanations, planning further investigative activities, and making decisions about what to do and how to proceed is extremely important. A teacher who controls the sequence and flow of all activities and who controls the dissemination of knowledge can inadvertently damage students' understanding of the nature and conceptual content of science. By preparing yourself for a number of possible eventualities and by developing your own understandings of the concepts, you can guide the students through the inquiry process and challenge them to probe further into their ideas.

Now, to throw a monkey wrench into this whole plan, you need to consider how children generally react to a challenging task, like the challenge of building a particular ship and developing a portfolio. In the midst of their excitement, they may not want to sit down and go through a lot of activities and patiently wait for the opportunity to start on their project. What do you do? If you try to hold to your plan (even a more general sequence of events), you may end up with a classroom full of frustrated, angry, or bored children. Remember that science proceeds in many directions, with failed attempts and mistakes along the way. A recommendation is to *let students start on the project*. When they run into dead ends and make mistakes, this is the prime opportunity to start introducing some of the sequences of activities that address the concepts behind the problems they have encountered. But remember to get them involved in identifying the problems and some ways in which they can set up experiments or other activities to explore these problems. Your knowledge of the sequence of activities will allow you to guide them through this process.

**Develop activities that address the integration of subject matter areas.** Since you need to be concerned about the relevance, meaning, and complexity of children's learning, it is important to consider how you need to develop an integrated unit. Integrated activities can arise basically in three different ways: (a) as a teacher-imposed approach that, for lack of a better word, is rather stilted (i.e., may not be particularly meaningful or relevant); (b) as a teacher-initiated approach that takes into account the fundamental relationships between similar patterns and concepts in science and those in other subject matter areas and other relevant contexts; or (c) as a response to children's ideas, questions, and interests.

The first approach (i.e., teacher imposed) is rather common and certainly the easiest to implement. In this approach, the class may be studying insects. So, the teacher hands out sheets of paper with drawings of insects on them and asks the students to color in the drawings with the intent of integrating art. However, such an approach is rather trivial and really does not capture the essence of art as a creative endeavor for the expression and communication of a particular insight about one's own experience of the world.

The second approach (teacher initiated) involves identifying particular patterns and concepts that share similar meanings across subject matter areas and contexts of personal experience. For instance, the teacher may be planning a unit on animals with an initial inquiry focused on earthworms. As the teacher explores the concepts involved with earthworms, she notices that earthworms are basically tubes. She realizes that one particular characteristic of tubular shapes is that they provide for the ability to penetrate, much like a meat thermometer, hypodermic needle, knitting needle, drill bits, submarines (that penetrate water and provide aerodynamic form), fingers (for digging in the soil), and so forth. At the same time, she notices that the movement of an earthworm involves a cycle of muscular contraction, which is similar to human and other animal movement. Such movement cycles are similar to all forms of movement, from bicycles to airplanes. In addition, the notion of cycle as a way of maintaining some system is shared in many aspects of our daily experiences, including pond ecosystems, weather patterns, daily sleep and eating cycles, arithmetic (e.g., cycles of steps in solving 2 and higher digit multiplication problems), and so forth. So, as she plans the unit, she includes inquiry and theorizing questions that could initiate investigations that naturally extend the children's understandings in multiple contexts and subjects.

The last of these three approaches to integration is more or less the flip side of the second approach. In this approach, the teacher stays on alert for comments and questions from her students, which could lead to personally meaningful and relevant avenues for integration. For instance, if you are working with the topic of electricity, you can include an exploration of Thomas Edison's life and work with electricity. On the other hand, if a student makes a joke about something being "an electrifying experience," you can capitalize on the comment by having children explore different meanings of words associated with electricity. Such an exploration can lead to creative writing, artistic expressions, or dramatic performances that elaborate upon and describe alternative meanings. Such integrated activities can lead to discussions of how the scientific meanings differ from those we use in our everyday lives and different contexts of use.

As a starting point for planning this aspect, you can construct a context map or brainstorm a list of possible directions (see Chapter 7 for a more complete treatment and examples of context maps). Some useful categories of integrated components can include

a. Historical developments, which emphasize how scientists and other scholars have approached the topic, as well as how various cultures have developed folk explanations around the topics

b. Fundamental patterns and concepts that span disciplines (see Appendix D for examples)

c. Contemporary uses and issues (e.g., social, environmental, political)

d. Issues related to how science, technology, and society affect one another

e. Related literature (e.g., poems, stories, novels)

f. Related artistic expressions (e.g., music, paintings, photographs, drama)

In addition, you should generate a list of possible reactions and personal constructions (in terms of contexts of meaning) children may generate. These may include (see Chapter 4 for more detailed explanations and examples of the following):

a. **Personal experiences** related to the topic

b. **Metaphors**

c. **Emotions, values, and aesthetics** reactions

d. Various **interpretive frameworks** or beliefs

e. Various **personal stories and imagery**

Once you have generated the two lists (integrated components and contexts of meaning), you need to think about how the items in both lists are related or connected to each other, how they may influence the way in which children have constructed their pre-unit meaningful understandings, and how they might influence their developing understandings during the unit. You also should identify the important concepts and relations that you want to help your students explore during the unit. Children's personal contexts of meaning also present possibilities for the development of concepts and various products. For example, metaphors can lead to interesting explanatory models for the phenomena they are studying. Metaphors also can lead to the development of poems or stories. Anthropomorphic frameworks, on the one hand, can be useful in developing conceptual understandings, or on the other hand, they can interfere with such development. They can lead to interesting possibilities for stories as well. Try to anticipate some of these different perspectives (metaphors, anthropomorphism, etc.) to get a feel for how they can be developed or challenged when they arise during the unit.

4. **Organize—clusters, sequences, and other activities.** The final stage is to start organizing all of the information and activities you have amassed. The organization will probably be a combination of clusters of information and activities around the various concepts, relationships, and directions (integrated perspectives), and of sequences of activities and events. You also should think about possible field studies, films, readings, computer software, resource people, and so forth, that can be incorporated into the unit. As you

develop a sense of how to organize these clusters, you may want to look at the E-7 model, in Section 8.3, for further ideas on organizing. In addition, you need to consider flexible timelines for inquiry units and for the entire year (see the end of this chapter for more details).

5. **Correlate your unit with the mandated standards or curriculum.** At this point, your planning has been based primarily upon your own concerns, ideas, and knowledge of the material. However, most teachers have to address mandated curricula and standards. In order to avoid a restricted approach to curriculum, it is best to put off addressing the mandated content until this point. Now you can look at the curriculum documents and indicate where you have addressed the mandated content. If you are missing a large number of specific content objectives, you can look for places where these objectives can be inserted, or develop another unit or time period where you can address the objectives. However, as you gain experience, you probably will find that you have addressed most of the skills during the year and will not have to spend much if any time addressing missed skills and objectives.

6. **Design assessment and evaluation strategies.** You also need to consider how you want to assess your students' growth in their abilities and understandings. The culmination of the unit should provide your students with a means of communicating their findings and understandings in the form of a meaningful project and other tasks (see Chapter 7). Such tasks and projects should allow students to express and demonstrate their understandings. From their completed work, you can look at the nature of their understandings and how they correspond to your initial conceptual objectives and other goals.

7. **A final note about planning.** Once you have established your plan on paper, do not view it as written in stone. The preplanning should be seen as a way of providing you with a framework that enables you to work with the classroom dynamics. You also should start your pre-unit assessment (see Chapter 7) at some point during your planning. The insights you gain about children's understandings (whether accurate or inaccurate) will help you design more effective activities. Such activities can address your students' inaccurate understandings, as well as extend and elaborate on their accurate understandings. In addition, you should be prepared to modify the course of events and activities at any time during your unit as you uncover new insights into your students' understandings. In fact, you may find that as you engage children in a particular investigation and discussion, you will get ideas for other activities that follow up on their interests and questions (see Example 8.3). Be flexible!

---

**Example 8.3**

A teacher explains:

As the students worked with the Cartesian divers, they were coming up with explanations that made sense to them, but were pretty much off the mark. They kept talking about the air escaping from the tube when you pushed on the balloon. Even when they measured the height of the water in the test-tube diver and observed the diver several times, they persisted with this notion. We had worked with a home-made manometer for measuring water pressure at various depths, and had done quite a bit with density, but they just weren't getting the connection with pressure. So, in the middle of this class, I began thinking about combining the manometer activity with the Cartesian diver. After class, I started to gather some equipment and put together an apparatus with the manometer tube going through the opening of a balloon. I cut off the other end of the balloon and stretched it over a 1-liter beaker with a test-tube Cartesian diver in it. The result was that when you pushed down on the balloon, the diver sank and the manometer showed an increase in pressure. It worked perfectly. Of course, when we did it in class, Murphy's law presided with most of the groups' equipment! Everything from the balloons popping off the beakers to the divers not sinking.... It has potential though. I think it's the right kind of transitional activity between water pressure and how a Cartesian diver works.

---

## 8.3   A Simple Model for Planning: E-7

Although there are many different models for planning instruction, the E-7 model takes into account recent advances in constructivist learning theory. In addition, the model provides a practical way to conceptualize and implement instruction. The following components of the model (the seven E's, explained in the list below) appear in one particular sequence.[1] However, it is very important to keep in mind that you can play with this sequence. You may find that starting somewhere else is useful for certain children and certain topics. As the class progresses and children become involved in certain ways, you may need to skip around and cycle through a smaller sequence more often. In addition, you may find this model useful for designing an individual activity or sequence of activities (microlevel) and for designing a whole unit or larger chunk of activities or lessons (macrolevel).

**Elicit:**    Elicit children's ideas and understandings about the topic and concepts you are about to explore. You can do this with various tasks, such as drawings, written definitions, concept maps, context maps, small-group conversations, individual conversations, and so forth. The intent is to gain insight into children's understandings, so that you can direct instruction to address their understandings.

**Engage:** Use an activity, set of materials, or other setup that engages student interest and curiosity.

**Explore:** Provide students with an opportunity to explore a particular phenomenon. Encourage them to generate their own explanations and concepts and to test them through experimentation and observation.

**Encounter:** Challenge the knowledge claims and explanations that the students have generated. You can do this with activities that challenge these ideas and with questions that pose alternative situations in which the students' explanations have to apply. You also can make a general comment like "I'm not convinced. Think more about it and try to convince me and everyone else." The ideal situation involves students challenging each other's knowledge claims and explanations in the form of group or class arguments.

**Explain:** Students can reiterate their explanations with supporting evidence. The teacher also can state the explanation or knowledge claim, although you have to be careful about doing this. The "teacher as authority" types of behavior can adversely affect student willingness to take risks, challenge their own and others' ideas, and take responsibility for their own learning.

**Elaborate:** Provide students with opportunities to (a) explore different aspects of the topic, (b) apply what they have learned to novel situations, or (c) apply their knowledge to realistic problems.

**Evaluate:** Students can evaluate the status of the explanations and knowledge claims they have generated. Do they make sense? Do the explanations have supporting evidence? Is the evidence sound? You also can have students evaluate what they have learned through group or class discussions or through more specific tasks or activities.[1]

## 8.4 Instructional Plans

When you think of planning, you usually think of lesson plans. However, the notion behind lesson plans is that a teacher can plan a set of lessons with an activity addressing a particular concept or idea over a particular linear sequence. However, if you want to do real inquiry with your students, you may not or even should not be able to predict exactly where the inquiry will lead. So, rather than thinking in terms of a specific lesson and a linear sequence of lessons, you need to consider alternative formats for planning. Instead of lessons, you may want to think in terms of longer-term instructional periods. So, rather than planning for 10:00 to 10:45 on Monday, you should think about how a particular inquiry can unfold over a period of several days.

---

Make arrangements to observe some classes (can be a university class) and look for the different components of the seven E's.

+ Which components are not evident?

+ How can any missing "E" components be included?

+ How can the omission or inclusion of a component affect learning and the classroom dynamics?

---

During a period of teaching, try to include each of the seven E components. Pay attention to students' reactions, as well as your own. (Audio- or videotaping this period of time may be very helpful for prompting your own reflections.)

+ In what order did they occur?

+ Did you find yourself backtracking and cycling through the components?

+ What prompted such backtracking and cycling?

+ How did you feel about the way teaching proceeded?

+ Were there times when you missed the opportunity to include a component?

+ How did the students react to instruction based on the seven E's?

Example 8.4 provides an example format for planning instruction based on inquiry. This particular example format is filled out with the types of information that can be used to explore the concepts related to density within a larger unit on floating and boat design. As is apparent, the major focus is on the conceptual content that a particular inquiry will emphasize. In planning, you need to identify a particular problem or conceptual area, then specify the concepts involved. Once you have done that, you need to develop problems or questions that will drive the investigations. At this point, you need to find or develop sets of activities (actual observations or experiments) that will provide students with the data to formulate explanations and develop the concepts. Of these sets of concepts, problems, and activities, you can select one with which to begin. After the first investigation, children may generate other questions that may lead in other directions. So, when you develop these sets of concepts along the left side of the page, you should be thinking of the possible directions (and concepts) that the children's inquiry may take. In a way, this process of planning is planning for the uncertainty of inquiry. On the right side of the example, you can add specific skills (e.g., measuring temperature in Celsius, designing an experiment, etc.) required in completing these investigations.

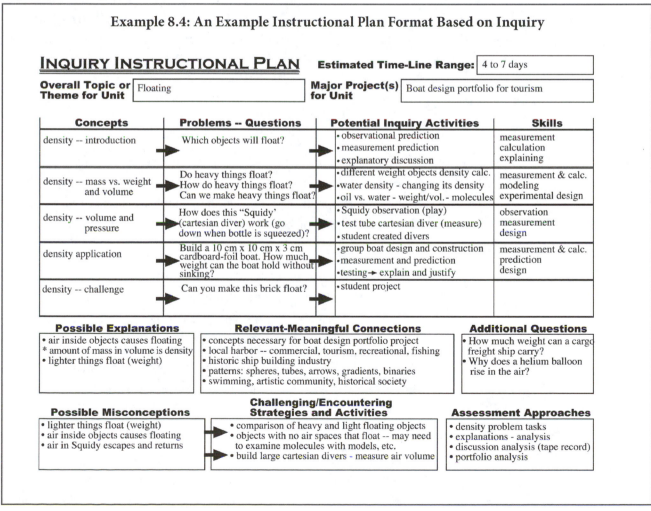

**Example 8.4: An Example Instructional Plan Format Based on Inquiry**

## INQUIRY INSTRUCTIONAL PLAN

**Estimated Time-Line Range:** 4 to 7 days

**Overall Topic or Theme for Unit:** Floating

**Major Project(s) for Unit:** Boat design portfolio for tourism

| Concepts | Problems -- Questions | Potential Inquiry Activities | Skills |
|---|---|---|---|
| density -- introduction | Which objects will float? | • observational prediction<br>• measurement prediction<br>• explanatory discussion | measurement<br>calculation<br>explaining |
| density -- mass vs. weight and volume | Do heavy things float?<br>How do heavy things float?<br>Can we make heavy things float? | • different weight objects density calc.<br>• water density - changing its density<br>• oil vs. water - weight/vol.- molecules | measurement & calc.<br>modeling<br>experimental design |
| density -- volume and pressure | How does this "Squidy' (cartesian diver) work (go down when bottle is squeezed)? | • Squidy observation (play)<br>• test tube cartesian diver (measure)<br>• student created divers | observation<br>measurement<br>design |
| density application | Build a 10 cm x 10 cm x 3 cm cardboard-foil boat. How much weight can the boat hold without sinking? | • group boat design and construction<br>• measurement and prediction<br>• testing → explain and justify | measurement & calc.<br>prediction<br>design |
| density -- challenge | Can you make this brick float? | • student project | |

**Possible Explanations**
• air inside objects causes floating
* amount of mass in volume is density
• lighter things float (weight)

**Relevant-Meaningful Connections**
• concepts necessary for boat design portfolio project
• local harbor -- commercial, tourism, recreational, fishing
• historic ship building industry
• patterns: spheres, tubes, arrows, gradients, binaries
• swimming, artistic community, historical society

**Additional Questions**
• How much weight can a cargo freight ship carry?
• Why does a helium balloon rise in the air?

**Possible Misconceptions**
• lighter things float (weight)
• air inside objects causes floating
• air in Squidy escapes and returns

**Challenging/Encountering Strategies and Activities**
• comparison of heavy and light floating objects
• objects with no air spaces that float -- may need to examine molecules with models, etc.
• build large cartesian divers - measure air volume

**Assessment Approaches**
• density problem tasks
• explanations - analysis
• discussion analysis (tape record)
• portfolio analysis

In addition, it is important to consider the information for the boxes at the bottom of the example page. What possible explanations for the results of these investigations could the children generate (of course, the currently accepted explanation should be highlighted)? What are the relevant and meaningful connections of these investigations to the children's lives? Are these activities important to developing the necessary understandings for a larger project? Are there local environmental or other issues that are being addressed? You also may find that generating additional related questions may be useful in the heat of the moment. These questions help to stimulate divergent investigations or activities that can impact on children's engagement and integrated understandings. Another important area to consider is the possible misconceptions that children may bring into the investigation, which may need to be addressed through further inquiry activities. As you gain experience with children and their misconceptions, filling in this area of the page will become quite a bit easier. Of course, you need to consider how you will assess the children's understandings, inquiry skills, and so forth.

Other possible instructional plan formats appear in Appendix E. However, you can make your own to fit the needs of your classroom and your goals. The important point is not to take a one-shot or one-activity-for-one-concept approach. Think about how real engagement in learning can unfold over a period of time, then plan accordingly.

## 8.5 Alternative Sequencing for a Restricted Curriculum Situation

If you happen to be teaching in a situation that requires covering specific content in a certain amount of time and requires students to prepare for standardized testing, how can you plan instruction that takes into account children's construction of knowledge? The traditional pattern over a period of three classes may go something like this:

1. Introduce concepts and content (lecture format).
2. Expand on content and work through examples.
3. Have students work through laboratory-type activities to confirm that they understand what has been presented.

In this sequence, the mode of delivery takes on the characteristics of transmitting knowledge to the students. The construction of knowledge is not addressed specifically, and if it occurs, it is left entirely up to individual students.

An alternative approach that can take place in the same amount of time might look something like this:

1. Introduce a problem that requires students to come up with their own explanations (best done in small groups around a table), then

have students work with laboratory-type activities to solve the problem and generate one or more potential explanations.

2. Engage students in a discussion in which they defend and support their particular explanations. Have students evaluate the strengths and weaknesses of each explanation.

3. Have students compare their explanations to the scientific explanation and evaluate the similarities and differences. Further discussions can be initiated that expand on the concepts and examples.

   ■ It is important to note that having students compare their explanations to the "correct" answer may have negative effects. Students may disregard the process they go through in constructing explanations if they think that their ideas do not count. They may insist that you just give them the correct answer. If you choose this route, you should proceed with caution.

Although the previous sequence occurs within the same time frame, you have allowed students to engage in constructing their own understandings. At the same time, students have engaged in processes that are similar to those used by scientists.

## 8.6 Taking into Account Children's Ability Levels (But Not Selling Them Short!)

Traditionally, we have assumed that children's abilities to think to various degrees of complexity and abstractness are tied to developmental stages. However, recent research has been questioning this assumption. What seems to make more sense is that children's thinking abilities are more dependent upon their previous experiences and prior knowledge. What does this mean for planning instruction?

1. Remember: Do not underestimate children's abilities. Little children can surprise you with their ability to come up with amazing explanations of various phenomena.

2. Provide a lot of opportunity for children to explore phenomena freely. Although they may not be able to verbalize much of what they are learning, their playing with phenomena (e.g., magnets) allows them to develop much needed experience that serves as a basis for further learning.

3. Oversimplifying your content and approach can lead to boredom and can certainly limit the extent of the children's learning. You should set your sights and expectations high. Such expectations should focus on student explanation and theory building, analysis and evaluation of knowledge claims, and developing in-depth conceptual understandings.

4. The older the children, the more resistant they may be to higher expectations and the challenge of engaging in real inquiry. They

may have more experience getting by while doing minimal work in school. You need patience and perseverance to get through the layers of resistance. Be consistent with your expectations and encourage their efforts.

Ideally, children should be involved in active inquiry into topics or aspects of topics that interest them. However, true inquiry takes time, and the direction it takes may change as time goes by. As you get to know your students—which ones need more direction, which need more structure, which need less structure, and so forth—you can plan according to these needs and characteristics. At all times, though, you need to be flexible and aware of what is happening with each child. If most children are winding up a unit topic, but a few are still going strong, you need to find a time and way to accommodate their continued inquiry.

## 8.7 Teaching and Working with Children: Implementing Instruction

So far, we have looked at ways of integrating instruction, facilitating classroom talk, encouraging creativity, conducting inquiry, paying attention to how children learn, thinking and reflecting about our practice, and planning for instruction. However, what do you do when you walk into the classroom? How do you translate all of this information into practice?

Teaching is not a prescriptive process. No one can say, "Do such and such, and then you will be a great teacher." It is for this reason that teacher reflection is so important (see Chapter 10 for a detailed discussion of critical and analytical reflection). You have to be able to think on your feet and reflect about what has occurred in your classroom. Every child and class is different. In fact, classrooms change continually. Tomorrow's class may be quite different from today's. The students may be completely engaged and well behaved before lunch, but appear to be completely different when they return. Depending on the context and dynamics of the classroom, your best plans may or may not work.

When you are teaching as a reflective practitioner, you will undoubtedly confront a number of dilemmas concerning both management and instruction. The interesting aspect of confronting dilemmas is that there usually is no right decision. For instance, you may have your own agenda for what is to take place during a certain class, but you find that the students are engaging in a heated debate about one part of the topic. What do you do? Do you bring the debate to a close and continue with the intended activities, or do you encourage the debate? Either choice has negative and positive aspects. Sometimes the choice may involve the question of whether to align oneself with the implicit or explicit values or goals of the school system or with your personal values and goals about learning, teaching, and the nature of science. You may need to think about a clear and well-thought-out justification for your particular action. Or you may try to find a middle ground between the extremes.

You have to make a decision (even not making an explicit decision to act is a decision), and at the initial time you confront the dilemma, you do not have a lot of time to consider all of the possibilities. However, time is on your side. Make a decision when you first confront a dilemma, then reflect on the situation in more detail after school. Develop support for a decision, which can be different from the one you made, so that when you confront the dilemma again, you can make the decision based on a rationale and on goals you have set for your students. Below is a list of some dilemmas that a teacher/researcher confronted while teaching:[2]

1. Control over the curriculum versus encouraging quality discourse
2. Maintaining intellectual engagement versus complying with time constraints
3. Confidence with the subject matter versus engaging children in discussions
4. Managing classroom arguments successfully versus providing answers

In each of these dilemmas, the teacher may struggle with a decision. You may feel limited by your own understandings of the content or by various internal and external pressures. However, examining these dilemmas will allow you to hone your skills in dealing with the changing dynamics of classroom teaching. Further information on dilemmas and reflection is available in Chapters 1 and 10.

The items listed below are not intended to provide a cookbook approach to teaching, but are guidelines for thinking about teaching and taking action.

**Be flexible and adaptable.** Be ready to change plans at any time:
- When classroom dynamics and the atmosphere do not appear to be conducive to the sort of activities you have planned.
- When children are not responding to the particular activity. Do not be afraid to change your plans and move to a new activity. Go back and regroup. Reflect on what factors may have affected the response to the activity. Could the activity be restructured in a way that engages the students?
- When opportunities for genuine and relevant inquiry or discussion arise from children's comments and questions. If children come up with an intriguing question or insight into a problem or issue, take advantage of the opportunity to engage the children.

**Be prepared to explore and build on children's personal experiences and ideas.** As in the previous item, be ready to adapt to new circumstances. Many opportunities for integrated activities arise during classroom discussions and activities. Be alert for potential avenues of relevant and meaningful explorations of topics arising from children.

**Be aware of your own teaching agenda and be open to exploring the children's agendas.** Sometimes we are so caught up in our own plans and what we want to accomplish that we miss golden opportunities to engage children in important discussions and investigations. This item is similar to the previous two, but focuses more on how we tend to proceed with our own plans no matter what happens. We tend to control what takes place and what information can be introduced into the discussion. By dismissing, not responding, or responding minimally to a child's question or comment, we send a message that what the child said was not relevant or important. Rather, we should be encouraging children to take more control over their learning.

■ In Example 8.5, we see that the teacher dismisses David's idea that the higher release angle and resulting faster speed of travel will be offset by a greater distance to travel, and therefore will make no difference on the period of the swing. David's idea jumped ahead of where the teacher wanted to be. She ignored David's comment in favor of the more simplistic one. In addition, we also see that David succumbs to the pressure and control of the teacher and conforms to the simpler answer.

---

**Example 8.5**

A teacher is leading a discussion about pendulums. They have been talking about what affects the period of the swing and have just begun discussing the effects of raising the angle at which the bob is released. As you read through the segment, try to identify the parts where the teacher's agenda dismisses the ideas of one child in favor of a more simplistic idea by another student:

**Teacher: What sort of difference, Jonathan, do you think? If I held it up here? [Teacher holds pendulum bob away from the support.]**

*Jonathan:* Well, it might make a difference.

*David:* I don't think it'll make a difference. I know it's got further to go but …

*Jonathan:* It's got faster.

*David:* But it's going faster; and so it won't …

**Teacher: Go faster.**

*David:* Make any difference because it's equal.

*Antony:* Well, I think it'll go slower because it's got further to go.

**Teacher: So if it goes up here; right, and we let it go, you reckon it'll go much slower?**

*David:* Miss, it's got more power than if you did it from about there.

**Teacher: So you think it'll go …**

*David:* Faster.

**Teacher: Faster. What do you think, Karen?**

*Karen:* I think it'll go faster as well.

**Teacher: Why?**

*Karen:* 'Cause if you can bring it up there it's bound to go faster because it's going to drop down faster.[3]

---

**Engage in scaffolding.** Build on children's previous knowledge and experience and on previous activities.

- **Provide continuity.** Try to connect one day's lesson and activities to previous lessons with summaries and recaps of what you have done before. Both children and teacher can initiate this process.

- **Participate in shared talk and activity.** Work and talk through processes with the class. Help the children see how to approach certain tasks or think about problems and issues. Make sure that the terms and ideas being discussed are understood in the same way by everyone. If a child says, "The pressure is making the object sink," make sure that the child explains what he or she means by pressure. If you are introducing the concept of adaptation, make sure that everyone has a similar understanding. For example, we may say that when we go to a higher altitude, we adapt to the decreased oxygen levels by producing more red blood cells, but this meaning of adaptation is not what is meant from a biological point of view. Adaptation is something that occurs genetically over generations of a species; acclimatization is what an individual does in response to an environmental change.

**Talk less. Encourage children to do more of the classroom talk.** Be aware of how much you are talking. Is what you are saying necessary? Are you preventing children from expressing their own ideas and engaging in the process? Sometimes your talk as the teacher is extremely important, but at other times it can be counterproductive. If you are introducing a new skill, like how to operate a microscope, you need to talk through the process with the children. At other times, you may talk on and on about how a particular object works without allowing the children to express their own ideas and engage in discussion.

**Encourage children to work independently.** Teaching should be a process that helps children learn how to work and learn independently. However, we often assume that either a student knows how to do a particular task or procedure, or a student needs to have each step of a procedure prescribed every time it is used. When learning a new procedure, you need to teach students how to do it, so that they can use the procedure independently. Talk while showing children through procedural processes, and encourage them to comment on the procedure as they are doing it. Make each step and process explicit. After guiding students through a procedure, encourage them to work through the process on their own. Offer additional help, if needed, but slowly withdraw your assistance on any further occasions when students ask for help with the same procedure.

On other occasions, when students are working on a task, resist immediately answering their questions. Answer their questions with questions that help children think through the problem or that point them to other sources of information.

**Make sure you approach procedures and thinking processes differently.** The learning of certain procedures needs to become automatic and routine. How to use a microscope, calculate volume, use a stopwatch, and so forth, as well as the names of specific objects and concepts, can be "routinized." Spending time rethinking how to do certain tasks or looking up commonly used terms can be very time-consuming. If we, as teachers, along with our children, talk through step-by-step procedures and repeat these procedures frequently, the procedural knowledge can become automatic. Like learning how to drive, we do not think about each step and process; we do all of them and rarely think about them once we have learned and practiced how to do them. It is efficient and effective. However, we occasionally find ourselves trying to teach certain skills that should not become or cannot be automatic in the same way that we would teach skills that need to become automatic. The traditional version of the scientific method is often approached in the same way, when in fact there is really no prescribed step-by-step approach to doing science. Students learn to think through the inquiry process. Each problem may require a different approach, and children need to consider the best ways to approach each one. The guiding principles for thinking about how to approach problems should be emphasized. (More information on these principles and thinking skills can be found in Chapter 4.)

**View student errors and mistakes as positive learning opportunities.** Mistakes have always been a major impetus for learning. We see examples of this in manufacturing, science, and technology. A car manufacturer may have to recall all of its cars from a particular year when a newly designed part for its vehicles is added. Once the manufacturer realizes its mistake, it is not going to continue making the faulty item in the same way. In a classroom, a group may have designed an experiment with pendulums that included some faulty procedures (e.g., used only one trial for each measurement, or did not keep certain variables constant). To say they made a mistake and leave it at that does not provide an opportunity for further learning. Instead, the group needs to re-evaluate its design, come up with improvements, and then repeat the experiment. You may have to lead them through this process, but this is an opportunity to teach the basics of doing science and to see how mistakes can lead to new discoveries.

**Avoid providing all of the answers to children's questions.** Determine what information is necessary to proceed with an investigation and what information the children can construct from their own inquiry. For information that is necessary and not easily accessible through inquiry, lead children to appropriate source materials or provide that information directly. For information that can be determined and constructed by the children, try to ask questions or make comments that

- Challenge students' claims or provide counter-evidence for their claims
- Create links to their prior knowledge and experience
- Create links to other observable evidence in their investigations
- Ask students to clarify their terms, claims, and so forth

**Provide opportunities for children to take ownership over their ideas and actions.** Much of what has been discussed so far in this list is geared toward helping children assume more control and ownership. Respect their ideas and explanations and allow them to develop further these ideas. You can challenge their ideas, but avoid being the knowledge authority. You probably know more than they do, and they know this, but you can create an atmosphere that provides respect for their ideas. Give them opportunities to explore, test, express, and evaluate their own ideas.

## 8.8 Some Example Unit Topics and Themes

You may find that using a science topic is a convenient way for building an integrated unit. The lists below provide a few ideas for such unit topics. Certain familiar topics have been left out: (a) seasonal topics that tend to be used year after year and (b) topics for which inquiry activities are difficult to provide.

The second list of topics is much broader and can serve for semester- or year-long themes. Each of these can be broken into subtopics. However, throughout the year, from subtopic to subtopic, you and your students can go back and make links with what you have worked with previously.

In considering the topics below, it is important to realize that they serve as a point of departure for addressing both broad conceptual themes and specific concepts. So, if you decide to design a unit around cockroaches, you can address (a) adaptation, (b) structure–function relationships (i.e., how specific structures are adapted for specific functions), (c) patterns of reproduction, growth, and development, and (d) communication.

### Specific Topics

| | | |
|---|---|---|
| Air: Breathing and respiration | Flight: Birds, planes, and kites | Ponds and lakes |
| Ants | Floats, boats, and submarines | Reproducing, developing, and growing |
| Behavior | Food: Finding and digesting | Rivers, lakes, soil, and rocks |
| Body | Fossils, dinosaurs, evolution | Science and sports |
| Bones and muscles | Frogs, toads, and salamanders | Senses |
| Cells | Gases, liquids, and solids | Sight and light |
| Cockroaches | Greenery (plants) | Snails |
| Color | Insects | Sound, hearing, and music |
| Conservation | Inventions | Space |
| Critters without backbones | Kitchen chemistry | Spiders |
| Earthworms | Light, lenses, prisms, mirrors | Spineless critters |
| Electricity and magnets | Mealworms | Toys and machines |
| Fields and forests | Nature in the school yard | Traces, tracks, and clues |
| Fish | Oceans and lakes | Water |
| Flies | Pendulums | Weather |

Refer to Section 8.7.

When you have an opportunity to work with children or observe another teacher working with children in a classroom setting, take an opportunity to review the previous points, including teaching dilemmas. Then observe how children react to certain actions taken by the teacher.

- What actions were conducive to children's learning, thinking, and taking control over their own learning and work?
- What actions were not conducive and why?
- What points from the above list were most difficult to do and why?
- What can you do to alleviate the difficulty?
- At what points did you feel that you confronted a dilemma?
- What was of concern in the dilemma?
- How did you resolve the situation?
- What were the consequences?

### Longer-Term, Broader, and More Challenging Unit Topics

| | | |
|---|---|---|
| Change | Energy | Sequences and time |
| Communication | Form and function | Structures, forces, and strength |
| Communities | Locomotion and movement | Survival |
| Competition | Patterns and shapes | Territory and space |
| Continuity | Protection | Variation |
| Cycles | Relationships, interrelationships | |

## 8.8.1 Broad Unit Topic Examples

Below are some examples of the subtopics involved in the broader units listed above. As shown in the examples above, such broad topics can be used to relate your own list of topics or those of mandated curricula to one common, year-long theme. In looking through the lists of subtopics, you may notice that some of these topics are not appropriate for all age groups. You may also find that you and your students can generate much better lists of subtopics.

### Communication

| | | |
|---|---|---|
| Auditory Information exchange | Hormones | Tactile |
| Chemical (internal/external) | Olfactory | Telephone |
| Codes Language | Radio | Television |
| Computers and modems | Rituals | Visual |
| Genes, DNA | | |

### Locomotion and Movement

| | | |
|---|---|---|
| Amoebas to mammals | Phloem and xylem in plants | Seeds and seed pods |
| Circulation—blood, etc. | Planets, stars, comets | Tides and currents |
| Continental drift | Planes, rockets, and boats | Transport |
| Inventions | Plants | Wind |
| Motor vehicles | | |

### Structures, Forces, and Strength

| | | |
|---|---|---|
| Acceleration | Buildings | Inventions |
| Architecture | Diameter–height relations | Surface area–volume relations |
| Bones | Endo- and exoskeletons | Tension and compression |
| Bridges | Friction and resistance | Trees and plants |
| Bubbles | Gravity | Work |

### Change

| | | |
|---|---|---|
| Caterpillars to butterflies | Energy transformations | Life cycles |
| Chemical reactions | Erosion | Life and death |
| Continental drift | Evolution | Seasons and weather |
| Cycles | Growth and development | States of matter |
| Earthquakes and volcanoes | Human effects on environment | Technologically initiated |

### Energy

| | | |
|---|---|---|
| Chemical | Fossil fuels | Nuclear |
| Conservation | Heat | Photosynthesis |
| Ecosystem, habitat | Kinetic and potential | Solar, wind, geothermal |
| Food conversion | Light | Work |
| Food web, food pyramid | Mechanical | |

## Protection

| | | |
|---|---|---|
| Adaptations to habitats | Clothing, housing | Of habitat, environment |
| Alertness, awareness | Coloration, shape, camouflage | Of self, young, species |
| Behavior | Hair, scales, mucous | Safety |
| Bones, shells, etc. | | |

## 8.9  Yearly Planning

Planning over the term of a year requires some flexibility. If your students are motivated and interested in a particular topic, you need to be prepared to extend topics. When students are really engaged in an investigation, you do not want to pass up the opportunity to help them go further. However, in terms of a broad plan for the year, you may want to consider a number of options.

In planning for the year, you may have to consider specific curriculum guidelines from your school, school board, or provincial or state department of education. However, you may find that you are afforded much more flexibility in the elementary school. Mandated guidelines should not prevent you from exploring important and intriguing topics with your students. You also may find that your own plans for science instruction address mandated guidelines, but not in the form or sequence suggested. In addition, you may find ways of adjusting your own weekly plans to accommodate special topics and investigations, while still addressing mandated topics at other times during the week. In the following paragraphs, we will move from how a weekly plan can be constructed to how we can plan for the year.

In Example 8.6, a typical arrangement of a weekly plan is shown. Although the times for each subject may vary, you get a sense of how a weekly schedule looks. Such a weekly plan provides blocks of time for each subject. However, sticking to such a schedule may be difficult for a number of reasons. Some activities may take longer than expected. In order to capitalize on your students' interests and enthusiasm for a particular activity or project, you may want to extend the designated time. On the other hand, you may feel obliged to cover all of the mandated curricular content, along with the expectations

---

### Example 8.6: A Typical Weekly Schedule

| | | | | |
|---|---|---|---|---|
| R | Reading | | | |
| Ma | Math | | | |
| PE | Physical Education | | | |
| S | Science | | | |
| SS | Social Studies | | | |
| A | Art | | | |
| W | Writing | | | |
| QT | Quiet Time | | | |
| Mu | Music | | | |
| O | Other | | | |
| P/I | Project/Individual Help | | | |
| CM | Classroom Meeting | | | |

| 9:00 | | | | | |
|---|---|---|---|---|---|
| R | Ma | R | W | Ma | 9:30 |
| W | R | W | Ma | R | 10:00 |
| S | S | QT | Ma | PE | 10:30 |
| Ma | PE | O | R | S | 11:00 |
| | | QT | | 11:30 |
| | | LUNCH | | 12:00 |
| Mu | SS | Ma | SS | W | 12:30 |
| O | W | Mu | A | QT | 1:00 |
| SS | | | | SS | 1:30 |
| QT | O | S | O | O | 2:00 |
| A | QT | | | A | 2:30 |
| CM | P/I | P/I | CM | P/I | 3:00 |

of your principal and school board to spend a specific amount of time on each subject area.

In Example 8.6, the subject areas are obvious. The "other" category has been inserted to accommodate specific topic areas, such as a foreign language (i.e., French, in most parts of Canada) or computers. However, three additional time slots are included: (a) quiet time, (b) project and individual help, and (c) classroom meeting. Quiet time can be inserted as a daily time slot for quiet reading or other activity. Time can be set aside for individuals or groups to work on projects in their area of interest or for individuals and groups to work on remedial activities and receive more individualized attention from the teacher. Classroom meetings (discussed further in Chapter 9) are times during which students can discuss issues of concern to them in the classroom or school.

An alternative approach to a weekly schedule is shown in Example 8.7. Here, flexibility is built into the schedule by combining subject areas in blocks of time. Although you may not actually follow the combinations at all times, such a weekly plan allows for the changing of combinations in ways that still address time requirements. At the same time, you can develop thematic units across all subject areas. A science unit can address the teaching of writing, reading, math, art, and so forth. Stories involving mathematical concepts, such as patterns and ratios, can lead to math activities. However, in order to justify your subject area coverage while working from such a weekly plan, you may need to keep track of how much time you spend on each subject area and what was covered.

---

### Example 8.7: An Alternative Weekly Schedule

**Legend:**

| | |
|---|---|
| R | Reading |
| Ma | Math |
| PE | Physical Education |
| S | Science |
| SS | Social Studies |
| A | Art |
| W | Writing |
| QT | Quiet Time |
| Mu | Music |
| O | Other |
| P/I | Project/Individual Help |
| CM | Classroom Meeting |

**Schedule:**

| Time | Day 1 | Day 2 | Day 3 | Day 4 | Day 5 |
|---|---|---|---|---|---|
| 9:00–9:30 | S W | Ma R W | R W | Ma | Ma SS |
| 9:30–10:30 | | | QT | R W | |
| 10:30–11:00 | A Ma | | O | SS | R S W |
| 11:00–11:30 | | PE | | QT | |
| 11:30–12:00 | | | LUNCH | | |
| 12:00–12:30 | Mu | S SS | Mu | A SS | A S |
| 12:30–1:00 | R SS | | | | QT |
| 1:00–1:30 | QT | | Ma S | O | O |
| 1:30–2:00 | O | O | | | |
| 2:00–2:30 | | QT | | | PE |
| 2:30–3:00 | CM | P/I | P/I | CM | P/I |

---

With a sense of how a weekly plan may look, you can extend your view to long-range plans. Example 8.8 shows a possible yearly plan for science instruction based on the general categories described in the *National Science Education Standards* of the United States. Although schools may block off each unit of instruction for a specific period of time, the plan below provides opportunities to extend and combine units throughout the year. In addition, other topics of your and your students' choice can be added. Such additional investigations can be inserted during the weekly plan options of "projects" and "other" (as noted in Examples 8.6 and 8.7).

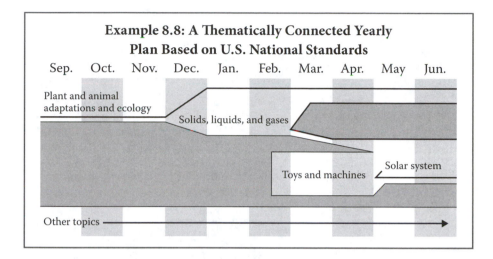

**Example 8.8: A Thematically Connected Yearly Plan Based on U.S. National Standards**

Sep.  Oct.  Nov.  Dec.  Jan.  Feb.  Mar.  Apr.  May  Jun.

Plant and animal adaptations and ecology

Solids, liquids, and gases

Toys and machines     Solar system

Other topics

♦ From the subtopics suggested in Example 8.7, what themes or concepts can be addressed across two or more of these subtopics?

♦ What relationships do you see between certain aspects of the subtopics listed in the example (e.g., does something in one subtopic affect something else in another subtopic)?

♦ What kinds of activities can you think of that will allow students to investigate each subtopic and describe the relationships between subtopics?

Without too much difficulty, you can see a common theme running through the topics listed in Example 8.8. As can be seen in this example, each of these topics share a sense of change. Adaptations change through the process of evolution. Environments change in different ways over different periods of time. Some of these changes are due to the influence of humans and their societies. Societies, as well, change over time. States of matter change. Force and energy describe real or potential changes (which may relate to changes in the states of matter). The earth and solar system have changed during the course of history and change in different ways all of the time. Taking such a broad view of the mandated content can allow us to identify an overarching conceptual theme, which can become a theme for the year. Activity sequences in each of these areas can be introduced and followed for a period of time. Different subtopics can be investigated concurrently and related to one another. Such an approach can provide students with opportunities to make connections to their world across diverse and seemingly different phenomena.

If you have the luxury of designing your own curriculum for the year, you can use either of the possible planning formats in Examples 8.6 and 8.7. What you need to keep in mind is a plan that allows for flexibility and that provides opportunities to go beyond your expectations. As we have seen in previous chapters, children are capable of thinking and learning at much higher levels than you may have assumed previously. Sticking too closely to curricular guidelines may prevent children from going much further with their learning. As teachers, we need to be concerned with helping each child grow to his or her fullest potential. Therefore, we need to plan for such possibilities.

## Advanced Reading

Davis, B., Sumara, D., & Luce-Kapler, R. (2000). *Engaging minds: Learning and teaching in a complex world*. Mahwah, NJ: Lawrence Erlbaum Associates.

Doll, W. E., & Gough, N. (Eds.). (2002). *Curriculum visions*. New York: Peter Lang.

Eisner, E. W. (1994). *Cognition and curriculum reconsidered* (2nd ed.). New York: Teachers College Press.
    Describes how you can address multiple ways of representing and understanding concepts through different sensory experiences.

Fleener, M. J. (2002). *Curriculum dynamics: Recreating heart*. New York: Peter Lang.

Marshall, H. (Ed.). (1992). *Redefining student learning: Roots of educational change*. Norwood, NJ: Ablex.

Monk, M., & Osborne, J. (Eds.). (2000). *Good practice in science teaching: What research has to say*. Philadelphia: Open University Press.

Pearce, C. R. (1999). *Nurturing inquiry: Real science for the elementary classroom*. Portsmouth, NH: Heinemann.
    Great description of how to plan, implement, and assess in an inquiry classroom (written by a practicing teacher).

Polman, J. L. (2000). *Designing project-based science: Connecting learners through guided inquiry*. New York: Teachers College Press.

Wallace, J., & Louden, W. (Eds.). (2002). *Dilemmas of science teaching: Perspectives on problems of practice*. New York: Routledge-Falmer, Taylor & Francis Group.

Wellington, J., & Osborne, J. (2001). *Language and literacy in science education*. Philadelphia: Open University Press.

## Notes

1. The E-7 model described here is an expanded and modified version of the five E's described by L. W. Trowbridge and R. W. Bybee in *Teaching Secondary School Science: Strategies for Developing Scientific Literacy*, 6th ed. (Englewood Cliffs, NJ: Merrill, 1996), p. 228.

2. See D. Tomanek, A case of dilemmas: Exploring my assumptions about teaching science, *Science Education*, 78, 399–414, 1994.

3. From D. Edwards & N. Mercer, *Common Knowledge: The Development of Understanding in the Classroom* (New York: Routledge, 1987); format changed from the original.

*Chapter 9*

# The Classroom as a Community of Young Scientists

In the previous chapters, we have examined a number of issues related to teaching and learning science. Although you may have gained some insight into what a social constructivist and inquiry-based classroom may look like, this chapter will examine the context of the classroom as a community. The notion of community is particularly important in terms of developing our conception of the basic purpose of schooling. Is schooling about learning sets of specified facts, skills, concepts, and so forth? Is schooling about helping children to develop into decent, socially responsible human beings? Is it about helping children learn how to participate in a democratic society? Is it about helping children develop a vision of the possible for what they might do in the future? Sometimes it appears as if schools focus only on the acquisition of specific skills and subject matter content. However, the role of schools should be, if it is not already, to focus on the points in each of the previous questions.

The problems evoked by these questions are that we may find it very difficult to teach children how to be decent and socially responsible, how to participate in a democracy, and how to develop visions of the possible through the typical teacher-directed approaches to instruction. Rather than teach *about* being decent, *about* being socially responsible, *about* participating in a democracy, and *about* developing a vision of the possible, you need to *do* all of these. In other words, you need to model these goals and help to make them manifest in the everyday lives of children in the classroom. The sense of a classroom as a community of learners, inquirers, and visionaries provides the context for manifesting meaningful and relevant learning and thinking within the context of working as a caring and responsible democratic community.

We all belong to multiple communities, such as our neighborhood (if the people in our neighborhood actually relate to one another), our job (e.g., community of professionals or community of laborers), our church or other religious organization, our recreational community, and so forth. All communities have some sort of shared purpose, which brings everyone together. However, communities that function well, that do not marginalize their members, and that effectively engage people in participating are not that common. Part of the problem in establishing and maintaining highly functional communities has to do with the way they are structured. Almost all of our experiences have been in hierarchical communities. A structure with power and control at the top is potentially problematic. Those who are being controlled tend to get resentful and may even rebel. All sorts of conflicts occur, including between people at lower levels of the hierarchy as they compete for the attention and good graces of their superiors or as they compete for a limited number of opportunities to move up in the hierarchy. The other possibility is that people become complacent in their positions in the hierarchy and move along the path of least resistance (or go through the motions). We see such reactions to communities from students in classrooms all the way to citizens within nations.

The alternative to a hierarchical structure for communities is one in which power and control do not move from the top down, but rather are shared and negotiated among all of the participants within the community. Such a system is called a holarchy or embedded layers, as opposed to the top-down layering of hierarchies. Figure 9.1 depicts an elementary classroom community as a holarchy of embedded layers. The center is the layer of full participation. When children begin the year in such a classroom, they may enter around the periphery. As they begin to engage in various aspects of the functioning of the community, they work their way toward the center as they move through layers of increasing participation. The details of this model will be elaborated upon throughout the rest of this chapter.

## 9.1 Developing the Classroom as a Community of Learners, Inquirers, and Young Scientists

The process of developing a classroom community requires a great deal of patience and perseverance on the part of the teacher. A functional community takes time to develop. The children need to go through a process of socialization consistent with the goals and characteristics of such a community. As the teacher, you need to have a firm grasp of these goals and characteristics. From the first day of school and throughout the year, the teacher needs to model these goals and help guide children through the process of functioning in such a community.

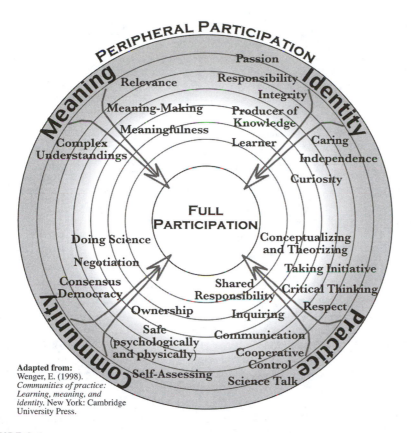

Adapted from:
Wenger, E. (1998). *Communities of practice: Learning, meaning, and identity.* New York: Cambridge University Press.

**FIGURE 9.1**

Take some time to think about communities in which you have been or are involved (such as a school classroom, a job, a club, etc.).

◆ Try to describe how each community fostered (or did not foster) a sense of identity, meaning, practice (or participation), and community.

◆ How do or did you feel in this community?

◆ Did you ever feel marginalized or feel that you were always on the fringe? Why do you think you felt this way?

◆ What can you learn from this experience in terms of what you can and should not do in creating a classroom community?

In Figure 9.1 and Table 9.1 four major dimensions of communities are depicted around the periphery with arrows moving toward the center. Etienne Wenger considers these dimensions to be the key components of any type of community. She identified these dimensions or components from her extensive investigations of a variety of communities of practice, including apprenticeship communities in a variety of past and present cultures, occupations, and other social contexts. These dimensions are important to keep at the forefront of one's thinking as classroom communities are planned and implemented. A brief description of these dimensions follows

### 9.1.1 The Basic Dimensions of Participation in a Community

These basic dimensions of communities need to be used as a framework for designing one's own classroom community. In the beginning of the design process, you need to brainstorm the specific characteristics and activities that need to be a part of each of these dimensions. The lists in the section below show some of the possible specific characteristics and activities.

### 9.1.2 Characteristics of Functional Classroom Communities

Many of the points listed above, as well as related goals and characteristics, appear in previous chapters. These points provide a general framework for guiding our work toward establishing democratic classroom communities. Although the notion of democracy in classrooms has been discussed for most

**TABLE 9.1** The Four Dimensions of Communities (according to Ettienne Wenger, 1998)

| | |
|---|---|
| Identity | "Who am I in this community?" Developing an identity as a member of the classroom community is critically important. Children need to see themselves as (a) active learners and producers of knowledge, (b) inquirers (amateur scientists), (c) valued members of the community with responsibility for running the community, (d) collaborators, and (e) caring and honest members of the community. Without the development of such an identity, a functional and cohesive community cannot develop. |
| Meaning | "What does it mean to be a member of this community?" Meaning not only concerns the purpose and functioning of the community, but also the necessary knowledge and skills. The meaning of a classroom community involves the notion of producing knowledge for some purpose (not just knowledge for knowledge's sake), such as for communicating the students' findings to a larger audience (e.g., on the classroom community's website, articles for local newspapers, performances or displays for parents, etc.). |
| Practice | "How do I participate in the classroom community?" The practices of the community range from what members do individually to what the group (community) does together. Participation includes developing characteristics, such as taking initiative, respecting others, sharing responsibilities, cooperating with others, and building consensus. In addition, participation involves activities that are specific to the classroom community. Such specific activities include talking science (or talking as inquirers and producers of knowledge), thinking critically, thinking creatively, communicating in ways that promote learning, inquiry, and self-governance, and conceptualizing and theorizing for producing knowledge. |
| Community | "What is the purpose, function, and nature (or feeling of) this classroom community?" The classroom community needs to be defined and described in some detail in order to develop and maintain a cohesive and functional classroom. Defining the community draws on the previous three components, but also involves looking at the whole context, including the underlying assumptions that guide everything that is done. For instance, if you consider that all students need to feel ownership over the community, then everything that is done must be consistent with the sense of ownership. You should never take an action that undermines student ownership, such as imposing an arbitrary rule. Children need to see a purpose for their communities, which may be closely tied to identity. Have children develop a name for their community, such as, Ms. Collins' Science Investigators (CSI). They could design and make T-shirts for all community members (including parents). |

- ✦ **Reflect on your experiences as a student or as a teacher.**
- ✦ **Describe specific examples of how schools implement a corporate model of education (through emphasizing conformity, efficiency, obedience, and unchallenged acceptance of authority).**
- ✦ **What effect do these emphases have on children's actions and thinking in the classroom?**
- ✦ **Are these emphases consistent with an instructional approach that asks students to engage in inquiry and the social construction of knowledge?**

of the 20th century (especially in the work of John Dewey), recent concern for this issue has resurfaced across North America. The notion of democratic classrooms does not just mean majority rule, but rather it suggests the kind of participation and attitude needed in a democracy (see Table 9.2).

Current practices in schools tend to de-emphasize democracy in lieu of a more corporate approach to schooling. Such a corporate approach emphasizes *conformity, efficiency, obedience, and unchallenged acceptance of authority.* From this perspective, students are expected to conform to standards of behavior and thinking set by the expectations of teachers and administrators. Instruction is to be delivered efficiently, with an emphasis on acquiring the intended content knowledge set out in curricular documents. Students are expected to obey the authority of the teacher and not challenge arbitrary rules of conduct or content knowledge claims.

On the other hand, an emphasis on democratic education contains five principles for empowering students (and teachers):

1. Believe in the individual's right and responsibility to participate publicly
2. Have a sense of political efficacy, that is, the knowledge that one's contributions to community life are important

**TABLE 9.2** Characteristics of a Classroom Community

| | |
|---|---|
| Responsibility | Children take responsibility for their own actions, including learning, participation, and behavior. They also take responsibility for the actions of their classmates and for running the classroom community. |
| Independence | Children become independent learners and inquirers. They develop their own goals and work toward them. |
| Leadership | Children take on roles of leadership in conducting investigations, managing classroom activities, and governing different aspects of the classroom community. |
| Collaboration | Children collaborate with others during classroom activities and the governance of the community. |
| Communication | Children actively communicate with one another about their work and the running of the classroom community. They are sensitve to the needs of all individuals to participate in group and classroom discussions. They actively listen and consider the opinions and concerns of others even if they disagree. |
| Consensus building | In a democratic classroom community, students need to develop the skills of building consensus, rather than voting on particular issues (see Section 7.2.1 in Chapter 7 for a more complete discussion of voting). When people vote, there are always a lot of individuals who lose and consequently feel marginalized. By building consensus and negotiating particular stands on issues (and knowledge claims), you can avoid marginalizing any of your children. You may want to have nonbinding votes just to see where individuals stand, but consensus needs to be the goal. If consensus cannot be reached, it is better to table the issue and try to reach consensus later, or at least agree to disagree. |
| Self-governance | Children need to take on roles in the governance process, including chairing classroom meetings that deal with specific issues. They participate in developing rules and patterns for working and participating in the classroom community. |
| Caring and support | An environment that fosters caring and that supports each individual is critical to developing a safe classroom where students can feel they can take risks and be a part of the community. Children need to care about the feelings, needs, and uniqueness of their classmates, and offer emotional and intellectual support for one another. |
| Relevance | Activities and tasks are relevant to the needs and interests of individuals and the group. This relevance applies to what is being investigated and studied, as well as to what decisions need to be made in terms of the classroom community. |
| Ownership | Each child feels that the classroom is his or hers. By taking on such a sense of ownership, they do not want to do anything that would jeopardize their classroom community. |

3. Value the principles of democratic life—equality (equity), liberty, community

4. Know that alternative arrangements to the status quo exist and are worthwhile

5. Gain the requisite intellectual skills to participate in public discourse[1]

These principles have numerous implications for how we view children's learning and how we view the process of teaching. In order for children to participate democratically in a classroom community, the way you relate to students needs to take these principles into account. You need to view each child as a unique human being with something to offer the community—individuals who do not need to conform to arbitrary standards, who challenge authority, and who act as responsible participants in a community rather than being blindly obedient. Although these types of actions may seem somewhat radical, they are the basis for a functioning democracy. To challenge authority does not imply belligerence, but suggests that children can be critical of claims made by some authority. For instance, a claim made by a book or by the teacher can result in a response by children like the following: "I don't agree with that. It doesn't make sense, because I've seen [a certain event] and that's not what happens." Thinking and talking like this promotes critical participation in a democratic community. In addition, such thinking is a major goal of scientific communities, where knowledge claims are not taken at face value. We are being bombarded constantly by knowledge claims of all sorts. Television commercials claim that a particular product has been proven to be effective. News programs report that scientists have proven that a certain process works in a specific way. As teachers, we want children (and adults) to be able to say, "Wait a minute … first of all, science can't prove anything. And furthermore, I wonder how they conducted their study. Did they account for [this or that] variable?"

As is apparent from the previous discussion, many teachers are beginning to view teaching and learning from the perspective of education for democracy. This perspective also involves the relationship between children and knowledge. Typically, schools tend to emphasize students as consumers of knowledge, rather than as producers of knowledge (see Example 9.1). In most classrooms, students are expected to remember facts and concepts delivered by the teacher. Even when students are engaged in hands-on activities, the expectation is that students will be able to recall specific information for the teacher. The teacher's role is that of knowledge authority. Challenging that authority is rarely done. However, when students are engaged in the production of knowledge, the teacher is no longer viewed as the knowledge authority. Students engage in inquiry that is of interest and relevance to them. The outcome is the production of knowledge that is shared publicly with the classroom or in the local community or beyond.

What is being suggested here is quite different from what takes place in most schools. Teachers and researchers involved in education for democracy see their efforts as going against the current tendency to corporatize schools. The corporate ideas and values that are evident in much of schooling (as mentioned earlier) include (a) an emphasis on *conformity*—that children learn the same thing and behave in similar ways; (b) *competition*—collaborative learning is not valued; (c) *memorization*—learning material quickly with a resulting conformity of knowledge; (d) *efficiency*—teach in ways that minimize downtime and inessential material; and (e) *teaching as a mechanistic process*—teachers follow a set agenda, procedures, and curriculum, in other words, following a teacher-proof curriculum.

The notion of a community of scientists, as described here, involves two conflicting perspectives. Typically, philosophers and sociologists of science have depicted scientific communities as not necessarily democratic. Normal science, as described by Thomas Kuhn, and stable inquiry, as described by Joseph Schwab, tend to be characterized by conformity, efficiency, and acceptance of authority. From this perspective, scientists conform to the standards and views of the science community. Their work is based on the efficient churning out of data in studies that fit with the prevailing views. Challenging

**Refer to Example 9.1.**

◆ What are the differences in the two approaches?

◆ What is the nature of the learning in both classrooms?

◆ What is the source of motivation for the students in both schools?

◆ What are the differences in the two classes between student involvement in inquiry and student control over their actions, thinking, and learning?

◆ What are the differences in how children are prepared for participation in a democracy?

---

**Example 9.1: Classroom Approaches:
Consuming Knowledge versus Producing Knowledge**

## Classroom Approach 1

A teacher is doing a unit on the environment. Many activities are conducted, including field trips to a local river to take samples and monitor pollution. The teacher carefully plans each class with specific concepts and facts to be learned. He presents this information to the students with colorful posters, overheads, videos, and even classroom discussions. Each of the activities, which include experiments and field trips, is used to demonstrate these concepts. The presentation of the information clearly demonstrates that pollution is bad and that everyone should follow the three R's (reduce, reuse, recycle).

## Classroom Approach 2

A teacher is doing a unit on the same topic. She has a number of possible activities planned, but her intent is to involve the children in doing their own research on the topic. The central focus of the study becomes the local river downstream from the major industrial area of their city. After a class discussion of the environmental concerns about the river, the students begin regular visits to the river. When on site, they collect samples and perform a number of simple tests. They also investigate the life in the river. In class discussions, they question what the information they have collected means and decide that they need to compare the river results with samples taken from another part of the river upstream from the city. They begin finding major differences between the two collection sites. As they continue to analyze their data, all of the students feel increasingly upset by their findings. As a group, they decide to write an article for the local newspaper, so that they can share their results with the general public. The article draws so much attention to the problem that the city council is forced to take action. (Although this is a fictional story, similar stories actually have taken place in a number of schools and communities across North America.)

---

◆ What characteristics of a democratic classroom community do you see in Example 9.2?

◆ How can you describe the notions of identity, meaning, practice (participation), and community (from Figure 9.1) as they have manifested in this example?

◆ In addition to the characteristics of classroom communities listed earlier in this chapter, what other aspects of this classroom are conducive to and supportive of classrooms as communities?

◆ How does this classroom compare to others you have seen and experienced?

◆ How do you see yourself working toward creating such a classroom community?

◆ What strengths, abilities, and personality characteristics do you have that will support your efforts in creating such a community?

◆ What aspects of yourself do you need to monitor in order for them not to interfere with the goals of creating a classroom community?

the accepted views and theoretical frameworks can result in being ignored and, in the extreme case, banishment from the community. There are many historical and contemporary examples of such cases (e.g., Galileo is a prime example; the Roman Catholic Church has only just recently exonerated him for insisting on a sun-centered, rather than earth-centered view of the heavens). Science does not progress in ways that are particularly nice and orderly. However, in the past several years, the Environmental Protection Agency in the United States has stated that science should be democratized. The public should have access to the knowledge of science. The decisions based on scientific knowledge should no longer be left entirely to the scientific community, but should involve an informed public. From this perspective, the classroom scientific community, described in this chapter, combines the positive attributes of the nature of science with the vision of education for democracy.

**Example 9.2: Observations of a Day in a Classroom Community**

The following observations took place during a one-day visit to a public school classroom in a major urban area. The classroom (depicted in Example 9.4) consisted of 25 grade 4 students of mixed ethnic backgrounds, including a range of abilities in speaking English. This visit took place in mid-April, well into the school year, and after six or seven months of work on establishing the classroom community.

The day started with children wandering into the classroom during the 15 to 20 minutes before school started. As the children settled into the room, they talked with each other, examined some of their ongoing experiments with plant growth, played with blocks, or played with one of the two birds in a cage near the teacher's desk in the corner. Some students engaged in short conversations with the teacher, whom they addressed by her first name (we will call her Jane). (The teacher said that in her first teaching position, the principal told her that the children would not respect her if they called her by her first name. She replied, "I'll keep that in mind. And if that happens, I'll change." She never has.) Everyone was very relaxed as the beginning of the school day approached.

With only a quiet indication by the teacher (I was not aware of any overt signal), the students gathered in the small carpeted area set aside for group gatherings. The teacher had been absent the day before. She had arranged for a substitute so that she could make her appointment with a doctor; however, the substitute was canceled due to an administrative mistake.

Jane started, "I hear you didn't have a substitute yesterday?"

The children in near unison asked, "Yeah, where were you?"

After explaining, Jane asked, "So, what did you do?"

One girl said, "I took the attendance, then took it to the office. When I got back, we all decided that we'd continue reading [a book they were reading]. So, we all took turns reading and then we discussed it."

Jane, half laughing, said, "Well, what do you need me for? The office was impressed that you really didn't need a teacher."

Following this interaction, another girl took the attendance with their bird mascot sitting on her shoulder. When she was ready to take the attendance to the office, she started to return the bird to the cage, but Jane said, "Why don't you take him with you. Everyone likes to see him."

Then, almost seamlessly, the first instructional activity of the day began. Jane briefly explained that she was going to pass around a sealed plastic sandwich bag with very moldy bread inside. As the bag was passed around, each child made one observation. Throughout the entire activity, the only sound besides the one child talking was the screeching of a bird from across the room. All of the children were listening intently to what each child had to say:

"It's green."
"It feels like clay."
"Looks like moss."
"Some of it feels hard."
"Some of it looks like fried pistachio nuts."

After this session, the children went off to work in groups on several of their plant study activities and experiments. They started examining a number of plastic baggies of different kinds of mold, which they had grown by placing fruit, bread, sandwiches, and so forth, in different locations around the room. As they finished this activity, they took measurements of their plant growth experiments and sketched and made observations of various kinds of stems.

Throughout this time, I wandered around the room talking to and observing the children. I noticed after one circuit of the room that a group I had spoken with was no longer the same. The group members had changed. Then I began to notice that all of the groups changed from time to time, as children got up and joined different groups. I also noticed that all of the talk taking place among the students was about the work in which they were engaged. They shared observations, argued about results, and negotiated explanations. As some children finished with all of their plant activities, they began other activities. A group of boys started playing on the computer. A group of girls took out a box of geo-blocks and began making different kinds of patterns. Another group of boys constructed buildings out of blocks. When all of the students were finished with the plant activities, they gathered on the carpet and shared the results from their plant experiments and activities.

The schedule for the day was written on the chalkboard:

| 8:20 | Plants |
|------|--------|
| 9:20 | Social Studies |
| 9:45 | Gym |
| 10:30 | Science Talk |
| 11:00 | Quiet Time |
| 11:30–12:15 | Lunch |
| 12:30 | Math |
| 1:15 | Cleanup |
| 1:30 | Meeting |

However, social studies never happened. I overheard one child say to others at the table as 9:30 approached, "Aren't we supposed to be doing social studies?" Another boy said very quietly, "It doesn't matter. We'll do it another time."

After gym, the students and Jane gathered together on the carpet. Everyone sat on the floor in a big circle with a small tape recorder in the center of the circle. Jane began by saying, "Well, we haven't done this for a while, so we'll see how it goes [referring to doing science talks]. We've been studying plants for a while and I thought it might be a good time to try to answer this question: How did plants begin?" Almost all of the children started talking at the same time. But as soon as one child established that he or she had the "floor", everyone else immediately stopped and listened intently. Only occasionally did Jane speak, and usually to ask a clarifying question. Throughout the science talk session, she took notes and listened carefully to every point made by the students. The content of the science talk turned very quickly to the issue of how plants moved onto the land. One boy brought up the notion of increasing complexity ("algae doesn't have that many parts"). Before long, a disagreement emerged about the dispersion and origin of plants on different continents. As different students stated their point and supporting rationale, everyone else listened very carefully. Finally, one girl reminded the others that all of the continents were "smushed together" a long time ago. From start to finish, all of the children were very supportive and encouraging of one another. Those who did not talk as much were supported with cheers and comments by the others, showing their interest in what the quieter individuals had to say. At one point, Jane added that one quiet girl's comments were "very important and could have fit in after earlier comments." She continued by explaining this girl's comments could have led to a new theme to be followed.

Two of the ESL (English as a second language) students were almost always sitting together. One could speak and understand virtually no English, while the other was capable of functioning in

English. Apparently, from the beginning of the year, these two boys paired up on their own, one acting as the translator for the other. Through the entire science talk, the two boys sat next to each other, whispering translations and comments.

At the end of the day, the children conducted a classroom meeting. One child acted as the moderator, while others brought up points or added to others' comments. One child brought up a concern that after quiet time "it gets too noisy. And, some of us still want to read." Other children suggested ways of accommodating the needs of those who wanted to play and those who wanted to read. Another child brought up an issue: "[A girl in another class] is always picked last when we play kick ball at recess. And now she's crying a lot. And I don't think it's fair." Both boys and girls added comments about how it feels to be picked last and generated some options for picking teams so that the same person would not always be picked last.

This day in the classroom was characterized by the teacher's and students' genuineness. Although energetic, the environment had a quality of being very laid back. Smiles and laughs were frequent on the faces of the teacher and children. Jane cared deeply about her students. She treated them each as respected citizens of the community—each with something important to offer. Her dealings with the children were marked by gentleness, as she prodded, guided, and supported the children. At one point, a group of children was making fun of someone, and with an almost lighthearted but obviously serious approach, Jane said very gently, "Thank you, I don't need imitators over here."

Her gentleness and caring seemed to be adopted by the children. The children treated everyone with respect. They cared how others felt and celebrated in each other's successes. Jane admits that the year did not start off this way. It was only in the last month or so that the children had settled into a stable and functional community.

## 9.2 Establishing a Classroom Community

At this point, you should have some sense of the nature of a classroom community. However, who exactly are the members of this community? Of course, you, as the teacher, and your students are members, but the community should not be limited to you and your class. As shown in Figure 9.2, it is important to involve parents as key members in this community. Parental support and involvement are critical to the development of a successful community. Such support and involvement can extend from simple understandings of and support for what you are trying to accomplish in the classroom to active involvement in the everyday functions of the classroom community. If you do not involve parents in the community, there is a great potential for conflict between what you are trying to accomplish and what parents may see as the goals for their children. However, by involving parents, this potential for conflict is greatly reduced, if not eliminated.

In addition to parents, it is important to involve the principal and other school administrators, other teachers, other school personnel (custodians, secretaries, etc.), school district and school board personnel, and people from the local community. Although these people may not be involved as much as parents, they are equally important to the success of the classroom com-

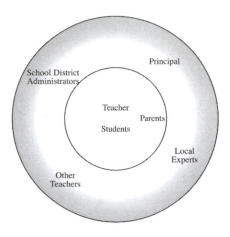

**FIGURE 9.2**

munity. Of course, without the support of the school principal, any efforts to establish and maintain an inquiry community are going to be difficult to accomplish. In general, all members of the classroom community should be viewed as having something to offer. The school custodian may be involved in flying model airplanes. The school secretary may be an amateur photographer. Your car mechanic obviously has expertise with mechanical systems. Other teachers in your school may have particular hobbies or areas of academic expertise that can be utilized in your classroom. The possibilities are endless for the potential expertise that can be invited into your classroom community from the local area. But you do not want to forget that each student in your classroom also has special strengths, interests, and abilities that can be useful to the work of the community.

As mentioned earlier, Etienne Wenger and her colleague Jean Lave drew on apprenticeship models in developing the notion of communities of practice. In this sense, the classroom community involves the teacher as mentor and the students as apprentices. From the model in Figure 9.1, we see student apprentices entering the community from the periphery, then moving toward the center where they can begin taking on the role of mentor in a variety of circumstances. One student may help another with a math problem or with editing a paper. As other people enter into the classroom community, they too may start from the periphery and move more quickly into mentorship roles. The mechanic or doctor may not have much expertise in working with young children through inquiry and knowledge production. So, your role as mentor extends to them as you induct them into mentorship roles.

Figure 9.3 provides an overview of the process of establishing and maintaining a classroom community. The planning process may begin as a fantasizing approach, where you try to paint a picture of what your ideal classroom will be like. As you work through this process, you will need to specify the attributes of the classroom, along with the types of activities and procedures involved. These attributes and other characteristics become the goals and objectives for your classroom community. In a similar approach to that described in Chapters 7 and 8, you need to specify exactly what you mean by

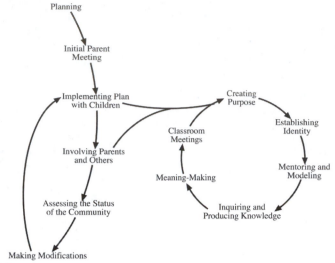

**FIGURE 9.3**

each attribute. For instance, you want your students to take on responsibility. But what does responsibility mean in terms of how it is to be manifested in the classroom? For this particular attribute, there are a number of contexts upon which one can be responsible, such as socially responsible, morally or ethically responsible, economically responsible, environmentally responsible, and so forth. Certainly, you want your students to develop a sense of responsibility in a wide variety of contexts, both within your classroom community and beyond this community. In more general terms, we think of someone who is responsible as (a) being able to answer for one's actions, (b) taking action in a particular situation, rather than defer to someone else, and (c) in related senses, taking initiative, being ethical, not avoiding tasks, and being straightforward and honest. As we can see, the simple notion of fostering responsibility takes on more depth of meaning and complexity once we begin to define it. At the same time, we have a better notion of how we can help students more fully develop a sense of personal and social responsibility (among others) within our classrooms.

Once you have a plan in place, it is important to get parents involved from the beginning. Before school starts, or at least during the first week of school, invite parents to a meeting with refreshments. At this meeting, make sure all of the parents have a chance to get to know each other, then introduce what your goals are for the children, how you will be approaching teaching and learning, how you will be establishing a learning and inquiry community, and why you are approaching teaching, learning, and community from the approach of inquiry, problem solving, and projects. Involve parents in coming up with suggestions for how they can help and for what other sources of expertise exist in the community. It may be a good idea to do a simple inquiry activity with the parents that demonstrates how the approach works and how they have learned from this approach. In addition, you may want to schedule a few additional meetings throughout the year. These meetings can focus on fund-raising to buy equipment or to pay for extended field studies, on specific projects the children are going to be working on, and on children's displays or performances that are the final products of their work in class.

As you implement your plans for a classroom community, you will need to focus on how to create a purpose and how to establish identity as a group member. Both of these aspects may take some time to develop. Although you should talk with your students about the purpose of "our community" and "who they are in this community," the real impact will come from manifesting purpose and identity. As students begin to acquire more responsibility, feel a sense of ownership, see that their ideas are valued, and so forth, they will begin to internalize a sense of purpose and identity.

As the community begins to take shape, parents and others need to be involved as much as possible in the daily workings of the classroom. Even stopping in to visit for a few minutes every so often helps to establish their membership in the community. However, visits with a purpose are essential. Parents can help with a field study, with developing final products, or with teaching students how to do something with which they have expertise.

Throughout the year and on a continual basis, you will need to assess how the community is developing and working. Are students acquiring ownership? Are they taking on responsibility? Are they developing identities as inquirers and knowledge producers? Constantly ask yourself these types of questions, and then make observations or collect other types of data that may help you answer these questions. If you see particular problems, brainstorm possible solution strategies, and then make modifications.

## 9.3 Setting up Your Classroom

This section will explore some of the issues involved in creating a physical space that is conducive to a functional classroom community of learners and inquirers. The overall layout and specific components of classrooms are important considerations when designing a classroom. The layout and components are important in creating an atmosphere and a functionality that facilitate the development of democratic, social constructivist, and inquiry-based communities in the classroom.

### 9.3.1 The Physical Arrangement

The physical arrangement of your classroom can have a big impact on the atmosphere of the room and the functioning of the community. There is no one right way to arrange a classroom. In fact, the arrangement of the classroom should be a combination of elements that reflect your personality, your vision of the atmosphere you want to create, the kinds of activities you want to have occur, and the practicalities of movement, storage, and access to materials and work spaces.

The arrangement of your room, including the position of the teacher's desk, the types of student work spaces, the arrangement of student work spaces, and so forth, *sends implicit messages to the students*. The teacher's

- ◆ **What messages about the role of the teacher and interactions among the students are conveyed in the arrangement of the classrooms in Examples 9.3, 9.4, 9.5 and 9.6?**
- ◆ **What kinds of activities can take place in these classrooms? Which kinds are easily accommodated? Which kinds would be difficult to do?**
- ◆ **How do 25 children fit into each of these rooms? What does this imply about children's work spaces?**
- ◆ **What kind of atmosphere is created in each of these classrooms?**
- ◆ **What kinds of movement patterns and access to materials can take place in each classroom?**

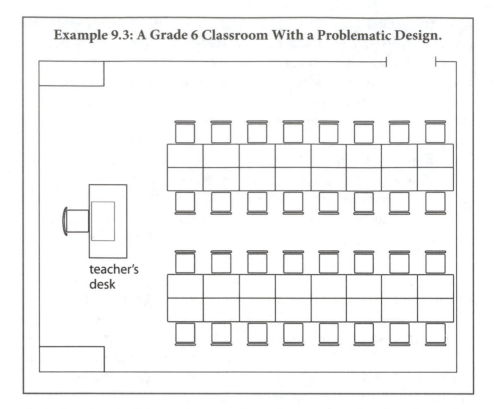

**Example 9.3: A Grade 6 Classroom With a Problematic Design.**

teacher's desk

desk placed at the front and center of the classroom implies that the teacher is at the center of attention and is in a position of authority. Student desks in rows facing the front of the room imply that the teacher is the source of knowledge and that talk among students is not valued. As you consider how you want to design your classroom, you need to think about how your classroom arrangement can send messages that are consistent with your goals for a classroom community.

At the same time, you need to consider the kinds of activities you expect to occur. Do you want students involved in group discussions and projects? Do you want to allow children opportunities to work alone? Do you want to work with the class as a whole group? Do you want to provide areas where students can store their work and ongoing experiments? Do you want to provide areas where students can have access to specialized equipment? Answering these questions will help you decide on the kinds of spaces you need. Once you have a sense of the spaces you need, you can proceed with coming up with some possible arrangements.

You also need to pay attention to the practicalities of movement and access. Students need to be able to move about the room for various activities and to access materials. The locations of supplies and materials need to be easily accessible.

Examples 9.3 to 9.6 show four actual classrooms. The first of these examples depicts a problematic design, while the remaining three show designs of successful classroom communities. As you look at these examples, try to imagine what it would be like to teach (or be a student) in such a classroom. What would it feel like? What kinds of activities can you imagine happening

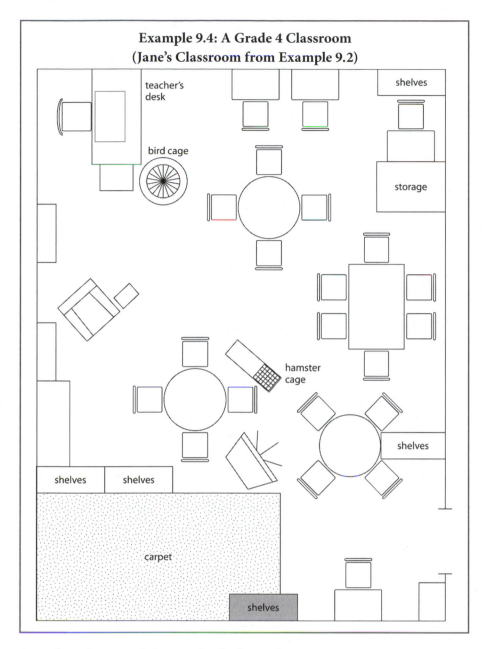

**Example 9.4: A Grade 4 Classroom
(Jane's Classroom from Example 9.2)**

teacher's desk

bird cage

shelves

storage

hamster cage

shelves

shelves    shelves

carpet

shelves

in such a classroom? As you think about these questions, start to come up with your own ideas of how you might want to arrange a classroom.

In Example 9.3, the teacher seems to be caught between wanting to control the action of the classroom and be the authority and wanting to facilitate some communication between students. However, the design is very limiting in the types of activities and interactions. The more formalized structure does not create an atmosphere conducive to a classroom community. At the same time, the boy sitting at the lower right side of the room (as in the last question in the sidebar), from my own observations, climbed over the desks to reach the door.

In Examples 9.4 to 9.6, you see a variety of classroom arrangements that facilitate the development of learning communities. In each of these arrangements, student work, books, materials, posters, and so forth, add to the visual

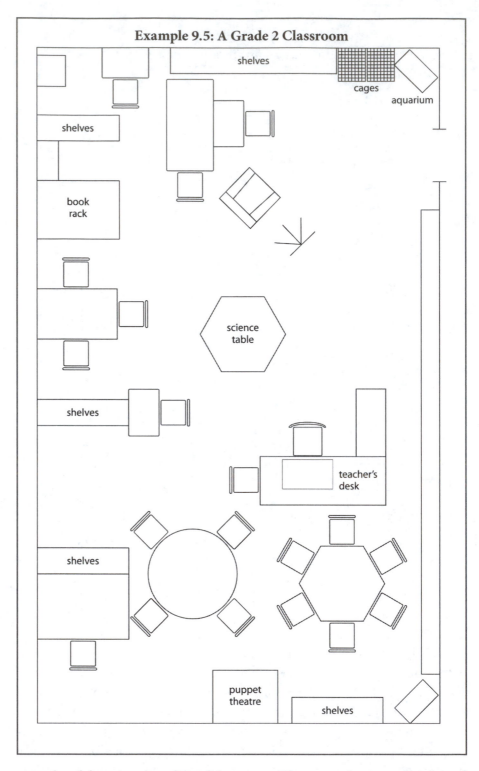

**Example 9.5: A Grade 2 Classroom**

appeal and functional quality of the rooms. The atmospheres are bright and cheerful. Walking into each of these classrooms brings a sense of excitement and stimulation, within an overall relaxed atmosphere.

Each of these classrooms also has specific areas for different types of activity, which promote flexibility and active participation in the classroom community. Ready accessibility to materials and supplies allows children to find

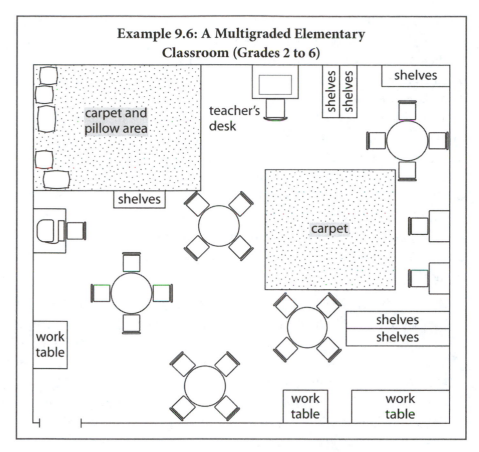

**Example 9.6: A Multigraded Elementary Classroom (Grades 2 to 6)**

carpet and pillow area

teacher's desk

shelves

shelves

shelves

carpet

shelves

shelves

shelves

shelves

work table

work table

work table

what they need during activities and to return these materials when they are finished with them. There are places for the class to meet as a whole, for small groups to work, and for individuals to find a quiet place to read or work alone. In Example 9.6, the carpeted and pillowed area provides a location where children can read, work in groups, or find a quiet place to relax if they are having a bad day. The needs of the children are accommodated and even become the central focus of each of these classroom arrangements.

### 9.3.2 Specific Areas and Centers

Depending on your own goals and needs in the classroom, you need to consider the specific areas and structures you want to include in your room design. An inquiry-based classroom should have plenty of easily accessible storage areas for supplies, equipment, resource materials, and books, as well as *room to keep the children's ongoing experiments and projects.* Bookshelves (which you can build) with plastic see-through containers or boxes can provide an easy way to organize and store many of your supplies and equipment (a list of some of the supplies and equipment is provided in Appendix K). Shelves or book racks can store a variety of books from optional readings to reference materials. The tops of shelves can be used for animal cages, aquaria, terraria, plants, and children's experiments.

Other areas you may want to include are a computer center and a construction center with simple tools (e.g., saws, hammers, screw drivers, etc.)

for building displays or experimental equipment (e.g., a mouse maze, passive solar-heated house models, ramps for testing toy car acceleration). Some teachers have built reading lofts from 2-in. by 4-in. boards, 0.75-in. plywood or particleboard, and carpeting. Reading lofts expand the usable space in your classroom and provide a cozy area for children to relax and read.

A science-and-technology exploration table may be a nice addition. You can start the year by placing a variety of objects, which can be related to a future topic, on the table along with any equipment that may aid children's exploration (e.g., hand lenses, forceps). As the year progresses, children should be encouraged to start bringing in their own discoveries to share with the class. However, successful incorporation and use of such a table requires that the items and topics be changed on a regular basis. Watch for waning interest, then rework the table. Some examples of what can be placed on a science exploration table include

- **Magnets**—A number of different kinds of magnets; a variety of metals, such as steel, aluminum, copper, and a variety of other common substances and materials found around the home. Children can be encouraged to bring in their own materials to test.
- **Birds**—A number of different kinds of birds' nests, abandoned eggs, a variety of feathers, bird skeleton or bones (if you find a dead bird, you can bury it in a can, with wire mesh over the top, for a month or so—when you dig it up the skeleton will be clean; see Appendix I.1.11 for more details on cleaning and mounting skeletons), hand lenses, and forceps.
- **Outer space**—An assortment of space fantasy toys, including those from Star Wars, Star Trek, and so on; star maps; a moon map; photos of astronomical objects and events; and any materials you can obtain from NASA or the Canadian Space Agency.
- **A take-apart center**—Old radios, small kitchen appliances, VCRs, telephones, and so forth, and a variety of tools, such as different sizes and kinds of screw drivers (flat head, Phillips head, Robertson head), different sizes of wrenches, monkey wrenches, wire cutters, and pliers.

At least one computer center is important to include in your classroom. Of course, children will want an adequate supply of games, so you may want to choose those with some educational value. However, the most important uses are going to involve telecommunications (e.g., e-mail and web-browsing capabilities), word processing, graphics, databases, spreadsheets, and, if possible, some simulation software for engaging students in investigations that are not feasible to conduct in the classroom. Of course, there are other kinds of software, but you need to be selective about what you include. Drill and practice software and programs geared toward passive, rote learning are not as valuable in classrooms geared toward active inquiry. Look for programs that will facilitate the children's investigations, the sharing of knowledge they have constructed, and the creation of high-quality products that allow them to share proudly their understandings with others. You may want to consider having the children design their own classroom web page (software packages are available that allow you to develop web pages with minimal knowledge of the more technical aspects of web page construction). Parts of such a web page can be devoted to sharing the results of the children's investigations. (See Appendix J for more information on incorporating technology in the classroom.)

## 9.4 Working with Children

The process of socializing children into a classroom community may take months. Throughout this process, you likely will encounter many ups and downs, successes and failures. There may be times when you think the approach is not working, and you want to exert more control and return to a more traditional approach. However, you need to view your work with children as a long-term process and one that will produce important results in children's social skills, independence, responsibility, and self-esteem. As in Example 9.2, after months of hard work with the children, Jane's classroom demonstrated their independence and responsibility by carrying out the class activities in her (and any adult's) absence. Patience, perseverance, and consistency are all needed in order to see a realization of the expectations and goals involved in establishing an inquiry community.

However, you may find the metaphors listed in Table 9.3 helpful in developing a sense of the roles you may assume as a teacher.

In addition to the actions you can take with children, it also is very important to involve children in the running of the classroom community. Rules of conduct should be negotiated among the entire classroom community (i.e., children and teacher). The children may want to develop their own bill of rights or constitution. Routines (such as taking attendance, cleaning the room, organizing presentations for parents, caring for animals, etc.) can be the responsibility of the children. The children need to develop a sense of ownership—that the classroom community is their community and they are responsible for what happens there.

As a final point, you may want to consider some of the work that has been done with creativity. Schools, as well as many businesses, tend to stifle creativity. However, many schools and businesses all over the world are beginning to address ways of nurturing and maximizing creativity. The list in Table 9.4 provides some ideas about how creativity is stifled—referred to as creativity killers in a book and PBS television series called *The Creative Spirit*, by Daniel Goleman, Paul Kaufman, and Michael Ray.

From a positive perspective, you need to keep in mind that creativity in any kind of endeavor, including science, operates from passion. Passion is the intrinsic motivation. People who operate from a basis of passion tend to set very high standards for themselves, to be persistent in reaching their goals, and to be willing to take risks. Your work with children needs to encourage and support the development of these characteristics.

❋

✦ **Can you think of any other examples of the metaphors listed above?**

✦ **What other metaphors can you think of that describe the roles of the teacher in a classroom community?**

✦ **What are some metaphors that describe the roles of teachers in more traditional classrooms?**

**TABLE 9.3** Teacher Roles in a Classroom Community

| | |
|---|---|
| Teacher as mentor | Mentor is the primary metaphor or role describing the teacher in a classroom community. Mentors are experts within a particular community of practice. Their key function is to help students become experts as learners, inquirers, problem solvers, knowledge producers, communicators, and participants in democratic communities. |
| Teacher as coach | As children struggle with ways of acting and talking in a classroom community, the teacher needs to coach the children. When a child makes fun of another child's comment during a discussion, the teacher needs to coach the child gently in more appropriate ways of reacting. Example: "Johnny, a comment like that can hurt someone's feelings. What is it that you don't agree with? Maybe you can just state your reasons for why you don't agree with his comment." |
| Teacher as guide | When children are struggling with an activity or problem, the teacher can help guide the child through the process. In many instances, we, as teachers, may not take the time to guide a student, but will just do the task for them. However, children need to struggle through the problem or task in order to gain the knowledge and skills. Guiding the children involves supporting them in their attempt and helping them go through the process. Example: Cathy is having trouble constructing a soda straw bridge between two chairs. She's getting quite upset and wants to quit, saying, "I can't do this! I'm not going to …" The teacher comes by and says, "I think you can build as good a bridge as anyone. Let's see what we can do." She helps Cathy see the problem and what steps are needed to come to a solution. |
| Teacher as model | The teacher needs to model the kinds of behavior, talk, and thinking that are central to an inquiry community. Such modeling can involve asking probing questions, asking clarifying questions, caring about the children, listening carefully to children's comments, appreciating the contributions of all children, being cheerful and kind, being curious about everything, being patient, and so forth. |
| Teacher as facilitator | The teacher needs to be prepared to help make things happen. If children ask an interesting and meaningful question, although the teacher may not have planned on addressing this topic, she or he needs to take the time to find ways of exploring this question. Such an effort may involve (a) seeking out an expert in the field to lead some activities in the classroom, (b) building an apparatus to help investigate the question, or (c) finding the necessary materials and supplies needed to explore the topic. |
| Teacher as orchestrator | Several different groups and individuals may be interested in several different topics or activities. The teacher may need to find ways of accommodating each group and individual, so that in various parts of the room different groups are working on very different activities. The teacher needs to orchestrate the routines of the varied activities and groups. |

**TABLE 9.4** Creativity Killers

| | |
|---|---|
| Surveillance | Children feel they are constantly being watched and criticized. The result is that creativity and risk-taking are repressed. |
| Evaluation | Excessive evaluation that is not constructive can result in children worrying about what others think to the point that they are never satisfied with their own work. |
| Rewards | The excessive use of prizes can deprive children of experiencing the intrinsic pleasure of creative activity. |
| Competition | Putting children in win-lose situations with only one winner can prevent them from making progress and feeling that they can work at their own rate. |
| Overcontrol | Telling children exactly how to do a particular task can make them feel that any originality is a mistake and that exploration is a waste of time. |
| Restricting choice | Telling children in which activities to engage can dampen their curiosity and sense of ownership. You should be supporting children in allowing them to be led by their curiosity and passion. |
| Pressure | Imposing grandiose expectations that are way beyond children's abilities can create an aversion to the subject area. |
| Time limits | Limiting children's time on tasks can prevent the cultivation of creativity. Children need open-ended time to explore, savor the experience, and take ownership. They also need downtime. Creativity does not always arise on call. |

## 9.5 Working with Parents and the Extended Community

Successful classroom communities require the support of parents. Much of what you will be doing in a classroom of this sort may be very different from the typical expectations of parents. So, in order to gain the support of parents, you need to be proactive—that is, communicate with and involve parents from the very beginning. However, before you begin this process you need to be well prepared. This book should help you with the beginnings of developing a strong theoretical and practical understanding of what your goals and expectations are. Although it is unfortunate that many teachers do not value theory, it is the theory that will allow you to communicate clearly and thoroughly what you want to do and what you are doing in your classroom. Table 9.5 includes some ideas of actions you can take to gain the support of parents.

Getting the parents on your side early in the school year will prevent many problems from arising. All too often, an adversarial relationship develops between parents and teachers primarily because of different sets of expectations and a lack of communication. This kind of problem can be avoided by developing a positive relationship right from the start. Such positive relationships with parents can help develop the atmosphere of the classroom community, as parents help to reinforce and extend your goals and expectations.

Extending the positive relations outside of the classroom can go beyond the parents as well. Local business people and others with interests and expertise of potential value in your classroom can be recruited to help. Some of these people may donate goods or services. Others may be willing to work with your class in their business or professional location or in your classroom. A doctor may bring some simple diagnostic equipment (e.g., stethoscope) and show children how to use the equipment and how to interpret what they see or hear.

You also may want to involve the administrators in your school. Some principals may not understand what you are trying to achieve. In such cases, you need to communicate your goals and rationale. In addition, inviting them into your classes to share their expertise may be a skillful way to gain their support.

When involving anyone in helping with class activities, you need to be prepared to train them in working from an inquiry approach. Prior to their involvement, you need to talk with them about how you want to engage your students in asking questions, formulating explanations, and so forth. Often such an approach will be a great relief to many non-teachers, who may be quite nervous about speaking to a classroom full of children. When they find that they are to be there as guides and resource people, they will feel much more relaxed and willing to participate.

- ✦ Have you experienced any of these creativity killers as a student at any level of education?
- ✦ How did you feel when you experienced these creativity killers?
- ✦ Did you ever experience situations where creativity was supported? How did you feel?
- ✦ What implications do these creativity killers have on your developing notions of a classroom community?

- ✦ From Example 9.2, how do you see that creativity was supported?
- ✦ How do you think you, as a teacher, can support creativity?

**TABLE 9.5** Activities for Gaining Parent Support

| | |
|---|---|
| Parent in-service | Begin the year with an early-evening in-service workshop for parents. Introduce the parents to the goals and expectations of your program and classroom community. Be sure to state a clear rationale for each point. Show parents how they can help reinforce some of the goals at home. Parents will also appreciate specific information on what kinds of books to get or read to their children (i.e., what will help children learn to read), how to respond to their children's questions, how to help them with homework projects, what kinds of science activities they can do at home, and so forth. You may want to include a sample inquiry activity in which the parents can engage. This meeting also can serve as a time to find out about the parents' interests and expertise, and to enlist volunteers for specific events or classroom activities. Of course, serving tea, coffee, and cookies may help parents relax and feel welcome in your classroom community. |
| Classroom newsletter | A monthly newsletter to parents describing your goals and expectations and the results of children's work is very helpful. Involve your students in writing and publishing this newsletter. You can provide material for the "Teacher's Corner" or a column that you write. Be sure to include samples of children's work and a calendar of events and things to remember (e.g., pizza day). |
| Parent volunteers | A classroom community should welcome visitors just to come and observe or to help out with various activities. Parents may agree to volunteer to help with field studies, student productions (e.g., a play about Galileo's conflict with the Church), building a reading loft or shelving, or providing help with particular activities in which they have expertise (e.g., helping students construct a web page, teaching children how to program, leading a bird-watching trip). Near the beginning of the year, it is important to find out about the parents' interests, skills, and expertise, as well as their willingness to volunteer. Areas in which you may not have much expertise may be supplemented with those of your children's parents. |
| Student presentations | As children complete a unit topic, they can share their newly gained knowledge and understanding with a larger audience, which should include their parents. For instance, some children may wish to communicate their understandings or completed projects through a dramatic performance, a scientific demonstration, a dance performance, a reading of a story they wrote, and so forth. The class can construct a museum and guide visitors (e.g., parents, other classes, etc.) through the displays. Such presentations are a wonderful way to show off the creativity, knowledge, and sophistication of your students. As described in Chapter 6, the parents can even take on a more active role. If your students have worked on group portfolio projects, in which a business or governmental committee must evaluate the portfolio proposals, the parents can be asked to play the role of the committee. |

## 9.6 Working with Yourself

The most important point to keep in mind is that *a working classroom community will not occur from the beginning of the school year.* The children's expectations and intentions are going to be very different from your goals and expectations. As with any other goal you set, there is a process in which you and your students must engage before achieving that goal. Throughout this process, patience with your children's bumpy road toward the goal and perseverance with maintaining your expectations are essential. All too often, teachers will give up on an approach to teaching or on achieving particular goals. For some reason, we, as teachers, give up too soon on new approaches when we do not see immediate positive results. Part of the problem with not persevering may be due to the nature of schooling. Teachers may feel that they are under scrutiny from administrators, who may expect orderly and efficiently run classrooms. Preconceptions of teaching based on previous experiences of attending school may affect your views of what classrooms should look like. These and many other factors may influence how teachers react to new approaches, which may take a lengthy period of time to implement effectively.

In order to persevere through the process of implementing a classroom community, you need to develop some strategies such as those listed below:

- **Find support among like-minded educators**. Make alliances with other teachers in your school or in other schools who share your goals and expectations in developing classroom communities. Meet on a regular basis to discuss your successes and difficulties. Brainstorm solutions to problems. Support one another in your attempts to develop working classroom communities.

- **Set aside time every week to reflect on the successes and difficulties you have encountered**. Look at the progress of individual students and the class as a whole.

- **Read books and articles**. Search for materials that describe other teachers' experiences in setting up classroom communities or in implementing instructional approaches consistent with the idea of the classroom as community.

- **Take on a role of teacher-as-researcher**. Audio- or videotape class sessions. Then analyze these tape recordings in terms of student learning, talking, and engagement. Look for effective and ineffective actions or actions that are consistent or inconsistent with the development of classroom communities. Investigate the process.

## Additional Reading

Gallas, K. (1995). *Talking their way into science: Hearing children's questions and theories, responding with curricula*. New York: Teachers College Press.
> This book is a must for all teachers. As a teacher-researcher, Karen Gallas describes her classroom, in which she conducts regular science talks about very complex ideas with very young children. It is an extraordinary book, not to be missed.

Reddy, M., McCrohon, C., Rupert Herrenkohl, L., & Jacobs, P. (1998). *Creating scientific communities in the elementary classroom*. Portsmouth, NH: Heinemann.

Rogoff, B., Goodman Turkanis, C., & Bartlett, L. (2001). *Learning together: Children and adults in a school community*. New York: Oxford University Press.
> This book is a description of a whole school that has become a community of learners. Written by researchers, teachers, and parents, this book is a must-read.

Wenger, E. (1998). *Communities of practice: Learning, meaning, and identity*. New York: Cambridge University Press.
> A must read. This book provides a great examination of the nature and development of communities of practice.

## Advanced Reading

Marshall, H. H. (Ed.). (1992). *Redefining student learning: Roots of educational change*. Norwood, NJ: Ablex.
> Examines the broad range of factors affecting our view of learning and the implications for how we view classrooms.

## Other Resources

http://www.oise.utoronto.ca/ICS/site_LabSchool/default.shtml: The Laboratory School, the Institute of Child Study, Ontario Institute for Studies in Education, University of Toronto

The Laboratory School (which draws students from its inner-city location) is another school that has been developed around the notion of community. Each classroom takes deep learning seriously. They take longer to cover material, but across the board the children's test scores skyrocket.

## Notes

1. See G. H. Wood, Teachers as curriculum workers, in J. T. Sears and J. D. Marshall, *Teaching and Thinking about Curriculum: Critical Inquiries* (New York: Teachers College Press, 1990), pp. 97–109.

## Chapter 10
# Reflective Practice

## 10.1    Background to Professional Thinking and Learning

As a teacher, particularly at the elementary school level, you are faced with a huge task. Not only are you supposed to teach every subject matter area, but you also have the responsibility for helping shape young people's lives in their formative years. What you do with your students can have a huge impact on them. This book is an attempt at creating a vision of how you can teach in ways that not only engage children in doing and learning science, but also engage children in participating in democratic communities. Engagement, in this sense, is not just participating in activities, but also participating out of a desire (including curiosity) to learn and work toward some goal. If you want to approach your teaching in the ways suggested in this book, you will face many obstacles. Some of these obstacles will be addressed in the next chapter, but the one that is the focus of this chapter has to do with your own learning as a teacher.

Most of what we have experienced as students throughout our schooling has been that of rather passive learners. We listen to our teachers, we take notes (maybe), we study, then we take a test. We all have been quite successful at this approach. However, when we move into becoming a professional educator, we really do not have anyone to tell us what to do and what to learn. At the same time, if we take the ideas in this book seriously, we are confronted with learning a whole new approach to teaching. When confronted with something completely different from what we are used to, we may find it difficult to take the leap or to transform the way we think about that something, which in this case is teaching.

Figure 10.1 depicts levels of learning and cognition. When we read something, experience something, or hear about something, we generally have an emotional reaction. We like it. We hate it. It's boring. These reactions are important in forming a sense of our own meaning and engagement. However, these reactions also can interfere with progressing to deeper levels of understanding. As we develop deeper understandings, we move through an understanding of the words and meanings of whatever it is we are trying to understand. Up to this point, however, our learning is fairly superficial. The next level is analytical, which is where we examine the relationships between the object of our learning and other things we know about already. We also uncover underlying assumptions, so that we know from what position the writer or speaker or doer is coming. As an experienced teacher has said, "A reflective teacher will learn never to assume anything!" The last level is one of transformation. At this level, what we are learning can have a huge impact in transforming our lives, our understandings, our beliefs, and so forth. If we are approaching teaching from a completely new perspective, we may need to reach this level of transformation before we become entirely comfortable with the approach to the point where it becomes a part of who we are, how we think about teaching and learning, and how we make everyday decisions in the classroom. In addition, this figure is interesting to contemplate in terms of how we may view learning among our own students. We may not have the ethical right to expect our students to enter into transformative levels of thinking, but we have an ethical obligation to provide our students with opportunities to transform.

The rest of this chapter is based on what is known as reflective practice. Reflective practice focuses on learning on our own and in ways that emphasize the analytical and transformative levels of learning and cognition in Figure 10.1.

## 10.2    An Overview of Reflection

Critical reflection is probably the single most important skill for teachers. By critically reflecting on your classroom experiences, you enable yourself to continue to grow professionally, to solve problems, and to extend children's learning. Throughout this book, reflective questions have been used to focus your thinking on specific issues. These questions have been inserted as a theme of this book. If these questions have stimulated you to consider various problems and issues, then you have already been engaging in critical reflection. This particular chapter will help to put critical reflection into a broader perspective of teacher thinking and will provide you with further opportunities to practice this skill.

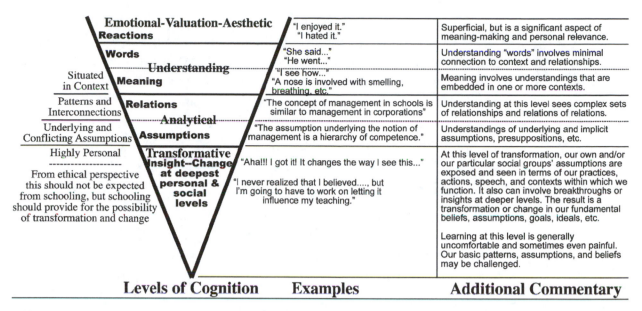

| Levels of Cognition | Examples | Additional Commentary |
|---|---|---|
| **Emotional-Valuation-Aesthetic** Reactions | "I enjoyed it." "I hated it." | Superficial, but is a significant aspect of meaning-making and personal relevance. |
| Words Understanding | "She said..." "He went..." | Understanding "words" involves minimal connection to context and relationships. |
| Situated in Context — Meaning | "I see how..." "A nose is involved with smelling, breathing, etc." | Meaning involves understandings that are embedded in one or more contexts. |
| Patterns and Interconnections — Relations Analytical | "The concept of management in schools is similar to management in corporations" | Understanding at this level sees complex sets of relationships and relations of relations. |
| Underlying and Conflicting Assumptions — Assumptions | "The assumption underlying the notion of management is a hierarchy of competence." | Understandings of underlying and implicit assumptions, presuppositions, etc. |
| Highly Personal -------------------- From ethical perspective this should not be expected from schooling, but schooling should provide for the possibility of transformation and change — **Transformative Insight—Change at deepest personal & social levels** | "Aha!!! I got it! It changes the way I see this..." "I never realized that I believed...., but I'm going to have to work on letting it influence my teaching." | At this level of transformation, our own and/or our particular social groups' assumptions are exposed and seen in terms of our practices, actions, speech, and contexts within which we function. It also can involve breakthroughs or insights at deeper levels. The result is a transformation or change in our fundamental beliefs, assumptions, goals, ideals, etc. Learning at this level is generally uncomfortable and sometimes even painful. Our basic patterns, assumptions, and beliefs may be challenged. |

**FIGURE 10.1**

There are basically two types of reflection:

1. *Reflection on action* is the process of thinking about past experiences in the classroom. When you return home after school, you may start thinking about a particular issue or problem that occurred that day. You analyze the situation, consider the implications, and generate a list of alternative actions. When you return to your class the next day, you have a plan or several alternative plans of action to implement.

2. *Reflection in action* takes place while you are in the midst of a particular situation in the classroom. You can be standing there with a group of children thinking about what you should do. You feel that you do not have the luxury of waiting until tomorrow, but that you need to come up with an immediate plan of action—you must make a decision.

Both of these types of reflection take some practice. Ordinarily, our thinking about a particular event in our lives tends to be a rehashing of events. Either we are elated or upset about something that happened, and we dwell on the emotional intensity. At times like this, we tend not to have a goal in mind (other than maybe making a painful memory disappear). Critical reflection, on the other hand, has a goal. We need to solve a problem or extend children's learning. Although we may experience intense emotional reactions to some kinds of problems in the classroom, we need to move beyond dwelling on this part of our experience and move toward reaching a creative solution. There is always tomorrow, even if you decide that your in-action decision was not the best one.

Basically, critical reflection is the practice of inquiry. As situations arise in the classroom, the reflective practitioner asks questions, analyzes events (e.g., disruptive behavior, a child's thinking, etc.), and comes up with possible courses of action. As with any inquiry, there may not be a clear-cut answer or solution. You need to combine the best of your theoretical and practical understandings in order to make sense of your experiences. At the same time, you need to be genuinely inquisitive and confident in your ability to gain an understanding of the situation and come up with solutions. Hopefully, you will draw on your creativity, empathy, personal experiences, and theoretical knowledge as you contend with the example situations.

## 10.3 Working with Yourself

The work of a teacher can appear to never end. You can devote nearly all of your waking hours to planning, considering the needs of each child, assessing students' work, and catching up on your content knowledge. Teachers can easily become workaholics. However, following such a path can be extremely detrimental to your own health and your working relations with children and peers, as well as to your personal relationships with friends and family. You need to be sure to devote time for yourself, your family, and your friends. There are no hard-and-fast rules for how to do this, but you may want to reflect on how you might schedule your life and on what guidelines you can develop. You may have to break this schedule and your guidelines from time to time.

### 10.3.1 Some Ideas to Consider for Developing Personal Schedules and Guidelines

- Stay late at school to do your planning and assessing.
- Devote your evenings and weekends to relaxing or engaging in enjoyable activities. Of course, the occasional weekend or evening parent meeting or school event may need to be accommodated.
- Get plenty of rest.
- Although summers provide ideal times to take courses or plan a special unit, be sure to allow plenty of time to engage in enjoyable activities and travel.
- Develop efficient routines to accomplish paper work and planning.
- Avoid situations where you are in a group of teachers complaining about work, the students, and so forth. Seek out like-minded teachers with whom you can share and discuss your successes, difficulties, goals, and feelings in a supportive environment.

The problem, as well as the positive aspect, of teaching is that it is a profession. As opposed to vocations, professions are not limited to a 9-to-5 day. As professionals, we think about our work throughout our lives. We take our responsibilities seriously. We also should feel passionate about our work with children. Our passion and creativity do not shut off when we leave the school. So, we need to work hard at finding a balance. Visiting a museum or traveling to a new location may be a nice activity for ourselves, but we are not going to be able to avoid thinking about how our experiences may fit with a potential instructional unit. However, having a good time, while we jot down ideas in a little notebook (which we always carry with us) is a nice way to combine our personal and professional agendas. The bottom line is to keep a reasonable perspective on how to devote time for yourself, while continuing to grow professionally.

Working with yourself as an aspect of the reflective process is particularly important when you have experienced difficult situations and are feeling emotionally raw. The experience of teaching can often leave you feeling as if you are on an emotional roller coaster. At one moment you may feel completely inadequate and depressed. At another moment, you may feel on top of the world—confident and elated. The idea here is to even out the severity of the ups and downs, especially to flatten the valleys of the roller coaster. However, before reflecting on your own experiences and feelings, you may find it useful to engage in some completely different activities, which will help you settle down and gain some perspective. Trying to reflect on your experiences while feeling particularly emotional about specific or generalized issues may not be very productive.

So, you may want to go for a walk in a quiet area. Listen to the sounds, feel the wind, and try to take in an expansive view of your surroundings. Lie or sit down in a comfortable spot. Close your eyes and try to listen to all of the sounds—near and far. Let yourself drift out toward the sounds. Then, after five minutes or so, open your eyes, continue to listen, but add your visual perceptions. Let any of your feelings and emotions just be there, but see them as only one part of all the space that surrounds you. (This technique is based on "acclimatizing" from Steve van Matre's earth education materials and is similar to some meditation techniques. This is the same technique describe in Chapter 2.) You also can take in a movie (a comedy would be great) or an enjoyable television program. Listen to uplifting music. Work on a hobby or engage in a favorite sports activity. The point is to give yourself some time to recover from any emotionally intense experience. Such emotional experiences can be very claustrophobic psychologically, so providing yourself with opportunities to feel a greater sense of spaciousness is especially important.

In addition, throughout your teaching career, you should develop and maintain a sense of humor. If children laugh at a mistake you make, laugh along with them, and make a little joke about yourself. See the humor in situations.

Once you have come to a point where you feel that you have gained some perspective on the situation, you can begin to reflect on specific problem areas. The problem areas on which you can focus are described in the next section.

## 10.4 The Focus of Reflection

The following areas of personal and professional inquiry are not necessarily discrete categories. You often will find a great deal of overlap between two or more of these areas as you begin to reflect on your experiences in the classroom. Keep this point in mind as you read and think about each area and the example questions.

### 10.4.1 Classroom Organization and Children's Behavior

Teachers are often confronted with issues concerning the behavior of individual children or the group. The following questions and commentaries will provide a sense of the range and types of questions you can ask yourself as you encounter problems in the classroom:

**What is the problem?**

It is important to define the problem. Defining the problem does not mean assigning blame, but means describing the situation and patterns that might be contributing to the behavior. You may find it useful to keep track of student behaviors along with a description of when they occurred and a brief description of what was taking place at the time.

**Is it an individual or group problem?**

In order to address the problem effectively, you need to know whether it is a problem of the group dynamics in the classroom or a problem of an individual child.

**Does it require a short-term or a long-term process toward a solution, or both?**

You also need to have some sense of how long it will take to address the problem at a causal level rather than from a symptomatic level. You may find that many situations require both a short-term and a long-term solution plan. For instance, suppose two children are always getting into fights in the classroom. The teacher may want to make sure the two children stay away from each other. She can lay down the "law" that they have to stay apart. From the long-term solution plan perspective, the teacher may develop activities that will address issues of how to get along with others. The activities can be used with the whole class. As they gain more understanding, the rest of the class can begin to model appropriate behavior.

**What potential strategies (long-term and short-term) can I use to address this problem?**

Using more than one approach for reaching a solution is advisable. Develop a list of possible strategies, prioritize them, and group together those that are compatible.

**Can an instructional action be responsible for the problem?**

Giving instructions that are unclear or confusing often can lead to problems with children's behavior, especially if it occurs frequently. The way in which a teacher reacts to children's questions or comments communicates unintended messages.

**Can the organization of the classroom or of instructional activities be a possible causal factor?**

If materials are not readily available or difficult to find, children may not act in appropriate ways. In some cases, the organization and flow of one activity into another may appear to the children as a lot of disconnected busywork, which is not very meaningful or relevant.

**What is the child's background? What is he or she experiencing outside of school? How would it feel to be this child?**

Try to be empathetic. Imagine what it might be like to be this child. Have you felt the same way in your own life? Are the overt actions in the classroom a reaction to some stress or confusion the child is experiencing?

**Do I need to act soon, or can I take the time to ponder the problem and find out more about the nature of the problem?**

In many cases, although it may not be very comfortable, you can take some time before acting. In fact, it is probably better to wait, reflect on the problem, and come up with some sensible solution strategies, rather than acting too hastily and creating an even bigger problem. An angry word can do more damage to the long-term condition of the classroom community than a day of chaos. Patience definitely can be a virtue.

**How can I find out more about the problem?**

What kind of research strategies can be used to uncover more information? You can talk to the child, to other children in the class, to the parents, to other teachers, and to other school personnel, such as the principal or school counselors. More detailed observations, and even audio- or videotape recordings, can be extremely helpful in gaining a better understanding of the situation. In some cases, you may need to seek help in understanding the problem and possible solution strategies from a professional counselor, social worker, or psychologist. Do not be afraid to seek help from a professional. Teachers are not trained to be psychotherapists, yet many of the problems you confront may require such expertise.

The development of critical reflection skills can lead to more effective actions in the classroom. By inquiring into the underlying causes and thinking about possible actions and their implications, you can become extremely skillful teachers. However, problems, especially those involving children's behavior, will never cease to exist. Becoming a reflective practitioner will allow you to continue to learn and grow professionally. Each new difficulty becomes an opportunity to inquire and to become an effective problem solver.

In some cases, you may find it helpful to work with a colleague. If you have developed a trusting friendship with another teacher, you can work together in basically one of two ways. One way can simply be reflecting on problems together. Another person's perspective may often allow you to see a pattern that, for one reason or another, you have not seen. However, when working together, it is important that you do not make judgments of each other's teaching style or approach. The second way of working together involves what has been referred to as clinical supervision. This term sounds a bit daunting, but simply refers to having another set of eyes in the classroom. If you sit in

- ✦ **What kind of problem did this teacher encounter (individual or group)?**
- ✦ **How did this teacher deal with the problem?**
- ✦ **What kind of attitude did this teacher try to maintain?**
- ✦ **How did this teacher's strategy fit with his goals for the classroom?**
- ✦ **What might have happened had the teacher reacted quickly and angrily?**
- ✦ **What other strategies could have been used with equal effectiveness?**

✳

**The following scenario happened to a teacher in a school in a very large metropolitan area: Mr. Smith was sitting drinking a cup of tea, talking to several students during a break. Another, rather hefty student (whom he did not know very well) walked into the room. The student picked up a pair of scissors, then used the scissors to pick up a tea bag. As he squeezed the tea bag with the scissors, he looked at Mr. Smith and said with a snarl, "Mr. Smith, this is your head."**

- ✦ **What would you do in response to this action?**
- ✦ **What is at stake here?**
- ✦ **What might be the long-term results of your action?**

---

### Example 10.1: A Teacher's Reflections and Actions

I started teaching in this class in the middle of the year. My welcome was the traditional introductory treatment of a substitute teacher. I didn't know the students' names, so I asked them their names. It quickly became apparent that their group creativity was at work as they switched names. They even used the wrong names on their class work. The temptation was to get angry and tell them to straighten up, but I was determined not to fall into that trap. I shrugged off their game and kept going. I figured that time was on my side, so I put off considering this problem until I got home after school.

After school, I talked to one of the students I knew from outside the school context. He was very helpful in straightening out the correct names and faces. The second day of class, the same boys started their name-switching routine. However, I had already spent some time thinking about the situation. I was prepared! I knew that I had to play their game better than they played it. So, as they called themselves the wrong names, I corrected them with totally new and suitably weird names I had made up the night before. They didn't like my names at all, and quickly corrected me with their real names. After that, they would occasionally call each other the switched names, but it was all in fun … like some sort of an "in joke" we could all laugh about.

I basically felt that the notion of community in the classroom was more important than the momentary discomfort I felt and the feeling of control I might get from acting as the disciplinary authority. Had I come down on them initially, I would have blown it. An animosity could have developed between me and them. By circumventing a clash and making the whole situation into an "in joke," we managed to come away with a feeling of mutual respect. I showed respect for their creativity by not getting angry with them and by playing their game. They gained respect for me as a teacher. I wasn't an easy mark, and I didn't treat them unreasonably.

---

on your colleague's class, you can take notes or collect data on what is taking place at different points during class. Afterwards, the two of you can sit down together and analyze the results, then generate a list of alternative strategies to deal with the particular problem. For example, during a reading lesson in a grade 2 classroom, a teacher was reading a book. From time to time, she would stop and call on students or mildly reprimand those who were not paying attention or distracting the others. Another teacher started noting which children were being called on to answer the questions. At the end, the observing teacher handed over the sheet of notes. As the classroom teacher looked at the notes, she said, "I can't believe it! I've been calling on all of the boys! I've got to stop that right away." The extra pair of eyes allowed the teacher to see something she had not been able to notice herself. However, one of the problems that needs to be overcome is the tendency of teacher's protective or defensive reactions. With the intense pressure of accountability, compounded by high-stakes testing, teachers often keep their doors closed and fear any sort of observation of their teaching. Chapter 11 will provide a view of how to create professional communities where colleagues and others are an integral part of your classroom.

## 10.4.2 Instruction and Children's Learning and Thinking

A majority of your reflecting will probably be focused on children's learning and thinking and how you can respond with instructional talk or activities. The example questions below will provide you with the nature and extent of the kinds of questions you might ask before, during, and after classroom activities and instruction. Following these examples, you will have an opportunity to reflect on a variety of classroom examples, and then reflect on this process.

- What do the children's understandings look like?
- What kinds of ideas might the children have that are making it difficult for them to understand this concept?
- What alternative strategies could I use to involve children in inquiry on this topic?
- In looking back at the way I handled this discussion, were there other questions I could have asked?
- In looking back at the way I sequenced today's activities, could I have used a different sequence or different activities?
- Should I have provided the children with a source for obtaining an answer to their questions, or should I have asked different questions or used different activities?
- Did I try to control this lesson too much? How was I controlling it? What alternative approaches could I have used?
- Was this activity too disorganized and chaotic? Could I have structured it better?
- Did the structure of the activities optimize student ownership over their ideas and explanations?
- Was the concept I introduced today inaccurate? How can I check on its accuracy?
- What sources of information can my students access for their work on this topic?
- Was this activity too highly structured, so that the children did not engage in active inquiry? Did they not feel ownership over the problem and the results? How could this problem be approached differently?

☞

In case you are curious about the action of the teacher in the scenario described in the previous sidebar, he responded by quietly picking up a wooden tea stirrer. He broke off a little piece about 2 cm. long, looked at the boy, and told him, very matter-of-factly and using the technical term, that it was a certain part of his (male) anatomy (important to a pre-adolescent). The other children in the room laughed and hooted as the boy slowly backed out of the room, muttering insults. Days later, the same boy came up to the teacher, patted him on the back, and asked if he needed any help in his science room. Although this type of action is not recommended in most situations, the teacher managed to play the child's game better than the child. In other situations, such an action could backfire and lead to legal difficulties. Essentially, the teacher intuitively read the situation and context and responded with what he thought was appropriate to the circumstances. The boy, who thought of himself as being tough, found his match in Mr. Smith. He gained a respect for the teacher and ended up being the teacher's helper, rather than a constant source of difficulty.

♦ What further questions could the teacher have asked to extend the theory building that had begun in this sequence (to the right)?
♦ What other activities could have been introduced to explore the concept of gravity and the issue of where the lid was located?

The following is an excerpt of a dialogue between a teacher and a few students during an activity focusing on spinning tops. The children had made tops with sticks and plastic lids from different kinds of cans.

*Child:*    The lid has to be near the bottom or it won't work.
**Teacher:**  **Why does the lid have to be near the bottom?**
*Child:*    Because of gravity …

At this point, the discussion of this issue stopped and moved on to other issues. Later in this session on tops, the children were playing with tops that used markers as the spinning point. Two comments from the children included:

*Child:*    Mine makes big circles.
*Child:*    Mine only makes small circles.

♦ How could you help the children to figure out why there is a difference in the size and patterns of circles made by the tops?

The examples in the previous activity are common events in the day-to-day experience of teachers. In the midst of the buzzing noise and activity in a classroom, teachers will miss many potential situations where children's thinking and inquiry can be extended. It is almost a given that many opportunities will be missed. However, with practice, you can increase the number of times you do take advantage of such opportunities. The best way to practice reflection is by looking at instructional events (i.e., audiotape recordings and partial transcripts of class sessions or videotape recordings) and looking for points at which further questions could have been asked or other activities could have been introduced. As you practice in this way, you will begin to come up with appropriate questions and activity ideas more quickly. In other words, your reflection on action can move toward reflection in action.

♦ In this last activity, what difficulties did you have in generating answers to the questions?
♦ If you had difficulties, what do you think is the source of this difficulty?
♦ Sitting down and trying to think of what to do can sometimes be very difficult. What would help you to come up with ideas for how to extend the inquiries and explanation building in the previous activity?

At the same time you are modeling the process of asking more probing questions and formulating new inquiry activities, your students will begin to learn how to ask the same sorts of questions and devise new experiments. This skill of reflecting on instruction is not just for your benefit as the teacher (and indirectly for the students as the recipients), but also for the students. Your children should be learning how to inquire. Asking probing questions and devising experiments to answer questions that arise during classroom activities is the basis for active inquiry.

As you think about instruction, you really need to focus on the four basic types of questions and activities that can:

1. **Extend** children's discussion, thinking, and inquiry
2. **Clarify** their explanations
3. **Elaborate** on their ideas
4. **Make connections** between different concepts or across disciplines

The questions asked in the activity above fall into these categories of questions, as do some of the questions listed in the example questions (see above). The point of these categories is to focus on questions that have a direct impact on children's inquiry. Basically, you are asking how you can help children learn and understand more and how you can help children develop their thinking skills.

Example 10.2 lists questions that can be asked of the children. Most of these questions help to extend the inquiry and ask children to elaborate on their understandings. The intent is to help the children explore the topic in more depth and in more detail. Enriched and more elaborate understandings will more likely be remembered for a much longer period of time than more superficial understandings. So, the point in asking these types of reflective questions is to develop ways of developing more elaborate investigations and discussions of particular topics.

---

**Example 10.2: Instructional Questions
Based on a Classroom Event**

The following sequences took place while a grade 3/4 class was involved in dissecting clams. Each statement or sequence is followed by the kinds of questions that can be asked.

*Child:*  Wow, it feels like jello.
- Do all parts feel like jello?
- Why is there a difference in the way different parts of the clam feel?

*Child:*  Gosh, these things are strong.
- What part of the clam is strong?
- Why do you think they need to be so strong?
- Is there any way we could figure out how strong the clam is?
- What muscles does a clam have?
- Where are the muscles located?
- What is the purpose of each of the muscles (or what is the function of each muscle)?

**Teacher: Why do you think they have shells?**

*Child:*  They have shells so that they can have a home.
- How are their shells like a home?
- What other things can you think of that are like a home?
- What makes a home a home, or what are the characteristics of a home?
- Can you think of any other reasons why shells are important? For what else are they useful?
- Are any of these reasons or ways of being useful similar to those of a home?
- What do all of the different kinds of homes we have listed have in common?

---

A grade 3/4 class is exploring insects. As the children are observing some of these insects in a jar, one child says, "He can't climb up, it's too slippery."

✦ How can this statement be turned into further inquiry?

✦ What equipment or supplies would you need to engage in this inquiry?

A grade 3/4 class is investigating the notion of balance. After the conversation has turned to talking about cats and balance, the following discussion takes place:

**Cory:** Maybe it's 'cause they have four legs, you know ... like paws and feet and they're all the same, and they land right.

**Diane:** They have a long tail, too. I think that balances them.

**Dave:** Yeah, but dogs have tails, too, and they can't do that.

This sequence is a nice example of how children can engage in an argument and provide counter-evidence to the claims of others.

How can you extend this discussion into inquiry?

The questions following the last sequence in this example (starting with the teacher saying "Why do you think they have shells?") help children to make connections with different concepts. These questions also can provide ways of making connections across disciplines. As children explore the notion of homes, they can develop different ways of representing their ideas. So, the notion of home starts to take on richer and more explicit meanings. In fact, such an exploration could grow into a tangential avenue of exploration and inquiry. As the exploration continues, children can look at how people's homes differ within and across different cultures. They can also explore the notion of animals' homes, such as nests, burrows, and stables. At some point, they can consider what all these different senses of homes (i.e., people's homes, animals' homes, and clams' shells) have in common.

---

**Example 10.3: Excerpt from a Reflection Paper by One of Two Student Teachers Working with a Group of Grade 3 Children**

We also examined other ways plants reproduce. Tom [student teacher] began a discussion with the question "How would one plant get its seeds to another plant if the wind didn't do it?" Tom gave them a hint to start their thinking.

**Tom:** **Think of bees. What do bees do?**

*Fred:* They take pollen from the … Oh, I know, maybe … maybe, oh … bees you know that thing in their head, not off their head, but pollen in their thing, the bees come and get it, and put it in the bird's nest.

**Tom:** **So, if a bee lands on a flower, what does it do when it's going to a flower—a bumblebee, what is it getting?**

*Fred:* Pollen.

**Tom:** **Okay. And it's going to go back to its beehive and make—what do bees make?**

*Fred:* Honey.

**Tom:** **But now let's say that a bee comes to a flower and it gets pollen all over its legs and stuff. Right? If pollen is like a nutrient that helps other seeds grow …**

*Fred:* Oh …

**Tom:** **So, remember …**

*Fred:* Maybe, when they're, like, on hairs, some of that drops and it goes on the ground, and then when they leave, it goes into the ground and then it makes more.

**Tom:** **Ashley, what about when the bee flies to another flower, what would happen? [Pause] If a bee goes to one flower and gets that stuff on its legs, the pollen, and it flies to another flower, where would the pollen go?**

*Annie:* To another flower.

**Tom:** **So, that might help some other seed to grow from that flower.**

## 10.5 Reflection Examples and Activities

The following examples and activities are included here for you to have an opportunity to see how different teachers and student teachers have thought about specific classroom events. As you read through the examples, you may find it helpful to imagine the situation and how you might react if it were happening to you.

In Example 10.4, the student teacher attempted to embed her thinking in a broader framework based on her reading of Karen Gallas's book *Talking Their Way into Science*. Drawing on a theoretical framework helps you to make sense of what you see and experience in the classroom. Without such a framework, you risk losing a consistency to how you think about your teaching and how you implement your instruction. In this case, the

**Refer to Example 10.3.**

**Before reading on, think about the following questions:**

✦ **What is your reaction to the previous conversational sequence?**

✦ **How did Tom's (the student teacher's) talk affect the discussion?**

✦ **Who is in control of this discussion? Whose ideas are at the forefront of the conversation? What characteristics of this discussion are indicative of control?**

✦ **What questionable scientific content assertion in Tom's talk could adversely affect the children's understanding?**

✦ **What alternatives to Tom's approach could you have taken in leading this discussion?**

---

### Example 10.4 Student Teacher's Reflection on Example 10.3

I felt this conversation was much too directed by Tom. We were leading a discussion the children could have had themselves. They had some great ideas, but they could not direct them toward an answer, namely because there was no clear-cut question to work their answers around. Fred could not elaborate on his great ideas because he, like Alice and Annie, were asked more questions. Fred, though, did grab an opportunity to try another idea when Tom gave him a suggestion of what pollen was. However, his idea did not lead into what could have been a discussion with Annie. Gallas in Chapter 11 explains that questions have to be carefully phrased so children are able to understand the context of the discussion. Asking questions about specific terms, which Tom was doing in this conversation and I was doing in the previous, does not go very far.

As Gallas points out, children's use of a term does not imply they understand what the word means. This happened with Fred—he used the word *pollen*, but as seen in the conversation I transcribed, he was not quite sure what it meant. When he was given an idea of what it meant, he got quite close to the truth about how pollen travels. However, this conversation would have worked out better if we had just thrown out a question to the children and let them work out an answer themselves. Looking at the list of the questions in the back of Gallas's book, none of her questions begin with *what* because it does not produce a discussion. Usually, it produces an answer from a few children who feel confident they will give the right answer. On the other hand, a *how* or *why* question produces ideas, none of which are wrong. All of the ideas generated contribute to an illumination of a phenomenon the children want to know more about. As Gallas suggests, the children's discussion is much more productive if the children suggest something they are interested in. Our role is to give them an open-ended question to get them started, or to encourage them to pursue a question they have asked in response to something they are curious about.

In Chapter 11, Gallas notes that *why* questions tend to be more difficult for children to solve. Sometimes it is best for the children to establish a theory on a *how* question before tackling the *why*. In our discussion, a question such as "How does pollen get from one flower to another?" might have produced more ideas from the children and given them the freedom to try answering this question on their own.

*Note*: In the transcript sequence, Tom's suggestion that pollen is a nutrient can be problematic. Pollen contains the male genetic material used in the sexual reproduction of flowering plants.

**See Example 10.4**

✦ How does this student's reflection on the previous transcript sequence differ from yours?

✦ What is the major point of this student teacher's reflection?

✦ Although the excerpt in Example 10.5 is rather short, what does this student teacher's reflection suggest about the teacher's role in classroom discussions?

**See Example 10.6**

✦ How did this teacher deal with the problem of his students' difficulty in generating an accurate explanation for the function of a Cartesian diver?

---

### Example 10.5: A Student Teacher's Reflection of Her Work with a Small Group of Children

A major mistake that I made during the meeting was to get overly excited when I realized that the child had begun to grasp the concept. When I thought that the child had brought up a good point, perhaps not necessarily connected to the topic, I wanted to jump on it. Sometimes I felt as though I had jumped on the child's comment too eagerly and therefore suffocated his thought process, because he would not elaborate any further. I have to learn to be more patient.

---

student teacher was able to extend her thinking in a way that was in line with a particular theoretical framework.

In Example 10.6, the teacher was acting as a co-participant and inquirer in the unit. Although he understood the concepts, his approach was to think of ways of designing experiments that would allow students to look at the

---

### Example 10.6: A Teacher's Reflection on Addressing Children's Faulty Explanations

(See also Example 8.3, where this particular problem and the teacher's approach to it were first described. The teacher in this example is reacting to his students' explanations of how a Cartesian diver works. After observing and investigating a toy Cartesian diver called a Squidy and another made from a partly filled and inverted test tube, the students came up with an explanation: "When pressure is put on the bottle, water rises through the tube, forcing air out of the top and causing the 'pus [short for octopus] to sink.")

How can the ideas expressed be addressed? The test tube Cartesian diver allowed them to see what was happening to the air in the tube, yet they seemed to insist that the air was being forced out. The air can't escape. Do we revisit the Cartesian divers again? I began thinking that there has to be a way of showing the relationship between the increase in pressure when you push down on the rubber and the decrease in the volume of air in the diver. As I mulled over this idea, I got the idea of combining a manometer [for detecting pressure changes] and a Cartesian diver setup. In terms of measuring the pressure while using a Cartesian diver, I might try cutting off the closed end of a balloon, putting the narrow opened end around the manometer tubing and sealing it with a rubber band, and putting the rest of the balloon over a large graduated cylinder. This way, the students can see the relationship between depth and pressure in conjunction with the changes in water level in the Cartesian diver.

---

> **Example 10.7: A Grade 5 Teacher's Reflective Talk about a Unit on Machines**
>
> OK. If I were to start again … I think … if I were doing a unit on simple machines and trying to implement that, I think I would try to have someone oversee the whole unit [five teachers developed different parts of the unit, then combined them]. I felt that was not an effective unit at all. I think it was so many different categories there. There wasn't a continuity as far as creative thinking or, you know, critical thinking or any of those skills. Some units had it, some units didn't [she is referring to the different sets of activities developed by the five teachers]. And I found that some of the instructions for the kids … it was all a game to them. But then when you asked them what they learned from it, they couldn't tell you. They had no idea. They did not pick up the information that we wanted. Yet, they did the entertainment and the activities and they had fun with it. But they did not walk away with the information. And I think in that way, there had to be more of a follow-up route particularly, like the pulleys and the inclined plane particularly. When I spoke to students about it, they really didn't have, they couldn't put it into words what they had learned or the reasoning behind it. There has to be more constructive.… The application of the theory I think would have been far better.… Some parts of the unit, though, I found allowed them to take the information and apply it. Well, the wheels were excellent. I think, you know, it works if you did have the experiment where they had to pull a brick along and they tried to use pencils to pull it.… But, I found with a centered approach [she is referring to the notion of learning centers—each set of activities developed by the different teachers functioned like a separate center] like that, the kids took a lot longer with that particular assignment. They whipped through the other ones. They'd do two or three in 15 minutes and no longer … they didn't really pick up a lot of the information. That's why I found the whole unit sort of fell apart.

- ◆ What were this teacher's concerns about the unit?
- ◆ How did the teacher characterize the children's engagement in the unit?
- ◆ What does this characterization suggest about designing classroom instruction?
- ◆ From what you have learned so far in this book, how could the unit be done differently? How would you design a unit on machines?

relationships from different perspectives. The teacher's curiosity and inquisitiveness helped to extend the inquiry of the whole class.

## 10.6  Dilemmas

One of the most common situations to arise as you teach, especially when you are first starting to teach, can be referred to as dilemmas. You come to a point where you have two choices, with no clear path to follow. You may feel that you need to let the children do most of the talking during classroom discussions, and you end up at a point where you feel hesitant about saying anything. Do you say something or do you not? The answer is not clear. The

◆ How did this teacher contend with his dilemma?

◆ How might the alternative decision to control the flow of the argument have affected the discussion, the children, and the teacher?

◆ How would you have handled the situation?

**Example 10.8: A Teacher's Reflection about a Dilemma of Control**

The argument that took place during today's class was great, but I felt conflicted throughout the entire time. I kept getting images of my past experiences of the official version of what classrooms should look like. At the same time, I knew that the argument was exactly what should be happening. I have seen these kinds of arguments taking place among researchers … just as much shouting, but probably more hostile. In a way, the students were being much nicer to each other than most adults I've seen in similar situations. Also, the argument was quite substantive. These were real issues for the children. It was actually great to see them so passionate over a conceptual topic. However, I kept going back and forth in my mind … should I try to control the children's behavior during the argument or should I let it go and see what happens? It was uncomfortable for me. I knew in my heart what I should do, but all my past history as a student and a teacher kept nagging away in the back of my mind. It's really too bad that schools can be such limiting places, and so unreal. It's as if the rest of the world can be one way, but schools have to be another. Anyway, for the most part, I let them go. Only after they seemed to be getting bogged down in back-and-forth accusations did I take steps to refocus the discussion. However, I tried to avoid making such steps into a big thing. I just tried to make the transition to the next stage of getting everyone to look at the points that had just been made and analyze the content and process.

best way to approach such situations is to make a decision and watch very carefully what happens. Add a comment or a question and see how students react. Or let the discussion go and see what happens. Whatever choice you make, you need to feel that time is on your side. Everything does not have to be perfect. In fact, you should look at teaching as an opportunity to inquire about teaching, as an opportunity to learn and grow professionally. Experiment, try out different approaches, try asking that difficult question, and see what happens.

Dilemmas arise all the time in the classroom. You encounter situations where you have choices of what to do. You must come to terms and make a decision. Although you may have a few moments to sit on the edge, you need to make a choice. At first these choices may seem to be very difficult. However, as you gain experience over time and continue to observe, inquire, and reflect, you begin to react to situations in ways that are consistent with the community approach you are taking in the classroom. In addition, the notion that *making mistakes* provides us with great opportunities to learn may help put teaching and the process of reflection into a more useful perspective. If you make a decision that does not appear to work out all that well, take the opportunity to analyze the situation and reflect on what you could do differ-

> **Example 10.9: A Teacher's Reflection about a Dilemma of Content**
>
> Whenever my students get into a discussion over a particular explanation or idea, I feel like I should either give them the right answer or let them keep arguing. It's funny that I should get stuck in this back-and-forth thinking about should I or should I not give them the answer. I've been through this a million times, but I always seem to go through the same conflict. I know that getting the students involved in hashing out their ideas is much more important than my telling them what is right. I suppose that the conflict keeps me on my toes. There may be times when I do need to introduce an accurate concept, and going through this internal battle with myself may help me not to miss the times when I do need to introduce specific content. It almost seems like some sort of self-checking mechanism.

+ How did this teacher contend with his dilemma?
+ As pointed out by this teacher, what are the implications of having to deal with dilemmas?
+ How does this relate to similar kinds of dilemmas you may have experienced in different situations?

ently next time. Feedback from the children can provide useful information as well. For example, if a child says, "But it isn't fair," in referring to some action you have taken, such a statement can be very useful in pointing to issues in the way you may be relating to the children. Children seem to be endowed with some sort of fairness radar. If they feel or perceive that they are not being treated fairly, then either some further communication about the reasons for your actions is needed or more attention needs to be paid to the concerns of the child.

## Additional Reading

Farrell, T. S. C. (2003). *Reflective practice in action: 80 reflection breaks for busy teachers*. Thousand Oaks, CA: Corwin Press.

Henderson, J. G. (1992). *Reflective teaching: Becoming an inquiring educator*. New York: Macmillan.
    A good introduction to reflective inquiry into professional practice. Covers a broad range of applications and includes a good chapter on leadership in a democratic classroom community.

Posner, G. J. (1989). *Field experience: Methods of reflective teaching* (2nd ed.). New York: Longman.
    A straightforward approach to organizing your thinking about reflective practice.

Tomanek, D. (1994). A case of dilemmas: Exploring my assumptions about teaching science. *Science Education, 78*, 399–414.
    A self-examination of dilemmas encountered while teaching science.

## Advanced Reading

Connelly, F. M., & Clandinin, D. J. (Eds.). (1999). *Shaping a professional identity: Stories of educational practice*. New York: Teachers College Press.

Loughran, J. (Ed.). (1999). *Researching teaching: Methodologies and practices for understanding pedagogy*. Philadelphia: Falmer Press.

Loughran, J., & Russell, T. (Eds.). (2002). *Improving teacher education practices through self-study*. New York: Routledge-Falmer, Taylor & Francis Group.

Schön, D. A. (1991). *Educating the reflective practitioner*. San Francisco: Jossey-Bass Publishers.
    The classic source for contemporary thinking about reflective practice.

Wallace, J., & Louden, W. (Eds.). (2002). *Dilemmas of science teaching: Perspectives on problems of practice*. New York: Routledge-Falmer, Taylor & Francis Group.

## Other Resources

Teacher Research, as a form of reflective practice (George Mason University), http://gse.gmu.edu/research/tr/TRreflective.shtml

Reflection and Reflective Practice (Open University, UK), http://www4.open.ac.uk/Mendeval/modile6/default.htm

*Reflective Practice* (journal from Routledge)

Developing Reflective Practice (University of Alberta), http://www.uofaweb.ualberta.ca/fieldexperiences/nav02.cfm?nav02=25846&nav01=25772

# Chapter 11

# Where to Go from Here: Participating in the Professional Community

Throughout this book, you have been exposed to a great number of ideas about how to approach the teaching of science in elementary school. However, your work is far from over. Teaching is a lifelong (at least career-long) process of continual learning. Every year, advances in our understandings of the teaching and learning processes grow. You need to keep up-to-date with these developments. In addition, you need to continue to reflect upon your own teaching and the specific circumstances of the context in which you teach. At the same time, you need to continue to learn more about science and to develop further understandings of science concepts. This chapter will discuss some of the ways you can continue to grow professionally and work toward full participation in the professional community of teachers.

## 11.1  Participating in the Professional Community

When you initially thought of entering the field of teaching, you began your journey toward participating in the professional community of teachers. This journey may have begun for a wide variety of reasons—from practical reasons for choosing an occupation to a passion for working with children. However, for whatever reason you began the journey, you need to understand the extent and nature of the professional community, which is depicted in Figure 11.1.

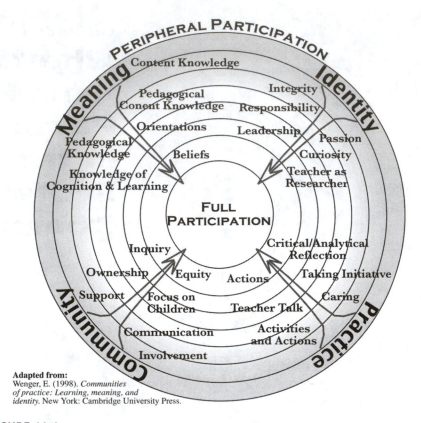

Adapted from:
Wenger, E. (1998). *Communities of practice: Learning, meaning, and identity*. New York: Cambridge University Press.

**FIGURE 11.1**

In order to grasp what is involved in entering into and participating in the professional community, the following tables are an outline of the implications for each of the aspects contained in Figure 11.1.

---

**TABLE 11.1** Identity

**Who am I as a teacher? Who am I as a participant in the community of teachers? How can I be true to myself and be a professional at the same time?**

*Identity in the context of the professional community involves*

1. Our personalities and how they manifest genuinely in our practice.

2. Our passions for learning, teaching, and working with children.

3. A sense of integrity—adhering to one's well-defined ethical and professional standards.

4. An insatiable curiosity about teaching, learning, and objects and phenomena in our world (within science, social studies, the arts, literature, mathematics, etc.).

5. A sense of responsibility for our own learning, professional growth, and well-being, as well as toward children's welfare and our professional community.

6. A sense of ourselves as leaders (or potential leaders) in the professional community.

7. A sense of being researchers into our own practice and children's learning and development.

8. A sense of holding multiple roles as teachers of children, including mentor, facilitator, orchestrator, guide, and so forth.

9. Confidence along with an ability to honestly assess our practice.

10. Openness to new ideas, critiques, children's expressions of individuality, and so forth.

11. How we see ourselves as members of the professional community.

---

**TABLE 11.2** Meaning

**What does it mean to me to be a teacher? How is my work as a teacher meaningful to me, to my students, and to the professional community? What kinds of knowledge do I need as a teacher?**

*Meaning in the context of community participation involves*

1. Our interests, beliefs, orientations, and values and how they relate to our practice

   What are my personal and academic interests, and how can I take advantage of these in my teaching?

   What beliefs do I hold about teaching, learning, and the world that could interfere with or support my teaching?

   What are my orientations toward teaching and curriculum (mechanistic, holistic, sequential, etc.) that can interfere with or support my teaching?

   What values do I hold that need to become my guiding principles and which values do I need to keep separate from my teaching?

2. Content knowledge needed in order to teach at the elementary school level, which includes knowledge in literature and writing, mathematics, science, social studies, art, music, drama, and physical education.

3. Pedagogical knowledge, which includes the theories and practical implications of learning and cognition, teaching and curriculum, schooling, philosophy, and so forth.

4. Pedagogical content knowledge, which is an understanding of what content is appropriate and of how we teach the content of a variety of subject matter disciplines.

5. Meaning also is embedded in the political, social, cultural, and environmental concerns and issues we are facing (i.e., embedded in relevant contexts).

---

**TABLE 11.3** Practice

**What are the actions, activities, thinking, and discourse of a teacher? What do I do as a teacher that defines my practices as a professional? How can my practice extend and contribute to the professional community?**

*Practice in the context of the professional community involves:*

1. Critical and analytical reflection is a key component to growing as a professional.

2. Taking initiative, being pro-active, and making decisions throughout our everyday lives as teachers are critically important to our practices.

3. We need to care for and about children as human beings with all of the needs, aspirations, concerns, and special qualities.

4. The actions we take in working with children need to be consistent with our philosophical orientations to teaching and learning.

5. The way we talk to children, parents, and colleagues differs, but makes up the discourse of the profession.

6. The activities in which we engage both in and out of school have an impact on our professional thinking and growth.

7. We need to strive for excellence in all aspects of our professional practice and not be satisfied with going through the motions or doing just enough to get by in our careers.

8. We need to read and learn in a variety of subject matter disciplines, teaching and curriculum, psychology, issues of schooling, politics, etc.

9. We need to participate in the professional community in a variety of ways.

10. We need to analyze and inquire into student learning, our own teaching, the politics of schooling, etc.

> **TABLE 11.4** Community
>
> **What is the nature and extent of the professional community? What is my role and situation in the professional community? How can I contribute to the professional community?**
>
> *The notion of professional community involves*
>
> 1. Viewing the profession as a community of inquiry, which looks at critical issues of teaching, learning, and schooling.
> 2. Feeling a sense of ownership for the welfare and continuity of the professional community, including taking on leadership roles, communicating through talk and writing to other professionals, assisting and supporting other teachers, and so forth.
> 3. Seeing children's learning, growth, and welfare as the bottom line of everything we do.
> 4. Seeing equity as a central concern, in terms of opportunity and treatment for children.
> 5. Expanding the vision of purpose of the community beyond children's learning and welfare to include what is beneficial for parents, the local community, and the whole of schooling and society.
> 6. Communicating with policy makers and the general public.
> 7. Doing whatever is necessary to help maintain the professional status of teachers..

The previous outline of what comprises the professional community of practice may be somewhat overwhelming. However, it is just this complexity that makes teaching an exciting endeavor. Obviously, there is no way to attain even a reasonable level of expertise in all areas of the profession during one's training to be a teacher. So, the bulk of the work needs to be done as you progress through your career. The notion of a professional community provides a context for how you can view your continuing development as a teacher. However, you need to realize that not all communities (of teaching or any other profession) are functional or positively supporting. Many of us may end up in schools where the focus of teacher-to-teacher conversations is on complaining about children, the administration, parents, and so forth. In such cases, you may need to find even one teacher in your school with whom you can develop a professional relationship. You can extend your search to other teachers in other schools in your area. The Internet provides a way to communicate with teachers anywhere in the world. In addition, there are a number of professional organizations that have annual or more frequent meetings, e-mail listservs, and other electronic forums. Your participation in the professional community is important, so extending that vision of your participation may be necessary.

In reading through the previous outline, you may notice that many of the details are not presciptions for what to do and how to do it. Although there is a push to teacher-proof much of teaching in some areas, to be a professional means that you need to make decisions about what to do and how to do it. You need to formulate your approach to teaching that is consistent with your philosophy of teaching, with who you are as a caring human being, and with the concerns of the professional community (in both the local situation and the larger national or international professional community). In the following sections, a few approaches to what you can do to continue your professional development are described. However, many other opportunities exist. In addition, you can take the initiative to start a discussion and support group of like-minded teachers or to start any number of other activities that can help you and your colleagues.

## 11.2 Continuing to Learn about Science

Knowledge of science content and the nature of science are critically important to increasing your effectiveness at facilitating science inquiry and science talk in the classroom. Although you can get off to a good start at creating a classroom community of young scientists with minimal science content knowledge, you need to learn more so that you can ask effective questions and design challenging activities and experiments. The following suggestions provide a variety of ways of developing further understandings. In pursuing any of these, you should always be looking for ways of incorporating what you learn into your teaching. You should also see these opportunities to extend your own learning as enjoyable challenges. You should not feel that science is beyond you. Although some of the terminology may be unfamiliar and daunting, try not to let such obstacles prevent you from getting involved in science learning and teaching. Just overlook what you do not understand and keep trying to make sense of science material and construct your own understandings, as well as continuing to help your students construct their understandings.

---

**A Science Educator's Experience of
Confronting a Daunting Science Task**

As a professor of science education, I was asked to act as an external examiner of a master's of science thesis in quantum chemistry. I tried to explain to the supervising professor that I had a degree in biology and that it had been years since my last chemistry course, which was far from being at the level of quantum chemistry. He attempted to set my concerns aside and insisted that I do it. I gave in to his demands and agreed to look at the thesis. When I received the thesis in the mail, my worst fears were confirmed. I flipped open the thesis to a page full of very complicated equations. My heart stopped. After a few expletives, I pulled myself together and said, "This is just science. I can do this. Just skip the pages of equations and read everything else." My advice to myself worked. As I read through the thesis, methodically skipping page after page of equations (it made the read much shorter!), I found that I could extract a basic understanding of the logic of the student's argument. I was able to pick up on points where her logic became a bit shaky and where she made quantum leaps in her logic. After the thesis defense, I felt relieved that I had succeeded in not making a complete fool of myself. I also left feeling that I had a greater appreciation of what elementary teachers must feel like when they first encounter situations where they must learn and teach science.

---

### 11.2.1 Reading Popular Science Books and Magazines

One of the easiest and more enjoyable ways to start the task of learning science is to start reading the vast assortment of books and magazines that deal with science. *Natural History, Discover, Scientific American, Equinox, National Geographic,* and *Canadian Geographic* are all relatively easy-to-read magazines that will keep you abreast of current ideas in science. Getting subscriptions to a couple of these may provide you with a readily accessible source of information, which you can read at your leisure.

A great number of very good books are available in libraries and bookstores (always check out used bookstores!). As mentioned previously, some of my favorite authors include Stephen Jay Gould, Diane Ackerman, Lewis Thomas, Jane Goodall, Stephen Hawking, and Richard Feynman. However, the choice is yours.

Some newspapers have science columns, as well as special reports on specific scientific discoveries. However, you need to be somewhat cautious of information from the newspapers. The frequency of misinformation is rather high. If you do see an interesting story in a newspaper, you can try to track down further information on the topic. The same caution holds true for information obtained through the Internet and its exponentially growing number of websites. Some of this information is excellent, while other information may be highly suspect.

As you read through such sources, you may not see the immediate relevancy to your own teaching of science. Some ideas will seem much too complicated for young children. However, the point is to develop an understanding of the major concepts of science and the logic of how ideas are linked together. As you continue to read, you will develop a greater understanding of how science works and of broader concepts. When you are in the midst of teaching, from the approach suggested in this book, you also may find that children are quite capable of dealing with some of the more complicated ideas in science. We just never really give them the chance.

### 11.2.2 Working and Talking with Scientists

As mentioned in one of the activities in Chapter 3, you can volunteer to work with scientists. This is an excellent way of learning not only more science content, but also a great deal about how science works. Developing a relationship with a scientist in this way can result in a powerful source of assistance when you need to understand more difficult concepts.

You can learn a great deal about the process of doing experiments, analyzing data, and formulating explanations. Another great learning opportunity involves the continual encounters with unexpected problems. Doing science always involves experimental failures, problems with equipment, data collection, and so forth. Experiencing these obstacles and how scientists deal with them can be incredibly valuable, since the same sorts of problems will occur in your classroom. The question, then, is how can such obstacles be turned into valuable learning experiences for the children.

Although finding the time to engage in such an activity may be difficult, you may find that doing something like this for a few hours a week during part of the summer is both enjoyable and rewarding. Be creative with your time, and see what you can manage to do to accommodate such opportunities.

### 11.2.3 Taking Courses

Take courses in science at a local college or university. In the beginning, you may want to take courses designed for teachers or those designed for nonmajors. As you build up your confidence, you can try taking more advanced courses. You also may want to focus on those courses with a heavy emphasis on laboratory or field experiences. Such courses more than likely will prove to be more valuable to you as a teacher. During such courses, you should find that many of the experiments you do can be adapted (or simplified) for children in elementary school. While you are taking such courses, you should keep a journal in which you can add reflections of the applicability of what you learn to your teaching.

### 11.2.4 Playing Around in Science

Whenever you have the opportunity, you should play around in science. You can do this at home, while taking walks, on vacation, and so forth. Such activities can involve simply pondering why a swarm of mayflies just seems to hover in one position, how a piece of dead electronic equipment works, or whether you can design a paper plane that flies the longest and straightest. The entire idea of playing around in science is based on being curious and following up on your curiosity.

This approach to adding to your scientific knowledge is a great companion to each of the previous ways of developing further understandings. After working with a scientist, reading, or taking a course, you can elaborate on your understandings by investigating questions you might have or by testing out some of the explanations to which you have been exposed. If you have children of your own, this is a great way to involve them in enjoyable activities. At the same time, you can learn a lot about how your own children approach coming up with explanations, designing experiments, and arguing about their ideas.

## 11.3  Continuing Your Professional Development

In addition to continuing to develop your own understandings of science, you need to keep up with developments in general approaches to teaching and to teaching science. If at all possible, you should subscribe to teacher journals (or at least visit the library on a regular basis). You also should keep an eye out for interesting professional and more advanced books on teaching, learning, science education, and so forth. Spending a few hours a week reading and reflecting on such readings can provide a continual source of inspiration and insight. A list of good journals and selected books is provided in Appendix L and at the end of each chapter in this book.

### 11.3.1 Networking with Colleagues Nationally and Internationally

Join one or more teachers' professional organizations. Such organizations usually have at least one conference a year. These conferences provide a wide selection of paper sessions and workshops, which can provide additional perspectives on teaching. In addition, networking with other teachers can prove to be extremely valuable. The conversations you have with your colleagues at conferences can be extended throughout the year by continued e-mail communication. You can share ideas and concerns with those with whom you have developed good working relationships.

The Internet offers a number of ways of connecting with a wider group of colleagues as well. There are many listservs and online forums, which provide for ongoing interactive conversations around specific topics of interest. However, you may find that you are overwhelmed by the amount of e-mail you get. So, enter into such listservs with caution, and do not be afraid to take yourself off the list if you find it to be too much. The Internet allows you to pick and choose your sources of information. There are many sites that deal with teaching, science teaching, and so on. As you find useful sites, you can bookmark them with your web browser and return to them whenever you want.

### 11.3.2 Forming a Science-Teaching-in-Elementary-School Discussion Group

The last suggestion involves a long-term commitment to working with a group of colleagues. As opposed to most in-service workshops, which occur during one day's time, the notion of developing an elementary science teachers' group can be much more rewarding. You need to find other teachers in your school and neighboring schools who are interested in continuing their professional development in teaching science. Once you have put together this group (it can be small to start), decide on a reasonable timetable for meetings. You may decide to meet once a month for a late afternoon and early evening pizza-and-pop workshop. There are many ways of organizing such a group, but you may want to start off by having everyone read an article or a book. The first session can start off with a discussion of the implications of the reading for teaching science. Then you may want to consider developing a format in which each person tries some new approach or activity before the next meeting. At that meeting, everyone can share their experiences. Problems can be put forth for group reflection and discussion. Successes can be analyzed for their applicability to other activities. Over the long term, such groups can be powerful sources of both information and support for continued professional development.

The fundamental idea expressed in this chapter is that you need to look for ways of supporting and continuing your development as a teacher. Going into your classroom every day, closing the door, working with your students, and then returning home can be a very lonely experience. You need to find time to talk with other adults, preferably colleagues, about teaching in positive ways. The talk and support found in many teachers' lounges in schools can be very negative, if not downright depressing. A lot of teachers avoid these lounges just for that reason. So, you need to look for better ways of finding the support you need. On the other hand, some teachers can transform the teachers' lounge into a more exciting, stimulating, and supportive place. Maybe you can bring in strange creatures or simple but intriguing science activities and transform your teachers' lounge.

## Additional Reading

**Note:** The following books cover a variety of topics, but represent some intriguing ideas that relate to some of what was discussed in this chapter.

Achinstein, B. (2002). *Community, diversity, and conflict among schoolteachers: The ties that blind*. New York: Teachers College Press.

Apple, M. W. (1999). *Power, meaning, and identity: Essays in critical educational studies*. New York: Peter Lang.

Bateson, M. C. (1989). *Composing a life: Life as a work in progress—the improvisations of five extraordinary women*. New York: Plume/Penguin.

Bateson, M. C. (1994). *Peripheral visions: Learning along the way*. New York: Harper Collins.

Bell, B. (2005). *Learning in science: The Waikato research*. New York: Routledge-Falmer.

Burke, J. (1999). *The knowledge web: From electronic agents to Stonehenge and back—and other journeys through knowledge*. New York: Touchstone/Simon & Schuster.

Christensen, L., & Karp, S. (Eds.). (2003). *Rethinking school reform: Views from the classroom*. Milwaukee: Rethinking Schools.

Davis, B., Sumara, D., & Luce-Kapler, R. (2000). *Engaging minds: Learning and teaching in a complex world*. Mahwah, NJ: Lawrence Erlbaum Associates.

Dillard, A. (1974). *Pilgrim at Tinker Creek*. New York: Bantam Books.

Doll, W. E., & Gough, N. (Eds.). (2002). *Curriculum visions*. New York: Peter Lang.

Fleener, M. J. (2002). *Curriculum dynamics: Recreating heart*. New York: Peter Lang.

Gallas, K. (2003). *Imagination and literacy: A teacher's search for the heart of learning*. New York: Teachers College Press.

Gould, S. J. (2003). *I have landed: The end of a beginning in natural history*. New York: Three Rivers Press.

Hatton, S. D. (2005). *Teaching by heart: The foxfire interviews*. New York: Teachers College Press.

Hodson, D. (1998). *Teaching and learning science: Towards a personalized approach*. Philadelphia: Open University Press.

Hyman, I. A., & Snook, P. A. (1999). *Dangerous schools: What we can do about the physical and emotional abuse of our children*. San Francisco: Jossey-Bass Publishers.

Johnson, E. B. (2004). *The dismantling of public education and how to stop it*. Lanham, MD: Scarecrow Education.

Lachs, J. (2003). *A community of individuals*. New York: Routledge.

Monk, M., & Osborne, J. (Eds.). (2000). *Good practice in science teaching: What research has to say*. Philadelphia: Open University Press.

Palmer, P. J. (1998). *The courage to teach: Exploring the inner landscape of a teacher's life*. San Francisco: Jossey-Bass.

Peery, A. B. (2004). *Deep change: Professional development from the inside out*. Lanham, MD: Scarecrow Education.

Polakow, V. (Ed.). (2000). *The public assault on America's children: Poverty, violence, and juvenile injustice*. New York: Teachers College Press.

Swope, K., & Miner, B. (Eds.). (2000). *Failing our kids: Why the testing craze won't fix our schools*. Milwaukee, WI: Rethinking Schools, Ltd.

Wenger, E. (1998). *Communities of practice: Learning, meaning, and identity*. New York: Cambridge University Press.

Wink, J. (2000). *Critical pedagogy: Notes from the real world* (2nd ed.). New York: Longman.

# Part III
Appendixes

*Appendix A*
# Safety

## A.1 Physical Safety

Being safety-conscious should permeate every activity you do in the class-room, but it should not keep you from doing interesting things with your students. The important point is to keep your children safe and to help them learn how to be safety-conscious.

### A.1.1 General Safety Precautions

Read and keep up-to-date with all safety information from your school board or district and from the Ministry or Department of Education.

- Try out all activities ahead of time. Look for potential hazards. Think about potential hazards before doing activities in class.
- Alert children to potential hazards.
- Get children involved in thinking about safety. Involve children in brainstorming ways to avoid dangers.
- Get into the habit of listing potential dangers in your planning.
- Be alert.
- Proper behavior is important during some activities. Horsing around can result in children getting hurt to a much greater degree than what might happen in relatively safe surroundings.
- Do not rush activities.
- Do not be careless.

- Never leave students unsupervised when handling potentially hazardous materials or equipment.

When working with potentially hazardous materials or equipment, keep a panoramic view of the whole class—do not get involved in a deep discussion with some children to the point where you are not aware of the rest of the class.

Set up a safe physical environment:
- Work with water or other liquids on floors or floor coverings that will not be slippery when wet.
- Make sure traffic-flow areas are wide and clear of obstructions.
- Make sure work surfaces are clear of any unnecessary materials.

Store all potentially dangerous equipment and supplies out of reach of children.

Teach children how to handle and store potentially dangerous equipment (e.g., scissors, knives, garden tools, etc.).

Always have a first-aid kit in your classroom. (See components of a first-aid kit described in Appendix F.)

Take a first-aid and CPR class.

If possible, take a laboratory safety course.

If possible, take a water safety course.

### A.1.2 Safety Supplies and Equipment

Always have a supply of

- Safety glasses
- Rubber gloves (or disposable vinyl—avoid latex, since many people are allergic to latex)
- Cotton work gloves
- Hot-pad gloves

Use safety glasses if there is any possibility of flying splinters, dust, liquids (other than cold water), or particles of any kind.

Use rubber gloves when working with specimens or hazardous chemicals.

Use cotton gloves when handling steel wool or sharp objects.

Use cotton gloves on field trips where children are picking up materials that could be potentially harmful (e.g., poison ivy, crayfish, sharp objects).

Watch out for:
- Long hair that can get caught in mechanisms, catch fire, or get into chemicals. Tie up or otherwise confine long hair. Have a supply of hair bands, strips of cloth, or yarn for tying up hair.
- Clothing that can get caught in mechanisms, catch on fire, or get into chemicals. Tie up or otherwise confine loose clothing.
- Jewelry, such as necklaces, can get caught in mechanisms. Rings on fingers also can get caught in mechanisms.

### A.1.3 Working with Flames and Heat

Avoid using open flames. *Never* use alcohol burners—you cannot see the flame.

If you need to heat something, use candles or hot plates. Make sure you have an appropriate fire extinguisher readily available.

Avoid heating test tubes, if at all possible. If heating a test tube (not generally necessary at the elementary level), make sure that (a) the test tube is being held in a test tube container, (b) the test tube is pointing away from the person holding it and away from anyone else, and (c) the test tube is being held with a test tube holder designed for this purpose. Heating materials in test tubes can result in the material in the test tube exploding out of the top of the tube.

### A.1.4 Working with Chemicals

Avoid using dangerous chemicals, such as strong acids (e.g., hydrochloric, nitric, acetic) and flammable liquids (e.g., gasoline, alcohol). You may need to use rubbing (isopropyl) alcohol from time to time. Keep it in a cool, dry place, away from heat and flames, as well as out of reach of children. We use chemicals every day (e.g., bleach, ammonia, alcohol, vinegar (an acid), etc.). They may seem innocuous, but should be handled with care.

- *Never mix bleach with anything other than water.* Mixing bleach with acids or with ammonia can produce *highly toxic* chlorine gas.
- Teach children *not* to mix chemicals "just to see what happens."
- Make sure there is adequate ventilation when using substances with noxious or potentially harmful fumes. Environmental sensitivities are becoming much more common. Avoid "smelly" materials whenever possible. Avoid using perfume and scented deodorants for personal use.
- Clearly label all substances.
- Do not store or use chemicals near food.
- Do not eat while working with chemicals.
- Avoid touching your face when handling chemicals.
- Do not inhale over a container of any chemical.
- Wash your hands thoroughly after handling chemicals.
- If you pour a chemical into a container for class use, do not use the container for other purposes, such as for drinking or keeping living specimens.
- Use digital thermometers or nonmercury thermometers, if possible. (If thermometers break, and they usually do, spilled mercury is toxic.)
- Familiarize yourself with the hazard symbols commonly used on chemical products.

### A.1.5 Equipment and Containers for Classroom Use and Storage

- Store shellac, alcohol, charcoal, and similar substances in jars or bottles with plastic tops.

**CHEMICAL HAZARD SYMBOLS.**

Toxic or poisonous

Corrosive

Reactive of explosive

Flammable or Inflammable (both terms mean the same)

- Use plastic or metal containers instead of glass whenever possible. Avoid glass, which can break.
- If you use glass (e.g., mirrors), smooth sharp edges or cover with electrical or duct tape.
- If you use glass to cover aquaria, and so forth, use safety glass or Plexiglas, if possible.
- Do not use directly reflected sunlight to illuminate microscopes. The sun's rays can damage the retina.

### A.1.6  Working with Electricity

When using batteries, be sure children are taught not to open them or tamper with them in any way. Treat batteries as toxic materials (they contain mercury and acid). Dispose of them through your local hazardous waste collections.

- Teach children to unplug electrical devices by pulling on the plug, not the cord.
- Use battery-operated or low-voltage (may plug into wall outlet, but use a converter to lower the voltage) devices whenever possible.

### A.1.7  Working with Dead and Living Animals

- Be careful about the animals you bring into the classroom.
  - Turtles and other reptiles may not be allowed in most classrooms because of the potential of *Salmonella* infections (potentially fatal dysentery).
  - Some animals bite. Be careful of hamsters, guinea pigs, birds, and some kinds of snakes (gerbils and rats tend not to bite). This does not mean that you should not have these animals in the classroom. Just be cautious. Some animals that are raised and handled a lot from just after birth are less likely to bite.
- Keep animal cages clean.
- Wear a safety mask when cleaning cages. Airborne bacteria and viruses can be very dangerous.
- Avoid touching your face when handling animals.
- Wash hands thoroughly after handling animals or cleaning cages.
- If you purchase preserved specimens, try to avoid those that are preserved in formaldehyde.

### A.1.8  Field Studies

- Wear long-sleeved shirts, hats, and so forth, for protection against the sun and for protection from mosquitoes, poison ivy, etc. Take along insect repellent.
- Wear appropriate footwear, for example, sneakers that can be worn in and out of the water.
- Remember to take along cotton gloves for each child.
- Be sure to bring along a first-aid kit.
- Take along rubbing alcohol for washing off hands after handling animals or other potentially hazardous materials.

■ Take sunscreen (SPF rating for 15 or more) for use by students. How-ever, purchase a *hypoallergenic* form. Many people have allergic reac-tions to some of the ingredients in sunscreens and skin creams.

### A.1.9  Allergies

Be careful of potential allergic reactions:

■ Are any of your students allergic to pollen?
■ Are any of your students allergic to particular foods?
■ Are any of your students allergic to bee stings?
■ Do any of your students have asthma?

Make sure children have any special medications, such as EpiPens (bee sting kits) or asthma inhalers, if you are going to be in areas or situations in which there is a risk.

## A.2  Personal, Psychological, and Social Safety

The categories of personal (i.e., physical violence between individuals), psy-chological, and social safety are very closely intertwined. Fights or other forms of physical violence often arise from social problems. So, as you read through the points below, keep these interconnections in mind.

### A.2.1  Personal

Physical violence from fighting and bullying through acts of extreme violence (i.e., killing students and teachers) are rooted in the social fabric of the child's home and community and of the classroom and school. Although numerous psychological factors may be at play, social factors play a major role.

■ Physical violence should not be tolerated, but it is a sign of social and psychological problems.
■ Zero tolerance is problematic in that it does not take into account the context.
  ■ In a typical fight, two children have a disagreement about some-thing. They have not yet found ways of resolving conflicts other than through fighting. So, you have an opportunity to help them develop alternative approaches to conflict resolution.
  ■ A conflict may arise between two children that leads to a fight. Although the fight is a problem, you have an opportunity to help these children learn and grow socially and emotionally. A *reality therapy* approach that involves working with each individual to take responsibility by describing exactly what happened, then proceed-ing to have each child propose other approaches to conflict resolu-tion can be an incredible learning experience.
  ■ If there are deep-seated psychological problems involved, where fighting is a regular pattern, then the child needs to be referred to a psychologist.

- A principal told one couple that their son "needed to toughen up." This was said during a meeting with the parents after the boy uttered a global threat and stormed out of school. The boy uttered the threat out of complete frustration after numerous days of severe teasing and physical abuse by other students during class time with no teacher intervention. Such an attitude toward "being tough" is not at all appropriate. No child should have to "toughen up."
- Be alert to signs of behavior that may lead to extreme acts of violence, such as
  - Repressed anger
  - Extreme withdrawal
  - Signs of abuse (emotional or physical)
  - Signs of having witnessed violence at home
  - Access to weapons
  - Extreme needs for attention or respect along with sense of low self-worth
  - Abnormal attraction to violence, weapons, and so forth, or to deviant peer groups
  - Antisocial behaviors

Of course, as human beings, we all may exhibit some of these behaviors, but we need to look for patterns that may indicate a problem. If you have questions or doubts, seek advice from your principal, school counselor, or psychologist. Dressing in gothic (black clothes, long overcoats, etc.) does not mean the child is deviant or antisocial. Look for deeper emotional qualities and patterns of behavior. Be sure to read and ponder the implications of the material in the following section.

### A.2.2 Psychological and Social

Schools should be safe places for children to learn. Such safety includes being safe not only from physical harm, but also from what we can consider to be emotional or physical violence. However, all too often schools are not emotionally safe places to be. Children are teased and taunted (more viciously than teasing that occurs among friends) and subjected to harshly negative criticisms from teachers and other types of behaviors from peers and adults that negatively affect children's curiosity, creativity, senses of humor, feelings of self-worth, confidence, openness, and other important qualities of being a child and human being. Even high-stakes tests can be acts of psychological violence. A teacher in New York City worked all year to get her students to develop higher levels of self-esteem. Just as the students had made significant gains, the tests came with all of their consequences (such as ending up in programs that were known by all to be for the "failures"). All the gains by the students were destroyed within two weeks, even though all of her students passed the test.

Consider the following points in contending with what may be very subtle acts of psychological and social violence against children.

- What you say to a child can have long-lasting effects, especially if it is part of a pattern in the way you relate to any particular child. Dismissing out of hand a child's idea can have negative effects on the child's self-esteem, creativity, and so forth.

- Children are growing psychological and socially; they need support and guidance.

- Children make mistakes, as we all do. These mistakes should be seen as opportunities to grow and learn, not as an opportunity for punishment.

- A clique within a classroom or school can have terrible consequences for those children not in the clique. Both girls and boys in elementary school form cliques, which then act to gang up on other children through vicious taunting and teasing. You need to work at developing interpersonal understanding and empathy.

- In relating with children, you need to remember to act in ways that create connections and not in ways that disconnect. Any top-down relationship tends to disconnect, such as rule by intimidation or authoritarianism. Competitive relationships also disconnect, such as in situations where the teacher and students are vying for control. On the other hand, relationships that focus on a sense of shared humanity and that engage in reciprocity or negotiation tend to create connections. Feeling a sense of compassion for our students, as opposed to pity (which is a disconnected top-down approach), allows you to share in their experiences. This compassionate attitude is simply a way of identifying with what they may be feeling. You do not have to openly discuss the way you identify with them, but just feel the connection. Based on this identification, your actions will reflect your connections with them. The "acid test" can involve questions you ask yourself, such as, What would it feel like if someone said or did this to me?

## Resources

Block, A. A. (1997). *I'm only bleeding: Education as the practice of social violence against children.* New York: Peter Lang.

Epp, J. R., & Watkinson, A. M. (Eds.). (1996). *Systemic violence: How schools hurt children.* Washington, DC: Falmer Press.

Polakow, V. (Ed.). (2000). *The public assault on America's children: Poverty, violence, and juvenile injustice.* New York: Teachers College Press.

"Safety in the Elementary Science Classroom" (from the American Chemical Society) at http://membership.acs.org/c/ccs/pubs/K-6_art_2.pdf

"Science Safety" (from the Connecticut State Department of Education) at http://www.state.ct.us/sde/dtl/curriculum/currsci_safety1.htm

# Appendix B
# Summary of the United States' National Science Education Standards

This appendix provides a brief list of the National Science Education Standards in the United States and how they correspond to the information in this book. However, for discussions of the issues involved in the standards, please see Chapters 6, 7, and 8.

## B.1  Principles (Chapter 2)

- Science is for all students.
- Learning science is an active process.
- School science reflects the intellectual and cultural traditions that characterize the practice of contemporary science.
- Improving science education is part of systemic education reform.

## B.2  Science Teaching Standards (Chapter 3)

### B.2.1  Assumptions

- The vision of science education described by the standards requires changes throughout the entire system.
- What students learn is greatly influenced by how they are taught.
- The actions of teachers are deeply influenced by their perceptions of science as an enterprise and as a subject to be taught and learned.
- Student understanding is actively constructed through individual and social processes.

- Actions of teachers are deeply influenced by their understanding of and relationships with students.

### B.2.2 Teaching Standard A

**Teachers of science plan an inquiry-based science program for their students. In doing this, teachers**

**TABLE B.1** Teaching Standard A

| Specific Standards | Chapters and Appendixes | | | | | | | | | | | |
|---|---|---|---|---|---|---|---|---|---|---|---|---|
| | 1 | 2 | 3 | 4 | 5 | 6 | 7 | 8 | 9 | 10 | 11 | Appendixes |
| Develop a framework of yearlong and short-term goals for students | | | | | | I | I | I | | | | D, E |
| Select science content and adapt and design curricula to meet the interests, knowledge, understanding, abilities, and experiences of students | I | I | | I | I | I | I | I | I | | | D, E, F, G |
| Select teaching and assessment strategies that support the development of student understanding and nurture a community of science learners | I | | I | I | I | I | I | I | I | I | I | |
| Work together as colleagues within and across disciplines and grade levels | I | | | | | | | | | I | I | |

### B.2.3 Teaching Standard B

**Teachers of science guide and facilitate learning. In doing this, teachers**

**TABLE B.2** Teaching Standard B

| Specific Standards | Chapters and Selected Appendixes | | | | | | | | | | | |
|---|---|---|---|---|---|---|---|---|---|---|---|---|
| | 1 | 2 | 3 | 4 | 5 | 6 | 7 | 8 | 9 | 10 | 11 | Appendixes |
| Focus and support inquiries while interacting with students | | | | I | I | I | | I | I | | | D, E, F, G |
| Orchestrate discourse among students about scientific ideas | | | | | I | I | | I | I | | | |
| Challenge students to accept and share responsibility for their own learning | | | | | | I | I | I | I | | | |
| Recognize and respond to student diversity and encourage all students to participate fully in science learning | | | | | | I | I | I | I | | | J |
| Encourage and model the skills of scientific inquiry, as well as the curiosity, openness to new ideas and data, and skepticism that characterize science | I | I | I | | I | I | | I | I | I | I | D, E, F, G, H, I |

## B.2.4 Teaching Standard C

**Teachers of science engage in ongoing assessment of their teaching and of student learning. In doing this, teachers**

**TABLE B.3** Teaching Standard C

| Specific Standards | Chapters and Selected Appendixes | | | | | | | | | | | |
|---|---|---|---|---|---|---|---|---|---|---|---|---|
| | 1 | 2 | 3 | 4 | 5 | 6 | 7 | 8 | 9 | 10 | 11 | Appendixes |
| Use multiple methods and systematically gather data about student understanding and ability | I | | I | I | I | | I | | I | I | | |
| Analyze assessment data to guide teaching | | | I | I | I | I | I | I | I | I | | |
| Guide students in self-assessment | | | | | | I | I | I | | I | | |
| Use student data, observations of teaching, and interactions with colleagues to reflect on and improve teaching practice | | | | | | | I | | I | I | I | |
| Use student data, observations of teaching, and interactions with colleagues to report student achievement and opportunities to learn to students, teachers, parents, policy makers, and the general public | | | | | | | I | | I | I | I | |

## B.2.5 Teaching Standard D

**Teachers of science design and manage learning environments that provide students with the time, space, and resources needed for learning science. In doing this, teachers**

**TABLE B.4** Teaching Standard D

| Specific Standards | Chapters and Selected Appendixes | | | | | | | | | | | |
|---|---|---|---|---|---|---|---|---|---|---|---|---|
| | 1 | 2 | 3 | 4 | 5 | 6 | 7 | 8 | 9 | 10 | 11 | Appendixes |
| Structure the time available so that students are able to engage in extended investigations | | | | | | I | | I | | | | D, E, F |
| Create a setting for student work that is flexible and supportive of science inquiry | | | | | | I | | I | I | | | |
| Ensure a safe working environment | | | | | | I | | | I | | | A |
| Make the available science tools, materials, media, and technological resources accessible to students | | | | | | | | | I | | | H, I, J, K,L |

*-- continued*

**TABLE B.4** Teaching Standard D

| Specific Standards | Chapters and Selected Appendixes | | | | | | | | | | | |
| --- | --- | --- | --- | --- | --- | --- | --- | --- | --- | --- | --- | --- |
| | 1 | 2 | 3 | 4 | 5 | 6 | 7 | 8 | 9 | 10 | 11 | Appendixes |
| Identify and use resources outside the school | | | | | | I | | I | I | | I | F |
| Engage students in designing the learning environment | | | | | | I | | I | I | | | |

### B.2.6 Teaching Standard E

**Teachers of science develop communities of science learners that reflect the intellectual rigor of scientific inquiry and the attitudes and social values conducive to science learning. In doing this, teachers**

**TABLE B.5** Teaching Standard E

| Specific Standards | Chapters and Selected Appendixes | | | | | | | | | | | |
| --- | --- | --- | --- | --- | --- | --- | --- | --- | --- | --- | --- | --- |
| | 1 | 2 | 3 | 4 | 5 | 6 | 7 | 8 | 9 | 10 | 11 | Appendixes |
| Display and demand respect for the diverse ideas, skills, and experiences of all students | I | | I | I | I | | | I | I | | | D |
| Enable students to have a significant voice in decisions about the content and context of their work and require students to take responsibility for the learning of all members of the community | I | | | | | I | I | I | I | | | |
| Nurture collaboration among students | I | | | I | I | I | I | I | | | | |
| Structure and facilitate ongoing formal and informal discussion based on a shared understanding of rules of scientific discourse | I | | | | I | I | | I | I | | | |
| Model and emphasize the skills, attitudes, and values of scientific inquiry | I | I | I | | I | I | | I | I | | | H, I, J |

### B.2.7 Teaching Standard F

**Teachers of science actively participate in the ongoing planning and development of the school science program. In doing this, teachers**

**TABLE B.6** Teaching Standard F

| Specific Standards | Chapters and Selected Appendixes | | | | | | | | | | | |
| --- | --- | --- | --- | --- | --- | --- | --- | --- | --- | --- | --- | --- |
| | 1 | 2 | 3 | 4 | 5 | 6 | 7 | 8 | 9 | 10 | 11 | Appendixes |
| Plan and develop the school science program | | | | | | | | | | | I | |
| Participate in decisions concerning the allocation of time and other resources to the science program | | | | | | | | | | | I | |
| Participate fully in planning and implementing professional growth and development strategies for themselves and their colleagues | | | | | | | | | | I | I | L |

Teachers who are enthusiastic, interested, and who speak of the power and beauty of scientific understanding instill in their students some of those same attitudes.

## B.3 Standards for Professional Development for Teachers of Science (Chapter 4)

### B.3.1 Assumptions

- Professional development for a teacher of science is a continuous, life-long process.
- The traditional distinctions between targets, sources, and supporters of teacher development activities are artificial.
- The conventional view of professional development for teachers needs to shift from technical training for specific skills to opportunities for intellectual professional growth.
- The process of transforming schools requires that professional development opportunities be clearly and appropriately connected to teachers' work in the context of the school.

### B.3.2 Professional Development Standard A

**Professional development for teachers of science requires learning essential science content through the perspectives and methods of inquiry. Science learning experiences for teachers must**

**TABLE B.7** Professional Development Standard A

| Specific Standards | Chapters and Selected Appendixes | | | | | | | | | | | |
|---|---|---|---|---|---|---|---|---|---|---|---|---|
| | 1 | 2 | 3 | 4 | 5 | 6 | 7 | 8 | 9 | 10 | 11 | Appendixes |
| Involve teachers in actively investigating phenomena that can be studied scientifically, interpreting results, and making sense of findings consistent with currently accepted scientific understanding. To meet the standards, all teachers of science must have a strong, broad base of scientific knowledge extensive enough for them to | | I | | | | I | | | | | | D, F, G, H, I |
| Understand the nature of scientific inquiry, its central role in science, and how to use the skills and processes of scientific inquiry | | I | I | | | I | | I | I | | I | F, G, H, I, J |
| Understand the fundamental facts and concepts in major science disciplines | I | | I | | | I | | | | | I | D |

*-- continued*

**TABLE B.7** Professional Development Standard A

| Specific Standards | Chapters and Selected Appendixes | | | | | | | | | | | |
|---|---|---|---|---|---|---|---|---|---|---|---|---|
| | 1 | 2 | 3 | 4 | 5 | 6 | 7 | 8 | 9 | 10 | 11 | Appendixes |
| Be able to make conceptual connections within and across science disciplines, as well as to mathematics, technology, and other school subjects | I | | I | I | I | I | I | I | | | | D, E, J |
| Use scientific understanding and ability when dealing with personal and societal issues | I | | I | | | I | | I | I | | I | J |
| Address issues, events, problems, or topics significant in science and of interest to participants | I | | I | I | I | I | I | I | I | | | D, E |
| Introduce teachers to scientific literature, media, and technological resources that expand their science knowledge and their ability to access further knowledge | | | | | | | | | | | I | I, J |
| Build on the teacher's current science understanding, ability, and attitudes | | I | I | | | | | | | | I | L |
| Incorporate ongoing reflection on the process and outcomes of understanding science through inquiry | I | | | | | I | | | I | I | | |
| Encourage and support teachers in efforts to collaborate | | | | | | | | | I | | I | J, L |

## B.3.3  Professional Development Standard B

Professional development for teachers of science requires integrating knowledge of science, learning, pedagogy, and students; it also requires applying that knowledge to science teaching. Learning experiences for teachers of science must

**TABLE B.8** Professional Development Standard B

| Specific Standards | Chapters and Selected Appendixes | | | | | | | | | | | |
|---|---|---|---|---|---|---|---|---|---|---|---|---|
| | 1 | 2 | 3 | 4 | 5 | 6 | 7 | 8 | 9 | 10 | 11 | Appendixes |
| Connect and integrate all pertinent aspects of science and science education | I | I | I | I | I | I | I | I | I | I | I | D, I, J |
| Occur in a variety of places where effective science teaching can be illustrated and modeled, permitting teachers to struggle with real situations and expand their knowledge and skills in appropriate contexts | I | | | | | | | | | I | I | |
| Address teachers' needs as learners and build on their current knowledge of science content, teaching, and learning | | | | | | | | | | I | I | |
| Use inquiry, reflection, interpretation of research, modeling, and guided practice to build understanding and skill in science teaching | | | | | | | | | | I | I | |

## B.3.4 Professional Development Standard C

**Professional development for teachers of science requires building understanding and an ability for lifelong learning. Professional development activities must**

**TABLE B.9** Professional Development Standard C

| Specific Standards | Chapters and Selected Appendixes | | | | | | | | | | | |
|---|---|---|---|---|---|---|---|---|---|---|---|---|
| | 1 | 2 | 3 | 4 | 5 | 6 | 7 | 8 | 9 | 10 | 11 | Appendixes |
| Provide regular, frequent opportunities for individual and collegial examination and reflection on classroom and institutional practice | | | | | | | | | | I | I | |
| Provide opportunities for teachers to receive feedback about their teaching and to understand, analyze, and apply that feedback to improve their practice | | | | | | | | | | I | I | |
| Provide opportunities for teachers to learn and use various tools and techniques for self-reflection and collegial reflection, such as peer coaching, portfolios, and journals | | | | | | | | | | I | I | |
| Support the sharing of teacher expertise by preparing and using mentors, teacher advisers, coaches, lead teachers, and resource teachers to provide professional development opportunities | | | | | | | | | | I | I | |
| Provide opportunities to know and have access to existing research and experiential knowledge | | | | | | | | | | | I | L |
| Provide opportunities to learn and use the skills of research to generate new knowledge about science and the teaching and learning of science | | | | | | | | | | I | I | |

## B.3.5 Professional Development Standard D

**Professional development programs for teachers of science must be coherent and integrated. Quality pre-service and in-service programs are characterized by**

**TABLE B.10** Professional Development Standard D

| Specific Standards | Chapters and Selected Appendixes | | | | | | | | | | | |
|---|---|---|---|---|---|---|---|---|---|---|---|---|
| | 1 | 2 | 3 | 4 | 5 | 6 | 7 | 8 | 9 | 10 | 11 | Appendixes |
| Clear, shared goals based on a vision of science learning, teaching, and teacher development congruent with the National Science Education Standards | | | | | | | I | I | | | I | |
| Integration and coordination of the program components so that understanding and ability can be built over time, reinforced continuously, and practiced in a variety of situations | | | | | | | I | I | | | I | |
| Options that recognize the developmental nature of teacher professional growth and individual and group interests, as well as the needs of teachers who have varying degrees of experience, professional expertise, and proficiency | | | | | | | | | | I | I | |
| Collaboration among the people involved in programs, including teachers, teacher educators, teacher unions, scientists, administrators, policy makers, members of professional and scientific organizations, parents, and business people, with clear respect for the perspectives and expertise of each | | | | | | | | | | | I | |
| Recognition of the history, culture, and organization of the school environment | | | | | | | | | | | I | J |
| Continuous program assessment that captures the perspectives of all those involved, uses a variety of strategies, focuses on the process and effects of the program, and feeds directly into program improvement and evaluation | | | | | | | | | | | | |

## B.4 Assessment in Science Education (Chapter 5)

### B.4.1 Components of the Assessment Process

The four components can be combined in numerous ways. For example, teachers use student achievement data to plan and modify teaching practices, and business leaders use per capita educational expenditures to locate businesses. The variety of uses, users, methods, and data contribute to the complexity and importance of the assessment process.

**TABLE B.11** Four Components of the Assessment Process

| Data Use | Data Collection | Methods to Collect Data | Users of Data |
|---|---|---|---|
| • Plan teaching<br>• Guide learning<br>• Calculate grades<br>• Make comparisons<br>• Credential and license<br>• Determine access to special or advanced education<br>• Develop education theory<br>• Inform policy formulation<br>• Monitor effects of policies<br>• Allocate resources<br>• Evaluate quality of curricula, programs, and teaching practices | • To describe and quantify:<br>  • Student achievement and attitude<br>  • Teacher preparation and quality<br>  • Program characteristics<br>  • Resource allocation<br>  • Policy instruments<br>  • Paper-and-pencil testing | • Performance testing<br>• Interviews<br>• Portfolios<br>• Performances<br>• Observing programs, students, and teachers in classroom<br>• Transcript analysis<br>• Expert reviews of educational materials | • Teachers<br>• Students<br>• Educational administrators<br>• Parents<br>• Public<br>• Policy makers<br>• Institutions of higher education<br>• Business and industry<br>• Government |

## B.4.2 Decisions and Action Based on Data

*B.4.2.1 Assessment Standard A* Assessments must be consistent with the decisions they are designed to inform.

**TABLE B.12** Assessment Standard A

| Specific Standards | Chapters and Selected Appendixes | | | | | | | | | | | |
|---|---|---|---|---|---|---|---|---|---|---|---|---|
| | 1 | 2 | 3 | 4 | 5 | 6 | 7 | 8 | 9 | 10 | 11 | *Appendixes* |
| Assessments are deliberately designed | | | | | | | I | | | | | |
| Assessments have explicitly stated purposes | | | | | | | I | | | | | |
| The relationship between the decisions and the data is clear | | | | | | | I | | | | | |
| Assessment procedures are internally consistent | | | | | | | I | | | | | |

*B.4.2.2 Assessment Standard B* Achievement and opportunity to learn science must be assessed.

**TABLE B.13** Assessment Standard B

| Specific Standards | Chapters and Selected Appendixes | | | | | | | | | | | |
|---|---|---|---|---|---|---|---|---|---|---|---|---|
| | 1 | 2 | 3 | 4 | 5 | 6 | 7 | 8 | 9 | 10 | 11 | *Appendixes* |
| Achievement data collected focus on the science content that is most important for students to learn | | | | | | | I | | | I | | |
| Opportunity-to-learn data collected focus on the most powerful indicators | | | | | | | I | | | | I | |
| Equal attention given to the assessment of opportunity to learn and to the assessment of student achievement | | | | | | | I | | | | I | |

B.4.2.3 *Assessment Standard C*  The technical quality of the data collected is well matched to the decisions and actions taken on the basis of their interpretation.

**TABLE B.14** Assessment Standard C

| Specific Standards | Chapters and Selected Appendixes | | | | | | | | | | | |
|---|---|---|---|---|---|---|---|---|---|---|---|---|
| | 1 | 2 | 3 | 4 | 5 | 6 | 7 | 8 | 9 | 10 | 11 | Appendixes |
| The feature that is claimed to be measured is actually measured | | | | | | | I | | | | | |
| Assessment tasks are authentic | | | | | | | I | | | | | |
| An individual student's performance is similar on two or more tasks that claim to measure the same aspect of student achievement | | | | | | | I | | | | | |
| Students have adequate opportunity to demonstrate their achievements | | | | | | | I | | | | | |
| Assessment tasks and methods of presenting them provide data that are sufficiently stable to lead to the same decisions if used at different times | | | | | | | I | | | | | |

B.4.2.4 *Assessment Standard D*  Assessment practices must be fair.

**TABLE B.15** Assessment Standard D

| Specific Standards | Chapters and Selected Appendixes | | | | | | | | | | | |
|---|---|---|---|---|---|---|---|---|---|---|---|---|
| | 1 | 2 | 3 | 4 | 5 | 6 | 7 | 8 | 9 | 10 | 11 | Appendixes |
| Assessment tasks must be reviewed for the use of stereotypes, for assumptions that reflect the perspectives or experiences of a particular group, for language that might be offensive to a particular group, and for other features that might distract students from the intended task | | | | | | | I | | | I | | |
| Large-scale assessments must use statistical techniques to identify potential bias among subgroups | | | | | | | | | | | | |
| Assessment tasks must be appropriately modified to accommodate the needs of students with physical disabilities, learning disabilities, or limited English proficiency | | | | | | | I | | | | | |
| Assessment tasks must be set in a variety of contexts, be engaging to students with different interests and experiences, and must not assume the perspective or experience of a particular gender, racial, or ethnic group | | | | I | I | | I | | | | | |

*B.4.2.5 Assessment Standard E* The inferences made from assessments about student achievement and opportunity to learn must be sound.

**TABLE B.16** Assessment Standard E

| Specific Standards | Chapters and Selected Appendixes | | | | | | | | | | | |
|---|---|---|---|---|---|---|---|---|---|---|---|---|
| | 1 | 2 | 3 | 4 | 5 | 6 | 7 | 8 | 9 | 10 | 11 | Appendixes |
| When making inferences from assessment data about student achievement and opportunity to learn science, explicit reference needs to be made to the assumptions on which the inferences are based | | | | | | | I | | | I | | |

## B.5 Science Content Standards (Chapter 6)

### B.5.1 Rationale

- Unifying concepts and processes in science
  - Systems, order, and organization
  - Evidence, models, and explanation
  - Change, constancy, and measurement
  - Evolution and equilibrium
  - Form and function
- Science as inquiry — Engaging students in inquiry helps students develop
  - Understanding of scientific concepts
  - An appreciation of "how we know" what we know in science
  - Understanding of the nature of science
  - Skills necessary to become independent
  - The dispositions to use the skills, abilities, and attitudes associated with science
- Physical science
- Life science
- Earth and space science
- Science and technology
- Science in personal and social perspectives
- History and nature of science

### Changing Emphases

| Less Emphasis On | More Emphasis On |
|---|---|
| Knowing scientific facts and information | Understanding scientific concepts and developing abilities of inquiry |
| Studying subject matter disciplines (physical, life, earth sciences) for their own sake | Learning subject matter disciplines in the context of inquiry, technology, science in personal and social perspectives, and history and nature of science |
| Separating science knowledge and science process | Integrating all aspects of science content |
| Covering many science topics | Studying a few fundamental science concepts |
| Implementing inquiry as a set of processes | Implementing inquiry as instructional strategies, abilities, and ideas to be learned |

### Changing Emphases to Promote Inquiry

| Less Emphasis On | More Emphasis On |
|---|---|
| Activities that demonstrate and verify science content | Activities that investigate and analyze science questions |
| Investigations confined to one class period | Investigations over extended periods of time |
| Process skills out of context | Process skills in context |
| Individual process skills, such as observation or inference | Using multiple process skills — manipulation, cognitive, procedural |
| Getting an answer | Using evidence and strategies for developing or revising an explanation |
| Science as exploration and experiment | Science as argument and explanation |
| Providing answers to questions about science content | Communicating science explanations |
| Individuals and groups of students analyzing and synthesizing data without defending a conclusion | Groups of students often analyzing and synthesizing data after defending conclusions |
| Doing few investigations in order to leave time to cover large amounts of content | Doing more investigations in order to develop understanding, ability, values of inquiry, and knowledge of science content |
| Concluding inquiries with the result of the experiment | Applying the results of experiments to scientific arguments and explanations |
| Management of materials and equipment | Management of ideas and information |
| Private communication of student ideas and conclusions to teacher | Public communication of student ideas and work to classmates |

## B.5.2 Unifying Concepts and Processes

*B.5.2.1 Developing Student Understanding*

■ The concepts and processes provide connections between and among traditional scientific disciplines.

■ The concepts and processes are fundamental and comprehensive.

■ The concepts and processes are understandable and usable by people who will implement science programs.

■ The concepts and processes can be expressed and experienced in a developmentally appropriate manner during K through 12 science education.

*Standard*: As a result of activities in grades K through 12, all students should develop understandings and abilities aligned with the following concepts and processes:

**TABLE B.18** Unifying Concepts and Processes in the Science Content Standards

| Specific Standards | 1 | 2 | 3 | 4 | 5 | 6 | 7 | 8 | 9 | 10 | 11 | Appendixes |
|---|---|---|---|---|---|---|---|---|---|---|---|---|
| Systems, order, and organization | | I | | | | I | | I | | | | D, E |
| Evidence, models, and explanation | | I | I | | | I | I | I | | | | D, E |
| Constancy, change, and measurement | | I | | | | I | | I | | | | D, E, H |
| Evolution and equilibrium | | | I | I | | I | | I | | | | D, E, H, I |
| Form and function | | I | | | | I | I | I | | | | D, E |

## B.5.3 Content Standards: K through 4

*B.5.3.1 Science As Inquiry: Content Standard A* As a result of activities in grades K through 4, all students should develop

**TABLE B.19** Content Standard A—Science as Inquiry

| Specific Standards | 1 | 2 | 3 | 4 | 5 | 6 | 7 | 8 | 9 | 10 | 11 | Appendixes |
|---|---|---|---|---|---|---|---|---|---|---|---|---|
| Abilities necessary to do scientific inquiry | | I | I | | | I | | I | I | I | I | F, G, H, I, J |
| Understanding about scientific inquiry | | I | I | | | I | | I | I | I | I | F, G, H, I, J |

*B.5.3.2 Physical Science: Content Standard B* As a result of the activities in grades K through 4, all students should develop an understanding of

**TABLE B.20** Content Standard B—Physical Science

| Specific Standards | 1 | 2 | 3 | 4 | 5 | 6 | 7 | 8 | 9 | 10 | 11 | Appendixes |
|---|---|---|---|---|---|---|---|---|---|---|---|---|
| Properties of objects and materials | | | | I | I | | | I | | | | D, G |
| Position and motion of objects | | | | | | I | | I | | | | D, G |
| Light, heat, electricity, and magnetism | | I | | I | | I | | I | I | | | D, G, H, I |

*B.5.3.3 Life Science: Content Standard C* As a result of activities in grades K through 4, all students should develop an understanding of

**TABLE B.21** Content Standard C—Life Science

| Specific Standards | 1 | 2 | 3 | 4 | 5 | 6 | 7 | 8 | 9 | 10 | 11 | Appendixes |
|---|---|---|---|---|---|---|---|---|---|---|---|---|
| The characteristics of organisms | | I | | I | | I | | I | | | | D, G, H, I |
| Life cycles of organisms | | | | | | | | I | | | | D, G, H, I |
| Organisms and environments | | I | | I | | I | | I | | | | D, G, H, I, L |

*B.5.3.4 Earth and Space Science: Content Standard D* As a result of their activities in grades K through 4, all students should develop and understanding of

**TABLE B.22** Content Standard D—Earth and Space Science

| Specific Standards | Chapters and Selected Appendixes | | | | | | | | | | | |
|---|---|---|---|---|---|---|---|---|---|---|---|---|
| | 1 | 2 | 3 | 4 | 5 | 6 | 7 | 8 | 9 | 10 | 11 | Appendixes |
| Properties of earth materials | | | | | | | | | | | | D, G, H, I, L |
| Objects in the sky | | I | I | I | | I | I | | I | | | D, G, H, I, L |
| Changes in earth and sky | | I | | | | | I | | | | | G, H, I, L |

*B.5.3.5 Science and Technology: Content Standard E* As a result of activities in grades K through 4, all student should develop

**TABLE B.23** Content Standard—Science and Technology

| Specific Standards | Chapters and Selected Appendixes | | | | | | | | | | | |
|---|---|---|---|---|---|---|---|---|---|---|---|---|
| | 1 | 2 | 3 | 4 | 5 | 6 | 7 | 8 | 9 | 10 | 11 | Appendixes |
| Abilities of technological design | | | I | | | | | | | | | D, J, L |
| Understanding about science and technology | | | I | | | | | | | | | D, H, I, J |
| Abilities to distinguish between natural objects and objects made by humans | | | | | | | | | | | | D |

*B.5.3.6 Science in Personal and Social Perspectives: Content Standard F* As a result of activities in grades K through 4, all students should develop understandings of

**TABLE B.24** Content Standard F—Science in Personal and Social Perspectives

| Specific Standards | Chapters and Selected Appendixes | | | | | | | | | | | |
|---|---|---|---|---|---|---|---|---|---|---|---|---|
| | 1 | 2 | 3 | 4 | 5 | 6 | 7 | 8 | 9 | 10 | 11 | Appendixes |
| Personal health | | | | | | I | | | | | | A, D |
| Characteristics and changes in populations | | I | | | | I | | | | | | D, G, H, |
| Types of resources | | | | | | | | | | | | F, G, H, I, J, K, L |
| Changes in environments | | I | | | | I | | I | I | | | D, F, G, H, I |
| Science and technology in local challenges | | | I | | | I | | I | | | | G, J |

*B.5.3.7 History and Nature of Science: Content Standard G* As a result of activities in grades K through 4, all students should develop understandings of

**TABLE B.25** Content Standard G—History and Nature of Science

| Specific Standards | Chapters and Selected Appendixes | | | | | | | | | | | |
|---|---|---|---|---|---|---|---|---|---|---|---|---|
| | 1 | 2 | 3 | 4 | 5 | 6 | 7 | 8 | 9 | 10 | 11 | Appendixes |
| Science as a human endeavor | | I | I | I | I | I | | I | I | | | G, H, I, J |

## B.5.4  Content Standards: 5 through 8

*B.5.4.1 Science As Inquiry: Content Standard A* As a result of activities in grades 5 through 8, all students should develop

**TABLE B.26** Content Standard—Science as Inquiry

| Specific Standards | Chapters and Selected Appendixes | | | | | | | | | | | |
| --- | --- | --- | --- | --- | --- | --- | --- | --- | --- | --- | --- | --- |
| | 1 | 2 | 3 | 4 | 5 | 6 | 7 | 8 | 9 | 10 | 11 | Appendixes |
| Abilities necessary to do scientific inquiry | | I | I | I | I | I | | I | I | I | I | D, F, G, H, I, J |
| Understanding about scientific inquiry | | I | I | I | I | I | I | I | I | I | I | D, F, G, H, I, J |

*B.5.4.2  Physical Science: Content Standard B*  As a result of their activities in grades 5 through 8, all students should develop an understanding of

**TABLE B.27** Content Standard B—Physical Science

| Specific Standards | Chapters and Selected Appendixes | | | | | | | | | | | |
| --- | --- | --- | --- | --- | --- | --- | --- | --- | --- | --- | --- | --- |
| | 1 | 2 | 3 | 4 | 5 | 6 | 7 | 8 | 9 | 10 | 11 | Appendixes |
| Properties and changes of properties in matter | | | | I | I | I | | | | | | D, G, H, I |
| Motions and forces | | | | I | I | | | | | | | D, G, H, I, J |
| Transfer of energy | | | I | | I | | | | | | | D, G, H, I, J |

*B.5.4.3  Life Science: Content Standard C*  As a result of their activities in grades 5 through 8, all students should develop an understanding of

**TABLE B.28** Content Standard CcLife Science

| Specific Standards | Chapters and Selected Appendixes | | | | | | | | | | | |
| --- | --- | --- | --- | --- | --- | --- | --- | --- | --- | --- | --- | --- |
| | 1 | 2 | 3 | 4 | 5 | 6 | 7 | 8 | 9 | 10 | 11 | Appendixes |
| Structure and function in living systems | | I | | I | I | | I | I | | | | D, G, H, I, J |
| Reproduction and heredity | | | | | | | | | | | | D, G, H, I, J |
| Regulation and behavior | | I | | | | | | | | | | D, G, H, I, J |
| Populations and ecosystems | | | | | | | | | | | | D, G, H, I, J |
| Diversity and adaptations of organisms | | | | I | | I | I | I | | | | D, G, H, I, J |

*B.5.4.4  Earth and Space Science: Content Standard D*  As a result of their activities in grades 5 through 8, all students should develop an understanding of

**TABLE B.29** Content Standard D—Earth and Space Science

| Specific Standards | Chapters and Selected Appendixes | | | | | | | | | | | |
| --- | --- | --- | --- | --- | --- | --- | --- | --- | --- | --- | --- | --- |
| | 1 | 2 | 3 | 4 | 5 | 6 | 7 | 8 | 9 | 10 | 11 | Appendixes |
| Structure of the earth system | | I | I | | | I | I | I | | | | D, G, H, I, J |
| Earth's history | | | | | | | I | I | | | | D, G, H, I, J |
| Earth in the solar system | | I | I | | | I | I | I | | | | D, G, H, I, J |

*B.5.4.5  Science and Technology: Content Standard E*  As a result of activities in grades 5 through 8, all students should develop

**TABLE B.30** Content Standard E—Science and Technology

| Specific Standards | Chapters and Selected Appendixes | | | | | | | | | | | |
|---|---|---|---|---|---|---|---|---|---|---|---|---|
| | 1 | 2 | 3 | 4 | 5 | 6 | 7 | 8 | 9 | 10 | 11 | Appendixes |
| Abilities of technological design | | | | | | | | | | | | D, G, H, I, J |
| Understandings about science and technology | | | | | I | I | | | | | | D, G, H, I, J |

*B.5.4.6 Science in Personal and Social Perspectives: Content Standard F* As a result of activities in grades 5 through 8, all students should develop an understanding of

**TABLE B.31** Content Standard F—Science in Personal and Social Perspectives

| Specific Standards | Chapters and Selected Appendixes | | | | | | | | | | | |
|---|---|---|---|---|---|---|---|---|---|---|---|---|
| | 1 | 2 | 3 | 4 | 5 | 6 | 7 | 8 | 9 | 10 | 11 | Appendixes |
| Personal health | | | | | | | | | | | | A, H, I |
| Populations, resources, and environments | | | I | | | I | | | | | | L |
| Natural hazards | | | | | | | | | | | | L |
| Risks and benefits | | | I | | | | | | | | | |
| Science and technology in society | | | I | | | | | | | | | D, G, H, I, J |

*B.5.4.7 History and Nature of Science: Content Standard G* As a result of activities in grades 5 through 8, all students should develop an understanding of

**TABLE B.32** Content Standard G—History and Nature of Science

| Specific Standards | Chapters and Selected Appendixes | | | | | | | | | | | |
|---|---|---|---|---|---|---|---|---|---|---|---|---|
| | 1 | 2 | 3 | 4 | 5 | 6 | 7 | 8 | 9 | 10 | 11 | Appendixes |
| Science as a human endeavor | | | I | | | I | | | | | | F, G, H, I |
| Nature of science | | | I | | | I | | | | | | H, I, J |
| History of science | | | I | | | | | | | | | |

The National Science Education Standards can be accessed at http://books.nap.edu/books/0309053269/html/index.html.

*Appendix C*

# Canadian Common Framework of Science Learning Outcomes: Pan-Canadian Protocol for Collaboration on School Curriculum

## C.1 A Vision for Scientific Literacy in Canada

The framework is guided by the vision that all Canadian students, regardless of gender or cultural background, will have an opportunity to develop scientific literacy. Scientific literacy is an evolving combination of the science-related attitudes, skills, and knowledge students need to develop inquiry, problem-solving, and decision-making abilities, to become lifelong learners, and to maintain a sense of wonder about the world around them.

Diverse learning experiences based on the framework will provide students with many opportunities to explore, analyze, evaluate, synthesize, appreciate, and understand the interrelationships among science, technology, society, and the environment that will affect their personal lives, their careers, and their future.

## C.2 The Scientific Literacy Needs of Canadian Students and Society

Science education aims to

- Encourage students at all grade levels to develop a critical sense of wonder and curiosity about scientific and technological endeavors
- Enable students to use science and technology to acquire new knowledge and solve problems, so that they may improve the quality of their own lives and the lives of others

- Prepare students to critically address science-related societal, economic, ethical, and environmental issues
- Provide students with a foundation in science that creates opportunities for them to pursue progressively higher levels of study, prepares them for science-related occupations, and engages them in science-related hobbies appropriate to their interests and abilities
- Develop in students of varying aptitudes and interests a knowledge of the wide variety of careers related to science, technology, and the environment

Science education must be the basis for informed participation in a technological society, a part of a continuing process of education, a preparation for the world of work, and a means for students' personal development. (Science Council of Canada, 1984)

## C.3 Foundation Statements for Scientific Literacy in Canada

In light of the vision for scientific literacy and the need to develop scientific literacy in Canada, four foundation statements were established for this framework. Curriculum developers should note that these foundation statements delineate the four critical aspects of students' scientific literacy. They reflect the wholeness and interconnectedness of learning and should be considered as interrelated and mutually supportive. The learning outcomes in this framework are stated in relation to these foundation statements.

### C.3.1 Foundation 1: Science, Technology, and the Environment (STSE)

**Students will develop an understanding of the nature of science and technology, of the relationships between science and technology, and of the social and environmental contexts of science and technology.**

**TABLE C.1** Foundation 1—Science, Technology, and the Environment (STSE)

| Specific Standards | Chapters and Selected Appendixes | | | | | | | | | | | |
|---|---|---|---|---|---|---|---|---|---|---|---|---|
| | 1 | 2 | 3 | 4 | 5 | 6 | 7 | 8 | 9 | 10 | 11 | Appendixes |
| The nature of science and technology | | | I | | | I | | | | | | H, I, J |
| The relationships between science and technology | | | I | | | | | | | | | H, I, J |
| The social and environmental contexts of science and technology | | | I | | | I | | I | I | | | D, I, J |

### C.3.2 Foundation 2: Skills

**Students will develop the skills required for scientific and technological inquiry, for solving problems, for communicating scientific ideas and results, for working collaboratively, and for making informed decisions.**

**TABLE C.2** Foundation 2—Skills

| Specific Standards | Chapters and Selected Appendixes | | | | | | | | | | | |
|---|---|---|---|---|---|---|---|---|---|---|---|---|
| | 1 | 2 | 3 | 4 | 5 | 6 | 7 | 8 | 9 | 10 | 11 | Appendixes |
| Initiating and planning | | | | | | I | | I | | | | E, H, I |
| Performing and recording | | | | | | I | | I | | | | E, H, I |
| Analyzing and interpreting | | | | | | I | | I | | | | E, H, I |
| Communication and teamwork | | | | | | I | | I | I | | | E, H, I, J |

## C.3.3 Foundation 3: Knowledge

**Students will construct knowledge and understandings of concepts in life science, physical science, and earth and space science, and apply these understandings to interpret, integrate, and extend their knowledge.**

**TABLE C.3** Foundation 3—Knowledge

| Specific Standards | Chapters and Selected Appendixes | | | | | | | | | | | |
|---|---|---|---|---|---|---|---|---|---|---|---|---|
| | 1 | 2 | 3 | 4 | 5 | 6 | 7 | 8 | 9 | 10 | 11 | Appendixes |
| Theories, models, concepts, and principles | | | I | | | I | | I | | | | D |
| Life science — Growth and interactions of life forms within their environments, in ways that reflect their uniqueness, diversity, genetic continuity, and changing nature | | I | | I | | I | | I | | | | D, E, F, G, H, I |
| Physical science — Encompasses chemistry and physics; deals with matter, energy, and forces | | I | | I | I | I | | I | | | | D, E, F, G, H, I |
| Earth and space science — Brings global and universal perspectives to students' knowledge; earth, solar system, and universe exhibit form, structure, and patterns of change | | I | | I | I | I | | I | | | | D, E, F, G, H, I |
| Creating linkages among science disciplines — Use unifying concepts, key ideas that underlie and integrate different scientific disciplines; integrate big ideas as a way to provide a context for explaining, organizing, and connecting knowledge: | | | | | | I | | I | | | | D, I, J |
| Constancy and change | | | | | | I | | I | | | | D, E, H |
| Energy | | | | | | I | | I | | | | D, E, H |
| Similarity and diversity | | | | | | I | | I | | | | D, E, H |
| Systems and interactions | | | | | | I | | I | | | | D, E, H |

## C.3.4 Foundation 4: Attitudes

**Students will be encouraged to develop attitudes that support the responsible acquisition and application of scientific and technological knowledge to the mutual benefit of self, society, and the environment.**

**TABLE C.4** Foundation 4—Attitudes

| Specific Standards | 1 | 2 | 3 | 4 | 5 | 6 | 7 | 8 | 9 | 10 | 11 | Appendixes |
|---|---|---|---|---|---|---|---|---|---|---|---|---|
| Appreciation of science | I | I | | I | I | I | | I | | | | |
| Interest in science | I | I | | I | I | I | | I | | | | D |
| Scientific inquiry | I | I | I | | | I | | I | | | | G, H, I, J |
| Collaboration | I | | I | | | I | | I | I | | | J |
| Stewardship | I | | | | | | | | | | | |
| Safety | | | | | | | | | I | | | A |

Growth of understandings may involve each of the following elements:

- **Complexity of understanding**: From simple, concrete ideas to abstract ideas; from limited knowledge of science to more in-depth and broader knowledge of science and the world.
- **Applications in context**: From contexts that are local and personal to those that are societal and global.
- **Consideration of variables and perspectives**: From one or two that are simple to many that are complex.
- **Critical judgment**: From simple right or wrong assessments to complex evaluations.
- **Decision making**: From decisions based on limited knowledge, made with teacher guidance, to decisions based on extensive research, involving personal judgment and made independently, without guidance.

## C.4 Development of the Four Foundation Statements

Student learning is affected by personal and cultural preconceptions and prior knowledge. Students learn most effectively when their study of science is rooted in concrete learning experiences, related to a particular context or situation, and applied to their world where appropriate. Science activities, therefore, occur within a sociocultural context, are interpreted within that context, and are designed to extend and challenge existing views.

The ideas and understandings that students develop are progressively extended and reconstructed as students grow in their experiences and in their ability to conceptualize. Learning involves the process of linking newly constructed understandings with prior knowledge and adding new contexts and experiences to current understandings.

Learning is enhanced when students identify and solve problems. Through such learning, students develop attitudes, skills, and a knowledge base that allow them to explore increasingly complex ideas and problems, especially if these are placed in a meaningful context.

Students learn to understand the world by developing personal conceptions, constructing mental images, and sharing these with others using everyday language, in diverse situations that respect a wide variety of learners.

## C.5  Teaching of Science

This framework of outcomes is designed to support the development in students of the attitudes, skills, and knowledge needed for developing problem-solving and decision-making abilities, for becoming lifelong learners, and for maintaining a sense of wonder about the world around them — in short, to develop scientific literacy.

Development of scientific literacy is supported by instructional environments that engage students in active inquiry, problem solving, and decision making. Diverse learning experiences involve designing activities so they are set in meaningful contexts. It is through these contexts that students discover the significance of science to their lives and come to appreciate the interrelated nature of science, technology, society, and the environment.

To facilitate instructional planning, examples of instructional contexts (called illustrative examples) are provided in the section that presents learning outcomes by grade. The selection of particular contexts and their development will likely vary with the local situation, and reflect factors such as the prior learning of the students, the dynamics of the classroom, the nature of the local environment, and available learning resources.

Although the particular contexts may vary, the overall scope and focus will normally include the following broad areas of emphasis:

- Science inquiry emphasis, in which students address questions about the nature of things, involving broad exploration as well as focused investigations
- Problem-solving emphasis, in which students seek answers to practical problems requiring the application of their science knowledge in new ways
- Decision-making emphasis, in which students identify questions or issues and pursue science knowledge that will inform the question or issue

Each of these three areas of emphasis provides a potential starting point for engaging in an area of study. These studies may involve a variety of learning approaches for exploring new ideas, for developing specific investigations, and for applying the ideas that are learned. Specific ways of encouraging students to explore, develop, and apply ideas are modeled in the illustrative examples.

To achieve the vision of scientific literacy, students must increasingly become engaged in the planning, development, and evaluation of their own learning activities. In the process, they should have the opportunity to work collaboratively with other students, to initiate investigations, to communicate their findings, and to complete projects that demonstrate their learning.

## C.6  General Learning Outcomes

### C.6.1  Science, Technology, Society, and the Environment

**By the end of grade 3, it is expected that students will**

| Specific Standards | Chapters and Selected Appendixes | | | | | | | | | | | |
|---|---|---|---|---|---|---|---|---|---|---|---|---|
| | 1 | 2 | 3 | 4 | 5 | 6 | 7 | 8 | 9 | 10 | 11 | Appendixes |
| Investigate objects and events in their immediate environment, and use appropriate language to develop understanding and to communicate results | | I | | I | I | I | | I | | | | D, F, G, H, I, J |
| Demonstrate and describe ways of using materials and tools to help answer science questions and to solve practical problems | | | | | | I | | | | | | G, H, I, J |
| Describe how science and technology affect their lives and those of people and other living things in their community | | I | | | | | | | | | | J |
| Undertake personal actions to care for their immediate environment and contribute to responsible group decisions | | | | | | I | | | | | | |

By the end of grade 6, it is expected that students will

| Specific Standards | Chapters and Selected Appendixes | | | | | | | | | | | |
|---|---|---|---|---|---|---|---|---|---|---|---|---|
| | 1 | 2 | 3 | 4 | 5 | 6 | 7 | 8 | 9 | 10 | 11 | Appendixes |
| Demonstrate that science and technology use specific processes to investigate the natural and constructed world or to seek solutions to practical problems | | I | I | | | I | | I | | | | D, F, G, H, I, J |
| Demonstrate that science and technology develop over time | | | I | | | I | | | | | | |
| Describe ways that science and technology work together in investigating questions and problems and in meeting specific needs | | | I | | | | | | | | | D, H, I, J |
| Describe applications of science and technology that have developed in response to human and environmental needs | | | I | | | | | | | | | J |
| Describe positive and negative effects that result from applications of science and technology in their own lives, the lives of others, and the environment | | | I | | | I | | | | | | |

## C.6.2 Skills

By the end of grade 3, it is expected that students will

**TABLE C.7** Skills, by the End of Grade 3

| Specific Standards | Chapters and Selected Appendixes | | | | | | | | | | | |
|---|---|---|---|---|---|---|---|---|---|---|---|---|
| | 1 | 2 | 3 | 4 | 5 | 6 | 7 | 8 | 9 | 10 | 11 | Appendixes |
| Ask questions about objects and events in their immediate environment and develop ideas about how those questions might be answered | | I | I | I | I | I | I | I | | | | D, F, G, H, I, |
| Observe and explore materials and events in their immediate environment and record the results | | I | | I | I | I | | I | | | | D, E, F, G, H, I, J |
| Identify patterns and order in objects and events studied | | I | I | I | I | I | | I | | | | D, H, J |
| Work with others and share and communicate ideas about their explorations | | | | I | I | I | I | | I | | | H, J |

**By the end of grade 6, it is expected that students will**

**TABLE C.8** Skills, by the End of Grade 6

| Specific Standards | Chapters and Selected Appendixes | | | | | | | | | | | |
|---|---|---|---|---|---|---|---|---|---|---|---|---|
| | 1 | 2 | 3 | 4 | 5 | 6 | 7 | 8 | 9 | 10 | 11 | Appendixes |
| Ask questions about objects and events in the local environment and develop plans to investigate those questions | I | I | | I | I | I | | I | | | | D, E, F, G, H, I |
| Observe and investigate their environment and record the results | I | I | | I | I | I | | | | | | D, F, G, H, I, J |
| Interpret findings from investigations using appropriate methods | | I | | I | I | I | | | | | | D, H, J |
| Work collaboratively to carry out science-related activities and communicate ideas, procedures, and results | I | | | I | I | I | | | I | | | H, J |

## C.6.3 Knowledge

**By the end of grade 6, it is expected that students will**

**TABLE C.9** Knowledge, by the End of Grade 6

| Specific Standards | Chapters and Selected Appendixes | | | | | | | | | | | |
|---|---|---|---|---|---|---|---|---|---|---|---|---|
| | 1 | 2 | 3 | 4 | 5 | 6 | 7 | 8 | 9 | 10 | 11 | Appendixes |
| Describe and compare characteristics and properties of living things, objects, and materials | | I | | I | I | I | I | I | I | | | D, H, J |
| Describe and predict causes, effects, and patterns related to change in living and nonliving things | | I | | I | I | I | | | | | | D, H, J |
| Describe interactions within natural systems and the elements required to maintain these systems | | I | | | | I | | | | | | D, H, J |
| Describe forces, motion, and energy and relate them to phenomena in their observable environment | | I | | I | I | I | | | | | | D, G, H, I, J |

## C.6.4 Attitudes

### In K through 3, it is expected that students will be encouraged to

**TABLE C.10** Attitudes, Grades K – 3

| Specific Standards | Chapters and Selected Appendixes | | | | | | | | | | | |
|---|---|---|---|---|---|---|---|---|---|---|---|---|
| | 1 | 2 | 3 | 4 | 5 | 6 | 7 | 8 | 9 | 10 | 11 | *Appendixes* |
| Recognize the role and contribution of science in their understanding of the world | I | I | I | I | I | I | | | | | | D, H, J |
| Show interest in and curiosity about objects and events within their immediate environment | I | I | I | | | I | | I | | | | D, G |
| Willingly observe, question, and explore | I | I | | I | I | I | | I | I | | | D, F, G, I |
| Consider their observations and their own ideas when drawing a conclusion | | I | | I | I | I | | I | | | | D, H, I, J |
| Appreciate the importance of accuracy | | | | | | I | I | | | | | H, J |
| Be open-minded in their explorations | I | I | | | | I | | | | | | |
| Work with others in exploring and investigating | I | | | | I | I | | | I | | | J |
| Be sensitive to the needs of other people, other living things, and the local environment | I | | | | I | I | | | I | | | D |
| Show concern for their safety and that of others in carrying out activities and using materials | | | | | | | | | I | | | A |

**In grades 4 through 6, it is expected that students will be encouraged to**

**TABLE C.11** Attitudes, Grades 4 – 6

| Specific Standards | Chapters and Selected Appendixes | | | | | | | | | | | |
|---|---|---|---|---|---|---|---|---|---|---|---|---|
| | 1 | 2 | 3 | 4 | 5 | 6 | 7 | 8 | 9 | 10 | 11 | Appendixes |
| Appreciate the role and contribution of science and technology in their understanding of the world | I | I | I | | | I | | | | | | D, H, J |
| Realize that the applications of science and technology can have both intended and unintended effects | | | I | | | I | | | | | | D, J |
| Recognize that women and men of any cultural background can contribute equally to science | | | I | | | | | | I | | | |
| Show interest and curiosity about objects and events within different environments | I | I | I | I | I | I | | | I | | | D |
| Willingly observe, question, explore, and investigate | I | I | | I | I | I | | | I | | | D, E, F, G, H, I, J |
| Show interest in the activities of individuals working in scientific and technological fields | | | I | | | | | | | | | |
| Consider their own observations and ideas as well as those of others during investigations and before drawing conclusions | | I | I | I | I | I | | | I | | | H, J |
| Appreciate the importance of accuracy and honesty | | | | | | I | | | | | | H, J |
| Demonstrate perseverance and a desire to understand | I | | | I | I | I | I | | I | | | G, H, I |
| Work collaboratively while exploring and investigating | | | | I | I | I | | | I | | | J |
| Be sensitive to and develop a sense of responsibility for the welfare of other people, other living things, and the environment | I | | I | | I | | | | I | | | D, F, G |
| Show concern for their safety and that of others in planning and carrying out activities and in choosing and using materials | | | | | | | | | I | | | A |
| Become aware of potential dangers | | | | | | | | | | | | A |

The Canadian Common Framework of Science Learning Outcomes are available online at http://www.cmec.ca/science/framework/.

*Appendix D*
# Learning for Complexity

One of the many challenges we face as teachers involves the pressures to cover a broad array of content. As discussed in Chapter 10, some of these pressures arise from the increasing emphasis on high-stakes tests and state or provincial standards, as well as the continuing historical patterns of schooling with its emphasis on textbooks and factual content. Although the *National Science Education Standards* in the United States and the *Common Curriculum* in Canada place greater importance on conceptual learning, these overriding pressures undermine the national vision for science teaching and learning.

The fundamental problem of teaching to specific standards, which is often referred to as teaching to the test, is that the knowledge we are attempting to teach becomes disconnected and fragmented. Students are faced with trying to remember bits and pieces of knowledge that are devoid of context (i.e., they do not fit within any meaningful and relevant framework). These bits and pieces of knowledge do not even fit together. As we have seen throughout this book, real learning is not a rote memory process, but rather is a process of making sense of various kinds of information and of constructing complex sets of interrelationships. Research has shown that rote memory has a very short half-life (i.e., the ability to recall memorized material drops off very quickly), whereas material learned through sense-making processes tends to have a much longer half-life. Assessment experts seem to agree that teaching to the test (e.g., using drill-and-practice and rote memorization) definitely increases test scores, but has no effect on learning.

So, if we are interested in student learning (rather than simply teaching to the test), how can we promote more complex learning? How can we survive in our careers when faced with pressures on student achievement as measured by standardized tests? These certainly are important questions. However, before we begin to explore how to teach for complex learning, we need to come to terms with how to face the apparent risk to teaching for complexity. In general, we need to think about the basic premise that in-depth learning will not only result in more meaningful and relevant knowledge, in greater motivation, and in students' abilities to learn on their own, but also in increased test scores. In schools and classrooms where such learning is emphasized, test scores have increased, such as in the Laboratory School (a school of the Ontario Institute of Studies in Education, University of Toronto). Another interesting example involves a former teacher, Jim Manley, in an elementary school in Mesa, Arizona. He focused his entire curriculum on science. His students would go into the field every week to collect data on water quality in a local river, research what was needed to build a pond on the school property, and then build the pond; and construct a garden and conduct an inquiry into plant growth. Within these activities, he would address mathematics, social studies, art, drama, language arts, and so forth. Although his principal avidly supported his work, other teachers became increasingly upset, thinking that he was going to bring down the school's test scores and adversely affect their potential for salary increases. In the end, he received the Arizona Teacher of the Year Award for the greatest increase in student test scores. He never taught to the test.

When we think of teaching for complexity, we may think that such a task is going to be more difficult for us and for students. In some ways, it may require more work on our part, but the greatest difficulty for children involves changing their approaches, their game plans for engaging in the classroom. The older the students, the more work it will take to help them adapt to the new approach. However, in the end, the task is simpler in that what they are learning makes more sense—it is more relevant to their lives, more meaningful, and much more exciting.

The primary characteristics of complex learning involve a focus on the following:

- Relationships and interrelationships
- Patterns and broad concepts
- Relevant and meaningful connections across disciplines (i.e., mathematics, writing, reading, art, drama, etc.)
- Problematizing instruction (see Chapter 6)
- Situating all activities in a variety of contexts
- Incorporating children's prior knowledge and contexts of meaning (see Chapters 4, 5, and 8)

These characteristics describe the fundamental framework for designing curriculum and implementing instruction and are, in a way, the background for our goals for student learning.

## D.1 Systems

We examine a variety of patterns and other broad concepts, in order to develop understandings of systems. This type of understanding is emphasized in both the United States *National Science Education Standards* and the Canadian *Common Framework of Science Learning Outcomes*. To develop such understandings, we need to think about

- How these patterns function
- How these patterns interact with each other
- How they describe parts of systems

Systems are active, fluid processes that interact with one another to create a self-sustaining whole. Although systems are a significant part of science, they also are significant across subject matter areas and in our everyday lives. Some examples of systems appear below:

| Natural Sciences | Social Sciences | Arts and Literature |
| --- | --- | --- |
| Ecosystem | Political systems | Writing processes |
| Solar system | Social systems (family, communities, cultures, etc.) | Artistic processes |
| Global ecological system | Mind and mental systems | Stories as systems |
| Plate tectonic systems | Business systems | Works of art as systems |
| Mechanical systems | Economic systems | Musical compositions and band-orchestral systems |
| Circulatory system | Systems of interactions and communication | Dramatic performances as systems (including movies, TV shows, etc.) |
| Respiratory system | Institutional systems (schools, organizations, etc.) | |
| Muscular and skeletal systems | Marketing systems | |
| Endocrine system | Language systems | |
| Nervous system | | |
| Electrical systems | | |
| Digestive system | | |

The above examples are but a few of the more common systems. In addition, systems interact with each other in a variety of ways that create much more complex situations. For instance, if we think about global warming, we find that the global ecological system, political systems, social systems, economic systems, business systems, and psychological systems interact with one another to create a complex global system. When we think about addressing this particular issue, we find that the situation is very complex. Finding a solution is equally complex, with no clear right answer. However, if we want our children to understand systems and contemporary issues, we need to examine how systems interact and work at generating possible solutions. One possible approach to engage children in an ongoing simulation about resolving a particular issue or problem is to divide your students into groups representing different systems (e.g., politicians, corporate CEOs, different social or cultural groups, and environmentalists). Then have them research their roles and begin to negotiate. One or two students can act as moderators, mediators, and organizers of these sessions. They may never reach a resolution, but a post-simulation debriefing can point out the difficulties of finding solutions to major issues, where so many different interests are involved.

## D.2 Patterns, Metapatterns, and Other Broadly Connecting Concepts

The term *metapattern* was coined by Gregory Bateson (1979) in his attempt to understand the fundamental interconnectedness of ecology and psychology. However, a number of other people have explored an array of fundamental patterns, including Tyler Volk (1995) in his book *Metapatterns: Across Space, Time, and Mind.* The following list of metapatterns includes those discussed by Volk, as well as some additional patterns.

Metapatterns are patterns that appear across a variety of biological, physical, technological, cultural, and psychological contexts. They share common fundamental meanings, even though specific meanings can vary within different contexts and usages.

### D.2.1 Metapatterns (Broad, Fundamental Patterns)

- Spheres
- Sheets
- Tubes
- Layers
- Borders and pores
- Centers
- Binaries
- Arrows
- Time and calendars
- Breaks
- Cycles
- Clusters
- Rigidity and flexibility
- Gradients
- Emergence
- Webs
- Triggers

**TABLE D.1** Spheres

### Spheres

**Background and Meanings**

Spheres and the tendency toward sphericity are common forms in the sciences, as well as in other disciplines. As physical forms they maximize strength and durability, have a reduced surface area-to-volume ratio, and minimize environmental contact. In more general terms, the fundamental meanings underlying this form involve equanimity, omni-directionality, simplification, and containment. Spheres and sphericity can be actual physical forms as well as invisible and metaphoric senses of form. In contending with the sense of sphericity, the forms can range from near-perfect spheres to partial spheres to squared-off and box-like forms. When nested together, spheres can form holarchic layers.

**Examples**

***Science:*** Cells, many fruits, planets, stars, eyes, droplets, heart, skulls, eggs and spores, bubbles, biosphere, ecosystems, inflated puffers, jellyfish, etc.

***Architecture and design:*** Domes, geodesic domes and spheres, atria, light bulbs, etc.

***Art:*** Halos in Renaissance paintings, spherical forms in paintings and sculpture, etc.

***Social sciences:*** Spheres as communities, as context, as schemata (as in schema theory), etc.

***Other senses:*** Sphere of influence, of friends, of consciousness, sphere as neighborhood, etc.

**TABLE D.2** Tubes

## Tubes

### Background and Meanings

As physical forms, tubes seem to have four fundamental aspects, which, in some cases, appear as one aspect and, in other cases, are combined in one form. One aspect involves the notion of strength and support along a linear dimension. The second aspect is that of bidirectional or unidirectional transport of energy, materials, or information. The third aspect involves the ability to penetrate, extend, or grow along a linear dimension. The fourth aspect involves the connections in relationships as in semantic webs or in the two-way conversation between two people. In biological forms, they increase the surface area-to-volume ratio compared to spheres, but not to the extent of sheets. In a more general sense, tubes involve the concepts of linear strength, linearity, extension or bridging, transfer or flow of information, and connection or relationship.

### Examples

**Science:** Nerve cells, blood vessels, appendages, phloem and xylem, stems and branches, hair, cilia, flagella, digestive tract, streams and rivers, lava tubes, pine needles, eels, snakes, worms, spider webs (tubes making sheet), bodies of airplanes, rockets, etc.

**Architecture and design:** Hallways, internal support structures, elevator shafts and stairwells, highways, trails, tunnels, bridges, electrical wires, pipes, networking cables, utility poles, suspension bridges (traffic flow, support structures, support cables), etc.

**Art:** Shape, brushes, pottery forms, sculpting forms, etc.

**Social sciences:** Relationships between people, connecting lines in concept maps, patterns of interaction, lines of communication, patterns of movement, support mechanisms, etc.

**Other senses:** Tobacco pipes, cigars, syringes and needles, etc.

---

**TABLE D.3** Sheets

## Sheets

### Background and Meanings

As physical forms, sheets maximize transfer across surface areas, maximize surface area-to-volume ratio, and extend or grow two-dimensionally. In general terms, sheets represent capture, contact, and movement across a plane. In addition, when put together, they can form layers and can act as borders. Spheres and tubes can be made of sheets.

### Examples

**Science:** Leaves, surface tension, membranes, individual layers of the earth and atmosphere, fins, airplane wings, skates and rays, films, snow coverage, movement of amoebas, etc.

**Architecture and design:** Walls, open areas as in large convention centers, fans and windmills, sails, turbines, etc.

**Art:** Canvas, shapes, etc.

**Social sciences:** Movement within a space, separation, etc.

**Other senses:** Clothing, rain coming down in sheets, bed coverings, parking lots, etc.

---

**TABLE D.4** Layers—General Characteristics

## Layers

### Background and Meanings

Layers point to increasing complexity as sheets, spheres, tubes, and other fundamental patterns combine in linear or nested layers. The process of layering is a building up of order, structure, and stabilization.

Layers in social systems create order and stability. However, in social systems, do all layers create self-sustaining stability? Can certain types of layering lead to a collapse of the system? What assumptions underlie different types of layered systems? What relationships arise from different types of layering systems? In addition to social systems, layers can be used to describe layers of knowledge, meaning, values, emotions, types of activity, types of thinking, resistance, openness, and so forth. So, we ultimately can have systems of layered knowledge and meaning residing within and affecting a layered social system. How does one system of layers affect systems of layers within it? How does one system of layers affect the system of layers within which it resides?

The following tables discuss hierarchies, holarchies, clonons, and holons—specific types of layering systems.

**TABLE D.5** Hierarchies (Layering)

## Hierarchies

### Background and Meanings

Hierarchies tend to be depicted as pyramidal arrangements of sheets. Hierarchies are identified as the relationships between layers become evident. In most cases, hierarchies are exemplified by power or control moving downward. In other cases, the top layers may indicate greater importance or significance. Information, materials, or energy move upward. They tend to create stratified stability. However, this stability may depend upon the types of binary relationships and other patterns that are created within the overall structure.

### Examples

**Science:** Trophic layers, phylogenetic trees, animal societies, etc.
**Architecture and design:** Pyramids, building design and layout, etc.
**Art:** As form, etc.
**Social sciences:** Governmental and organizational structures; classrooms, schools, and schooling; some learning theories; etc.
**Other senses:** Information trees, branching decision trees, etc.

**TABLE D.6** Holarchy (Embedded Layers)

## Holarchies

### Background and Meanings

A holarchy is a nested system of layers in which the units (wholes) within one layer are parts for the wholes in the next larger, encompassing layer. Holarchic layers can be used to describe certain types of social, political, and institutional organizations, as well as structures in science and other disciplines. In holarchies the wholes at each level have particular kinds of relationships with the other wholes on that same level, and these relationships change as we move up the nested layers from physics to organisms to social systems. The relationships between layers in holarchies tend to be ambiguous and more difficult to describe.

### Examples

**Science:** Rose flowers, the earth and atmosphere, atoms, bodies of organisms, holarchic layers of complexity in organisms (from DNA/RNA components to the whole), solar system, galaxies, etc.
**Architecture and design:** Some building and community designs, etc.
**Art:** Forms as depicted, etc.
**Social sciences:** Communities (as described by Jean Lave and Etienne Wenger), many tribal societies, democracy in its purest form, etc.
**Other senses:** Mandalas, apprenticeships, etc.

**TABLE D.7** Clonons (Layers)

# Clonons

## Background and Meanings

The notion of clonons falls within the scope of holarchies, in that specific objects or ideas are repeated to create embedded layers. As with the process of cloning, a specific object can be replicated. Clonons can build wholes, and each whole can be a clonon of a larger set.

## Examples

**Science:** Identical cells in layers of tissue, protons, neutrons, electrons, worker ants, each fish in a school; identical atoms in a molecule (e.g., two clonons of hydrogen joining a holon of oxygen to form a holon of a water molecule, which in turn becomes a clonon of water molecules in a cup of water); etc.

**Architecture and design:** Bricks in a wall, tiles on a floor, each light fixture in a ceiling, each office or room on a floor, windows in a skyscraper, each house in a subdivision, etc.

**Art:** Each brush stroke in a painting, each decorative design unit in a pottery bowl, each point in a pointillism painting, etc.

**Social sciences:** Each individual in a community or society, each client in a business, each factory worker at a specific point in an assembly line, etc.

**Other senses:** Each tomato on a tomato plant, each tomato plant in a tomato garden, etc.

---

**TABLE D.8** Holons (Layers)

# Holons

## Background and Meanings

Holon, as mentioned previously, refers to a whole, which is often comprised of clonon parts or sets of clonon parts. Holons themselves can become clonons of even greater wholes. The idea of holons (in contrast to indistinguishable clonons) is that holons are functionally and structurally distinct parts on the level of a holarchy. Holons are like organs, on different scales of wholes. Thus, the body's holons are heart, lungs, brain, and so forth, which themselves are composed of many clonons, the relatively indistinguishable heart cells, etc.

## Examples

**Science:** A planet; a solar system; an atom is a holon of three fundamental types of clonon particles; atoms become clonons of larger holon molecules, etc.

**Architecture and design:** Buildings, a community, etc.

**Art:** Subjects, figures formed from points or strokes, a sculpture, etc.

**Social sciences:** A concept, a community or society, an action holon of component clonon actions, a family, a class of students, etc.

**Other senses:** A wall or fence, an archway made of stone clonons, a gang or clique, etc.

**TABLE D.9** Borders and Pores

### Borders and Pores

#### Background and Meanings

Borders involve the concepts of protection, separation of inside from outside, containment, and barrier or obstacle. With pores, borders regulate the flow and exchange of materials, energy, or information. Small pores heighten regulation and reduce flow, while larger pores decrease regulation and increase flow. Borders can be visible entities, fuzzy, or invisible. Physical borders tend to be built of sheets of repeating parts (clonons).

#### Examples

*Science:* Cell membranes and osmosis, skin and pores, eyes, ears, nose, mouth, stomata, the earth's crust and volcanoes, clouds with fuzzy borders, atmosphere, edge of a pond, etc.

*Architecture and design:* Walls with doors and windows, roof and skylight, etc.

*Art:* Depicted forms, frame with canvas as opening pore to another world, pottery bowl or vase with circular pore, etc.

*Social sciences:* Personal space, psychological and social obstacles, problem as border with paths to solutions as pores, physical space divisions and openings, social barriers, racism and other biases as barriers, propaganda as a barrier to truth, borders between countries with border crossings, etc.

*Other senses:* Borders and openings in Feng Shui, borders between properties, airline security, etc.

---

**TABLE D.10** Centers

### Centers

#### Background and Meanings

Centers act to stabilize the whole, provide resistance to change, and provide for organization of the whole. They can act as attractors for autopoietic (self-generating, self-sustaining) systems. In a more general sense, they can imply importance or significance and a sense of centricity. As such, centers can radiate relations to other centers, information, etc.

#### Examples

*Science:* Nucleus, strange attractor, queen ant or bee, fulcrum, dominant male in primate societies, center of gravity, heart in circulatory system, brain in nervous system, etc.

*Architecture and design:* Main office, central meeting places, central structural supports (such as elevator shafts in skyscrapers), etc.

*Art:* The central figure or object as subject; the organizing principle or emotional focus of a piece of art, etc

*Social sciences:* President, dictator, leader, teacher, principal, heart as center of individual in many indigenous cultures, brain as center of individual in most technologically developed cultures, organizing principles of societies and other groups, focus of life or activity (e.g., individuals may consider self, family, work, sport, hobby, or spiritual efforts as center), ego, anthropocentrism, conceptual prototype, conceptual defining characteristics, etc.

*Other senses:* Altar in a church, shrine in a temple, a deity or deities, sacred sites (Mecca, Bodhgaya, Jerusalem), shopping center, etc.

**TABLE D.11** Binaries, Trinaries, and More Complex Sets of Relationships

**Binaries... plus**

### Background and Meanings

Binaries are the simplest form of complex relations. More complex relations involve increasing numbers of components (e.g., trinaries, quaternaries, etc.). Such binary relations are the most economical (in a variety of senses) way to generate complex wholes with significant new properties. Binaries involve senses of separation or unity, duality, and tension. They also provide for a synergy between parts and wholes.

### Examples

***Science:*** Bilateral symmetry; positive and negative particles, ions, electrodes, etc.; male and female; opposing forces; diurnal and nocturnal; dorsal and ventral; space and time; acid and base; DNA with component pairs and paired helices; inhale and exhale; respiration and photosynthesis; mass and volume; perception as the recognition of difference; form and function; acceleration and deceleration; etc.

***Architecture and design:*** Inside and outside and the associated dynamics between them in buildings; entrance and exit; up and down passages; etc.

***Art:*** Light and dark; monotone and multicolored; tensions between parts; attraction and repulsion (emotionally); etc.

***Social sciences:*** Report talk and rapport talk; leader and follower; positive and negative attitudes; consumer and producer; passive and aggressive; trust and distrust; unity and disunity or separation; etc.

***Other senses:*** Near and far; all or nothing; night and day; open and closed; on and off; asleep and awake; old and young; love and hate; etc.

---

**TABLE D.12** Types of Binary Relationships

| Gregory Bateson | Complementary | Symmetrical | Reciprocal |
|---|---|---|---|
| **Metapattern specific** | Disparate binary | Competitive binary Commiserate binary | Collaborative binary |
| **Metapattern general** | Divergent binary Separating binary | Divergent binary Separating binary | Convergent binary Unifying binary |
| **Other descriptors** | Dominant-submissive Controlling-subservient Directive-passive | Dominant-dominant Submissive-submissive Vying for control Oppositional | Cooperative Mutuality Supportive |

---

**TABLE D.13** Arrows

**Arrows**

### Background and Meanings

Arrows indicate flow, progression, directional links and relationships, and directionality in general. Arrows are often linked to time (as an arrow) and sequences. Arrows of time are equivalent to tubular relations in space. Arrows also depict specific directional relations between binaries.

### Examples

***Science:*** Chemical reactions, acceleration, nerve transmission, vectors, velocity, osmosis, rivers, currents, wind, volcanic flow, bird flight, force, etc.

***Architecture and design:*** Traffic flow, sequences in construction, escalators, directionality in lighting and décor, structural strength in supporting weight, etc.

***Art:*** As objects, as eye movement in looking at a piece of art, choreography, drama, etc.

***Social sciences:*** Directional relations, movement, flow, stages and sequences, etc.

***Other senses:*** Journeys and pilgrimages, travel plans, agenda, etc.

**TABLE D.14** Time, Calendars, and Clocks

## Time and Calendars

### Background and Meanings

Time can be considered a binary of movement and memory and can be observed by connecting several spaces. Time can be seen as an arrow or cycle. Time also is evident as counting, progression, and sequences.

### Examples

***Science:*** Biological clocks, velocity, acceleration, time-space phenomena, etc.

***Architecture and design:*** How time is defined and related to in particular contexts; at Arcosanti (an environmentally situated desert city in Arizona) all buildings are multiuse in order to minimize building use downtime; etc.

***Art:*** In drama, music, dance, and other performance arts time is the fundamental organizing pattern, as well as fundamental to the perceptual experience; etc.

***Social sciences:*** Calendars, clocks, history, sequences and stages in development, etc.

***Other senses:*** Time to kill, wasting time, time management, timeliness, etc.

---

**TABLE D.15** Breaks

## Breaks

### Background and Meanings

Transformations, change, leaps, shifts, sequences of stages, dilemmas and decisions

### Examples

***Science:*** Chemical reactions, metamorphosis, evolutionary change (punctuated equilibrium), energy transformations, change from action to reaction, waterfalls, branching, etc.

***Architecture and design:*** Divisions of space and activity, vehicle brakes, etc.

***Art:*** Perceptual shifts, design changes, etc.

***Social sciences:*** Insights, stages in development, events that change psychosocial states, etc.

***Other senses:*** Divorce, death, birth, marriage, crashing waves, breakthroughs, etc.

---

**TABLE D.16** Cycles

## Cycles

 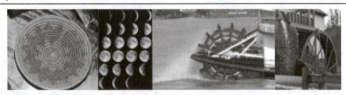

### Background and Meanings

Cycles are repetitions in space or time, such as circulations, waves, repetitive routines, etc. Interactions of cycles and arrows create spirals or helices. Fundamentally, cycles serve to maintain a system. Cycles in a system can be as simple as a feedback loop in a thermostat or as complex as multiple interacting cycles within the biosphere or whole earth system. Conversations and arguments involve at least one cycle acting as a feedback loop.

### Examples

***Science:*** Kreb's cycle, earth's rotation and revolution, lunar phases, animal movement, biological rhythms, breathing, water cycle, carbon cycle, nitrogen cycle, seasons, tides, bird songs, light, sound, feedback loops, etc.

***Architecture and design:*** Heating and cooling systems, movement patterns in buildings, etc.

***Art:*** Perceptual movement, musical compositions, choreography, etc.

***Social sciences:*** Repetitive actions, routines, rituals, helical patterns of themes running through discourse and other psychosocial situations, etc.

***Other senses:*** Laps in a race, wheel of karma, etc.

---

**TABLE D.17** Clusters and Clustering

### Background and Meanings

Clusters refer to the accumulation or movement of objects or ideas to positions of proximity to one another. Such clustering may involve one or more center attractors. Clustering seems to involve some sort of attraction that brings objects or ideas together.

### Examples

**Science:** Plant growth in a particular location, clusters of stars, lichen growth on a particular part of a rock, mold and bacterial growth, bird flocks, colonial organisms, etc.

**Social sciences:** Town and city development; tribal, community, and nation development; clustering of ideas within a conceptual space; family structures; cliques; gangs; etc.

**Art:** Movement apart and together in drama and dance, pictorial representations of alternating space and clusters, etc.

**Architecture and design:** Building plans that provide space for people to gather, office spaces or rooms in a home that come together around a common space, automobile controls and feedback dials on dashboards, placement of plants and objects in landscape design, etc.

**Other senses:** Cultural and religious events and gatherings, parties, groupings of people in a variety of settings and contexts, etc.

---

**TABLE D.18** Rigidity and Flexibility

### Background and Meanings

Rigidity and flexibility can be binaries of space, time, and relationship. Rigidity implies strength and impenetrability, while flexibility implies adaptability and change. In a spatial sense, a tube, sphere, sheet, border, or layer can be rigid or flexible. Boundaries of time can be rigid sequences of steps or stages or can delimit actions and activities. Binary relationships can be rigidly established or provide for flexibility. Both flexibility and rigidity can serve to protect.

### Examples

**Science:** Adaptation, acclimatization, organism tolerance to environmental change and variation, cell walls versus cell membranes, etc.

**Social sciences:** Rules, mores, cultural borders, national borders, social layering, personality typologies, institutions and organizations, etc.

**Art:** Rigid and flexible representations in dance and theater, moving versus static sculpture, etc.

**Architecture and design:** Flexibility in skyscrapers, rigid versus flexible interior designs, car crumple zones and unibody construction, springs, etc.

**Other senses:** Athletic protective wear, yoga, martial arts, letter of the law versus spirit of the law, rigid versus flexible writing styles, flexible scheduling, open-minded versus close-minded, etc.

**TABLE D.19** Gradients

## Gradients

### Background and Meanings

Gradients refer to continuums and shades of gray rather than rigid binaries of black and white. Both hierarchies and holarchies can be described as clearly defined and fuzzy demarcations along a continuum. Size, color, light, temperature, speed, quantity, amounts, elevations, and distances refer to continuums. Most choices for humans and other animals do not manifest as a clear binary, but as multiple choices along a continuum with no clear right or wrong.

### Examples

***Science:*** Speed; acceleration; temperature gradients; slopes; density; solubility; salinity; statistical degrees of freedom; levels of hurricanes, tornado, earthquakes; etc.

***Social sciences:*** Population densities, public opinion, intelligence, economic trends, from traditional to modern allegiances in tribal and cultural groups, intensity of emotions, etc.

***Art:*** Use of color, light, and shading; pace of action in dance and drama; curvatures in sculpture; tempo in music; etc.

***Architecture and design:*** Walkway design, handicap ramps, elevators, lighting of spaces, plumbing design, landscape drainage, golf course design, etc.

***Other senses:*** Mixed emotions, degrees of friendship, closeness of families, types of lies, etc.

**TABLE D.20** Emergence

## Emergence

### Background and Meanings

Emergence refers to beginnings and to the arising of new themes and other patterns. Patterns can emerge out of seeming chaos, from cyclical patterns of self-generation, or from breaks or branching. The notion is a sense of some property or pattern arising at a new level of complexity.

### Examples

***Science:*** Birth, mutation, Big Bang theory, weather pattern formation, new evolutionary lineages, plant growth on bare rock, speciation, star formation, etc.

***Social sciences:*** New trends, city formation, new organizational patterns in social groups, argument formation, etc.

***Art:*** Novelty, new techniques and materials, representations of emergence, etc.

***Architecture and design:*** New design property, new design leading to unanticipated effect, spatial arrangements to allow for creative gatherings, etc.

***Other senses:*** Insight, invention, etc.

**TABLE D.21** Webs

## Webs

### Background and Meanings

Webs are physical, biological, social, psychological, and virtual networks of relationships. Where spheres can represent a context, webs describe complex sets of interrelationships of a particular context. A complex lattice of tubes, like a sheet, can involve capture, support, or multidirectional movement. In sheets, such movement is within a plane, whereas movement in webs can become three-dimensional. Webs also involve a sense of complex organization.

### Examples

**Science:** Spider webs, food webs, lattice-like structures in biological and physical forms, retae (networks of blood vessels), endoplasmic reticulum, lattice structures of crystals, etc.

**Social sciences:** Semantic webs, concept and context maps, hegemony, street layout in cities, social and political contexts, relationships in organizations, matrices, etc.

**Art:** Patterns, sculpture design, etc.

**Architecture and design:** Beam structures in buildings, safety nets, etc.

**Other senses:** Web of deceit, fishing nets, electric grids, the Internet, The Matrix, etc.

---

**TABLE D.22** Triggers

## Triggers

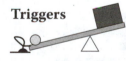

### Background and Meanings

Triggers are much like centers except that there is a sense of initiating some sort of action. As in the trigger of a gun, some event or substance can initiate one action or a set of actions.

### Examples

**Science:** Fight-or-flight reaction mechanism, catalysts, reflexes, mechanisms in chain reactions, etc.

**Social sciences:** The notion of pushing someone's buttons involves triggering an emotional reaction; cognitive dissonance can trigger emotions and result in a variety of questions or concerns; 9/11 triggered deep emotional, military, and political actions; etc.

**Art:** A particular event, experience, or thought triggers an image or idea for a painting; in writing, the use of a metaphor can trigger sets of ideas or emotions in the reader; etc.

**Architecture and design:** Skidding triggers the antilock brake system; a change in temperature triggers the feedback loop of the thermostat; etc.

**Other senses:** A particular smell triggers memories; a comment in a conversation triggers new thoughts and connections; a word, phrase, or sentence can trigger memories, emotional reactions, etc.

Now, try doing the activities in Appendix G.8.

**TABLE D.23** Other Broad Concepts

### Community (related to clusters, holarchies, etc.)

Communities generally involve the metapatterns of clusters, holarchies, cycles, tubular relationships, borders and pores, spheres, and so forth. However, the notion of community can provide the context for examinations of human communities (e.g., residential, tribal, business, professional, teams as communities, etc.); animal, plant, and other living organism communities; and communities as represented in the arts and literature.

### Regulation

Regulation is related to borders and pores. It is important in terms of maintaining a balance in all kinds of systems. Regulation is a major concept in engineering, chemistry, physics, biology, and ecology, as well as in politics and society. Regulation of body temperature, water, blood pressure, population, and other biological and biochemical processes is critical to understanding other major concepts in biology and ecology. Hormones help to regulate numerous systems with a living organism, including temperature, blood pressure, reproduction, growth, etc. In politics and society, including all businesses and other types of organizations, there are regulations (laws, rules, etc.) to control people's behavior and work. Such regulations can be explicit (e.g., written laws, rules, procedures, etc.) or implicit (e.g., as in the mores of a particular culture or society). A painter (either the artist or artisan) regulates the amount and flow of paint. The photographer regulates the amount of light entering the camera. The creative writer regulates the amount of information provided at any given point in a story or novel.

### Variation

Variation is important in understanding evolution and ecology as well as social systems, art, music, mathematics, psychology, and literature. Diversity and difference are aspects of variation. Variation provides the raw material for the emergence of something new: a new species, a novel idea, or a unique perspective. Variation as difference allows us to perceive—without difference we would be unable to see. Difference, variation, and diversity also provide for a sense of healthy continuity. Marriage among members of the same family is illegal in most parts of the world, so that genetic inbreeding can be avoided. Many breeds of dogs are plagued by genetic diseases because of the degree of inbreeding that has taken place.

### Energy

Energy is needed for any action. In science, the major source of energy comes from the sun. The sun, in turn, contributes to the perpetuation of systems that create other sources of energy, such as the wind. Water flow in streams and rivers, as well as tidal fluctuations, provides other sources of energy. Geothermal energy from deep within the earth is a source that is not connected with the sun. In biological systems, energy is produced and stored through biochemical cycles. However, plants also provide the initial source of energy in the form of food production through photosynthesis. Nuclear energy involves the inherent subatomic energy of all matter. Einstein's $E = mc^2$ essentially states that all matter is fundamentally energy. From a Newtonian physics point of view, energy is the ability to do work, and work is defined as a force that acts on an object to move or displace it. Beyond the scientific, energy can be used to describe a variety of situations in more literary or metaphoric ways. We may say that a particular child has a lot of energy. Although the child probably has no more energy than any other child in the scientific sense, we use the word to describe the activity of the child as energetic. We can use energy to describe a work of art, the quality of a relationship, a literary work, and so forth. In all of these nonscientific contexts, the meaning of energy is different from that in science. Where energy is the source of "fuel" for activity in science, energy is often used to describe the quality of activity or a feeling of intensity in nonscientific contexts.

### Force

In science, force is defined as mass that is accelerating (force = mass × acceleration). However, in other contexts force is used to describe a variety of qualities, such as a forceful personality or statement, "the Force" in the *Star Wars* movies as a source of energy, applying force to a situation, and so forth. This difference in meaning between scientific and other contexts is the source of a lot of confusion and difficulty in understanding the scientific meaning of force. However, force can be depicted as an arrow (as a mass accelerating or a forceful person influencing others).

**TABLE D.23** Other Broad Concepts

## Power

In physics, specifically mechanics, power is the amount of work (see energy, above) done in a particular period of time. In terms of electricity, power is measured in watts as the amount of current (amperes) times the potential difference across a particular component of the electrical system (volts). In optics, power is the ability of a lens or another type of device to focus light at different powers of magnification. In mathematics, power is the number of times a number is multiplied by itself, which is referred to as an exponent (e.g., $10 \times 10 \times 10 = 10^3$). In other senses, power has to do with strength and control. A particular leader has a lot of power when he or she is able to control others in a particular situation. A book or work of art can be powerful when it is influential or expresses an idea in a way that has a great impact on the reader. In general, a shared meaning of power involves a sense of action that has a particular impact.

## Distribution

Distribution can involve the metapatterns of clusters or binaries (or greater numbers of relationship. In ecology and population biology, distribution of species is important in understanding how the locations of specific organisms change over time and what factors in the environment affect such changes. Such understandings of the processes that affect the distribution of species can lead to greater understandings of evolution, such as the creation of new species, causes of extinction, and so forth. In other senses, distribution has to do with scattering, spreading, dividing up, or delivering something. Many cars still have distributors, which distribute electricity to each spark plug in a specific order. However, electronic ignition systems (basically a simple computer) have been replacing the mechanical system of a distributor. In a sense, distribution refers to how a particular system distributes information, materials, or objects. In hurricanes and other natural and human-initiated disasters, political, social, and organizational systems will try to distribute food, water, and other emergency services to the victims. In a general sense, distribution has to do with descriptions of how something is spread out (species or dots on a graph of some event) or with the processes of how something is spread or delivered. In both cases, the importance of distribution may involve answers to the questions of how such distribution affects the particular situation (e.g., the survival of the species, the propagation of new species, the survival and welfare of victims, the running of an engine, etc.).

## Communication

Communication has to do with the sending and receiving of information. However, communication is not just a one-way process, but rather a cycle or feedback loop of sending, receiving, reacting to, and responding to information. Many animals communicate with a variety of sounds (e.g., birds chirping, frogs croaking, cicadas buzzing, etc.). However, visual communication is another major means of communication among animals with eyes (e.g., bees "dance," many birds and mammals use various postures, etc.). Earthworms, insects, and other more complex animals use chemicals to communicate. Human beings, of course, have highly developed language systems, but body language, facial expressions, and physical gesturing are quite significant in communication, as are touch and smell. Communication also involves technology (telephones, radio, television, and the Internet). However, communication refers to how the nervous system and hormones work in coordinating various bodily functions. RNA molecules provide information for cellular functions. DNA provides information for the transferring and building of whole new individual organisms from generation to generation. Communication also occurs across multiple systems. In a simple sense, when I walk by my neighbor's house at night, my movement is sensed by his motion detector, which then turns on a light. In a more complex sense, when I drive my car, I receive messages from the environment (e.g., I see a bump in the road, I feel the tires slipping due to the ice on the road, etc.) to which I respond by moving the steering wheel or pressing on the brake or accelerator pedal. At very complex levels, changes in the physical environment on earth are received by organisms, which in turn respond. In fact, in the early days of life on earth, bacteria responded to changes in the earth's environment, which resulted in changes to the environment (i.e., developing photosynthetic capabilities, thereby producing oxygen, which created further changes to the environment, etc.).

**TABLE D.23** Other Broad Concepts

## Locomotion and Movement

The ideas of locomotion and movement are important related concepts in science and other subject matter areas. They relate to a number of metapatterns, including arrows (that can depict movement as relationships over time), binaries (as spatial relationships, such as in the contraction of opposing muscles for movement to occur), cycles (as the coordination of muscular contractions to accomplish movement), and so forth. Movement can deal with physics, such as Newton's three laws of motion: 1. Law of inertia: A body at rest stays at rest or a body in motion stays in motion in a straight line, unless acted upon by a force. 2. Law of dynamics: The acceleration of an object is the total of the force acting upon it divided by the object's mass. 3. Law of reciprocal reactions: For every force there is an equal and opposite force, or for every action there is an equal and opposite reaction, and that momentum cannot be created or destroyed, but only transferred from one object to another. In biology, movement and locomotion are related to transferring materials and energy at the cellular levels, as well as within various systems (e.g., circulatory system, etc.). In addition, movement and locomotion are important aspects of how various species are adapted for survival in terms of acquiring food (or other energy sources) and water, protection (e.g., fight or flight), and reproduction. In the social sciences, movements of populations and individuals are important in understanding broader patterns of establishment and growth of communities, town, and cities, as well as nations. Movement in these cases is often determined by geographical features. Prior to motorized transportation systems, movement of people was determined initially by characteristics of the terrain, then by locations of rivers and oceans for transportation by boat. Older cities were established for their locations as ports along bays and rivers. In the arts, movement is certainly critical to choreographed dances and dramatic performances. However, a painting may provide a feeling of movement, as well as guide one's eyes in certain patterns through the painting. Music also provides a sense of movement, which, in the classical sense, is even referred to as movements. Across all of these contexts, there is a metaphoric sense of Newton's law of action and reaction or of feedback loops (cycles that communicate information).

## Protection

Protection is an obviously important concept in biology. Animals are adapted in a variety of ways for protection from environmental factors and from predators. However, the term protection may be somewhat misleading. As human beings, our sense of protection may arise from a sense of fear. We may be afraid to fly in an airplane, walk down the street at night, or live in an area that could be attacked by terrorists or that is subject to frequent environmental hazards. Although recent research in animal behavior shows that some more complex animals, such as some mammals, may experience a variety of emotions, including fear, most animals do not think in ways that perpetuate a life of fear. Protection for nonhuman animals is mostly concerned with environmental factors and avoidance of predators. The shape of a snail's shell can serve to protect it from some predators, but not all. The tough but flexible body of a sea anemone, which can be withdrawn into a sphere shape, allows it to be flexible when in crashing waves. The skulls of animals provide protection for the brain. Abilities to blend into the surroundings, to hide quickly, or to run are behaviors that provide protection from predators. Some animals build structures that provide protection. The larvae of caddis flies build tubular structures from sand and other materials in which to live, many birds build nests, gophers dig extensive tunnels, bees build hives, and humans build homes and make clothing for protection. Beyond the biological, protection in the social sciences is concerned with the psychology and sociology of fear, warfare and armed forces, and so forth. The notion of protection as behaviors in reaction to fear is a major focus of novels, movies, television shows, and plays, as well as some artwork.

## Adaptation and Acclimatization

From a biological perspective, adaptation has to do with genetically acquired traits that provide for the survival of the species (not necessarily individuals). A trait is an adaptation for one particular function. Some traits may have secondary functions, which are not necessarily adaptations. For example, a giraffe's neck may have been an adaptation to reach and eat the leaves in tall trees. The added advantage of seeing distant predators is not an adaptation, just a fortunate side effect. In everyday usage, we use adaptation in ways that are not aligned with the biological meaning. We travel from sea level to the top of a mountain (10,000 ft, or about 3,000 m) and we say that we will adapt to the altitude change after a few days. We are not adapting in the biological sense, but rather we are acclimatizing. However, our ability to acclimate to a change in altitude (and to other changes) may be an adaptation. Acclimatizing is what an individual organism does in response to environmental changes (e.g., changes in salinity for marine organisms, in temperature, etc.). The notion of acclimatization also appears in psychology and other social sciences. People acclimate or adjust (or not) to changes in conditions, from a long-distance move, to a new culture, and so forth. Such difficulties to adjusting to change are often the focus of novels, movies, and artwork.

**TABLE D.23** Other Broad Concepts

## Competition and Cooperation

In the biological sciences, competition for food, sun (among plants), and other resources has long been seen as a major factor in understanding ecological relationships. However, this view is being challenged as one that arose from male-dominated science. Although competition is still a factor, the notion of cooperation among organisms is gaining greater acceptance. The same sorts of conflicts appear in the social sciences and in everyday life experiences. Schools have promoted competition as a necessary skill for succeeding in adult life. However, cooperative skills are increasingly seen as important in working as a team in a number of occupations. In global politics, competition for natural resources often leads to wars and other conflicts. Competitive relationships among individuals in intimate partnerships will generally fall apart, whereas cooperative relationships will tend to last (see binaries under metapatterns). Examining the dynamics and effects of competition and cooperation can be intriguing for children as they develop their understandings of their personal experiences, of events in the world, and of biological phenomena.

## Continuity

Continuity is a key concern for systems of all sorts. In biology, continuity of the species is of obvious importance, as is continuity of ecosystems. However, continuity is important to maintaining particular cultural traditions. The loss of cultural traditions and languages is of great concern to Native American/First Nations peoples throughout North America, as well as to many aboriginal peoples around the world. Although nothing is permanent, we all buy cars, appliances, and other technological devices with the hope that they will not break down, at least in the near future. However, we often encounter problems in hoping for permanence when faced with impermanence. In Western societies, we avoid discussions of death and have underlying expectations of things lasting. Politicians and political leaders may engage in actions that will perpetuate their rule. The intent is to force a continuity of power, rather than developing systems that will naturally provide for a reasonable continuity (of shared or cooperative power).

## Survival and Extinction

Survival and extinction are ideas that extend from continuity. Survival of the species is important, but so is extinction. If the dinosaurs had not become extinct, it is very unlikely that human beings would have emerged on the scene. If no plants, animals, or other organisms had ever become extinct, we would have been overrun with organisms. The cycles of survival and extinction are important to healthy ecological systems. However, an increase in extinction rates, as is now evident, can be problematic for the overall continuity of the biosphere. In other contexts, the same pattern of survival and extinction is apparent with particular ideas or technologies. Vinyl records have almost reached extinction (they are still available in secondhand stores) since CDs emerged (and they are likely to become extinct as well). The "earth as the center of the universe" has become virtually extinct as a guiding framework for understanding our world.

## Territory and Space

Territory and space are important notions in biology and ecology. Animal territoriality is important among some species, while not in others. However, the notion of space is important beyond that of territory, which involves some sense of ownership and competition. The distribution of organisms in a particular area or space may be important to survival and continuity. On individual levels, such as birds sitting on a wire, there tends to be a regular pattern of space around each individual. Although birds may sit far apart, they will never get too close. People in North America tend not to get closer than 2 ft (60 cm) when in conversation, unless they are in an intimate relationship or packed into a crowded elevator or subway car. When people are forced to be closer than 2 ft apart, they react in a variety of ways, including crossing arms, looking up or facing a different direction, fidgeting, and so forth. The use of space in schools, offices, homes, and other settings has a variety of effects. If you walk into an office where the person is sitting behind a desk and you are on the other side of the desk, there is a sense of distancing and separation. There is a border (see metapattern) preventing contact. If you walk into an office where the desk is against the wall, there is a sense of openness and closer contact. Pharmacies often have not only the separation of a counter, but also an elevated floor behind the counter. The pharmacist is higher than the customer, signifying a greater sense of power and authority. A teacher's desk at the front of the classroom signifies authority and power. The functions and effects of spatial and territorial arrangements are important not only in the natural and social sciences, but also in the visual, musical, and dramatic arts. We may think of music as a solid and continuous construction, but the space between notes may even be more important than the notes themselves. Try listening to the spaces rather than the notes. Even literature plays with notions of space. Beyond the purely descriptive nature of space and context in stories, literature creates a sense of space between events. Such spacing of critical events creates variations in intensity.

### D.2.2 Other Broad Concepts

### D.3 Teaching and Learning for Complex Understandings

Specific information on planning, which is compatible with complex learning, appears in Chapter 8. A metapatterns instructional plan format is provided in Appendix E. Examples of curriculum unit outlines appear in the book's support web site. However, the points below are important to keep in mind when designing instruction.

- The patterns and concepts discussed previously should be viewed as themes that can extend over long periods of time. Although you may start with an emphasis on a particular pattern or concept, you should plan in ways that will allow this pattern or concept to re-emerge throughout a particular unit or even throughout the year.

- Always do activities that explore children's experiences of these patterns and concepts in their everyday lives at the beginning. So, if you are going to introduce cycles, have children explore the cycles they experience in their everyday lives, followed by discussions of how cycles function and what is important about cycles (e.g., maintaining a particular system). From this point, you can extend cycles to the particular topic under investigation.

- As you proceed through your instructional topic, start incorporating comparisons with other contexts. Again, if you have introduced cycles within a study of animal movement, you can compare these cycles to geological cycles, mechanical cycles, other biological cycles, and, of course, to the everyday experiences of cycles that the children explored initially.

- Gradually increase the depth of understandings of these patterns and concepts. In a way, this is a cycle of examining patterns and concepts, with each iteration going into greater depth. For cycles, this may be looking at how binaries or trinaries of relationships may perpetuate the cycle (e.g., opposing muscles for locomotion, firing and exhaust in an engine, day and night for sleep and wake cycles, etc.). Keep asking about the function or purpose of the pattern, such as cycles maintaining a particular system.

- Pay particular attention to the shared meanings of these concepts and patterns across different contexts and subject matter areas. However, always examine how certain meanings vary across contexts (e.g., how force differs between physics and everyday uses, even though there is still some deeper sense of shared meaning). This examination of meanings and contexts is important to help deal with the typical confusion and misunderstandings that plague much of science learning.

- Finally, the following table shows how you can use metapatterns to represent a variety of processes and situations.

**TABLE D.24** Metapatterns and What They Can Represent

| Metapatterns | Can Be Used to Represent: |
| --- | --- |
| Sphere | Context, environment, situation, object, organism, containment, layer in holarchy |
| Tube | Relational connection (two-way), two-way flow |
| Sheet | Layer in hierarchy, two-dimensional movement in all directions, capture, border or barrier |
| Borders and pores | Obstacle, barrier, regulatory openings, protection |
| Layers—hierarchy | Stacked layers of some social situation or organization, levels of energy in ecology |
| Layers—holarchy | Layers of earth and atmosphere, nonhierarchical social or organizational layers, object layers |
| Layers—clonons | Identical parts comprising wholes, building blocks, structures |
| Layers—holons | Nonidentical, individualized parts comprising wholes; wholes that become clonons in even greater wholes |
| Centers | Organizing factors, attractors, etc. |
| Binaries, plus | Units in relationship (organisms, numbers, balance in mechanical or chemical systems, etc.) |
| Arrows | Force, motion, actions, pathways, directions, directional relationships, sequences and stages, etc. |
| Time, clocks, and calendars | Biological clocks, progression of time (as an arrow), repetitive sequences of time (as cycles) |
| Breaks | Changes, transformations, branching, diversions, etc. |
| Cycles | Biological cycles, mechanical cycles, geological cycles, geochemical cycles, feedback loops (mechanical, social, etc.), political/historical cycles, etc. |
| Clusters | Social groupings, astronomical and physical groupings, biological groupings, etc. |
| Rigidity and flexibility | Psychological and social rigidity and flexibility, physical and technological flexibility and rigidity, biological tolerance limits, acclimatization, etc. |
| Gradients | Continuums, shadings, sloping (physical and in data), acceleration, etc. |
| Emergence | Birth, beginnings, psychological and social innovation, etc. |
| Webs | Structures, large sets of relationships, networks (organizations, communication, transportation, biological, etc.), etc. |
| Triggers | Initiators, events that start other events, stimuli, etc. |

## Additional Sources of Information

Bateson, G. (1979). *Mind and nature: A necessary unity*. New York: Bantam Books.

Bateson, M. C. (1994). *Peripheral visions: Learning along the way*. New York: Harper Collins.

Burke, J. (1999). *The knowledge web: From electronic agents to Stonehenge and back—and other journeys through knowledge*. New York: Touchstone/Simon & Schuster.

Burke, J. (2000). *Circles: 50 round trips through history, technology, science, culture*. New York: Simon & Schuster.

Capra, F. (1996). *The web of life: A new scientific understanding of living systems*. New York: Anchor/Doubleday.

Davis, B., Sumara, D., & Luce-Kapler, R. (2000). *Engaging minds: Learning and teaching in a complex world*. Mahwah, NJ: Lawrence Erlbaum Associates.

Doll, W. E., & Gough, N. (Eds.). (2002). *Curriculum visions*. New York: Peter Lang.

Fleener, M. J. (2002). *Curriculum dynamics: Recreating heart*. New York: Peter Lang.

Johnson, S. (2001). *Emergence: The connected lives of ants, brains, cities, and software.* New York: Touchstone/Simon and Schuster.

Morowitz, H. J. (2004). *The emergence of everything: How the world became complex.* New York: Oxford University Press.

Volk, T. (1995). *Metapatterns: Across space, time, and mind.* New York: Columbia University Press.

Volk, T. (1998). *Gaia's body: Toward a physiology of earth.* New York: Copernicus/Springer-Verlag.

Complexity and Education Group and their free online journal, *Complicity: An International Journal of Complexity and Education,* http://www.complexityandeducation.ualberta.ca

*Appendix E*
# More on Planning

The following instructional plan formats can be used to focus on particular types of activities or goals. Be sure to read Chapter 8, particularly Section 8.4. An inquiry instructional plan format is provided in this particular section (Example 8.4).

## E.1 Seven E's Instructional Plan

Be sure to read Section 8.3 in Chapter 8 for an understanding of each of the seven E's.

| 7 E'S INSTRUCTIONAL PLAN | Estimated Time-Line Range: |
|---|---|
| **Unit Topic or Theme:** | **Major Unit Projects:** |
| **Concepts:** | **Skills:** |
| | |

**Eliciting Strategy or Activity:**

| PRIMARY ACTIVITIES | Questions |
|---|---|
| Engaging | |
| Exploring | |
| Encountering/Challenging | |
| Explaining Strategies/Activities | |
| Elaborating/Extending Activities | |
| EvaluationStrategies/Activities | |

Curriculum/Standards Addressed

**FIGURE E.1**

## E.2 | Field Study Instructional Plan

Be sure to read Appendix F for a complete treatment of field studies.

**FIELD STUDIES INSTRUCTIONAL PLAN**    Estimated Time: [____]

| | |
|---|---|
| **Unit Topic or Theme:** | **Major Unit Projects:** |
| **Concepts:** | **Skills:** |
| **Pupose/Goals:** | **Fit with Unit Inquiry:** |
| **Location:** | **Contact People and Others:** |

| Inquiry and Other Activities | Questions |
|---|---|

**Follow-Up Activities, Projects, and/or Products**

| Curriculum/Standards Addressed: | Safety/Emergency Measures: |
|---|---|

**FIGURE E.2**

Metapatterns Instructional Plan

Be sure to read Appendix D for a more thorough treatment of metapatterns and other broad concepts. The following two figures provide a blank form and an example of a completed form on the topic of locomotion and movement.

| METAPATTERNS INSTRUCTIONAL PLAN | Estimated Time: |
|---|---|

| Unit Topic or Theme: | Major Unit Projects: |
|---|---|

**Conceptual Content:**

**Metapatterns:**

**Links and Relationship Across Subject Matter Areas:**

**Initial Activities:**

**Inquiry Initiating Problems and Questions:**

**Inquiry Activities:**

**Potential Knowledge Sharing Products:**

**Assessment Strategies:**

**Science Curriculum Standards:**

**Other Curriculum Standards:**

**FIGURE E.3**

## METAPATTERNS INSTRUCTIONAL PLAN  Estimated Time: [            ]

**Unit Topic or Theme:** Locomotion and movement

**Major Unit Projects:** [            ]

**Conceptual Content:**

Physiology of locomotion; Adaptive value of movement; Structure/Function; Territoriality; Transport and circulation; Growth as movement; Dispersion; Energy; Force; Laws of motion; Inertia; Velocity; Acceleration; Transport and culture interrelationships; Transformation.

**Metapatterns:**

Cycles-patterns of movement; Binaries-appendages, muscle contraction, etc.; Tubes, Sheets-aerodynamics, structures, etc.; Centers-gravity, control, organization; Arrows-directionality, velocity, acceleration; Breaks-erosion, transformations; Time-patterns in time.

**Links and Relationship Across Subject Matter Areas:**

Animals, protozoans-types of locomotion, purposes, adaptations, etc.; Technological-clocks, vehicles, etc.; Earth science-plates, air and oceanic currents, streams, revolution, rotation, etc.; Sociological/anthropological-movement of peoples, technological effects, etc.; Literature-movement of characters, character/story development, etc.; Visual Arts-representation of movement and psychological impacts, dynamic sculptures, etc.; Dramatic and musical arts-choreography, psycho-social effects, etc.; Experiential-daily routines, sports, moving, traveling, etc.; Psychological-eye movement, thinking as movement, etc.

**Initial Activities:**
- Context maps of "movement" and "locomotion."
- Scavenger hunt for movement and evidence of movement.

**Inquiry Activities:**
- Observe how people move – compare to observations of other animals (dogs, squirrels, birds, earthworms, fish, etc.).
- Pendulum inquiries.
- Classifying and mapping locomotion, movement.
- Technologies of transport and how they have affected cultures and societies throughout history.
- Force, energy, and motion experiments with a variety of objects (e.g., rockets, paper airplanes, toy cars, marbles, toy boats, paper helicopters, etc.).
- Experiments with water and wind erosion.
- Observational studies of animal locomotion along with structure/function, symmetries, etc.
- Observations and experiments with plant adaptations for dispersal of seeds.

**Inquiry Initiating Problems and Questions:**
- How fast does a crow fly?
- What effects has movement/transport had on societies and cultures, as well as on ecosystems (including transport and introduction of non-native species).
- What affects pendulum movement, airplane flight, toy car movement?
- What are the advantages to a variety of animals for their adaptations for movement?
- What are the similarities and differences between the movement cycles in a variety of animals, weather systems, and technologies?

**Potential Knowledge Sharing Products:**
- Video documentary of movement, motion, locomotion.
- "Car" construction and races.
- Paper airplane construction and contest.
- Movement, motion, locomotion website.
- Movement, motion, locomotion museum.
- "Perpetual" motion machine.

**Assessment Strategies:**

Discourse analysis; Context and concept maps; Problem focused portfolios; Informal interviews; Student artifact analysis, including major project products; Observations (with and without rubrics); Rubric-based observations of specific task performance.

**Science Curriculum Standards:** [            ]

**Other Curriculum Standards:** [            ]

**FIGURE E.4**

*Appendix F*
# Field Studies

Extending inquiry beyond the confines of the classroom can provide exciting and worthwhile experiences for you and your students. However, you want to make sure that such excursions move beyond the typical field trip to become field studies. Field trips tend to be "look, see, and listen" experiences. Students are not actively engaged in inquiry. On the other hand, field studies actually continue the inquiry that has already begun in the classroom or begin an inquiry that continues back in the classroom. You and your students should see a real need to extend your work into other settings. Table F.1 provides a comparison between field studies and field trips. With a little bit of imagination, you can design field studies to complement just about any topic you are exploring with your students.

## F.1 Types of Field Studies

Determining field settings depends upon your topic and the availability of appropriate settings in your area or within a reasonable distance. In planning field studies, you have three basic options:

1. **Local** trips to the school yard or areas to which you can walk
2. **Day** trips to which you would need to take either a bus (or other public transportation) or a car (i.e., recruit parents to help drive)
3. **Extended** trips to locations where you will want to stay anywhere from one night to four or more nights

**TABLE F.1** A Comparison between Field Studies and Field Trips

| Field Studies | Field Trips |
|---|---|
| Specific goals for the experience | Goals, if any, are general and superficial |
| Students are active participants | Students are passive receivers |
| The experience is relevant, meaningful, and engaging for students | The experience may not be at all relevant, meaningful, or engaging for students |
| Field studies continue the emphasis of the characteristics and personal and social skills that are a part of community membership | Students are typically kept under tight control, with little or no focus on responsibility, ownership, mutual control, and so forth |
| Students are involved in complex thinking and knowledge production | Students are generally not involved in thinking beyond the superficial |
| Students involved in inquiry and other research skills: interviewing, observing, experimenting, note taking, and so forth | Students are generally asked to listen to someone and ask questions |
| Students may interact with professionals at the field site | Little or no interaction is present with professionals at the field site |
| Field study is an integral part of the unit of study | Field trip is tangential to the unit of study |
| Student identity is that of researcher | Student identity is not focused and sees trip as opportunity to get out of school |

* **How do your experiences with field trips compare to the information provided in Table F.1?**
* **What did you learn from participating in field trips?**
* **If you have participated in field studies, how did your experiences and learning differ from field trips?**

Table F.2 provides a few examples of topics, possible field study sites for each topic, and the type of trip required for each site.

**TABLE F.2** Examples of Topics and Potential Field Study Sites

| Topic | Potential Field Sites | Type |
|---|---|---|
| Oceans | Coastal locations | Day; extended |
| | Aquarium | Day; extended |
| | Oceanographic or marine engineering laboratory | Day; extended |
| | Boat trip (e.g., chartered boat, whale watching) | Day; extended |
| Machines | Ship builder or other equipment construction site | Day |
| | Factory | Day |
| | Mechanic | Day |
| | Engineering firm | Day |
| | Museum of science and technology | Day |
| Flight | Zoo (flight of birds and other animals) | Day; extended |
| | Aviation school (flight simulator) | Day |
| | Local airport (charter flight) | Day |
| | Museum of science and technology | Day |
| | Aircraft manufacturing company | Day |
| | School yard or other local site (bird flight) | Local |
| Forests | Local woods or forest | Local; day |
| | Remote forest (programs by camps or at campground, etc.) | Extended |
| | Logging or forestry company | Day |
| | Zoo or nature park | Day; extended |
| | Museum of natural history | Day; extended |
| Communication | Telephone company | Day |
| | Advertising or public relations company | Day |
| | Computer communications company | Day |
| | Zoo (animal communication) | Day; extended |
| | Sites where people gather/communicate | Local; day |
| | Neurologist's or physiologist's laboratory | Day |
| | Television and radio stations | Day |

From Table F.2, we get the sense of how each topic can lead to a variety of field studies in quite different settings. Field studies do not necessarily need to be outdoors. The point is to link our inquiry to appropriate sites and to provide our students with opportunities to extend their understandings of and engagement in the topic under study.

Field studies can be divided again into three categories based on the planning required. The first involves taking our class to an established organization where the employees (i.e., experts) handle the activities. In this situation, the teacher's planning is minimal. However, you will need to make travel arrangements and visit the site ahead of time and meet the people with whom you will be working. In such cases, the experts generally tend to be somewhat apprehensive about working with a group of children. It is your task to help make them feel comfortable and to provide them with details on how you want the field study to work. In other words, you need to train them on how to engage children in inquiry and in the tasks that take place at the site. Some examples are a physiologist's laboratory, an aviation school, a factory, or an advertising agency.

The second type of planning category involves taking students to a pre-established educational setting, such as an environmental program conducted by a summer camp during the off-season, a zoo, or museum. Your planning, in this case, is focused on communicating your needs with the educational staff and arranging for funding and transportation.

The third category involves planning an extended (overnight) trip in its entirety. These trips require the most work, but can be very rewarding. Planning such an extended field study needs to begin well in advance. In fact, starting your preparations a year ahead is ideal. Details of planning such an excursion are provided in the next section.

This local field study allowed students to develop an understanding of the physical context of the pond from which they collected specimens and to engage in a variety of data collection procedures typical of what scientists would do. Back in the classroom, the information and the pond water samples and specimens they collected provided the basis for their continued study of ponds.

---

### Example F.1: Examples of Local, Day, and Extended Field Studies

■ **A Teacher's Local Field Study Based on Pond Ecology**

John, a grade 6 teacher, began a pond study by taking his class to a pond located near his school. The children began the study with a few acclimatizing activities. These activities were followed with some art activities (i.e., drawing the area surrounding the pond without using manufactured implements, such as pencils or markers). Then the children collected specimens using a variety of nets and strainers, as well as their hands.

As the children collected and observed their specimens, they generated many questions and commentaries about the pond and the organisms, many of which were recorded either in the students' notebooks or by the teacher. After the initial collections and observations, the students drew maps of the pond and recorded observations linked to specific parts of the pond (i.e., where they collected specimens,

*-- continued*

Bernoulli's principle states that the faster air moves, the lower the pressure. This occurs because air flowing over the top of an airplane's wing has to travel a longer distance over the curvature of the wing and must travel faster to keep up with the air below the wing; the faster air on top of the wing creates a lower pressure, and therefore lift is created by the higher pressure under the wing.

In this excursion, the children were provided with an experience of flying. Not only did the children fly, but they had an opportunity to see how the plane worked and to talk with the pilot about each aspect of the flight. The motivation and interest generated by this experience carried over to the rest of the unit, which resulted in products of much higher quality than any others done in the school at that grade level.

During this extended field study, children had the opportunity to engage in thorough investigations of a number of different habitats and geological features of a coastal environment. The depth of study made possible by this excursion allowed the class to develop more sophisticated understandings than would have been possible had the topic been studied exclusively in the classroom. An unexpected result of the field study arose the following fall, when the parents (who had not been known for coming to school meetings) decided that they wanted to meet every two weeks and raise money to support the program.

types of vegetation in or along the edge of the pond, etc.). Additional data on temperature, pH, and dissolved oxygen were collected and recorded, along with the time and date of collection.

As the field study came to an end, each group of students saved enough pond water and organisms to fill their own 1-gallon aquariums back in the classroom. Observations of their pond water aquaria continued over the next several weeks.

Although the major focus of the unit was completed in four weeks, the children continued to visit the pond throughout the year. By the end of the school year, the students had collected data on temperature, pH, dissolved oxygen, and pond organisms during the fall, winter, and spring and were able to compare their results and note changes over time.

### ■ A Student Teacher's Day Field Study Based on Flight

Molly, a student teacher, had been exploring flight with her grade 2 class in a school located in an economically deprived neighborhood. The children had been designing and flying paper airplanes, investigating Bernoulli's principle, the effects of center of gravity, and so on. Then Molly arranged for an air charter service to take the children on flights around their city.

After getting signed releases from all but one of her students' parents, they went to the airport. At the site, one child decided not to go and remained with the one child without parental permission. During the flight, the pilot engaged each child in discussions about how the plane worked. Upon returning to the classroom, the very excited children continued their work in developing elaborate displays on airplane flight.

### ■ Two Teachers' Combined Extended Field Study to the Coast

Two teachers from schools about 160 km (100 miles) apart met at a conference. A friendship ensued with regular communications. At one point in the spring, they began discussing the possibility of doing a joint field study, which would bring together students (spanning grades 4, 5, and 6) from both schools. During the summer, they continued planning. One teacher traveled to the coastal field location and began exploring potential field sites and accommodations. Throughout the rest of the summer, they continued to share ideas and formulate plans for a trip the following spring (including when to catch low tides at the field sites).

Because of the large number of students, they planned two trips, each of which consisted of 40 students, 12 parents, 2 biology graduate students, and the 2 teachers. The students engaged in observations and collecting at a variety of sites, including the beach, sand dunes, tidal streams, mud flats, and marshes. Throughout each of the three days, the students had opportunities to write in their journals, see local historic and natural history sites, and play games. The last evening included a campfire with skits (on what they had learned) performed by the children.

## F.2 | Planning an Extended Field Study

Extended field studies provide students with unique opportunities to engage in intensive in-depth investigations in ways that are not possible in the classroom. Any scheduled activity can be changed, so that if students are enthusiastically involved in an investigation, you can allow them to continue. In addition, for both you and your students, such excursions allow you to get to know each other outside of the school setting. Not only do the students see you first thing in the morning (desperately seeking coffee, etc.), but they also see you as their major connection with home and security. You see them throughout the day and night, as young people not operating under the unwritten rules of how to get by in school. Your relationships with students can undergo a lasting change that extends back into the classroom community.

### F.2.1 Coordinate the Field Study with Your Unit of Study and Begin Initial Planning

Be sure that your field study is an integral part of your unit. Plan the trip so that it occurs at a point when students have necessary skills and knowledge to take full advantage of the experience. In other words, try not to plan the trip at the beginning of the unit, but somewhere near the middle or end of the unit, unless you are beginning the unit with collecting data, such as a pond study. However, you do need to make sure that your class will have enough time after the field study to develop projects on what they learned during the field study, as well as the rest of the unit.

The points you need to address in planning extended field studies are provided in the subsection below.

#### F.2.1.1 Pretrip Planning

1. Start planning far enough in advance (at least six to eight months for extended field studies).
   - Early planning will help you avoid many problems and develop a more cohesive and intensive field study.
2. List a number of potential field sites.
   - Explore the area you intend to visit. Look for good sites that will provide some variety of habitats (or other experiences, depending on the topic and location).
3. Start considering the following questions for each site (details on each of these questions are provided later):
   - How will the children and adults be housed (cabins, motel, tents, etc.)?

- Who will supply the staff with expertise?
- How will we get there?
- How long will it take to get there?
- What types of clothing, equipment, supplies, and so forth, will we need to take along?
- What equipment, supplies, and so forth, will be supplied at the field site?
- What types of safety precautions need to be taken?
- What and where are the nearest emergency facilities?
- How will meals be provided?

4. Visit the site.
- Plan to spend a day or more visiting the site as far in advance as possible.
- List and describe possible sites where children can investigate different types of habitats, and so forth.
- Look for all the potential *hazards* (e.g., potential for flash floods along a stream, slippery or unstable rocks, areas where unexpected large waves can occur, quicksand or a similar situation) and list each in detail.
- Get maps of the site and surrounding area, or make your own. Topographic maps, as well as detailed local road maps, can be very helpful (many of which are available on line, including aerial photos, such as at http://maps.google.com).
- Locate hospitals, the police station, doctors' offices, and so forth. Get phone numbers and addresses of all emergency facilities. Clearly indicate their locations on the map. Drive different routes to the hospital. Indicate the easiest and fastest route on the map.
- If you have children with physical disabilities, you should plan on ways to accommodate them.

5. Plan for emergencies.
- Although you already should have identified potential hazards, do more safety planning. Brainstorm and list all the possibilities: physical hazards, weather, illnesses, injuries, and so forth. Talk to local people, especially the local police, about any hazardous situations of which you may not be aware.
- Plan courses of action for various emergencies. For example, if you are on low ground by a stream, can you get to high ground quickly? If an accident happens at a particular field site, what course of action will you take to get the student (or adult) to the hospital?
- List any protective clothing that could prevent injury or illness (e.g., sneakers for wading in streams, ponds, beaches, or marshes; long-sleeved shirts for protection against sunburn and insects).
- Put together at least one first-aid kit. A minimal first-aid kit should contain the following:

As a teacher was exploring a potential field site, he sank up to his thighs in the muck in a marsh. Fortunately, a [quite panicked!] friend followed his instructions to throw him some scrap lumber that had washed up along the bank. The teacher managed to pull himself out of the muck using the wood as a base. Then he walked back to the bank stepping on the wooden planks. Later, after warning the children about going into the muck, two girls thought they would find out for themselves. They were quickly and easily rescued and quite embarrassed as the teacher took pictures of them being rescued.

| Various sizes of Band-Aids | Scissors | Sunscreen |
|---|---|---|
| Thermometer (digital is best) | Alcohol | Forceps |
| Acetaminophen (Tylenol) (only use with signed permission from parents) | Insect repellent | Ice pack |
| Various sizes of sterile gauze | Burn ointment | Eye wash |
| Topical antiseptic | Adhesive tape | Petroleum jelly |

- Take a first-aid and CPR course, if you have not already taken one.
- Make copies of emergency phone numbers, maps to emergency facilities, and so forth. Distribute this information to staff and chaperones.
- Plan how you will handle personal medications of students. You should keep all medications (with the exception of inhalers or insulin needles, which the child has been trained to administer to himself or herself).
- Make sure students bring (and always have with them) their inhalers for asthma, bee sting kits, insulin kits, and so forth. Always double-check at every point of departure for field site trips and other excursions.
- Bring a cellular phone if you have one. If not, ask chaperones to bring theirs. If you are going to be in an area where cell phones do not work (this is where visiting the site is important), find the locations of the nearest phones and where cell phones do work. Locate and indicate these locations on your map.
- Make sure that each student's parents have signed the necessary permission forms and documents that are required by your board. Example F.2 provides a sample emergency release form. You *must* have a *signed and notarized* form for each student, if possible. If a student needs hospital attention and the parents cannot be contacted, hospitals will not attend to the injury or illness unless it is life threatening. The completed form gives you the right to authorize medical treatment in the event that the child's parents cannot be contacted. In any case, always be sure to check with your own school for specific forms designated for use by your school board. Example F.3 provides a sample medical information form. This permission slip will offer you some legal protection. However, if you are negligent, nothing will protect you. Again, be sure to check with your school for the specific forms required by your school board.

6. Accommodations
- Staying in buildings, as opposed to camping, is more expensive. However, staying inside is safer and more comfortable.
- Buildings should have a large room for meetings and project work. A large meeting room also can provide you with a location for setting up a laboratory for the children. Aquaria, microscopes, and other equipment can be set up so that your students can continue their inquiry back at the home base.

**Example F.2: Emergency Form**

## Emergency Form

Child's name:_____

In case of emergency, please notify (parent or guardian):

Mother's name:_____

Father's name:_____

Address:_____

_____

Home phone:_____

Work phone: father:_____  mother:_____

Other phone numbers:_____

The above student has the following allergic reactions to medications:


In case of emergency, please provide health insurance number which covers medical treatment for your child:


Doctor's name, address, and phone number:

_____

_____


I, _____, hereby grant to _____ the right to act
            parent                                  teacher

on my behalf in case of an emergency, to take any necessary action to secure the safety and well-being of my

child, including the right to authorize medical treatment if I or my spouse cannot be contacted.


_____        _____
             parent signature                                      date

Witnessed and notarized by:

- A kitchen may be necessary if the management does not supply food. If a kitchen is not available and food is not supplied, you should plan accordingly. With coolers and borrowed camping stoves, you can provide simple foods, such as cereal for breakfast, sandwiches, hot dogs, and hamburgers.

7. Food
- Eat inexpensively. Plan on foods that are simple to store and prepare.

**Example F.3: Permission Slip and Health and Safety Information.**

**Permission Slip and Health and Safety Information**

I hereby grant permission for my child, _____, to participate in the field trip described below. I furthermore release the teacher-in-charge, school, and school board from any responsibility, except for negligence, for the injury and sickness of my child incurred during this field trip.

_____     _____

parent or guardian signature                                            date

Description of field trip (include purpose, location, and date[s]):

*[you must provide this information for parents]*

My child has the following allergic or other medical conditions (include name and dosage of medications, if necessary).

Unless precluded by any information provided above, the chaperones and /or teacher will dispense simple medications such as acetaminophen or cough syrup for the treatment of minor cold symptoms, simple headaches, and other minor aches, pains, and discomforts. Other first-aid medication also will be available. Please indicate specific recommendations or circumstances of which the teacher and chaperones should be aware:

I grant the teacher or other designated staff member(s)
_____ to dispense the following medication(s):

_____     _____

parent or guardian signature                                            date

My child has permission to go swimming, at the discretion of the teacher and if a lifeguard is present.

_____     _____

parent or guardian signature                                            date

---

- Involve parent chaperones in food purchasing and preparation.
- Be sure to look into any potential food allergies that can affect your students. To be safe, avoid some of the more common food allergens, such as peanuts, sesame, and shellfish.

8. Transportation
   - For overnight field studies, you will probably have to charter a bus. If your school will not provide one, shop around for the best deal.
   - *Important*: Take at least one car in case of emergencies, such as taking a child to the doctor or hospital (see Example F.4).
   - Make sure that any drivers (e.g., parents and teachers) have high liability coverage on their cars. Check with your school to find out the recommended minimum coverage.

9. Staff
   - Search for your own experts at local universities. Graduate students can usually be talked into helping out, if persuaded by a meager honorarium. Such experts allow you not to be at the center of attention. In addition, the children will view the experts very differently than they view teachers.
   - Whenever possible, meet with the expert staff to discuss your expectations of how to engage the children in hands-on inquiry, the field sites (e.g., descriptions of each site, types of activities for each site), learning goals for the students, and other possible activities.
   - Plan a tentative sequence of activities at various field sites and at the home base.
   - Recruit parent volunteer chaperones. Parents can help with driving and meal preparation. They also can help with getting the children to sleep. (The first night is very crazy! Getting them to sleep can be very difficult. However, by the second night, they are so tired they usually beg to go to bed earlier than you have planned.) Heavily recruit any parent who is a nurse or doctor.

---

**Example F.4**

On a two-night field study to a coastal site, a grade 4 child cut his ankle on some shells. A nurse/parent who was chaperoning was able to assess quickly the severity of the cut and apply first-aid treatment. She recommended that the boy be taken to the hospital for stitches. Having an extra car helped in getting the child to the hospital. A couple of hours later, he was able to rejoin the group. Although he was hobbling a bit, he was able to participate in the rest of the activities.

---

10. Cost analysis
    - Plan a budget that includes transportation costs, accommodations, food, staff honoraria and fees, materials, and any other costs you can determine.
    - Determine how much, if any, the school or district will contribute toward the costs.
    - Figure the cost per student. Can parents afford the trip? Are they willing to pay for the trip?
    - Plan fund-raising activities to lower the cost per student or to subsidize students whose parents cannot afford it.
11. Make a list of the equipment and materials that need to be taken along.
    - Can students make some of the equipment (dip nets, etc.)?
    - From where can such things be borrowed?
12. Make a list of all the things that each student needs to bring along.
    - Examples include insect repellent, sunscreen, canteens, flashlights, bedding, toiletries, a journal notebook, pens, pencils, specific

**Example F.5**

A teacher's recounting of a near disaster, where planning for the unexpected would have helped:

In late May, we took 90 students on a five-day trip to an environmental program at a summer camp in the Adirondack Mountains. The first day was extremely hot. Black flies were eating everyone alive! The second day was cool and rainy. Twelve of the children departed on a three-day survival trip with one of the staff. All of the children were wearing sneakers and light clothing. At 5:00 A.M. the next morning, one of the camp's staff woke me up. He said, "I just wanted you to know that there's 18 inches of snow on the ground. The phone and power lines are down … and no one has been able to get out to the main road. Just be prepared when the boys wake up."

Later in the morning, the 12 children on the survival trip made it back to the cabins. All of them had hypothermia. However, the rest of the students pulled together and rounded up extra blankets in which to wrap the 12 survival trip children. The entire trip turned into a survival trip! We all survived and had a great time, but the situation could have been disastrous.

clothing (e.g., cold- and warm-weather clothes, rain gear, protective clothing such as sneakers and cotton gloves, caps or hats).

13. Communication with parents.
    - Be sure to sell the field study as an important learning experience that allows students to engage in inquiry and apply their understandings and knowledge.
    - Communicate all the safety precautions you have taken. Be sure to address the importance of filling out the emergency and medical history forms.
    - Try to involve them in the field study. Some parents can help chaperone. Others can help with planning and fund-raising. You also may find that some parents have expertise that may complement your field study.
    - For younger children, dispel fears of homesickness. The children are usually far too busy and having too much fun to think about home. If they do get homesick, plan with the parents how you can address their needs. If a child has a history of becoming homesick, then you may suggest that the parents come along as chaperones.

14. The trip
    - Do not forget the emergency release and health and safety information forms.
    - It is usually a good idea to have the children write in journals at specified times. Journals are not diaries. They are tools for reflecting on the goals, processes, and content of the field study. Journals should contain thoughts that analyze, interpret, evaluate, describe, and so

forth, as well as research notes, new insights, new things learned, and so forth. Creative expression (poetry, drawings, sketches, etc.) can be included and encouraged. Students can include their own personal or emotional reactions to the trip, the activities, and so forth. Staff could spend time at the end of each day discussing some of the nonprivate entries in small-group discussions.

- The first night is the worst from an adult's point of view. The children are wound up — be prepared for a long night!
- Watch out for negative interactions among the children: confront situations immediately and help the children work out their own differences.
- Be ready to change scheduled activities. Evaluate the field study with staff and make modifications when necessary.
- Skits are good events for the last night around a campfire, if you can have one. Children can work in groups on ways to communicate what they have learned or experienced during the field study.

## F.3 Summary

One of the key advantages to using field studies as a complement to your students' inquiry involves *time*. In the classroom, we are lucky to devote an hour or maybe two to intensive investigations. However, field studies allow for in-depth study over longer periods of time. For day and extended trips, you and your students can focus on one topic. Longer and more varied observations can be accommodated, as well as more thorough investigations.

In addition, field studies can incorporate activities that allow children to develop understandings and skills that cross subject area boundaries. Language arts, visual and dramatic arts, history and social studies, math, and physical education activities can all be incorporated into the focus of the field study. Children also can be provided with the time needed to develop cross-disciplinary understandings, such as how a particular stream being studied affects environments and people downstream and how the stream can be understood through art, poetry, stories, history, and mathematics.

At the same time, the nature of the classroom inquiry can develop through the shared experiences of you and your students. Taking the community outside of the classroom can deepen the relationships among the children and between you and your students. The roles students take on within the community can include more opportunities to care and look out for one another, to work together on daily chores and activities not generally associated with school (e.g., preparing food, making campfires), and to take on different sorts of leadership roles (e.g., wake-up calls, clean-up, and other chores). In general, the field study experience can lead to deeper and more meaningful relationships, as well as a more cohesive sense of community.

- How do you see field studies contributing to an inquiry community in the classroom?
- What kinds of field studies can you imagine doing with your students?
- What kinds of activities, in addition to those focusing on inquiry, could you include to help build a sense of community?
- What kinds of activities could you include to develop integrated understandings?
- What problems might you encounter in planning and conducting a day-long or extended field study? How would you deal with these problems?

## Additional Reading

Durrell, G. (1989). *A practical guide for the amateur naturalist.* New York: Alfred A. Knopf. (out-of-print, but available from on line book sellers)

> A must-have guide for investigating a variety of environments. Includes information on how to collect, keep (grow and breed), and identify plants and animals, as well as on conceptual content.

Stokes guides to bird behavior, observing insects, animal tracking and behavior, amphibians and reptiles, etc. Available from Stokes Nature Company (http:// www.stokesbirdsathome.com).

van Matre, S. (1990). *Earth education: A new beginning.* Greenville, WV: Institute for Earth Education.

> This book provides a strong background for conducting field studies focused on the environment. Other books from the same publisher provide practical information and activities.

Other field guides including the Peterson field guides, Audubon field guides, Golden Book guides, and so forth.

*Appendix G*
# Activity Sampler

This appendix provides an assortment of sample activities. Try doing these activities in order to extend your experience with scientific inquiry. You can build on these activities to develop larger inquiry units.

## G.1 Structures

Using soda straws (cut in consistent 8- to 10-cm. (3- to 4-in.) lengths) and little L-shaped pipe cleaners (cut to 2- to 3-cm. (1-in.) lengths), make a bridge between two chairs or tables.

■ Use only the materials described.
■ The L-shaped pipe cleaners are to be used to connect two or more straws. Insert one end of the L into one straw and the other end of the L into another straw, as shown in the diagram below.

**FIGURE G.1**

- The span of the bridge should be between 50 and 75 cm. (about 20 to 30 in.).
- The bridge must be able to sustain a weight of no less than 50 g (about 2 oz).

As a follow-up activity, make a stronger bridge that can hold even more weight!

✦ **Refer to the activity in Appendix G.1. When you are done, answer these questions:**

✦ **What difficulties did you encounter?**

✦ **How did you deal with these difficulties?**

✦ **What did you learn from dealing with these difficulties?**

✦ **Sketch a picture of your final bridge design.**

✦ **Did you design a bridge that did not work? Sketch a picture of it.**

✦ **What characteristics of the bridge design contributed to the bridge working or not working? In other words, why did your bridge work or not work?**

✦ **How would you redesign your bridge?**

✦ **How are real bridges designed?**

✦ **Where did the original designers of bridges get their ideas?**

✦ **What non-human-made objects are similar to bridges in function or design?**

## G.2 Marble Collisions

Set up a marble track (e.g., flexible plastic corner molding or piece of foam pipe insulation cut in half) between two tables or two chairs. You may want to use tape to hold each end in place.

Get an assortment of different-size marbles or ball bearings. Next, play around letting marbles roll down the track.

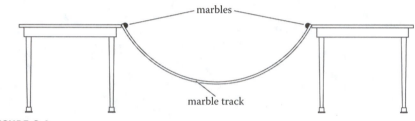

**FIGURE G.2**

- Try letting them go from each end of the track at the same time and at different times.
- Try using different-size marbles. Try using a marble and a metal ball bearing, and so forth.
- You may also want to use a balance scale, stopwatch, and tape measure.
- What happens when two different-size marbles collide?
- What happens if you put one marble at the bottom of the arc and hit it with different-size (larger or smaller) marbles?
- What other questions can you ask?
- Try designing some experiments that will answer some of these questions.
  - What other variations of experiments can you try? Make a list.
  - What explanations can you generate to describe the reactions of colliding marbles?

## G.3 Pendulums

Use the diagram below to help you design a pendulum apparatus out of scrap materials.

There are many variations to the above apparatus, which you can try. You also can hang pendulums from the ceiling or from other tall structures.

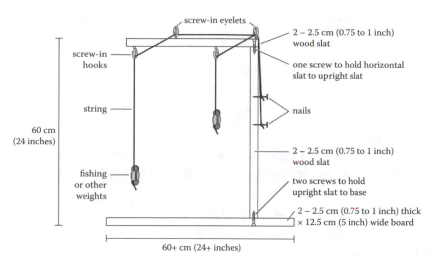

screw-in eyelets

screw-in hooks

string

60 cm (24 inches)

fishing or other weights

2 – 2.5 cm (0.75 to 1 inch) wood slat

one screw to hold horizontal slat to upright slat

 nails

2 – 2.5 cm (0.75 to 1 inch) wood slat

two screws to hold upright slat to base

2 – 2.5 cm (0.75 to 1 inch) thick × 12.5 cm (5 inch) wide board

60+ cm (24+ inches)

**FIGURE G.3**

- Take five minutes or so to play around with the pendulum apparatus or the pendulum hanging from the ceiling. What do you notice about the behavior of pendulums?

- Describe some of the factors that affect pendulums and that describe the behavior of pendulums. Generate some questions that involve two or more of these factors.

- Design and conduct experiments that will answer the questions listed in the sidebar, as well as any of your questions. What factors will you control? What factors will you manipulate? What factor will you measure? How will you measure this factor?

- What factors determine the period (the length of time to make one swing) of the swing?

- What factors determine the distance of the swing?

## G.4 Balancing Act

Cut pieces of pegboard into different shapes. A couple of examples are shown below. Each piece should be about 60 to 75 cm. (2 to 2.5 ft) across. You will need a generous supply of cubic-inch (2.5 × 2.5 × 2.5 cm) blocks or large metal washers.

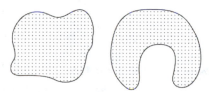

**FIGURE G.4**

Place a pegboard piece on the ball and can as in the diagram below. How would you get the example shown on the right side, above, to balance on the ball?

Make sure the pegboard balances evenly.

※

◆ Once you have completed the activity in Section G.3, try answering the following questions:

◆ What did you find out?

◆ What difficulties did you have?

◆ Are your data accurate? How can you increase the accuracy of your data?

◆ Are pendulums used for anything? List some examples.

◆ Can you invent a real device that uses a pendulum to accomplish a particular task?

◆ Can you invent a science fiction device that uses a pendulum?

◆ Would a pendulum work underwater?

◆ Would a pendulum work on a space shuttle orbiting the earth?

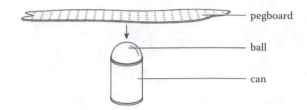

FIGURE G.5

- With two or more people, try placing the cubic-inch blocks or large metal washers on the pegboard. Be careful not to tumble the board.
- Try gently tossing the blocks.
- Try doing it quickly; pick up the pace.
- Try a different-shape piece of pegboard.
- Try using different kinds and sizes of objects at the same time.
- Try testing out some of these ideas on an adjustable beam balance (a rule that can slide along the fulcrum (balancing point) and from which you can hang weights, as shown below).

- ◆ What did you discover about balance?
- ◆ What factors influenced the balance of the board? Can you make any generalized statements or rules about balancing?

- ◆ In what phenomena is the concept of balance important?
- ◆ In what other topics of investigation can the concept of balance be incorporated?
- ◆ Could you create a story where all the rules of balance were changed? What would life be like?

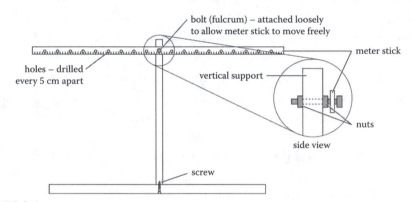

FIGURE G.6

## G.5 Batteries and Bulbs

FIGURE G.7

1. Use one piece of wire to connect a battery and a bulb so that the bulb will light. Draw a diagram of this setup. (Use the drawing of the bulb below, but add your own drawings of one battery and one piece of wire.) Use arrows, diagrams, and words to explain how you think your setup works.
2. Light the bulb by adding drawings of two pieces of wire that connect the battery and the bulb in the diagram below. Use arrows, words, and anything else to explain how you think your setup works.

**FIGURE G.8**

3. Now try testing out each of your ideas with a battery (1.5-V D cell), a bulb (1.5 to 3.0 V), and two pieces of bare copper (or aluminum) wire. What happened? Record your observations. Consider the following questions:

    a. How would you express your understanding of the way in which a battery and bulb work, as in a flashlight?

    b. What is necessary for a circuit to work? Try writing a definition of an electrical circuit.

**FIGURE G.9**

    c. If your setup does not work, what other ways could the battery and bulb be connected that might work? Try them. Why do you think each of them did or did not work?

    d. Try reworking your definition of a circuit.

4. Now try constructing a circuit with a switch. Use as many pieces of wire as you need.

5. Try changing the position of the switch in the circuit. Does it make any difference?

6. Add a second bulb to the circuit so that the switch turns on both lights.

7. Try changing the circuit so that one bulb stays lit all the time and the switch turns the other bulb on and off.

8. Try adding a second switch so that each switch controls a separate light bulb.

9. Try changing the circuit so that one switch turns on both bulbs.

10. Try changing the circuit so that both switches must be on for the bulbs to light and so that either switch will turn off the lights.

11. Try reworking your definition of circuit.

12. How are electrical circuits cycles (see Appendix D) similar to and different from other types of cycles?

❄

✦ Reflect on your experiences in trying to understand electrical circuits:

✦ What prior knowledge and other ideas seemed to interfere with or make it more difficult to make sense of your attempts to make a working circuit?

✦ What did you find useful in working through some of these obstacles and constructing a more meaningful understanding?

✦ How could you use these insights in developing strategies for teaching children?

## G.6   Construct a Boat to Hold a Specific Cargo

Build a boat out of aluminum foil and a piece of cardboard. Cut a piece of cardboard about 10 cm² (4 in.²). Use the cardboard to provide strength to the bottom of your boat. Wrap aluminum foil around the cardboard, while extending the sides of your boat about 2 cm. (0.75 in.) high.

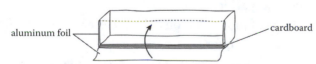

aluminum foil —      — cardboard

**FIGURE G.10**

The task is to predict how much cargo (mass) your boat will hold without sinking. You need to calculate the relative density of the boat by measuring its dimensions in order to get the volume and its mass. The formula for density is

Density = mass (measured as weight on earth) ÷ volume

Once you have calculated the density of your boat, weight a washer or other object of which you have a supply. Then predict how many washers or objects your boat can hold without sinking.

**Weight of washers:**

Diameter: _____ Weight: _____

Boat design:

Length: _____ Width: _____

Height: _____ Weight: _____

Calculate the relative density of the boat:

Density = mass (weight) ÷ volume = _____

Sketch of boat (label size of each dimension):

Predict the number of washers the boat can hold: _____

Predict the total weight of washers the boat can hold: _____

Tested result of the actual number of washers the boat can hold: _____

Actual total weight of washers the boat can hold: _____

✦ **Did your predictions fit with your results?**

✦ **How did this activity affect your understanding of density?**

✦ **What other activities can you design to address the concept of density?**

## G.7   Forest or Open-Field Study

Sit down in a comfortable spot and relax, close your eyes, listen, feel, experience the spot. Open your eyes and relax your gaze. Take in as much of the scene in front of you as possible without moving your eyes. Continue to listen and feel. Do this in the middle of the open field, then crawl in under the fir trees and repeat. How do you feel in each spot? How is each area different?

### G.7.1   Field

✦ **Sketch any of the plants and animals you find during the following activities.**

✦ **A quick sketch of the study area may also be helpful.**

✦ **Always record any questions that arise.**

✦ **Record you observations in each area (field and different types of forest habitats).**

1. Describe the vegetation you see.
   - Are the plants all the same height?
   - What colors are evident?
   - Do the colors of the vegetation change closer to the ground?
   - What could account for the changes in color?
   - How are these plants adapted for their particular habitat?
2. Get down close to the ground and carefully explore; use your fingers to carefully spread apart the vegetation.
   - What is the area like near the ground?
   - How deep do you have to go before reaching the soil?

3. Pick up some of the soil. Close your eyes. What does it smell like?
   - What does it feel like when you rub it between your fingers?
   - Describe in detail what it looks like.
   - Dig deeper into the soil. Does it change in color, texture, smell?
4. Do you see any animals?
   - What do they look like?
   - What are they doing?
   - Do you see any evidence that animals have been there?
   - How are these animals adapted for the places they are living?

### G.7.2   Hardwood Forest

1. Are any other types of vegetation growing in the hardwood stand?
   - Where is the vegetation located?
   - What kind of vegetation is it?
   - Why do you think it is growing there?
   - What types of competition may occur between the large hardwoods and the smaller vegetation.
2. Carefully look through some of the leaf litter and soil beneath it.
   - What types of animals seem to live in the hardwood stand only?
   - Do you see any evidence of other animals? Describe this evidence? What type of animal contributed that evidence?
   - Are there different levels (actual height above the ground) of animal activity?
   - What types of relationships might there be between the animals, plants, and soil in the hardwood forest?
3. What kinds of trees make up the forest?
   - Which species of tree is most common?
   - Are the trees in the forest close together or far apart?
   - How tall are the trees (figure a way to estimate the height)?
   - Measure the circumference of the tree. What is the ratio between the circumference and the height?
   - Now find six smaller trees or tree-like shrubs of different heights with a main trunk. Measure their height and circumference, then figure the ratio.
   - Compare the ratios.
   - What patterns do you see?
   - What would happen if the large hardwoods had a circumference half of what it is?
   - What would happen if the branches of any of the trees had a circumference or diameter that was twice as big?
   - What if your leg bones had a diameter twice what they are?

### G.7.3   Fir Tree Forest

1. Crawl into the middle of the fir trees.
   - Are there any other plants growing? Why or why not?

- What do the fir trees feel like? (Close your eyes. Use different parts of your body.)
- What do they smell like?

2. Describe in detail the floor of the woods.
3. Do you see any animals?
   - What are they or what do they look like?
   - What are they doing?
   - Do you see any evidence that animals have been there?
   - What kind of animals could they have been?
   - What were the animals doing?

### G.7.4 Comparisons of the Different Habitats

1. How are the three areas different?
2. Compare the plants, animals, soil, vegetation, textures, smells, appearance, temperature (relative), tastes, etc.
3. What is the area between the field and the firs trees like?
4. Are the plants different from those in the middle of the field?
5. Do different animals seem to live there than in the firs or the field?

### G.7.5 Patterns and Relationships

1. For each area (field and woods), draw a context map (see Chapter 7, Section 7.4.1) that shows all the variables (living and nonliving things in each particular habitat, any of the sense observations, and any other ideas that help to describe the context of the habitat).
2. After completing the variables or multiple perspectives portion, draw connecting lines between the various items that seem to be related in some way.
3. Label each of these relationships with a word or phrase that describes it.
4. What relationships and patterns can you identify? How can these relationships be investigated further? Can any integrated activities (e.g., poetry, art) be used to describe these patterns and relationships in different ways?

## G.8 Exploring Metapatterns

Throughout this book the idea of learning about complex ideas has been a major theme. These ideas not only are important in science, but are important in many subject matter areas. The following activities take a more general focus on how to explore and use metapatterns while inquiring into a variety of topics. Therefore, it is important that you read the material in Appendix D and make a list of metapatterns to refer to as you proceed with these activities. (In the classroom, you can have your students design a poster for the wall.) However, a brief list is provided here without explanations.

Before we proceed, it is important to realize that even though some of the words describing metapatterns may be big, children are already familiar with

| | | | | |
|---|---|---|---|---|
| • Spheres | • Sheets | • Tubes | • Borders & Pores | • Layers: |
| • Centers | • Binaries++ | • Arrows | • Time-Calendars | • hierarchies |
| • Breaks | • Cycles | • Clusters | • Rigidity- | • holarchies |
| | | | Flexibility | • clonons |
| • Gradients | • Emergence | • Webs | • Triggers | • holons |

**FIGURE G.11**

these patterns by the time they enter school. Our task is to help children begin to formalize their understandings of these patterns, then to help them:

a. Understand the functions and meanings of these patterns
b. Understand how these patterns interact with one another in various systems and situations
c. Use these patterns to analyze a variety of phenomena
d. Use these patterns to investigate similarities between diverse phenomena and contexts
e. Use these patterns to inform their work in writing, math, scientific inquiry, art, and other areas

So, with younger children, we may be emphasizing (a) and maybe move on to (b), (c), and (d). With older children, we may need to start with (a) and move on through the entire list. The following activities are intended to help you move through these levels (layers) of understanding metapatterns and provide some ideas for how these concepts can be utilized in your own classroom.

### G.8.1 Scavenger Hunt

■ After familiarizing yourself with the basic meanings of the metapatterns, take the list with you for a period of time (30 min up to 24 h). Find as many examples of each metapattern as you can. (In the classroom, you may want to group similar metapatterns together and do several scavenger hunts over several days or weeks. Do a short scavenger hunt around the school, then ask children to continue at home.) For those examples that you cannot collect, make a sketch, take a photograph or video, or describe the example. (Answer the following questions yourself or in discussions with others. However, in the classroom, you can have children discuss the questions as a whole class or in small groups and then as a whole class. It may be helpful for children to develop group displays of their findings along with charts that contain the answers to these questions.)
■ Discussion questions:
  ■ What is the function of each metapattern example for the particular organism or situation?
  ■ For each metapattern, how are the examples similar in terms of their function? In what ways are they different?
  ■ What examples contain more than one metapattern? How do the metapatterns in these examples interact with one another?

### G.8.2 Going Deeper: Earthworms

- Get a live earthworm, either by digging up one in a garden or by purchasing some from a store that sells them for fishing bait. Place the earthworm in a tray with or without some soil. Be sure to keep the earthworm moist by sprinkling or spraying water on it every 5 or 10 min. [You can do similar activities for just about any organism, object, or phenomenon.]
    - Examine the earthworm's movement. You may want to start with a more general question like: What metapatterns are evident in the movement?
        - How is the earthworm's movement a cycle?
        - How is the earthworm's movement a binary? (How do muscles work as binaries?)
        - How is the earthworm's movement an arrow?
        - How do these binaries, cycles, and arrows work together?
    - Examine the earthworm's overall structure for evidence of metapatterns. Use a hand lens. Gently rub the earthworm with your fingertip along its length in each direction and along each side.
        - What is the advantage of the tubular shape for the earthworm (or how does the tubular shape help the earthworm)?
        - Can you find tubular structures inside the earthworm (they are somewhat translucent, so you do not need to cut them open)? What do you think these tubular structures are?
        - How do the cycles of movement affect the internal tubular structures?
        - What structural binaries do you notice in the earthworm? Can you find a front and back? Can you find a top and bottom? Can you find its setae (short hair-like structures on each side of the earthworm and slightly down from the horizontal midpoint)?
        - How do the binaries and tubular shape of the earthworm work together with the cycles and binaries of movement?
- Extensions:
    - How is the earthworm's flexibility an advantage? How is it a liability?
    - What would be the problems for earthworms, if they were more spherical or more sheet-like?
    - Can you find other metapatterns in the earthworm, such as types of layering, borders and pores, breaks (any change, transformation, etc.), gradients, and so forth? How do these patterns function to the advantage of the earthworm? How do they interact with the binaries, cycles, and tubular shape of the earthworm?
- Discussion questions (and further extensions):
    - How are the binaries, cycles, and arrows of earthworm movement similar in function to our own bodies' binaries, cycles, and arrows of movement? How are they different?

- How are the binaries, cycles, and arrows of movement of earth-worms and human beings similar to and different from those of bicycles, cars, airplanes, fish, birds, bees, millipedes, and so forth?

- How are these kinds of structural binaries similar to and different from relationship binaries (how two people relate to one another)? How are they similar to other structural binaries, such as sense organs (eyes, ears)? How do these binaries act to unify or maintain a particular process or system of processes?

- How are these structural, relational, and process binaries similar to and different from the binaries you find in stories (books, movies, etc.; good and evil, hero and villain, etc.), in mathematics, politics, school, and so forth?

### G.8.3 Some Points to Consider

- After introducing and exploring all or a group of metapatterns, you should continue to use them throughout the rest of the school year in a variety of subject matter areas, including science. You may find that children will bring them up automatically. However, if they do not, you may need to ask questions that refocus them.

- When you introduce metapatterns, it is essential that you spend a good deal of time exploring them in children's experiences of their every-day lives. As they identify metapatterns, move toward examining their functions so that they begin to construct the basic understandings as described in Appendix D. Then introduce new examples to expand their understandings.

## G.9 Challengers: Jumping into What Scientists Experience

The following activities have been designed to allow you (and your students) to experience the kinds of problems and emotions experienced by scientists. When scientists are engaged in their work, they may not have a clear idea of how to proceed. They may have to develop a new technique or piece of equipment for a field or laboratory observation or experiment. After constructing this new piece of equipment or using a new technique, they may find that it does not work as expected. In the midst of collecting data, they may encounter all sorts of problems, which need to be addressed. Their emotions during investigations may range from total elation to utter frustration and anger. Some of their work may be tedious and boring, while other aspects can be completely engaging and exciting. So, as you approach these activities, be sure to keep a journal in which you can record descriptions and reflections on your experiences, as well as descriptions of your methods and approaches, your data, and your interpretations. (If you have not read Chapter 3, you should do so before proceeding.)

In contrast to the previous activities, where explicit instructions are provided, the following activities do not have such instructions. You will need to draw on your own creativity, imagination, and resourcefulness. Keep in mind that coming up with a right answer is not necessarily the most important aspect of these activities. What you should be learning about involves

- The nature of scientific inquiry and what scientists experience
- The processes of approaching and solving problems and conducting inquiry
- How your mind works as you encounter and solve problems, deal with emotions, collect data, interpret your data, and so forth

When using these activities in your own classroom, you may wish to do one of them (or one of your own design) as a starting point for a particular unit or at some point during a particular unit. You also may want to introduce them as a unit in themselves, where you emphasize examinations of the nature of science. In such a case, you may divide up the class into groups, then have each group work on one task at a time, while making sure the students assume the roles of *competing laboratories*. In this scenario, they will need to be cautious of "industrial espionage" and keep their work secret. Another alternative is to introduce all of the activities as a *lottery*. The rules for each of these latter two scenarios and the more general rules and guidelines that can be used with your students are described below. These guidelines are for you and should be adapted for particular classroom use.

### G.9.1   Competing Laboratory Rules and Guidelines

- Each group is a separate scientific lab competing to come up with a solution to the problem. Watch out for corporate spies from the other labs!
- Each lab has two weeks to complete their task and come up with a solution.
- At the end of two weeks, each lab will be asked to present their results to an audience. These presentations are formal and should include visual aids (videos, photographs, drawings, graphs, charts, etc.). The presentations should utilize PowerPoint or another presentation software program, an overhead projector, or large posters that are readable from a distance.

*Time limits* are an important part of these activities. Scientists are often put under pressure to complete an investigation within a specified time to meet the deadlines of grants, and so forth.

*Competition* is common in science, as scientists vie to be the first to come up with a particular idea or theory, product, process, and so forth. The results of their research are used in competing for additional grant funding.

*Espionage* is of great concern, especially in corporate laboratory settings. However, spying on and stealing others' ideas can be problematic in any scientific setting. Watson and Crick, who were awarded the Nobel Prize for determining the structure of DNA, "stole" the idea of a double helix from Linus Pauling.

The audience may include outside evaluators. *External evaluators* are often used during grant work to assess the quality of the research being conducted.

However, all scientific work is evaluated by other scientists prior to publication or presentation at conferences. Parents can be used to act as evaluators during an evening conference presentation. Other children from upper grades can be asked to attend and act as evaluators. The external evaluators should be asked to evaluate each presentation with positive comments and constructive criticism.

### G.9.2 Lottery Approach Rules and Guidelines

- Each group will be responsible for completing each topic lottery.
- Each group will blindly draw a topic lottery card.
- Once drawn, each group may have the option to trade in its card for another from the teacher (if additional cards are available), but the second card must be kept (you cannot backtrack and go with your first card *and* you cannot draw a third card).

*Risk taking and risk management* are a part of doing science. Scientists apply for grants, which involve a great deal of time and effort. Do they take a risk to apply for one grant competition (highly competitive, but more money) or another competition (less competitive, but less money)? However, other risks are quite common as well. Do you proceed with one line of inquiry, which could yield valuable results, but which is time-consuming, expensive, and highly risky in terms of actually producing results? Or do you proceed with a tried-and-true line of inquiry, which may not yield the potentially exciting results of the other line of inquiry.

### G.9.3 General Rules and Guidelines

- You must complete the task as stated and keep a regular log and reflection.
- The teacher may or may not answer your questions. Any answers will not be intentionally misleading or erroneous. Questions about the final answer, and so forth, will not be answered.
- The intent of working on these tasks is to provide a problem to solve, which may involve experiencing a variety of emotions (e.g., frustration, anger, joy, etc.). In addition, each of these tasks incorporates certain aspects of what is encountered in doing science.
- All tasks most likely can be solved within the physical setting of the school or home and surrounding areas.
- You must do the task (not find the results from other sources).
- Do not look up information from secondary or tertiary sources, such as websites, textbooks, articles, encyclopedias, and so forth, unless told to do so in the task instructions.
- *You must follow all rules.* Following rules means following the rules as stated. You may add other rules, but keep in mind that the important part of rules is what is not included in the rules. Grant competitions have strict rules and guidelines. The scientific community has both explicit and implicit rules for conducting valid inquiry. However, we often unconsciously impose rules on ourselves in the form of particular

assumptions. "Thinking out of the box" involves not being constrained by our assumptions. Creativity often arises from not being constrained in this way and is a major factor in being a successful scientist.

### G.9.4 The Tasks

*G.9.4.1 How Fast Does a Crow or Raven (or Other Large Bird) Fly?*

Develop two or more procedures to measure how fast a crow or raven flies. Provide a clear description of these procedures along with data to support your claim. Be sure to include a personal log (what you did and thought about in chronological order) and reflection on how science works and the experience of scientists.

*G.9.4.2 What Is the Relationship between the Circumference and Height of Different Tree Species?* Measure the circumference of 10 trees of at least five different species. Devise one or more procedures for measuring the height of these trees. What is the ratio of circumference to height? Does the ratio change with height? Is the ratio different between species? What does this ratio or relationship suggest about why such a relationship exists. Provide a clear description of these procedures along with data to support your claim. Be sure to include a personal log (what you did and thought about in chronological order) and reflection on how science works and the experience of scientists.

*G.9.4.3 How Much Weight Does a Pine Tree's Trunk and Branches Hold?* Select a pine tree (or another approved tree). How much weight (of its pine needles) does this tree hold? Devise one or more procedures for estimating the weight of the needles. Provide a clear description of these procedures along with data to support your claim. Be sure to include a personal log (what you did and thought about in chronological order) and reflection on how science works and the experience of scientists.

*G.9.4.4 Build a Straw and Pipe Cleaner Structure That Is at Least 2 m. Tall and Takes Up No More Than 0.5 × 0.5 m. of Floor Space (Also, It Has to Hold at Least 10 g. of Weight at Its Summit).* Straws can be any length. Pipe cleaners can be only about 2 cm. long, bent into an L shape, and can only be inserted into the ends of the straws. No other materials can be used. Provide a clear description of this structure and a scientific explanation of why it is stable and has vertical strength (holds the 10-g. weight). Be sure to include a personal log (what you did and thought about in chronological order) and reflection on how science works and the experience of scientists.

*G.9.4.5 What People Have Better Hygiene after Using Public Restrooms? Corollary Questions:* What age ranges and sexes wash their hands more often after using restrooms? What is the range and mean time spent washing hands? How many use soap? How much time is needed to wash hands to reduce bacteria by 90% with and without soap (this answer can be investigated or obtained from outside sources)? (At least 15 people in each category need to be observed, i.e., 15 men, 15 women, 15 boys, and 15 girls). Provide a clear description of your procedures along with data to support your claims. Be sure to include a personal log (what you did and thought about in chronological order) and reflection on how science works and the experience of scientists.

*G.9.4.6 Build a Pendulum That Will Swing for at Least 12 h. (24 h. Is Even Better).* Your pendulum cannot receive help from any outside electrical, magnetic, or mechanical source. It can be started with no more than a 30° angle from the vertical. You must provide a scientific explanation for why this pendulum works. Provide a clear description of your procedures along with data to support your claim. Be sure to include a personal log (what you did and thought about in chronological order) and reflection on how science works and the experience of scientists.

*G.9.4.7 What Fish in Our Aquarium (or Another Aquarium) Have the Most Rapid Breathing Rate? What Factors Affect the Breathing Rate of These Fish?* Is there any relationship between breathing rate and other factors, such as size, species, type of activity, and so forth? You can explore other factors, but you *cannot* (a) remove or touch the fish, (b) affect or adjust the water in any way, or (c) do anything that may harm or cause stress to the fish. Construct scientific explanations for your claims. Provide a clear description of your procedures along with data to support your claims. Be sure to include a personal log (what you did and thought about in chronological order) and reflection on how science works and the experience of scientists.

*G.9.4.8 Build a Vehicle (Car) That Will Travel at Least 20 m. and Not Be Powered by Electricity.* Your car can be built with any of a variety of materials, but cannot use any kind of electricity for power. Your car must be no longer than 30 cm. and no wider than 15 cm. The car cannot use a ramp or any kind of initial push. It must lie flat on the floor or ground. You must provide a scientific explanation for why this car works. Provide a clear description of your procedures along with data to support your claim. Be sure to include a personal log (what you did and thought about in chronological order) and reflection on how science works and the experience of scientists.

*G.9.4.9 Build a Working Kite.* Build a kite that will reach at least 15 m. high and stay in the air for at least 5 min. You cannot purchase a kite or use one that is made professionally. The kite can be any size. You must provide a scientific explanation for why your kite works. Provide a clear description of your procedures along with data to support your claim. Be sure to include a personal log (what you did and thought about in chronological order) and reflection on how science works and the experience of scientists.

*G.9.4.10 Determine the Number of Each Kind of Seed in the Jar.* The liter or 4-liter (or 1-gallon) jar contains a variety of birdseeds. Remember that you have a limited amount of time to complete this task. Provide a clear description of your procedures along with data to support your claim. Be sure to include a personal log (what you did and thought about in chronological order) and reflection on how science works and the experience of scientists.

*G.9.4.11  How Much Water Does a Plant Leaf Contain?*  State your claim as the amount of water in grams or milliliters per gram of leaf. You must present convincing evidence for your claim. Use any plant leaf or leaves that are not a cactus or succulent. You can use a succulent, but these leaves can be used only as comparison to the other leaves. Provide a clear description of your procedures along with data to support your claim. Be sure to include a personal log (what you did and thought about in chronological order) and reflection on how science works and the experience of scientists.

*G.9.4.12  What Are the Percolation Rates of Different Soils in Our Area?*  Determine the percolation rates for at least four different soils in our area as liters per square meter per minute. What are the implications for flooding and agriculture or gardening. Provide a clear description of your procedures along with data to support your claim. Be sure to include a personal log (what you did and thought about in chronological order) and reflection on how science works and the experience of scientists.

*G.9.4.13  What Color Car Is the Coolest in the Summer?*  Summers are hot. If you intend to buy a car, what color would be the coolest? Provide your own convincing scientific evidence to support what color, if any, your car should be (if you want the coolest car to get into after it has been sitting in the sun). Provide a clear description of your procedures along with data to support your claims. Be sure to include a personal log (what you did and thought about in chronological order) and reflection on how science works and the experience of scientists.

*G.9.4.14  How Can You Wire a Room So That Switches at Either End of the Room Will Turn a Light On and Off?*  You have a room with two doors at either end and a switch at either end (you can build a model room). You need to wire the room so that the switches on either side will turn the light on and off (so, if one switch is in the "on" position, the other switch will turn off the light and vice versa). Build a battery (one D cell)-operated model and provide a wiring diagram and explanation. Provide a clear description of your procedures along with data to support your claims. Be sure to include a personal log (what you did and thought about in chronological order) and reflection on how science works and the experience of scientists.

After completing one or more of these tasks, think about and discuss with others answers to the following questions:

- What do you think would be the difference between doing these tasks as stated and doing these tasks with explicit instructions on how to do these tasks? Would your learning be any different? Would your understanding of science be any different?

- How do you think children will respond to these tasks in terms of (a) their engagement, (b) their abilities to complete the tasks, and (c) their learning?
- How can your assumptions about children's abilities limit your thinking about doing these activities in your classroom?
- What did you experience and learn about doing science and what scientists experience in their work?
- How can such experiences be used to discuss the nature of science with children?

*Appendix H*

# Data Collection and Analysis Techniques

This appendix is designed to help teachers acquire some of the practical skills required in doing scientific inquiry, particularly in terms of the skills children should develop in collecting and analyzing data. Part H.3 focuses on techniques you can use to analyze data children collect as part of their inquiry.

## H.1  Background

There are two basic types of scientific inquiry: (a) *observational* and (b) *experimental*. There also is a third type, which we can think of as *theoretical*; it includes thought experiments and computer simulations (this area is typical in the areas of quantum chemistry and describes much of the work of Albert Einstein). However, the primary focus in elementary school is with observational and experimental. Although experiments are actually a subset of observations, we will draw a distinction between them based on the descriptions below.

a.  **Observational inquiry** involves the collection of data based on observations of some phenomenon. The data can be numerical, descriptive (i.e., written notes), or diagrammatic (e.g., maps, drawings or sketches, etc.). The data also can be audio or video recorded.

b.  **Experimental inquiry** involves designing an experiment (see Chapter 6 for more details on experimental design), where most variables (or factors) are controlled while one variable is measured as a result of manipulating another variable. An example is measuring how far a toy car pushes a box after running down a ramp. In this case, the slope of the ramp is varied (and the angle is measured as the *independent variable*) and the result (*dependent variable*) is measured as the distance the box has moved.

Even though these two categories of inquiry may seem distinct, some inquiries may be rather fuzzy in terms of whether it is purely observational or purely experimental. For instance, if you and your students are observing the behavior of squirrels around a bird feeder, a student may decide to put a boom box with a CD of rap music playing under the bird feeder to see what happens. It is an interesting idea, where a variable is introduced, but it may or may not be an experiment depending on what data are collected. If the number of attempts by the squirrels to reach the bird feeder are counted before and after the introduction of music are counted, it would be an experiment. However, if the student plays the music and watches what happens to the behavior without collecting clearly defined observational data before and after, it would be more of an observational (playing around) study. When students get an idea and try it out (as playing around), it can provide for the groundwork of designing a more controlled experiment. Other examples of activities typically done in classrooms, which tend to be observations rather than experiments, include (a) egg drop—students build a container to hold an egg, then drop it from some height; (b) placing a hard-boiled egg with its shell removed over the opening of a juice jar after a match has been placed in the jar; (c) measuring the temperature increase of water being heated on a hot plate every 30 s until it boils; (d) building an electrical circuit with a battery, bulb, and pieces of wire; and (e) using a lemon "battery" to light a bulb.

It is important to keep in mind that the questions students or teachers ask will determine what kind of inquiry is required. Please be sure to read Section 6.1 of Chapter 6 for descriptions of types of questions and how they relate to different types of inquiry and other activities.

## H.2 Collecting Data

The following tables provide examples of the types of data that can be collected for particular topics or questions. The information here is only a sampling of the possibilities. However, the tables will provide you with a sense of how to match particular focuses of inquiry to the types of data collection that may be necessary. Keep in mind the difference between qualitative or descriptive data (i.e., data based on observational descriptions), quantitative data (i.e., numerical data based on counts or measurements), and data collected as a result of conducting an experiment (i.e., data that results from controlling many variables while manipulating one variable and measuring or counting the resulting change in another variable).

## H.2.1  Earth Sciences

**TABLE H.1** Apparent or Real Motion of Sun, Moon, and Planets

| Observational | |
|---|---|
| *Descriptive* | *Quantitative* |
| Sky maps | Observation time |
| Visual descriptions | Angle in arc |
| Sketches | Angle from southern horizon |
| | Rise and set times |

**TABLE H.2** Soil Characteristics

| Observational | |
|---|---|
| *Descriptive* | *Quantitative* |
| Descriptions (color, etc.) | Weight per volume |
| Separation by particle size (soil sieves) with description | Weight and volume, then percentage of total sample |
| Soil cores with descriptions, including separation of particles in each layer | Water saturation capacity (total and for each particle size) |
| | Percolation rate (rate for an amount of water to seep into soil over a particular surface area) |

**TABLE H.3** Minerals

| Observational | |
|---|---|
| *Descriptive* | *Quantitative* |
| Descriptions of color, texture, etc | Hardness |
| Reactivity to acid | Mass (weight per unit volume, i.e., grams per cubic centimeter) |
| Crystalline structure, if present | |

**TABLE H.4** Landscape

| Observational | |
|---|---|
| *Descriptive* | *Quantitative* |
| Feature mapping (rock outcroppings, soil differentiation, vegetation, etc.) | Measurement of slopes |
| Soil sampling (see above) | Topographic mapping |
| Satellite images and photographs | |

**TABLE H.5** Erosion

| Observational |
|---|
| *Descriptive* |
| Stream table studies with descriptions and mapping |
| Satellite images and photographs |

| Experimental |
|---|
| Stream table studies with measurements of soil loss while varying soil composition, vegetation, slope, rate of water flow, etc. |

**TABLE H.6** Stream Studies

| Observational | |
|---|---|
| *Descriptive* | *Quantitative* |
| Feature mapping, including locations of rocks, vegetation, bottom features, etc.<br><br>Stream cross section (includes measurements of depth at regular intervals across the stream) (See "Life Sciences," below)<br><br>Satellite images and photographs | Quantitative data mapping, which can include the items below:<br><br>Slope measurements<br><br>Flow rate at different points: (a) surface rate from different locations and (b) estimated volume per minute<br><br>Depth measurements at different locations (See "Life Sciences," below) |

## H.2.2 Life Sciences and Ecology

**TABLE H.7** Animal (and Human) Behavior

| Observational | |
|---|---|
| *Descriptive* | *Quantitative* |
| Mapping, including movement, behaviors, etc.<br><br>Description of naturally occurring behaviors in natural or classroom settings (written descriptions, sketches, videotapes, audio recordings of sounds)<br><br>Locomotion/movement: Description, videos, purpose/activity, anatomical analysis | Behavior occurrence counts (can be combined with mapping and descriptions)<br><br>Reproductive behaviors: Counts of various stages<br><br>Space and distance relationships among individuals of the same species in different situations (e.g., birds on a wire, birds in a flock, birds in a nest, etc.) |
| **Experimental** | |
| Stimulus-response: Introduce variable (stimulus), measure, or describe a particular response<br>Food preference: Food types vs. attraction to food, etc. | |

**TABLE H.8** Anatomy and Physiology (Animals)

| Observational | |
|---|---|
| *Descriptive* | *Quantitative* |
| External anatomical descriptions and sketches (comparative among species is useful), including underlying muscle and bones (as felt on humans)<br><br>Pulse locations (human)<br><br>Nerve ending type (pain, touch, cold, hot, discrimination) mapping (human)<br><br>Heart sound descriptions<br><br>Dissections (as needed of simple animals): Sketching, describing (compare across animal species) | Measurement of sizes and ratios of body parts (see Table H.11)<br><br>Heart rate or breathing rates of different types and sizes of animals |
| **Experimental** | |
| Pulse (and blood pressure) vs. position (lying, sitting, standing)<br>Pulse (and blood pressure) vs. exercise amounts and types (including per minute recovery)<br>Breathing rate vs. position and exercise (including per minute recovery) | |

**TABLE H.9** Anatomy and Physiology (Plants)

### Observational

| Descriptive | Quantitative |
|---|---|
| Plant leaf, flower, stem, root descriptions, sketches, rubbing, photos/scans | Stem/trunk diameter/circumference-to-height ratios |
| Seed dissections with descriptions, sketches | Leaf and fruit shapes with surface-to-volume ratios |
| Chromatography: Grind leaves, mix in alcohol, place 1 to 4 drops on vertical filter paper or hang filter paper strip in solution; describe color separations | |

### Experimental

Aquatic plant photosynthesis: Air bubbles produced (number per minute) vs. light color, intensity, etc.


**TABLE H.10** Reproduction and Growth

### Observational

| Descriptive | Quantitative |
|---|---|
| Descriptions and sketches of snail egg development (under microscope) | Analyses of large variety of animals and the number of offspring per reproductive cycle vs. size and type of organism |
| Descriptions and sketches of egg growth and development stages in insects and other arthropods (butterflies, moths, cockroaches, mealworms, or other available invertebrates, frogs, etc.) | |
| Descriptions and sketches of plant seed dispersal mechanisms | |

### Experimental

Plant seed germination rate under different conditions

Plant growth from seed to various stages of growth under different influences (water, light, temperature, various fertilizers, chemicals, etc.)

**TABLE H.11** Adaptation and Structure-Function Relationships

## Observational

| Descriptive | Quantitative |
|---|---|
| Comparative description of similar structures across a wide variety of animal and plant types—variation in structure versus function for specific organism types (e.g., eyes with cones and rods in humans, multilens eyes in insects, light-sensitive eye spots in flat worms (planaria), immovable eyes in owls, eyes on sides of heads in birds and many fish vs. in front) | Size (length, width, surface area, volume, etc.) of various structures versus their functions and adaptive value (e.g., ears in elephants, humans, dogs, birds, frogs, as well as lack of ears in snakes, etc.); see tubes, sheets, spheres, borders and pores, and so forth, in Appendix D |
| Descriptions of primary and secondary functions (the elephant's nose is used for breathing, picking up food and water, spraying water—which is the adaptation?); human eyes are not an adaptation since eyes are present in a large variety of organisms; primate opposable thumbs are an adaptation for holding and fine-motor manipulation of objects | Appendage shape and size versus speed, maneuverability, and so forth |
| Shape of structures for specific functions (e.g., mouth size and shape, teeth size and shape, etc., vs. food acquisition and ingestion) | |

**TABLE H.12** Ecology (Related to Adaptation and Behavior)

## Observational

| Descriptive | Quantitative |
|---|---|
| Food web observations, descriptions, relationship sketches, and so forth | Population sizes of various organisms within a particular community (count numbers in a particular sample, then apply to whole); dominant species populations in niches |
| Plant and animal structures, functions versus niche (i.e., function and activity within an ecosystem) | Environmental factors (temperature, moisture, pH, etc.) versus species present in various ecosystems |
| Descriptions of interspecies competition and cooperation within an ecosystem or community | Number of different species in different locations (habitats, ecosystems, etc.)—(a) local or regional (from field studies) or (b) from secondary data (online and other sources)—biodiversity |
| Mapping, descriptions, and so forth, of various ecosystems and habitats (focus on definite vs. fuzzy borders as containment, etc.) | Description and counts of habitat diversity and change from maps, satellite imagery, and so forth |
| | Population counts and estimates in various habitats within ecosystem (zonation, etc.) |

## Experimental

Ecological factors (temperature, light, pH, chemicals, numbers of individual species at start-up (e.g., snails, plant species, beetle species, etc.) vs. population growth, population cycles, population survival, etc. (e.g., several pond water aquaria, several terrariums, etc.), subjected to different variables); use invertebrates and plants only

## H.2.3 Physical Sciences

**TABLE H.13** Mechanics, Motion, Forces

### Observational

#### Descriptive

Descriptions of various motions, actions and reactions, collisions, feelings (when experiencing certain motions on playground equipment, etc.)

### Experimental

Force versus motion (speed, direction, distance) of various objects (e.g., toy cars, pendulum bobs, marbles, paper airplanes, toy rockets, etc.)

Force versus motion (reactions) in collisions of different masses (pendulum bobs, marbles, etc.)

Force versus mass in different mechanical systems (ramps, pulleys, gears, wheel and axles, etc.)

Force versus mass versus shape versus velocity (and other variables) in different media (air, water, varying viscosity liquids, etc.)

Frictional forces in mechanical systems—sliding blocks with variables: surface, slope, distance traveled, pulling force, and so forth

Buoyancy versus gravity—variable densities, masses, etc.

**TABLE H.14** Electricity and Magnetism

### Observational

| Descriptive | Quantitative |
|---|---|
| Circuit building and diagramming | Measurement of magnetic forces |
| Descriptions of static electricity effects | Measurements of resistance and conductance (of different materials, etc.) |
| Descriptions and sketches of magnetic effects, lines of force, and so forth | |
| Descriptions of magnetic and nonmagnetic objects | |
| Descriptions of attraction and repulsion of magnets, static electricity | |

### Experimental

Electromagnetic—number of coils versus strength (maximum weight of object lifted)

Electromagnetic—number of coils versus distance of attraction

**TABLE H.15** Light

### Observational

| Descriptive | Quantitative |
|---|---|
| Description of light spectrum (using prisms or simple spectrometers) | Descriptions and sketches of light paths through series of mirrors with angles of reflection |
| Descriptions of color filter interactions | Focal lengths of various lenses |
| Descriptions of lens effects | Ray box—draw lines of light rays to mirrors, lenses, and prisms, then from exit points (extrapolate lines within lenses and prisms) |
| Descriptions of effects of pinhole camera | |

### Experimental

Magnification of light intensity—time to initiate burning of paper versus magnification of lens

Measurement of refraction through various media

Sunlight heat absorption of various materials (color, etc.)

**TABLE H.16** Sound

| Observational | |
|---|---|
| *Descriptive* | *Quantitative* |
| Descriptions of sound from various sources (loudness, pitch, etc.) | Diagram sound wave reflection in tray of water, measure angles |
| Descriptions of sound conductance through various media (liquids, solids, air, string (that is attached to cans at either end—string-can phones)) | |

| Experimental |
|---|
| Sound frequency (with speaker or tuning fork) versus length of wave (measured in tray of water) |
| Pitch versus tautness or length of string (match pitch to tuning forks) |
| Pitch versus volume of air in bottles (blow over top of bottle, match to tuning forks) |
| Different pitch drums and effect on candle flame (placed in opening of drum) or piece of tissue paper hanging from end (measure angular displacement) |

## H.2.4  Metapatterns

Many of the previous data collection approaches are applicable to metapatterns. And many of the data collection approaches below are applicable to the previous areas, as well. See Appendix D for more details on metapatterns.

**TABLE H.17** Structural and Spatial: Sphere, Tubes, Sheets, Border and Pores, Layers, Centers

| Observational | |
|---|---|
| *Descriptive* | *Quantitative* |
| Descriptions of forms, where they occur, their functions, and so forth | Comparisons of surface area–to-volume ratios of different forms |
| | For particular borders, size of pores versus amounts or rates of transfer through pores |

| Experimental |
|---|
| Comparison of strengths of spheres, tubes, sheets (amount of weight to break forms made of same materials) |
| Center of gravity effects on airplane flight, balance, and so forth |

**TABLE H.18** Relational and Contextual: Spheres, Tubes, Sheets, Border and Pores, Layers

| Observational | |
|---|---|
| *Descriptive* | *Quantitative* |
| For a particular situation: Descriptions of spheres as contexts, tubes as relations, sheets as individual layers in hierarchy, layers of functionality, centers as organizers, and so forth | Counts of types and occurrences of interactions as tubular relations |
| | Obstacles or barriers to communication or relationship versus number of occurrences (of interaction, etc.) |

| Experimental |
|---|
| Reaction type to invasion of invisible borders (e.g., standing certain distances from people vs. their reactions) |

**TABLE H.19** Structural and Relational: Centers, Binaries, Breaks, Clusters, Gradients, Webs, Rigidity and Flexibility

| Observational | |
|---|---|
| *Descriptive* | *Quantitative* |
| Description of systems (organisms, social, mechanical, stories, etc.): Specific descriptions of relations between centers (organizers, power centers, etc.); binaries or more complex sets of units (people, ants, etc.); clusters, continuums, and densities (and other aspects that manifest as gradients); webs of relations; rigidity and flexibility in relations and centers; and breaks as transformations and changes | Counts or measurements of centers, numbers in relationships, degree of change, numbers in clusters, degree of gradient, numbers of relationships within web, degree of flexibility or rigidity |

| Experimental |
|---|
| Change or vary some factor in center, binary, and so forth, and describe or measure result to system, and so forth |


**TABLE H.20** Relational: Binaries, Arrows, Triggers

| Observational |
|---|
| *Descriptive* |
| In this case, arrows are directional relationships: Describe or sketch relationships in terms of effects of particular units (organisms, objects) in a particular situation (arrows can be related to power, control, attraction, repulsion, force, etc.) |
| Description of systems and their initiating factors (triggers) in relation to parts (binaries or more complex sets of units) |

| Experimental |
|---|
| Triggers as initiators: Degree of a particular factor versus particular reaction or action |


**TABLE H.21** Temporal and Procedural: Arrows; Time, Calendars, and Clocks; Breaks; Cycles; Emergence; Triggers

| Observational | |
|---|---|
| *Descriptive* | *Quantitative* |
| Descriptions of systems in terms of regularity of time | Measurements of timing, speed, direction of particular events or systems (as arrows or cycles) |
| Descriptions of events in terms of arrows, cycles, and breaks | |
| Descriptions of triggers (initiating factors) for events | |
| Descriptions of emergence of new events or organisms | |

| Experimental |
|---|
| Effects of particular factors (i.e., that cause transformation or change [breaks]) on timing or directions of events or systems (arrows or cycles) |

## H.3 Analyzing Data

There are several approaches to analyzing data that children collect during their investigations in science. Almost all data analysis approaches are attempts to find patterns. However, the first approach, analyzing patterns, is intended for use with broad patterns, such as metapatterns. In fact, metapatterns themselves are useful tools in analyzing data. They can be used to symbolize or represent particular objects, events, and so forth.

### H.3.1 Analyzing Patterns

Our whole world is defined by patterns (including the words you are reading right now). The skills of recognizing and analyzing patterns are important not only in science, but also in all aspects of our lives (e.g., mathematics, reading, writing, social studies, art, etc.). After analyzing patterns of a particular situation or object, children should engage in comparing the patterns to similar patterns in different situations or objects.

**Example:**

**TABLE H.22** Examples of Using Metapatterns to Analyze Various Phenomena

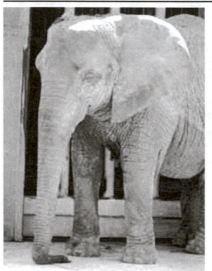

Ears = sheets: capture sounds, surface area
   exposure for cooling
Trunk = tube: transfer of air and water
Trunk = flexible tube: holding, grasping
Legs = tube: vertical structural strength
Body = sphere: containment, reduce surface area
   exposure per volume
Eyes = sphere: allow mult-directional movement

Child: We planted our seed sprouts upside down, but the leaves still grew up and the roots grew down. The leaves must be attracted to the sun and the roots must be attracted to water. (These "attractions" are called tropisms: phototropism and gravitropism.)

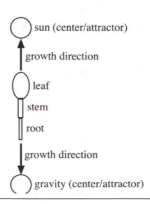

## H.3.2 Categorizing, Classifying, and Grouping

As observational data (descriptions, sketches, photos, or numerical) are collected, they can be sorted into categories, clustered around themes, grouped in a variety of ways, or classified as hierarchical sets of relationships. We typically use these processes in our everyday lives as we try to make sense of our worlds. However, with refinement they can become powerful tools in analyzing scientific data.

**Example:**

**TABLE H.23** Example of a Classification Scheme Based on Beak Structures and Types of Food

| Categorizing and Grouping | Beaks | Food | Bird Examples |
|---|---|---|---|
| Birds with sharp, pointy beaks | Sharp, pointy | insects, worms | robin, woodpecker |
| Birds with bulky, stubby beaks | | fish | tern, cormorant |
| Birds with large, curved beaks | Large, curved | rodents | owl, hawk, eagle |
| Birds with flat, long beaks | Bulky, stubby | seeds | sparrow, finch |
| Birds that eat insects and worms, and so forth | Flat, long | aquatic plants | duck, flamingo |
| Birds that eat rodents | | | |
| Birds that eat aquatic plants | | | |
| Birds that eat fish | | | |
| Birds that eat seeds | | | |

### Classifying

One possible classification of organisms in a pond water aquarium, which were collected from a local pond. In this example, the focus is on understanding the organisms in terms of their subhabitats in relation to their structures and movement. So, the purpose here is not to understand evolutionary relationships, but to understand ecological relationships and adaptations.

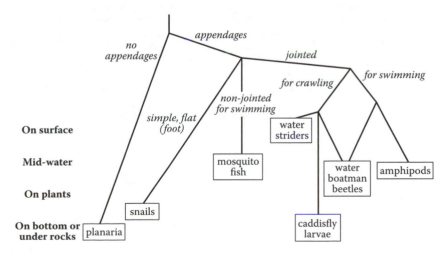

**FIGURE H.3**

## H.3.3 Representing Processes and Systems (Flowcharts, etc.)

The ability to analyze processes and systems is critical to developing complex understandings of our everyday experiences, as well as concepts in science and across the curriculum. Flowcharts and other diagrams can be used to track sequences of steps or stages, cycles, and other processes.

**Example:**

**TABLE H.24** Examples of Flowcharts that Represent Processes and Systemsl

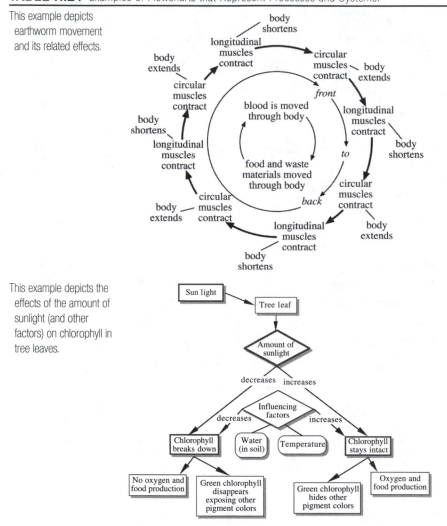

This example depicts earthworm movement and its related effects.

This example depicts the effects of the amount of sunlight (and other factors) on chlorophyll in tree leaves.

## H.3.4 Graphing

Graphing is a powerful, but abstract way of representing data. In order to develop understandings of graphs, it may be helpful to have students begin with physical representations that take them through stages from concrete to abstract representations. For example, if you run cars down a ramp, have students measure the starting distance up the ramp with a piece of string, then use another piece of string to measure the distance traveled from the bottom of the ramp. Draw the vertical and horizontal axes of the graph on a white board, chalkboard, or large piece of butcher paper. Place the start distance strings horizontally from the vertical axis, and then place the distance traveled strings from the right end of the corresponding horizontal strings to the horizontal axis. Label the strings and the points along the axes. Draw a line that connects the intersection points of the strings.

**Example:**

**string graph**

In addition, it is important to use specific types of graphs to represent specific kinds of data. The following is a list of graph types and the data that are most appropriate for each type of graph, along with an example. Remember that it is important to always label graphs.

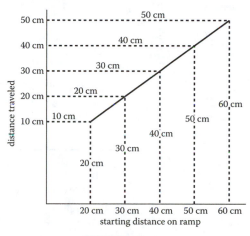

**FIGURE H.6**

**TABLE H.25** Three Common Types of Graphs

Bar Graphs
Used to represent data that involve categories (sex, species, etc.) and
the number of units in categories.

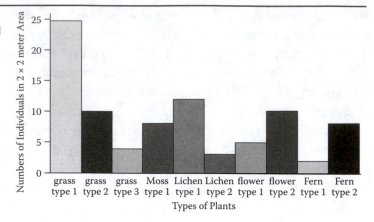

Line Graphs
Used to represent data that are continuous. You may record specific
points, but such graphs can indicate where other points could occur
along the continuum. Data are plotted as points that intersect from
the x-axis and y-axis. It is important to place the dependent variable
(the variable that is measured as a result of varying the independent
variable) along the y-axis. The independent variable is placed along
the x-axis (horizontal line).

Population of earthworms in classroom worm farm:

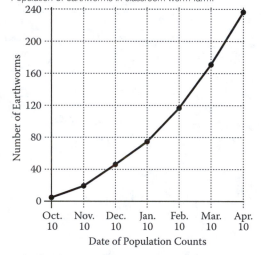

Pie Charts
Used to represent data that involve categories (see "Bar Graphs,"
above). However, rather than numbers in each category, pie charts
represent the data as percentages of the whole.

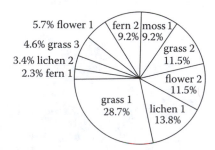

## H.3.5  Diagramming and Drawing

Diagrams provide a way to simplify and represent data from a variety of inquiry activities.

**Example:**

**TABLE H.26**  Examples of Drawings and Diagrams that Represent Data

Sketch of a hydra with labels

Electrical circuit diagram:

Flashlight beam reflection diagram:

## H.3.6 Mapping

Mapping can be used to analyze patterns of behavior of organisms, as well as geological and ecological patterns. Students can draw their own maps or use commercially available maps, depending upon the particular inquiry.

**Example:**

Topographic map that students can create:

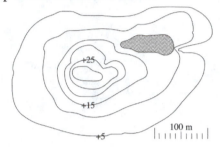

Map of squirrel behavior over 15 min:

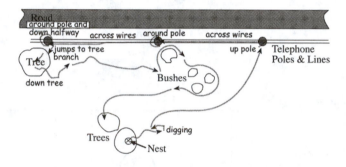

## H.3.7 Analyzing Relationships

Developing organizational schemes for analyzing the relationship among various groups of data or information is important. There are many ways of organizing data. However, one simple approach is a grid, as depicted below.

**Example:**

**TABLE H.27** Example Grid for Analyzing Relationships (Tubular Structures and Functions)

| Tubular Structures: / Functions: | Lengthwise Strength | Transport of Materials | Transport of Information | Penetration | Moderate Surface Area Exposure for Volume | Other |
|---|---|---|---|---|---|---|
| Earthworm body | | | | X | X | |
| Snake body | | | | X | X | X |
| Plant root | | X | | X | X | X |
| Pine needle | | | | | X | X |
| Telephone pole | X | | | | | X |
| Telephone wire | | | X | | | |
| Sink drain pipe | | X | | | | |
| Highway | | X | | | | |
| Elephant trunk | | X | | | | X |

In this example, you can add codes for other characteristics, such as flexibility, rigidity, biological, technological, and so forth. As you work with these kinds of arrays or grids of information, you begin to see patterns that may not have been evident beforehand.

## H.3.8 Modeling

As discussed in a number of chapters, modeling is a process we all use to make sense of our world. However, the real power of models in terms of analyzing data and learning needs to be addressed more explicitly. Models are useful in describing processes, such as the electrical circuit shown above. Models can be drawn, constructed as three-dimensional representations, or constructed as scaled-down working representations. Developing such models can provide a way of testing one's explanations for how a particular system works.

**Example:**

**TABLE H.28** Examples of Models

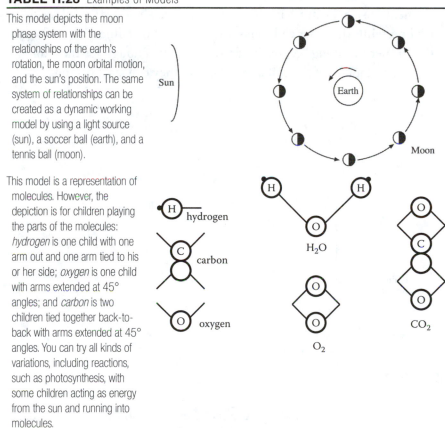

This model depicts the moon phase system with the relationships of the earth's rotation, the moon orbital motion, and the sun's position. The same system of relationships can be created as a dynamic working model by using a light source (sun), a soccer ball (earth), and a tennis ball (moon).

This model is a representation of molecules. However, the depiction is for children playing the parts of the molecules: *hydrogen* is one child with one arm out and one arm tied to his or her side; *oxygen* is one child with arms extended at 45° angles; and *carbon* is two children tied together back-to-back with arms extended at 45° angles. You can try all kinds of variations, including reactions, such as photosynthesis, with some children acting as energy from the sun and running into molecules.

## H.3.9 Calculating and Simple Statistics

For many science inquiries, we work with measurements and counting. Working with numbers is an important part of trying to find patterns in the data. The following information not only is important for doing science, but also provides relevance for learning particular mathematics skills.

*H.3.9.1 Measurement Error* Measurement error plagues all of science. Such errors are dealt with in one of two ways: (a) highly refined instruments that reduce but do not eliminate measurement error and (b) repeated measurements in multiple trials of experiments, from which the mean (average) value is then determined. In the classroom you can demonstrate measurement error, then have children think about how they can reduce the error (of course, the highly refined instruments are not going to be an option).

### Example 1:

Provide meter sticks to each student or group of students, then have them measure the height of the same table to the nearest 0.5 mm.

### Example 2:

Go outside and have one child run a particular distance (20 or 30 m). Provide the other children (individually or in groups) with stopwatches or watches with second hands. Have them measure how long it takes the runner to reach the finish line. Have two children hold a string at the finish line, while the other children stand near the finish line. You can start the runner by saying "get ready, get set, go" loud enough for the runner to hear and for all of the children to hear so they can start timing.

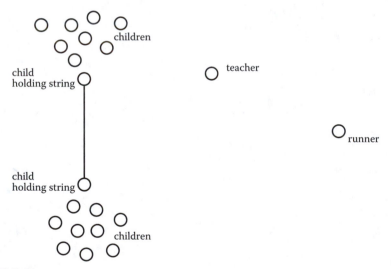

**FIGURE H.12**

*H.3.9.2 Estimating* Estimating numbers, heights, and distances is a useful skill. Estimating numbers is useful in determining how many birds are in a large flock, how many plants are in a large area, and so forth. Estimating heights of large objects and large distances is helpful when involved in field studies, where you may be interested in determining the heights of trees, the distances between particular land features, and so forth.

*H.3.9.2.1    Estimating Numbers*    Make a little viewer out of cardboard, with several different-size squares cut out. The sizes could be about 2.5 × 2.5

cm. and 6 × 6 cm. The two sizes can be used for different types of situations (counting a cluster of small organisms in a sample of water or counting the number of blackbirds in a large flock). Count the number of objects or organisms in one of the squares, then estimate how many squares worth of objects or organisms there are.

*H.3.9.2.2   Estimating Heights and Distances*   Take an object (could be you or a child) of known height (or width, where the height of a person is the same as the distance from fingertip to fingertip with arms outstretched). Stand fairly far away, then use your hand or part of your hand to measure against the known object to estimate the height or distance.

### H.3.9.3  Simple Statistics

*H.3.9.3.1     Measurements of Central Tendency*

Mean, median, and mode can provide some interesting information on how numbers are skewed. It is interesting that claims, such as "the mean income has increased in the past year," can be misleading. The mean can increase, but the median could decrease. In such a case, the rich may have gotten much richer, while there was a big increase in the number of people whose incomes decreased. The points at the top of the income scale vastly increased in income, but the numbers of individuals making less increased. The increase in income offsets the increase in numbers of people making less.

**TABLE H.29** Example Mean, Median, Mode Calculations

**An example set of data:**
**Bean plant growth after 4 weeks (measured in centimeters and from 20 bean plants):**
**2, 5, 7, 7, 9, 10, 10, 11, 12, 13, 13, 13, 15, 16, 16, 16, 16, 17, 20, 24 cm**

Mean

The mean is the average. Divide the sum of the numbers by the number of incidences. Means are useful in reducing the effect of measurement errors by doing the same experiment several times (the more the better). The mean also is useful in determining the central point in a range or spread of numbers.

Total (of data set) = 253253 ÷ 20 = 12.65 (the mean)

Median

The median is the halfway point in the range of numbers. Half of the results are above and half are below the median. In contrast, the mean may be skewed higher or lower, depending upon how many points (numbers) are clustered higher or lower. If the median point on an even set of numbers comes out between two numbers, select the midway point between the two numbers (e.g., in our data set of 20 numbers, the median is 13, but if the 10th number was 12 and the 11th number was 15, then the median would be 13.5).

The 10th number is 13 and the 11th number is 13; therefore, median = 13

Mode

The mode is where the most points occur. In our data set we can show our points as

```
                              16
                  13          16
        7    10   13          16
   2  5 7  9 10 11 12 13 15 16 17 20 24
```

Mode = 16

The mode is interesting in seeing just how and where numbers are clustered. In a bimodal skew, where there are two modes at either end of the spectrum, the mean or median may not tell us as much about the skew as seeing the two modes at either end with very little in between. In the case of the increased mean income, the mode is at the lower salary scale.

*H.3.9.4 Probability*  How likely is it that some particular thing is going to happen? This question refers to probability. Determining the probability of something happening provides us with a tool for predicting what may happen given certain conditions. The examples below will help to clarify how you can use probability.

### Example: Eye Color in Offspring

B = brown, which is dominant; b = blue (lack of pigment), which is recessive:

| mother / father | B | b |
|---|---|---|
| b | Bb | bb |
| b | Bb | bb |

| mother / father | B | B |
|---|---|---|
| b | Bb | Bb |
| b | Bb | Bb |

**FIGURE H.13**

In the left grid, the mother has a recessive gene for blue pigment, but her eyes are brown, since brown is dominant. The father has blue eyes (two recessive genes for blue). They have a 50:50 probability of having children with blue eyes. In the right grid, the mother has two genes for brown eyes. The probability of having children with blues eyes is zero.

### Example: Flipping Two Coins

H = heads; T = tails:

|  | H | T |
|---|---|---|
| **H** | H-H | H-T |
| **T** | H-T | T-T |

**FIGURE H.14**

In this grid, we see that the following probabilities occur: 25% heads-heads, 50% heads-tails, and 25% tails-tails. You can extend this grid to dealing with three, four, or more coins or whatever types of variables you wish to analyze in terms of probability.

The interesting aspect of probabilities is that the probability of something happening in a particular situation is the same for each instance. For example, with coin flipping, you toss two coins and you get a heads and a tails. What is the probability of getting a heads and a tails on the next try? It is the same—a 50% chance to get a heads and a tails. Over many tries, you would expect to get a distribution close to 25% heads-heads, 25% tails-tails, and 50% heads-tails.

## H.4 | Formulas and Conversions

The formulas and conversions provided here may be useful to introduce to students as they work with a variety of inquiries. Although the math involved may be beyond their current learning, if their questions lead them to needing to know how to calculate something, then you should provide them with the appropriate formula. For instance, if they need to know how to calculate the volume and surface area of a sphere to compare with that of a tube, you can provide them with the formulas.

### Formulas:

A = area; V = volume; P = perimeter; C = circumference; l = length,; w = width; b = base; h = height; r = radius; d = diameter; $\pi$ = pi (3.1416).

### Area:

**TABLE H.30** Some Common Formulas for Calculating Area

| | | |
|---|---|---|
| Triangle: $A = 1/2\, bh$ | Rectangle: $A = lw$ (square $= w^2$) | Circle: $A = \pi r^2$ |
| Sphere: $A = 4\pi r^2$ | Cylinder (tube—including ends): $A = \pi dh + 2\pi r^2$ | Cube: $A = 6w^2$ |

For irregular shapes, like a leaf, place the object on graph paper. Trace the shape, then count the squares. For the partial squares, make estimates by combining them into complete squares.

### Perimeter/Circumference:

**TABLE H.31** Formulas for Calculating the Perimeter or Circumference

| | | |
|---|---|---|
| Polygons: Add length of each side | Circle: $C = 2\pi r$ | For irregular shapes, use a piece of string to go around the shape, then measure the length needed to go around the shape. |

### Volume:

**TABLE H.32** Some Common Formulas for Calculating Volume

| | | |
|---|---|---|
| Sphere: $V = (4/3)\, \pi r^3$ | Cylinder: $V = \pi r^2 h$ | Cube: $V = lwh$ (or w) |
| Cone: $V = (1/3)\, \pi r^2 h$ | Pyramid: $V = 1/3Ah$ (A = area of 1 side) | |

For irregular shapes or for any shape, place a container large enough to hold the object in a large tray, bucket, or tub. Fill the container completely with water to the point where it starts to overflow. Sponge up any of the water that overflows. Then place the object into the container. If the object floats, press down (with a very thin object, such as a pin) until the object is completely submerged. Pour the water that overflowed into a graduated cylinder or measuring cup with the finest gradations possible.

**Conversions:**

A = area; V = volume; P = perimeter; C = circumference; l = length,; w = width; b = base; h = height; r = radius; d = diameter; π = pi (3.1416).

**Length/Distance:**

**TABLE H.33** Metric and U.S. Standard Measurements of Distance Conversions

| | | | |
|---|---|---|---|
| 1 cm. = 0.39 in. | 1 in. = 2.54 cm | 1 m = 1 yd + 3.37 in. | 1 yd = 0.91 m |
| 1 m = 39.37 in. | 1 ft = 30.48 cm | 1 km = 0.62 mile | 1 mile = 1.609 km |

**Area:**

**TABLE H.34** Metric and U.S. Standard Measurements of Area Conversions

| | |
|---|---|
| 1 m² = 10.76 ft² | 1 ft² = 929 cm² |

**Volume:**

**TABLE H.35** Metric and U.S. Standard Volume Measurement Conversions

| | | |
|---|---|---|
| 1 liter = 1.057 quarts | 1 quart = 0.946 liter | 1 U.S. gallon = 3.785 liters |

**Temperature:**

**TABLE H.36** Freezing and Boiling Points of Water in Celsius and Fahrenheit.

| | Celsius | Fahrenheit |
|---|---|---|
| Freezing point of water at sea level = | 0°C | 32°F |
| Boiling point of water at sea level = | 100°C | 212°F |
| | 1°C | 1.8°F |
| | 10°C | 18°F |

**Weight:**

**TABLE H.37** Metric and U.S. Standard Weight Measurements and Conversions

| | | | |
|---|---|---|---|
| 1 g = 0.036 oz | 1 oz = 28 g | 1 lb = 16 oz | 1 kg = 1000 g |
| 1 kg = 2.2 lb | 1 lb = 453 g | | |

## H.5 Summary

With all of these approaches to data collection and analysis, you need to gain experience using them. As you work on planning a variety of inquiry projects, try using the material in the appendix prior to implementing instruction with children. As they encounter situations in their investigations, you will then be able to guide them to the appropriate techniques.

*Appendix I*

# Science Techniques

## I.1   Collecting and Keeping Organisms

The following techniques for making equipment and conducting inquiry are some of the more common ones you may find useful in facilitating your classroom inquiry community. Although explicit instructions are provided, you may want to experiment with the designs and procedures. Local conditions and available tools and materials may require that you make modifications. Also, if you have Native American students or students from other cultural backgrounds, please make sure that the animals you keep in the classroom will be permissible within the culture.

### I.1.1   Finding and Keeping Spiders

*I.1.1.1   Collecting*   House and garden spiders are probably the easiest to collect and keep. Make sure the kind you collect are web-spinning spiders. If a spider is dangling from a silk thread, run your hand above the spider so that the thread sticks to your hand. Carry the spider to a jar and lower the spider into it. If the spider is on a web, gently knock the web and spider into a jar.

*I.1.1.2   Keeping*   You can use a leaky aquarium with a glass or screen top as a cage, or you can try building a cage from scrap lumber and screen. The cage should be large enough to accommodate a large web, at least 30 × 30 × 30 cm.(1 ft³). Whatever type of cage you come up with, make sure there are no cracks through which the spider can escape. Place a piece of foam rubber in a jar lid and soak with sugar water (this provides water for the spider to drink) on the bottom of the cage. Add tree branches if you want. Feed the spiders with live houseflies or fruit flies.

### I.1.2 Finding and Keeping Mealworms

*I.1.2.1 Collecting*  Mealworms are the larvae of the *Tenebrio* beetle. Look for the *Tenebrio* beetle in corn cribs or granaries. Or, if you prefer, buy some at your local pet store.

*I.1.2.2 Keeping*  Put 5 to 10 cm. (2 to 4 in.) of bran meal and a potato (for moisture) in the bottom of a plastic tub. As the potato dries out, replace it with a fresh one. Place a thin layer of shredded paper over the bran meal on which the beetles can crawl. Add 25 to 50 beetles and cover the tub. The beetles start laying eggs 7 to 10 days after they emerge. The eggs hatch in about two weeks. The larvae can be used for fish and other vertebrate food or for study in class. When the larvae grow to about 2.5 cm, they pupate. Adults emerge in two to three weeks.

### I.1.3 Finding and Keeping Earthworms

*I.1.3.1 Collecting*  There are two methods of collecting earthworms. One way is to dig carefully through leafy, rich soil. The second way is to go out at night after a rain to a grassy area. While standing, use a flashlight to spot earthworms stretched out along the surface of the ground. As you crouch down, point the flashlight slightly off to the side so that the beam is not directly on the worm. Grab the worm firmly and pull gently until the worm loosens its hold in its burrow. Collect only undamaged worms. A third alternative is to go to a bait store and buy worms.

*I.1.3.2 Keeping*  For short periods (i.e., overnight) you can keep worms in a closed container (with holes in the lid) along with some freshly cut grass. For longer periods, set up containers with at least a cubic foot of the following soil mixture for every 50 worms. The soil mixture should contain equal parts of old leaves and leafy loam soil (from the woods). The soil in your container should be 20 to 30 cm. (8 to 12 in.) deep. Keep the soil moist but not saturated. Worms eat the leaves, so you do not have to feed them. Check and remove any dead worms every week or so. Ideally, keep the worms in a cool room (10 to 15°C). Keep the container covered, but not airtight.

### I.1.4 Keeping Houseflies

The instructions below are a bit complicated. Try using easily available items and not separating eggs and larvae. See what happens. Make the project a class investigation into the life cycle and appropriate conditions for houseflies.

You will need a screen cage to hold the houseflies. It should be at least 30 cm. (12 in.) in each dimension. See the diagram below for an example.

Food and water should be available at all times. A simple food (dry mixture) can consist of 10 g. sugar, 10 g. powdered milk, and 2 g. dried yeast all

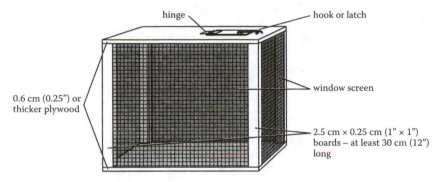

Labels on figure:
hinge
hook or latch
0.6 cm (0.25") or thicker plywood
window screen
2.5 cm × 0.25 cm (1" × 1") boards – at least 30 cm (12") long

**FIGURE I.1**

mixed together. Put this mixture in a petri dish or other flat dish and place it in the cage. For a water mixture, pour 2.5% sugar solution over 1 cup of wood shavings in a shallow tray. The solution should not cover the shavings, but it should be reachable.

*I.1.4.1   Raising Houseflies*   The flies will need a medium in which to lay eggs. You can provide such a medium by placing a small amount of baking soda in a depression in the center of the wood shavings (in the shallow tray on the bottom of the cage). The larvae (maggots) will require their own medium, which may be created by following these instructions:

1. Thoroughly mix together some powdered milk, bran, and pine shavings.
2. Add corn syrup at 50 ml. (3 tablespoons + 1 teaspoon) per liter of dry mixture.
3. Add water to make a moist mash (too much water makes the medium too heavy and can drown the larvae).
4. Put the medium in a wide-mouthed 4-liter (1-gallon) jar.
5. Place the eggs on the medium and cover with a few wet shavings.

The larvae should hatch and mature in 7 to 10 days at room temperature. Pupation will occur in the larval container if allowed to dry a little. Then the pupae can be collected by floating them in water. Allow the pupae to air-dry, and then place them in the screen cage. A life cycle takes 19 days at 21°C or 12 days at 27°C.

## I.1.5   Finding and Keeping Ants

*I.1.5.1   Collecting*   Look under large rocks for ants. The ones found there develop colonies near the surface, so they are easy to dig up. Dig down deeply to be sure to get the entire colony, especially the queen. Put the soil and ants into a large bucket or tub. Use a small hobbyist paint brush to pick up ants and transfer them to a closed container. You can use a kitchen strainer to assist in sifting through the soil. Make sure you have the queen ant (the largest), above all others.

Place as large a jar as possible inside a wide-mouthed 4-liter (1-gallon) jar (keeps ants near the glass). Surround the jar with black construction paper, which can be lifted off to view the ants. Fill the gallon jar with a mixture

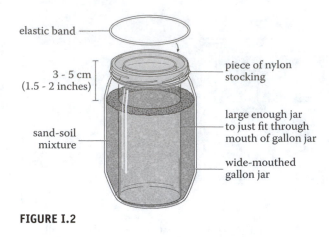

elastic band

3 - 5 cm
(1.5 - 2 inches)

sand-soil
mixture

piece of nylon
stocking

large enough jar
to just fit through
mouth of gallon jar

wide-mouthed
gallon jar

**FIGURE I.2**

of sand and soil. Keep the soil slightly moist. Leave 3 to 5 cm. (1.5 to 2 in.) of space at the top. Place a small piece of foam rubber cut to fit in a small lid (4 to 5 cm. (1.5 to 2 in.) in diameter) and wet with sugar water (a water source for your ants). Be sure to keep this sponge wet. Place food scraps or dead insects on top of soil mixture. Place ants inside. Cover with a piece of nylon stocking and an elastic band.

### I.1.6   How to Make a Terrarium

Use a wide-mouthed 4-liter (1-gallon) jar or aquarium of any size. Set it up according to the diagram below, then add small plants, ferns, mosses, lichens, decorative rocks, and so forth. If you are using a larger aquarium, you also can put in a small lizard, frog, land snail, or salamander. Be sure to embed a small bowl into the soil, so that there is a small pond. Do not keep the terrarium in direct sunlight if you are keeping animals in it. Place a sheet of clear, heavy plastic or Plexiglas (the lid of a 4-liter or gallon jar) over the top. Animals in terraria require some care, such as feeding and replacing water in the pond; otherwise, terraria are pretty much self-sufficient.

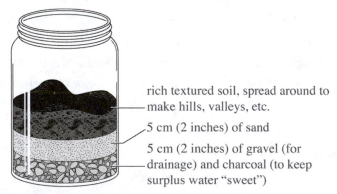

rich textured soil, spread around to
make hills, valleys, etc.

5 cm (2 inches) of sand

5 cm (2 inches) of gravel (for
drainage) and charcoal (to keep
surplus water "sweet")

**FIGURE I.3**

### I.1.7   Setting up a Balanced (or Semibalanced) Aquarium

Natural, balanced aquaria not only are easy to set up and maintain, but are fascinating arenas for observation and investigation. Clean any size aquarium or gallon jar. Collect enough clear water from a pond to fill the aquarium. Collect snails and vascular plants (duckweed and elodea with long leafy strands and roots). You also can collect small fish. Keep enough fish so there is no more than one small fish per 2 to 4 liters of water. Collect some bottom material (sand and gravel). Use kitchen strainers to sift through vegetation and bottom muck for aquatic insects and other tiny organisms.

The populations of aquatic organisms will change over time. Some water beetles may last for several weeks or months; others will die off rather quickly. The mosquito fish are common and much like guppies. You may need to feed them a few times a week with commercial fish food. Try not to overload the aquarium with any one kind of plant or animal. The idea is to find a balance. Finding this balance is a good project for you and your students to work on. Remember that the plants supply the oxygen and the snails help clean the aquarium.

## I.1.8 Setting up and Maintaining a Simple Marine Aquarium

Marine aquaria are more difficult to maintain than freshwater aquaria; however, if you live in an area near the ocean, you can set up a simple and easy-to-maintain aquarium with local specimens.

*I.1.8.1 Initial Setup and Planning* Before collecting specimens for your aquarium, you need to do some preplanning. Make sure you have a large, all-glass aquarium. The larger the better, but a 38-liter (10-gallon) tank is fine to start with (smaller ones will work, but will only allow for a few specimens). Make sure the aquarium is clean.

- For a small aquarium, you can use a filter that hangs over the side. Purchase bio-balls, which are made of layers of plastic with spaces between each layer. Place these into the filter container, then place the included sponge on top. Both the bio-balls and sponge provide places for bacteria to grow and act as biological filters. The sponge also will catch other particular matter. Clean the sponge every month by squeezing and rinsing it out with water from your aquarium (never use tap water, which will kill the bacteria). For a larger aquarium, you should add a canister filter. These filters will sit on the floor, with an intake and output hose going into the aquarium. Fill this filter with the same types of materials. Do not use charcoal in a marine aquarium. For both types of filters, you will need to take apart the filters and clean the impellers (a propeller with a magnetic shaft). The impellers get dirty with use and will stop working. Remove the impeller and clean in tap water.
- Make sure the gravel has been cleaned prior to purchase. If not, rinse and boil the gravel.
- Place a cover over the aquarium. If you do not purchase one that fits, make one out of Plexiglas or other type of plastic (glass can be dangerous and should be avoided, if possible).
- You also may find it useful to have a thermometer, a hydrometer (for measuring the salinity), a couple of aquarium nets of different sizes, and an aquarium scraper or scrubby made for aquarium cleaning (not the kitchen variety, which contains chemicals that will kill your organisms).
- Find an area where you can find some safely accessible tidal pools. Ask around or do some exploring.

- Buy a tide table (or find one online) and find the times when it is convenient to schedule a collecting trip at low tide. Note that the times in many tide tables are in standard time, so add an hour to the times during the summer (some tide tables use Greenwich mean time, which you will need to adjust to your particular time zone).
- Gather together enough containers (4 to 20 liters (1 to 5 gallons)) with tight lids to carry water to fill your aquarium. Use a number of small containers rather than one or two big ones—water is heavy! If possible, take back more water than you need. Keep the extra water as a reserve and store it in the dark. Then change about 5-10% of the water every couple of weeks.
- Take along a slightly larger container for transporting specimens. If it is hot when you make your collecting trip, you may want to transport specimens in a large plastic or foam cooler. Add an ice pack if your drive is longer than an hour.

*I.1.8.2   Collecting*

☞

**Some of the best specimens to collect are:**
- ✦ Starfish
- ✦ Sea anemones
- ✦ Sea urchins
- ✦ Hermit crabs (and other kinds)
- ✦ Snails (e.g., periwinkles)

*I.1.8.2.1      Equipment*
- Plastic kitchen strainers (with handles)
- Purchased or home-made nets (long handles may be very useful)
- Assorted plastic trays and containers

*I.1.8.2.2      Safety*   Be careful when working around tidal pools:
- Waves can come up without warning and knock you over and drag you into the rocks.
- The rocks can be very slippery, especially ones that appear greenish, reddish, or black.
- Barnacles and mussels are sharp and can produce extremely nasty cuts.
- Protect yourself from the sun.
- Take some cotton garden gloves (to protect your hands against cuts from barnacles, sea urchins, rocks, etc.).
- Wear old sneakers you do not mind getting wet (to protect your feet).

Collect just enough specimens for the size of your aquarium. The general rule for fish is about 3 cm. of fish for 16 liters of water (1 in. of fish for every 4-5 gallons of water). You can probably get by with more specimens than that for slow-moving invertebrates. The tendency when you are out in the field is to collect the biggest specimens and a lot of them. Keep the size and numbers down. Do not overcrowd. You can always add more later. *Do not* collect any kind of plant (algae). Saltwater plants are very difficult to keep alive. They die quickly and poison the aquarium. Keep in mind that crabs will devastate any kind of pretty setting you might want to create in your aquarium. Be prepared. Snails are helpful in keeping the aquarium clean, as are clams. However, clams are a favorite food of starfish. Sea anemones eat fish. If you have a few different kinds of fish, you will soon find out which ones eat other fish.

Be sure not to let your newly collected specimens sit out in the sun too long before you transport them. In fact, you may want to keep them in a net that is tied off or hung over the tidal pool water. Rapid rises in temperature may kill your specimens. Also, warmer water holds less dissolved oxygen than cooler water. Collect the water in which the specimens are to be transported just before you leave.

*I.1.8.3  Maintaining*  When you return to your classroom, fill the aquarium and place your specimens in the tank. Specimens collected from tidal pools tend to be quite hardy and tolerant of changes in temperature and salinity. However, you will need to keep both of these factors fairly constant. Keep the aquarium out of direct sunlight—this will reduce the chances of the water temperature rising too high and will cut down on algae growth. You can tape a piece of black paper on the back side of the aquarium if it is sitting near a window. As soon as you set up the aquarium, mark the water level on the outside of the glass with a wax pencil or marker. As the water evaporates, you can add dechlorinated tap water to keep the level constant. By regulating the water level, you are keeping the salinity relatively constant (the water evaporates and leaves the salt, thus raising the salinity). If you have a hydrometer, you should record the level when you first set up the aquarium, in order to keep a more accurate record of salinity (you could write this on the glass as well). In general, the salinity, which is read as the specific gravity, should be between 1.018 and 1.022. The low range is usually healthier for the organisms. Also, it is highly recommended that you change about a quarter of your aquarium water every month. Remove the water with siphons, jars, or buckets, then add freshly collected salt water. Be sure to allow the water temperature of the new water to change to within a couple degrees of the aquarium water. If you cannot collect fresh seawater, you can purchase sea salt from an aquarium store. Mix the salt with dechlorinated tap water that has been allowed to sit long enough to change to room temperature. Make sure the salinity is the same as the aquarium water.

☞

**As time proceeds, be sure to remove any dead specimens immediately. The first few days are critical. Any specimens that live beyond the first few days to a week are likely to last.**

You can feed the invertebrate specimens a couple times a week and fish every day with small pieces of (frozen) fish (avoid oily fish like mackerel). Store-bought fish food (flakes and pellets) may work as well. Place a piece of fish in the tentacles of sea anemones. Be careful not to overfeed. After a few hours, remove any uneaten fish pieces or other food. If you have barnacles, you can raise some brine shrimp and add them to the tank every week. You can purchase brine shrimp eggs in a pet store. They will give you instructions for growing them.

If you want to set up a more complex marine aquarium, you will need to spend a good deal more money.

## I.1.9   How to Make Hand Nets

A simple item for collecting an assortment of freshwater organisms is an adapted kitchen sieve. The large size works best. See illustration for details.

**FIGURE I.4**

Other nets can be constructed from a variety of netting materials. Each type of material (differing mesh sizes) will be effective in catching different types of organisms. For the handles, use varying lengths of dowels or broomsticks. The loop can be made of old lamp shade loops, clothes hangers (however, they tend to bend too easily), or sturdy but pliable metal strips. Attach the loop to the handle by bending the loop to fit halfway across the diameter of the handle. Use heavy-duty staples in a staple gun or U-shaped nails to attach. You may want to wrap the joint with bare copper or aluminum wire.

Some possible netting materials are plastic screening and varying mesh sizes of netting from marinas, sporting goods stores, or hobby shops. Sew netting onto loop with dental floss, fishing line, or nylon thread. Make several nets with different types of netting materials and different-length handles.

### I.1.10   How to Make a Plankton Net

Purchase bolting cloth (used in silk-screen printing, plankton nets, etc.) or another type of cloth that does not stretch. Find an old lamp shade and remove the metal ring from either the top or bottom of the lamp shade. Find a wide-mouth jar that is 1 liter (1 quart) or smaller. Cut the cloth in a V shape so that the top will fit around the lamp shade ring. The bottom should fit loosely around the top of the jar. Sew the two sides of the V-shaped cloth together. Then place the ring inside of the top of what is now a cone-shaped piece of cloth. Wrap the cloth over the ring and sew together. Fold the bottom cloth inward (about 1 cm. (0.5 in.)) and sew together (a hem). Then cut three or four pieces of nylon cord (3 to 5 mm. (1/8 to 3/16 in.) in diameter) that are about 60 cm. (2 ft.) long. Poke holes through the cloth near the lamp shade ring at equal distances from one another and tie one end of each string to the ring. Tie the other ends of the strings together, so that if you hold the ends and lift the net, the opening of the net will be parallel to the ground. You may want to tie these ends to a key ring or similar metal loop.

Purchase a heavier roll of nylon cord (at least 6 mm (¼ in.) in diameter) that is at least 20 m. (60 ft.) long. Tie one end to the joined cords or ring at the end of the plankton net. The last piece you will need is a metal hose clamp that is big enough to go around the collecting jar. Place the jar inside the small end of the net so that the cloth extends past the screw grooves on the top of the jar. Attach the hose clamp so that it holds the jar at the bottom of the net.

You are now ready to use the plankton net. Start by folding the jar into the net (as shown in the Figure I.5) so that you have a kind of net frisby. Hold on to the end of the heavy cord (tightly) and toss the net (as you would a frisby) out into the water. Be careful to toss the net to a location where there are no protruding rocks, branches, or other obstacles that can snag it. Allow the net to sink until it is just under the water surface, then pull the net in as fast as you can.

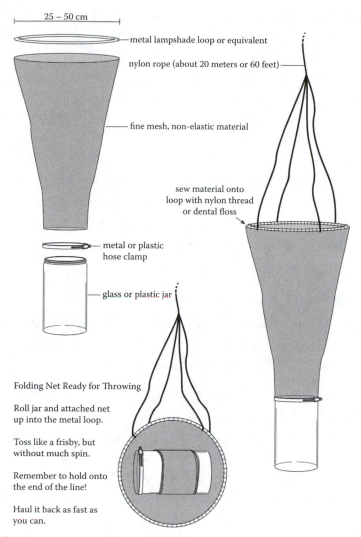

25 – 50 cm

metal lampshade loop or equivalent

nylon rope (about 20 meters or 60 feet)

fine mesh, non-elastic material

sew material onto loop with nylon thread or dental floss

metal or plastic hose clamp

glass or plastic jar

Folding Net Ready for Throwing

Roll jar and attached net up into the metal loop.

Toss like a frisby, but without much spin.

Remember to hold onto the end of the line!

Haul it back as fast as you can.

**FIGURE I.5**

When you get the net back, hold it up from the ring where the cords join and pour water from a bucket so that you wash anything sticking to the net into the jar. Remove the jar from the net by loosening the hose clamp. You should see lots of little organisms swimming around inside the jar. You can pour the jar into another container for closer inspection with hand lenses and microscopes.

## I.1.11  Preserving Specimens

From time to time you may wish to preserve an animal specimen (e.g., a fresh road kill) or a part of an animal (e.g., a cow's eyeball obtained from a butcher). Killing an animal in order to preserve it may not be something you wish to do, but you may come across a recently dead animal that you think your students may want to look at or dissect. The best preservative for relatively complex animals is formaldehyde, but formaldehyde (formalin) has been suggested as a possible carcinogen (cancer-causing agent). There are a variety of other preservatives on the market; however, the easiest and safest to use is alcohol. Methyl alcohol is probably the most effective, although rubbing (isopropyl) alcohol also can be used.

For smaller organisms, such as earthworms and jellyfish, you can just drop them into a container filled with alcohol. However, for more complex organisms or parts of organisms, you should try to inject alcohol into any cavities. A syringe (10 cc or bigger) and a 2.5-in. needle can be purchased at a drug store or through a scientific supply house (they are very inexpensive). Fill the syringe with alcohol and inject it into as many different parts of the organism as possible. When you are finished, put the organism into a container filled with alcohol.

Note that alcohol is not a great preservative. You should use specimens as quickly as possible. In addition, alcohol evaporates very quickly. When you take the organism out of the container of preservative, it will dry out very quickly. Keep the specimen moist by pouring or spraying water over it every 5 to 10 min.

### I.1.12  How to Clean and Mount a Skeleton

Obtaining a complete skeleton of an animal is not very difficult. When you find a dead animal (e.g., a road kill that has not been crushed), the flesh can be removed and the bones cleaned without very much difficulty.

1. If you want to mount a complete skeleton, be sure to measure the carcass (length, height, etc.). Recording these measurements will be helpful when you start to put the bones together.
2. The next task is to remove the flesh from the bones. The easiest way to proceed is to place the carcass in a can or tub (depending on the size of the animal) and cover it with wire mesh screening. The mesh in window screens is too fine. Use mesh with openings of about 6 mm (1/4 in.).
3. Dig a hole big enough to bury your container. Cover the container with soil (it is okay if some soil gets in the container, but you may not want to force soil into the container—too much soil in the container may make extracting the bones more difficult). The container should remain buried for at least three or four weeks. After this period of time, check to see if the bones are clean. If not, replace the container in the ground and wait a couple more weeks. If you live near salt water, you can attach rope to your can or tub and lower it into the water off a dock or pier. Check the container every couple of days. Tiny organisms (amphipods, etc.) will eat the flesh off the bones in a relatively short time.
4. Carefully remove all the bones. Be sure to look for the tiny vertebrae of the spine and tail.
5. If you want bones that are whiter, you can place the bones in a mixture of one part chlorine bleach in two parts of water. For small animals, soak the bones for a few minutes, then remove and rinse thoroughly in water. The bones of larger animals can be soaked in the solution for an hour. If you leave the bones in the bleach too long, they will become brittle and break very easily when you handle them.

6. If you want to put the skeleton together, you should start by laying the bones out in the correct order. This task is challenging, but may be a great project for your students. Once you have the bones arranged, you can put the vertebrae together by threading a piece of fairly rigid wire through the holes in the center. Attaching other bones may be somewhat more difficult. You can try using super glue or a similar fast-drying cement.

## I.2  Science Techniques and Procedures

### I.2.1  Dissecting

Dissection is generally not a part of the elementary curriculum. In addition, there is a move away from dissecting in schools. However, you may find that your inquiry can be enhanced greatly by dissecting particular organisms, especially if students ask questions that can be addressed through dissection. Students may find a recently dead animal in the school yard and ask questions that could be answered by dissecting the animal. On the other hand, you may wish to order some specimens from a scientific supply company. In either case, there are some basic techniques that can help make for a successful activity.

*I.2.1.1  Basic Equipment*

- Forceps—One of the most important tools. (Those with fairly sharp points are particularly useful.)
- Probe—An important tool.
- Teasing needle—An important tool.
- Scissors—With sharp points.
- Scalpel—Occasionally useful.
- Dissecting pins—May be useful for certain specimens (regular straight pins can work).
- Dissecting trays—These can be the size of a baking pan or a cookie sheet for large specimens. (You can get dissecting trays with wax in the bottom for pinning down specimens when they are cut open, but you may find that a sheet of Styrofoam will serve the same function.)

*I.2.1.2  Techniques*  Dissection is not a process of mutilating the specimen (something a lot of children might like to do). Rather, it is a process of carefully exploring and exposing different tissues and organs. Proceeding in this way, you will find forceps, probes, and teasing needles to be the most useful tools. Scissors are useful in cutting through the first layer of skin but are not used that often afterwards. Scalpels are useful in cutting through thick, tough skin or through cartilage. Depending on the organism, the following steps may differ:

1. Carefully cut through the top layer of skin with the scissors. Pull up skin slightly with the lower blade of the scissors as you cut, in order to avoid cutting through an underlying muscle or other tissues. For an organism like a frog, you may want to make an H-shaped cut, then fold back or cut off the flaps of skin.

2. Use the probe, teasing needle, or forceps to expose various muscles and to clean away any thin, transparent connective tissue.

3. You can follow each muscle and locate the origin (its anchoring point on a bone) and its insertion (point where the muscle attaches to the bone it moves). Have children try to figure out which muscles are responsible for which movements.

4. If you have purchased specimens with blood vessels filled with colored latex, you can have children carefully follow and expose these vessels. At this point, any muscle tissue that is in the way can be removed. After the muscles have been explored, they can be cut through or removed to expose the internal organs. Again, proceed carefully so that underlying organs are not damaged.

5. The same procedures apply to cleaning away connective and fatty tissue.

6. Children may find it interesting to look at the contents of the stomach and intestines. Follow the same procedures for cutting through the outer layer of skin.

### I.2.2 Caring for and Using Microscopes

The use of microscopes in elementary school is not generally a part of the curriculum. However, as with dissection, microscopes can allow children to extend their inquiry in meaningful ways. The most useful microscope for your classroom is a stereo microscope (often referred to as a dissection microscope). They range in magnification from 20× to 50×, and allow you to view solid objects in more detail. You also can view pond water or transparent objects. The model shown in the diagram below is an inexpensive scope, which is ideal for elementary classrooms. More expensive models provide a number of additional features, including the ability to adjust the magnification.

- Always carry the microscope by grasping the arm firmly with one hand and placing your other hand under the base.
- Use petri dishes or other shallow dishes to view liquids.

The compound microscope allows you to magnify objects from 40× up to 400× or more. This scope can be used for viewing small organisms and single cells. The model shown below is an inexpensive student microscope. These scopes tend to be less expensive than the stereo microscopes shown previously.

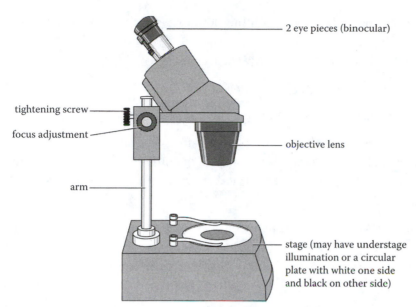

2 eye pieces (binocular)

tightening screw

focus adjustment

arm

objective lens

stage (may have understage
illumination or a circular
plate with white one side
and black on other side)

**FIGURE I.6**

### I.2.2.1 Using a Compound Microscope

- Always start viewing an object with the lowest-power objective lens. Otherwise, you risk damaging the lenses.

- Once an object is in focus, you can move the next higher-powered lens into place. To be sure that you do not damage the higher-powered lenses, watch from the side as you slowly move the next lens into place.

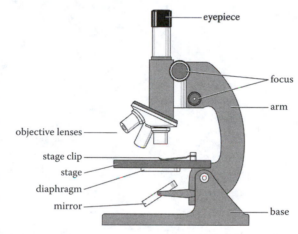

eyepiece

focus

arm

objective lenses

stage clip

stage

diaphragm

mirror

base

**FIGURE I.7**

- Always use a slide or shallow dish to view objects. Never put objects directly on the stage.

- Use the diaphragm to adjust the amount of light passing through the object and lens.

- Do not use direct sunlight to illuminate your microscope. You can damage the retina of your eye.

- Always carry the microscope by grasping the arm firmly with one hand and placing your other hand under the base.

### I.2.2.2 Caring for and Storing Any Microscope

- To clean your microscope, wipe off all nonglass parts with a soft, damp cloth.

- Clean lenses with lens paper.

- Cover your microscope with the cloth or plastic cover that came with it (or a plastic bag).
- Store microscopes on a sturdy shelf.

### I.2.3   Making Slides

You can use two types of slides for viewing very small objects:

1. Flat slides: Use with a cover slip to view drops of water and single cells.
2. Well slides: Use to view larger objects that are visible to the naked eye; well or depression slides are thicker and have a concave depression in the middle.

In addition, you may want to consider using plastic slides and cover slips. Glass slides and cover slips can break and cause nasty cuts. However, plastic slides can scratch more easily and are not as sturdy.

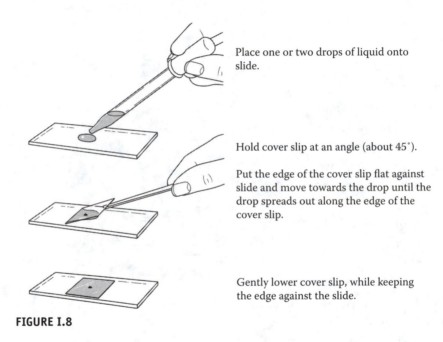

Place one or two drops of liquid onto slide.

Hold cover slip at an angle (about 45°).

Put the edge of the cover slip flat against slide and move towards the drop until the drop spreads out along the edge of the cover slip.

Gently lower cover slip, while keeping the edge against the slide.

**FIGURE I.8**

### I.2.4   Separating Pigments Using Simple Paper Chromatography

Cut strips of filter paper (coffee filters should work fine) about 1 cm. wide and 10 to 15 cm. long. Cut two indentations (about 3 mm deep) from each side at about 1 cm. from one end of each strip. Get some tall, narrow jars (e.g., olive jars) or rig up a way to hang filter paper into shorter jars (see diagram).

With your students, collect a variety of green leaves (not fall colorations) and bring them back to the classroom. Grind each type of leaf in 20 to 30 ml of ethyl (grain) or isopropyl (rubbing) alcohol. Let the leaf sit in the solution overnight. The resulting solution should be dark green.

You can try two ways of separating the pigments:

1. Place a drop of the green solution between the two notches of filter paper. Let it dry. Place three more drops in the same way. Then hang filter paper in a clear solution of alcohol (in a shallow dish or small cup).

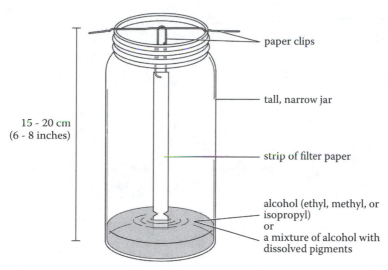

paper clips

tall, narrow jar

15 - 20 cm
(6 - 8 inches)

strip of filter paper

alcohol (ethyl, methyl, or
isopropyl)
or
a mixture of alcohol with
dissolved pigments

**FIGURE I.9**

2. Hang filter paper in the green solution of alcohol, so that about 6 mm.
(0.25 in.) of the filter paper is submersed in the liquid.

In either case, wait until the solution has risen almost to the top of the filter
paper. Remove the filter paper and let it dry. You should be able to see different colors separated into lines across the filter paper. (The heavier molecules
of pigment stop rising sooner—thus separation). Let the kids play around
with different leaves and substances.

For water-soluble pigments (e.g., some marking pens), use water instead
of alcohol.

### I.2.5    Making Contour or Local Topographic Maps

Topographic maps use lines to show the elevation of landforms. Each line
represents a specific elevation. In official topographic maps, the elevations
are from sea level (0 elevation). However, you are studying a particular pond
and its surrounding environment or any other local environment. You can
select an elevation from which to work, such as the pond or another low
point (your elevations can proceed as positive elevations above this point and
as negative elevations below this point).

*I.2.5.1    Materials*

■ Meter sticks (it may be helpful to have a stick that is longer (2 m.), which
you can mark at each meter or centimeter)
■ Long tape measure (6 m. (20 ft.) or longer; not necessary, but very
helpful)
■ Trundle wheel (not necessary, but very helpful; a trundle wheel is a
wheel with a circumference of 1 m attached to a handle, and it clicks
for each meter)
■ Bubble level (preferably one that is cylindrical and can attach to and
slide along a string)
■ Right-angle bubble level
■ Protractors

- Lots of thin wood, metal, or plastic stakes
- String (with as little elasticity as possible)
- Graph paper
- Pencil

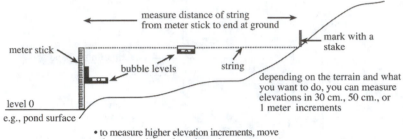

measure distance of string from meter stick to end at ground

mark with a stake

meter stick

bubble levels

string

level 0

e.g., pond surface

depending on the terrain and what you want to do, you can measure elevations in 30 cm., 50 cm., or 1 meter increments

• to measure higher elevation increments, move the meter stick to the stake and repeat

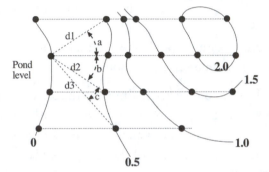

Pond level

d1

a

d2

b

d3

c

2.0

1.5

1.0

0

0.5

measurements for contour map along the lines (transects)

dot indicates elevation increment measurement (stakes) to make sure the contours are consistent with first transect, measure the angles (a, b, c) from the 1st stake to the 2nd stakes on the other transects and measure the distances (d1, d2, d3) from the 1st stake to the second stakes of the other transects

**FIGURE I.10**

## I.3   Science Equipment and Measurement

### I.3.1   How to Make Hand Lenses

Try obtaining discarded lenses from opticians or other industries that make or use lenses. If all else fails, cheap assorted lenses can be purchased from some scientific supply companies (see Appendix K for addresses and write for free catalog).

For each hand lens, cut out two small squares of heavy, but somewhat pliable, plastic or cardboard. The squares should be 2 to 4 cm. larger than the diameter of the lens. Cut circles in the center of each square. These circles should be slightly smaller than the lens. Put the lens between the two squares and cement the squares together.

**Plastic holders glued together with epoxy type cement will produce a waterproof hand lens.**

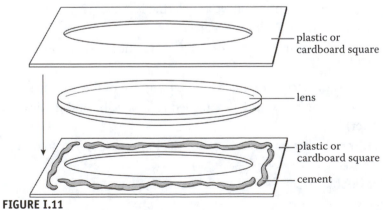

plastic or cardboard square

lens

plastic or cardboard square

cement

**FIGURE I.11**

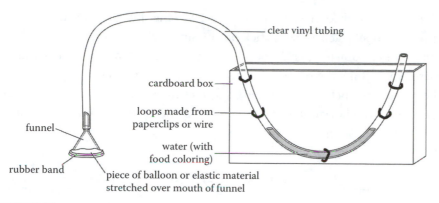

FIGURE I.12

## I.3.2  Making a Simple Manometer for Measuring Water Pressure

You can make a device, called a manometer, for measuring the relative pressure of fluids. The following diagram shows how to construct this device. Once you have finished construction, add enough water (add food coloring to the water, if you want) to the vinyl tubing so that the bottom of the U is filled.

Once you have completed the manometer, try immersing the funnel into a bucket of water and watch what happens to the water in the U. Mark the level of water for your normal readings in the air.

## I.3.3  Measuring Large Heights and Distances

You can use the same technique for measuring distances. Measure the height of a student. Have the student stand at the end of the distance you want to measure, for example, at the other side of a pond or lake. Put his or her height into the ratio as B. Solve the formula for the distance, A.

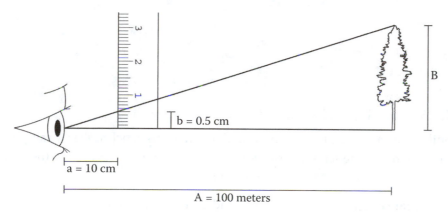

FIGURE I.13

## I.3.4  Clinometer (Measuring Angles— Moon, Sun, or Slopes on Land)

This clinometer can be used to determine the positions of the moon and sun in their arcs across the sky. It can also be used to measure the inclinations of the moon and sun from the southern horizon (which change seasonally). In addition, you can use this clinometer to measure the heights or distances of objects as described in Section I.3.3, as well as the slopes of the land. To measure the slope, place a meter stick on the slope with its edge on the ground. Turn the clinometer upside down and place along the upper edge of the meter stick. Take the reading from where the string hangs straight down. If the slope reads between 0 and 90°, subtract the reading from 90° to get the slope from the horizontal. If the slope reads between 90 and 180°, subtract 90° from the reading.

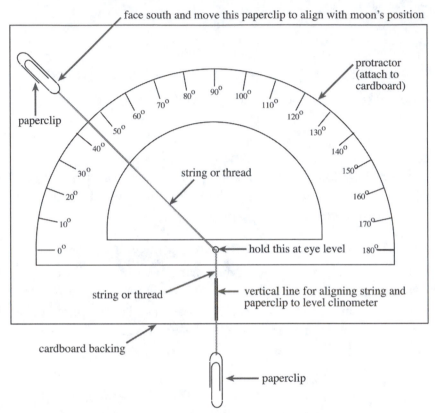

face south and move this paperclip to align with moon's position

paperclip

protractor (attach to cardboard)

string or thread

hold this at eye level

string or thread

vertical line for aligning string and paperclip to level clinometer

cardboard backing

paperclip

**FIGURE I.14**

### I.3.5 Making and Using Soil Sieves

Soil sieves are useful in separating different-size particles in soil samples. You can make one set of soil sieves or enough sets for each group of students. The list of materials below is for one set of sieves:

■ Six coffee cans—Remove the tops and bottoms of each can
■ Six different-size openings of nylon or metal mesh (large enough to fit around the base of the coffee cans):
  ■ Mesh, very fine, 1/64 in. or smaller, about 60 counts or higher per inch (will take some hunting—search the web for "screen mesh" or explore art supply stores)
  ■ Mesh, fine, about 1/32 in., about 30 counts per inch (will take some hunting—search the web for "screen mesh" or explore art supply stores)
  ■ Window screening, 1/16 × 1/16 in. mesh, about 15 counts per inch—Metal or nylon (available from hardware stores)

- Hardware cloth, 1/8 × 1/8 in. mesh—Metal (available in hardware stores)
  - Hardware cloth, ¼ × ¼ in. mesh—Metal (available in hardware stores)
  - Hardware cloth, ½ × ½ in. mesh—Metal (available in hardware stores)
- Spool of thin, flexible wire
- Hammer
- Nail
- Block of wood
- Pliers
- Wire cutter

Put the edge of the can on top of the block of wood. Use the hammer to punch at least eight small holes around the perimeter of one end of the can. Wrap the piece of screen around the opening and use the thin wire to attach the screen to the can. You may want to use a pair of pliers to flatten the edges around the holes that were punched into the can.

When you dig up a soil sample, place your sample into a bucket or other large container. Remove a smaller sample (about 1 liter) and place it in another container. Spread out a large sheet of butcher paper, then hold the smallest sieve over a specific spot. Pour your small sample into the can and shake until all of the small particles have gone through the sieve. Place the next biggest sieve over another spot on the butcher paper and pour the remaining sample into the can and shake. Repeat until you have the largest particles left in the last sieve. You can dump the largest particles onto the butcher paper. At this point, you can examine the particles in each pile with hand lenses and write descriptions of the color, shape, and size of the pile. You can weigh each pile to determine the percentage of each particle size in the soil sample. Compare soils from different areas or depths in a deep hole.

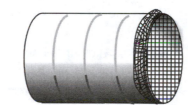

**FIGURE I.15**

### I.3.6   Making a Stream Table

A stream table is a great way to study erosion patterns of various types of soil both with and without vegetation or with a variety of other variables (e.g., objects). The design below is for making your own stream table from scratch, but you can use other things for the table itself, such as plastic sleds or long plastic planters without holes in the bottom. Depending on how much work you want to devote to making your stream table, you can make a simple one or go for increasingly complex designs. However, the basic design is fairly simple.

The components include the following:

- A table that is long enough to accommodate your stream table. (An old coffee table with a shelf underneath is ideal.)
- Stream table (of whatever form) with a drainage hole about 2 to 3 cm. below the top of the bottom end. Drill a hole that will accommodate the tubing in the next step.

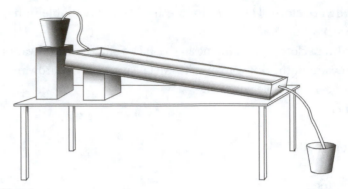

**FIGURE I.16**

- If the stream table is not made of a rigid material, place the stream table on a board that is a little longer than the stream. Nail or screw a piece of 2 × 2 in. or similar piece of wood across the bottom of the board to keep the stream table from sliding off the board

- Place one end of the stream table on wooden blocks. You can add or subtract these wooden blocks to change the slope.

- A length of plastic tubing (a fairly large diameter is better to allow for rapid drainage) that will fit snuggly into the hole at the bottom end of the stream table. The length of the tubing should be based on going from the bottom of the stream table to a large bin that will catch the water on the shelf (or floor) underneath the stream table. Use plastic glue or silicone caulking to seal and keep the tubing in the stream table hole. Allow no more than 0.5 cm. (¼ in.) of the tubing to protrude on the inside of the stream table.

- For the water source you can do one of the following:
  - Place a gallon (4-liter) or larger bucket on a solid wooden box or other object so that the bottom of the bucket is higher than the raised end of the stream table. Get a length of plastic tubing (the same as that at the bottom of the stream table) that will reach from the bottom of the bucket to just past the top of the stream table at its lowest height (or smallest slope). Attach string or wire that will hold the tubing to the stream table: poke or drill two holes into the middle of the top edge of the stream table. Loop a piece of wire or string through the holes, so that the tubing can fit through and be held snuggly in place. When you are ready to start, fill the tubing with the water in the bucket (submerge it completely). While the tubing is still submerged, place a finger over one end of the tubing, then remove that end from the water and put it into your loop of wire at the top of the stream table. Make sure the other end of the tubing is touching the bottom of the bucket. If you want, add a hose clamp to the tubing to easily shut off or adjust the flow. (Use a hose clamp that is basically shaped like an E—the tubing fits between two of the parallel pieces of metal; a screw through the other end of the E adjusts the middle piece of metal.)

- Add an aquarium pump. Place a submersible pump with a fairly low volume flow into the bucket or tub that catches the drained water. Run a piece of tubing from the output of the pump up and through the wire loop at the top end of the stream table. The best kind of pump to use is one that will allow you to adjust the flow of water.

*Appendix J*
# Technology

This appendix provides a summary of the types of technology that can be used in teaching and learning science. This is a huge topic worthy of a separate book. However, a brief overview of the possibilities is provided in this appendix.

Although you can teach science through inquiry with materials that are inexpensive or free (be a good scrounger and dumpster diver), you can enhance your science program with a variety of technological tools. If you want to add to your technological resources, you may be able to raise funds with the help of parents or write grants to a variety of agencies. There are many sources of grants for teachers from state or provincial and federal agencies (not just those directly involved in education), private foundations, and corporate foundations.

## J.1 Uses of Technology

- Tools for inquiry
  - Collecting and organizing data
  - Analyzing data
- Tools for production
  - Developing products that communicate the results of inquiry
- Tools for communicating
  - Communicating with scientists (asking questions, etc.)
  - Collaborating on inquiry projects with students from schools around the world

- Participating in discussion groups and forums on specific topics
- Tools for recording group work and events and enhancing the sense of community
  - Keeping track of the classroom community
- Tools for finding content information
- Tools for teachers (along the same lines of the previous uses)
  - Inquiring into your learning
  - Inquiring into student learning
  - Producing materials for your classroom
  - Keeping track of assessment data on your students
  - Communicating with colleagues from around the world
  - Recording your teaching experiences
  - Finding content information for your own learning

## J.2   Computers and the Internet

Almost all schools have computers and access to the Internet. Although some schools have computer labs, which can be useful, the best arrangement is to have at least one computer in the classroom. One computer for each group of children is ideal.

### J.2.1   The Internet

The amount of information available on the Internet is increasing exponentially every year. However, keep in mind that there is a lot of junk, misinformation, and ethically questionable material on the Internet. Be an informed and critical user, and help your students become informed and critical users. Always check the information you find from at least one other source, and try not to rely entirely upon the Internet—print materials are still valuable and provide information not available online.

Students can use the Internet as a source for the following:

**TABLE J.1**  Some Uses of the Internet

| | |
|---|---|
| Data and raw information | Examples include:<br>• Moon and sun rise and set times<br>• Tide tables<br>• Photos and images of earth landforms (from on land to satellites)<br>• Live or pre-recorded video feeds on a wide variety of topics from around the world<br>• An incredible range of data about all kinds of natural and social science phenomena<br>• Geographical Information Systems (GIS) |
| Online inquiry activities and simulations | Examples include:<br>• Use of video and animation to engage children in conducting inquiries on line<br>• Physics simulations<br>• Ecology simulations<br>• Biology simulations<br>• Earth science simulations |

**TABLE J.1** Some Uses of the Internet

| | |
|---|---|
| Discussion groups and forums | Examples include:<br>•Discussion forums for children on science-related sites<br>•Set up you own discussion groups and forums on your classroom website |
| Content information | Science content information from a wide variety of sites |

In addition, students can develop products that can be put onto their classroom community web page.

Teachers can use the Internet for the following:

- Science content information
- Science inquiry activities
- Science teaching news and information
- Professional organizations
- Communicating with colleagues, scientists, and other professionals

Specific links to web-based materials are provided in Appendix L.

**TABLE J.2** Uses for Different Types Software

| Software | Uses |
|---|---|
| Word processors | Organizing data and information in tables<br>Producing documents, charts, and so forth, for communicating knowledge |
| Spreadsheets | Organizing and analyzing numerical data<br>Producing graphs of numerical data |
| Databases | Storing and organizing text, images, and numerical data<br>Analyzing text data |
| Presentation software (e.g., PowerPoint) | Communicating results of investigations and other science projects |
| Graphics software | Creating models, diagrams, and other graphics for analyzing data and communicating results |
| Organizational software (e.g., Inspiration) | Graphically organize (and text outline) information<br>Flowcharts, concept maps, context maps, and so forth |
| Web design software | Producing web pages to communicate and share results of projects |
| Movie editors | Collect and edit video data<br>Produce video films for sharing results (e.g., documentaries, news shows, etc.) |
| Video analysis software (e.g., Measurement in Motion) | Videotape motions of objects, then analyze the motions (speed, velocity, acceleration, etc.) |
| Sound software | Record sounds (physical or biological), then analyze frequencies, and so forth<br>Record and manipulate frog, cricket, or bird sounds, then play back to organisms to investigate reactions |
| Simulations | Investigate simulated scientific phenomena<br>Game forms allow students to manipulate situations that simulate complex real-world systems |
| Games | Children can play games that involve science concepts |
| Science content | There is a wide range of software that allow children to explore science topics (not particularly recommended at the beginning of units, but great once children want to know more) |

## J.2.2 Computer Software

For specific science-related software, read reviews and try using demos prior to purchasing. Make sure the software is suitable for your children, scientifically accurate, and consistent with your approach to inquiry. In addition, much of the generic software applications are useful for teachers in terms of grading, organizing and storing assessment information, and producing materials for the classroom. See Table J.2 on the previous page.

## J.3 Photography

Although any type of camera is useful, digital cameras are the best. You can obtain fairly inexpensive digital cameras that will be great to have available for your students' use. In the "old" days, we had to wait several days to get the film developed (not to mention spending money for developing and printing). With digital cameras, the photos are available immediately, with no additional expenses.

The following list provides some examples of photographic-related equipment and their potential uses in the classroom.

**TABLE J.3** Cameras and Other Photographic Equipment and Their Uses

| Equipment | Uses |
|---|---|
| Cameras (digital or film) | Record series of events over time (somewhat like time-lapse photography) to see changes—plant growth, animal growth, animal movement (with more rapid sequences), field study environment throughout the year (analyze seasonal changes), stream table erosion patterns over time sequences and with different variables, and so forth |
| | Record and collect examples of natural patterns for comparison and analysis later |
| | Record specific aspects of any short- or long-term investigation for analysis |
| | Use photos for final products (web pages, books, etc.) |
| USB microscopes | Relatively inexpensive and attach directly to a computer's USB port |
| | Groups of children can view the same image of microorganisms and other small objects at the same time; images can be recorded for further analysis and for use in final products |
| Scanners | Scan flat and three-dimensional objects: |
| | Place a clear piece of plastic or overhead film onto the scanner's glass surface to protect the scanner |
| | Place an object on top of the plastic |
| | Close scanner top for flat objects (leaves, etc.) or cover object with a piece of white or black cloth (try both) |
| | Scan the object |
| | Use in the same way as taking photos |
| | Scan photographs from various print resources for use as data, such as for comparing geological or architectural structures from around the world with those that children are investigating locally |
| | Scan student sketches, drawings, and other work for inclusion in final products |

## J.4 Video

Video cameras are great tools for investigating a variety of phenomena. Although digital video is the easiest to utilize, any type of video camera is useful. With digital video, you can take a sequence of some phenomenon, then plug it into a computer, upload sequences, edit, and view the movie on the computer. You also can record the edited movie back onto a tape, then transfer it to a VHS tape for easy distribution to other users. Using any kind of video allows students to view sequences over and over again, as well as frame by frame in order to capture fairly rapid action in a step-by-step sequence.

**TABLE J.4** Video Cameras and Their Uses

| Equipment | Uses |
| --- | --- |
| Video camcorder | Record animal movement, then analyze step-by-step sequences. Compare a variety of critters. |
| | Record mechanical motion for analysis. |
| | For any type of motion, the frame rate (frames per second) provides a way for measuring speed, especially if a ruler is placed next to the object that is moving while videotaping. Most video-editing software provide an on-screen timer, so that precise times can be used in analysis. |
| | Extract frames in a sequence. Open frames in a photo-editing software application. Use line tools in the photo-editing software to trace positions of legs, earthworm bodies, or other objects, then delete photo leaving the lines. The movement can be analyzed without actual details of the images interfering, including measurement of angle changes in jointed appendages, and so forth. |
| | Some cameras can be set for time-lapse photography. Set camera on tripod. Set timing, then videotape slow action, such as plant or mold growth. |
| | Record various types of animal (including human) behavior for analysis in the classroom. |
| | Students can use cameras to record interviews with scientists or other experts and with people during investigations of opinions or knowledge. |
| | Students can use video as ongoing or final products, such as weekly science news shows for the whole school, a video documentary on their investigations, and so forth. |
| | As a teacher, use video to study your children's learning and classroom talks, as well as your own teaching. (Prior to videotaping your students, make sure you get signed consent forms from parents.) |
| USB macro/micro cameras | These cameras connect directly to a computer's USB port. They are generally adjustable for different levels of magnification and may be able to attach to a microscope. |
| | • Record close-up events or details of smaller objects and organisms, such as a snail's mouth movements while eating, earthworm movement in close-up detail, sand grains, skin, and so forth. |
| | • Analyze sequences as you would with video, as discussed above. |

## J.5 Audio

Audio recording can be very useful in taping a variety of sounds, which can then be put into a computer and analyzed. As mentioned previously, animal sounds can be analyzed, manipulated, and played back to animals (crickets, birds, etc.) to see how they react to changed beats, changed frequencies, an so forth. Children also can use recorded natural sounds to produce "music" along with sounds they produce. When interviewing people (experts or the general public), a tape recorder allows children to capture the entire interview verbatim. As a teacher, tape recorders are useful in investigating children's talk during small-group or whole-classroom discussions and science talks, as well as inquiring into one's own teaching.

## J.6 Laboratory Probeware

Laboratory probeware allows students to record data and graph the data in real time. Probeware includes a base, which can be connected directly to a computer (or specific types of calculators) as you collect data, or can be used to record data in the field and then be connected to the computer for data retrieval and analysis. A variety of probes can be connected to the base for

**TABLE J.5** Some of the More Useful Laboratory Probes

| | |
|---|---|
| Temperature probe | Measure temperate change and rate of one or more specific situations, for example, heating of tap water, salt water, oil |
| Light sensor | Light intensity for photosynthesis experiments<br>Use two to measure speed or four for acceleration (put light source behind where objects are moving or try using to detect variation of light as large objects pass by)<br>Use to analyze light absorption or reflectivity of various materials, and so forth |
| Photogate | Use to measure speed and acceleration of small toy cars, marbles, and so forth (use three or four for acceleration down a ramp) |
| Motion detectors | For large object motion speed and accelerationUse two to get speed of large objects |
| Sound level meter | Analyze animal sounds<br>Analyze musical sounds<br>Analyze sounds produced by manipulating different materials in different ways |
| Heart rate monitor | Analyze heart rates before, during, and after various forms of exercise |
| Blood pressure sensor | Analyze blood pressure before, during, and after various forms of exercise |
| Respiration monitor belt | Analyze respiration rates before, during, and after various forms of exercise |
| Flow rate sensor | Analyze the flow rate in streams or currents in ponds |
| Magnetic field sensor | Analyze the magnetic fields of various kinds of magnetics, including those used in speakers, phones, electric motors, and so forth |
| Barometer | Measure and keep track of barometric pressure changes during units on weather |
| Relative humidity sensor | Measure and keep track of humidity changes during units on weather<br>Collect data on the humidity of a closed-system terrarium (day and night variations, and so forth) |
| UV sensors | Collect data of changes in ultraviolet light intensities throughout the school year |

use in collecting specific types of data. Some of the more common and useful probes include:

PASCO
10101 Foothills Blvd.
Roseville, CA 95747
800-772-8700 or 916-786-3800
Website: http://www.pasco.com

Vernier Software and Technology
13979 SW Millikan Way
Beaverton, OR 97005-2886
888-837-6437
E-mail: info@vernier.com
Website: http://www.vernier.com

Other science education suppliers carry these two manufacturers' products as well.

## J.7   Other Science Equipment

See Appendix K for lists of other equipment and materials that are useful to have in your classroom.

**TABLE J.6**   Other Useful Science Equipment

| | |
|---|---|
| Volt-ohm meter with ammeter | Measures volts (electromotive force causing electricity to flow), ohms (resistance), and amperes (electrical current) (1 volt creates a current of 1 amp through a material with a resistance of 1 ohm) <br> Useful in analyzing circuits, resistors, conductivity of various materials, checking batteries, and so forth. |
| Balance scales | Developing understandings of mass (including mass–volume relationships) <br> Weighing objects, liquids, and so forth |
| Spring scales | Measuring the weight of objects that can be attached to the hook <br> Measuring force, including buoyancy (attach object that will sink in water, then measure weight out of water, then when object is submerged in water); attach object to hook, then attach loop at other end of spring scale to a string, which can then be swung like a pendulum—see difference in force at different parts of swing; and so forth |
| Spectroscopes | Simple and inexpensive spectroscopes can be used to analyze wave length distribution of various light sources |
| Stethoscopes | Inexpensive stethoscopes can be used to listen to the heart, but also to other sounds through a variety of mediums (e.g., wood, metal, water, etc.) |

*Appendix K*

# Equipment, Supplies, and Materials

## K.1 Basic Science Equipment and Materials for the Classroom

### K.1.1 Safety Supplies

- Rubber or vinyl gloves
- Cotton gloves
- Safety goggles
- Hot pads or gloves
- Hair bands or cloth to tie up long hair
- First-aid kit
- Sunscreen

### K.1.2 Containers

- Assorted cardboard boxes
- Buckets
- Cans
- Glass and plastic jars
- Plastic containers
- Plastic tubs and bins
- Plastic storage containers

### K.1.3 General Supplies

- Alcohol (isopropyl or rubbing)
- Aluminum foil
- Baking soda
- Ball bearings
- Balloons
- Balls (rubber, tennis, golf, beach, ping-pong, etc.)
- Broken guitar strings
- Candles
- Cardboard (sheets, tubes)
- Cellophane (assorted colors)
- Cheese cloth
- Clay (modeling, plasticine)
- Clothes hangers
- Clothes pins
- Corks
- Corn starch
- Cotton
- Dowels
- Egg cartons
- Eye droppers (pipettes)
- Filter paper (coffee type is fine)
- Fishing line
- Fishing weights
- Flower pots
- Food coloring
- Glass plates
- Glue and cement
- Gravel
- Marbles
- Matches
- Metal baking trays
- Metal sheets and scraps
- Nails
- Netting
- Nuts and bolts
- Oil (vegetable, mineral, etc.)
- Old motors
- Paper clips
- Paraffin
- Pie tins
- Pipe cleaners
- Plastic bags (sealable and others)
- Plumb bobs or other weights
- Rubber and vinyl tubing

- Rubber bands
- Rubber stoppers
- Salt
- Sand
- Sandpaper
- Screening
- Screws
- Sponges
- Steel wool
- Strainers (with handles)
- Straws
- String and rope
- Sugar
- Tape (cellophane, masking, duct)
- Thread
- Tongue depressors
- Toothpicks
- Vinegar
- Washers (various sizes)
- Wax paper
- Wood (assorted)
- Yarn

### K.1.4 Basic Equipment

- Aquariums and terrariums
- Balance scales (equal-arm and other types)
- Battery charger with rechargeable batteries
- Cages
- Compasses (circle)
- Electric hot plate
- Flashlights
- Forceps (tweezers)
- Funnels
- Graduated pitchers
- Levels (bubble and other)
- Magnetic compasses
- Magnifiers (hand lenses)
- Meter sticks
- Metric rulers
- Nets
- Protractors
- Scalpels or knives
- Scissors
- Spring scales
- Stopwatches or timers
- Tape measures (retractable, sewing)

- ■ Thermometers (various scales, types, uses)
- ■ Trundle wheel

### K.1.5   Tools

- ■ Garden trowels
- ■ Hammers
- ■ Metal shears
- ■ Pliers
- ■ Saws (cross-cut, coping, etc.)
- ■ Screw drivers (multiple-head types)
- ■ Shovels
- ■ Volt-ohm meter
- ■ Wire cutters
- ■ Wrenches

### K.1.6   Topic-Specific Items

- ■ Batteries (AAA, AA, D, C, 9-volt)
- ■ Battery holders
- ■ Gears
- ■ Iron filings
- ■ Lenses
- ■ Lightbulb receptacles (for 1.5- to 3-V bulbs)
- ■ Lightbulbs (1.5 to 3 V)
- ■ Magnets
- ■ Mirrors
- ■ Prisms
- ■ Pulleys
- ■ Switches (knife, household, etc.)
- ■ Toys (cars, mechanical, etc.)
- ■ Wire (insulated, bare, assorted thicknesses)

### K.1.7   Wish List Items

- ■ Anemometer
- ■ Barometer
- ■ Blood pressure monitor (sphygmometer)
- ■ Compound microscope(s)—slides, cover slips
- ■ Digital camera(s)
- ■ Digital video camera(s)
- ■ Laboratory probeware
- ■ Rain gauge
- ■ Stereo dissecting microscope(s)
- ■ Stethoscope

Many of the items listed here can be obtained for free. Ask parents for donations. Go dumpster diving. Ask businesses, repair shops, mechanics, and so forth, to save potentially useful throwaways.

## K.2 Sources of Science Supplies and Equipment

**TABLE K.1** Some of the Suppliers of Scientific Equipment and Materials

| United States Suppliers | | |
| --- | --- | --- |
| Carolina Biological | 2700 York Rd.<br>Burlington, NC 27215 | 800-334-5551 (U.S. costumers)<br>877-933-7833 (Canadian customers)<br>http://www2.carolina.com |
| Delta Education | 80 Northwest Blvd.<br>Nashua, NH 03061-3000 | 800-258-1302<br>http://www.delta-education.com |
| Edmund Scientifics (now owned by Science Kit-Boreal) | 60 Pearce Ave.<br>Tonawanda, NY 14150 | 800-728-6999—orders, catalogs, product information, educational discounts<br>http://www.scientificsonline.com |
| NASCO | 901 Janesville Ave.<br>Fort Atkinson, WI 53538<br>4825 Stoddard Rd.<br>Modesto, California 95356 | 800-558-9595<br>http://www.enasco.com |
| Science Kit–Boreal Laboratories | 777 E. Park Dr.<br>Tonawanda, NY 14150 | 800-828-7777<br>http://www.sciencekit.com |
| Ward's Natural Science | P.O. Box 92912<br>Rochester, NY 14692 | 800-962-2660<br>http://www.wardsci.com |
| Canadian Suppliers | | |
| Boreal-Northwest | 99 Vansickle Rd.<br>St. Catharines, Ontario L2S 3T4 | 800-387-9393<br>http://boreal.com/Default.asp? |
| Merlan Scientific | 247 Armstrong Ave.<br>Georgetown, Ontario L7G 4X6 | 800-387-2474<br>http://www.merlan.ca/index.html |

*Also see Carolina Biological, under United States suppliers (above)*

*Appendix L*
# Resources

Since the first edition of this book, the resources available to teachers, children, and parents have grown exponentially. This growth is, in large part, due to the increase in information and materials available on the Internet. The information in this appendix obviously cannot list all of the good resources. Instead, the appendix contains some important and relevant links and other resources, as well as a sampling of the types of information you may find useful in teaching and learning.

The problem with listing Internet sites is that the URLs (Internet addresses) change or cease to exist. If you try one of the links provided here and it does not work, try deleting the information after the first single slash (/). If that does not work and you are sure you have entered the correct URL, do a search for the organization or topic that you are trying to access.

## L.1 Professional Organizations

### L.1.1 State and Provincial Associations

**TABLE L.1** Professional Organizations

| **The Association for Science Education (ASE)** |
| --- |
| http://www.ase.org.uk |
| United Kingdom—with international members<br>Annual conference; journals (*Education in Science, Primary Science Review, School Science Review*, and *Science Teacher Education*); other materials |

| **International Council of Association for Science Education (ICASE)** |
| --- |
| http://icase.unl.edu/ |
| International |

| **National Association for Research in Science Teaching (NARST)** |
| --- |
| http://www.educ.sfu.ca/narstsite (linked from http://www.narst.org) |
| United States—with large international membership<br>Annual meeting; journal (*Journal of Research in Science Teaching*); monographs |

| **National Science Teachers Association (NSTA)** |
| --- |
| http://www.nsta.org |
| United States and Canadian chapters—with international members<br>Produces a great deal of useful materials; regional and national conferences; journals (*Science and Children, The Science Teacher*, et al.) |

| **School Science and Mathematics Association (SSMA)** |
| --- |
| http://www.ssma.org |
| United States—with international members<br>Annual conference; journal (*School Science and Mathematics*); other print resources; grant program for teachers |

Most of these are affiliated with NSTA, listed above.

**TABLE L.2** State and Provincial Associations

| | |
| --- | --- |
| Alberta | http://www.atasc.ab.ca |
| British Columbia | http://www.bctf.bc.ca/bcscta |
| Quebec | http://www.apsq.org |
| Saskatchewan | http://education.uregina.ca/mathed/SSMSTS/home.html |
| Manitoba | http://www.stam.mb.ca |
| Ontario | http://www.stao.ca |
| Alabama | http://www.asta.auburn.edu |
| Alaska | http://www.aksta.org |
| Arizona | http://www.azsta.org |
| Arkansas | http://www.aristotle.net/~asta |
| California | http://www.cascience.org |
| Colorado | http://www.mines.edu/outreach/cont_ed/cast/cast1.htm |
| Connecticut | http://www.csta-us.org |
| Delaware | http://www.k12.de.us/science/dts |
| Florida | http://www.fastscience.org |
| Georgia | http://www.georgiascienceteacher.org/index.htm |
| Hawaii | http://home.hawaii.rr.com/hasta |

**TABLE L.2** State and Provincial Associations

| | |
|---|---|
| Idaho | http://www.uidaho.edu/ista |
| Illinois | http://www.ista-il.org |
| Indiana | http://www.hasti.org |
| Iowa | http://ists.pls.uni.edu |
| Kansas | http://kats.org |
| Kentucky | http://www.ksta.org |
| Louisiana | http://www.lsta.info |
| Maine | http://www.mainescienceteachers.org |
| Maryland | http://emast.org |
| Massachusetts | http://www.mast.nu |
| Michigan | http://www.msta-mich.org |
| Minnesota | http://www.mnsta.org |
| Mississippi | http://www.ms-msta.org |
| Missouri | http://www.stom.org |
| Montana | http://www.opi.state.mt.us/msta |
| Nebraska | http://www.neacadsci.org/nats/index.htm |
| Nevada | Nevada State Science Teachers Association (no website) |
| New Hampshire | http://www.nhsta.net |
| New Jersey | http://www.njsta.org |
| New Mexico | http://www.nmsta.org |
| North Carolina | http://www.ncsta.org |
| North Dakota | http://www.ndsta.k12.nd.us/index.htm |
| Ohio | http://www.secoonline.org |
| Oklahoma | http://www.angelfire.com/ok3/osta |
| Oregon | http://oregonscience.org |
| Pennsylvania | http://www.pascience.org |
| New York | http://www.stanys.org |
| Rhode Island | Rhode Island Science Teachers Association (no website) |
| South Carolina | http://www.scscience.org |
| South Dakota | http://www.sdsta.org |
| Tennessee | http://www.uu.edu/tsta |
| Texas | http://www.statweb.org |
| Utah | http://www.usoe.k12.ut.us/curr/science/usta/ustadir.html |
| Vermont | http://www.uvm.edu/vsta |
| Virginia | http://www.vast.org |
| Washington | http://www.wsta.net |
| West Virginia | http://www.wvsta.org |
| Wisconsin | http://www.wsst.org |
| Wyoming | http://wsta.1wyo.net |

## L.2 Science-Related Organizations

**TABLE L.3** Science-Related Organizations

| | |
|---|---|
| **AIMS Education Foundation** | http://www.aimsedu.org/<br>Integrating science and mathematics curriculum and materials, and so forth |
| **Canadian Space Agency (CSA)** | http://www.space.gc.ca/asc/eng/default.asp<br>Space, space travel, satellites, and so forth |
| **Environment Canada** | http://www.ec.gc.ca/<br>Agency overseeing air, water, climate, wildlife, and other environmental concerns |
| **Institute for Earth Education** | http://www.eartheducation.org/<br>Earth and environmental education, acclimatizing activities, and so forth |
| **Geological Survey of Canada** | http://gsc.nrcan.gc.ca/index_e.php |
| **Meteorological Service of Canada** | http://www.msc-smc.ec.gc.ca/ |
| **National Aeronautics and Space Administration (NASA)** | http://www.nasa.gov<br>Space, space travel, satellites, and so forth |
| **National Oceanic and Atmospheric Administration (NOAA)** | http://www.noaa.gov/<br>Weather, oceans, moon and sun rise and set times, fisheries, satellites |
| **Science Service** | http://www.sciserv.org/<br>Science news, science fairs, scholarships, and other activities and information |
| **United States Geological Survey (USGS)** | http://www.usgs.gov/<br>Earth and space sciences |

## L.3 Internet Resources by Science Topic or Resource

### L.3.1 Maps, Aerial Photos, and Satellite Photos and Images

**TABLE L.4** Internet Resources: Maps, Aerial Photos, and Satellite Photos and Images

| | | |
|---|---|---|
| EarthNet | http://envisat.esa.int | Photos and images |
| Google earth | http://earth.google.com | 3D (Three-dimensional) interactive images |
| Google maps | http://maps.google.com | Maps, satellite photos |
| MapTech | http://mapserver.maptech.com | Topographic, historical |
| Multimap | http://www.multimap.com/ | International maps |
| NOAA satellite | http://www.noaa.gov/satellites.html | Satellite photos, images |
| Real-time science data | http://solar.physics.montana.edu/tslater/real-time/ | Images, data, interactions |
| Space Imaging | http://www.spaceimaging.com/gallery/default.htm | Photos and images |
| Space Science | http://www.ssec.wisc.edu/data/#rtsat | Real-time images |
| TopoRama | http://toporama.cits.rncan.gc.ca/ | Canadian topographic maps |
| TopoZone | http://www.topozone.com/ | U.S. topographic maps |

## L.3.2 Earth and Space Sciences (Including Weather)

**TABLE L.5** Internet Resources: Earth and Space Sciences (Including Weather)

| | |
|---|---|
| Amazing Space | http://amazing-space.stsci.edu/ |
| Astro WebCam Philippines | http://www.angelfire.com/space/jkty5597/webcam.html |
| Australia —— IPS Radio and Space Services | http://www.ips.gov.au/ |
| Canadian Space Agency | http://www.space.gc.ca/asc/eng/default.asp |
| Challenger Center for Space Science Education | http://www.challenger.org/ |
| China National Space Administration | http://www.cnsa.gov.cn/main_e.asp |
| Earth Watch | http://www.earthwatch.com/ |
| Earthquake activity | http://gldss7.cr.usgs.gov/neis/qed/qed.html |
| European Space Agency (ESA) | http://www.esa.int/esaCP/index.html |
| Indian Space Research Organisation | http://www.isro.org/ |
| Kennedy Space Center Video Feeds (NASA) | http://science.ksc.nasa.gov/shuttle/countdown/video/video.html |
| NASA EdSpace | http://edspace.nasa.gov/ |
| NASA television | http://www.nasa.gov/multimedia/nasatv/index.html |
| National Aeronautics and Space Administration | http://www.nasa.gov/home/index.html?skipIntro=1 |
| National Space Development Agency of Japan | http://www.nasda.go.jp/index_e.html |
| NOAA climate | http://www.noaa.gov/climate.html |
| NOAA weather | http://www.noaa.gov/wx.html |
| Puckett Observatory | http://www.cometwatch.com/ |
| Real-time science data access page | http://solar.physics.montana.edu/tslater/real-time/ |
| Russian Space Agency (RSA) | http://liftoff.msfc.nasa.gov/rsa/rsa.html |
| Space Education | http://www.eagle.ca/~matink/themes/Solar/spaceedu.html |
| Space Weather (NOAA) | http://www.sec.noaa.gov/ |
| Space.com | http://www.space.com/ |
| Space.cweb—Netherlands | http://space.cweb.nl/space3d_iss.html |
| Students for the Exploration and Development of Space | http://www.seds.org/ |
| Weather Online | http://www.weatheronline.co.uk/ |
| Weather Underground | http://www.wunderground.com/ |

## L.3.3 Oceanography, Marine Biology, and Coastal Information

**TABLE L.6** Internet Resources: Oceanography, Marine Biology, and Coastal Information

| | |
|---|---|
| Bedford Institute of Oceanography (Canada) | http://www.bio.gc.ca |
| Bimini Biological Field Station | http://www.miami.edu/sharklab/news.html |
| Hawaii Institute of Marine Biology | http://www.hawaii.edu/HIMB/ |
| Monterey Bay Aquarium | http://www.mbayaq.org/ |
| National Oceanography Centre, Southampton | http://www.soc.soton.ac.uk/ |
| NOAA coasts and oceans | http://www.noaa.gov |
| Scripps Institute of Oceanography | http://sio.ucsd.edu/ |
| Sea Grant Ocean Sciences Education Center | http://www.vims.edu/bridge/ |
| Vancouver Aquarium | http://www.vanaqua.org/home/ |
| Woods Hole Oceanographic Institute | http://www.whoi.edu/ |

## L.3.4 Physics and Chemistry

**TABLE L.7** Internet Resources: Physics and Chemistry

| | |
|---|---|
| Chemistry.org | http://www.chemistry.org/portal/a/c/s/1/acsdisplay.html?DOC=kids\index.html |
| Internet- accessible machines | http://www-cse.ucsd.edu/users/bsy/iam.html |
| Internet campus | http://www.eoascientific.com/campus/ |
| Minds-on physics simulations | http://www.hal-pc.org/~clement/science.htm |
| Museum of Science and Technology | http://www.most.org/ |
| Ontario Science Centre | http://www.ontariosciencecentre.ca/scizone/ |
| Schlumberger Excellence in Educational Development | http://www.seed.slb.com/ |
| The Exploratorium | http://www.exploratorium.edu/ |

## L.3.5 Life Sciences and Ecology

**TABLE L.8** Internet Resources: Life Sciences and Ecology

| | |
|---|---|
| Ant Cam | http://www.antcam.com/ |
| Bug bios | http://www.insects.org/ |
| Bug Scope | http://bugscope.beckman.uiuc.edu/ |
| Deformed frogs in Minnesota | http://www.pca.state.mn.us/hot/frogs.html |
| Earthlife web | http://www.earthlife.net/ |
| Interactive biology | http://serendip.brynmawr.edu/sci_edu/biosites.html#4 |
| National Wildlife Federation | http://www.nwf.org/ |
| Try Science | http://www.tryscience.org/ |
| Whale net | http://whale.wheelock.edu/Welcome.html |
| X-ray for kids | http://www.uhrad.com/kids.htm |

## L.3.6  Live Streaming Videos

**TABLE L.9**  Internet Resources: Live Streaming Videos

| | |
|---|---|
| Beluga cam | http://www.vanaqua.org/belugacam/index.html |
| Exploring Science Site (related to this book) | http://elsci.coe.nau.edu |
| Fisheye View cam | http://www.fisheyeview.com/FVCamStream.html |
| James Reserve cams | http://www.jamesreserve.edu/ |
| Monterey Bay Aquarium cams<br>Outer bay, birds, sharks, sea otters, kelp forest, Monterey Bay, and large video collection | http://www.mbayaq.org/efc/efc_outerbay/outerbay_cam.asp<br>http://www.mbayaq.org/efc/efc_sandy/sandy_cam.asp<br>http://www.mbayaq.org/efc/efc_smm/smm_cam.asp?bhcp=1<br>http://www.mbayaq.org/efc/efc_otter/otter_cam.asp<br>http://www.mbayaq.org/efc/efc_mbay/mbay_cam.asp?bhcp=1<br>http://www.mbayaq.org/efc/video_library/video_library.aspx |
| Mote Marine Laboratory | http://camcoder.mote.org/icam/default.htm |
| National Zoo cams | http://nationalzoo.si.edu/animals/webcams/ |
| Panda cam | http://www.sandiegozoo.org/pandas/pandacam/index.html |

## L.3.7  General Science Teaching Resources

**TABLE L.10**  Internet Resources: General Science Teaching Resources

| | |
|---|---|
| Annenberg Media | http://www.learner.org/ |
| Exploring Science Site (related to this book) | http://elsci.coe.nau.edu |
| Franklin Institute online | http://sln.fi.edu/ |
| Franks Potter's Science Gems | http://www.sciencegems.com/ |
| National Geographic | http://www.nationalgeographic.com/index.html |
| Pro Teacher | http://www.proteacher.com/ |
| Science Learning Network | http://www.sln.org/ |
| Smithsonian Institute Education | http://www.smithsonianeducation.org/ |
| Think Quest | http://library.thinkquest.org |

### L.3.8   Internet Projects

**TABLE L.11** Internet Resources: Internet Projects

| | |
|---|---|
| The World Weather Watch Project | http://www.cyberbee.com/weatherwatch/ |
| Classroom Feeder Watch | http://birds.cornell.edu/cfw/ |
| The Jason Project | http://www.jason.org |

##  Teacher Professional Journals and Children's Magazines

**TABLE L.12** Teacher Professional Journals and Children's Magazines

| | |
|---|---|
| *Science and Children* | http://www.nsta.org/elementaryschool#journal |
| *National Geographic Kids Magazine* | http://www.nationalgeographic.com/magazines/ |
| *Audubon* | http://magazine.audubon.org/index.html |
| *Chickadee Magazine* | http://www.owlkids.com/ |
| *Discover* | http://www.discover.com/ |
| *Owl Magazine* | http://www.owlkids.com/ |
| *Odyssey* | http://www.odysseymagazine.com/ |
| *Ranger Rick (and others)* | http://www.nwf.org/kids/ |
| *Science Weekly* | http://www.scienceweekly.com/ |
| *Yes Magazine* | http://www.yesmag.bc.ca/ |
| *Popular Science* | http://www.popsci.com/popsci/ |

## L.5   Books for Teachers

For a more extensive list of books, please see the readings lists at the end of the chapters, as well as in Appendix D.

Achinstein, B. (2002). *Community, diversity, and conflict among schoolteachers: The ties that blind.* New York: Teachers College Press.

Atkins, P. (2003). *Galileo's finger: The ten great ideas of science.* New York: Oxford University Press.

Axelrod, A. (2003). *Science A.S.A.P. (as soon as possible, as simple as possible).* New York: Prentice Hall.

Bransford, J. D., Brown, A. L., & Cocking, R. R. (Eds.). (2000). *How people learn: Brain, mind, experience, and school.* Washington, DC: National Academy Press.

Brookman, J. (Ed.). (2004). *Curious minds: How a child becomes a scientist.* New York: Vintage Books.

Bruner, J. (1990). *Acts of meaning.* Cambridge, MA: Harvard University Press.

Calabrese Barton, A., & Osborne, M. D. (Eds.). (2001). *Teaching science in diverse settings: Marginalized discourses and classroom practice.* New York: Peter Lang.

Calder, N. (2005). *Einstein's universe: The layperson's guide.* New York: Penguin.

Davis, B., Sumara, D., & Luce-Kapler, R. (2000). *Engaging minds: Learning and teaching in a complex world.* Mahwah, NJ: Lawrence Erlbaum Associates.

de Campos Valadares, E. (2006). *Physics, fun, and beyond: Electrifying projects and inventions from recycled and low-cost materials.* Upper Saddle River, NJ: Prentice Hall PTR.

Duckworth, E. (Ed.). (2001). *"Tell me more": Listening to learners explain.* New York: Teachers College Press.

Duschl, R. A. (1990). *Restructuring science education: The importance of theories and their development.* New York: Teachers College Press.

Evans, P., & Selina, H. (2001). *Introducing evolution.* Roystan, UK: Icon Books.

Feynman, R. P. (1985). *"Surely you're joking, Mr. Feynman": Adventures of a curious character.* New York: Bantam.

Feynman, R. P. (1988). *"What do you care what other people think?": Further adventures of a curious character.* New York: Bantam Books.

Feynman, R. P. (J. Robbins, Ed.). (1999). *The pleasure of finding things out: The best short works of Richard P. Feynman.* Cambridge, MA: Helix Books/Perseus Publishing.

Gallas, K. (2003). *Imagination and literacy: A teacher's search for the heart of learning.* New York: Teachers College Press.

Gurstelle, W. (2001). *Backyard ballistics.* Chicago: Chicago Review Press.

Hart-Davis, A. (2005). *Why does a ball bounce: 101 questions you never thought of asking.* Buffalo, NY/Richmond Hill, ON: Firefly Books.

Hatton, S. D. (2005). *Teaching by heart: The foxfire interviews.* New York: Teachers College Press.

Highfield, R. (2002). *The science of Harry Potter.* New York: Penguin.

Hodson, D.(1998). *Teaching and learning science: Towards a personalized approach.* Philadelphia: Open University Press.

Ingram, J. (2003). *The velocity of honey and more science of everyday life.* Toronto, ON: Penguin Canada.

Jargodzki, C. P., & Potter, F. (2001). *Mad about physics: Braintwisters, paradoxes, and curiosities.* New York: Wiley.

Kakalios, J. (2005). *The physics of superheroes.* New York: Gotham Books.

Lambros, A. (2002). *Problem-based learning in K-8 classrooms: A teacher's guide to implementation.* Thousand Oaks, CA: Corwin Press.

Marton, F., & Tsui, A. B. M. (Eds.). (2004). *Classroom discourse and the space of learning.* Mahwah, NJ: Lawrence Erlbaum Associates.

McGill, I., & Brockbank, A. (2004). *The action learning handbook.* New York: Routledge-Falmer.

Moring, G. F. (2004). *The complete idiot's guide to understanding Einstein* (2nd ed.). New York: Alpha Books.

Newton, D. P. (2000). *Teaching for understanding: What it is and how to do it.* New York: Routledge-Falmer.

Newton, D. P. (2002). *Talking sense in science: Helping children understand through talk.* New York: Routledge-Falmer.

Ramsland, K. (2001). *The forensic science of C.S.I.* New York: Berkeley Boulevard Books.

Roberts, S. M., & Pruitt, E. L. (2003). *Schools as professional learning communities.* Thousand Oaks, CA: Corwin Press.

van Matre, S. (1990). *Earth education: A new beginning.* Greenville, WV: Institute for Earth Education.

Wolf, F. A. (2005). *Dr. Quantum's little book of big ideas: Where science meets spirit.* Needham, MA: Moment Point Press.

# INDEX

scientists', 36–39, 41, 44, 46–48, 50–54, 60, 284, 375

students' learning how to design, 9, 78, 138, 210, 216, 217, 270

Explanations

addressing inaccurate, 216–217, 222, 274

alternative, 26,  39, 74, 96, 114, 130, 161, 224

children's, 76, 77, 78, 110, 209, 221, 231; *see also Chapters 4 and 5*

children's views of scientific, 66

constructing, 4, 9–10, 26, 112–113, 138–140, 142–143, 188, 190, 219, 222–225

evaluating, *see Assessment approaches, explanations and definitions; Evaluation*

negotiating, 9, 11, 69, 107, 112, 161, 186, 216–217,  225, 245

science education standards emphasis on children's, 309, 310, 311

scientific, 11, 38–42, 47–48, 53, 57, 68, 88, 90, 96, 284

supporting, 11, 161, 222

testing of, 35, 151, 154, 161, 285, 399

## F

Facts

learning, 4, 36, 237, 242, 243, 303, 310, 325

nature of scientific, 38, 44, 46, 48, 50, 52–53, 54, 55, 58, 167

and science teaching, 132, 210

views of science as a collection of, 36, 69

Fantasy, 81, 92, 94, 104, 254; *see also Contexts of meaning*

Field studies, 22–23, 219, 248, 249, 294–295, 347, 370–372, 388, 430; *see also Appendix F*

Field trips, xvi, 23, 243, 292, 351, 352

Floating; *see also Concepts and topics, science*

argument about, 116–126

children's understandings of, 67, 92–93, 174–175, 177–179, 180, 182, 185–186, 188, 190, 197–198

unit of study, 193–196, 214–215, 216, 223–224

Flowcharts, 394, 429

Formulas

area, 403

density, 119, 370

perimeter, 403

triangles (for determining height or distance), 421

volume, 403

## G

Galapagos Islands, 37

Goals

affecting our work and effort, 173

for assessment, 160–162, 167–168, 220; *see also Goals, in planning*

children's, 80, 110, 141, 196, 257, 258, 361

children working towards, 141, 196, 208–209

for classroom communities, 164, 237–243, 247–248, 255

in classroom design, 253

consistency of and with, 250, 255, 268

defined, 162–164

defining specific, 163–164; *see also Objectives*

discourse, 108, 113, 127, 128, 161, 187–188

for field studies or trips, 352, 360

general, affective, 160

inquiry, 127, 145–146, 161, 162

learning, 160–161, 162, 226, 306, 326

parents', 246, 257

in planning, 95, 160–162, 208–209, 210, 224, 227, 300, 306, 345

of portfolios, 192–193

psycho-social, 161–162

of reflection, 261, 263

of schooling, 226

of science and scientists, 41, 47, 49–50, 63

of science education, 9–11

sharing, with children, 113

as student products, 196, 208–209, 210

of and for teachers (self), 168, 261

and testing, 201

thinking, 80, 161

as visionary statements, 163

working towards, 258–259

Greek and Latin roots in scientific names, *see Names and naming*

## H

History, 334, 362

earth's, 184, 235, 313

human, 56, 69, 91, 165, 167

local and school, 306

natural, 13, 45, 97, 137, 138, 143, 194, 355

of science, 7, 45, 70, 309, 310, 312, 314; *see also Nature of science,*

teachers' personal, 276

Homology, 94, 146

Humor, 102, 110, 196, 212, 265, 296; *see also Contexts of meaning*

Hypotheses, xv, 36, 38, 39, 53, 58, 67, 68, 154

## I

Imagery, *see Contexts of meaning*

Imagination

children's, xiii, xiv, 13, 65, 83, 86–87, 137, 138, 180

goals and, 163

scientists', 45, 47–48, 54

teachers', 273, 351, 375–376

Independence, 54

in classroom communities, 241, 255

of learners and thinkers, 4, 8, 9, 11, 110, 229, 241

in science education standards, 309, 318

Inferring (Inferences), 6, 47, 74–75, 83, 148, 149, 161, 167; *see also Thinking*

Inquiry, 4–5; *see also Science; Chapter 6*

activities, *see Activities and investigations*

assessment of, 170, 187–188, 191, 193, 198–200

children's engagement in, 10, 31–32, 69, 76, 81, 85, 110, 169, 326

classroom community focus on, 13, 107, 113; *see also Chapter 9*

collecting and analyzing data, *see Appendix H; Data analysis; Data collection*

field studies and, *see Appendix F; Field studies*

goals of, *see Goals, inquiry*

and learning, 92, 99, 102, 119, 120, 125, 127, 165, 189, 190

planning for and implementing, 93, 95, 120, 167; *see also Chapter 8*

pitfalls of teaching through, 131–133

play and, 96–98

process of, 31, 127

resources for, 12, 439; *see also Appendix L*

in science education standards

Canada, 315, 316, 318, 319

United States, 300, 301, 302, 303, 304, 309, 310, 311, 312, 313

scientists', xv, xvi, 37, 39, 44, 46, 47, 48, 54

teachers' engagement in, 12, 19–20, 21, 69, 112–113, 127, 281, 282, 283; *see also Chapter 10, Reflection*

Inquisitiveness, *see Curiosity*

Instructional plans, 222–224; *see also Appendix E*

Integration; *see also Metapatterns; see also, Curriculum, integrated*

assessment of, 170, 174–176, 177, 183, 196

planning for, 208, 217–219, 226, 227, 231–233

in science education standards, 304, 305, 306, 310, 317
types of, 217–218
of understandings (learning), xviii, 10, 84, 100–101, 104, 162, 224
Internet, *see Technology tools and uses*
Interpretive frameworks, *see Contexts of meaning*
Issues; *see also Activities, controversial issues; Assessment, issues; Concepts and topics, evolution; Culture(s)*
of accountability, *see Accountability*
in classroom communities, 234, 241, 246
as focus for activities, 69, 137, 163, 193, 208, 219, 224, 227, 229, 327
as focus for discourse, 116, 119, 122, 125
gender, 18–19, 48, 56–57, 179, 308, 315
in science, 36, 41, 44, 45, 48, 61
in science education, 41, 66, 76, 137, 200–205
in science education standards, 304, 316, 319
in teaching, 9, 49, 104, 120, 249, 281, 282; *see also Chapter 10; Reflection*

## J

Justification of knowledge claims, 130, 164–165, 170; *see also Knowledge, claims*

## K

Knowledge
authority, 4, 117, 120, 132, 231, 242
claims; *see also Arguments, about density*
advertising, 61, 143, 242
challenging of, *see Challenging, knowledge claims*
evaluation of, 7, 9–10, 187–188, 222, 225
negotiating, 9, 11, 80, 142, 161, 179, 199, 209
portfolios focused on, 192–196
questioning, 129–130
science, 37, 38–39, 48–50, 57, 113, 210
students', 114, 164–165
support for, 11, 113, 114, 130, 157, 161, 164–165, 170, 210; *see also Evidence; Justification of knowledge claims*
testing and, 201
consuming vs. producing, 10, 141, 240, 242, 243, 247, 249, 256, 333, 352
construction, *see Chapters 4, 5, and 6*
decontextualized, 165, 203

experiential, *see Contexts of meaning*
fragmented, 48–49, 98–99, 102–103, 109, 197, 325
personal, experiential, *see Contexts of meaning*
prior, 369
children's, 74, 75, 77, 79, 81, 231, 318, 326
in planning, 95, 168, 225
scientists', 37
school-type, *see Contexts of meaning*
as tentative, xiii, 13, 38, 39, 210
transfer of, 80, 103, 105n. 5, 196–198, 199

## L

Leadership, 52, 59, 99, 103, 332, 333, 339
student, 161, 187, 191, 241, 362
teacher, 280, 282
Listening
to children, 112, 125, 126, 132, 187, 190, 256
skills, 10, 112, 113, 114, 115–116, 163, 241, 244, 245

## M

Magnifiers, *see Hand lenses*
Maps
concept, *see Concept maps*
context, *see Context maps*
contour, 148, 419–420
as data, 148–149, 150
in data analysis, *see Data analysis, mapping*
sources of, 444
Meaning, *see Contexts of meaning*
Measurement; *see also Data collection*
errors, 143, 152–153, 154–155, 400
estimating, 400–401
of large heights and distances, 421–422
Memorization, 4, 15, 36, 42, 141, 160, 192, 202, 242, 325
Metapatterns
arrows
explanations and examples of, 101, 328, 333, 334, 338, 340
inquiries on, 343, 374–375, 391–392
binaries, 101
explanations and examples of, 125, 126, 127, 330, 333, 334, 335, 336, 339, 340
inquiries on, 374–375, 391
borders and pores (barriers, obstacles, etc.)
explanations and examples of, 101, 328, 329, 332, 335, 338, 341
inquiries on, 343, 374, 388, 390
breaks (transformation, change, etc.)

explanations and examples of, 101, 125–126, 328, 334, 336
inquiries on, 343, 374, 391
centers, 101, 328
explanations and examples of, 40, 125–126, 127, 165–166, 238–239, 243, 250, 332, 335, 337
inquiries on, 343, 390–391
clonons
explanations and examples of, 330, 331, 332
inquiries on, 343, 373
clusters
explanations and examples of, 101, 174–175, 328, 335, 338, 339
inquiries on, 343, 391
cycles, 101, 197, 311, 328
examples, 55, 100, 142–143, 157, 203
explanations, 8, 100, 102, 125–126, 167, 218, 334, 338–343
inquiries, 100, 232, 369, 373, 374–375, 387, 388, 391, 394
inquiry questions, 27, 100, 102, 139
understandings of, 100, 102, 181
emergence
explanations and examples of, 7, 101, 126, 156, 175, 328, 336, 338, 341
inquiries on, 343, 373, 391
gradients
explanations and examples of, 101, 328, 336
inquiries on, 343, 373, 374, 391
hierarchies
explanations and examples of, 204, 238, 330
inquiries on, 343, 373, 390, 393
holarchies
explanations and examples of, 238–239, 280, 328, 330, 331, 336, 338
inquiries on, 343, 373
holons
explanations and examples of, 330, 331
inquiries on, 343, 373
layers
explanations and examples of, 101, 226, 238, 328, 329–330, 331, 335
inquiries on, 343, 373, 385, 390
rigidity and flexibility
explanations and examples of, 101, 328, 335, 336
inquiries on, 343, 373, 391, 398–399
sheets
explanations and examples of, 82, 101, 328, 329, 330, 332, 335, 337
inquiries on, 343, 373, 374, 388, 390, 392
spheres, 40, 98

explanations and examples of, 101,
126, 165, 328, 329, 335, 337, 338,
340
inquiries on, 343, 373, 388, 390, 392,
403
time, calendars, and clocks
explanations and examples of, 101,
333, 334
inquiries on, 343, 385, 389, 391
triggers
explanations and examples of, 45,
101, 238, 337
inquiries on, 343, 373, 391
tubes
explanations and examples of, 101,
218, 328, 329, 335, 337
inquiries on, 343, 373, 388, 390, 392,
403
webs
explanations and examples of, 101,
131, 165, 232, 328, 329, 337, 405
inquiries on, 343, 373, 388, 391
Metaphors, *see Contexts of meaning;
Analogies*
Misconceptions, 21, 36, 38, 58, 59, 70, 224
Mistakes, working with and value of, 210,
212
students', 5, 6, 123, 151–152, 154, 217,
230, 256, 297
teachers', 8, 9, 117, 132–133, 212, 265,
274, 276
Models, modeling
children as, 266
children's intuitive, 123
in data analysis, *see Data analysis,
modeling*
of learning, 112, 142
as learning tools, 25, 26, 28, 137,
165–166, 167, 186–187, 199, 219,
429
as learning tools in science education
standards, 309, 311, 317
scientific, 40, 45, 57
teachers as, *see Roles of teachers*
of teaching, 142, 208, 220, 221–222,
238–239, 304
Motivation, 6, 49, 55, 148, 171, 242, 257,
326, 354

## N

Names and naming
Greek and Latin, 17–18
of organisms, 17–18
Native Americans (and aboriginal peoples),
*see Culture(s), Native North
Americans*
Nature of science, 7, 9–10, 24, 110, 113,
120, 160, 226, 243, 283; *see also
Chapter 3*

in science education standards, 309,
312, 314, 316, 319
in teaching, 375–381
Negotiation
in communities, 193, 198, 238, 241, 297,
327
of knowledge claims, *see Knowledge,
claims, negotiating*
of rules, 255
Networking, 286, 343
Normal science, 39, 40

## O

Obedience, 110, 240
Objectives, 162, 167, 187–188, 220, 241, 247
behavioral, 164, 165
conceptual, 165, 214–215, 220
defined, 164–165
Observation
based on theory, 37, 38, 54, 58
children's, 77, 78, 81–82, 85, 95, 125, 148,
221, 271, 274
children's understandings of, 67, 68
components of, 18, 21, 81
as inquiry approach, 9, 26, 52–53, 56,
130, 139, 143–151, 156
and learning, 104
nature of scientific, 38, 39, 40, 41, 48–49,
51–52, 54, 60, 154–155, 212–213
in science education standards, 321,
322, 323
of scientists, 62–63
as a skill in science, 11, 17, 37, 161, 164–
165, 199, 210, 211, 222, 353–354
of students, 123, 244–246, 267, 268–269,
276, 301; *see also Assessment*
techniques and approaches science, 69,
78, 147–151, 154–155, 383–391,
393
technological aids for, 150–151, 430–433
Off-task, 112
Ownership, children's; *see also Control,
children's*
and behavior, 123
and children's identities, 249
of classroom community, 92, 163, 240,
241, 249, 255
and engagement, 116, 126, 141
of learning and work by children, 6,
31–32, 69, 76, 112, 121, 127, 138,
231, 269
and motivation, 6, 92
obstacles to, 132, 151, 256
and passion, 121

## P

Parents, 135

communicating with, 159, 162, 173, 184,
202, 205, 361
expertise of, 211, 361
fear of, 90
in-service for, 248, 258
learning from, 3, 59, 79, 107, 151
as members of the classroom
community, 246, 248–249, 282
permissions from, 354, 357, 358, 359
science education standards emphasis
on relating to and working with,
301, 306, 307
socialization by, 18
support of, xiv, 57, 150, 249, 257–258,
427, 438
working with, 196, 205, 240, 257–258,
267
volunteers, 97, 196, 351, 360, 377
Passion, xiv, 257
children's, 47, 116, 121, 122, 123, 126,
160, 175, 256, 276
scientists', 47, 48, 68
teachers', 5, 12, 20, 264, 279, 280
Patterns; *see also Metapatterns*
in data analysis, 28, 29, 30, 392–403
in science, 7–8, 126, 183, 210, 213
integrated, 146, 175, 217, 218–219, 231,
232, 326–327, 338–341
investigating, 130, 142, 144–145, 148,
149, 245, 270, 342, 372, 423
knowledge (understandings) of      10,
11, 96, 99–103, 145–146, 161, 165,
199
in science education standards, 317, 321
types (formal, spatial, temporal), 146
Pedagogical knowledge and content
knowledge, 281
People
Ackerman, Diane, 71, 284
Bateson, Gregory, xvi, xx, 72n. 1 and 2,
328, 33, 328, 333, 343
Bateson, Mary Catherine, xviii xx,
13–14, 98, 105n. 4, 287, 343
Bateson, Nora, xx
Bauer, Henry, 58–59, 71, 72n. 22
Begay, Fred, 59–60, 72n. 23
Burke, James, 57–58, 71, 72n. 21, 287,
343
Copernicus, 40, 42
Cori, Gerty Radnitz, 56
Curie, Marie, 54
Darwin, Charles, 52–54, 70, 71, 72nn.
15, 16
Descartes, 57
Dewey, John, 240
Driver, Rosalind, 71
Duschl, Richard, xvi, 71, 206, 448
Edwards, Derek, 133, 236n. 3

in assessment, 170, 171, 197, 204
children's determining of, as skill, 114, 187
children's perception of, 80, 91–92, 215
in children's thinking, 180, 187, 196–197
of content knowledge, 210, 217, 325–326
and context, 80, 97–98, 164–165, 203, 237–238, 241
of field studies, 352
and inquiry, 136–138, 224, 227–228, 242, 352
in learning, 93, 196–197
of complex, integrated concepts, xix, 10, 100–103, 139, 200, 217–218, 325–326, 399
of science concepts, 160–161, 164–166
and passion, 116
of school, 91, 92
in teachers' professional development and communities, 281, 284
in teaching, xix, 9, 35, 80, 138, 196–197, 203, 207, 228, 266–267
and theories, 167
Religion (and religious symbolism), 41, 49, 52, 88, 89–90
Reprimands, 268
Resistance, 330, 332
to change by students, 225–226, 238
complacency and, 238
of ideas to change, 104, 123
to science, 22
Respect
for environment and organisms, 11, 160
of others by students, 114, 187, 231, 240, 246, 296
of students by teachers, 231, 246, 268, 296, 302, 318
of teachers, xvi, 244, 268, 269
Responsibility, 57, 237
as classroom community characteristic, 163, 237–238, 240–241, 249, 255, 352
definition of, 248
as professional community characteristic, 18–19, 280
in science education standards, 300, 302, 317, 320, 323
student, xvi, 6–7, 107, 110, 161, 170, 171, 191, 198, 222
teacher, 3, 204–205, 261, 264
in working with problematic behaviors, 295
Revolutionary science, see Science, types
Risk(s)
health, 19, 295, 314
in science, 47–48, 377
-taking, 257, 377

students', 6, 112, 128–129, 172, 222, 241, 256
teachers', 4–5, 9
for teachers, 4–5, 121, 204, 205, 209, 273, 326
Role model, teachers as, 5, 18–19, 136
Roles of students, 97, 110, 142, 161, 187, 241, 327, 362, 376
Roles of teachers, 5, 8, 161, 204, 259, 280; see also Knowledge, authority
in classrooms, 7, 95, 116, 136, 246, 250, 256, 273, 404
coach, 113, 188, 256
co-participant, 114, 117
facilitator, 4, 5, 7, 107, 117, 120, 124–127, 280, 283
guide, 5, 112, 117, 151–152, 154–156, 167, 170, 188, 216–217, 238
mentor, 112, 117, 247, 280
model, 112, 113, 114, 129, 136, 171, 237, 270, 300, 302; see also Role model, teachers as
orchestrator, 117, 280, 300
in professional communities, 282
in science education standards, 300, 301, 304, 305, 307

## S

Safety; see also Appendix A
on field studies, 356, 357, 358, 359, 361, 409, 410
physical and health, 19, 301, 323, 413
psychological. 6, 128–129, 172, 241, 301
supplies and First Aid kits, 435
as a topic, 233, 318, 322, 323, 337
Scaffolding, 229
Science; see also Inquiry
aesthetics of, 41, 45, 52, 56, 60, 175
ambiguity in, 9, 46
assumptions and beliefs in, 37, 38–39, 40, 41, 49–50, 52, 57, 58, 60
biases, 36, 37, 42–43, 52
as body of knowledge, 36, 51, 69
as business, 49–50
concepts, see Concepts and topics
creativity in, xv, 39, 44, 45, 47–48
curiosity, 44, 49–50, 53, 60
discovery in, 36, 42, 44, 45, 46, 47, 52, 53, 54, 57, 58, 61
doubt in, 38–39, 51, 52, 56, 125
economics of, 49–50
and emotions, 41, 42, 46–47, 52–53, 54, 55–56, 57, 375, 376, 377
and imagination, xiv, 45, 47–48, 54
influence on (and of) gender, race, and ideology, 48
objectivity in, 36, 37, 42, 45, 55, 58, 147, 155
passion in, 47–48, 52–57, 68

patience and perseverance in, 50, 53, 54
proof, see Proof
risk-taking in, 47–48
as social enterprise, 37–38, 48, 49–50, 57–58
and society, 35, 38, 41, 44, 48, 50, 57–58, 61
subjectivity in, 37, 44
surprise in, 46
talks, see Discourse
and technology, 35, 43, 44, 48, 58
and technology, in science education standards, 304, 309, 310, 312, 313–314, 315, 316, 317, 319–320, 323
theories, 35, 36, 37–41, 44, 45, 46–47, 52–54, 57, 58–59, 60
topics, see Concepts and topics
types of (normal and revolutionary), 37, 39
uncertainty in, 45–46, 51
worldviews, 52
Science organizations, 306, 444
Science techniques; see also Data, analysis; Data, collection; Measurement
chromatography, 387, 418–419
collecting and keeping organisms, 16, 20, 149, 405–415
contour (topographic) mapping, 148, 419–420
dissecting, 76, 77, 179, 271, 386, 387, 413, 415–416
mapping, 26, 148–149, 150, 356, 385, 386, 388, 398, 419–420
mounting and cleaning skeletons, 254, 414–415
preserving specimens, 413–414
slides, making microscope, 418
soil sifting, 422–423
Socialization (of students), 18, 32, 238, 255
Software, see Technology, software
Standards, science, 102–103, 160, 200–203, 205, 208, 220
in Canada, 12, 70; see also Appendix C
in United States, 12, 70, 135, 234–235; see also Appendix B
Stories and learning, 11, 47, 81, 82–83, 97, 104, 175, 219, 234, 327; see also Contexts of meaning

## T

Talk (-ing), see Discourse
Teachers
characteristics of excellent, 5–6
expectations of, see Expectations, teachers'
identity, 5, 6, 240, 267, 280–282; see also Roles of teachers
roles, see Roles, of teachers